Late Prehistoric Florida

Florida Museum of Natural History: Ripley P. Bullen Series

UNIVERSITY PRESS OF FLORIDA

Florida A&M University, Tallahassee
Florida Atlantic University, Boca Raton
Florida Gulf Coast University, Ft. Myers
Florida International University, Miami
Florida State University, Tallahassee
New College of Florida, Sarasota
University of Central Florida, Orlando
University of Florida, Gainesville
University of North Florida, Jacksonville
University of South Florida, Tampa
University of West Florida, Pensacola

Late Prehistoric Florida

Archaeology at the Edge of the Mississippian World

EDITED BY

Keith Ashley and Nancy Marie White

University Press of Florida
Gainesville · Tallahassee · Tampa · Boca Raton
Pensacola · Orlando · Miami · Jacksonville · Ft. Myers · Sarasota

Copyright 2012 by Keith Ashley and Nancy Marie White
All rights reserved
Printed in the United States of America on acid-free paper

First cloth printing, 2012
First paperback printing, 2015

Library of Congress Cataloging-in-Publication Data
Late prehistoric Florida : archaeology at the edge of the Mississippian world / edited by Keith Ashley and Nancy Marie White.
p. cm.
Includes bibliographical references and index.
ISBN 978-0-8130-4014-1 (cloth: alk. paper)
ISBN 978-0-8130-6187-0 (pbk.)
 1. Mississippian culture—Florida. 2. Excavations (Archaeology)—Florida. 3. Florida—Antiquities. I. Ashley, Keith H. II. White, Nancy Marie.
E99.M6815L37 2012
975.9'01—dc23   2012000879

The University Press of Florida is the scholarly publishing agency for the State University System of Florida, comprising Florida A&M University, Florida Atlantic University, Florida Gulf Coast University, Florida International University, Florida State University, New College of Florida, University of Central Florida, University of Florida, University of North Florida, University of South Florida, and University of West Florida.

University Press of Florida
15 Northwest 15th Street
Gainesville, FL 32611-2079
http://www.upf.com

Contents

List of Figures   vii
List of Tables   ix
Preface and Acknowledgments   xi

1. Late Prehistoric Florida: An Introduction   1
   Keith Ashley and Nancy Marie White

2. Southwest Florida during the Mississippi Period   29
   William H. Marquardt and Karen J. Walker

3. Mississippian Influence in the Glades, Belle Glade, and East Okeechobee Areas of South Florida   62
   Robert S. Carr

4. The Indian River Region during the Mississippi Period   81
   Thomas E. Penders

5. Early St. Johns II Interaction, Exchange, and Politics: A View from Northeastern Florida   100
   Keith Ashley

6. The Alachua of North-Central Florida   126
   Vicki Rolland

7. An Overview of the Suwannee Valley Culture   149
   John E. Worth

8. Safety Harbor: Mississippian Influence in the Circum–Tampa Bay Region   172
   Jeffrey M. Mitchem

9. Fort Walton Culture in the Tallahassee Hills   186
   Rochelle A. Marrinan

10. Fort Walton Culture in the Apalachicola Valley, Northwest Florida   231
    Nancy Marie White, Jeffrey P. Du Vernay, and Amber J. Yuellig

11. Defining Pensacola and Fort Walton Cultures in the Western
    Panhandle 275
    Norma Harris

12. The Mississippi Period in Florida: A View from the Mississippian
    World of Cahokia 296
    John E. Kelly

    References Cited 311
    List of Contributors 363
    Index 365

Figures

1.1. Areas covered by volume chapters 2
1.2. Location of major Florida rivers, lakes, and bays 5
1.3. Florida and the Mississippian world 11
2.1. The Charlotte Harbor–Pine Island Sound–San Carlos Bay estuarine system 30
2.2. Climatic fluctuations, sea-level episodes, and cultural chronologies for southwest Florida and the greater Southeast, ca. 100 B.C.–A.D. 1700 32
2.3. Topographic map of Mound Key 48
2.4. Topographic map of the Pineland Site Complex 50
2.5. Topographic model of the Pineland Site Complex before twentieth-century land modification 52
3.1. Map of southeastern and south-central Florida depicting principal sites 63
3.2. Late Woodland– through historic-period chronology of southeastern and south-central Florida 65
3.3. Nicodemus Earthworks 74
3.4. Shell-mask gorget uncovered in Palm Beach County 77
3.5. Shell gorget vulture uncovered at 8Da1081 in the Everglades 78
4.1. Indian River region 82
4.2. Major sites discussed in the chapter 91
4.3. Known radial and arc burial sites in Florida 94
5.1. Mill Cove Complex and Mt. Royal archaeological site locations 102
5.2. St. Johns II site locations in northeastern Florida 103
5.3. Copper long-nosed maskettes recovered from Grant Mound by C. B. Moore in 1895 105
5.4. Spatulate celt #1 recovered from Shields Mound by C. B. Moore in 1895 106
5.5. Spatulate celt #2 recovered from Shields Mound by C. B. Moore in 1895 106
5.6. Mill Cove Complex showing location of Grant Mound, Shields Mound, and Kinzey's Knoll 108

5.7. Broad view of the greater Southeast 113
6.1. Location of Alachua heartland and greater distribution of Alachua ceramics 128
6.2. Gainesville-area sites 129
6.3. Examples of Prairie Cord Marked rim treatments 131
6.4. Alachua period pottery 131
7.1. Map showing major Suwannee Valley and Suwannee Valley–related sites and site clusters 153
7.2. Ceramic types associated with the Suwannee Valley culture 160
8.1. Core of the Safety Harbor culture area in central peninsular Gulf coast Florida 173
8.2. Englewood Incised pottery from Tatham Mound 177
8.3. Partial Safety Harbor Incised vessel from Tatham Mound 177
9.1. Tallahassee Hills region and adjacent territory 191
9.2. Diagrammatic representation of the Lake Jackson site (8Le1) 197
9.3. Chert projectile points excavated from Mound 3, Lake Jackson 210
9.4. Fort Walton Incised ceramic rim sherds from Mound 3, Lake Jackson 211
9.5. Ceramic disks excavated from Mound 3, Lake Jackson 212
10.1. Map of Fort Walton sites in the Apalachicola/lower Chattahoochee Valley 232
10.2. Schematic map of Fort Walton mound sites in Apalachicola/lower Chattahoochee Valley 234
10.3. Celts from Fort Walton burials at the Corbin-Tucker site 236
10.4. Fort Walton ceramic types 238
10.5. Fort Walton Incised partial vessels 239
10.6. Lake Jackson rims showing attributes 240
10.7. Relative frequencies of Lake Jackson rim attributes 245
10.8. Fort Walton Incised design styles classified by Yuellig 250
10.9. Copper disks from the Corbin-Tucker site cemetery 254
10.10. Test Unit G at the Corbin-Tucker site, showing elite burials 255
10.11. Yon mound and village site 257
11.1. Western Florida panhandle 276
11.2. Counties of the western panhandle surrounding Pensacola, Choctawhatchee, and St. Andrews bays 277
11.3. Geographic limits of Fort Walton and Pensacola pottery 278
11.4. Bowls with similar incised decorations from Pensacola and Choctawhatchee bays 289

Tables

4.1. Recorded radial and arc burial patterns in peninsular Florida 95
6.1. Commonly accepted Alachua chronology and associated pottery types 130
6.2. Calibrated radiocarbon dates from Alachua sites 134
6.3. Frequency of Alachua surface treatments from Rocky Point 135
7.1. Calibrated radiocarbon dates for Fig Springs, South End Village (8Co1) 157
7.2. Ceramic types identified within the Suwannee Valley series at Fig Springs, 1990 159
7.3. Decorative overtreatments identified within the Suwannee Valley series at Fig Springs, 1990 161
7.4. Rim profile distribution by ceramic type at Fig Springs, 1990 163
7.5. Indigenous food taxa identified from all Suwannee Valley contexts, including mission-era Jefferson components, Fig Springs, 1988–1990 168
9.1. Radiocarbon dates cited in text 194
9.2. Archaeological history of the Lake Jackson site (8Le1) 198
9.3. Overview of the Lake Jackson mounds 200
9.4. Summary of site development and ceramic chronology at the Lake Jackson site 203
9.5. Summary of mortuary data from Lake Jackson Mound 3 205
9.6. Mound sites in the Tallahassee Red Hills area 213
10.1. Details of Fort Walton radiocarbon dates discussed in this chapter 242
10.2. Temper in two diagnostic Fort Walton ceramic types in the Perry Collection, Curlee site (8Ja7) 248
10.3. Maize from Fort Walton sites in the Apalachicola/lower Chattahoochee Valley 264
11.1. Total Mississippi-period sites in five northwest Florida counties 280

11.2. Calibrated radiocarbon date information for sites discussed in chapter   282
11.3. Sherds recovered from the Hickory Ridge site   287
11.4. Naval Live Oaks Cemetery Lazarus Collection, National Park Service, Southeastern Archeological Center   288

Preface and Acknowledgments

The aboriginal inhabitants of Florida were the first people of what is now the United States to be encountered and described by sixteenth-century Old World explorers. As a consequence, their cultures were severely impacted and their numbers decimated by these foreign invaders. While we know a lot about some Florida groups, we know next to nothing about others. This volume focuses on what late prehistoric societies in Florida were like in the five centuries or so leading up to the moment of first contact and the rapid and irrevocable changes that followed.

This book came about after talking to colleagues and realizing that no up-to-date synthesis or comprehensive picture of late prehistoric life throughout Florida existed, particularly with regard to how the various Florida cultures related to the rest of the greater Southeast. In the last few centuries before contact, large and powerful political systems had developed across the Southeast. These Mississippian societies lived in large villages and associated agricultural hamlets, built platform mounds, and engaged in long distance trade. Florida, while positioned along the periphery of the Mississippian heartland, was not isolated from the social, economic, and ideological developments of the interior Southeast, as we hope readers will see in this volume.

We have tried to produce a book that is accessible and clearly written and provides researchers with our current state of knowledge on late prehistoric Florida, including descriptions of new data and syntheses of past work. The chapters shed light on the state's varied native groups, societies that ranged from coastal and riverine fishers and shellfish collectors to cleared-field maize farmers. The volume presents both a general overview of Florida during the late prehistoric period and details from specific areas of the state. Social complexity among nonagricultural fisher/foragers, unique ceramic complexes, temple-mound ceremonialism, regional settlement systems and political organizations, exchange or gifting of exotic artifacts, and even consequences of early European contact are among the topics explored by the contributors.

We are grateful to all the hard-working contributors in this book, who initially responded to the original symposium invitation and later to the request to be part of the (long, long!) process of turning it all into a printed volume. Many of them did extended research into original sources and collections to bring their material all together with fresh perspectives. We believe the results to have been improved considerably also because they were able to provide some peer review on each other's chapters.

We also thank Victor Thompson, Adam King, and another anonymous reviewer for the University Press of Florida (UPF) for their comments and recommendations, and other professionals and students who shared their thoughts on various chapters or aspects of this volume. It is wonderful to have colleagues in Florida and beyond who are willing to share their efforts and data completely and to offer tough but friendly critiques. We thank the staff at the UPF for all their help, guidance, and patience; we particularly appreciate the efforts of editors John Byram, who got the ball rolling, and Kara Schwartz, who helped bring it to completion. And thanks to all the many others who were willing to take a chance on us and then help turn raw words into a finished product. We also appreciate Karen Mayo's production of the index.

Keith Ashley thanks his family—Angela, Avery, and Kyle—for their tremendous support and for allowing him the time to work on this book. Nancy White thanks Adela and Tony White for continual inspiration and encouragement.

1

Late Prehistoric Florida

An Introduction

KEITH ASHLEY AND NANCY MARIE WHITE

The archaeological record of late prehistoric Florida is often bypassed or devalued by scholars outside the state, many of whom tend to view Florida natives as somehow cut off from the supposedly more complex and important developments of the interior Southeast. To some extent, Florida occupies a geographically marginal position as North America's southeastern appendage. But it is not an island separated from the mainland by hundreds of miles of ocean waters. Still, Florida societies, particularly those of the peninsula, have been largely ignored or given minor consideration in overviews on the Mississippian Southeast (A.D. 1000–1600). Perhaps the omission is nothing more than the by-product of gross generalizations focused on cultures that fit the "Mississippian" mold. Yet at times there appears to be an underlying sense of indifference, allowing researchers to cast "non-Mississippians" aside as inconsequential. But just how different were Florida societies from those of the Mississippian world? And does being different render Florida societies irrelevant or culturally inferior and justify exclusion from the social landscape of the Mississippi-period Southeast? We think not.

This volume attempts to shine a light on late prehistoric cultures in Florida, from the northwestern panhandle to the southern tip of the peninsula, and to explore the degree to which Florida's inhabitants distilled the ideas and trends of the broader Mississippian world (figure 1.1). As detailed in the following chapters, labeling Florida societies as either Mississippian or non-Mississippian pigeonholes them and distorts the reality of the native world. Agriculture was not needed for political complexity, nor was it a prerequisite for active participation in long-distance exchange. Our aim is not to recast Florida societies as Mississippian wannabes pleading

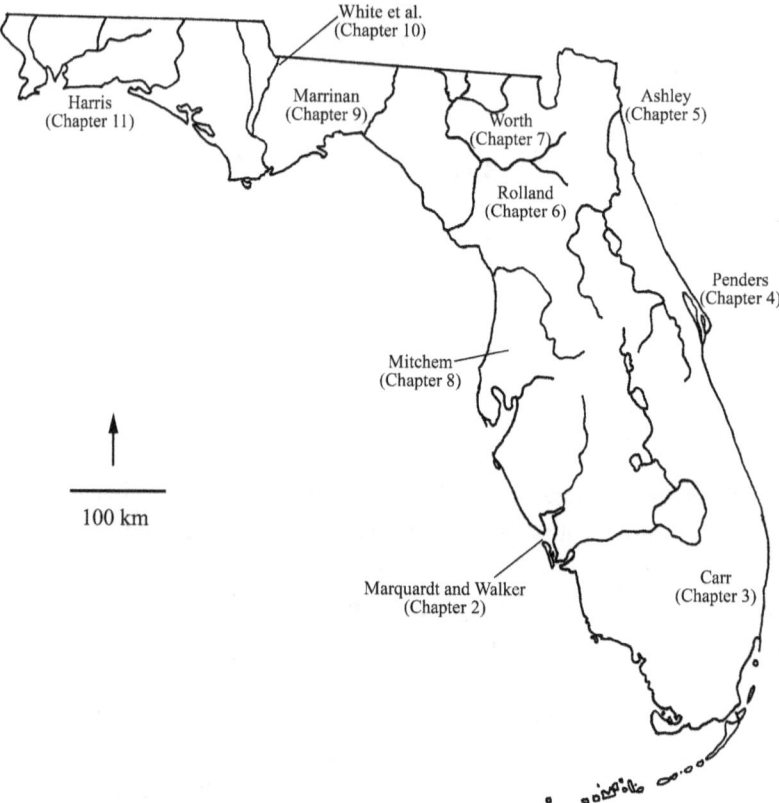

Figure 1.1. Areas covered by volume chapters.

for acceptance into the in-crowd, although arguments can be made that more-northerly Florida groups such as the historically known Timucua, Apalachee, and ethnically uncertain Fort Walton peoples of the Apalachicola River valley and points westward fall easily within the span of variation in Mississippian culture. The importance of Florida's aboriginal peoples lies in their own cultural traditions and histories that often intersected with those outside their territorial boundaries. By lifting the veil of cultural uniformity frequently draped over Florida in Mississippian literature, we expose a diverse and vibrant collection of intensive maize farmers, part-time gardeners, hunter-gatherers, and coastal and riverine fishers and shellfish collectors. In this light, Florida was to a degree a microcosm of the broader Southeast, and its study has a lot to offer those outside the state (Weisman 2003: 210).

Florida's Spatial Boundaries and Natural Diversity

The state of Florida, like many other peninsular political entities such as modern Italy, consists of both a slender coastal segment attached to the continent and a thin peninsula that juts into the sea. The current Florida peninsula extends some 650 km south into warm subtropical waters, dividing the Gulf of Mexico from the Atlantic Ocean. It is so narrow (240 km wide) that from Tampa along the Gulf coast you could see the space shuttle take off from Cape Canaveral on the Atlantic coast; nobody is far from the sea. Florida's coastline is dotted with islands of varying sizes, including many barrier islands and the Keys, an archipelago of more than 1,500 islands dangling in a south-southwest arc from the peninsula's southern tip.

Although the state is encircled on three sides by ocean waters, Florida's northern border is arbitrary, formalized by the U.S. government not even two centuries ago. Thus, we should not expect the modern state line to be congruent with native territorial boundaries, which themselves were fluid over the more than 12,000-year history of indigenous occupation. For those late prehistoric societies living in northern peninsular and panhandle Florida, cultural boundaries likely extended up or across rivers and overland into Alabama and Georgia as population sizes waxed and waned through time. For this volume, however, our geographical area of inquiry will be confined to the state of Florida.

Florida emerged from the sea, having surfaced within the past 30 million years as limestone deposits and marine sands gradually accrued atop igneous and metamorphic basement rocks (Schmidt 1997: 2). Guided by global climatic conditions, sea levels have advanced and retreated, alternately covering and exposing land, while at the same time building and reworking the surface contours and shores. Marine processes driven by sea-level fluctuations have played a primary role in forming the Florida we know today, a dynamic landscape that continues to be shaped by ongoing depositional and erosional actions.

Outsiders who travel through Florida often leave with the impression that the state is flat, sandy, and humid. Although they are not wrong, the state is not nearly as uniform as many assume. It is relatively flat with little relief, particularly compared to the continental interior, but deep ravines with high walls and highland features occur throughout the northern half of the panhandle. The horse country that forms the spine of peninsular Florida is marked by rolling hills. Found throughout the state are sand ridges aligned parallel to the present coast, which represent dunes that once fronted earlier shorelines. Elevations range from sea level to a high of 105 m in the coastal plain uplands of the western panhandle (mean elevation of the state is 30 m). The southern third of the peninsula, however, is less than 15 m in elevation.

Because of Florida's great north–south length (720 km), its climate varies by latitude: temperate in the north, subtropical in the south, and tropical in the Keys (Chen and Gerber 1990). Temperatures, greatly influenced by oceanic conditions, can vary throughout the state, especially along a north–south gradation. Vis-à-vis other areas of the world that share the same latitudinal position, one might expect Florida to be a desert, but its enclosure on three sides by warm ocean waters creates conditions that support lush vegetation (Ewel 1990: 4). In fact, Florida has more biological diversity than any other state in the eastern United States; a recent inventory documented 69 natural upland and wetland biomes across the state (FNAI 1990). Ecosystems in temperate northern Florida contrast sharply with those of subtropical southern Florida.

Upland native ecosystems in Florida during Mississippian times would have included pine flatwoods and dry prairies, xerophytic scrub and high pine lands, temperate woodlands, panhandle ravines and river bottomlands, maritime forests, coastal dunes, and the tropical hardwood hammocks of the southern peninsula. Wetland communities consisted of freshwater marshes and swamps as well as coastal salt marshes and mangroves. Today, Florida has 2,172 km of coastline, more than the entire Atlantic U.S. coast from Florida to Maine (2,092 km) (Humphreys et al. 1993: 1). The shoreline includes dunes fronted by sandy beaches pounded daily by high-energy waves. In areas of low-energy wave and wind action, the coast takes less of a beating. There, mud floors develop, which support sea grass marshes along the panhandle shores, the central Gulf coast area, and the northern two-thirds of the Atlantic coast; dense mangrove swamps thrive along the peninsula's southern tip (Johnson and Barbour 1990: 429).

Florida holds more than 17,700 km of interior and near-shore rivers, streams, and waterways, 7,700 lakes larger than 4 ha, and 600 springs (Miller 1997). Figure 1.2 displays the location of some of the larger rivers in Florida, most of which are oriented north–south. With the exception of the lower Chattahoochee-Apalachicola system, Florida rivers lack extensive alluvial floodplains, locales that provided interior Mississippian

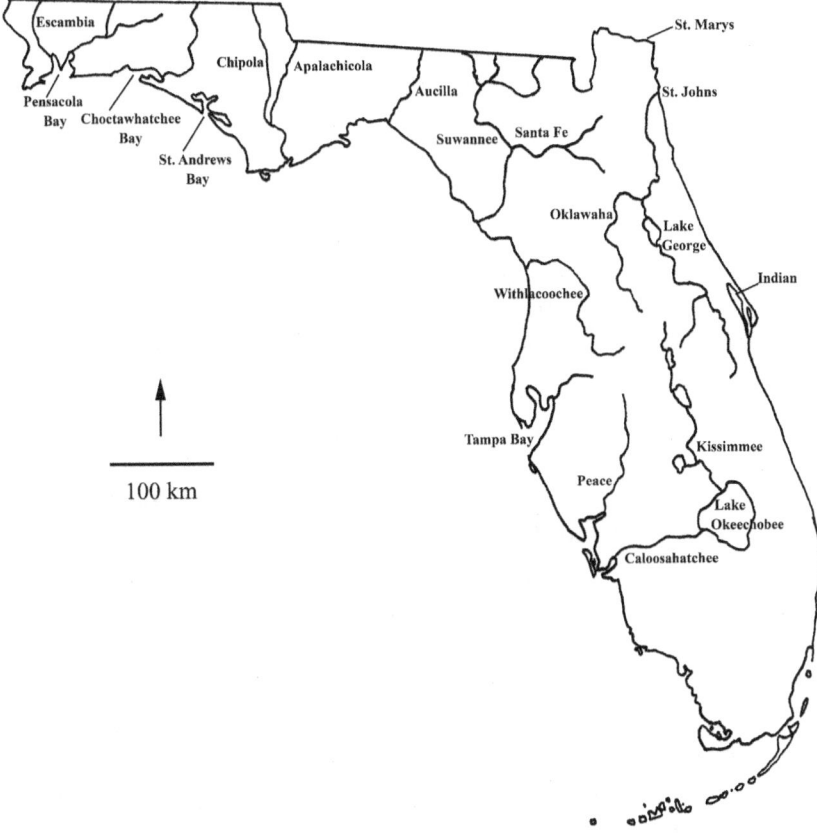

Figure 1.2. Location of major Florida rivers, lakes, and bays.

agriculturalists with nutrient-rich and seasonally replenished farmland. By modern agricultural standards, most Florida sands are often considered porous and infertile, although the red clay and loamy soils in the northern part of the state are more conducive to agricultural pursuits (Ewel 1990: 3). Precipitation provides the source of all fresh water in Florida, although much of the rainwater is lost to runoff and evaporation (Miller 1997: 69). Both interior and coastal wetland habitats significantly shaped precolumbian settlement and subsistence patterns, particularly in areas lacking fertile soils favorable for farming (Milanich 1994: 415). The archaeological cultures of Florida were as diverse as the natural environments in which they existed. Even during the Mississippi period it is not possible to paint all Florida societies with the same brush.

Distinguishing Mississippi Period and Mississippian in Florida

The chapters in this volume cover the time from about A.D. 1000 to 1600, a chronological interval in southeastern prehistory known as the Mississippi period. Although archaeologists generally have been reluctant to couple the terms *Florida* and *Mississippian,* John Goggin (1949a: 17, 1952: 64) recognized "Florida Mississippian" as one of his 10 Florida cultural traditions. He further commented that in the panhandle "the culture in Fort Walton times represents a blend of the Floridian elements of the [Woodland-period] Weeden Island culture plus a strong Mississippian influence" and that "a strong Middle Mississippian influence" also was seen in certain Safety Harbor pottery types (Goggin 1947: 117–18, 1949a: 39). Other than these sweeping statements and noting that Florida Mississippian straddled the prehistoric-historic divide in northwest and Gulf coast Florida, Goggin offered little insight into the tradition.

John Griffin (1949: 45–47, 1952a: 325–27), like Goggin, observed that the Fort Walton period in northwest Florida and the Safety Harbor period on the central Gulf coast both displayed "a pronounced Mississippian flavor" between the mid-fifteenth and early seventeenth century, an influence that diminished from north to south. At this time, the consensus among Southeastern archaeologists was that Mississippian was a protohistoric phenomenon. Gordon Willey (1949a: 569–70) took it a step further and proposed the movement of people from the Mississippi Valley to explain the appearance of agriculture, temple mounds, and other Mississippian traits in the Fort Walton region of the Florida panhandle (see Marrinan, chapter 9, and White et al., chapter 10, this volume). His explanation was not surprising given that most archaeologists of the day viewed migration as the prime factor responsible for the spread of the Mississippian culture across the Southeast landscape.

Connections to the interior were not lost on Goggin (1947: 125), who astutely noted that "Florida's peripheral position by no means excluded it from the broader aspects of the general southeastern prehistoric picture." Specifically, Goggin (1949a: 27–28, 1949b, 1952: 123–24) and John Griffin (1952a: 331, 1952b) called attention to the presence of "Southern Cult" (Southeastern Ceremonial Complex or SECC) artifacts and stylistic motifs on sites throughout the state. In particular they pointed to copper repoussé plates, long-nosed god maskettes, and spatulate celts taken by C. B. Moore from Mt. Royal and Grant and Shields mounds (Mill Cove Complex) along the St. Johns River (Ashley, chapter 5, this volume; Milanich 1999). By the mid-twentieth century, a link between Florida and the greater Southeast during late prehistoric times in the form of exotic mortuary goods was recognized by a host of other archaeologists (e.g., Ford and Willey 1941; James Griffin 1967; Larson 1958; Waring and Holder 1945; Williams and Goggin 1956). However, other than acknowledging (or implying) acquisition through contact and raising important questions about trade with the interior Southeast, little effort was made to explain what these high-profile items were doing on Florida sites.

Perhaps the boldest statement regarding Mississippian culture in Florida came in the 1980 landmark publication *Florida Archaeology*. In it Milanich and Fairbanks (1980: 92) explicitly stated that Mississippian peoples inhabited parts of Florida, namely, the same two areas identified earlier by John Griffin. In the *Archaeology of Precolumbian Florida*, published 14 years later, Milanich (1994: 355) reaffirmed his position that "Fort Walton was a Mississippian culture," a claim bolstered by salvage excavations by Calvin Jones at Lake Jackson in the mid-1970s. There, high-status Mississippian burials with classic SECC artifacts (such as engraved copper plates) were uncovered, placing Lake Jackson on a par with Cahokia, Moundville, and Etowah in the Mississippian pantheon (Jones 1982, 1994; Marrinan, chapter 9, this volume; Payne 1994).

But Milanich (1994: 387) altered his stance on Safety Harbor in light of new data, stating that "the Safety Harbor culture . . . like Pensacola [culture of the western panhandle], apparently was influenced by Fort Walton developments in the eastern panhandle but was not a true Mississippian culture" (see Harris, chapter 11, and Mitchem, chapter 8, this volume). In some ways, Safety Harbor seemed like a continuation of the distinctive Fort Walton culture evolving in situ farther south, with some other distinguishing ceramic characteristics such as more bottles and beakers, for example. This Gulf coast culture, however, lacked a key Mississippian characteristic: an agriculture-based economy. Besides Safety Harbor, the St. Johns II culture of northeastern Florida has been touted as influenced to some degree by Mississippian culture, particularly three large mound sites—Mt. Royal, Grant, and Shields—known to contain exotic stone and copper artifacts (Milanich 1994: 247, 268–70). Bense (1994: 205) went further and used these same data to label St. Johns II an "early Mississippian culture."

It is worth noting that over the past half century, terms such as *Mississippian influence, Mississippian-related,* and other like qualifiers have been commonly used to refer to Florida cultures such as St. Johns, Pensacola, and Safety Harbor. These terms usually indicate nothing more than the manifestation of some Mississippian characteristic and imply a degree of interaction with the interior Southeast. In certain instances, however, the reference is more specific and highlights burials that contain artifacts or exotica derived from the Mississippian world to suggest some form of localized (and diluted) religious expression (i.e., SECC) or prestige-goods economy gained through involvement in Mississippian exchange networks.

At this point, we are compelled to make an important distinction in nomenclature, one recently awakened by Kidder (2007: 196–97). The terms *Mississippi period* and *Mississippian* are not synonymous. The former is a specific unit of time, whereas the latter identifies a particular way of life or cultural pattern. We use the term *Mississippi period* to remove the connotation of Mississippian and denote the era from about A.D. 1000 to 1600, a time in which not all natives of the Southeast fit the conventional definition of Mississippian. Among researchers, the terminal date for the Mississippi period tends to vary along a sliding temporal scale, from A.D. 1450 to 1700. Some bring the era to an abrupt halt with the De Soto *entrada* through the Southeast, beginning in 1539. We have chosen A.D. 1600 as the ending date, thus providing authors the opportunity to incorporate documentary and archaeological information from the early years of European contact.

Native societies that flourished during the Mississippi period are among the most intensely studied by southeastern archaeologists, and a good portion of the twentieth century was spent haggling over the concept of Mississippian. (In earlier archaeological systematics, the time interval that would effectively become the Mississippi period was known as Temple Mound I and II, thus invoking an immediate bias against Florida, where temple mounds were known only for Fort Walton, Pensacola, and Safety Harbor cultures.) The history of this discourse followed the general trends of Americanist archaeology. Early arguments focused on developing trait lists for Mississippian societies, whereas later emphasis was placed on the evolutionary and adaptive qualities of Mississippian chiefdoms (e.g., Deuel 1935; Ford and Willey 1941; James Griffin 1967, 1985; Peebles and Kus 1977; Phillips et al. 1951; Smith 1978).

Recent research has begun to emphasize the historical trajectories of individual chiefdoms and other communities throughout the Southeast, exposing considerable variability beneath the veneer of Mississippian uniformity (e.g., Blitz 1993a, 2010; Blitz and Lorenz 2006; Cobb 2000, 2003; Cobb and Garrow 1996; King 2003; Knight and Steponaitis 1998; Lorenz

1996; Maxham 2000; Nassaney 1992; Pauketat 1994). Because of the diversity, some have gone so far as to suggest even discarding the concept of the "chiefdom" as too essentialist a notion to encompass this great variety of Mississippian political systems (e.g., Pauketat 2007). Nonetheless, we believe that the term, however flawed, serves a useful purpose as a convenient shorthand label for a "rough level" of political organization (Muller 1997: 41). Moreover, its use as a heuristic device fosters comparison and does not prevent the study of social process or cultural change (Zeitlin 1996: 65).

So then, what is Mississippian? Winnowing the morass of characteristics forwarded over the years, including shell-tempered pottery, maize farming, temple mounds, and wall-trench houses, reveals a few salient cultural features that stand out. Mississippian societies possessed an economy based on intensive maize agriculture, maintained institutional inequality and chiefdom-level political organization, and participated in long-distance interaction and exchange networks that involved the movement of exotic items of stone, shell, and copper, often embellished with recurrent motifs and religious iconography (see Blitz 2010; Cobb 2003; Griffin 1967, 1985; Smith 1986; Steponaitis 1986). But even these core features have been shown to vary among Mississippian groups in the wider Southeast. While these defining characteristics may have coalesced during the Mississippi period, their seeds germinated during earlier times in southeastern prehistory, and each followed its own developmental trajectory. Moreover, the timing, extent, and tempo of the "Mississippianization" process across the Southeast were uneven and affected by local cultures, histories, and environments (Blitz and Lorenz 2002: 120; Cobb and Garrow 1996: 21–22).

No doubt many Mississippian societies shared some general cultural features, organizational as well as material and ideological, as a result of contact and interaction. But the southeastern United States was far from being a socially and politically homogenous landscape during the six centuries prior to European arrival. This was a dynamic time marked by the rise and fall of chiefdoms and the movements of different peoples across the landscape. In addition, located along the periphery and established within the frontiers and backwaters of the Mississippian world were non-Mississippian hunter-gatherers, fishers and shellfish collectors, and gardeners (Jenkins and Krause 1986: 82–85, 2009; King and Meyers, eds. 2002; Muller 1995: 320; Stephenson et al. 1996). So if we are to achieve a more realistic and thorough understanding of the Mississippi-period Southeast, we must not only focus our attention on those varied groups that fall within the broadly accepted range of Mississippian but also showcase those who do not. In doing so, however, we must refrain from viewing societies as ahistorical and isolated entities, for throughout prehistory those societies were interconnected in webs of ever-changing interaction. As we begin to understand variation at the local level, we can ultimately strive to comprehend why both broad similarities and variations developed across the greater Southeast during the Mississippi period (Cobb 2003: 79; Blitz 2010: 25).

Florida Connections with the Mississippian World

The *Mississippian world*, as it has come to be known by archaeologists, typically encompasses a wide area extending from the Atlantic coast of Georgia and South Carolina westward to eastern Oklahoma and from the Gulf of Mexico north to central Illinois (figure 1.3). As drawn, it would include the Florida panhandle but omit the entire Florida peninsula. The Fort Walton culture (specifically, the Lake Jackson site, with its large platform mounds, chiefly burials, ritual accouterments, and dependence on maize farming) is often the lone Florida representative on many published maps of the Mississippian world (e.g., Barker 2002: 43; Cobb 2003: 64; Payne and Scarry 1998: 23).

We should point out that our use of the term *Mississippian world* is intended merely to reflect the wide geographical extent of Mississippian societies in eastern North America and does not carry the theoretical baggage that attends a world systems model. While Florida clearly holds a peripheral location in the Mississippian world, we should not presuppose that societies there were simple pawns under the political and economic control of more politically complex chiefdoms of the interior core. Assuming that peripheral groups always strive to be just like core groups also would be a mistake. Rather, we should expect the relationships between peripheries and cores to "vary under different structural conditions and historical contingencies" (Stein 2002: 906). Comprehension of the Mississippian world as an interconnected system ultimately will come about only through cumulative knowledge of the myriad relationships among societies both within and outside its edges (King and Meyers 2002: 115).

Southeastern archaeologists have long been aware of the presence of foreign artifacts and materials in late prehistoric Florida burial mounds, but these sites often serve as nothing more than a dot on some sort of

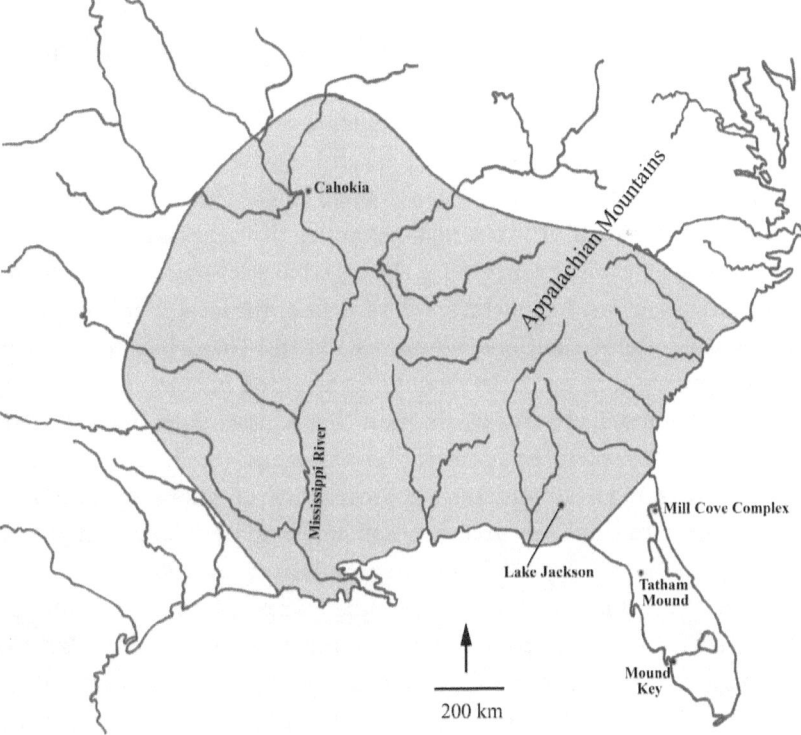

Figure 1.3. Florida and the Mississippian world (shaded).

artifact distribution map. And when lacking Mississippian trappings, Florida societies are rendered isolates. This perception is misguided, however, as ample evidence indicates that Florida natives actively communicated ideas and interacted with groups beyond their local catchment areas and social boundaries (Milanich 1994). But this does not mean that all Florida societies were engaged in sustained interaction with the Mississippian world. Visits to distant mound centers and direct involvement in exchange networks very well may have been sporadic and weakly structured for many Florida groups. Peoples of the southern peninsula may have found interaction with groups in the Caribbean (and beyond) more feasible (White 2005a), especially since water travel is usually easier than walking overland.

Indigenous Florida societies, as with all human cultures, were not closed systems sealed off from external contact, but rather open and dynamic social formations involved in an array of interactions that include intermarriage, emulation, trade, questing, gift giving, migration, alliance, warfare, and the diffusion of ideas and information (none of which are mutually exclusive). As such, they were open to the reception and transmission of cultural influences across social boundaries, although some appear to have been better able at times to resist the outside world. It is therefore a challenge for researchers to determine how and to what degree specific local events and developments were constrained or conditioned by processes operating at regional or macroregional scales (Kowalewski 1995). While maintaining an explicit concern for the external relations of Florida's late prehistoric societies, we must never lose sight of the local people and their history and cultural traditions. We must strive to "strike a balance between the recognition that no society can be understood in complete isolation from its neighbors and the assumption that contact with the outside is the main factor explaining a society's development" (Stein 1999: 4). What we are advocating is a multiscalar approach that permits a synchronized consideration of similarity and variation across space (Marquardt 1992a; Marquardt and Crumley 1987; Nassaney and Sassaman 1995).

It is in the realm of economic (and embedded political) interaction that Florida societies are most often linked to the interior Southeast. But the phenomena of long-distance contact and exchange were not exclusive to the Mississippi period. In midwestern and southeastern North America, including Florida, the far-flung movement of exotica appears to have been episodic, with three major periods of florescence: the Late Archaic, Middle Woodland, and Mississippi periods (Cobb 1991: 205–9; Johnson 1994: 100). From this, however, we should not infer that local societies lived completely insular lives during other periods of prehistory (Cobb and Nassaney 1995; Nassaney and Cobb 1991). Rather, these three intervals signify specific times of increased interregional contact and flow of unusual items outside their source areas.

The Mississippi period heralded the growth of wide-ranging spheres of social interaction that provided access to information and resources separated by tens, hundreds, and even thousands of kilometers (e.g., Brown et al. 1990). Taken as a whole, the widespread distribution of exotic materials across the Mississippian Southeast highlights the existence of complex connections that linked much of eastern North America. This should not be surprising, because Indian-authored maps of the early historic period indicate that southeastern natives possessed subcontinent-wide geographic knowledge (Lafferty 1994: 179; Waselkov 1989). Long-distance exchange is generally assumed to have been accomplished primarily in a down-the-line manner through an intricate web of short and overlapping trading links, some well orchestrated, others loosely connected (Brown et al. 1990; King and Freer 1995: 270; Muller 1995, 1997).

While this kind of trade certainly took place, we should not disregard other forms of interaction and exchange. For example, questing or direct acquisition by Florida groups may have resulted in trips to the interior and returns home with foreign materials, or perhaps representatives of Mississippian communities may have made their way to Florida with the same intent. There were likely many mechanisms and contexts for extralocal exchange. In fact, according to early historic accounts, gift giving was essential to native diplomacy, and such reciprocal relationships played a vital role in exchange partnerships, alliance building, and chiefly negotiations (Hall 2009; Smith and Hally 1992). There is no reason not to think that such factors motivated giving and receiving during the Mississippi period.

Items of frequent acquisition included marine shell from the Atlantic and Gulf coasts, copper from the Appalachian Mountains and Great Lakes region, and various other minerals from localized sources scattered throughout eastern North America (Brown et al. 1990; Griffin 1967). There is little doubt that Florida natives were directly involved in the collection and export of much of the marine shell (e.g., whelk, marginella, olive) that ended up in settlements throughout the greater Southeast, as discussed in several chapters in this volume. Whelks, for example, were popular because their large size and thick shell made them a suitable material for artistic expression and fine craftwork.

Florida societies of the Mississippi period were not the first to engage in shell trade. Abundant evidence indicates that their Woodland-period ancestors were heavily involved in exchange systems that sent whelk shells away from the coast to points as far north as Ohio and Michigan during Hopewell times (Brose and Greber 1979; Caldwell and Hall 1964). Indeed, Florida natives appear to have benefited for a long time from the demand for marine shells by groups living in the landlocked interior of southeastern and midwestern North America (e.g., Brown et al. 1990; Claassen and Sigmann 1993; Mitchem 1996b; Muller 1987, 1997; Phillips and Brown 1978: 206–8). As Mitchem (chapter 8, this volume) advises, sourcing studies of marine shell are needed to reconstruct specific points of origin and routes of exchange that covered broad areas.

With respect to Mississippi-period shell artifacts, a potential trend is emerging. Engraved gorgets, masks, and drinking cups, which would have required whole shells or very large sections of the outer whorl, are not as frequent in early Mississippian mounds as they are in mounds that postdate A.D. 1250. Moreover, these exalted and symbolically charged items appear to have been made from sinistral lightning whelks (*Busycon sinistrum*), a species with greater frequency (and larger size) along the Gulf coast (Abbott 1974; Hale 1976; Kozuch 1998: 3; Milanich 1979: 85–86). Kozuch (1998) argues that because most gastropods are right-handed (dextral, or spiraling in a clockwise direction), left-handed (sinistral, or counterclockwise spiral) whelks may have been targeted for their peculiarity. Moreover, she suggests that value or symbolism may have been tied to the direction of their spiral (Milanich 1979: 95). The knobbed whelk (*Busycon carica*), a stout dextral species, is abundant along the Florida Atlantic coast (Abbott 1974; Hale 1976: 68). While knobbed whelk would have been suitable for beads, it may not have possessed requisite features for cup and gorget manufacture. Thus, the Gulf waters of Florida might have become the preferred source location for whelks during middle and late Mississippian times. The greater demand for lightning whelks after A.D. 1250, combined with the eventual decline of Macon Plateau (and even Cahokia), might have negatively impacted the role of Atlantic coast St. Johns II communities as shell suppliers and dampened their involvement in Mississippian exchange (Ashley, chapter 5, this volume).

It is important to keep in mind, however, that simply because some Florida societies, such as in the Alachua and Suwannee Valley of northern peninsular Florida or the Indian River region of Atlantic coastal central Florida, lacked the exotica of the Mississippian world does not mean they did not actively communicate ideas and move utilitarian goods or even people beyond their local environments and territorial boundaries, as was the case in the Southeast during the Late Woodland period (Cobb and Nassaney 1995; Nassaney and Cobb 1991). In addition, a dearth of material evidence for contact and exchange does not automatically translate to isolationism, because such evidence may be relatively invisible owing either to the nature of interaction or to preservation biases (Brown et al. 1990: 252).

Florida Farmers

Maize agriculture, for many, has been the litmus test to qualify as Mississippian. In fact, a lack of dependence on maize farming appears to be the common denominator when one looks at the lot of archaeological cultures relegated to the status of non-Mississippian. The archaeological literature is relatively mute with regard to Mississippi-period foragers who may have lived in the recesses of the interior Southeast, so precisely how much smaller-scale gardening or plant encouragement, if any, was practiced by these groups remains unclear. There tends to be more mention of foragers along the coast, most notably the Guale of the Georgia Bight, who apparently added small-scale crop production (swidden gardening) to their fishing-hunting-gathering way of life less than a century prior to European arrival (Crook 1986; Reitz 1988; Thomas 2008). But farming, even in the Mississippian heartland, was always supplemented with collection and exploitation of many wild animals and plants.

Florida archaeologists have been plagued by dissatisfaction when it comes to precolumbian agriculture, best expressed by paraphrasing a catchphrase of the 1980s: "Where's the corn?" While details are typically lacking, textual references to corn farming among the Apalachee and Timucua of northern Florida are scattered throughout sixteenth-century Spanish and French documents (Hann 1996; Milanich 1996; Worth 1998a). The impression given by these direct accounts is that the Indians of panhandle Florida practiced rain-fed agriculture involving large cleared fields, whereas the Timucua of the north, north-central, and northeastern parts of the peninsula cultivated small plots or gardens that included maize. According to the earliest Mission-period documents of the late sixteenth century, the Atlantic coastal Timucua and Guale (Georgia) routinely produced enough surpluses to construct and use public granaries (Worth 1999: 3).

Preserved maize has been recovered from precontact Fort Walton sites in the Tallahassee Red Hills and Apalachicola River valley as well as from numerous seventeenth-century Mission-period sites throughout the central and northern parts of the state. But outside the eastern panhandle, direct evidence of maize is minimal, and the dearth of evidence for precolumbian agriculture in Florida remains perplexing in light of documentary evidence (Milanich 1994: 415). Even a high-profile site such as Mt. Royal, along the middle St. Johns River, which evinces clear connections to the Mississippian world during the period A.D. 1000–1300, has yet to yield evidence of precolumbian corn, although seventeenth-century Mission-period contexts at the site have produced charred corncobs and kernels (Ashley 2005a; Jones and Tesar 2001). The absence of corn agriculture is the number-one reason Florida cultures such as St. Johns, Safety Harbor, and Pensacola are typically ignored or at least downplayed in popular Mississippian summaries.

In terms of macrobotanical remains (cobs and/or kernels), the only incontrovertible proof for the presence of precolumbian corn in peninsular Florida comes from four sites at the mouth of the St. Johns River in northeastern Florida (Ashley 2009) and one site in north-central Florida (Rolland, chapter 6, this volume). Surprisingly, no other sites to date have yielded preserved corn in unequivocal precontact contexts. A possible exception is the Fig Springs site, a late precolumbian and Mission-period village in Columbia County (Weisman 1992; Worth, chapter 7, this volume). There, a charred cob was directly dated to the late sixteenth/early seventeenth century. In the northern part of the site, another feature with corn was radiocarbon-dated to the eleventh century. However, this assay was on charred hickory hull fragments, not corn. In addition, chinaberry seeds—a plant introduced to the region in the nineteenth century—were present in the feature, indicating postdepositional mixing.

Recent archaeological research in northeastern Florida may shed some light on the corn dilemma. There, corn has been recovered from precontact and Mission-period contexts, and radiocarbon dates (at the two sigma level) suggest maize was incorporated into the coastal Timucua subsistence economy no earlier than A.D. 1450 (Ashley 2009). The first appearance of preserved corn on archaeological sites in northeastern Florida is coincident with the emergence of San Pedro pottery, which includes a cob-marked type similar to Alachua Cob Marked of north-central Florida. This evidence suggests a much later date for the introduction of maize cultivation into the subsistence mix of the coastal Timucua than previously thought. On the Georgia coast, David Thomas's recent work, including AMS dates and isotope analysis, "point to very late maize; no more than a century prior to European contact" (Thomas, personal communication 2009).

Similarities in stylistic trends between San Pedro and Alachua pottery suggest that the late date (post–A.D. 1450) for the entry of maize in northeastern Florida might also apply to inland Timucua groups such as the Potano (see Rolland, chapter 6, this volume). In fact, in northern peninsular Florida the only radiometric assay on corn comes from a feature at the Ardisia site (8Mr2722) dated to A.D. 1430–1640; three additional radiocarbon dates on charcoal samples from contexts containing cob-marked pottery corroborate this late date (Wayne and Dickinson 2002; Rolland, chapter 6, this volume). Moreover, available carbon and nitrogen isotope ratios on human bone from a variety of sites suggest that C^4 plants such as corn were a minor constituent of native diets in peninsular Florida prior to Spanish mission times (Hutchinson et al. 1998, 2000; Larsen et al. 2001).

This also may be the case for coastal Fort Walton in the panhandle, where shell middens so far have turned up no evidence for agriculture, only reliance upon the same abundant aquatic resources that had provided a dependable living since at least Middle Archaic times (see White et al., chapter 10, this volume).

Most rivers in Florida are spring-fed, with little organic sediment. The absence of extensive floodplains annually replenished with fertile alluvium may explain the delayed spread of corn cultivation into the peninsula. Moreover, corn agriculture may have differed in Florida from that practiced in the interior Southeast. Corn very well may have been grown in small gardens, contributing little to the diet until the mid-fifteenth century or so, at which time its importance increased. The cultivation strategy of inland and coastal Timucua at the time of European contact was likely quite flexible and included a mix of farming and foraging that probably varied annually (and spatially) depending on environmental and social circumstances. The potential late date for the introduction of corn into peninsular Florida, combined with the lack of testing at contact-period villages, might account for its scarcity in the archaeological record there.

Broadly speaking, a mixed subsistence economy based primarily on hunting-fishing-gathering might characterize most Florida societies prior to the fifteenth century. Knowledge and use of the sea and inland waters were always crucial to Florida natives. Despite any environmental constraints, however, some Florida natives eventually turned to agriculture. With the adoption of maize farming and the rise in hereditary leaders controlling multiple communities, the contact-era Timucua clearly represent a regional variant of agricultural Mississippian chiefdoms (Worth 1998a and chapter 7, this volume). The reasons for and the cultural and political ramifications of the shift to agriculture at this late date provide fertile grounds for research with implications for Mississippian archaeology.

Florida Chiefdoms

By and large, archaeologists agree that the term *Mississippian* refers to ranked and hierarchically organized societies with institutionalized inequality and marked status distinction, time and again classified as chiefdoms (Cobb 2003; Smith 1986; Steponaitis 1986). Mississippian chiefdoms are often modeled to include a size ranking of different kinds of sites, ranging from paramount "towns" with massive and numerous earthworks and populations estimated to have been in the thousands, to midsized subsidiary mound centers, to small, numerous and dispersed rural farmsteads. Mound centers contained one or more platform mounds and other corporately constructed earthworks arranged around one or more large plazas (e.g., Lewis and Stout 1998; Smith 1978, 1986; Steponaitis 1986). Many towns were fortified with defensive walls to protect against raids launched for control over productive farmland (alluvial floodplains), revenge, or prestige building (DePratter 1991).

Most late prehistoric Florida settlements depart from this general image. There is currently no conclusive evidence in Florida for precontact villages guarded by palisades within either the archaeological or the documentary record. This is somewhat surprising given the raid-prone Florida landscape described in sixteenth-century Spanish and French accounts. Platform mounds, as used in the Mississippian world, do not seem to have figured prominently in Florida villages outside the Fort Walton and Pensacola communities of the panhandle (Harris, chapter 11, Marrinan, chapter 9, and White et al., chapter 10, this volume). What appear to be platform mounds and plazas occur at a few of the more nucleated Safety Harbor villages in the Tampa Bay area, but their function(s) is still unclear (Mitchem, chapter 8, this volume). The Early Mississippi–period Shields Mound in northeastern Florida seems to have had a flat summit, but there is currently no evidence to suggest it served as a platform for any structure; it was a mounded communal cemetery (Ashley, chapter 5, this volume). In southwest Florida, elevated midden-mounds were constructed, but to house domiciles and other buildings and keep them elevated above surging waters (Marquardt and Walker, chapter 2, this volume). A similar situation may have taken place in areas of southeastern and east-central Florida prior to or shortly after contact (Carr, chapter 3, and Penders, chapter 4, this volume).

According to documentary sources, by the late sixteenth century, societies throughout Florida exhibited "different levels of chiefly political complexity and practiced an array of economic strategies" (Milanich 1998: 245). Prehistoric Fort Walton groups and one of their contact-era counterparts (Apalachee) clearly maintained a chiefdom structure (Payne 1994; Payne and Scarry 1998; Scarry 1996), although details regarding many aspects of its political operation are still matters of discussion. The Calusa are no strangers to Mississippian studies, in which they are commonly presented as a foil to the archetypical Mississippian society—that is, a chiefdom-level society without agriculture. Living amid the spectacular richness of the estuaries of southwest Florida, which are among the state's most productive natural ecosystems, the historic Calusa maintained a tribute-based complex chiefdom and subsistence economy fueled by the harvesting of fish, shellfish, and other wildlife that inhabited or frequented the shallow, inshore coastal waters (Marquardt 1987a, 2001; Marquardt and Walker, chapter 2, this volume; Widmer 1988). But outside these groups and excluding studies predicated on historic documents, the political organization of Mississippi-period societies in Florida has been an underpursued topic of inquiry, and most interpretations derive from severely limited data.

The various contact-period Timucua of northern peninsular Florida, from the Suwannee River east to the Atlantic coast, present an interesting case, which may have an important bearing on Mississippi-period research. On the basis of ethnohistoric information, Timucua polities are modeled as simple chiefdoms, each consisting of a small cluster of villages (approximately 5–10), with a centralized political administration that included noble lineages and inherited positions of authority (Hann 1996: 73–84; Milanich 1996: 156–60; Worth 1998a: 86–92). Given the documented coupling of hereditary leadership and centralized decision making above the individual village level, one would be hard pressed to argue that sixteenth-century Timucuan societies did not "fall within the anthropological definition of chiefdoms" (Worth 1998a: 13). From an archaeological perspective, however, none of the Mississippi-period groups occupying the vast Timucua-speaking region appears to possess the settlement hierarchies, population levels, or material trappings characteristic of mainstream Mississippian societies in the interior Southeast. As Milanich (1998: 248) is quick to point out, "Were it not for the documentary record, we might not ever recognize that the Timucua were organized as simple chiefdoms" (see Worth, chapter 7, this volume).

For the Timucua, there was no formal political organization above the local multicommunity level, although one or more simple chiefdoms may have united to form regional alliances that at a glance resembled a complex chiefdom (Milanich 1998; Worth 1998a). Milanich (1998) believes that these alliances were ephemeral, military in nature, and misinterpreted by early French and Spanish explorers as a formalized and complex sociopolitical organization. The volatile Timucuan landscape, which in the sixteenth century included the European presence, may have caused simple chiefdoms to ally themselves and "act complex" when the need arose in order to thwart military aggression posed by other allied groups, complex chiefdoms, or European forces (Milanich 1998: 248–49). The apparent ability of sixteenth-century Timucuan polities to range from simple to short-term complex chiefdoms suggests that political systems were quite fluid, making it difficult to generalize polities as chiefdoms or not chiefdoms over the broad temporal range of the Mississippi period.

Unfortunately, little significant research has been aimed at examining how specific late prehistoric political systems in Florida formed, operated, and changed during the five centuries prior to European contact. When chiefly organization first emerged in each area of the state is still open to debate, and researchers have not yet determined how far back into the Mississippi period we can extend the social and political order seen in accounts penned by European explorers and missionaries. How much of what was documented was a postcontact phenomenon, a direct response to the European presence, is still not known. A typological debate over whether Florida societies were chiefdoms or not is not what is needed. We should start by asking, how were Mississippi-period societies complex and how did they get that way? We need to turn to the archaeological record and address political-economic questions through sound empirical evidence, multiple scales of analysis, and appropriate theories.

Shell-Tempered Pottery

An oft-cited characteristic of Mississippian societies is the production of shell-tempered pottery. However, little or no shell-tempered pottery occurs in Mississippi-period Florida except in the western part of the panhandle, within the Pensacola culture, located at a juncture with the rest of the Mississippian world (see Harris, chapter 11, this volume). The decided lack of shell-tempered pottery in Florida became enormously important to archaeologists quite early, especially in defining Fort Walton. There has been a recent flurry of activity in studying shell tempering in the eastern United States, including functional and historical explanations of its origin and use, technological and firing experiments, exploration of its origins, and documentation of its existence far earlier than the Mississippi period in a few regions (e.g., Feathers 2006; Feathers and Peacock 2008; Sabo and Hilliard 2008). Crushed shell appears in some Amazonian ceramics thousands of years earlier than in the eastern United States (Roosevelt 1995), and despite all the studies, it is anyone's guess how individual tempering agents were chosen in different times and places. Also, despite the intensive work, many other questions remain about shell-tempered ceramics. For example, why, of two sherds in the same context, does one have the shell leached away (leaving slit-shaped voids) and the other does not? Why do some have coarsely crushed shell and others, finely crushed? How are choices made between freshwater, marine, and fossil shell, and how can these be distinguished during laboratory sorting?

Now there is good documentation of other regions in the Southeast outside Florida where shell-tempered ceramics are not common during the Mississippi period, such as some Lamar areas (Williams and Shapiro 1990). Many researchers think temper is not important and potters used just what was lying around or easiest to get. Others embed the whole process of materials procurement and ceramic manufacture within deep, even sacred meaning, practice, and ethnic or other identification. We are still grappling with some basic questions, such as why a particular aplastic or tempering agent was used at any given time, let alone used in certain proportions in a pot or an assemblage. However, it is abundantly clear that potters of Mississippi-period Florida, by not using much or any shell, are doing something fundamentally different from most of the Mississippian world that surrounds them. They certainly had no lack of shell to use. Perhaps avoiding shell temper was a deliberate means of manifesting identity.

Volume Overview

This volume is the first statewide synthesis devoted exclusively to the Mississippi-period archaeology of Florida. Despite the burgeoning number of Mississippian studies over the past few decades, outside the Fort Walton culture area, the Mississippi period has never been a major research topic in Florida. Although Florida archaeologists have at times explored site-specific or local adaptations, reconstructed local events, and worked toward developing local ceramic chronologies that cover the five or so centuries prior to European arrival, little effort has been spent trying to bring it all together at the regional level and assess the development of Florida cultures in relation to their Mississippian neighbors. To address this lacuna, we organized a symposium entitled "A New Look at the Mississippi Period in Florida" for the sixty-third annual Southeastern Archaeological Conference. Expanded versions of all symposium papers are included in this volume, as is an additional paper on southeastern Florida.

The following chapters provide the most up-to-date information on the Florida Mississippi period, spotlighting a mosaic of cultures. A concerted effort was placed on reconstructing late prehistoric Florida from real archaeological data. Many of the volume's authors revisited original field notes and maps, site forms, and other primary sources, which often meant crawling around dusty shelves and boxes. In some cases, artifact collections were reexamined to address various stylistic, technological, or taxonomic issues. We believe a necessary first step is to come to grips with what archaeological information on the Mississippi period is actually available throughout Florida. We must assemble the array of pertinent archaeological evidence to build a solid empirical foundation that we can then draw upon to answer more complex, theoretically charged questions such as those of an ideological nature.

At present, many areas of Florida severely lack fine-scale data relating to the Mississippi period. Without relevant data, we believe interpretations can become contrived. Consequently, the majority of chapters lack extensive theorizing. For the most part, the general theoretical perspective employed in this volume, implicit if not directly stated, emphasizes a centralist position—combining interpretations based on empirical data in scientific fashion with more humanistic ideas to produce workable, imaginative models that nonetheless do not stray too far from the real evidence. Authors focus on a variety of issues but pay particular attention to infrastructural aspects of late prehistoric Florida societies such as subsistence economy and the timing and extent (if any) of maize-based farming; regional settlement structure as it relates to social and political organization; ceramics as chronological markers and potential means of identity; human-environment relationships; and exchange and possible involvement in broader networks of interaction, particularly those reaching beyond Florida. Such information is vital to regional comparative synthesis and interpretation.

A focus on regional coverage allows for comparison of broad patterns of similarity and diversity within Mississippi-period Florida and beyond. Though the artificial constructs of archaeological cultures and the multitude of local archaeological names used over the years have traditionally spotlighted mostly ceramic characterizations, the volume's authors are now able to add a great deal more information. Each of the main cultural regions in Florida is covered to some degree, although the societies highlighted may not reflect the entire region in time and space. For example, the St. Johns region is represented by groups living at the seaward end of the river, and the focus is on the Early Mississippi period. At present, archaeological knowledge of the Mississippi period is uneven across the state. We also must remember that Florida cultures were not static prior to the invasion from Europe; all were altered by time. Those living in Florida in A.D. 1000 differed from those of A.D. 1500, who themselves changed in the aftermath of European arrival. The chapters in this volume are arranged geographically, beginning in the south, farthest from the Mississippian world. The volume concludes with a perspective on Florida from deep within the Mississippian world.

In chapter 2, William Marquardt and Karen Walker trace the Mississippi-period cultural trajectory of the Calusa of subtropical southwest Florida against an environmental backdrop bolstered by climate and sea-level data from the Florida Gulf coast and beyond. The richness of the paleoenvironmental information allows Marquardt and Walker to identify short-term meteorological fluctuations in the mostly favorable environmental conditions of the southwest Florida estuaries. They then turn to the available archaeological record to assess the impact of these environmental oscillations on the native population and explore how the Calusa reacted. While lacking true platform mounds, shell-tempered pottery, and corn farming, the Calusa had social complexity and a scale of construction projects in the form of midden-mounds and a sophisticated system of excavated canals that rivaled those of any Mississippian chiefdom, save for perhaps Cahokia. As Marquardt and Walker rightfully state, "Calusa society was far from a depauperate reflection of Mississippian social formations."

In chapter 3, Robert Carr continues the focus on south Florida by examining the Atlantic coast and the interior Lake Okeechobee–lower Kissimmee River regions. His brief description of the south Florida environment summons an interior landscape that was topographically low and perennially wet prior to the major water diversion and drainage efforts of the past few centuries. Carr outlines three culture areas—Glades, Belle Glade, and East Okeechobee—in terms of ceramics, mound centers, and settlement distributions. Each area was characterized by a fishing-hunting-gathering subsistence economy predicated specifically on estuarine (coast) and freshwater (interior) aquatic resources. A conspicuous feature of Carr's study is the ample evidence of large-scale construction projects in the form of mounds, earthworks, and shellworks. Massive amounts of wet soil were moved as lengthy canals were cut through the interior wetlands, eventually linking Lake Okeechobee with the Caloosahatchee River and the Gulf coast. Water travel was key to human movement throughout south Florida, and the canal system represents an impressive display of engineering knowledge. Carr posits that ditches and ponds were constructed in the interior as weirs and impoundment areas for fish, suggestive of early aquaculture.

Moving up the Atlantic coast to east-central Florida, Thomas Penders in chapter 4 directs his attention to the Malabar II culture of the Indian River Lagoon. In the archaeological literature, this coastal area is often overshadowed by the nearby St. Johns region, to the extent that, at times, it is subsumed within St. Johns as a border or transitional area. Following the lead of earlier separatists, beginning with Irving Rouse in the 1950s, Penders argues that, although the two regions shared in the production of chalky St. Johns pottery, Malabar and St. Johns are not the same culture. Clearly, Indian River natives were fishers and shellfish collectors for millennia prior to and for a century or more after European arrival. The most sweeping changes in Malabar II culture appear to have been the result of contact not with outsiders from the Mississippian world but rather with foreigners from another continent. The historic Ais of the Indian River Lagoon took advantage of their fortuitous location along Spanish shipping lanes to become master salvagers of Spanish booty, parlaying its acquisition into increased political power among south Florida natives.

Chapter 5, by Keith Ashley, moves the volume's focus to St. Johns II groups in the far northeastern corner of the state. Perhaps nowhere in Florida were connections to the Mississippian world stronger during the opening centuries of the Mississippi period than in the St. Johns River valley. Highlighted by spatulate celts, copper long-nosed maskettes, and variously shaped small copper plates, the spectacular Mississippi-period artifacts of the Grant and Shields mounds (Mill Cove Complex) were first brought to everyone's attention by C. B. Moore in the 1890s. This impressive list of mortuary items, combined with the fact that these St. Johns II communities were not Mississippian farmers, presents somewhat of a paradox and often leads to the question, Why would a bunch of fishers and shellfish collectors have rare pieces of foreign artifacts such as spatulate celts and long-nosed god earpieces? Eschewing a traditional prestige-goods economy interpretation that views the high-profile exotic items in mounds as instruments of power flaunted by elites, Ashley focuses more on the communal nature of ritual and mortuary ceremony and views burial mounds and grave goods as an expression of corporate identity.

In chapter 6, Vicki Rolland tackles the Alachua culture of north-central Florida, which emerged in Late Woodland times and persisted into the Spanish Mission period. At present, Alachua components lack clear archaeological evidence of both long-distance interaction and chiefly organization. While indirect evidence of maize horticulture is revealed on cob-marked pottery surfaces, sparse macrobotanical evidence in the form of preserved corn has been recovered from precolumbian contexts. Moreover, limited available stable isotope data on human bone suggest a predominantly hunting-gathering way of life. Rolland draws attention to the fact that we have yet to pinpoint conclusively when maize farming was incorporated into the Alachua subsistence base, but it appears to have been a rather late addition. In fact, maize apparently did not become a significant part of the Alachua diet until a century or two prior to European contact, a time that may also have witnessed the rise of chiefly leaders.

In a complementary study, John Worth in chapter 7 provides a stunning look at a cultural manifestation that gives every indication of a small-scale society with a simple, nonhierarchical political organization in the archaeological record but is known historically to have been a complex chiefly society. The Suwannee Valley culture is a relative newcomer to the pages of Florida archaeology in that it was first defined in the early 1990s. Though rooted in the Mississippi period, Worth's study effectively draws on primary Spanish accounts to expose sociopolitical complexities not apparent in the archaeological record. The discrepancy between the documentary and archaeological records leads one to wonder whether the dearth of typical Mississippian material correlates is a result of a chiefly form of organization that emerged very late in precolumbian times, leaving little hard evidence, or was something qualitatively different. While present archaeological data are limited and hinder a solid interpretation of Mississippi-period political organization, Worth is optimistic and believes the rich documentary record combined with systematic archaeological research will allow archaeologists to explore the Suwannee Valley culture in greater detail.

Jeffrey Mitchem, in chapter 8, examines the Safety Harbor culture along the central peninsular Gulf coast. It developed in situ out of the local Manasota culture, a regional variant of Weeden Island, similar to the development of Suwannee Valley, Fort Walton, and some other Florida Mississippi-period cultures out of their local Woodland roots. Safety Harbor features platform mounds and plazas in nucleated settlements around Tampa Bay but more dispersed habitation to the north and south, with burial mounds farther from domestic areas. Ceramics include classic Mississippian jar and bottle forms but not enough similarities to indicate sustained interaction with the wider Mississippian world. There was no shift inland to grow maize, only continuity of coastal lifeways. Mitchem believes that whatever attenuated Mississippian influence is present, it is related to economic interaction: movement far into the continental interior of highly valued marine whelk shells in exchange for the ground stone, copper, and other nonlocal objects found at a few Safety Harbor sites. While perhaps not Mississippian in the strictest sense, Safety Harbor people were organized into chiefdoms in the Tampa Bay area when the Spanish first recorded them.

The Fort Walton culture of northwest Florida has clear Mississippian credentials, but understanding it is fraught with difficulty. In chapter 9, Rochelle Marrinan critiques questionable Fort Walton models, arguing that most are based upon meager data and have become very derived. She questions whether the Lake Jackson site was a paramount chiefdom on a par with Etowah and Moundville merely because it produced SECC artifacts. In the rolling Tallahassee Hills between the Aucilla and Ocklockonee rivers, Fort Walton settlement aligns with the multitude of lakes, in the absence of large alluvial streams, but soils were still good for agriculture. Platform mound–village complexes, abundant exotic artifacts, and ceramics in Mississippian forms (but not shell-tempered) indicate typical Mississippian political systems. Engraved copper plates at Lake Jackson with female burials even suggest the possibility of women chiefs in these likely matrilineal societies. Marrinan shows gaps in the field data for many sites and questions the continuity between prehistoric Tallahassee Fort Walton and the historic Apalachee encountered so early and changed so quickly by the Spanish. She further believes that Leon-Jefferson is a postcontact phenomenon, possibly a result of processes at work in the sixteenth century after Narváez and De Soto arrived.

In chapter 10, Nancy White, Jeffrey Du Vernay, and Amber Yuellig present Fort Walton in the Apalachicola–lower Chattahoochee Valley. They too question models emphasizing power, agency, and migration—speculations requiring empirical evidence. They describe mound sites, evidence for maize farming (but continuing foraging lifeways on the coast), and Fort Walton emergence from local Woodland foundations. New investigations at the Yon, Pierce, and Curlee sites provide details of ceramic chronology. The distinctive six-pointed open bowl, near-absence of shell temper, and unusual lack of chipped stone in Apalachicola Fort Walton may all mean maintenance of a specific identity within the greater Mississippian world. A few protohistoric dates suggest that Fort Walton peoples of unknown ethnicity retained their culture as something else moved in. No Spanish were in the region until the late Mission period, but their germs and a very small number of their artifacts did arrive. Rapid depopulation in the sixteenth century apparently left much of the valley empty. Lamar ceramics, now dated to around 1700, may represent Proto-Creeks moving downriver into the empty land. Remnant Fort Walton peoples may have already been gone when they arrived.

In the far western panhandle, Pensacola is the only Mississippi-period culture in Florida with traditional shell-tempered pottery—understandable given its location. In chapter 11, Norma Harris describes the Pensacola region and addresses the mixture of Fort Walton and Pensacola ceramics from the Apalachicola River westward. She reviews sites in the major estuaries: St. Andrew, Choctawhatchee, and Pensacola bays. There is some evidence for maize, most of which appears to be protohistoric, but the major adaptation is to coastal aquatic resources. Harris thinks the interior was abandoned during the Mississippi period, possibly because of infertile soils and increased communication along coastal waterways. A few mounds and many rich habitation and cemetery sites on the coast have high-profile goods such as copper, shell beads, and pottery with Mississippian iconography; some have European items. Harris points out the absence of ethnohistorical records. Research in this region could expand our knowledge of both prehistoric and protohistoric societies.

In chapter 12, John Kelly examines our work from the perspective of a Mississippian insider and a researcher uninfluenced by all the biases of Florida archaeology. It is from the stage of Cahokia that Kelly views Florida and the broader Southeast. Cahokia, in western Illinois, was the largest Native American mound complex north of present-day Mexico, reaching its zenith between ca. A.D. 1050 and 1200. It maintained a central precinct of some five square miles with more than a hundred earthen mounds rising above the artificially altered urban landscape (Milner 1990, 1996; Pauketat 1994). Away from the town center were farmsteads positioned along the fertile alluvial soils of the Mississippi River and its tributaries. While controversy reigns over the precise political structure of Cahokia and how chiefs there came to and wielded power, there is no doubting its size and scale of influence during the Early Mississippi period (see Milner 1996 and Pauketat 1994 for contrasting views). Aboriginal peoples of Florida must have been aware of Cahokia.

Kelly begins with a short primer on the concept of Mississippian, then delves into a discussion on what he sees as a Mississippian horizon, which he further subdivides into Formative or pre-Mississippian (A.D. 900–1050), Pre-Classic Mississippian (A.D. 1050–1200), Classic Mississippian (A.D. 1200–1400), and Post-Classic Mississippian (A.D. 1400–1539+). Focusing on the spatial and temporal aspects of these constructs, he explores a series of material trends and their behavioral implications. He touches on the Florida cultures most involved in interactions with (and directly influenced by) Mississippian societies. He speculates that the creation of social ties, perhaps through clan organization, structured the movement of materials and ideas across the Southeast and Midwest. Like others in this volume, Kelly views the availability of marine shell and the desire on the part of many Mississippians to acquire it as the primary conditions drawing Florida societies into interactions over broad distances during the Mississippi period.

The chapters in this book present significant new syntheses on the Mississippi period throughout Florida, altering some long-standing perspectives. But our collective effort is more an introduction on the subject than the final word, for we have only begun to scratch the surface. This volume issues challenges and clarion calls for systematic survey, excavation, and new research and perspectives on Mississippi-period Florida. The peoples represented were the first in the Southeast (and the entire United States) to see, react to, and be devastated by invading Europeans. It is imperative that we try to understand how they once were, so that we can then explain how they changed and all disappeared.

2

Southwest Florida during the Mississippi Period

WILLIAM H. MARQUARDT AND KAREN J. WALKER

This book focuses on the Mississippi period, ca. A.D. 1000 to 1500. In the archaeology of the southeastern United States, "Mississippian" generally means chiefdom-level societies that "practiced a maize-based agriculture, constructed (generally) platform mounds for elite residences and various corporate and public functions, and shared, to a considerable extent, a common suite of artifact types and styles, particularly in the realm of pottery (usually shell-tempered) and certain symbolic or prestige related artifacts" (Welch and Butler 2006: 2). Often implicit is an assumption that Mississippian chiefdoms represent the most complex cultural developments in the aboriginal southeastern United States.

In southwest Florida, their contemporaries had no maize agriculture, constructed no platform mounds, and made a rather undistinguished pottery. Even so, Spaniards who encountered the historic Calusa in the sixteenth century observed a stratified society divided into nobles and commoners, with hereditary leadership, tributary patronage-clientage that extended throughout south Florida, ritual and military specialists, far-ranging trade, an accomplished and expressive artistic tradition, complex religious beliefs and ritual practices, and effective subsistence practices that supported thousands of people and allowed a sedentary residence pattern (Fontaneda 1973; Hann 1991; Solís de Merás 1964). Furthermore, for nearly two centuries after contact, the Calusa maintained their identity and beliefs, effectively repulsing European attempts to conquer and convert them to Christianity, while many southeastern United States chiefdoms were in cultural ruin within a few decades (Hann 1991).

The Calusa heartland was in the coastal region encompassing Charlotte Harbor, Pine Island Sound, San Carlos Bay, and Estero Bay (figure 2.1). This

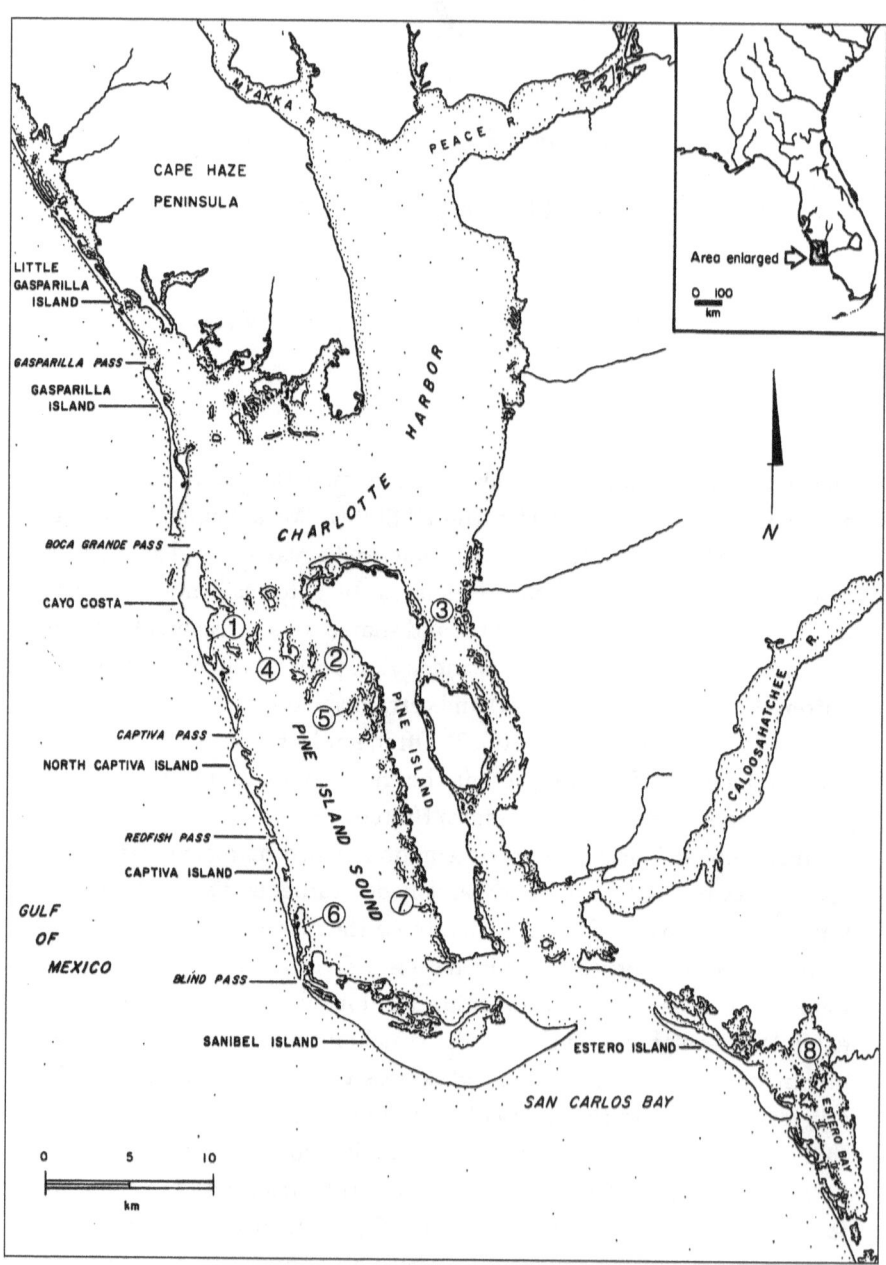

Figure 2.1. The Charlotte Harbor–Pine Island Sound–San Carlos Bay estuarine system. Numbers indicate sites discussed in text: (1) Mark Pardo; (2) Pineland Site Complex; (3) Indian Field; (4) Useppa Island; (5) Josslyn Island; (6) Buck Key; (7) Galt Island; (8) Mound Key. Drawing by William Marquardt.

estuarine region is fed by fresh water from the Myakka, Peace, and Caloosahatchee rivers and from lesser streams in the Estero Bay area. Centrally located within this complex estuarine system is Pine Island Sound, a broad, flat, shallow, grassy inshore body of water fringed by mangroves and protected by barrier islands. Because the large, linear landform of Pine Island acts as a barrier to freshwater streams emptying into Pine Island Sound, the latter's waters are more marine than are the estuaries of Charlotte Harbor and San Carlos Bay. The region is subtropical, characterized by warm winters, in contrast to the temperate greater southeastern United States. For this reason, here marine/estuarine fish and shellfish are available year-round and, at least in protohistoric and historic times, in great quantities. We now know that this productivity fluctuated through the past several millennia but was generally high during the tenth through sixteenth centuries, surely a factor underlying the emergence of the Calusa as a complex society.

In this chapter, we focus on southwest Florida and first sketch the environmental background against which cultural changes took place during the Mississippi period. We then discuss environmental and cultural changes during that period. Finally, because interregional connections, large-scale communal construction projects, and hierarchical social structure are all generally associated with Mississippian chiefdoms, we examine these topics in terms of southwest Florida and consider the evidence for influence on the area by Mississippian peoples.

Environmental Change in the Caloosahatchee Region during the Mississippi Period

To date, there is still an absence of highly resolved climate records from Florida. However, this void is no longer a barrier to our considering the role of climate in the state's cultural trajectory, even for the recent two millennia. This is because the many new climate studies of the past 20 years, concerning both modern and past climates, indicate that broad-scale regions are characterized by widespread atmospheric-oceanic teleconnections. Paleoclimatic records from within these regions indicate that change can occur relatively rapidly and synchronously in both low and high latitudes. The collective result of all this new research has been recognized as a paradigm shift in the field of paleoclimatology (NRC 2002: 1), characterized by the acceptance that climate can and does change rapidly and that it has done so at scales relevant to past ecosystems and human societies,

Time	Greater North Atlantic Climate	Southwest Florida Sea Level	Southwest Florida Chronology	Glades Area Chronology	Greater SE United States Chronology
AD 1800-1850			Creek/Seminole/ Miccosukee	Creek/Seminole/ Miccosukee	
AD 1750-1800					
AD 1700-1750					
AD 1650-1700			Caloosahatchee V AD 1500-1750	Glades IIIc AD 1600-1750	Protohistoric/Historic
AD 1600-1650					
AD 1550-1600	Little Ice Age AD 1200-1850	Sanibel II Low ca. AD 1200-1850			
AD 1500-1550				Glades IIIb AD 1400-1600	
AD 1450-1500					Late Mississippian AD 1400-1500
AD 1400-1450			Caloosahatchee IV AD 1350-1500		
AD 1350-1400					
AD 1300-1350			Caloosahatchee III AD 1200-1350	Glades IIIa AD 1200-1400	Middle Mississippian AD 1200-1400
AD 1250-1300					
AD 1200-1250					
AD 1150-1200				Glades IIc AD 1100-1200	Early Mississippian AD 1000-1200
AD 1100-1150					
AD 1050-1100	Medieval Warm Period ("Mississippian Optimum") AD 850-1200	La Costa High ca. AD 850-1200	Caloosahatchee IIB AD 800-1200		
AD 1000-1050				Glades IIb AD 900-1100	
AD 950-1000					
AD 900-950					
AD 850-900				Glades IIa AD 750-900	Late Woodland AD 500-1000
AD 800-850					
AD 750-800					
AD 700-850	Vandal Minimum ca. AD 500-850	Buck Key Low ca. AD 500-850	Caloosahatchee IIA-late AD 650-800		
AD 650-700				Glades I - late AD 500-750	
AD 600-650					
AD 550-600			Caloosahatchee IIA-early AD 500-650		
AD 500-550					
AD 450-500					
AD 400-450					
AD 350-400					
AD 300-350					
AD 250-300					
AD 200-250	Roman Warm Period ca. 350 BC-AD 500	Wulfert High ca. 100 BC-AD 500	Caloosahatchee I 500 BC-AD 500	Glades I - early AD 1-500	Middle Woodland 100 BC-AD 500
AD 150-200					
AD 100-150					
AD 50-100					
AD 1-50					
50 BC-AD 1					
100-50 BC				Pre-Glades	

Figure 2.2. Climatic fluctuations, sea-level episodes, and cultural chronologies for southwest Florida and the greater Southeast, ca. 100 B.C.–A.D. 1700.

sometimes as rapidly as within a decade. Additionally, in step with this research is the new recognition that sea level also can respond rapidly, within 50 years or less.

This research and its funding base continue to accelerate in part because of the National Research Council's (NRC 2002) call for a focus on "abrupt" climate change based on the recognition that sudden change increases the potential for societal and ecological impacts (see also Alley et al. 2003). So very relevant for Florida archaeology is the definition the NRC (2002: 14) provides of abrupt climate change from a societal and ecological view: "[A]n abrupt change is one that takes place so rapidly and unexpectedly that human *or* natural systems have difficulty adapting to it."

The greater North Atlantic atmospheric-oceanic region is the most relevant for thinking about the human-environment history of Florida and the greater southeastern United States. Whereas regional temperature patterns may be relatively synchronous, precipitation and storminess trends are much more geographically variable within the region. Drawing on an extensive literature review presented elsewhere (Walker 2012), we examine the A.D. 850–1500 portions of a group of records most relevant to southwest Florida and its archaeological periods, Caloosahatchee IIB, III, and IV. These periods correspond with the end of the greater Southeast's Late Woodland period and all of its Mississippi period, A.D. 1000–1500. We project our environmental context back to A.D. 850 (figure 2.2), a time prior to the beginning of the Mississippi period, because it is important for setting the stage for cultural change, and forward to 1850, the end of the Little Ice Age.

Several of the cited climate and sea-level records come from the subregion of the southwestern or tropical North Atlantic (Gulf of Mexico and Caribbean areas), areas closest to southwest Florida. Others are from more northern latitudes, illustrating the teleconnectivity of the greater North Atlantic region. The Florida Straits records (Lund and Curry 2004) offer the closest paleoclimate data, and the sea-level model of Stapor and colleagues (1991) is based on southwest Florida's beach ridges. For fluctuations in the records, the time spans and individual events are only approximations, as dates for the different records are expected to vary because of radiocarbon error ranges and variation in correction/calibration usage. The trends referred to below (warmer versus cooler, higher versus lower, and wetter versus drier) are relative in relation to previous and subsequent trends and for the most part are not quantified.

Climate and Sea Level, ca. A.D. 850–1200

A Sargasso Sea sea-surface temperature (SST) record (Keigwin 1996) shows a warming beginning at A.D. 850 that by A.D. 1000 reached the warmest temperature of the 3,000-year record. There was a subsequent cooling until A.D. 1050 followed by a slight warming at A.D. 1150 followed by another cooling. An SST record from off Puerto Rico (Nyberg et al. 2002) suggests a warm period between A.D. 700 and 950. A Chesapeake Bay SST record (Cronin et al. 2003) documents relative warmth from A.D. 800 to 1000. Sediment cores from the Florida Straits (Lund and Curry 2004) possibly record warmth for this time span, peaking in one core at about A.D. 900 and in another at about A.D. 1100–1150. A cooling follows. An SST record off the coast of western Africa (deMenocal et al. 2000) shows warmth until about A.D. 1150.

A precipitation record from the Cariaco Basin (coastal Venezuela) (Huag et al. 2003) indicates two wet subepisodes: one from about A.D. 900 to

1050 and a moderately wet one from about A.D. 1050 to 1200. A Yucatán precipitation record from Lake Punta Laguna (Curtis et al. 1996) reveals a highly variable time with dry conditions from A.D. 900 to 1050 and a major wet event between A.D. 1050 and 1150 followed by a relatively drier span until A.D. 1250. Another Yucatán record (Hodell et al. 1995) shows the wet event earlier, at A.D. 900, followed by relatively dry conditions until about A.D. 1350.

This time span correlates roughly with what has been variously named by climate historians as the Early Medieval Warm Epoch, Medieval Optimum, or Medieval Warm Period. In the recent climate literature, its signature of warmth has been extended both temporally, to roughly A.D. 900–1300, and spatially, although not uniformly. When compared with the preceding (Vandal Minimum, or VM) and subsequent (Little Ice Age, or LIA) cooler time spans (figure 2.2), the signature appears often enough now in climate records that it is commonly referred to by climate scientists as the "MWP" (Medieval Warm Period). Yet its temporal and spatial extent as well as its magnitude of warmth (especially this last item as compared with the twentieth-century record) have been topics of debate (Bradley 2000; Bradley et al. 2003; Broecker 2001; Crowley 2000; Mann 2000; Osborn and Briffa 2006). A well-known human-climate association with this episode is that of the Norse people who established settlements on the west coast of Greenland during this relatively warm episode but then experienced drastic depopulation during the subsequent LIA (McGovern 1994; Pringle 1997). In the context of the southeastern United States, and of relevance to this chapter, Gunn (1997: 144) uses the term *Mississippian Optimum* to refer to the MWP. However, this overall warm period was punctuated by periods of drought as well as periods of plentiful rainfall, which would have affected the fortunes of Mississippian chiefs and their followers. Dendrochronological data indicate a major drought along the Georgia coast at A.D. 1176–1220 (Blanton and Thomas 2008: 801–5). Anderson and colleagues (1995: 272–73) propose that the period A.D. 1056–1152 would have been difficult for Mississippian agriculturalists in the Savannah River valley, especially during the intervals A.D. 1056–61, 1076–90, and 1124–52. Harvest shortfalls also were likely during A.D. 1162–64 and 1359–77.

Tanner's (1993, 2000) Denmark sea-level record indicates a sharp rise beginning at A.D. 850. If accurate, this signature would push back the beginning of the MWP to A.D. 850. In this record, by A.D. 950, sea level was as high as it was during the late Roman Warm Period (RWP). It remained high until A.D. 1050. An abrupt regression followed, dramatically bottoming out at A.D. 1100. An alpine glacial record shows an eleventh-century advance (Haeberli and Holzhauser 2003: 14). Consistent with this pattern is the isotopic analysis of an A.D. 1050 oyster shell from southwest Florida (Blackwater River estuary), indicating winter conditions colder than those indicated by modern (1990s) oyster shells (Surge et al. 2003: 749). Another sharp rise in the Denmark record brought sea level to its former position by A.D. 1150. A Red Sea record (Siddall et al. 2003: 854) shows a higher sea level compared to previous and subsequent levels between A.D. 800 and 1200. A well-known record from South Carolina (Colquhoun and Brooks 1986: 276) documents a high sea level centered on A.D. 950.

Archaeological research in the Mayan area of the Yucatán indicates a sea level 1 m higher than the twentieth-century mean for the period between A.D. 800 and 1200, based on well excavations (Bruce Dahlin, personal communication 2002). Tanner's (1991, 1992) Gulf of Mexico record exhibits an overall high sea level for the period. Stapor and colleagues (1991: 815, 835) estimate that sea level began to rise around A.D. 850, reaching a level near the twentieth-century mean and possibly as much as 0.3 m above it. They name the associated beach-ridge sets "La Costa." Thus, in this chapter, we refer to the southwest Florida high sea-level episode as the La Costa High (figure 2.2).

Although details (timing and magnitude) of the environmental variability within the A.D. 850–1200 time span vary from record to record, this period, at least in the greater North Atlantic region, including the greater Southeast and southwest Florida, can be argued to have been characterized by general warmth and high sea level but punctuated with at least one shorter-term, but abrupt, cooler event with an associated abrupt sea-level regression. The time span is commonly referred to by both climate historians and paleoclimate scientists as the Medieval Warm Period, and, in southwest Florida, the overall episode of high water as the La Costa High (figure 2.2). Precipitation during this period varied from subregion to subregion. The Yucatán and Cariaco records indicate variable wetness and dryness for much of the tropical North Atlantic. However, Florida, like the greater Southeast, may have been wetter overall rather than drier during the MWP.

Sea-level records suggest a rise at least up to the twentieth-century mean and in the case of the Denmark record, an abrupt short-term regression centered on A.D. 1100. Tanner's (1993, 2000; see also Gunn 1997) Denmark record, despite its high-latitude origin, is consistent with the other sea-level and climate records (including the southwest Florida model), an important point because it is a sea-level record constructed at 50-year intervals, thus providing archaeologists with needed detail at a human and ecosystem time scale. Of particular relevance for the topic of this chapter is Tanner's (2000) presentation of the record for the A.D. 1–1850 time span. The record's consistency with or support by other records closer to southwest Florida indicates its validity for application in southwest Florida as well as other parts of Florida; thus, we emphasize it in our cultural change section below.

Climate and Sea Level, ca. A.D. 1200–1850

The Sargasso Sea record indicates that cooling began by A.D. 1150 and continued until it was interrupted by a warming spike at A.D. 1400–1550. Sea-surface temperatures (SSTs) again cooled, with the coolest temperatures of this period centered on A.D. 1650. After a slight warm-up, temperatures leveled off from A.D. 1750 to 1850. The Puerto Rico record exhibits a similar pattern. The Chesapeake Bay record documents three cool subepisodes between A.D. 1000 and 1900. All three Florida Straits cores record a cool period, and at least two of them show an intervening warm spell, as seen in the Sargasso record. The western African record is consistent with the Sargasso and Florida records. A coral core dating to the eighteenth and early nineteenth centuries collected from off of Puerto Rico indicates SSTs two to three degrees cooler than those determined for a 1980s core (Winter et al. 2000).

The Cariaco record shows a rapid drying event followed by an equally rapid wet event centered on A.D. 1250. From about A.D. 1300 to 1750, a general drying trend is recorded, with one wet spike at A.D. 1500 and three dry punctuations at A.D. 1575, 1650, and 1750. In the Lake Punta Laguna core, the period is marked by two subepisodes. The first is dominated by drying, with wetter punctuations at A.D. 1250, 1400, and 1500. After A.D. 1500, wetness dominates with three events at A.D. 1550, 1700, and 1800. In the Chinchacanab record (Curtis et al. 1996), the variability is less extreme. Both Yucatán cores record a wet event centered on A.D. 1450 coincident with the warm-up seen in the ocean cores. Another Yucatán sinkhole sediment core from Aguada X'caamal records an abrupt change in constituents between A.D. 1450 and 1500, indicating an increased salinity associated with a drier climate (Hodell et al. 2005). Dendrochronological data suggest prolonged drought periods on the southeastern U.S. coast, ca. A.D. 1564–71, 1585–95, and 1627–67 (Blanton and Thomas 2008: 805; Stahle et al. 1998).

The time span of roughly A.D. 1200/1300 to 1850 is known climatically as the Little Ice Age (LIA) because it was a time of cooler temperatures and glacial advances compared to the MWP. Three cool subepisodes are documented in the Haeberli and Holzhauser (2003: 14) alpine glacial record: A.D. 1250–1350, 1500–1650, and 1750–1850. The cooling subepisodes are generally thought to have been widespread if not of global occurrence. The LIA's initiation date varies depending on the data set being considered, but it is usually set anywhere from A.D. 1200 to 1300. The end date of A.D. 1850 is more often agreed upon, based on an undisputed rapid warming after this date. Even so, the solar history presented by Eddy (1994: 30) would suggest A.D. 1715, the end of the Maunder Minimum, as an end date. In his book on the LIA, Fagan (2000) brings together many well-known examples of historical events and processes (including the Black Plague and the French Revolution) intricately associated with the climate of the LIA.

Considering sea-level fluctuations, Tanner's Denmark record indicates a lowered level from ca. A.D. 1200 to 1850 that is less severe overall and less erratic than the one that characterizes the earlier Vandal Minimum (VM) episode. Of relevance for the topic of this chapter is that LIA sea levels were relatively uninterrupted by abrupt changes compared with the dramatic A.D. 1100 event. Minor short-term regressions were centered on A.D. 1350 and 1700. The South Carolina record documents a low stand centered on A.D. 1450. Tanner's Gulf of Mexico record, not as finely resolved as the Denmark record, exhibits a sea-level drop at around A.D. 1200/1250 that lasted to around 1800/1850. Stapor and colleagues (1991: 815, 835) estimate that the Gulf's sea level began to fall around A.D. 1450, reaching about 0.3 m to perhaps 0.6 m below the twentieth-century mean. They estimate its duration to have been as long as 400 years and name the associated beach-ridge sets "Sanibel II." Thus, in this chapter, we refer to this episode as the Sanibel II Low (figure 2.2). Isotopic analysis of an A.D. 1220 oyster shell from southwest Florida's Blackwater River estuary indicates winter conditions similar to those indicated by modern (1990s) oyster shells (Surge et al. 2003). The Puerto Rico salinity record indicates that the lowest values of the LIA centered on A.D. 1400.

While the timing and magnitude details of the environmental variability observed within this interval of A.D. 1200–1850 vary from record to record, the argument can be made that, for the greater North Atlantic region, including the greater Southeast and southwest Florida, the Little Ice Age was characterized by general coolness and lowered sea level but punctuated with shorter-term, slightly warmer events and small rises in sea level. The Denmark record, in particular, portrays an overall stable span of time. Of particular note, however, are two minor regressions, even though they do not come close to comparing with the magnitude of the MWP's A.D. 1100 and VM's A.D. 850 events. Precipitation during this period varied from subregion to subregion; the Yucatán and Cariaco records indicate general dryness for much of the tropical North Atlantic, and this may have been the case for Florida and the greater Southeast as well.

Cultural Change in the Caloosahatchee Region during the Mississippi Period

Caloosahatchee IIB, A.D. 800–1200

We begin this discussion at A.D. 850, environmentally a pivotal point in time, to set the stage for exploring change during that portion of southwest Florida's Caloosahatchee cultural sequence that corresponds with the Southeast's Mississippi period. People living during the first century of the Caloosahatchee IIB period (A.D. 800–900) likely were adversely affected by the most detrimental of three sea-level regressions associated with the VM climatic episode. The cooling event centered on A.D. 850, and its associated sea-level regression must have been devastating for a people who depended on shallow-water aquatic foods, especially being the third and most severe in a cascading series of such cooling/sea-level events (Marquardt and Walker 2012; Walker 2012). For example, given the shallowness of Pine Island Sound, residents along its eastern margin (Pine Island's western shoreline) at such sites as the Pineland Site Complex (8LL33, 34, 36, 37, 38, 757, 1612), Josslyn Island (8LL32), and Galt Island (8LL27, 81) would have abandoned their homes to seek better access to aquatic resources farther west, resettling on both the barrier islands (e.g., Cayo Costa, Sanibel Island) and the westernmost inshore islands (e.g., Useppa Island, Buck Key). The inshore marine fish populations would have been impacted first; the fish responded simply by moving to deeper waters. At that point, the collecting of shellfish would have intensified until either the diminishing water level could no longer sustain those populations or human collection pressure became too great, or both.

The Caloosahatchee IIB period tentatively has been assigned a beginning date of A.D. 800 by Cordell (1992: 168, 2012), largely based on pottery assemblages from Josslyn and Pineland. It is recognized by small amounts of Belle Glade Red and the eclipsing of sand-tempered plain by Belle Glade Plain as the dominant pottery. (Originally made in the Lake Okeechobee area ca. A.D. 200, Belle Glade Plain first appears in limited amounts in southwest Florida ca. A.D. 500.) Weeden Island pottery also is present, as are wares with chalky sponge-spiculate (St. Johns) and limestone-tempered (Pasco) pastes. As more assemblages from other sites are studied, A.D. 900 might emerge as a more accurate date for the appearance of the new IIB assemblage. An examination of the IIB radiocarbon dates from Pineland, Josslyn, and Galt reveals an absence of midden deposits securely dated to the ninth century. This void supports the idea that sites in shallow-water locales were sparsely populated or even abandoned between A.D. 800 and 900. In contrast, for example, Useppa Island's (8LL51) Shell Ridge has midden deposits dating predominantly to the IIB period (Marquardt 1999: 79, 89–91), with three dates falling securely within the ninth century (see figure 2.1 for site locations).

As the MWP began its rapid warming trend, sea level quickly responded so that by A.D. 900, the La Costa High was well on its way to refilling Pine Island Sound and other shallow areas. Between A.D. 900 and 950, the inshore waters were highly productive, with ample fish and shellfish for the taking. Sites in shallow areas were reoccupied, as evidenced by midden deposits dating to A.D. 900 to 1200 that exhibit faunal assemblages of high diversity and high salinity (characteristics likely due to a raised sea level) and indicate overall great abundances of fish and shellfish remains (deFrance and Walker 2012; Walker 1992). Technologically, the faunal assemblages and their associated artifacts (net weights, hooks, sinkers) reflect efficient net fishing as well as hook-and-line fishing, techniques that served the Calusa and their predecessors well for many centuries (Walker 2000).

Based on deposits at Pineland, we see a major change in settlement in the tenth century: a decisive shift from a more extensive settlement along the shoreline to a more intensive one, largely, if not completely, restricted to the summits of midden-mounds. Caloosahatchee IIB midden accumulation was intensive and spatially constrained, with midden-mounds at Pineland rising to seven meters in height by the end of IIB, ca. A.D. 1150 to 1200. (During the Caloosahatchee I and IIA periods [e.g., ca. A.D. 50 to 750 at Pineland], habitation had been extensive along the shoreline but had moved episodically inland or shoreward through the centuries in response to significant sea-level fluctuations; see Marquardt and Walker 2001, 2012; Walker et al. 1994, 1995.) Although not well supported by pottery assemblages, the radiocarbon-date sequence at one of Pineland's mounds (Randell Complex Mound 1) suggests that some purposeful mound building may have taken place during this time (Wallace 2012). Nonetheless, the timing correlation between an abruptly rising (over a 50- to 100-year interval) sea level and the intensive vertical growth of midden-mounds is impossible to dismiss, leading us to speculate that ever-higher water levels were a significant factor in a spatial reorganization of Pineland and other mound complexes, including Estero Bay's Mound Key (8LL2). In other words, whereas the pre-IIB settlement response to sea-level fluctuation was to move back (inland) and forth (shoreward) along the shifting shoreline, the new IIB response was to move upward in response to rising water levels. With the warming of SSTs (see above) during the MWP, tropical storms would have been more powerful, if not more frequent (Walker 2012), and their associated storm surges would have provided even more motivation for coastal peoples to build upward and live on elevated ground.

These Pineland IIB linear mounds were perpendicular to the shoreline, in contrast to earlier deposits, and they paralleled a canal situated between the highest two mounds. Centrally located, the canal was later extended beyond the site complex all the way across Pine Island, a distance of 4 km (see discussion below). The central canal section at Pineland (between the highest two mounds) may have been an altered natural waterway that once emptied into the sound and was fed in part by artesian water. Its location may have contributed to the IIB spatial reorganization, including the formalization of the central water court and the eastward extension of the canal. A rise in water levels (sea and freshwater) as abrupt as that indicated for the A.D. 850–950 period surely was a factor in the realization of a structural need for managing the ever-increasing amounts of water around and within Pineland and other settlements. In the absence of any absolute or relative dating, we hypothesize that the innovative beginnings of what later became an elaborate system of constructed waterways at Pineland were coeval with the early part of the IIB vertical mound growth, ca. A.D. 900 to 950, and that both changes were associated with the A.D. 850–950 sea-level rise. Additionally, this is the time when Belle Glade pottery, initially made in interior south Florida, became the predominant ware at

Pineland and elsewhere in the region. Higher water levels compared to those of the preceding few centuries would have facilitated travel to and from the interior, along constructed canals as well as natural waterways.

Just when things were going well, in the midst of the warm MWP, an abrupt reversal occurred in the temperature trend, resulting in a sudden (within 50 years) sea-level regression, centered on A.D. 1100. Although not as severe as the A.D. 850 event, it nonetheless may have disrupted the productive estuarine ecosystem enough to force a new move westward, following the aquatic resources. Despite extensive testing and dating of deposits across the Pineland Site Complex, no conclusive evidence has been found there for midden accumulations ca. A.D. 1100. A soil analysis (Scudder 2012) at Pineland's burial mound (known as Smith Mound, 8LL36) identified an A horizon that had developed along the top of the lowest of three major strata. In this lowest stratum was an in situ human burial radiocarbon-dated to cal A.D. 1020–1170. The A horizon indicates abandonment of the mound for a time before the second stratum began to accumulate and/or was deposited. This may be evidence for an abandonment ca. A.D. 1100. If that is the case, then the burial, and thus the earliest (so far that we know of) practice of mound burial at Pineland, may date sometime between A.D. 1000 and 1050. All of Pineland may possibly have been vacated during the severest part of the ca. A.D. 1100 short-term low-sea-level event. Radiocarbon-dated midden deposits at Josslyn and Galt, both in similar shallow-water locales, also present gaps in time centered on the twelfth-century low-sea-level event (as well as during the earlier VM low-water episode ca. A.D. 550–850). Such a significant lowering of the water would have presented a serious setback for the region's population. Pineland was reoccupied probably by A.D. 1150; Josslyn and Galt's reoccupation dates are closer to A.D. 1200 (Marquardt 1992b: 11, 14–25).

Dietler (2008: 437–42) has demonstrated that production of lightning whelk (*Busycon sinistrum*)[1] shell cutting-edged tools became more precise, standardized, and efficient during the Caloosahatchee IIB period (A.D. 800–1200), possibly to satisfy elite demand. The more favorable climatic conditions of the IIB period may have increased demand for shell tools to manufacture dugout canoes. During the same period, large-scale construction projects included the Pine Island Canal and the accumulation of midden deposits to form high mounds at such places as Pineland (8LL33) and Mound Key (8LL2). Increased quantities of Belle Glade Plain pottery probably indicate increased commercial and sociopolitical relations with the

Lake Okeechobee area. In sum, during a time of mostly favorable climatic conditions, the Calusa of southwest Florida experienced an overall period of prosperity and expanded their influence throughout south Florida.

Caloosahatchee III, A.D. 1200–1350, and IV, A.D. 1350–1500

Between A.D. 1150 and 1200, sea level began a moderate drop associated with the LIA climatic episode. Sea level continued in an overall lowered position until around A.D. 1850, roughly the end of the LIA. Relative to the MWP's La Costa High, the LIA's Sanibel II Low was clearly lower, but compared to the VM's Buck Key Low of ca. A.D. 550 to 850, it was neither as low nor as erratic. Rather, the LIA and its Sanibel II Low in coastal southwest Florida could even be considered comparatively stable, with little or no detrimental effect on the region's aquatic ecosystems and human populations.

The cultural transition from Caloosahatchee IIB to III occurred around A.D. 1200. Again, there was no radical departure from established subsistence practices or technology during this period. The accumulation and/or buildup of midden-mounds continued in a constricted spatial pattern as in the IIB period. On Josslyn Island and on Buck Key (Marquardt 1992b: 19, 35–36), significant deposits of large lightning whelk shells date to Caloosahatchee III, suggesting that environmental conditions during this time favored an abundant supply of these large shellfish. Production of cutting-edged tools continued as well. While Belle Glade Plain remained the dominant plainware and Weeden Island pottery lingered, St. Johns Check Stamped appeared in middens for the first time, marking the beginning of the III period. St. Johns Check Stamped was originally made in northeastern Florida as early as A.D. 750 (Milanich 1994: 246–48). At Pineland, about 90 percent of Safety Harbor–related pottery from mortuary contexts was of nonlocal "Lake Jackson" sherd-tempered paste, as defined by Cordell (2005: 107, 109; but cf. White et al., chapter 10, this volume, on Lake Jackson paste).

Caloosahatchee IV began at A.D. 1350, when sea level was at one of the two lowest points within the overall Sanibel II Low episode (nonetheless at a level much higher than those of VM [Caloosahatchee IIA] times). But between A.D. 1350 and 1400, it returned to its previous A.D. 1300 level. Again the basic fishing-gathering-hunting technology continued much as before. Zooarchaeological samples from Pineland document continued abundant molluscan and fish populations (deFrance and Walker 2012) but with a lowered diversity and salinity compared to IIB samples, likely because of a lower water level. At the Mark Pardo site (8LL606) on Cayo Costa (see figure 2.1), a deposit of large lightning whelk shells dates to Caloosahatchee IV, suggesting a continuation of an abundant supply and continued use of these large whelks during this period. Although again not conclusively supported by pottery assemblages (Cordell 2012), the radiocarbon-date sequences (Walker and Marquardt 2012) within two of Pineland's mounds (Brown's Complex Mounds 1 and 2) suggest purposeful mound building ca. A.D. 1300 to 1500.

Caloosahatchee IV is recognized archaeologically by the first appearance of Glades Tooled pottery and the relative decrease of Belle Glade Plain in favor of sand-tempered plain. This may indicate political realignments to the south (Ten Thousand Islands) and away from the east, or perhaps a reorganization of exchange relationships. Belle Glade Plain continued to dominate in the Lake Okeechobee area, even as it diminished in importance on the southwest coast relative to sand-tempered plainware. Lowered water levels may have hindered travel between the coast and the interior. Present in small numbers are grog-tempered sherds, with pastes similar to those associated with Lake Jackson and Baytown. Most Pinellas-style ticked rim sherds at Pineland are locally made and found in Brown's Complex Caloosahatchee IV strata. Most Caloosahatchee IV, nonlocal Safety Harbor–related pottery in Pineland's middens is of Pinellas paste (frequent to common quartz sand; laminated/contoured paste texture; frequent rounded clay lumps, no sherd inclusions). Minor amounts of shell-tempered pottery, not made in south Florida (Pensacola series), are found in mortuary contexts. The Caloosahatchee IV period lasts until the time of the first likely contacts with Europeans in south Florida ca. A.D. 1500 (Marquardt 1988: 176–79).

If one examines Tanner's (2000: 93) sea-level graph, an interesting correlation is the timing of fluctuations within the LIA/Sanibel II Low. A.D. 1350 marks the lowest point in sea level of the first series of drops between A.D. 1150 and 1350. Beginning at A.D. 1350, sea level rose back to where it had been in A.D. 1300, after which, very minor fluctuations occurred until A.D. 1650. Between A.D. 1650 and 1700, sea level dropped to its lowest point of the LIA before it rose again between A.D. 1700 and 1750. The A.D. 1150–1350 time span of the sea-level fall was closely coeval with Caloosahatchee III (A.D. 1200–1350). The A.D. 1350–1500 time span of the partial recovery was coeval with Caloosahatchee IV (A.D. 1350–1500). Later, during the Caloosahatchee V period (A.D. 1500–1750), the Maunder

Minimum–associated A.D. 1650–1750 drop in sea level may have reduced the inshore fish populations, placing the Calusa in a vulnerable position during a time of increasing political-economic pressure from European interests (see below).

Summary, A.D. 800–1500

In southwest Florida, the latter half of Caloosahatchee IIB and all of the Caloosahatchee III and IV periods coincide with the "Mississippi" period of A.D. 1000–1500. Generally speaking, the first part of this 500-year period, coeval with Caloosahatchee IIB, was warmer with higher sea levels, and the second half, coeval with Caloosahatchee III/IV, was cooler with lower sea levels, but fluctuations—especially the A.D. 1100 event—within these overall trends undoubtedly had local and regional effects, as discussed above. Before A.D. 800, habitation was more extensive, often along shorelines, and shifted position several times, sometimes within 50 years, as a result of shoreline transgressions and regressions. The most pronounced of three significant sea-level regressions took place ca. A.D. 850, perhaps finally leading to depopulation of sites situated in shallower parts of the estuary, such as at Josslyn Island and Pineland. After A.D. 900, as sea level recovered, renewed habitation at Pineland became more intensive, shifting to the tops of linear midden-mounds situated perpendicular to the shoreline. By A.D. 1000/1050, burials were placed in separate sand mounds not far from living areas; craft specialization became more pronounced; and large-scale public works, such as canals and mounds, were undertaken. Throughout this period, subsistence and technology remained conservative, and fish remained the main dietary staple. Although the III/IV periods (A.D. 1200–1500) correlate with LIA lowered sea levels, the latter were neither as severe nor as erratic as the IIA sea levels of the VM. In fact, the III/IV Calusa people of southwest Florida may have experienced the most stable and salubrious climatic and sea-level conditions of the preceding 2,000 years.

Analysis and Interpretation

Our perspective is that of historical ecology, the holistic study of social formations in their dynamic environmental contexts (for more on this theoretical orientation, see Balée 1998; Crumley 1994, 2007; Marquardt 2012). For us, culture and environment are historically situated, influencing one another in a basic and fundamental manner. Cultural changes cannot be fully understood in the absence of environmental context, nor can environmental conditions be considered the sole or even the principal drivers of cultural changes. In short, culture and environment are dialectically related and mutually constitutive (Marquardt 1992a) and form a totality that can be studied regionally and through time (Marquardt and Crumley 1987).

People interact not only with the physical structures of their environments (landforms, rivers, estuaries, forests, etc.) but also with sociohistorical structures that are built up by human actors in the course of interacting with physical structures and with one another. Sociohistorical structures include property relations and power relations that characterize a particular social formation (Marquardt 1992a: 104–8). Furthermore, physical structures are often conceived, approached, propitiated, and interacted with within the framework of belief systems. Finally, sociohistorical structures are not static; they emerge and mutate through time as impinging conditions offer opportunities and present challenges that must be responded to based on established knowledge systems. Although they may be cognized in terms of historically situated belief systems (religion, myth, and the like), climate changes and dramatic weather events, such as hurricanes, are significant impinging conditions.

With this orientation in mind, we now consider interregional connections, large-scale communal construction projects, and social complexity for southwest Florida during the Mississippi period because these phenomena are often associated with Mississippian chiefdoms. We also speculate on the degree to which developments among southwest Florida people were influenced by those of their contemporaries in the greater Southeast.

Interregional Connections

Based on extensive research on Pineland pottery by Cordell (1992, 2012), we think that southwest Florida people lived in relative cultural isolation until the Caloosahatchee IIB period. Ceramic technology was conservative, with plain, incurved bowls with rounded rims being made from local clays. Belle Glade pottery, first made in the Lake Okeechobee area about A.D. 200, made its way to the southwest Florida coast by A.D. 500 but was slow to become popular there. Not until the latter part (A.D. 650–800) of Caloosahatchee IIA did ceramic forms become more diverse, with outslanting bowls and vase or vertical forms being added to the inventory.

By Caloosahatchee IIB times (A.D. 800–1200), the latter part of which includes the Early Mississippi period, Belle Glade pottery had become the most prominent plainware. Small quantities of micaceous, chalky, and limestone-tempered wares were present along with Weeden Island pottery. These changes in pottery use signal much-increased interaction with other regions of the Florida peninsula. The higher water levels of the MWP may have facilitated exchange through improved travel routes, especially compared with the previous lows of the VM.

During Caloosahatchee III (A.D. 1200–1350, or middle Mississippian) times, interaction with other areas became even more pronounced. A check-stamped chalky ware (St. Johns Check Stamped) originally made in northeastern and eastern Florida was added to the inventory, as was Pinellas Plain from Florida's central Gulf coast. Interregional exchange within the Florida peninsula would have increased the possibilities for diplomacy, political alliance, formal trading agreements, and intermarriage. But trade and exchange were not limited to Florida. Exotic materials from the Midsouth and Midwest (e.g., quartz, galena) are also found in Caloosahatchee III contexts (Walker and Marquardt 2012).

For example, Stratum 19 in our excavation of Brown's Complex Mound 2 at Pineland partially documents a structure, and we tentatively interpret the stratum as a house floor. A date of cal A.D. 1270–1340 is associated with the floor, and its ceramics are consistent with Caloosahatchee III. Aside from the numerous pottery sherds, ark-shell net weights, shell tools, drilled shark teeth, and bone point/pin fragments, several unusual artifacts came from Stratum 19. They include a silicified coral hafted biface of a Marion or Putnam type; a utilized chert flake; a piece of quartz; a cone-shaped, chalky object, possibly of dolomite; a cube of galena; a possible net-mesh gauge of quahog clam shell; and a complete, finely pointed bone perforator. The quartz, galena, and perforator were found within 25 cm of one another, and the chalky object was about 80 cm from these. In addition, specimens of sandstone and ochre were recovered. A few of the former may have been used as sharpening stones. The quartz cannot have come from Florida and is likely to be from no nearer than the Georgia piedmont. Mass spectrometer measurements of lead isotopes revealed that the galena originated in southeastern Missouri (Austin et al. 2000). We interpret the house represented by Stratum 19 as a special structure in which ritual preparation took place.

It seems clear that the Calusa exchange network reached into the Midwest and Midsouth, at least indirectly, by middle Mississippian times, if not earlier. What could coastal people have offered in return? A possibility that immediately springs to mind is the lightning whelk shell, large, robust specimens of which are found along the southwest as well as northwest Florida coast. One need only think of the many thousands of lightning whelk and other marine-shell beads manufactured at Cahokia (Kelly 2006: 246), where some 18 species of marine shells were fashioned into artifacts by specialists and probably used in ritual and political displays, to imagine a significant demand for Gulf-coast marine shells. Indeed, the Caloosahatchee III/IV examples of concentrations of large whelk shells noted above may be related to such demand. Of course, some lightning whelk shells had moved into the Midwest much earlier, being found in burials of the Shell Mound Archaic of Kentucky and Tennessee (e.g., Webb 1974: 205–15; Webb and DeJarnette 1942: 197–98 and plates 222–23; see Watson 2005: 555). Nevertheless, the demand for marine shells, particularly the lightning whelk, in the Midsouth and Midwest during the Mississippi period may have drawn the coastal Calusa more firmly into the Mississippian world in spite of their geographic distance from major Mississippian centers where the beads, pendants, and engraved shell cups were ultimately produced.

Large-Scale Construction Projects

A hallmark of Mississippian societies is the flat-topped, rectangular platform mound. Both the number of mounds in Mississippian towns and the sheer volume of some of the larger earthworks are impressive. The largest mounds in Mississippian towns may have been the locations of chief's houses, rather than of temples or other ritual structures (Payne 2006: 96–97, 104). Towns in southwest Florida did not have truncated pyramidal mounds, but during Mississippian times Calusa people did create impressive linear midden-mounds that probably supported communal domiciles (in middle Mississippian times they may have redeposited older middens to build their midden-mounds higher), and they did use sand mounds for burying their dead. Perhaps more important, as early as the beginning of IIB times they began intrasite spatial reorganizations that during III/IV times became conventionalized village plans. Let us consider briefly the two largest known Calusa towns: "Calos" and "Tampa," today known as Mound Key and Pineland, respectively (figure 2.1).

Mound Key is an island in Estero Bay.[2] Archaeological deposits occupy most of the 51-ha island, although some parts of the island have been

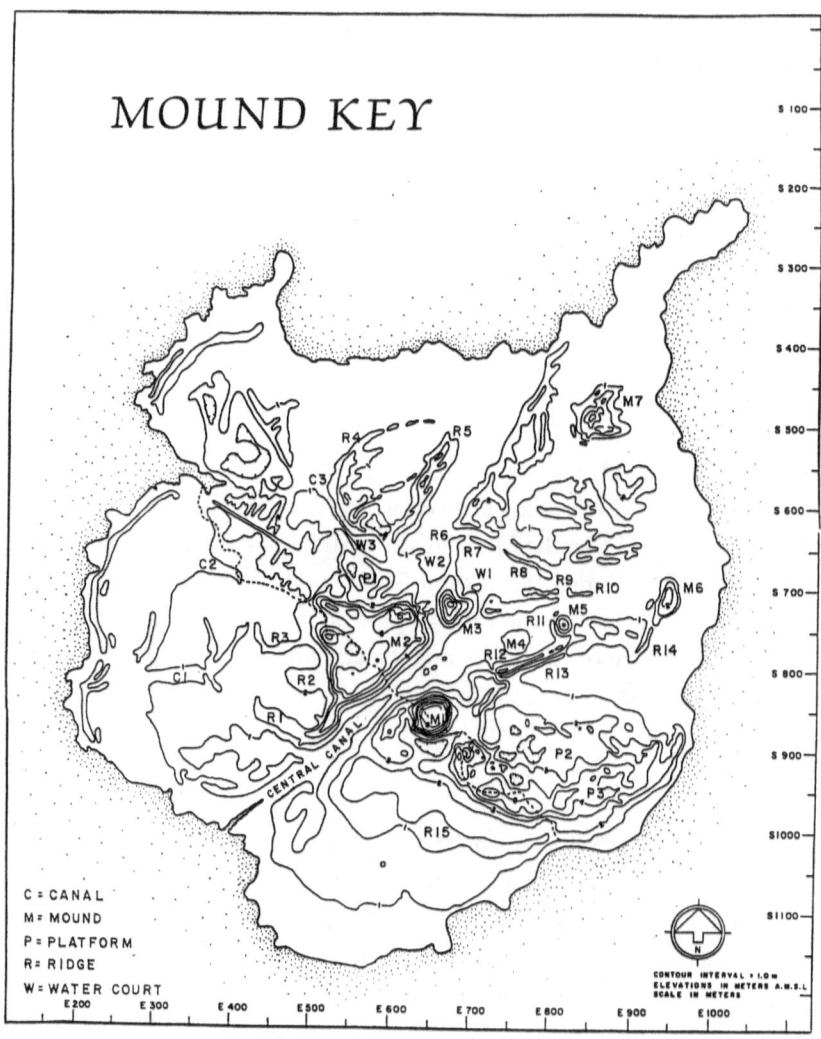

Figure 2.3. Topographic map of Mound Key (8LL2). Drawing by Corbett Torrence.

reduced by mining for road construction materials. Still visible are substantial midden-mounds (the largest about 10 m high), a large artificial canal, smaller midden ridges, and burial mounds (figure 2.3). Only limited mapping and testing of the site have been accomplished to date (Torrence et al. 1994), but radiocarbon dates (data on file, Anthropology Division, Florida Museum of Natural History) show that the island was inhabited by A.D. 300 and it was a major Calusa town during the protohistoric Caloosahatchee V period (Wheeler 2000b).

The two major mound groups of Mound Key are bisected by a substantial entrance canal; subsidiary canals probably branched off from it to reach other parts of the town. In the sixteenth century, Calos—almost surely the Mound Key site—was the capital of the Calusa polity, with more than one thousand inhabitants. The Spaniards report that in 1566, governor Pedro Menéndez de Avilés met there with Calusa king Caalus in a building large enough for two thousand people to stand without being very crowded (Solís de Merás 1964: 145). Inscribing a rectangle around the main mounds at the site yields an area of 30 ha, and the height of the tallest mound is 9.8 m (Torrence et al. 1994).

The Pineland Site Complex, known to the historic-period Calusa as Tampa,[3] is composed of multiple midden-mounds, some of which are grouped in spatially discrete mound complexes (figure 2.4). In addition, to the east and south, buried shoreline middens and other midden-mounds began to accumulate as early as A.D. 1. As discussed above, the habitation pattern before A.D. 900 was more extensive and shoreline oriented, and subsequent to A.D. 900 it was oriented to the tops of midden-mounds. Thus, what we envision as the late prehistoric manifestation of Pineland is in fact the result of as much as 1,700 years of aboriginal occupation, not just solely that of the Mississippi period. Today the peak elevation of Brown's Complex Mound 1 is 9.0 m, although it was probably somewhat higher before being reduced in the early twentieth century.[4]

Similar to the configuration of Mound Key, the two major mound complexes at Pineland are bisected by a large canal. It led into a central water court, and smaller canals led to water features, including a pond, a canal that surrounded a burial mound, and another canal that surrounded another mound. The principal canal continued eastward, running the entire width of Pine Island, about 4 km. Late nineteenth-century eyewitnesses recorded the width of the canal itself as 30 feet (9 m) and its depth as 6 feet (2 m), with a width of 50 feet (15 m) from berm to berm on either side of the feature. Luer and Wheeler (1997) estimate its width as varying between 18 and 23 feet (5.5–7.1 m), with channel depths of 3 to 5 feet (0.9–1.5 m). They confirm a total length of 2.5 miles (4.0 km) and identify several water-control structures and feeder ponds that allowed water to flow into or out of the canal as needed.

Excavating and maintaining a 4-km-long canal and its associated water-control features would have been a formidable task requiring much coordinated labor. To get a rough estimate of the amount of sediment that would have to be removed, using Luer and Wheeler's conservative figures,

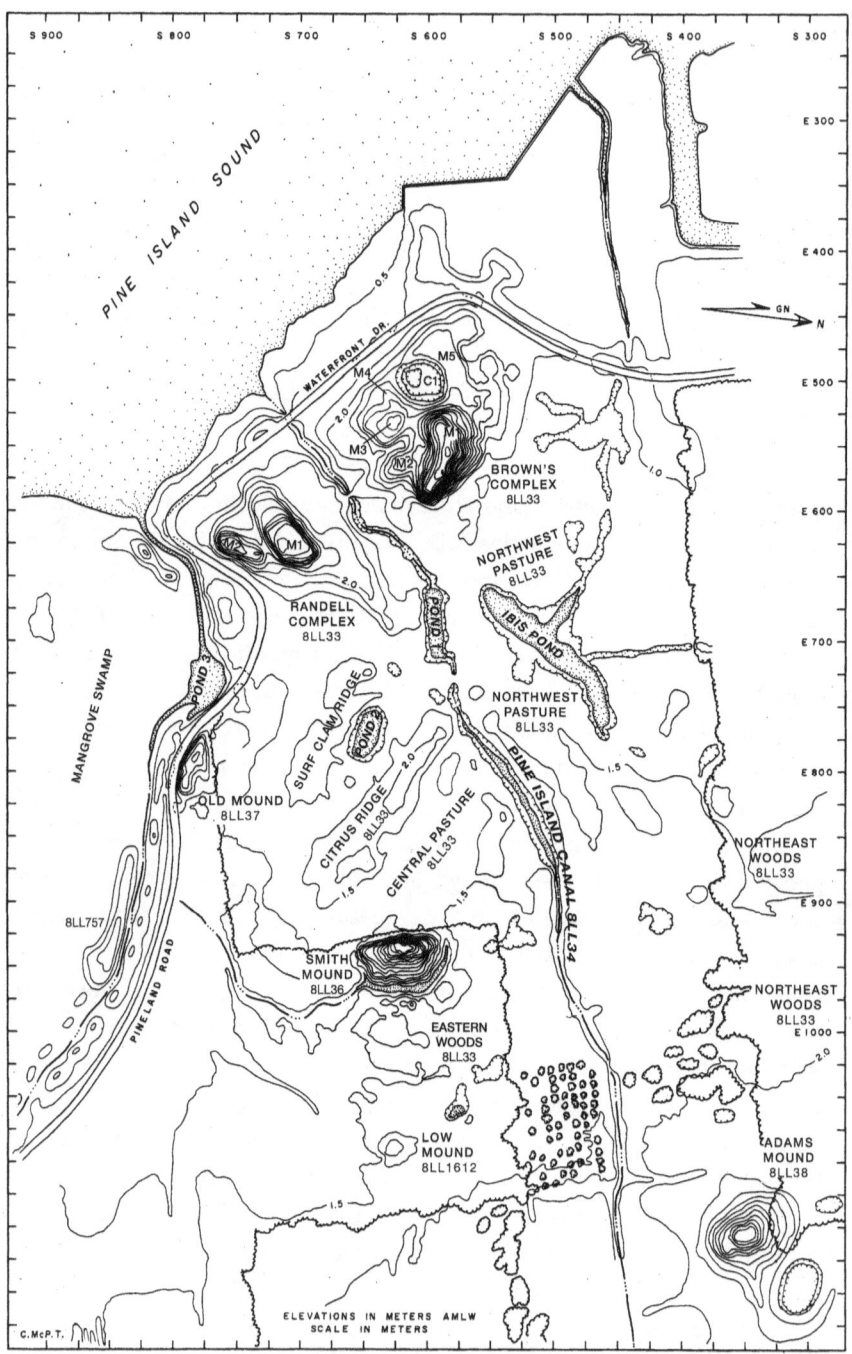

Figure 2.4. Topographic map of the Pineland Site Complex (8LL33, 36, 37, 38, 757, 1612). Drawing by Corbett Torrence and Sue Ellen Hunter.

one can multiply the width (20') by the depth (4') by the length (2.5 miles), yielding an estimate of 1,056,000 cubic feet, or 29,903 cubic meters. This figure for the canal sediments alone (not counting control structures and feeder ponds) compares favorably with the volumes of some of the larger mounds at major Mississippian sites such as Etowah and Moundville. For example, Mound A at the latter site is estimated to have occupied 30,150 cubic meters (Lacquement 2010: 348).

That the Pine Island Canal is an engineering achievement rivaling any in aboriginal North America seems clear, but why was it built? As a result of Luer and Wheeler's (1997) detailed analysis, we know how the canal was structured and how it worked. And thanks to the practical knowledge won through years of canoe-based exploration of the Pine Island Sound–Matlacha Pass area by Charles Blanchard (2002, 2008), we can confidently assert that the canal would have facilitated the movement of goods and people from the Calusa heartland to and from interior south Florida because it provided a strategic advantage "in avoiding the wildly variable navigational problems presented by wind, tide, and current at the northern end of Pine Island in order to reach Matlacha Pass" (Blanchard 2008: 62).

Although one tends to think of the canal in terms of trade goods, raw materials, and foodstuffs, the transport of people—diplomats, traders, leaders, warriors, captives—would also have been important to the Calusa and their client polities (e.g., the Tequesta, Mayami, Ais, Jeaga) and trading partners across south Florida. In addition to the strategic, practical advantage the canal provided, surely it enriched the prestige and personal wealth of the leaders who caused it to be built and maintained. Pineland on the western end and the Indian Field site (8LL40) on the eastern end would have been especially important as ports of entry and exit from the Calusa domain.

The canal must have had local ecological effects, but we imagine that it also had profound political-economic importance. Once built and put into use, it became a part of regional history and its presence had to be accounted for. Human-made, the Pine Island Canal functioned as a major waterway for transportation, much as would a natural river. The canal would have been aggrandizing for the individuals who created and controlled it, and undoubtedly its formidable presence on the landscape would have been noted by all.

Pineland's habitation mounds, composed of accumulated—and in some cases possibly redeposited—middens (shells, bones, ashes, charcoal, dirt, etc.), were also of noteworthy size in late prehistoric times. Widmer (2002:

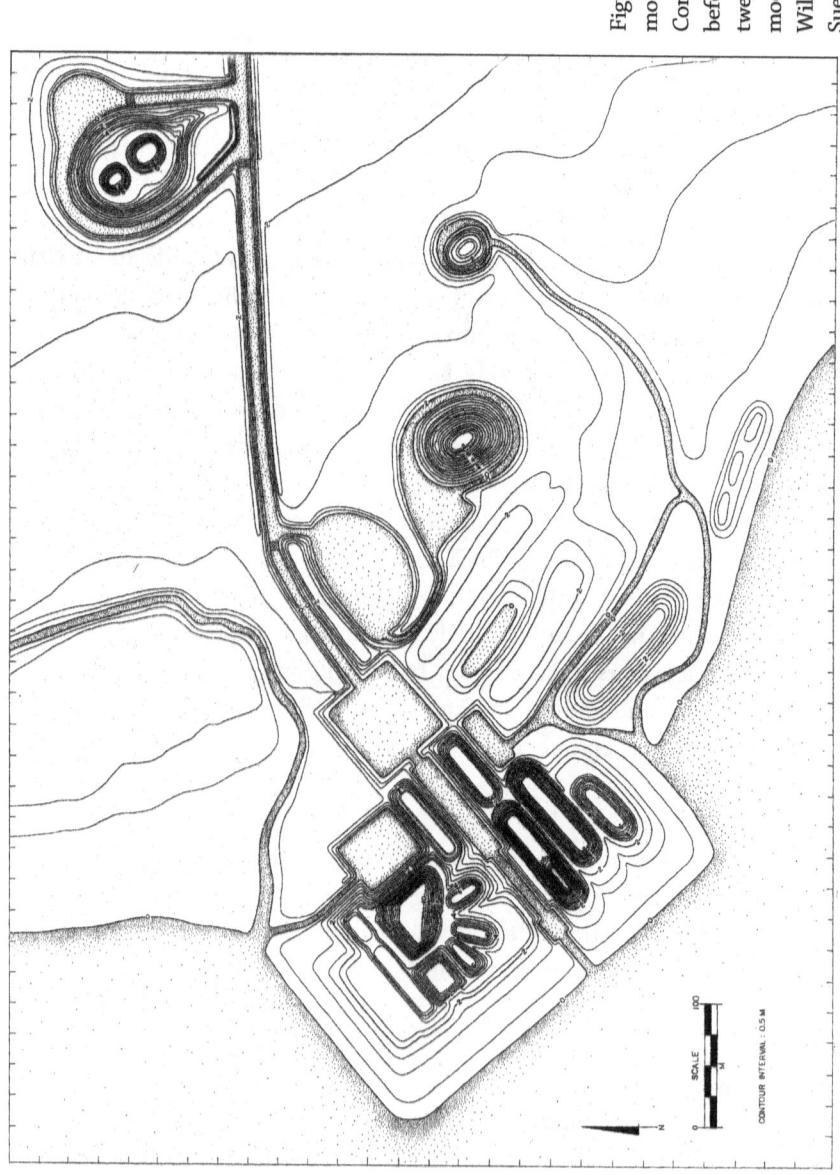

Figure 2.5. Topographic model of the Pineland Site Complex as it appeared before twentieth- and twenty-first-century land modification. Drawing by William Marquardt and Sue Ellen Hunter.

389) refers unequivocally to "temple mounds . . . at all large village sites in [southwest Florida]" by A.D. 800. Goggin and Sturtevant (1964: 194–95) mention "temple mounds" in a broader discussion of "extensive shellworks and earthworks" in Calusa sites but comment that "it is not clear whether [the shellworks and earthworks] gradually accumulated from refuse or were deliberately built by moving refuse from elsewhere in the site."

We are not sure what Widmer and others mean by "temple mounds." Our extensive investigations at the Pineland Site Complex suggest that the high mounds are in fact domiciliary midden-mounds. Based on extensive testing and auger surveys at Pineland, coupled with oral-history interviews with previous landowners, examination of all available aerial photographs, and extensive study of Frank Cushing's notes, diaries, and sketch maps (Kolianos and Weisman 2005a, 2005b), we have suggested a configuration (figure 2.5) for the Pineland Site Complex as it might have looked when abandoned by the Calusa in 1710 (Worth 2012). If we are correct, the site complex encompassed some 42 ha, or 104 acres. We have no archaeological evidence that anyone ca. A.D. 1500 lived anywhere but on top of the habitation mounds, although it is possible that some structures were built along the shoreline fronting the mound complexes (under today's Waterfront Drive) or on stilts over the water. Because archival evidence suggests that the historic Calusa lived in large thatched communal houses, and because several of Pineland's midden-mounds are linear, we imagine the domiciles as longhouses or perhaps as a series of long, narrow structures in a line on top of each of the habitation mounds.

Social Complexity

The postcontact Calusa social formation was hierarchical and tributary and functioned intermittently as a weak tribute-based state between A.D. 1500 and 1700 (Marquardt 1987b: 98–101). Inasmuch as the Calusa paramount leader inherited his position, had ultimate political and religious authority, commanded elite military specialists, and had the power of life or death over his subjects, he may properly be called a "king."

In the absence of firm evidence, it is impossible to know how far back in time to project this level of social complexity. Like their Mississippian contemporaries, the precontact Calusa were surely a chiefdom, but the degree of precontact Calusa organizational complexity is still a matter for discussion. One of us has argued elsewhere (Marquardt 1987b: 103–10, 2001: 166–68) that the intensity of the hierarchical and tributary system described by the Spaniards was at least partly a direct response to the Spanish invasion. In other words, the apparatus of kingship may have been an attempt to adapt to the new broader-scale political economy that had been thrust upon them by the European invasion. This is not to say that the Calusa were not a chiefdom, even a complex chiefdom, before the Spaniards arrived but simply that the statelike organization observed postcontact may have been in part a response to Spanish presence. Based on ethnohistoric sources, the postcontact period shows continuities in basic fisher-gatherer-hunter subsistence and a persistence of native ideology that confounded Spanish attempts to convert the Calusa into Christian agriculturalists (Hann 1991: 184–85, 420, 428).

The legitimacy of the Calusa king was intertwined with his presumed connections with the spirit world, as reported by Laudonnière (1975: 110) in 1564: "The king was held in great reverence by his subjects and . . . he made them believe that his sorceries and spells were the reason why the earth brought forth her fruit." In 1567, Rogel (Hann 1991: 247) commented, "[I]t is expedient for [the Calusa king] to show to his vassals and to his neighboring kings that he is the legitimate king . . . because to that end during his childhood they taught and instructed him in all the things that it is expedient for the king to know about the cult and veneration of the idols, and if he were suddenly to forsake the idolatry at the beginning of his reign, the aforementioned kings and vassals would say that he was not a legitimate king, as he did not know what kings are obliged to know."

A high priest, who was kin to the Calusa king, was keeper of the temple and its idols. Such priests were said to have the power to summon the winds (Sturtevant 1978: 148). If we assume that this was the case prior to contact, it is interesting to speculate on the possible effects of abrupt climatic fluctuations or short-term catastrophic weather on the leadership structure. Might the sea-level low of A.D. 1350 and its implied dampened fishery have had a destabilizing influence on leadership? We believe it is prudent to keep noncultural phenomena in mind when we are searching for explanations of the nature and timing of significant changes in social structure.

Mississippian Influences

Were southwest Florida chiefdoms influenced by developments in the Mississippian world? Surely they were. If they were drawn into the exchange networks that moved marine shells into Mississippian town centers, their awareness of broader-scale political economies and ideologies must have been heightened. The Calusa use of dedicated mounds for burial beginning in the eleventh century and the placement with the dead of pottery sherds from extralocal places may be indications of ideological shifts ca. A.D. 1000 that were at least in part stimulated by contact with Mississippian peoples.

If an alternative ideology with new ways of regarding the ancestors was adopted in the eleventh century by the Calusa, it need have come from no farther away than the central Gulf coast region to the north, where the Safety Harbor culture was established by A.D. 1000 (Milanich 2002: 369; and see Mitchem, chapter 8, this volume). Indeed, Weeden Island burial ceremonialism (interment in sand mounds with inclusion of ceramic vessels with the dead) had developed in the modern-day Tampa Bay area well before A.D. 1000 (Willey 1949a: 105–13). In Manatee and Sarasota counties, just to the north of Charlotte Harbor, burial mounds with inclusions of Weeden Island–series and St. Johns Check Stamped pottery were used after A.D. 700 (Luer and Almy 1982: 42, 46–47). Near Punta Gorda, the Aqui Esta mound (8CH68), which dates to the Englewood period (A.D. 1000–1200), included a number of Mississippian-influenced sherds as well as some chalky-paste pottery associated with late Weeden Island (A.D. 700–1000) (Luer 2002a: 105). Late Weeden Island pottery vessels are found in other mounds in northern Charlotte Harbor (Willey 1949a: 131–35, 344–45).

Some Mississippian-influenced vessels found in the central Gulf coast area are of nonlocal origin, while others were made by local potters who had knowledge of Mississippian-style vessel forms and decorative techniques (Luer 2002a: 105, 2002b: 157). Cordell (2012) found that much of the Safety Harbor–related decorated pottery of the Caloosahatchee IV period (A.D. 1350–1500) at Pineland was probably locally made using Pineland paste (frequent to common sponge spicules; common to abundant very fine to medium quartz sand, occasional coarse quartz; medium to fine paste texture; can be slightly laminated; sandy tactual quality). Based on her analysis, she proposes a dichotomy for Pineland's Safety Harbor pottery between sand-tempered and Pineland pastes on the one hand (local or proto-Calusa manufacture) and grog- and sherd-tempered wares on the other (Safety Harbor proper, or proto-Tocobaga manufacture). Some pottery found in Pineland's burial mound is sherd-tempered "Lake Jackson" paste, possibly originating in the Tallahassee Fort Walton area (see Marrinan, chapter 9, and White et al., chapter 10, this volume).

Burial in mounds is, of course, not exclusively a trait of the Mississippian period. Burial mounds had been used in the greater Southeast as early as Early Woodland times (1000–200 B.C.; Anderson and Mainfort 2002: 4–9). They are known in northeastern Florida during the Early Woodland St. Johns I period (500 B.C.–A.D. 100; Milanich 1994: 260) and in northern, northwest, and south Florida by the Middle Woodland period (100 B.C.–A.D. 500; Austin 1993; Dickel and Carr 1991; Milanich 2002: 359). Surely this was an idea not unknown to the Calusa in southwest Florida; yet they did not apparently adopt the practice until ca. A.D. 1000, when the influence of Safety Harbor culture in the modern-day Tampa Bay area spread to both the north and the south along the Gulf coast (Milanich 2002: 367).

We think it likely that the adoption of mound burial at Pineland and Mound Key was a reaction to the increasing political influence of the Safety Harbor culture in the central Gulf coast region. If establishing a burial mound is a way for a lineage to make claim to a region through links to founding ancestors, as many archaeologists surmise, then the adoption of this practice in southwest Florida may have been a response to the rising influence of a chiefdom located in the central Gulf coast region. By the sixteenth century, the Calusa of southwest Florida were said to be bitter enemies of the Tocobaga, who then controlled the central Gulf coast region (Solís de Merás 1964: 223–24).

In spite of these influences, we assert that southwest Florida chiefdoms never became fully "Mississippianized." Three hallmarks of Mississippian—maize agriculture, special-purpose nonmortuary earthworks, and the manufacture of shell-tempered pottery—were never adopted in south Florida. Maize agriculture was impractical and culturally unsavory (Hann 1991: 184–85) to Calusa fisherfolk. Fishing-gathering-hunting continued to be the dominant mode of production even as exchange relations and exposure to new ideas brought the Calusa and their neighbors more fully into the cultural realm of the greater Southeast. Calusa society was far from a pale reflection of Mississippian social formations farther north. In fact, as we have discussed above, the Calusa lived atop high domiciliary mounds and engineered intricate canals and waterworks that compare favorably in scope with coordinated civil projects anywhere in the Southeast. Although their pottery was unremarkable, their carving, painting, and engraving compare favorably with any art in aboriginal North America.

We do believe that the Calusa were influenced indirectly by developments in the Mississippian world. Their participation in broad-scale southeastern U.S. exchange networks brought extralocal goods to southwest Florida from the Midsouth and Midwest, and they integrated some

Mississippian ideas into their own belief system. Nevertheless, the Calusa maintained their traditions and never abandoned their fisher-gatherer-hunter subsistence strategy, even after being devastated by population loss and driven from their homeland in the eighteenth century (Hann 1991: 428; Sturtevant 1978: 147).

Conclusion

In this chapter, we have reviewed human-scale climatic and sea-level changes and considered their roles in Caloosahatchee IIB, III, and IV (A.D. 800–1500) cultural changes within southwest Florida during the time known in the greater Southeast as the Mississippi period (A.D. 1000–1500). The most noticeable pattern overall is the correlation in timing between Caloosahatchee IIB and the MWP/La Costa High and between Caloosahatchee III/IV and the LIA/Sanibel II Low. Similar correlations can be observed between early Mississippian times (A.D. 1000–1200) and the MWP and between middle/late Mississippian times (A.D. 1200–1500) and the LIA.

Environmental fluctuations—whether they were centuries-long episodes of an erratic or stable nature or individual abrupt or gradual events—would have impacted subtropical Florida's shallow-water estuarine ecosystems.[5] These impacts would primarily have been in the form of changing water levels, which would have affected availability and distributions of resources, primarily fish and shellfish. We think that especially pronounced low-sea-level events (those centered on A.D. 850 and 1100) caused population movements away from normally reliable shallow estuarine habitats (e.g., at the Pineland Site Complex) and toward deeper waters nearer the barrier islands (e.g., at Useppa Island). At the other extreme, abrupt rises in sea level, perhaps combined with short-term severe weather events such as hurricanes, likely contributed to a conscious effort to build high domiciliary midden-mounds rather than continue a pattern of extensive but shifting shoreline habitation.

We also suggest that environmental fluctuations may have influenced exchange, large-scale construction projects, social structure, and interactions with the broader Mississippian world. Inasmuch as the legitimacy of hereditary leaders was bound up with the productivity and predictability of a bountiful natural environment, we think it likely that climate, sea level, and even weather also profoundly influenced political developments.

The Calusa achieved levels of cultural complexity comparable to those of

Mississippian peoples, but neither was immune to environmental factors that provided both opportunities for and obstacles to continued prosperity. For example, in the Calusa heartland, the MWP's sea-level rise of A.D. 850–900 provided a productive fishery that contributed much to their development between A.D. 900 and A.D. 1050. Yet that fishery would have been adversely impacted by the A.D. 1050–1100 sea-level drop (although not to the extent of the earlier A.D. 800–850 event).

Meanwhile, Mississippian maize-agriculture-based societies prospered during the Warm Medieval Period (A.D. 850–1200), but some, such as Cahokia, faltered or underwent reorganization during the subsequent Little Ice Age (A.D. 1200–1850), which was less favorable to staple-crop agriculture. After ca. A.D. 1300 (and somewhat earlier in the environs of Cahokia), mound building and ritual display diminished while warfare increased among Mississippian societies, and some major mound centers were abandoned (Bense 1994: 197, 218; Milner 1996: 47–51; Williams 2001: 191, 193–95). The fifteenth century witnessed further turmoil and the virtual abandonment of previously heavily populated regions of the central Mississippi Valley (Bense 1994: 239–48; Mainfort 2001: 175, 188–89).

As the Little Ice Age unfolded, however, the Calusa were at a distinct advantage over more northern agriculturalists. Although it would have been cooler in southwest Florida, the Little Ice Age drew sea level in Pine Island Sound down only moderately, while lessening the frequency of severe storms. While Mississippian societies downsized and reorganized, the Calusa became stronger and expanded their influence southward. Thus, in 1513 and 1521, Ponce de León was met by well-organized and disciplined Calusa warriors, and in 1566 Pedro Menéndez de Avilés found in the Calusa king a shrewd and calculating paramount leader who controlled significant resources over a vast area. In the same century, Pánfilo de Narváez, Hernando de Soto, and others who ventured into the Mississippian Southeast often encountered little resistance and abandoned towns.

Following European contact, the Calusa kingdom bent but did not break, conserving its traditions and reasserting its control. From 1570 through the late 1600s, the Calusa chose to avoid both the English and the Spanish. In the end, a combination of environmental and cultural factors may have been to blame for their demise. A sudden drop in sea level between 1650 and 1700 (known in the climatic literature as the Maunder Minimum) may have left the Calusa in a vulnerable position just as native societies throughout the greater Southeast were succumbing to the slave-based political economy of the broader world system (Gallay 2002: 127–54). By the

1680s, the Tocobaga were no longer a threat and the Calusa had established patron-client relations with groups in the central Gulf coast, who protected them from surprise invasions from the north (Marquardt 2001: 170; see Hann 1991: 23–30). Those same patron-client relations would have guaranteed movement of supplies into southwest Florida in times of diminished resources.

Isolation from European colonial society allowed the Calusa to enjoy regional autonomy and consolidate political power, but it also left them and their clients dependent on the traditional military technology of bows, clubs, and throwing sticks. In spite of their reputation as fierce warriors, they were defenseless against the muskets of well-armed Creek and Yamassee slave raiders, who drove them from their lands and waters between 1704 and 1711, enslaving many and killing those who resisted (Hann 1991: 325–35; Marquardt 2001: 170–71).

In this chapter, we have used a historical-ecological method to characterize the dynamic interplay between environmental and cultural changes in southwest Florida ca. A.D. 850–1850, and we have situated the Calusa social formation in the context of developments elsewhere in Florida and the southeastern United States. We first outlined well-documented climate changes that influenced both the greater Southeast and Florida and suggested opportunities and challenges that may have influenced social formations in south Florida to change or to remain the same. Cultural intercourse with Mississippian peoples can be demonstrated—at least indirectly—so surely south Florida people were aware of other Mississippi-period social formations and how they differed from their own. Even so, they did not adopt iconic Mississippian traits such as shell-tempered pottery or flat-topped temple mounds.

Judging from the remarkable Pine Island Canal, the Calusa were obviously capable of mobilizing a work force and could have built extensive Mississippian-style temple mounds had they wished to. Only in the eleventh century did the Calusa begin to bury their dead in mounds, perhaps an imitation (or emulation) of Mississippian-influenced Safety Harbor people to the north, whose political power had begun to rival their own.

We firmly believe that consideration of political-economic changes must go hand in hand with consideration of environmental changes because the latter often provide significant challenges and opportunities that can impede or enhance cultural developments. Although they may be cognized within the social formation in terms of historically situated belief systems (myth, religion, and the like), climate changes and dramatic weather events, such as hurricanes, can be significant impinging conditions, facilitating or frustrating sociopolitical initiatives. Steponaitis (1991: 227) writes that "particular trajectories of chiefly development may be inexplicable unless they are considered in the context of broader political and economic processes that transcend the boundaries of any single region." We heartily agree, but to "political and economic" processes we would add "environmental." As Gunn (1997: 135) puts it, "[M]ost if not all regional landscapes have a global-scale environmental context that must be understood before any meaningful analysis of culture change can be undertaken." Global climatic fluctuations can have salutary or detrimental local effects, and these effects can be abrupt: on the order of 50 to 100 years, just two to three human generations. Thanks to remarkable advances in climate research over the past 20 years, we can now begin to consider the potential effects of climate changes at temporal scales relevant to human decision making. It makes no sense to ignore these formidable forces in the study of Mississippi-period culture, whether in Florida or elsewhere.

Notes

1. The scientific name of this animal has fluctuated during the past 20 years, from *Busycon contrarium* to *Busycon sinistrum* and now, because of recent genetic studies (Wise et al. 2004), to *Busycon perversum* L. Wise and his colleagues assert that all North American sinistral whelks are conspecific. Here we retain the *sinistrum* species name, the current official nomenclature at this writing. Wise and colleagues (2004) recommend that *Busycon perversum* be applied to all North American sinistral whelks, with subspecies qualifiers *perversum* for the Yucatán peninsula, *laeostomum* for the Atlantic coast, and *sinistrum* (Hollister 1958) for the northern and eastern Gulf of Mexico. All lightning whelks in southwest Florida waters would thus be *Busycon perversum sinistrum*.

2. Mound Key is an archaeological state park, situated in Estero Bay near Fort Myers Beach. The site is listed in the National Register of Historic Places. Mound Key is open from 8 a.m. to sundown daily and is accessible by boat. Private crafts are allowed to land, or visitors may patronize one of several tour-boat companies that travel regularly to the site. An unimproved path with interpretive signs traverses the island, leading the hiker through the main canal trench and up and over the highest mound. There are no docks or facilities (www.floridastateparks.org/moundkey/default.cfm).

3. On early maps, Charlotte Harbor was known as the "Bay of Tampa," named for the large Calusa town at present-day Pineland, while the large bay to the north was known variously as "Bay of Pooy" (Hann 1991: 12) or "Bay of the Holy Spirit." A mapmaker's error in the late seventeenth century transposed "Bay of Tampa" northward, hence the former Bay of Pooy is today known as "Tampa Bay." The modern place-name of Tampa is in fact the Calusa name for the Pineland Site Complex (Worth 2012).

4. The Pineland Site Complex is located on the northwestern shore of Pine Island in coastal Southwest Florida, near Fort Myers. First inhabited about 2,000 years ago, Pineland was occupied by Native Americans until 1710. The site was partially reduced in the twentieth century by the removal of portions of some midden-mounds for road material and fill dirt and by the filling of low areas. Nevertheless, enormous shell mounds still overlook Pine Island Sound, and remains of many centuries of Indian village life blanket the old pastures and groves. Remnants of the Pine Island Canal are still visible. The site is listed in the National Register of Historic Places. Thanks to a grant of land from Donald and Patricia Randell and funds raised from private donors, agencies, and foundations, in 1996 the Florida Museum of Natural History established the Randell Research Center at Pineland as a permanent program of archaeological and environmental research. The site is open to the public daily, and visitors may walk the Calusa Heritage Trail, a 3,700-foot path (about 0.7 miles, or 1,128 m) that winds among and over the mounds, wetlands, and canal. The trail includes museum-quality interpretive signs and wayside benches, as well as stairways to the top of both primary shell mounds, observation platforms atop the tallest mound, and a bridge and boardwalk over low-lying areas. Also available are public restrooms, a picnic area, and a teaching pavilion featuring interpretive materials and a bookshop (http://www.flmnh.ufl.edu/RRC).

5. We are mindful of the widely held contention that "the effects of climate change are likely to be most pronounced on societies heavily dependent on agriculture" (Anderson et al. 1995: 259), but we assert that effects of climate change on fishing-gathering-hunting societies can also be profound, depending on local physiographic conditions and established subsistence strategy.

3

Mississippian Influence in the Glades, Belle Glade, and East Okeechobee Areas of South Florida

ROBERT S. CARR

The effects of the sweeping tide of "Mississippianization" across the greater Southeast upon Native Americans in southeastern Florida (including the Lake Okeechobee area) have received little attention by scholars. Mississippian influences in the extreme southern end of the peninsula appear to have been ephemeral at best, but there are some important cultural manifestations dating to ca. A.D. 1000–1500 that suggest the pulse of Mississippian development may have reached south Florida. In this chapter I describe the principal site centers in the region and their relation to trade routes that favored the movement of ideas and materials into Lake Okeechobee and throughout southeastern Florida. I also detail certain cultural practices, such as earthwork and mound construction, and artifact types that appear to have developed (or became more pronounced) during the Mississippi period.

Environmental Setting

This chapter focuses on southeastern and south-central Florida, which includes both the Atlantic coast (Glades Area and the eastern part of East Okeechobee Area) and the interior Lake Okeechobee region (Belle Glade Area and the western part of East Okeechobee Area) (figure 3.1). This part of Florida encompasses major drainage features integral to understanding the movement of material goods, ideas, and people, both within the region and to points northward within the Florida peninsula.

The overall Kissimmee River–Lake Okeechobee watershed encompasses 720,000 km^2, of which the lake basin covers between 12,400 km^2 and

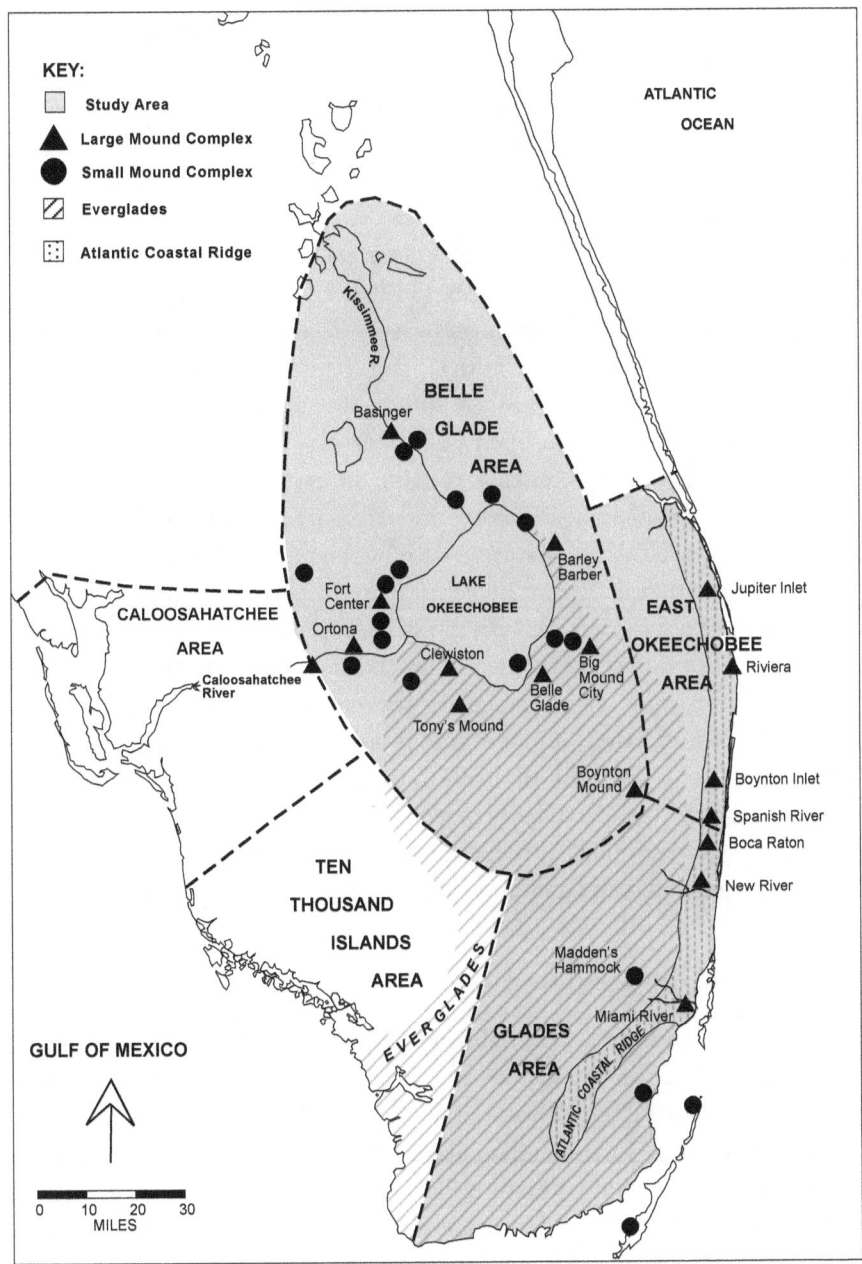

Figure 3.1. Map of southeastern and south-central Florida depicting principal sites.

15,000 km² , depending on water fluctuations (Brooks 1974). To the north is the Kissimmee River, which drains southward from central Florida into Lake Okeechobee. The lake also is fed by several smaller streams such as Fisheating, Taylor, and Van Swearingen creeks. Ground surface elevations continue their gradual decline from the north side of Lake Okeechobee south through the Everglades, descending from an elevation of about 3–4 m above sea level to less than 2 m over a distance of 80 km. This gradual southward flow has been characterized as a "River of Grass" as it fans across the Everglades (Douglas 1947), eventually emptying into the Gulf of Mexico. The flow also fingers eastward through the Miami River, Arch Creek, New River, Spanish River, and the myriad of waterways that traverse the Atlantic Coastal Ridge, spilling into Biscayne Bay, New River Sound, Lake Worth, and the open Atlantic Ocean.

By the early twentieth century, plans to drain the Everglades had been implemented, ultimately shrinking the expansive wetland to less than a quarter of its prehistoric character. Although most of the region was low and wet, the Atlantic Coastal Ridge presented a narrow upland along the east coast, as did the adjacent barrier islands, providing suitable and important areas for prehistoric habitation and settlement. In the wetlands, where uplands were scarce, habitation was confined to tree islands (Carr 2002). In the inundated prairies of the Okeechobee basin, earthworks were constructed for settlement, probably to provide sufficient elevation above the water level. The selection of these locations, particularly in the southern and western portions of the lake region, were likely in response to accessing major waterways and canoe trails, linking the interior to the coast.

Defining the Three Culture Areas

The *Glades Area* was originally defined by Mathew Stirling (1936: 355) as a distinctive culture area to include all of southern Florida. Shortly thereafter, John Goggin (1947) delineated more-specific boundaries and identified three inclusive subareas: the Calusa subarea in southwest Florida, the "Tekesta" subarea of southeastern Florida and the Florida Keys, and the Okeechobee subarea around Lake Okeechobee. These were defined on the basis of Goggin's (1947) recognition of distinctive natural environments, occupation by different historic tribes, and differences in the archaeological record. Another definition of the Glades culture area was proposed by Carr and Beriault (1984: 1–11), using the term *Everglades Area* to encompass only southeastern Florida. In 1988 Griffin followed suit and used the

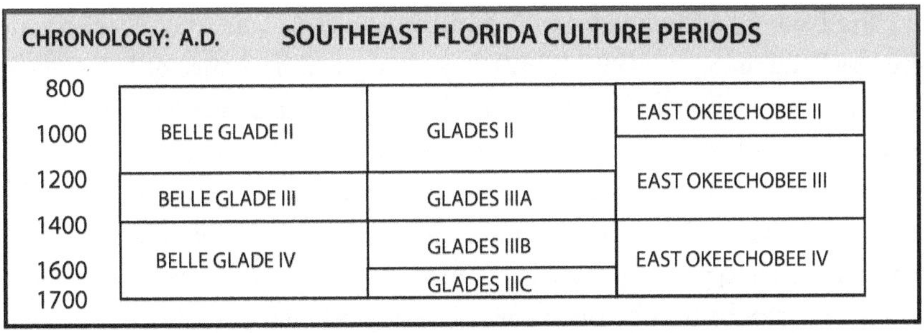

CHRONOLOGY: A.D.	SOUTHEAST FLORIDA CULTURE PERIODS		
800	BELLE GLADE II	GLADES II	EAST OKEECHOBEE II
1000			
1200	BELLE GLADE III	GLADES IIIA	EAST OKEECHOBEE III
1400			
1600	BELLE GLADE IV	GLADES IIIB	EAST OKEECHOBEE IV
1700		GLADES IIIC	

Figure 3.2. Late Woodland– through historic-period chronology of southeastern and south-central Florida.

designation *Everglades Area* in his synthesis of south Florida archaeology (Griffin 1988, 2002). Milanich (1994), however, retained the term *Glades Area* in his overview of Florida archaeology.

In this chapter, I use the designation *Glades Area* but confine it geographically to southeastern Florida and the Florida Keys (see figure 3.1). Its eastern and southern boundaries are easily defined by the Atlantic Ocean, but the exact locations of the other two borders are more difficult to determine. Carr and Beriault (1984) suggest a western boundary somewhere west of the Shark River and east of Turner River, probably near the eastern boundary of Big Cypress Swamp, and they place the northern coastal boundary near the Broward–Palm Beach County line.

Throughout prehistory the Glades Area was characterized by a fishing-hunting economy that Goggin referred to as the Glades Tradition. There is no evidence of intensive agriculture, although wild plant gathering and limited cultivation of gourds were likely. No macro-evidence of maize has been found on Mississippi-period sites, but it appears on eighteenth-century sites in this region with the arrival of the Seminoles. The Glades Area has a distinctive ceramic assemblage compared with those of the Indian River region to north and the Ten Thousand Islands, Caloosahatchee, and Belle Glade areas to the west (see Marquardt and Walker, chapter 2, and Penders, chapter 4, this volume). In the Glades Area, incised and punctated ceramics emerged sometime between A.D. 500 and 700. By A.D. 1200, ceramic assemblages were marked by an increase in St. Johns Check Stamped and Belle Glade Plain and the appearance of two new types: Surfside Incised and Glades Tooled. With the arrival of these new types, produced locally until the time of European contact, there was a dramatic decrease in the prevailing number of incised types typical of the Glades II period (figure 3.2).

The Lake Okeechobee basin is within the *Belle Glade Area*. First classified by William Sears (1967, 1982), based on the dominance of Belle Glade ceramics and what he believed was the occurrence of maize agriculture, the area also is distinctive because of its signature earthworks of raised earthen circles and crescents with outward extending, raised spokelike causeways (Carr 1975, 1985). Unlike the myriad of incised and decorated ceramic types typical of the Glades Area, the Belle Glade ceramic assemblage is characterized by plainwares, particularly Belle Glade Plain, which first emerged ca. A.D. 400–500.

Goggin (1949a) was the first to recognize that the area east of Lake Okeechobee, generally coinciding with Palm Beach County, was part of a culture area not well understood and without clearly defined boundaries. He defined it as the East Coast Region of the Okeechobee archaeological subarea and further noted that no "local" ceramic forms could be found there (1949a). Undoubtedly, this is a reference to the near absence of distinctive incised and decorated ceramic types in this part of south Florida. In addition, Goggin listed a number of nonlocal pottery types for the region that included St. Johns Plain and St. Johns Check Stamped (post–A.D. 750), which are more common on northern sites. In 1984 Carr and Beriault classified this region as the *East Okeechobee Area*.

Frequent interactions appear to have occurred with groups in the St. Johns, Indian River, and East Okeechobee regions. The presence of St. Johns pottery, *Busycon* shell adzes and Type X shell picks, and exotic trade goods such as ground stone celts and plummets in the East Okeechobee archaeological record demonstrates interactions with groups to the north (DuBois 1957; Goggin 1952; Kennedy et al. 1993; Rouse 1951). Thus, the main influence on the East Okeechobee Area after ca. A.D. 1000 seems to have come from the north, such as the Indian River and St. Johns areas, rather than from the Belle Glade Area to the west, although contact with the latter certainly occurred, as indicated by the presence of small amounts of nonlocal Belle Glade Plain pottery. Few of the signature decorated ceramic types of the Glades Area occur in the East Okeechobee Area.

Review of Principal Mound Centers

To understand the movement of exotic goods, information, and other cultural influences into south Florida requires knowledge of the principal mound centers throughout the Kissimmee River area, Lake Okeechobee basin, and southeastern Florida and how these sites may have functioned as redistribution centers of exotica and political and religious ideas. Providing an accurate inventory and assessment of these centers, particularly with respect to chronology, is constrained by a paucity of data resulting from minimal archaeological sampling and/or adverse site impacts due to development.

Principal mound centers are characterized by a complex of mound and earthwork architecture, habitation middens (often placed on constructed mounds), and excavated canals and ponds. In southeastern Florida, in present-day Broward, Miami-Dade, and Monroe counties, these larger centers tend to be on the coast, particularly at or near the mouths of major rivers or estuaries. Smaller complexes—many with accompanying burial mounds—occur upstream on these same drainage systems and on smaller creeks, as well as along the western edge of the Atlantic Coastal Ridge, including islands abutting the eastern Everglades, and on the Florida Keys. Resource procurement camps and smaller habitation sites are widely scattered along the coast, including on the barrier islands, on mainland shores of Biscayne Bay, and throughout the Keys and Everglades.

In Palm Beach County, an area that generally coincides with the southern portion of the East Okeechobee Area, large villages occur both on the coast and on the eastern edge of Lake Okeechobee. The county encompasses two principal culture areas: East Okeechobee and Belle Glade. The coastal area evinces pervasive influences from the north, while the western part of the county is marked by site types and artifacts representing influences from the Lake Okeechobee vicinity to the west.

In the Belle Glade Area, larger earthwork and mound complexes occur throughout the Lake Okeechobee basin, the upper Caloosahatchee River, and the Kissimmee River valley. Smaller earthwork complexes and habitation middens also occur, often associated with hammock islands and sometimes as isolated mounds and earthworks constructed within wet prairies, where high natural ground is scarce or nonexistent; sites are often placed near deeper sloughs and canoe trails.

Glades Area

It is near the present-day Broward–Palm Beach County line at Boca Raton Inlet where a change in ceramic assemblage composition appears to signal the southern end of the historic Jeaga territory and the northern boundary of the historically documented Tequesta. The domain of the latter was spread throughout the Everglades and extended south through the

Florida Keys, a region that coincides with the Glades Area. This is an area considerably larger than the Tequesta's principal town at the mouth of the Miami River, where most historic encounters with these people occurred. However, archaeological investigations indicate that the ceramic markers and other distinctive artifact types associated with the town of Tequesta also occur in similar frequencies south through the Florida Keys (Carr et al. 1988) and west through the Everglades (Carr 2002), suggesting that the overall area was part of the Tequesta sphere of cultural influence throughout much of the Glades period rather than the political domain of the Calusa, who dominated the Keys during the historic period (Hann 2003).

A large mound complex (8Bd3) was located on the New River in present-day Fort Lauderdale. Although mostly destroyed, 8Bd3 once encompassed a group of sand mounds and earthworks, including one mound with a zig-zag earthen causeway (Carr et al. 1991). All that remains today is an elongated midden-mound (8Bd87), about 150 m long, that parallels the north bank of the New River (Beriault and Carr 2000).

The largest mound complex in southeastern Florida, 8Da11 and 8Da12, was at the mouth of the Miami River, occupying both banks and abutting Biscayne Bay (Carr and Ricisak 2000; Griffin et al 1982; Wheeler 2000a). This was the center of the historic Tequesta chiefdom. The site was characterized by at least five constructed mounds and a large black-earth and shell midden that occurred on both the northern and southern sides of the river. At least two nonmounded cemeteries are documented, one on each side of the river. Prehistoric activity areas extend 500 m north and south of the river's mouth and continue 1 km west along the river on both banks. The entire area was probably not in use at any one time, as evidence suggests that habitation activities shifted through time, possibly to avoid the unhealthy conditions posed by decomposing shell and food refuse.

Unfortunately, all of these mounds have been destroyed, with only scant archaeological documentation (i.e., Douglass 1885; Eck 2000), so little information exists to determine mound chronology. But the little that has been reported, combined with information from similar mounds in the area, suggests that the mounds date to the Glades III period (ca. A.D. 1200–1600), with several of the mounds having European objects (Eck 2000).

One of the mysteries of the Miami River settlement is a habitation shift from occupying both the north and south banks to only the north bank, beginning about A.D. 1000 and continuing uninterrupted until European contact and Spanish mission efforts in the sixteenth and eighteenth century (Carr and Ricisak 2002). The settlement movement coincides with a change in regional ceramic assemblages, characterized by a decrease in the variety and quantity of local decorated wares, coupled with an increase in nonlocal St. Johns pottery, specifically, St. Johns Check Stamped and St. Johns Plain. Marquardt and Walker (see chapter 2, this volume) note a shift in settlement at Pineland in southwest Florida around the same time because of rising sea levels, but this interpretation does not explain the apparent abandonment of the south bank on the Miami River. A rise in sea level probably would simply have forced the settlement southward, where elevations increase to 3.5 m above sea level, but no evidence for such a movement has been found.

From south of the Miami River to Key West are numerous other smaller village-mound complexes including Cutler (8Da7, 8Da8), Sands Key (8Da3), Plantation Key (8Mo23), Key Largo (8Mo25,26), and Stock Island (8Mo2). One particularly significant site grouping is the Matecumbe Complex, which consists of a burial mound (8Mo13) and at least four middens abutting the Indian Key Channel separating Upper and Lower Matecumbe Key. None of the smaller sites in the Keys has yet provided evidence of having been a major town center, but exotic artifacts reported for the islands include chert and ground stone tools (Goggin 1949b).

East Okeechobee Area

In southeastern Florida the northernmost mound center is at Jupiter Inlet in far northern Palm Beach County. Two large sites occur there—one on the north side of the inlet mouth (8PB35) and one on the south side (8PB34). The Jupiter Lighthouse site (8PB35) is associated with a possible parabolic dune that extends 300 m east–west. The site is situated atop a moundlike hill near the western end of the dune, which is horseshoe shaped with its opening to the east. A shell midden deposit occurs across the southern dune, which rises up to 15 m above sea level. A sand burial mound, which has never been excavated, is reported to occur on the inside of the dune's westward apex (Douglass 1885). Midden deposits occur southward from the southern arm of the dune, where they are deepest near the inlet. Ceramic types range from fiber tempered to St. Johns Check Stamped, indicating occupations from the initial Late Archaic through East Okeechobee III–IV period. Exotic materials have not been reported from the site, but midden excavations have been limited and disturbances severe, as a result of more than a century of lighthouse and subsequent Coast Guard construction activities.

In contrast, exotic artifacts have been uncovered at the DuBois Midden (8PB34), located on a constructed shell midden ridge 5 m above sea level. Prior to shell borrowing, the midden ridge extended about 122–83 m east–west, paralleling the inlet shore (Wheeler, Pepe, and Kennedy 2002). Today, only a 90-m segment survives. This elevated midden was apparently intentionally constructed, as Wheeler observed clean shell and evidence of "basket loading" at the site (Wheeler, Pepe, and Kennedy 2002: 184). The shell ridge had other auxiliary features, including additional shellworks, one parallel ridge to the south, and at least one sand burial mound. Three radiocarbon dates were determined for samples uncovered by Florida Atlantic University (Kennedy et al. 1993; Wheeler and Pepe 2002; Wheeler, Pepe, and Kennedy 2002). Two of these dates have a two sigma range of A.D. 721–1253, placing occupation during the Glades II period.

Exotica from 8PB34 include ground stone celts and pendants (DuBois 1957). Recent investigations conducted on top of the surviving shell midden uncovered two nonlocal, sand-tempered shell-stamped sherds within a ceramic assemblage containing mostly St. Johns Check Stamped and sand-tempered plainwares (Carr et al. 2009). Historic accounts and recent articles have identified this site as the town of Jobe, where the Englishman Jonathan Dickinson was taken in 1696 after his shipwreck. A recovery of a likely seventeenth-century ship spike and glass bead reinforces this interpretation (Carr et al. 2009).

Located 24 km south of the Jupiter Inlet Complex are two principal sites associated with Palm Beach Inlet and Lake Worth. Goggin (1949b) reported a burial mound (8PB28) and midden (8PB29) on the barrier island on the southern side of the inlet. The site area is now covered by residential housing and roads. Archaeological monitoring of the midden site by the author and surface collections by a neighbor resulted in the recovery of numerous St. Johns Check Stamped sherds and a single nonlocal ground stone celt. In 2007, house remodeling about 200 m to the north uncovered the remnants of a sand burial mound that contained disarticulated human remains (Mueller 2007). No grave goods were observed.

Directly west of these two barrier island sites on the east shore of Lake Worth is the Riviera site (8PB30). This site was situated on an elevated shell midden ridge, not unlike that at the Dubois site. The Riviera site has been destroyed, but an early twentieth-century map of it was recently published by Wheeler, Kennedy, and Pepe (2002), who refer to these three sites collectively as the Riviera Complex. All three appear to have been occupied during the Glades III period. Wheeler and Pepe (2002) posit that the Riviera site is the historic village of Jeaga.

Twelve kilometers south of the Palm Beach Inlet is a group of mounds and middens known as the Spanish River Complex (Furey 1972; Wheeler, Kennedy, and Pepe 2002: 125–28). The grouping includes two sand burial mounds (8PB11, 8PB13), an unmounded cemetery, and at least three middens (8PB12, 8PB55, 8PB56). Most of these sites are located on the barrier island, although others occur along the Spanish River westward onto the mainland. The site group on the barrier island is now collectively referred to as 8PB9636 (Wheeler 1998). Ceramics recovered from these sites date to ca. A.D. 750–1783, so it is likely that many of the mounds were constructed during the Mississippi period (Wheeler, Kennedy, and Pepe 2002: 125).

Belle Glade Area

Large earthwork-mound complexes surround Lake Okeechobee and occur along the Kissimmee and Caloosahatchee river basins. Among the largest of the site complexes in south Florida is Ortona, located on the north side of the Caloosahatchee River between Fort Center and Estero Bay (see figure 3.1). The complex consists of earthworks that include sand mounds, midden-mounds, an "effigy" pond (8Gl43), and ridges or causeways that extend west from a large burial mound. The largest mound (8Gl5) is over 8 m high and is the highest in the area. The Ortona site is connected to the Caloosahatchee River by two canals that include western and eastern segments that, combined, are 5.9 km long, making them the longest prehistoric transportation canal in North America (Carr et al. 2002; Kenworthy 1883; Wheeler 1995).

Radiocarbon dates recovered from organic sediments deposited after construction suggest the canals were first built around A.D. 200 (Carr et al. 2002). These canals are similar to the one that traverses Pine Island on the Gulf coast near the mouth of the Caloosahatchee River (Luer 1989). The fact that the canals are so similar and that they combine to link the Caloosahatchee River to the Lake Okeechobee basin indicates a strong cultural and political affinity between the two areas through time. The Pineland mound center is discussed in chapter 2 (Marquardt and Walker, this volume).

Other large earthworks occur around Lake Okeechobee. Beginning on the west shore is Fort Center (8Gl13) at Fisheating Creek, followed clockwise by Barley Barber (8Mt19), Belle Glade Mounds (8PB45), and Big Mound City (8PB46) (Carr 1986). On the east side a large number of smaller mounds and earthworks dot the Kissimmee River drainage, including an important complex at Basinger (Carr 1985; Johnson 1996). Other large earthwork complexes, such as Tony's Mound (8Hn3), occur south of the lake in the northern Everglades. Smaller mound complexes often characterized by a single burial mound, some with parallel earthen causeways and a midden-mound, occur throughout the area. The southernmost example of the Belle Glade–style earthwork complex is the Boynton Earthworks (8PB100), located in the eastern Everglades, 15 km northwest of the Spanish River Complex (Carr 1973; Willey 1949b).

Archaeological testing and radiocarbon dating have been limited in the Belle Glade Area, so determining which sites were in use during the Mississippi period is difficult. However, by A.D. 1000–1200, mound construction appears to be characterized by new formats that included large flat-topped mounds, larger burial mounds, and new types of earthwork alignments (described below). Surveying of Lake Okeechobee earthworks was conducted by Carr (1985) and subsequently by Hale (1989) and Johnson (1996), all aiding in classifying earthwork sites by type.

The most comprehensive investigation of a single earthwork complex was conducted at the Fort Center site (Sears 1982), although earlier excavations were performed at Belle Glade and Big Mound City (Willey 1949b). The Fort Center investigations indicate a long history of mound building and earthwork construction, perhaps dating back to ca. 750 B.C. for the large circular ditch earthworks and some of the sand burial mounds. The large circular ditch measures more than 365 m in diameter and was hypothesized by Sears (1982) to be a drained field for maize cultivation, an interpretation based solely on the recovery of corn pollen (Sears and Sears 1976). No evidence of this ditch function has been fully demonstrated. I posit an alternative function in which the numerous circular ditches served as fish impoundments connected to adjacent creeks and rivers by an intricate weir and gate system. Fish populations could have been diverted into these impoundments and maintained for community subsistence.

The earliest manifestation of earthwork construction is during the Belle Glade I period (ca. 750–500 B.C.), with the creation of what I believe were large circular fish weirs associated with residential midden-mounds and a community burial mound. By the Mississippi period (A.D. 1000), Belle Glade earthworks had developed a new look. Large circular earthworks were constructed, 1–2 m above the surrounding wetlands and up to 300 m in diameter, with multiple linear causeways extending from a central crescent ridge. Each linear causeway terminated at a small sand mound. The exact function of these new earthwork complexes is unclear, but sand burial mounds and midden-mounds often occur in close association. It is likely that this architectural format, unique to North America, reflects an efficient community settlement layout designed to maximize water access and create elevated mounds for habitation, cemeteries, and possible gardens. However, elevated mound surfaces—all probably constructed to be above water—are relatively small in area, with little space available for maize or any type of intensive cultivation, let alone large numbers of people.

A typical example of the smaller earthwork-mound complex is the Nicodemus site (8G19), located south of Fort Center (figure 3.3). Other mound types are elongated, such as at the Pepper Mound (8Hn4). A similar example of an elongated flat-topped mound occurs at Ortona. Both are narrow platforms with small domiciliary mounds constructed on top. These scattered Okeechobee mound complexes may represent secondary villages, with alliances to leaders or even chiefs of larger complexes.

Exchange, Interaction, and Possible Mississippian Influences

The larger mound complexes described above probably represent principal settlements that served as hubs of exchange and political power during the late prehistoric period. Many of these towns are likely the same sites described during the sixteenth century by the Spanish, particularly in Escalante Fontaneda's list of Indian towns and villages (Hann 2003). Movements of people and goods followed major water routes often associated with larger mound complexes. For example, in the interior the Kissimmee River route to Lake Okeechobee linked north-central and south Florida, and the lake area in turn was connected to the Gulf coast by way of the Caloosahatchee River. This route allowed traffic to move from Fort Center to Ortona, and then by canal to the Caloosahatchee River and onward to Mound Key and Pine Island along Florida's southwest coast. The antiquity of this flow-way connection suggests strong cultural (and likely political) relations between these two areas, even prior to the Mississippi period.

It is hypothesized that the Miami River center (8Da11, 8Da12) was linked to the interior by a canoe route through the Everglades that probably followed the western edge of the Atlantic Coastal Ridge to the Democrat River, which would have provided access to the Belle Glade Mounds

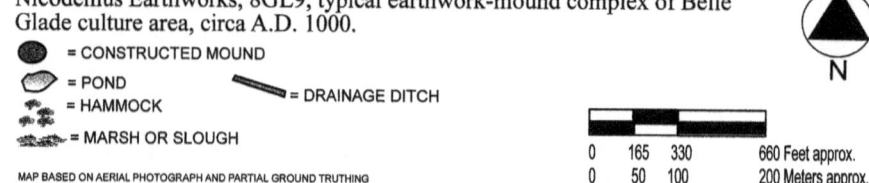

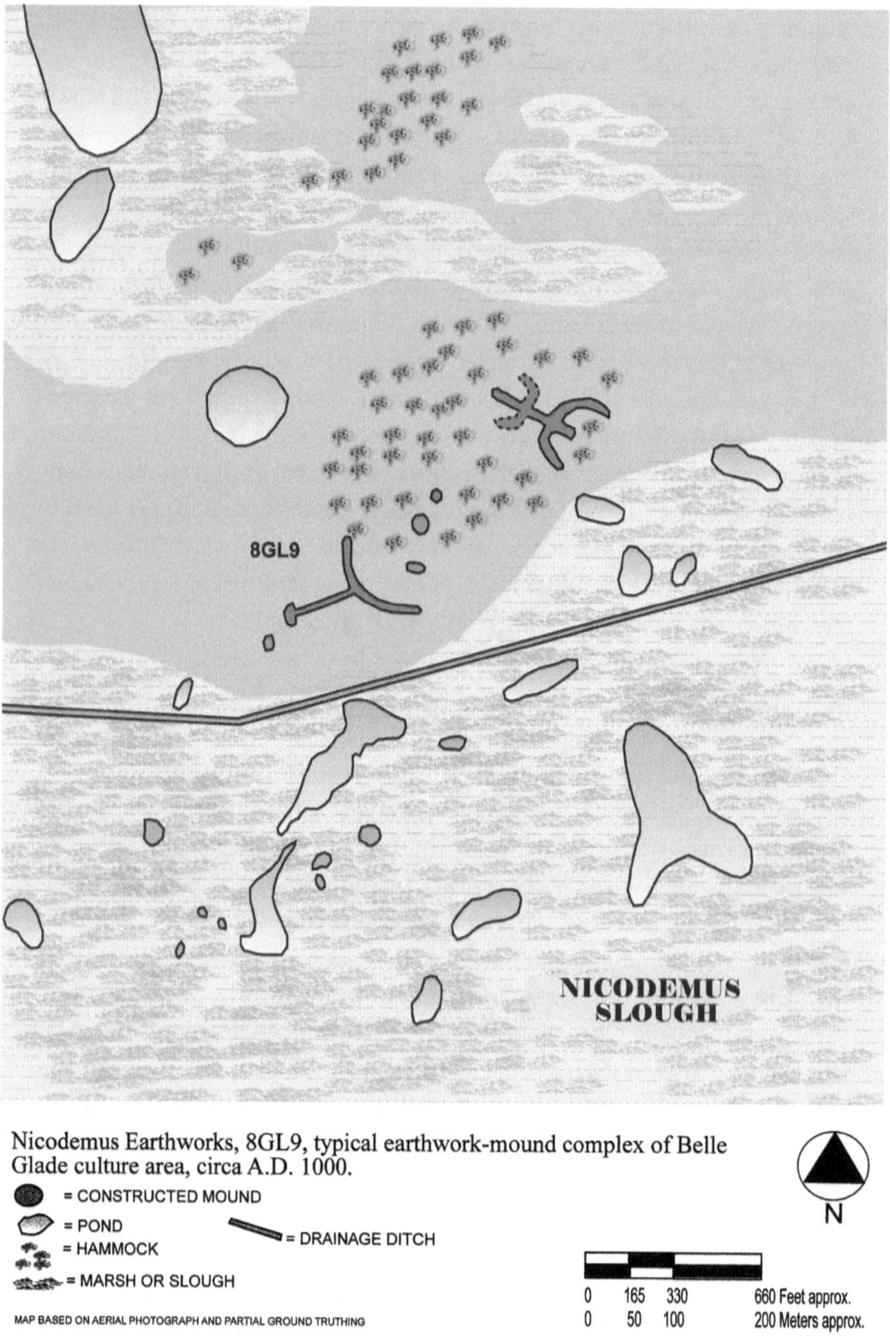

8GL9
NICODEMUS
SLOUGH
Nicodemus Earthworks, 8GL9, typical earthwork-mound complex of Belle Glade culture area, circa A.D. 1000.
= CONSTRUCTED MOUND
= POND
= HAMMOCK
= MARSH OR SLOUGH
= DRAINAGE DITCH
N
0 165 330 660 Feet approx.
0 50 100 200 Meters approx.
MAP BASED ON AERIAL PHOTOGRAPH AND PARTIAL GROUND TRUTHING

Figure 3.3. Nicodemus Earthworks (8Gl9).

(8PB45), a likely regional center. From there the water route would have touched Kramer and Ritta islands, where important satellite settlements offered strategic locations for the movement of materials across Lake Okeechobee (Davenport et al. 2011). Kramer Island, where large quantities of shell tools and ornaments were recently discovered by Davenport and colleagues, may have been a principal transit center during the late Glades II and III periods.

Northern and eastern routes from the lake followed smaller creeks and rivers to the Atlantic coast, although they may have been minor routes and possibly not well used, because they crossed what may have been cultural boundaries, at least during the contact period. There appears to have been some degree of stability between prehistoric Woodland- and Mississippi-period (Glades II–III periods) boundaries and later historic territorial boundaries, as suggested by continuity in distinctive ceramic assemblages in abutting areas through time. A north–south route along the Atlantic coast was likely along the bays, on the western side of the barrier islands, and on the Indian River, where access to northeastern Florida would have been easily gained.

With major corridors of transit and interaction well established in southern Florida by A.D. 400, as demonstrated by Hopewellian-like artifacts uncovered at various mounds (e.g., Austin 1993; Dickel and Carr 1991), exchange networks for the movement of goods and ideas continued during and probably throughout the Mississippi period. But what are generally lacking are artifacts or clear-cut evidence of influences from the broader Mississippian world. Large platform-like mounds may have been built in the area after A.D. 1200, but evidence is not conclusive. Moreover, none of these has survived intact. Candidates for larger, flat-topped mounds occur at Maddens Hammock (8Da45) along the eastern Everglades and the Rock Mound (8Mo25) on Key Largo (Newman and Tesar 1997). Evidence of ramps has been reported at both sites (Goggin 1949b), but their integrity has been compromised by destructive excavations by vandals, precluding a confident assessment of their exact function and format. Other large mounds in the region have been destroyed by modern construction and development.

At present there is no evidence to suggest that maize agriculture was practiced anywhere in south Florida during the Mississippi period. Not only were environmental conditions unsuitable for intensive maize cultivation, but also the subsistence opportunities afforded by the area's expansive wetlands, rivers, and coastal estuaries created an ample year-round source of food. Fishing technology had developed to include multiple strategies such as netting, weirs, and poisons—all designed to maximize the quantity of fish caught.

The abundance of marine resources is regarded as a key impetus for the development of social complexity and chiefdomship in south Florida, particularly with the Calusa (Goggin and Sturtevant 1964; Marquardt 1992b). The cooperation needed for constructing and maintaining fishing weirs and nets and, more important, the organization of community labor to construct and maintain earthworks, canals, and mounds might have required a principal chief or centralized decision-making structure. Griffin (2002) argued that such activities began earlier than A.D. 800, a temporal marker set by some archaeologists as the beginning of chiefdoms among the Calusa (Widmer 2002: 391). Griffin (2002: 320–21) also speculated that historic tribal areas such as Tequesta or Fort Center may have been secondary chiefdoms, as many of these tribes were reportedly providing tribute to the Calusa during the historic period. By the sixteenth century, Spanish accounts suggest the existence of at least seven distinct provinces or chiefdoms in coastal south Florida (Hann 2003: 10–11). Shoring up the ethnographic accounts is archaeological evidence that suggests at least four and likely five coastal areas of distinct archaeological assemblages in southern Florida.

New mound construction with an emphasis on larger mortuary mounds, both for interring human remains and acting as platforms for charnel houses, may characterize the period A.D. 1200–1600. The more complex earthworks typical of the Belle Glade Area also appear to have been constructed (or expanded) at this time; however, there is insufficient evidence to indicate whether these changes developed internally or as a result of outside influences.

Exotic artifacts such as ground stone celts and plummets and copper ornaments occur in the East Okeechobee and Glades areas. Several examples have been reported and observed from the Jupiter Inlet (Dubois 1957) and Riviera complexes. Numerous examples have been found in Miami-Dade County associated with deposits containing St. Johns ceramics, such as at 8Da12 (Carr 2009), reinforcing the idea that the materials arrived along routes from northern Florida; but much of this exotica dates to Woodland times and apparently represents Hopewellian influences. Willey (1949b: 128) believed that ground stone celts in southeastern Florida derived from the St. Johns area as a result of both Hopewellian- and Mississippian-influenced Weeden Island interactions. Candidates for materials moving out

Mississippian Influence in South Florida · 77

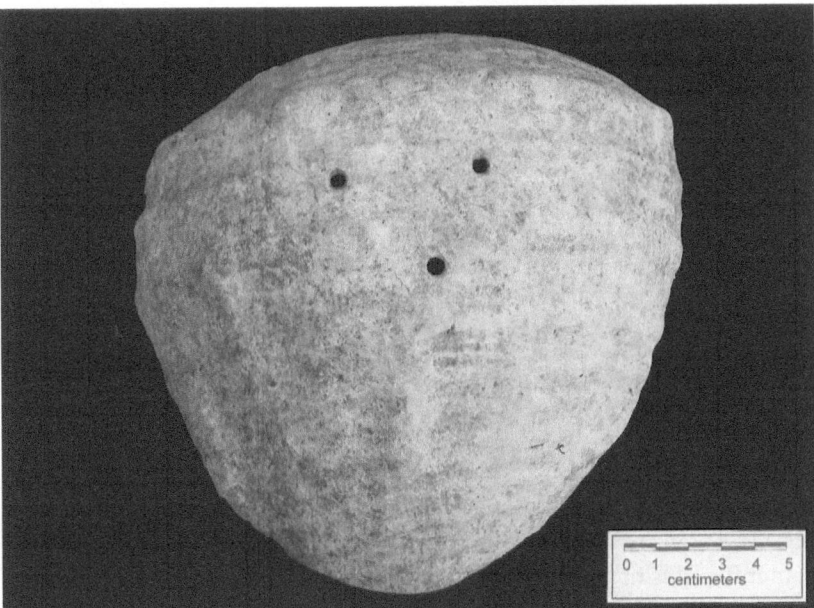

Figure 3.4. Shell-mask gorget uncovered in Palm Beach County.

of southern Florida to the north include shells, pumice, shark teeth, and feathers.

Three artifacts uncovered in south Florida deserve special attention because of their possible connections to the broader Mississippian world. The first is a shell-mask gorget recovered from a site (8Pb45) in Palm Beach County. The site has since been destroyed by sugar cane cultivation, but in the 1930s project supervisor Roswell Harrington collected several artifacts and human remains during canal dredging for a new bridge. Precisely what type of site once existed there is unclear, but it is located in Canal Point on the eastern side of Lake Okeechobee, an area that appears to have been a wetland marsh prior to drainage and cultivation (Carr et al. 2004).

The Canal Point shell gorget is ovoid in shape, suggestive of a mask, with a narrowing rounded "chin," though it is not a mask type specifically described by Smith and Smith (1989). The Canal Point gorget is comparable to other Mississippian shell masks, such as that from Nodena (Arkansas), though it lacks any incised designs or other decorative alterations. It measures about 20 cm by 20 cm across the "eye" area and is plain, without engravings, but with three drill holes, two possibly representing eyes and one a mouth (figure 3.4). It is the most southerly known occurrence of a possible shell-mask gorget. No other comparable specimens have been

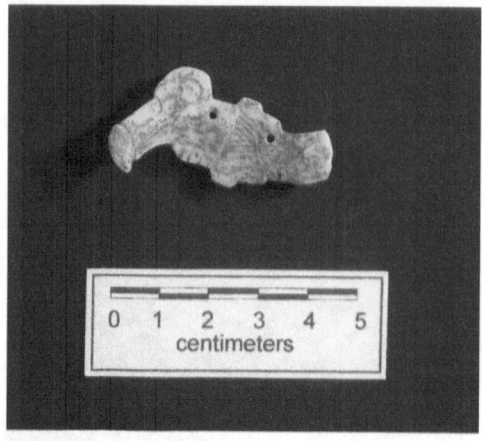

Figure 3.5. Shell gorget vulture uncovered at 8Da1081 in the Everglades.

reported in southern Florida. Most specimens have been found in Tennessee and Arkansas, and this single occurrence may represent late Mississippian influences in south Florida.

A second artifact of particular interest is a shell buzzard pendant (figure 3.5). The shell is carved into a naturalistic depiction of a vulture. It was found on a tree island site (8Da1081) in the eastern Everglades in a black-earth midden that included ceramics from the Glades II and III periods (ca. A.D. 1200–1600 [Coleman et al. 1983]). Although disarticulated human remains were uncovered nearby, there is no conclusive evidence that it was associated with any human burials. However, identifying such associations on tree islands is often difficult because of extensive disturbances. This artifact might be associated with the Mississippian "buzzard" motif, though it could be earlier as well.

The third artifact is a silver disk engraved with a clearly Mississippian design, a hand and eye motif, uncovered at the Fort Center site (8Gl13) on the west side of Lake Okeechobee (Sears 1986: fig. 5.2H). The weeping eye motif is rarely encountered in south Florida. The association of this disk with other artifacts obviously of European origin indicates a likely seventeenth- or eighteenth-century date for the disk.

During the Glades II and III periods, a major florescence of naturalistic art occurs in south Florida, with well-executed bone pin and wooden carvings, many with zoomorphic representations and intricate geometric motifs (Wheeler 1996a). In the Tequesta area, Wheeler and Coleman (1996: 50–55) define the Everglades tradition, represented on bone pins by intricate designs including knot-and-braid forms, punctates, zoned punctations, and zoned hatching (Wheeler 2004). The zoomorphic motifs, with the best-known examples excavated from Key Marco (Cushing 1897), include alligators, birds (particularly woodpeckers), snakes, and a panther as represented by the Marco cat. The bird is a particularly important motif during this period, with examples manufactured as *adornos* on ceramic pots and carved shell pendants and crested woodpeckers shaped from shipwrecked (salvaged) gold and silver. The cross is depicted as a design element on both shell and bone artifacts during the Glades III period (ca. A.D. 1200–1600) and is an important motif exhibited on metal tablets found throughout south Florida, with specimens made from ship-salvaged silver, copper, lead, and gold (Allerton et al. 1984; Goggin 1949c; Luer 2010).

These unique south Florida artistic and design themes depicted on ceremonial artifacts were first recognized by Goggin as manifestations of the "Glades Cult" (Goggin 1949c), also known as the South Florida Ceremonial Complex (Hann 2003: 192) and as the Terminal Glades Complex (Wheeler 2004). But the designs bear only partial similarities to those associated with the Southeastern Ceremonial Complex (SECC). Widmer (1989: 166, 168–71) points this out and notes that many of the SECC motifs, such as the winged serpent and the bilobed arrow, are absent from the south Florida artistic complex, as are certain artifact types such as ceramic water bottles and copper headdresses and breastplates, to name a few. Conversely, the crested bird and ceremonial tablets, as well as other metal ornaments that appear to be types created during the period of European contact, do not appear in the SECC.

Summary

Mississippian influences in the form of ideas and exotic objects probably reached south Florida on the same canoe corridors and routes that had heralded the appearance of earlier Middle Woodland–period Hopewellian influences. These routes amplified exchange opportunities and brought influences from multiple directions: southward along both the Kissimmee and Indian rivers and from the Gulf coast up the Caloosahatchee River to Lake Okeechobee. By A.D. 1200, large mound complexes had already been established across the area, and although comprehensive radiocarbon dating is lacking, large burial mounds, many with charnel houses, were likely constructed during this period. Other mound types of this period include flat, elongated mounds apparently used for domiciliary purposes in the Belle Glade Area. Exotic objects of copper and ground stone tools are reported in the same chronological context, including the appearance of "cult" objects such as the shell-mask gorget, as well as intricately carved shell, bone, and wood—some with cross motifs and bird designs suggestive of Mississippian influences. Although major Mississippian characteristics such as maize cultivation and the construction of platform mounds are lacking, archaeological evidence indicates that this was a period of vigorous cultural change and sociopolitical development in south Florida. These changes may be the result of some Mississippian influences reaching their most southerly locations in North America, attesting to the fluidity of the cultural conversation of ideas and materials between the greater Southeast and Florida.

4

The Indian River Region during the Mississippi Period

THOMAS E. PENDERS

The Indian River region of east-central Florida was inhabited by mobile fisher-hunter-gatherers for millennia prior to European arrival. Though they had contact with neighboring peoples during this time, Indian River populations were largely severed from intensive interactions with the broader Southeast by societies of northern peninsular and panhandle Florida, who were more actively engaged in widespread interaction networks. The sixteenth century, however, witnessed changes in native life as a somewhat steady flow of exotics made its way to the natives of the Indian River region. These foreign materials, however, did not derive from the Mississippian world but rather came from European shipwrecks, vessels grounded along the Atlantic seaboard of central Florida. This windfall brought power and increased sociopolitical complexity to the historic natives of the Indian River region, known to Europeans as the Ais, while they persisted as coastal foragers. Focusing on the Indian River Lagoon, this chapter provides an updated perspective on the Malabar II culture (A.D. 1000–1600) and explores changes wrought by European contact, including recent claims that the historic Ais (and perhaps their predecessors) constructed monumental architecture in the form of shell/earthworks.

Indian River Lagoon Environment

The Indian River is a restricted coastal lagoon with openings to the Atlantic Ocean at Ponce de Leon Inlet (north), Sebastian Inlet (central), and St. Lucie Inlet (south). It is part of a larger lagoonal system known as the Indian River Lagoon that includes Mosquito Lagoon and Banana River (Harbor Branch Oceanographic Institution 2001). Combined, this watershed

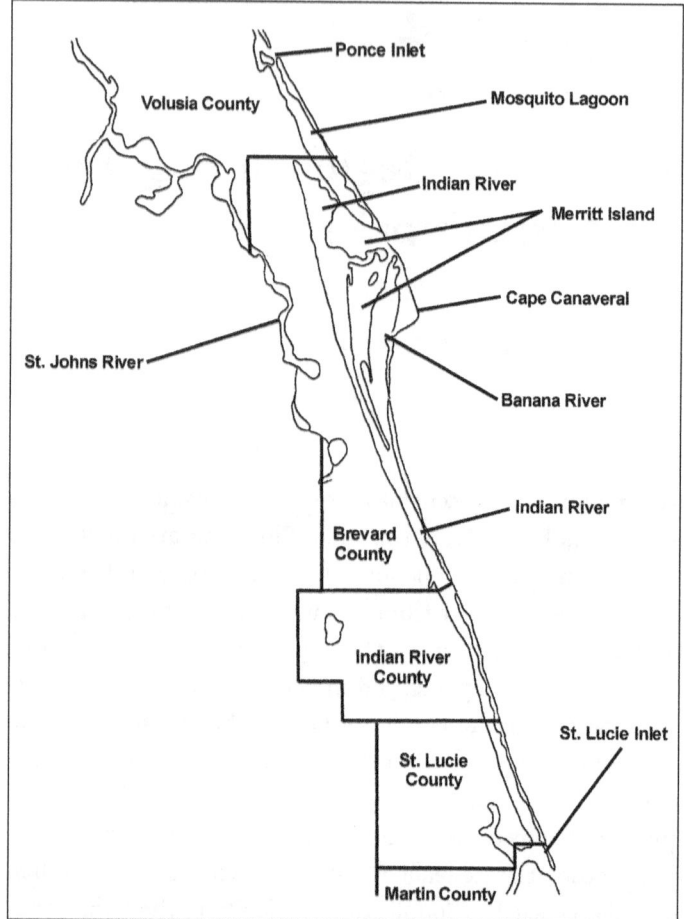

Figure 4.1. Major physiographic features and political boundaries of the Indian River region.

extends about 250 km along Florida's east coast, between the outer islands and the mainland peninsula. Water movement is typically wind driven and nontidal except at the inlets, where tides do play a role. The Indian River Lagoon varies in width from just less than 1 km to 5 km and averages only 1 m in depth, conditions that would have facilitated native canoe travel.

The Indian River Lagoon includes a chain of islands along the coast from St. Lucie Inlet north to Cocoa Beach, at which point the coastal geomorphology becomes more complex. Cocoa Beach has a series of islands within the Banana River known locally as the Thousand Islands. To the north are Merritt Island and Cape Canaveral, which are actually two barrier islands joined at the southern tip of Mosquito Lagoon (figure 4.1). The coastal area is a diverse mosaic of ecosystems that include mangrove and salt marshes, sea grass habitats, oak forest/maritime hammock, pine flatwoods, oak/saw palmetto scrub, and beach dune (Brech 2004; Breininger et al. 1994). The Indian River Lagoon touts among the highest levels of biodiversity of any estuary in North America, being home to more than 3,000 different plants and animals (Harbor Branch Oceanographic Institution 2001). It serves as a spawning ground and nursery for many different marine and freshwater fish species and has one of the most diverse bird populations in America (Breininger et al. 1994; NASA 2000; Virnstein and Campbell 1987). Because the Indian River Lagoon lies between temperate and tropical climatic zones, it is often viewed as an environmental transitional zone (Dickel and Doran 2002: 40).

Malabar Culture

The Indian River culture area was originally defined by Irving Rouse (1951: 51) as stretching from near the northern boundary of Brevard County south to St. Lucie Inlet, a distance of some 190 km. From east to west it extended from the Atlantic seaboard to the upper St. Johns River basin, an average distance of about 50 km (figure 4.1). Rouse (1951) further defined the post-Archaic Malabar culture of the region, the archaeological antecedent of the historic Ais, whose territory roughly mirrored that of the Indian River region. Relying primarily on the widespread distribution of the St. Johns ceramic tradition, Milanich and Fairbanks (1980) later opted to combine the St. Johns and Indian River regions to form the East and Central Lakes District, which covered nearly the entire eastern two-thirds of peninsular Florida. Following the results of a series of archaeological investigations in the 1980s, however, researchers again spotlighted the Indian River region as a distinct culture area or transitional zone between St. Johns to the north and Glades to the south and have continued to advocate the use of Malabar terminology (Brech 2004; Campbell et al. 1984; Milanich 1994: 243; Russo 1988; Sigler-Eisenberg 1985; Sigler-Eisenberg and Russo 1986).

Building upon earlier temporal sequences forwarded by Goggin (1947, 1948a), Rouse (1951) brought together all available archaeological data to establish the first comprehensive synthesis and chronology for the Indian River region. Although he viewed Indian River as a distinctive cultural region, he, like Goggin, labeled it a transitional area and appeared rather unimpressed with what he described as the rather "nondescript" and "simplistic" Malabar culture (Rouse 1951: 68–69). He divided the local post-Archaic period into Malabar I and II subperiods or phases. In the absence of radiocarbon dates, he assigned the Malabar II phase to the years A.D. 1000–1763 and noted that St. Johns Check Stamped pottery was diagnostic of the Malabar II phase (Rouse 1951: 237, 259).

Not much has changed in the past sixty years. The Indian River region still suffers from a dearth of radiometric dates, and St. Johns Check Stamped pottery is still viewed as a temporal marker for the Malabar II phase. On the basis of ceramic similarities, Malabar II is generally assumed to be coeval with St. Johns II and dated to A.D. 750–1565 (Milanich 1994: 250), making it temporally equivalent to the Late Woodland and Mississippi periods of the broader Southeast. In the following sections I use available data to provide an updated overview of pottery assemblages, site types and distributions, and subsistence strategies characteristic of the Indian River region during the Malabar II period.

Pottery Assemblages

One material characteristic that persisted in the Indian River region from the beginning of Malabar I times to at least the mid-seventeenth century was the ubiquity of plain ceramics. Unfortunately, the production of undecorated wares for more than two millennia has greatly handcuffed our ability to assess accurately the temporal affiliation of sites, particularly in the absence of radiometric dates (Brech 2004: 37). Archaeologists have relied mostly on the presence of minority or nonlocal types to help date sites. Following the lead of Rouse (1951: 246, 250), researchers typically define Malabar I pottery assemblages based on the presence of St. Johns (sponge-spicule-tempered) and sand-tempered plainwares along with small amounts of St. Johns Incised and Dunns Creek Red. Malabar II assemblages are highlighted by the addition of St. Johns Check Stamped, the occasional occurrence of nonlocal wares (or local copies of foreign types), and eventual discontinuation of St. Johns Incised and Dunns Creek Red (Rouse 1951: 254).

Throughout the Malabar I and II phases, the ratio between the two plainwares is thought to vary along a north–south gradation, with St. Johns Plain dominating to the north, sand-tempered plain to the south, and roughly equal amounts of the two in the middle (Rouse 1951: 250, 254; Sears 1958: 122). Because of this gradation, sand-tempered plainwares are frequently assumed to represent Glades Plain or Belle Glades Plain of south Florida (Rouse 1951: 246, 250). For this reason, Rouse and many subsequent researchers have viewed Malabar as a transitional pottery assemblage reflective of the area between St. Johns to the north and Glades to the south. In contrast, Espenshade (1983: 188) believes that "Indian River potters participated in the ceramic traditions of south Florida." Although many have acknowledged this interregional spatial trend, however, it has yet to be systematically tested (Dickel 1992: 32; Lanham and Brech 2007: 35). Following Russo's (1992a: 120) advice for the St. Marys region of extreme northeastern Florida (i.e., north of the St. Johns region), I believe the use of the term *transitional* undermines the distinct culture identities of the Indian River region.

Recent research allows commentary on a couple of the long-held temporal assumptions regarding Malabar ceramic assemblages. First, St. Johns Incised no longer appears to represent a reliable temporal marker, because Brech's (2004: 121) ceramic analysis has clearly shown that this ceramic type occurs in both Malabar I and II contexts. Second, and more important, the frequency of check stamping in Malabar II assemblages might be far less than that in St. Johns II assemblages to the north. Cordell's (1985) study of Malabar pottery assemblages from sites along the upper St. Johns River was the first to suggest such a trend. Brech's (2004: 123; Lanham and Brech 2007: 35) work appears to corroborate Cordell's findings that check-stamped wares typically made up between 8 and 20 percent of the pottery types in Malabar II assemblages.

This observation, however, is muddied by the fact that check stamping appears to decrease in assemblage frequency from north to south within the Indian River region. In fact, determining the precise percentage of check stamping within Malabar II assemblages is extremely difficult because of geographical variability and the frequent inability to separate Malabar I and II components in multicomponent shell middens. Suffice it to say that Malabar II middens include sand-tempered plain, St. Johns Plain, and St. Johns Check Stamped along with a smattering of minority types and nonlocal wares. Thus, as Brech (2004) astutely notes, Malabar is not a pottery type but a pottery assemblage in which St. Johns wares are a part. With this said, the paucity of radiocarbon dates from secure Malabar II contexts leads me to question whether the date of A.D. 750/800 for the advent of check stamping in St. Johns II pottery assemblages is applicable to the Indian River region. The emerging consensus argues against direct use of the St. Johns ceramic chronology for the Indian River region.

Assessing Indian River Subsistence and Settlement Models

Within the Indian River Lagoon, Malabar II sites (as well as Malabar I sites) range from shell or black-earth middens to low-density artifact and shell scatters. Faunal remains from these sites indicate that subsistence was geared toward the exploitation of estuarine lagoon resources through intensive fishing and the collection of shellfish (Milanich 1994: 252; Sigler-Eisenberg and Russo 1986). The Indian River Lagoon has long been known for its fisheries. In fact, Jonathan Dickinson in 1696 reported that an Ais fisher "in two hours time . . . got as many fish as would serve twenty men: there were others also fishing at the same time, so fish was plenty" (Andrews and Andrews 1981: 13). A fishing way of life was supplemented with the hunting of birds, mammals, and reptiles that inhabited marsh, coastal strand, or upland hammock environments.

Sites sampled within the Cape Canaveral Air Force Station (CCAFS) clearly demonstrated that bony fish made up more than 80 percent of the vertebrate diet and included sea catfish, seatrout, Atlantic croaker, black drum, redfish, porcupine fish, and mullet (Bellomo 1996; Deming and Horvath 1999). Cartilaginous fish, including shark and ray, constituted the second-largest vertebrate contributor to the Malabar diet. Mammal, reptile, and bird remains made up approximately 10 percent or less of these faunal assemblages (Bellomo 1996; Deming and Horvath 1999). Similar results were reported for the Blue Goose Midden (8IR15) in Indian River County to the south (Handley 2001: 1116–17).

Shellfish are at times the most conspicuous constituents within Malabar middens. Species exploited at the Cape Canaveral sites were predominantly quahog clam and coquina, with minor amounts of whelk, crown conch, and moon snail shell also taken. Other studies suggest that quahog clam and oyster were the primary shellfish collected in the northern Indian River Lagoon area, with a greater use of the cross-barred venus clam noted in the middle part of the lagoon system (Horvath 1995). In addition, a large number of coquina middens have been observed throughout the Indian River Lagoon (Bellomo 1996; Deming and Horvath 1999; Rouse 1951; Sigler-Eisenberg and Russo 1996). Several large features at the Sams site (8Br1872) on Merritt Island were filled with crown conch shells (Penders et al. 2009).

Site distributions and native land uses within the Indian River region have been the subjects of intermittent study over the past half century; most of this work has occurred within the realm of cultural resource management (Bense and Phillips 1990; Brech 2004; Campbell et al. 1984; Dickel 1992; Fandrich 1988; Lanham and Brech 2007; Pepe 2000; Rouse 1951; Russo 1985, 1988; Sigler-Eisenberg 1988). From Late Archaic times onward there appears to be a progressive increase in the number of archaeological sites on the barrier islands (including Merritt Island) and a concomitant decrease in sites within the upper St. Johns River basin (Brech 2004: 38–39; Rouse 1951).

Malabar II sites in the northern portion of the Indian River Lagoon are found along the eastern and western banks of Mosquito Lagoon and the eastern bank of the Banana River. Current data suggest that most sites recorded within the CCAFS appear along the Banana River (Bellomo 1996; Bense and Phillips 1990; Deming and Horvath 1999). According to the Florida Master Site File, sites on southern Merritt Island tend to be situated along the eastern bank of the Indian River and in the southernmost portion of the island facing the Banana River. In addition, few sites are currently recorded on the western (mainland) bank of the Indian River directly across from Merritt Island. South of Merritt Island, Malabar II sites are distributed along both the eastern and western banks of the Indian River as far south as St. Lucie Inlet. Brech (2004: 46, 49) further identifies an increase in Malabar II sites on barrier islands in the middle part of the Indian River Lagoon.

These settlement trends may have coincided with the rise in sea levels, temperatures, and precipitation reported for southwest Florida (Marquardt and Walker, chapter 2, this volume). If such sea-level changes also took place along the central-east coast of Florida, then we would expect heightened water levels in the Indian River Lagoon to have increased nearshore fish abundance, thereby attracting more people to the shoreline. At the same time, more precipitation would have increased flooding of the upper St. Johns River marshes.

A general, yet untested, settlement-subsistence model is emerging from available site distribution data for the Malabar II period in the Indian River Lagoon and inland upper St. Johns River basin. As described by Sigler-Eisenberg and Russo (1986: 23), coastal foragers in this model employed a logistical pattern of residential mobility that involved "central villages and burial mounds, satellite households, and a variety of small, collecting/fishing stations." Multicomponent sites distributed linearly along the east bank of the Indian River and coastal strand were identified as residential bases, while more numerous artifact scatters and low-density middens with few occupational components were considered special-use or short-term procurement camps. In effect, the coastal inhabitants of the Indian River Lagoon are portrayed as semisedentary collectors who made few residential moves, and those that were made were of a seasonal nature (see Binford 1980). Interestingly, the same logistic strategy is thought to have been practiced by groups living permanently along the upper St. Johns River (Sigler-Eisenberg 1988), suggesting permanent interior (St. Johns River and marshes) and coastal populations.

Sigler-Eisenberg and Russo (1986: 21–31) further argued for year-round occupation of barrier islands, although individual sites may have been occupied only seasonally. Such a strategy seems tenable for the Merritt Island–Cape Canaveral region. Although predominately a Malabar I site, Futch Cove (8Br170) was a black-earth midden with minor amounts of coquina; it is interpreted as a logistical fish-procurement site located within an estuarine setting on Merritt Island (Russo 1992b). Sea catfish was the dominant vertebrate species, and minor quantities of coquina were scattered throughout the black-earth midden. Other sites might have been occupied for the primary purpose of collecting shellfish. Besides fish and shellfish, deer populations on the island were once quite large, and today shark and sea turtles abound off the ocean side of the island.

A slight variant of the permanent coastal occupation model is based on the 1605 Spanish account by Alvaro Mexia (Higgs 1942; Rouse 1951). This interpretation claims that historic Ais towns were paired along the Indian River Lagoon. The main towns were occupied in the summer along the western (mainland) shore of the Indian River Lagoon, while "winter towns" were "satellites" on the barrier islands (Lanham and Brech 2007: 30). The former sites are fewer and were used repeatedly over a long period of time, while the latter are widely dispersed, more numerous, and often have less evidence of repeated use (Lanham and Brech 2007: 34). This model also argues for a logistical or semisedentary form of foraging.

It is important to note that Mexia apparently did not make landfall at the villages he mapped as he passed through the area in June and July of 1605. Lanham and Brech (2007) admit to problems with aspects of the map. Moreover, the Indian River region was abandoned during his expedition, so whether these "paired" villages were occupied concurrently or seasonally, as some have speculated, is uncertain. While the "paired town" model is intriguing and may have some bearing on early seventeenth-century Ais settlement patterns, the dearth of site testing and seasonality data renders it speculative at this time, particularly for the precontact period.

At this point, we still do not fully understand how the varied sites in the upper St. Johns basin (and the people who occupied them) articulated with the coastal sites. While I favor the interpretation that there were separate coastal and freshwater riverine/marsh populations, conditions south of Merritt Island, where the barrier island narrows, might have been different in the past. In this area, the distance between the coastal strand and the upper St. Johns River decreases significantly, and there are more waterways feeding into the western side of the Indian River. It might have been more feasible for coastal populations there to move inland seasonally to the nearby upper St. Johns River basin.

Sand Mounds

Shell and sand mounds were once a common feature of the Indian River landscape. In his synthesis of Indian River archaeology, Rouse (1951: 110–13, 252–53) depicts more than 40 burial mounds on his distribution maps but states that he only "identified 20." Failure on the part of past excavators to provide requisite provenience and context information makes it difficult to assign many of these mounds with any confidence to either Malabar I or II times (or both). For the most part, Malabar mounds tend to be low and constructed of sand or sand and shell, and almost all contain burials. The highly acidic nature of Florida soils, however, often results in poor bone preservation. It is worth noting that human interments also occur in Indian River middens. Perhaps middens were used for burial during times when mounds were not accessible.

Unlike other areas of Florida, where mounds are positioned away from coeval occupation sites, almost all sand mounds in the Indian River region are located adjacent to or in close proximity to habitation areas. For example, consider the geospatial relationship of the mounds at CCAFS and the nearby town of Cape Canaveral. The DeSoto Groves Mound (8Br83) is the northernmost mound on CCAFS, located 10 km north of Burns Mound (8Br85). Moving south, Holmes Mound (8Br86), Hammock Mound A (8Br88a), and Norris Mound (8Br89) are each approximately 1 km apart. Between these sites are several occupation sites. The Fuller Mound Group is located approximately 5 km south of the CCAFS mounds. Burials in Sams Mound, DeSoto Groves Mound, and Norris Mound were shallow and all thought to date to Malabar II times. All of these mounds are within or adjacent to large multicomponent permanent villages or residential sites along the Banana River, which would have provided a readily available supply of food throughout the year.

I believe each coastal Malabar burial mound constituted a "central place" and focal point for seasonal rituals and sociopolitical gatherings for specific lineages. These mounds may have further served to link the living to their dead ancestors (Buikstra and Charles 1999: 201). It has been suggested that mounds were created first by lineages or other kin groups to establish ownership of a cultural history tied to a territory, and later used as a place to inter the dead (Wallis 2008). By adding new burials or stages to the mounds over time, the fisher-hunter-gatherers of the Indian River region could have reaffirmed their claims to the past, the land, and its resources. Such a scenario would have required not a large, formally organized labor pool but rather a small-scale effort organized by a kin or community leader.

A review of burials in the region shows no individuals with a higher number of grave goods or segregation in the burials along age, gender, or other criteria. Moreover, when present, exotics appear in general mound contexts unrelated to individual burials. The lack of grave accompaniments appears to have been a long-standing practice in the Indian River region. In fact, it represents a pattern that can be seen as far back as the Early Archaic at the Windover site (Dickel and Doran 2002).

Claims of Monumental Architecture

In the middle part of the Indian River region, four sites recently have been described as containing terraced earthen (and possibly shell) ridges or platforms, some of which exhibit possible ramps (Lanham and Brech 2007: 24–27). All are located south of Merritt Island on the western (mainland) side of the Indian River at or near its confluence with a freshwater stream: 8Br1978 (possibly Summer Pentoaya) at Eau Gallie River, Trysting Stairs (8Br39) at Crane Creek, 8Br49–50 at Turkey Creek, and the Grant Mound site (8Br56 [this is not the Grant Mound, 8Du14, located at the mouth of the St. Johns River and discussed by Ashley in chapter 5 of this volume]). The location of these sites is shown in figure 4.2.

Despite claims to the contrary, there is no documentary evidence for the existence of monumental architecture at either Trysting Stairs or Turkey Creek. In addition, the descriptions of Grant Mound are dubious at best. Of note is the fact that all four sites are large occupation sites located adjacent to a creek or river that empties into the Indian River, a situation

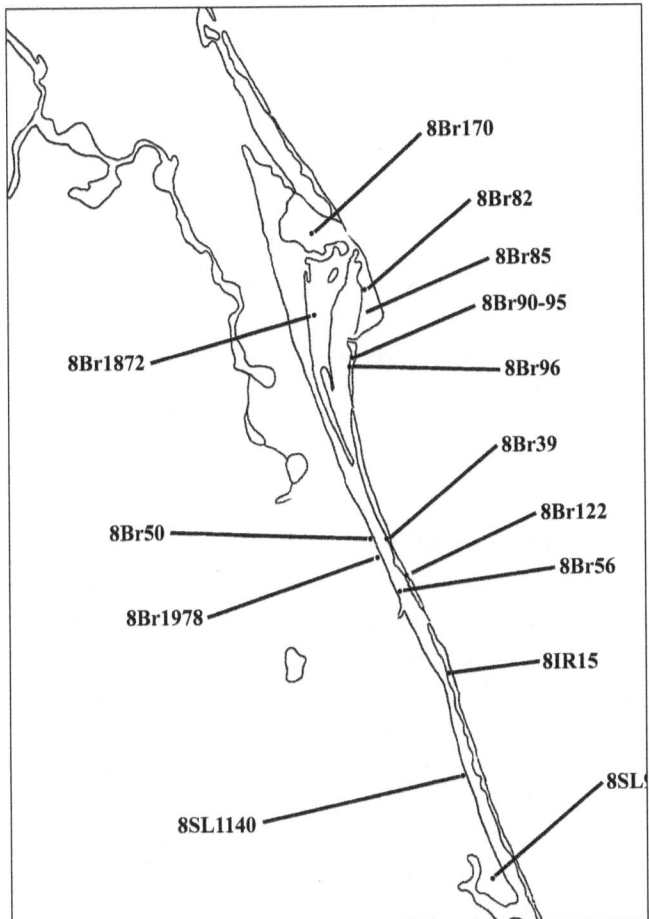

Figure 4.2. Major sites discussed in the chapter.

similar to that of large sites at the southern end of the Indian River region. Unfortunately, all of these sites have been impacted to varying degrees by modern development, and none has been subjected to extensive systematic excavation. Thus, it is still unclear whether these are true platform mounds, human-modified relic dune formations, or the result of twentieth-century construction activities. If they are legitimate native constructions, two questions arise: when were they built (prior to or after European contact) and what was their intended use?

The alleged location of the Ais village of Summer Pentoaya (8Br1978) is on the western bank of the Indian River in present-day Eau Gallie. It is reported to have staggered, descending platforms along with mounds/middens with ramps and a causeway (Lanham and Brech 2007: 24). The terraces and descending platforms depicted at the site mimic those reported for Grant Mound. No subsurface testing has been performed at the site to date, and Lanham and Brech (2007: 24) admit that the terraces and platforms "could be artifacts of modern development and/or midden removal, and not aboriginal constructions."

At the southern end of the Indian River region are Kings Mound (8SL9) and Deanne Browning Midden (8SL1140) in St. Lucie County. Kings Mound has yet to be tested, so its chronological position is uncertain. However, a "ramp structure on the mound's west side . . . is suggestive of a Mississippian-era temple mound" (Wheeler 1999). Deanne Browning Midden, which measures 50 m by 100 m and about 1 m in height, also exhibits a prepared platform summit (Wheeler 1997). Again, because of the absence of excavation, the precise nature and age of this artificial edifice are unknown.

Interestingly, within the Indian River region some of the mounds, constructed of sand, shell, or both materials, exhibit platform summits and/or remnants of what might have been ramps similar to those described for the Calusa region (Hann 2003: 37–40; Marquardt and Walker, chapter 2, this volume). While Hann (2003: 75) remarks that the Ais lacked temple mounds, Lanham and Brech's (2007: 24) recent study suggests the existence of causeways, ramps, and platforms that might have been anthropogenic features of Indian River landscape. There are no platform mounds or evidence of monumental architecture in Indian River County, and the number of these sites decreases as one travels north through the adjoining region into St. Lucie County. Perhaps they served merely as domiciliary mounds to elevate houses above rising waters and tidal surges, as hypothesized for southwest Florida by Marquardt and Walker (chapter 2, this volume).

Documentary evidence for such an interpretation is presented in Dickinson's 1696 journal, which mentions houses of the Ais on mounded shell middens and on the natural ground surface (Andrews and Andrews 1981: 12, 29, 32–33). Hann (2003: 74) suggests these elevated houses were occupied only during heavy rains and flooding, apparently based on Dickinson's reference to the Ais taking refuge in a house on an "oyster hill" from rising waters during a hurricane or tropical storm. Unfortunately, most sites exhibiting distinctive mounded shell/earthworks either have not been tested or were excavated prior to the advent of modern archaeological techniques, so precise contextual information is lacking. Thus, a definitive verdict on the intentional construction of monumental architecture and its use in ceremonial or political capacities must await additional research.

Unique Mortuary Practice

Three sites in the Indian River region show evidence of radial or wheel-spoke burials (see table 4.1). The Burns site (8Br85), also known as Burnham's Grove, is located on the eastern bank of the Banana River in CCAFS. Beginning with the work of LeBaron in 1884, this multicomponent site has been the subject of several investigations (Bellomo 1996; Cantley et al. 1994; Deming and Horvath 1999; Levy et al. 1984; Rouse 1951; Stirling 1931; Willey 1954). In addition to Malabar II pottery, more than 50 human skeletons "oriented with heads towards the center of the mound," a stone celt, a notched stone (or bone) weight, and "a silver pendant of cross-and-square design" were recovered (Rouse 1951: 193, 194). More recent investigations have recovered fragments of Spanish olive jar (Deming and Horvath 1999). The Little Manatee and Sarasota wares suggest a temporal range of A.D. 900–1250 based on dated sites in the St. Johns region to the north (Ashley, chapter 5, this volume), whereas the silver pendant and olive jar sherds point to postcontact site activities.

The Fuller Mound Group (8Br90–95) is located on the eastern bank of the Banana River, within the present-day community of Cape Canaveral. The map at the Florida Master Site File indicates that the Fuller Mound Group actually consisted of two clusters of mounds: Fuller Mounds B, C, and F made up the northern group, whereas Mounds A, D, and E formed the southern group. Rouse (1951: 196) and Willey (1954) indicated that Mounds A, B, and D all contained shallow burials. Two of the mounds (A and D) had burials "carefully oriented with the heads toward the apex of the mound very much like the spokes of a wheel." Extended and flexed burials were observed, as were other unspecified interment modes. Mound B displayed a shallow pit in the "apex of the mound" where 20 individuals were found "jumbled together." In addition, two interments placed outside the pit were buried with their feet toward the center of the mound (Rouse 1951: 198; Willey 1954: 83–85).

Taken from the fill of Mound A (8Br90) were St. Johns Plain and Check Stamped vessel fragments, as were "a grooved stone weight; two single-grooved, plummet-shaped pendants of stone; a perforated plummet-shaped pendant of quartz crystal; and fragments of four bone pins";

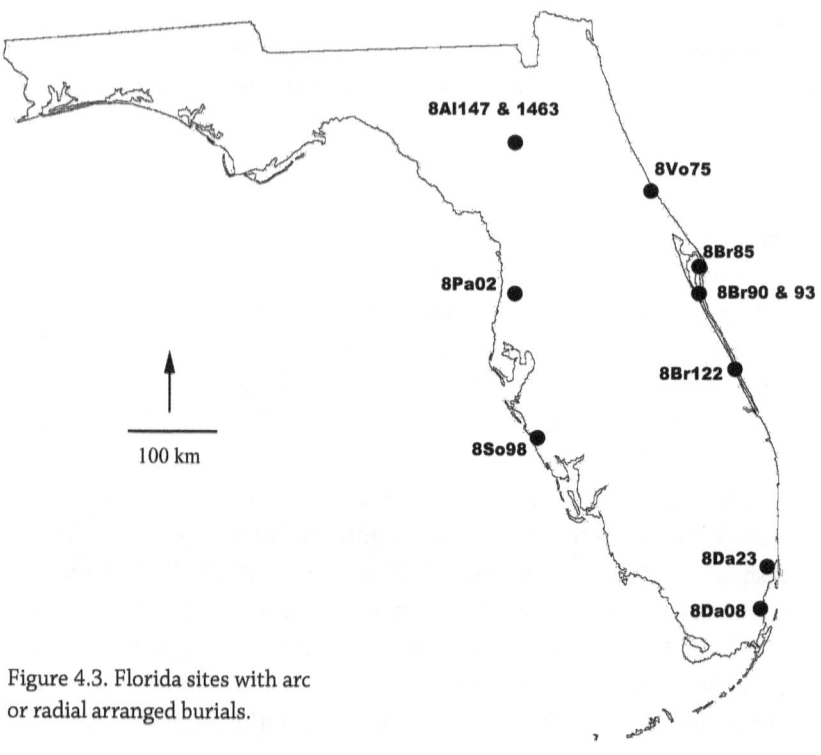

Figure 4.3. Florida sites with arc or radial arranged burials.

additional artifacts of shell and bone were recovered (Rouse 1951: 196; Willey 1954: 83–86). Also retrieved from the sand mound were an iron celt, glass beads, and several copper and gold objects described by Rouse (1951: 197) as being of "European manufacture." Of these, one is a unique copper pendant "of aboriginal manufacture, but of European-transported metal" exhibiting what Willey (1954: 85–86) describes as a rattlesnake motif. Whether any of these artifacts were directly associated with burials is unknown. Mound D (8Br93) yielded glass trade beads (Rouse 1951: 198; Willey 1954: 87).

Across the Indian River from the Grant Mound on the barrier island is the Casuarina Mound (8Br122). Excavations conducted between 1886 and 1907 identified more than 125 burials in "three superimposed groups"; the upper two groups were interred in the sand mound, whereas the lowest was at the base of the sand mound in shell (Rouse 1951: 207–8). Artifacts recovered included a copper bead from the uppermost group and a notched stone projectile point, a stone hone, and a stone pendant along with other shell and bone artifacts from unprovenienced mound contexts. It was reported that during highway construction in the 1940s "the crew found a

Table 4.1. Recorded radial and arc burial patterns in peninsular Florida

Site	Burial Pattern	Cultural Affiliation	European Goods	Possible Precontact Exotics
Arch Creek (8Da23)	Radial	Glades II	No	?
Burns site (8Br85)	Radial	Malabar II	Yes	Yes
Casuarina (8Br122)	Radial	Malabar II	Yes	Yes
Cutler Mound (8Da8)	Radial	Glades II	No	No
Fuller Mound A (8Br90)	Radial	Malabar II	Yes	Yes
Fuller Mound D (8Br93)	Arc	Malabar II	Yes	No
Henderson Mound (8Al463)	Arc	Hickory Pond	No	No
Laurel Mound (8So98)	Radial	Safety Harbor	No	Yes
Oelsner Indian Mound (8Pa2)	Radial	Weeden Island–Safety Harbor	No	Yes
Ormond Mound (8Vo75)	Circular	St. Johns	Yes	Yes
Woodward Mound (8Al47)	Arc	Hickory Pond	No	Yes

Source: Adapted from Luer and Almy 1987: 307, table 1.

circle of skeletons radiating like the spokes of a wheel" in a mound thought to be 8Br122 (Rouse 1951: 209). If true, this would make four Indian River mounds dated to Malabar II times that reportedly contained such a burial arrangement. Moreover, burial in a wheel-spoke or radial fashion is found only within the coastal sector of the Indian River region, with none reported on the mainland or along the St. Johns River.

Seven previously recorded sites in Florida have been identified as containing radial (wheel-spoke) or arc burials, and all appear to postdate A.D. 700 (figure 4.3; table 4.1). Luer and Almy (1987) described the presence of radial and arc-shaped burials in peninsular Florida at six previously recorded sites in Alachua, Dade, Pasco, and Sarasota counties. The Ormond Mound (8Vo75) contained two interments of individuals placed in a circular pattern around the apex of the mound in mass graves (Jennings et al. 1955). While the excavators suggested that the Ormond Mound was not a St. Johns II construction, they did report St. Johns Check Stamped and Little Manatee Shell Stamped sherds from mound fill. Goggin (1952) assigned the mound to both the St. Johns I and St. Johns II periods.

Of those mounds listed in table 4.1, only the Burns site, Fuller Mounds, Henderson Mound, Laurel Mound, and Ormond Mound are documented with respect to diagrams, maps, or detailed field notes. However, Garner (1992) suggests that although there is no such information for the Oelsner Mound (also known as the mound on the Pithlochascootie River), the pattern may indeed exist. It is worth noting that some of these mounds contained burials other than those laid out in the prescribed circular or arc fashion. The inclusion of both primary and secondary interments suggests that the mounds were used over a period of time with the overall layout of the mound in mind. When taken as a whole, the presence of radial (wheel-spoke) or arc burials is neither widespread nor common. Burial in a wheel-spoke fashion may "reflect a change of burial customs between the Malabar I and Malabar II periods" (Willey 1954: 89). Although the reason for burials being laid out in a spoke pattern is unclear, this unique practice may be a very late Malabar II manifestation somehow associated with the advent of European contact. However, this is not confidently documented, though all the Indian River mounds seem to be associated with European goods (but the European-period burials could be intrusive).

Why the Lack of Nonlocal Artifacts?

Rouse's (1951) review of Indian River burial mounds leaves one with the impression that exotic or nonlocal grave goods were infrequently encountered in mortuary contexts. Items recovered, though again hard to pin down as to period of deposition, include stone celts, stone plummets, quartz pieces, and rarely, copper. The presence of these materials indicates some ability on the part of coastal Malabar societies to acquire materials derived from far-off areas of the eastern United States, but I believe that this was never a major part of Malabar II culture.

Although widespread interaction networks were established during Woodland and Mississippian times, Indian River natives appear to have been largely marginalized by St. Johns River inhabitants to the north. During the Mississippi period, St. Johns mound centers such as Mt. Royal and Mill Cove controlled the flow of materials into and out of northeastern Florida (Ashley, chapter 5, this volume). The Indian River region may have been in effect shut out of the broader interaction networks dominated by St. Johns societies who moved marine shell and other coastal resources into the Mississippian world. This was also true of Fort Walton societies in the Florida panhandle, who possibly controlled the flow of goods down to the southwest coast of Florida. To the south, the Indian River region was on the periphery of the canal/canoe network that linked south Florida.

The ability of Florida's northernmost groups to gain the upper hand in interacting with the Mississippian world was largely the result of geographic proximity. They had access to Florida resources in demand, and they were located closer to the Mississippian world. After about A.D. 1520 or so, Indian River groups gained an advantage as exotic items from distant places began to appear along their shores in the form of European goods, so although Indian River groups had in the past been largely cut off in terms of access to more-northerly exotic material, this was no longer the case. This is the topic to which I now turn.

European Shipwrecks and Changes in Malabar II Culture

The current picture of the Malabar II culture is one of conservatism with little substantive cultural change following Archaic times, particularly with respect to material culture and subsistence. At present, whether this is a true characterization of the Malabar culture or simply a reflection of an incomplete archaeological record is unclear, because of inadequate systematic excavation and research as well as lack of preservation of perishable goods. The sociopolitical organization of Mississippi-period Malabar societies is difficult to comprehend with available archaeological data. For the precontact era, however, I see no reason to disagree with Milanich's (1998: 253) position that "[a]rchaeological evidence from the Ais and their neighbors all indicates simple chiefdoms or even autonomous village-level political integration." In fact, Davidsson (2001: 78) describes the Ais at the time of Ponce de Leon's landfall along the eastern coast of Florida as "subsistence-level, semi-nomadic hunters and gatherers." Other early Spanish accounts also imply that the natives of south Florida had an "unstructured society where the chief had very little effective control over the ordinary Indian," making him more or less a "first among equals" (Hann 2003: 71). But, admittedly, ethnohistoric references to Ais politics are at times ambiguous and conflicting.

The influx of European goods did have a major impact on the region. The Gulf Stream, a powerful current running northeast from the Caribbean, was the preferred shipping lane used by the Spanish galleons loaded with precious metals and other goods leaving Central America for Europe. While expediting the long journey, this route exposed ships to the catastrophic effects of tropical storms and hurricanes along the eastern coast of Florida during the summer and early fall (Davidsson 2001: 79–80). The Ais benefited from their geographic location along the main shipping channel to Europe, and they developed a "maritime salvor-wrecker culture" (Davidsson 2001: 78–79, 81–82, 87). While the Ais retained their fishing-hunting-gathering way of life throughout nearly two centuries of salvaging, the sudden and frequent appearance of exotic cargo on their doorstep clearly altered native alliances, trade routes, and power structures in their favor. When the Spaniard Pedro Menendez first met the Ais cacique, the chief's head was adorned with a gold headband, as were the heads of native men who accompanied him (Hann 2003: 72, 78). The shipwrecked Spaniard Hernando Escalante Fontaneda (1973: 18), who lived in Florida between 1542 and 1569, wrote that the "king of Ais and the king of Jeaga are poor Indians, as respects the land; for there are no mines of silver or gold where they are, and in short, they are rich only by the sea, from the many vessels that have been lost well laden with these metals" (Andrews and Andrews 1981; Davidsson 2001: 80–85; Hann 2003: 79–80).

The placement in mounds of shallow graves with associated European or exotic grave goods is common in the Indian River region, both coastal and inland, as well as along the St. Johns River to the north. Researchers have suggested that some of the low sand mounds above midden deposits were specifically created for late burials. Data to prove this are lacking, however, except in cases where European goods are present. During later Malabar II, the period of European contact, the effects of disease, warfare, and other problems resulted in an above-normal number of burials. Existing mounds were used for the placement of the dead. Graves were made shallow both to expedite burial and to avoid disturbing the ancestors. Furthermore, except for the Ormond Mound (8Vo75) to the north and coastal mounds in Brevard County, none of the sites with radial or arc burial patterns has European goods. The lack of rich graves or goods associated with an elite or high-ranking individual is commonplace within the Indian River region during the Malabar II Period, even in postcontact graves. Given the cultural conservatism of the area, this is not unexpected. The archaeological record of nonburial sites shows no indication of an elite group or complex chiefdom-level of organization.

While the presence of European goods did not have a significant impact on the daily lives of the Indian River Lagoon inhabitants, it apparently affected the political landscape. The suggestion has been made that the Ais were allies of the Calusa, and some have gone as far as to state that the Calusa chief was able to demand tribute from the Ais, at least during the early historic period (Hann 2003: 167; Milanich 1998: 252–53). But this latter portrayal, if accurate, underwent a startling metamorphosis during the sixteenth century, as the "chief of the Ais seems to have played a hegemonic role on the east coast somewhat akin to that of the Calusa ruler for much of the rest of south Florida" (Hann 2003: 167). The political sway that the Ais demonstrated among native populations along the eastern Florida seaboard appears to have been a rapid development that might have paralleled a similar sixteenth-century rise in strength among the already powerful Calusa as a result of Spanish presence in Florida (Marquardt 1987b, 1992). As Milanich (1998) argues, the Ais, like their Timucuan neighbors to the north, may have appeared to be complex because of the need to organize to protect their interests, whether from the Calusa or Europeans. Some researchers interpret the arrival of the Ais chief at the village of the Hobe to obtain his share of the loot from a shipwreck as evidence of his authority over a complex chiefdom (Lanham and Brech 2007: 24). I offer the following as an alternative explanation: the chief of the Ais, being from the Cape Canaveral area, which was closest to the Spanish, had an agreement with the Spanish regarding the salvage of wrecks and their materials. His proximity to the Spanish merely placed him as ranking chief in an alliance of simple chiefdoms that stretched along the east coast from St. Augustine to south Florida.

Summary

Current archaeological data indicate little evidence of Mississippian characteristics or influences in the Indian River region. Although exotic goods do occur in Malabar II contexts, they are neither frequent nor in large quantities. Pottery types from adjacent areas do occur on sites in the region, and regular contact between coastal groups and the interior upper St. Johns clearly transpired. Thus, while resources from the coast might have made their way to the upper St. Johns River basin, then northward to destinations unknown, coastal Indian River populations apparently received little for their efforts. As cultural changes of various sorts took place throughout other areas of Florida and the broader Southeast during the Mississippi period, the Indian River region appears to have undergone little modification, at least in terms of subsistence and material culture. When substantial changes finally did occur within Malabar II societies, we see that the source was in no way connected to the dynamics of the Mississippian world but instead was linked to the arrival of Europeans and their material culture, much of which came from ships that floundered along the coast or washed up on the shores of the Atlantic seaboard of Florida. Though the Ais thwarted attempts at missionization, their final century of existence was marked by disease, slaving, warfare, and eventual annihilation.

5

Early St. Johns II Interaction, Exchange, and Politics

A View from Northeastern Florida

KEITH ASHLEY

The presence of raw materials and Mississippian artifacts on sites far from their place of origin speaks of complex interaction networks that connected many mound centers and smaller communities across the greater Southeast. Natives living along the St. Johns River were clearly involved in these interregional exchanges, as indicated by the recovery of exotica from certain sand burial mounds (Moore 1894a, 1894b, 1895). But northeastern Florida still figures almost exclusively in Mississippian studies as a peripheral area and mere final destination for exotic items moved throughout southeastern North America. Even among Florida archaeologists the tendency has been to treat nonlocal materials simply as trade goods that loosely linked St. Johns sites in some unknown way to distant places or peoples. In fact, few efforts have been made to explore the social or political aspects of these connections, and those researchers who have done so simply perceive the presence of exotica in St. Johns II mounds as evidence of an elite-driven prestige-goods economy (Milanich 1994: 269, 1996: 10–11; Payne and Scarry 1998: 47; Phillips and Brown 1978: 207–8).

I believe a major reason for the lack of substantive discussion on the topic has been the paucity of archaeological data from St. Johns II contexts other than burial mounds excavated more than a century ago. The situation, however, is beginning to change as St. Johns II sites have become the subject of recent research and cultural resource management projects (Ashley 2002, 2003, 2005b, 2005c, 2008; Ashley and Hendryx 2008; Ashley et al. 2007; Dickinson and Wayne 1997, 1999; Hendryx and Smith 2002; Hendryx et al. 2008; Johnson 1988, 1996, 1998; Marrinan

2005; Parsons 2008; Penders 2005; Rolland 2004, 2005; Smith et al. 2001; Thunen 2005). As a result, 30 radiometric dates from 16 sites have been assayed, securely lashing the St. Johns II culture of northeastern Florida to ca. A.D. 900–1250/1300, making it the regional variant of the Early Mississippi period of southeastern North America. *Northeastern Florida* herein is used in a narrow geographical sense to refer to the extreme corner of the state that includes Nassau, Duval, and northern St. Johns counties. For the broader St. Johns River basin, archaeologists currently set the start of the St. Johns II period to A.D. 750 and extend it into the early Spanish colonial period (Milanich 1994: 247).

What is becoming clear from recent research is that St. Johns fisher-hunter-gatherers of northeastern Florida were among the earliest participants in Mississippi-period interactions, successfully acquiring exotic raw materials, high-profile finished goods, and nonlocal cord-marked pottery. Involvement in these far-reaching networks of contact and communication evidently wrought settlement and political changes throughout the St. Johns River basin, as certain communities emerged as major players in Early Mississippi–period exchange. Most notable were the Mill Cove Complex and Mt. Royal. In these St. Johns II communities, the imported trappings of the Mississippian world appear to have served more as items of mortuary ritual and cultural reproduction that ended their life histories in communal burial mounds and less as objects of elite power. Focusing on the Mill Cove Complex and other early St. Johns II communities near the river's mouth, this chapter considers old data in a fresh light and draws upon new archaeological information to address issues of long-distance contact and interaction, ritual, and the possible role of exotica within the St. Johns II political economy.

Social Landscape of the St. Johns River Basin

At the twilight of the Late Woodland period, northeastern Florida was inhabited by a seemingly small number of people affiliated with the local Colorinda culture. By the early tenth century, however, substantial change was under way, as evinced by the abrupt appearance of St. Johns II sites throughout northeastern Florida (Ashley 2003: 129–37; Goggin 1952: 55, 58; Milanich 1994: 263). St. Johns II pottery assemblages consist mostly of St. Johns Plain and Check Stamped wares, along with minor amounts of incised and punctated types, including Little Manatee and Papys Bayou, as well as Ocmulgee Cord Marked.

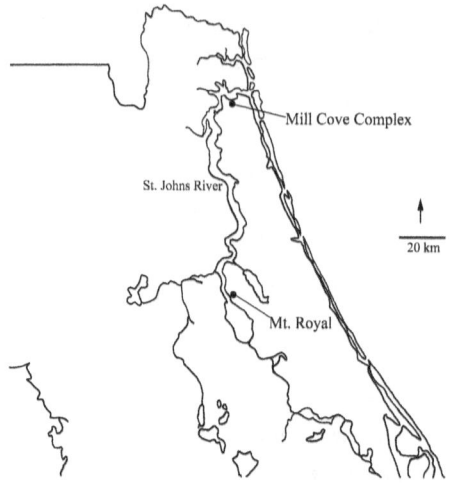

Figure 5.1. Mill Cove Complex and Mt. Royal archaeological site locations.

Discontinuity between the locations of most Late Woodland Colorinda and later St. Johns II sites suggests a demographic reconfiguration of the river basin in which some St. Johns II people from the south relocated to the north along the lower St. Johns (Ashley 2006). The St. Johns is a north-flowing river with its headwaters in central Florida and its mouth in northeastern Florida. What happened to the makers of Colorinda pottery is currently unclear, but they were likely absorbed into the burgeoning St. Johns II culture, which would dominate the northeastern Florida landscape between the tenth and late thirteenth centuries. This approximately 350-year period represents the only time when St. Johns pottery was the primary domestic and ceremonial ware manufactured throughout the entire St. Johns River basin and adjacent Atlantic coast.

By the eleventh century, two dominant settlement concentrations existed along the northern third of the St. Johns River (Miller 1998: 83–84), and each contained a mound center showing the strongest ties in Florida to the early Mississippian world. The Mill Cove Complex stood out among the northern settlements in the vicinity of the river's mouth, while Mt. Royal commanded the landscape to the south, immediately north of Lake George (figure 5.1). While St. Johns II sites are known for the 100-km stretch of river between the Mill Cove and Mt. Royal settlement clusters, no large burial mounds dated to the Early Mississippi period have been recorded (Ashley 2003: 130–32; Miller 1998: 83; Sassaman et al. 2000: 111). In fact, only five low earthworks in this intervening area have been loosely assigned to the St. Johns II period (A.D. 750–1500), and whether any were contemporaneous with the Mill Cove Complex and Mt. Royal is unknown.

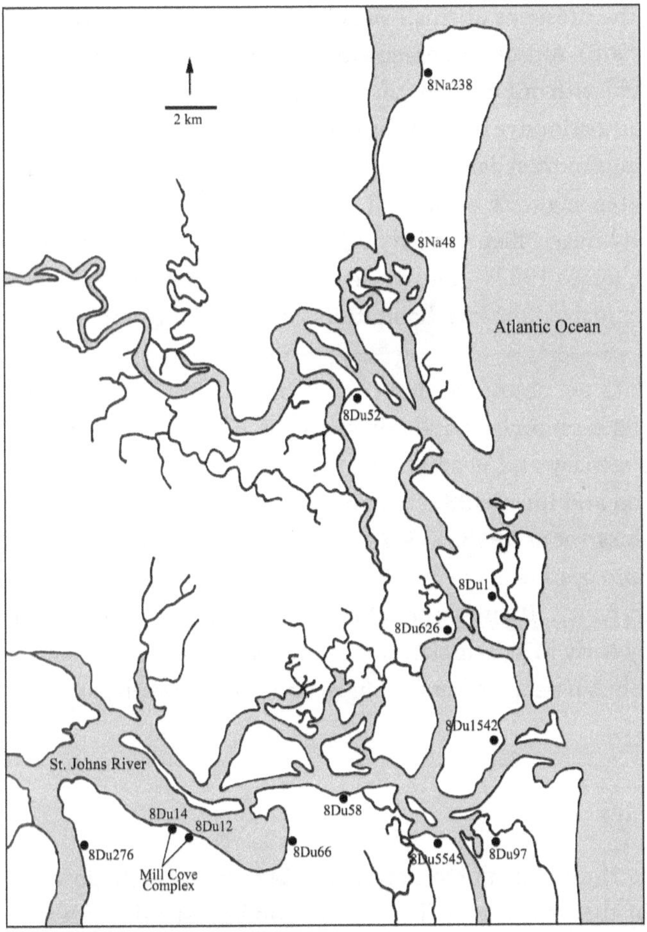

Figure 5.2. St. Johns II site locations in northeastern Florida.

The northern site concentration includes 12 potential St. Johns II settlements (figure 5.2). This is an increase over the nine and 11 villages reported in previous studies (Ashley 2002: 169, 2003: 182–208, 2005c: 294). Six are located on the south side of the St. Johns River (including Mill Cove Complex), and six are situated north of the river. All 12 include extensive midden deposits, and 10 contain a sand burial mound. The two (8Du276 and 8Na238) that currently do not have a mound probably did prior to pre-twentieth-century land-clearing activities. Available seasonality data for the Mill Cove Complex and the Grand Shell Ring (8Du1) indicate year-round settlements that likely served as residential hubs or villages (Ashley 2003: 137–207; Ashley et al. 2007; Marrinan 2005).

Hunting, fishing, and gathering forays undoubtedly took households or special task groups beyond mound settlements for short periods of time, as evidenced by the presence of small sites located away from settlement centers (Ashley 2008). Although a precise understanding of how these varied sites articulated with one another throughout the year currently eludes us, we do see some distinctive differences in the structure and composition of short-term versus more sedentary settlements. The present distribution of St. Johns II sites suggests a collector strategy of low residential mobility centered on linearly dispersed yet relatively stable settlements (see Binford 1980: 10; Russo 1992a). Clearly, settlement-mound sites were not vacant centers but loci of domestic habitation, ritual, and interment of the dead.

Subsistence data are abundant and convincingly define a fishing and shellfish-collecting economy squarely fixed on the rich aquatic resources of the St. Johns estuary and nearby Atlantic coast (Ashley 2008; Ashley et al. 2007; Hardin and Russo 1987; Marrinan 2005; O'Steen 1999; Russo 1992b: 118–19; Russo et al. 1993: 136–73). In fact, small to medium-sized estuarine fishes and oysters made up the bulk of their diet, along with wild plants, nuts, and fruits. Though undoubtedly aware of the maize-based economy of many early Mississippian communities of the interior Southeast, coeval St. Johns II peoples were not agriculturalists or even part-time maize farmers.

Mill Cove Complex

Of the St. Johns II sites in northeastern Florida, one overshadows all others because of the presence of the region's two largest sand mounds. Separated by only 750 m, the Shields (8Du12) and Grant (8Du14) mounds highlight what is now referred to as the Mill Cove Complex (Ashley 2005b; Thunen 2005; Thunen and Ashley 1995). Each earthwork was grafted onto a high relict dune along the south side of the St. Johns River, some 15 km west of the river's mouth. The Mill Cove Complex is unrivaled among Early Mississippi–period sites in Florida in its spatial extent, size of mounds, number of mound interments, and quantity and quality of exotica. Mt. Royal (8Pu35), located 100 km to the south, however, contained more nonlocal materials than either Shields Mound or Grant Mound.

Excavation of the Grant and Shields Mounds

The peripatetic and indefatigable mound digger C. B. Moore (1894b, 1895) excavated both Shields and Grant mounds in the 1890s. Moore spent more

Figure 5.3. Copper long-nosed maskettes recovered from Grant Mound by C. B. Moore in 1895. Photograph courtesy of the National Museum of the American Indian and the Smithsonian Institution.

than 50 days combined at the two mounds and, with the help of local laborers, moved considerable amounts of soil. With a height of more than 8 m and a base diameter of nearly 66 m, Grant Mound was the taller of the two Mill Cove earthworks. At the time of Moore's visit, the northern side of the mound was eroding into the river, while two low, parallel ridges extended a short distance south from the mound. In Grant Mound, Moore (1895: 485–88) recovered items of steatite, galena, quartz, and mica along with more than a hundred ground-stone celts and a variety of copper plates, two long-nosed god maskettes, a copper-sheathed, biconical ear plug of wood, and other copper-covered artifacts (see Ashley 2003: 139–44; Thunen 2005). Figure 5.3 shows the two maskettes as they exist today.

At 5.5 m in height, Shields Mound exhibited a more intricate design, incorporating a platform summit, a short ramp to the north, and a lengthy causeway and elongated, fishhook-shaped approach to the south (see Moore 1895: 453). Moore (1895: 461) unearthed fewer copper artifacts and stone celts in this mound, but he did recover two spatulate celts along with quartz crystals, galena cubes, mica, Archaic-looking bannerstones, and more than one hundred projectile points (see Ashley 2005b: 153–57). The spatulate celts are depicted in figures 5.4 and 5.5. From both Shields and Grant mounds he reported finding items of local material such as

Figure 5.4. Spatulate celt #1 recovered from Shields Mound by C. B. Moore in 1895. Photograph courtesy of the National Museum of the American Indian and the Smithsonian Institution.

Figure 5.5. Spatulate celt #2 recovered from Shields Mound by C. B. Moore in 1895. Photograph courtesy of the National Museum of the American Indian and the Smithsonian Institution.

whelk cups, marine shell beads, and other shell artifacts, along with pearls, shark teeth, and bone pins and implements; some bone, wood, and shell artifacts were covered with copper foiling.

Within the interior of the two mounds Moore (1894b, 1895) observed colorful layers of clean white, charcoal-laden black, and hematite-impregnated red sands that denoted distinct construction and/or burial episodes. Hundreds of primary and secondary human burials were encountered in each mound, suggesting that these were continuous-use, mounded community cemeteries and not mortuary monuments for elites (Ashley 2002: 171).

In terms of chronological placement, the spatulate celts, long-nosed god maskettes, and biconical ear spool fall firmly in the A.D. 900–1200 time frame (Brown et al. 1990: 264; Kelly 1991: 73–75; Sampson and Esarey 1993: 463–64). Moreover, the absence of motifs and Southeastern Ceremonial Complex imagery on stone, shell, or sheet copper supports a pre–mid-thirteenth century date for Grant and Shields mounds (see Brown and Kelly 2000; Kelly, chapter 12, this volume). Finally, seven calibrated radiometric assays from village contexts at Mill Cove are totally consistent with a date range of A.D. 900–1250 (Ashley 2005b: 155).

Site Testing and the Distribution of Exotica within the Mill Cove Complex

For the most part, testing of nonmound areas at Mill Cove has been spotty and restricted to 50-cm-square shovel tests and 1-m-square units excavated during separate, small-scale survey projects (Hendryx and Smith 2002; Johnson 1988; NEFAS 2001; Parks 2004). The results of these investigations indicate that St. Johns II refuse deposits and shell middens cover almost 15 ha (975×150 m) between Shields Mound on the east and Grant Mound on the west (figure 5.6). More systematic shovel testing and limited unit excavations have taken place near each mound (Ashley 2005b; Hendryx et al. 2008; Thunen 2005). The immediate vicinity of Shields Mound was marked by a diffuse spread of scattered shell and abundant pottery vessel fragments along with a few localized accumulations of dense shell midden closer to the mound (Ashley 2005b: 159–61; Ashley 2005c: 293). A similar situation might have surrounded Grant Mound, but modern residential impacts mar a clear understanding of refuse disposal patterns there (Ashley 2005b: 167–70; Thunen 2005).

Testing of the village area between the two mounds provided valuable information on the intrasite distribution of pottery and other craft items. To date, the only nonlocal items recovered from domestic middens were small amounts of lithic (chert) debitage, a few chert points (Pinellas type), and Ocmulgee Cord Marked pottery, all of which appear related to everyday household activities. There currently is no evidence of exotic craft production at the household level within the extensive spread of domestic

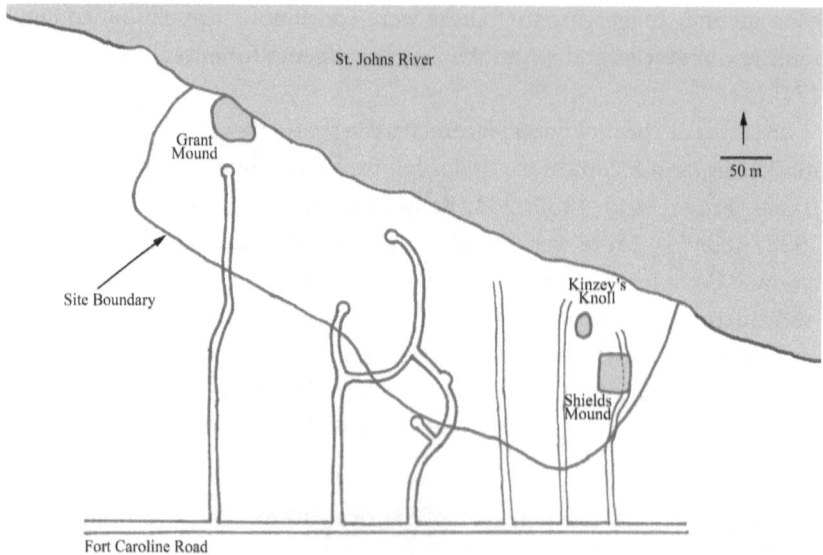

Figure 5.6. Mill Cove Complex showing location of Grant Mound, Shields Mound, and Kinzey's Knoll.

refuse at the Mill Cove Complex. Exotic materials, however, were spatially restricted to a few conspicuous, mounded shell middens closest to Shields Mound.

Most notable was Kinzey's Knoll, located 50 m northwest of Shields Mound, where large amounts of oyster shell, vertebrate fauna, and pottery were piled to a height of 80 cm during the late-tenth and eleventh centuries (Ashley 2005b: 161–64). The variety and sheer volume of refuse suggest activities related to the preparation, consumption, and disposal of food at Kinzey's Knoll (Dunbar 2001; Marrinan 2005). Fragments of more than 350 separate vessels were identified, and the vast majority of sherds displayed minimal evidence of surface wear and tear, perhaps owing to limited vessel use prior to discard (Rolland 2004, 2005). Well represented are typical St. Johns Plain and Check Stamped bowls along with Ocmulgee Cord Marked vessels. Sourcing and refiring studies indicate that some Ocmulgee vessels were imported from southern-central Georgia, while others were locally produced (Ashley 2003: 104–28; Rolland 2005: 135–50). Vis-à-vis other sampled midden loci at Mill Cove, Kinzey's Knoll exhibited the highest frequencies of both small and large bowls and greater amounts of decorated, burnished, and red-slipped wares (Rolland 2004, 2005). All told, the number of broken bowls, their size ranges, and the quality and condition of many vessels from Kinzey's Knoll suggest a special-event assemblage.

The shell midden at Kinzey's Knoll also contained other spectacular artifacts such as a variety of ornate bone pins, pendants, and beads; shell beads, pendants, and other ornaments; stone projectile points (including earlier Archaic forms); pieces of copper (both beads and scraps); and modified shark teeth (Bland 2001; Penders 2005). One small point recently has been identified as a Cahokia Side-Notched, which has been reworked (John Kelly, personal communication 2008). It is made of a nonlocal stone, perhaps Burlington chert from the midwestern United States. In addition, numerous nonlocal sandstone abraders, possibly associated with craft (e.g., lithic, bone, or even late-stage copper) production, were recovered. Hematite in the form of small nodules, ground powder, and residue adhering to certain artifacts and shell was encountered (Ashley 2005c: 291–92). A greenstone celt fragment with red staining might have been used to crush iron oxide nodules into powder. In Shields Mound, Moore (1894b, 1895) identified deposits and layers of hematite-laden sands, often associated with human burials. Interestingly, one large piece of bone within the Kinzey's Knoll shell midden was positively identified as human.

Their close spatial proximity combined with a striking similarity in material content suggests a processual link between Kinzey's Knoll and Shields Mound in the treatment of the dead. Elsewhere I have posited that the mounded shell midden at Kinzey's Knoll reflects the by-product of ceremony, feasting, corpse preparation, and the manufacture of grave goods and other ritual paraphernalia (Ashley 2005c: 292–93). At present, whether Kinzey's Knoll or the summit of the Shields Mound itself (or both) was the actual scene of ritual activity and feasting is unclear, but the former obviously represented an appropriate locus for the disposal of refuse resulting from such activities. Outside burial mound contexts, Kinzey's Knoll is the richest St. Johns II deposit excavated to date in northeastern Florida (and the broader St. Johns River basin).

Communities beyond Mill Cove

Turning to the 11 other St. Johns II settlements in northeastern Florida, we can see that all have (or likely had) an associated sand mound, suggesting that mounded cemeteries were an important feature of St. Johns community layout. Aside from Grant and Shields, all recorded sand mounds were less than 5 m in height and all but one (8Du58) are known to have yielded human skeletal remains. Field procedures, extent of excavation, and level of reporting associated with past mound investigations vary, but most are deemed inadequate by today's standards. Because the majority of excavated mounds were small in terms of size and burial numbers, they appear to have had shorter use lives (and smaller settlement populations) than either Grant or Shields. The most intriguing burial earthwork is the Goodman Mound (8Du66), which exhibited a high incidence of child burials compared to those of adults, including a centrally located interment of 10 subadults (Bullen 1963; Jordan 1963). In all, 13 subadults and three adults were identified. Drawing on ethnohistoric accounts of local Timucua practices, Adelaide Bullen (1963) concluded that the interment represented dedicatory sacrifices of first-born children. Although this "first-born" interpretation is open to debate, the burial composition and arrangement does hint at some form of staged event or ritual reenactment.

Most of the smaller St. Johns II mounds subject to excavation have produced low quantities of exotica in the form of copper, greenstone, graphite, hematite, or mica. Dug by Augustus Mitchell in 1875, the low and unassuming Mitchell Mound on Amelia Island, north of the St. Johns River, even yielded a spatulate celt similar to those from Shields Mound and Mt. Royal (Ashley 2003: 204–6; Goggin 1952: plate 10b). This mound also may be the same as the "Mound South of Suarez Bluff" excavated 20 years later by Moore (1895). Copper appears to be rare in the smaller mounds, having been documented only for the Mayport Mound. To date, no exotic materials have been reported from nonmound contexts at any of these St. Johns II village-mound sites, although some chert artifacts (points and flakes) along with Ocmulgee pottery are reported from most domestic middens. Several potential village sites (e.g., 8Du4, Du58, Du66, and Du97) are characterized by a diffuse and variable spread of refuse, with the thickest shell middens situated close to, and in some instances partly beneath, a burial mound. Though it is tempting to interpret these middens as the by-product of feasting, ritual, mortuary preparation, or other community-wide events, none has been adequately tested at this time to support such a claim.

Outside the Mill Cove Complex, the most extensive testing to date has taken place at the Grand site (8Du1) on Big Talbot Island, some 16 km northeast of Mill Cove (Ashley et al. 2007). The Grand site is a one-of-a-kind piece of St. Johns II architecture, consisting of a shell ring and sand burial-mound complex. The shell ring measures approximately 70 m east–west, 65 m north–south, and 1 m high. A 2-m-high sand burial mound surmounts its western arc. The intentional deposition of refuse in a large ring shape is unusual for this time period, and the presence of a contemporaneous sand burial mound atop a section of the shell ring seemingly bestows a degree of sacredness to the area. The complex is surrounded by an extensive, yet discontinuous, dispersal of St. Johns II middens (Ashley and Thunen 2008).

A 1-x-14-m trench was excavated through the southwestern arc of the shell ring, revealing a complex internal stratigraphy of more than 20 different zones, areas, and features (Ashley et al. 2007). Ring strata suggest the inclusion of both large, quickly piled accumulations of unconsolidated shell and well-packed layers of shell midden that might have accumulated gradually with no major hiatus in refuse deposition. Unlike Kinzey's Knoll at Mill Cove, no exotica or ornate artifacts of shell or bone were recovered. Testing outside the ring thus far suggests a settlement consisting of autonomous households dispersed over a broad area, with the Grand shell ring and sand mound complex serving as the central rallying point and public arena for both nonritual and ceremonial activities, including mound burial. However, if the Grand shell ring was the scene of ritual and feasting, its contents (or at least those from the sampled section) are qualitatively different from those of Kinzey's Knoll.

Possibly Shields and Grant are so much larger and contain more burials and more exotica than other St. Johns II mounds in the area simply because they were used as mortuary repositories over a longer span of time. In fact, save for the size and material contents of individual burial mounds, St. Johns II settlements consist of domestic middens containing relatively similar types and ranges of artifacts and zooarchaeological remains, suggesting that each community produced and traded for its own daily needs, although they may have been linked ceremonially to the Mill Cove Complex. At present, exactly when and how long each settlement was occupied is unclear, but it is unlikely that all were occupied at precisely the same time during the entire A.D. 900–1250 time range.

The Pull of Mississippianization

Although most southeastern archaeologists set the start of the Mississippi period at A.D. 1000, archaeological evidence clearly shows that the tenth century was a dynamic time in which interaction spheres were broadened and key Mississippian traits began to circulate along paths of communication and exchange that had been mostly dormant during the Late

Woodland period (Cobb and Garrow 1996; Cobb and Nassaney 1995; Smith 1990). But responses to these new ideas and developments were mediated by cultural traditions, which helped shape the variable and uneven rates and forms of Mississippianization, or what Cobb (2000: 200–201) calls the "pluralistic creation of Mississippian identities."

With this said, I view the emergence of St. Johns II communities in northeastern Florida (ca. A.D. 900) as an unanticipated and historically contingent outcome promoted in part by the intersection of a macroregional demand for a locally available resource(s). Today, marine shell is commonly assumed to have been the foremost item leaving Florida for the Mississippian world, as discussed below (and see Mitchem, chapter 8, this volume). The pull of involvement in emerging Mississippian exchange networks as suppliers of shell combined with the small resident population at the river's mouth might have precipitated the relocation of some St. Johns populations to extreme northeastern Florida to gain regular access to coastal resources. Perhaps Mt. Royal had already begun to establish itself as a regional center fostering emulation.

Involvement in these far-flung routes of contact and interaction should not be perceived merely as resulting from the centripetal pull of macroregional processes. It also entailed the specific decisions and actions of local individuals and social groups who actively took part in constructing their social milieu. One thing is for certain: St. Johns II societies at two strategic points along the river—Mill Cove and Mt. Royal localities—seized upon an opportunity in the tenth century to become engaged in long-distance exchange more successfully than any other groups along the Atlantic coast during the Early Mississippi period.

Patterns of Contact and Exchange

Once avenues of communication and exchange were established in northeastern Florida, with whom were St. Johns II communities interacting (directly and indirectly)? Nonlocal items such as copper, stone, galena, and mica reveal links to the north, and a connection upriver (south) to Mt. Royal also is undeniable. In fact, similarities between Mt. Royal and the Mill Cove Complex are so strong that the two appear to have shared aspects of culture, technology, and mortuary ritual (Ashley 2002: 169; Moore 1894b: 203–4). Ocmulgee Cord Marked pottery of southern-central Georgia is found on almost every St. Johns II site in northeastern Florida (typically accounting for between 2 percent and 18 percent of the St. Johns II pottery

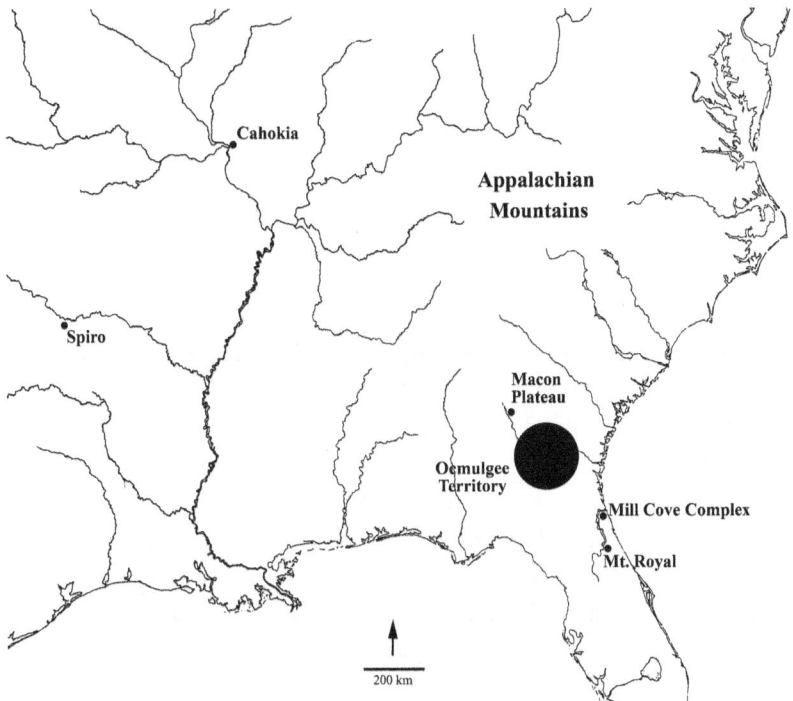

Figure 5.7. Broad view of the greater Southeast.

assemblage). Neutron activation analysis and sherd refiring studies demonstrate that cord-marked sherds from northeastern Florida include both trade wares and local copies, virtually indistinguishable from each other except at the chemical level (Ashley 2003: 104–27; Rolland 2004: 132–50). The stunning similarity between trade and local wares has been used to suggest that Ocmulgee potters may have married into St. Johns II communities to cement social alliances (Ashley 2002: 168). Ocmulgee pottery has been recovered from both sacred and secular contexts in northeastern Florida, and it also is present in midden deposits at Mt. Royal.

Taking a bird's-eye view of the Southeast, we can see that Ocmulgee hunter-gatherers were situated between northeastern Florida and Macon Plateau, which was the dominant early Mississippian chiefdom in the Deep South at the time (figure 5.7). Lake Jackson to the west had yet to reach its regional and interregional prominence (Marrinan, chapter 9, this volume; Payne 1994; Scarry 1996). It does not seem too large a stretch to assume that Mill Cove and Mt. Royal had connections to Macon Plateau, particularly given that St. Johns pottery and marine shell have been found at Macon Plateau (Fairbanks 1981; Richard Vernon, personal communication 2005). Some of the exotic rock, mineral, and metal that found its way to Mill Cove could possibly have come from, or at least passed through, Macon Plateau. Of particular interest here are the spatulate celts from Shields Mound and Mt. Royal, which might have a southern Appalachian origin and very well may have come directly from Macon Plateau (see Pauketat 1983).

Beyond Macon Plateau, the recovery of certain Early Mississippi–period items such as copper-veneered, wooden biconical ear plugs and long-nosed god maskettes from Grant Mound points to connections with the American Bottom and the Cahokia polity (Griffin 1946: 88; Kelly 1991; Kelly and Cole 1931: 322, 335; Sampson and Esarey 1993: 463–64). The recent identification of a Cahokia Side-Notched point from Kinzey's Knoll (Shields Mound) provides additional evidence for involvement in the Cahokia sphere of interaction. Moore (1894b: 21) also recovered what appears to be a Cahokia Side-Notched point from Mt. Royal. Results of trace element analysis of more than 20 copper artifacts from Grant Mound and Mt. Royal tie the metals to sources in both the Appalachian Mountains and the Great Lakes region (Goad 1978: 136–48).

Links to groups to the west are less obvious but still present. Gulf coast pottery types, identified by their nonlocal paste characteristics, occur infrequently on some St. Johns II sites (Rolland 2004: 67). Spiculate-tempered Papys Bayou, Little Manatee, and Sarasota Incised wares are found in mounds and middens in the Florida Gulf coast region, but whether these are tradewares or local reproductions is unclear (Goggin 1952: 108; Willey 1949a). It is quite possible that inspiration for the various St. Johns Incised and Punctated wares is rooted in the Weeden Island pottery tradition of the Florida Gulf coast (Mitchem, chapter 8, this volume). Interaction with Early Mississippi–period groups to the west in the panhandle of Florida is uncertain, although Goggin (1952: 110) mentions that a "few" Fort Walton–like sherds have been recovered from "larger river and coastal sites." The St. Johns River would have provided northeastern Florida natives with direct access to groups to the south and indirectly to the west and the Gulf coast. Finally, the recovery of two queen conch (*Strombus gigas*) shells from the Grant Mound in the late 1980s shows that St. Johns peoples also were able to acquire materials from far southern Florida.

The importation of copper and other exotica suggests that local materials left northeastern Florida as part of exchange, alliance, and/or gifting networks. If we widen the geographical scale out from the St. Johns River, we see no sites in Florida or Georgia during Early Mississippi times with as much copper as Grant Mound and Mt. Royal. Even Macon Plateau has yielded little copper to date, and the metal also is sparse at early Mississippian sites along the Apalachicola River drainage (White et al., chapter 10, this volume). Moreover, the metal is conspicuously absent on sites along or near the Atlantic and Gulf coasts, in areas that encompass the natural range of marine shells such as whelk, olive, and marginella. While shark teeth, pearls, yaupon leaves, bird feathers, and other nondurable items very well may have gone out of northeastern Florida, marine shell is likely to have been the principal export, given its ubiquity along the coast and popularity among Mississippian peoples (Ashley 2002: 167).

Marine shell was greatly desired among Mississippians of the greater Southeast, as evidenced by the sizeable numbers of artifacts made from it, particularly beads, found on interior sites situated great distances from ocean waters. Several archaeologists have implicated Florida communities such as the Mill Cove Complex and Mt. Royal in trafficking marine shells from the Atlantic and Gulf coasts to the interior Southeast (Ashley 2002: 167–68, 2005a: 282–83; Brown et al. 1990: 260; Milanich 1999: 10–11; Mitchem 1996b: 233–34, chapter 8, this volume; Payne and Scarry 1998: 46–47; Phillips and Brown 1978: 207–8). A major artery for the transportation of shell (as well as traders, questers, and other emissaries) out of Florida during the Early Mississippi period was through northern peninsular Florida, either along the Alachua Trail or the intracoastal waterway, then through the Ocmulgee territory into Macon Plateau, and then perhaps onward to Cahokia.

Clearly northeastern Florida natives profited from the popularity of marine shells among Early Mississippi–period societies. At present, however, there is no evidence of specialized or centralized production of shell artifacts for exchange. Based on their common association with local burials, shell bead production was likely embedded in the domestic economy, and shell procurement, along with the collection of other coastal resources such as pearls and shark teeth, could have been subsumed within the course of daily subsistence activities (see Brown et al. 1990: 271). Whole shells could have been collected from the beach following intensive storms and tidal surges, while usable fragments would have been ever-present along the seashore. Most shell appears to have left Florida in raw form. In sum, an amalgam of different kinds of social relations, engaged at local, regional, and macroregional levels, seems to have embodied St. Johns II life.

Politics of Exchange

How might we begin to interpret the above information within the context of the St. Johns II political economy? According to conventional thinking, St. Johns II societies received copper and other exotica in final form via down-the-line exchange as part of some local prestige-goods economy. There is no doubt that the residents of Mill Cove, as well as Mt. Royal to the south, were major consumers of exotica during the Early Mississippi period. Many pieces of copper along with artifacts of nonlocal rock/mineral ended their long journeys and life histories in St. Johns II burial mounds (Ashley 2002: 166, 2003: 301–2). Obviously, mortuary interment was the ultimate destination for most exotica in St. Johns II society. But I believe we should refrain from always interpreting nonlocal grave goods as life possessions reflective of an individual's wealth and social standing within society (King 2004). At this time, we cannot rule out the possibility that some grave goods were communally owned inalienable objects, gifts for ancestors, or props within mortuary displays or performances, particularly in light of what appears to be a staged burial of infants within the Goodman Mound.

Our refined chronology for northeastern Florida places St. Johns II communities such as Mill Cove and Mt. Royal at the forefront of incipient and early Mississippian interaction networks during the late tenth through twelfth centuries. Possession of finely crafted and potentially hard-to-obtain display goods such as long-nosed god maskettes and spatulate celts underscores the vital role Mill Cove and Mt. Royal played in Early Mississippi–period exchange. Of the seven known pairs of copper long-nosed god ear pieces, three have been taken from sites in the American Bottom (Kelly 1991: 73–74). The others have come from locations on the periphery of the Mississippian world: Aztalan in Wisconsin, Spiro in Oklahoma, Gahagan in Louisiana, and Grant in Florida (Williams and Goggin 1956).

Robert Hall (1989: 240–47, 1997: 148–53) draws a link between depictions of the long-nosed god and a semidivine Winnebago hero known as Red Horn or He-who-wears-human-heads-as-earrings (Kelly, chapter 12, this volume). It further has been suggested that the maskettes were part of an adoption ceremony that forged kinship relationships "between the powerful leader of a large polity and his political clients in outlying areas" (Duncan and Diaz-Granados 2000; Hall 1997: 51; Pauketat 2004: 116). Thus, Mississippian chiefs may have gifted these items directly to St. Johns representatives as part of an adoption or alliance ritual that bonded them as exchange partners. St. Johns communities perhaps were the primary brokers of shell and other coastal resources to early Mississippian chiefdoms such as Macon Plateau and Cahokia—an alliance that required direct diplomacy rather than down-the-line movement of certain exotica.

A pivotal region along the northward route into the Mississippian world was the Ocmulgee territory, which was positioned squarely between northeastern Florida and Macon Plateau. Ocmulgee hunter-gatherers, who occupied the area encompassing the confluence of the Altamaha, Ocmulgee, and Oconee rivers of southern-central Georgia, may have served as intermediaries or at least provided unencumbered access through their territory, in effect easing the flow of St. Johns peoples, goods, and information between the interior Southeast and the Atlantic coast (Ashley 2002: 167). However, findings of recent stable-isotope analysis of a small skeletal collection from two sites in the Ocmulgee-Blackshear region of southern Georgia suggest that if these riverine foragers were acting as go-betweens they were not receiving and consuming identifiable amounts of corn or marine resources as a result of their interactions (Tucker 2007).

Regardless of the specific roles held by the participants, direct interactions between St. Johns II communities and Ocmulgee foragers are evidenced by the presence of Ocmulgee Cord Marked pottery in St. Johns II contexts. Strong similarities between local copies and actual tradewares suggest the relocation of some Ocmulgee potters (women) to St. Johns II communities, perhaps a result of marriage alliances (Ashley 2002: 168, 2003: 307–12). Ocmulgee pottery served everyday uses in St. Johns communities, as demonstrated by its presence in domestic middens, but the ware also played a role in display and serving in public ceremonies, such as at Kinzey's Knoll near Shields Mound. Households may have contributed Ocmulgee pots to feasts or other presentations to convey publicly their family's link to a distant place or to Ocmulgee allies. Hinterland visitors also might have brought nonlocal pots directly to the site. In any case, it is clear that Ocmulgee pottery was pervasive within St. Johns villages and integrated into sacred and secular realms of life.

The nature of participation in long-distance trade systems is fundamentally tied to how labor is appropriated at the local level (Cobb 2000; Saitta 1994, 1997). The recovery of copper plates and other exotic artifacts from large St. Johns II mounds has led some researchers to infer social inequalities based on some form of prestige-goods economy (Milanich 1994: 269, 1996: 10–11; Payne and Scarry 1998: 47; Phillips and Brown 1978: 207–8). Within a prestige-goods model, elite power stems from their control over access to exotic goods/raw materials, items awarded high value through elite manipulation and gained only through external trade (Frankenstein and Rowlands 1978: 75; Peregrine 1992). Exotica within such economies serve as sumptuary goods and sources of power that bring to life and justify the superior social standing of those who possess them. Such display goods are then circulated among elites to establish and preserve social alliances at various geographical scales. Elites possessing prestige goods are able to appropriate surplus labor and goods to fund their own political agendas. As such, prestige goods are instruments of power (or symbolic capital) that allow the exploitation and control of others (Bourdieu 1977; Saitta 1999).

I disagree with past interpretations that consider exotica in local mounds evidence of a St. Johns II prestige-goods economy. Mere possession or even control of the distribution of exotica by elites does not automatically translate into power over surplus labor and goods, as stipulated in prestige-goods models. In addition, a tendency of prestige-goods models is to conflate all exotica under a single category and treat them in an undifferentiated manner that suggests they were equally valued and served the same roles (Lessure 1999). However, ethnographic research indicates that different kinds of social valuables are used in myriad ways and carry different meanings (Cobb 1993; Peregrine 1992; Saitta 1999).

There is little doubt that exotic materials such as copper, mica, and greenstone were highly valued mortuary goods among St. Johns II societies, because nonlocal materials occur in the largest and smallest of mounds. Their distribution across northeastern Florida suggests they were almost exclusively consumed in burial mounds and to a lesser extent in special "middens" (e.g., Kinzey's Knoll) adjacent to burial mounds; the latter have been interpreted as the by-product of public ritual rather than the domestic refuse of elites (Ashley 2005c; Marrinan 2005; Rolland 2005). The virtual absence of copper, mica, ground stone artifacts, and nearly all nonlocal items (save for lithic points and Ocmulgee pots) in any village area throughout the region is remarkable. The same situation has been observed at Mt. Royal (Ashley 2005a). Thus, the treatment and exhibition of copper and other exotica appear to have been confined to communally sanctioned arenas of group interaction and performance such as public feasting, ritual staging, and mound burial (Ashley 2005c: 292).

Our understanding of St. Johns mortuary practices is derived largely on the basis of evidence from Grant and Shields mounds, both excavated more than one hundred years ago by Moore (1894b, 1895). Because of his methodological and reporting deficiencies, we cannot say much about mound population demographics, the role of exotic materials or grave goods during each specific burial episode, or how individual interments related to one another in time and space. We do know that St. Johns mortuary customs included both primary and secondary burials; the latter often contained multiple individuals. Despite the inadequacies of Moore's work, some general statements about St. Johns mortuary practices are possible.

At Grant Mound, Moore (1895: 32, 33) reported that primary burials "largely predominated." Furthermore, he stated that "most burials were without accompanying relics when found [and] that shell beads, usually unassociated with other objects, were the most frequent tribute to the departed." Stone celts, of which he recovered 147, "occasionally" occurred with bones. At Shields, most burials showed "an unnatural juxtaposition" indicating that secondary burials predominated (Moore 1895: 13). It is unclear whether Moore's frequent references to finding "few human remains" mean intentional partial representation of bodies or the by-product of differential skeletal preservation. Though this is open to alternative interpretations, the impression I get is that nonlocal grave goods in these two accretionary mounds at times occurred in association with primary burials but more frequently were placed near secondary interments or in contexts unassociated with human remains (Ashley 2002: 171, 173n3).

Some items such as shell beads may have been personal possessions, whereas others may have been associated with social or clan position. It is worth noting that not all potentially wearable items were worn at death, because such items appear to have been placed apart from the body. This is especially true of the rectangular and square copper "plates," often found covered or wrapped in either bark or vegetal fiber (Moore 1894b: 139, 1895: 22, 40). Perhaps these objects were not regalia but pieces of far-off lands destined for the spirit world. The history of these objects and the journey they made bestowed them with power, and sending them to the spirit realm may have helped restore or maintain cosmic order.

Considering available St. Johns II settlement, craft production, and mortuary data, I am more inclined to see a fit with some form of communal political economy rather than support for institutionalized distinctions between elites and commoners (Ashley 2002: 171–72, 2003: 344–48). The latter comes more into focus in the sixteenth century, as corn becomes a dietary component and warfare becomes a facet of Timucuan life in northeastern Florida (Hann 1996; Milanich 1996; Worth 1998a). But we must keep in mind that inequalities exist within a communal political economy, as certain individuals may have benefited in their role as exchange broker, ritual specialist, or other communal functionary. In fact, Saitta (1997: 10) argues that a communal political economy does not necessarily deny instances of exploitation but only requires that "most of its surplus labor is collectively produced and distributed." Thus, my endorsement of a communal political economy for Early Mississippi–period St. Johns II societies in no way means I am labeling them egalitarian.

In attempting to interpret the St. Johns II political economy, we also need to consider their domestic economy. Midden data paint the St. Johns natives as generalized foragers in tune with the daily rhythm of life in an estuary and salt marsh environment. Fishing was the dominant subsistence activity, followed by shellfish collecting, hunting, and gathering. The ubiquity and richness of coastal habitats appears to have hindered the ability of local leaders to assume direct control over food supplies and means of production, meaning each community was economically autonomous (Ashley 2002: 165, 2003: 278–81). From a material culture standpoint, their tool kits were not flashy and are mostly recognized by informal bone and shell tools. In fact, their shell tool assemblages pale in comparison to those of the Calusa of southwest Florida (Marquardt 1992c; Walker 2000). Pottery consists of a limited range of bowl forms of various sizes (Rolland 2004, 2005). Stone tools are typically infrequent in midden context but, when recovered, include small Pinellas arrow points and/or chert debitage.

The rather basic quotidian material assemblage (at least in terms of nonperishable items) contrasts dramatically with the kinds of artifacts found in mortuary-related contexts. Exotica, stone points (including numerous scavenged Archaic types), smoking pipes, shell and pearl adornments, ornate bone pins, iron oxide (nodules and powder), and unique ceramic vessel forms (or freak wares, as C. B. Moore termed them) occur in sand burial mounds. Interestingly, bottle forms are completely lacking in St. Johns mounds. Again, because many of these same materials along with large amounts of food remains and at least one human bone fragment were recovered from Kinzey's Knoll, it seems reasonable to conclude that graveside feasting, mortuary preparation, and ritual acts involving the handling of more elaborate items were part of the burial interment process at Shields Mound. In other words, the use and display of exotica and uniquely crafted items was compartmentalized within St. Johns society and restricted to ritual and mortuary contexts.

At present there is no evidence for nonmound burials dating to local St. Johns II times (A.D. 900–1250), suggesting that all deceased were afforded burial in a sand mound. The monumentality of Grant and Shields mounds made them important features of the St. Johns cultural landscape. It has been speculated that burial mounds served as shrines dedicated to ancestors, those who had died recently as well as those dead for decades or even centuries (Buikstra and Charles 1999). As such, these visual edifices were daily reminders of community and common history, not monuments for rulers or elite families. In this light, sand mounds paid homage to dead kin, and the periodic nature of mortuary ritual provided recurrent opportunities to venerate and reaffirm ties to their ancestors and claims to the land (Buikstra and Charles 1999: 204–5). Death and ritual were public events as the deceased were laid to rest in a corporate repository. It is true that the dead were treated in different ways in St. Johns mounds, since some individuals were buried in the flesh shortly after death, while others went through a lengthy process involving defleshing and disarticulation. However, what such mortuary differentiation meant socially to St. Johns people is still unclear.

I propose that by the early years of the Mississippi period, St. Johns II communities had become enmeshed in exchange networks, thereby broadening the geographical extent of social relationships necessary for cultural reproduction. Essential to the process of social reproduction at this time was the maintenance of long-distance social relations and the acquisition of objects from far-off and potentially dangerous places. Exotica might have been conveyed directly to St. Johns representatives to create or maintain social alliances. In such a context, exchange, or more appropriately gifting, serves to bind individuals or communities in relationships of reciprocity and shared indebtedness (Mauss 1967; Sahlins 1972). While immediate payback of a gift is not expected, a bond between the parties is maintained as long as each fulfills the alternating role of giver and receiver. The nature of early Mississippian life in the interior Southeast and in northeastern Florida brought these distant communities together in relationships of social importance to each.

Once accepted into St. Johns life, exotic materials assumed a community-wide role in mortuary activities and rituals geared more toward the promotion of group identity and solidarity than the manifestation of the coercive power of elites (Ashley 2002: 172, 2003: 347). The objects, in this view, became physical markers of community success within networks of social relations that covered great distances. In the end, however, these culturally valued objects invariably came to be deposited in communal mortuary mounds, perhaps because no living person was worthy of possessing them. Exotica might have been offered or gifted to the ancestors to secure their favor. Perhaps in some instances individuals who played important roles in St. Johns society served as emissaries responsible for taking exotica (now imbued with culturally specific meaning and significance) to the land of their ancestors. Though the objects were leaving the world of the living, they were cementing a connection between the living, their ancestors, and the land. By placing exotic materials in burial mounds, the natives were intentionally taking them out of active use and circulation, thereby creating a continuous need to secure replacements through exchange, diplomacy, or perhaps pilgrimage (questing). The reproduction of society required constant work and negotiation of social relations beyond the salt marshes and estuarine waters of northeastern Florida.

At the Mill Cove Complex, the presence of two large, contemporaneous sand mounds, each replete with human burials, implies organization with two social groups (Ashley 2005c: 294). In moieties each division often assumes certain social, ritual, or political responsibilities that must be carried out for the benefit of the broader community. While Moore's (1894b, 1895) excavations at Shields and Grant mounds yielded the same categories of artifacts, differences in the quantity and quality of certain materials stands out. For instance, copper was far more prevalent in Grant Mound, and finished pieces such as biconical ear spools, long-nosed god maskettes, and repoussé plates were either lacking or absent in Shields Mound. While more than 140 ground stone celts were taken from Grant, Shields produced far fewer, but included the only two spatulate forms. Shields also yielded more than one hundred projectile points, many of which were large Archaic forms, whereas Grant contained only 15. An interesting aspect of the Archaic points from both Grant and Shields is that the majority exhibit far less evidence of retouch than is displayed on similar point types found on Archaic sites, suggesting that St. Johns II populations were preferentially selecting symmetrical and idealized forms of older lithic points for ritual and mound burial (Wilcox 2010: 81–82). Finally, primary burials were more common at Grant, while secondary burials were more frequent at Shields. Though these differences might represent nothing more than sampling bias, the possibility exists that distinct ceremonial obligations were maintained by two social groups and that specialized rituals necessitated distinct materials, highlighting the fact that not all display goods are the same.

A common practice in corporate societies is the mobilization of labor and goods for public ceremonies and construction projects that draw members together in community-avowing endeavors (Blanton et al. 1996: 6). In the St. Johns case, mortuary ritual and interment in a communal cemetery would have operated to establish and reinforce social ties between the living and dead and to promote a shared community identity through nonexploitative means. It further provided an important context for the mobilization of labor beyond kinship ties in St. Johns II societies. But we must keep two things in mind. First, even in communal societies not everyone participates or shares equally (Saitta 1994, 1997). Second, a communal political economy is a dynamic sociohistorical manifestation consisting of kinship definitions, social positions, and religious ideology constantly reproduced and contested through negotiation. In other words, we should not assume that the communal structure of St. Johns II society was static and free of internal challenge to the communal ethic during the period A.D. 900–1250.

Over its span of occupation, certain individuals or families at Mill Cove (and Mt. Royal as well) certainly may have attempted to use their strategic positions as communal elites to widen the social gap and assert more exploitative social relations (Ashley 2002: 172). In the absence of direct authority over the means of production, the potential for "power over" often lies in the control of exotic exchange and ritual knowledge and ideology, although such control is inherently tenuous because of the vicissitudes of long-distance relations (Cobb 2000; Pauketat 1994). Such actions would have required elites to manipulate communal symbolism and meaning embodied in exotic goods in order to uphold exploitative relations. In all likelihood any attempts to usurp societal constraints certainly would have been countered to some degree by the general populace, who would have resisted any efforts at exploitation (Ashley 2002: 172).

Communal ritual, while drawing members of society together, can also contain the seeds of alienation and provide a stage where certain individuals or groups attempt to use these events for personal power construction (Emerson 1997: 14). Quite possibly, those ritual specialists invested with the storage and handling of ceremonial paraphernalia and esoteric knowledge, supported voluntarily and needed by the general populace, were the ones most likely to promote change in social order and redefine the cultural meaning of display goods. Under certain historical conditions, some communal elites in St. Johns communities may have attempted just that.

The ability of Mill Cove Complex residents to host pan-community events on a regular basis would have enabled them to secure an advantage in social and political relations. Thus, the most potentially opportune context in which to challenge community ethos in St. Johns II societies would have been ritual settings at the Mill Cove Complex, the same public arena used to integrate society. St. Johns II social groups (e.g., clans, moieties) may have been ranked higher with respect to roles assumed during high-profile rituals, which drew a measure of distinction to them. Even if this ranking was ceremonial and not equivalent to "power over" in everyday life, such a hierarchical structure provides a fracture that, through manipulation, could potentially develop into relations of obligation and institutionalized social inequality (Knight 1990: 7).

Such differential participation in St. Johns life undoubtedly brought friction and constant negotiations between aspirant elites and the general populace over extent of control. Although temporary episodes of success on the part of particular elites (lineages or clans) may have occurred at Mill Cove (and Mt. Royal), attempts to transform communal politics and ideologies into exploitative tributary relations appear to have been unable to take hold in the face of a stronger communal political economy. Present evidence points to a decentralized regional economy, meaning that each village controlled its own internal and external operations, which would have worked against attempts by individuals or kin groups at the Mill Cove Complex to gain regional hegemony (Ashley 2002: 172). Thus, the Mill Cove Complex served as a regional ceremonial and ritual center, hosting a variety of events of a social and political nature (Ashley 2005c: 297). As such, it likely assumed a dominant and influential status among the St. Johns II villages of northeastern Florida, but it was not the capital of a complex chiefdom.

Conclusion

In the end, St. Johns II societies in northeastern Florida were unable to sustain themselves as historical circumstance changed the macroregional landscape. Their involvement in Early Mississippi–period interactions appears to have waned with the decline of Cahokia and the fall and abandonment of Macon Plateau, which brought about the proliferation of smaller rival chiefdoms across the Southeast. Such events may have set into motion shock waves that disrupted existing interaction networks and social alliances, creating conditions that St. Johns II societies in northeastern Florida could not overcome, leading them to abandon (or at least depopulate) the far corner of the state and move upriver by A.D. 1250–1300. By this time, the major artery for the flow of shell and copper and other materials into and out of Florida appears to have shifted to the Florida panhandle. Within two centuries or so, however, the introduction of corn farming and the shift from long-distance trading to territorial raiding created a volatile landscape that appears to have fostered stronger social divides and institutionalized inequalities, characteristics of the contact-era Timucua encountered by the earliest Spanish and French interlopers.

Acknowledgments

I would like to thank Nancy White, Vicki Rolland, and Jeff Mitchem for their valuable comments on this chapter. I also appreciate John Kelly's insights on Cahokia. Nichole Bishop helped draft several of the figures, and I thank her. Finally, figures 5.3–5.5 are used with the permission of the National Museum of the American Indian, Smithsonian Institution.

6

The Alachua of North-Central Florida

VICKI ROLLAND

North-central Florida was home to the sixteenth-century Potano Timucua, who, according to European documents, were maize farmers organized into simple chiefdoms (Hann 1996; Worth 1998a). From an archaeological perspective the Potano and their precolumbian predecessors are represented by the Alachua culture. Despite possessing two primary characteristics of Mississippi-period societies of the interior Southeast, the Alachua were far from archetypical Mississippian farmers and temple-mound builders. Rather, archaeological data are more suggestive of a Late Woodland way of life with a simple material culture inventory, a strong reliance on hunting and gathering, and a lack of obvious social stratification, nonlocal funerary goods, and monumental architecture. As such, the Alachua appear to have had a lifestyle similar to that of Suwannee Valley peoples immediately to their north. For that region, Worth (1998a, 2002, and chapter 7, this volume) has drawn upon Spanish documentary evidence to support the existence of a chiefly sociopolitical organization at contact, although material correlates for such a society are lacking. The same is true for the Alachua archaeological record.

At this time archaeologists have yet to recognize any Mississippian characteristics within the Alachua culture, including evidence for elite involvement in far-flung exchange networks. The absence of exotic stone or copper is noteworthy considering the fact that such materials have been recovered in earlier Woodland-period Cades Pond contexts and from contemporaneous Safety Harbor and St. Johns sites to the west and east, respectively. However, the presence of Safety Harbor and St. Johns wares in Alachua contexts indicates interactions with those neighboring societies. Their strongest relations, however, appear to have been with groups immediately to the north and northwest in the Suwannee Valley area.

Early Alachua groups (ca. A.D. 900–1250) formed the southern end of a geographical band of cord-marked pottery-making people that stretched from north-central Florida to the central Savannah River valley of Georgia and South Carolina. The overall structure and nature of sites across this area of the Southeast are strikingly similar, and their distribution appears to reflect the dispersal of regionally based Woodland foragers (Ashley 2005d; Stephenson 1990). No evidence exists at this time for elite individuals or kin groups having been involved in Mississippian exchange. Current information further suggests that maize farming did not become a conspicuous aspect of the Alachua economy until the mid-fifteenth century, a situation that may have fostered the eventual emergence of chiefly leaders, as described in early historic documents. This chapter focuses on the Alachua culture prior to European contact and presents an updated overview and assessment of current research.

The North-Central Florida Environment

Alachua and Marion counties form the heartland of the triangular-shaped Alachua culture region (figure 6.1), although both Prairie Cord Marked and Alachua Cob Marked pottery are found over a far broader area (Austin 2001; Brown et al. 1990; Johnson 1987; Kohler 1991). None of the Alachua boundary lines is distinct; rather, they are dotted in along geographical formations. To the north, sites within the Santa Fe River drainage system contain mixtures of Alachua and Suwannee Valley pottery types, suggesting that it served as a buffer zone between those two similar cultures (Milanich 1994: 332; Worth, chapter 7, this volume). To the east and southeast, the broad St. Johns River basin divided the Alachua and St. Johns culture areas. Throughout this basin, archaeologists find sites with pottery assemblages consisting of both Alachua sand- and grit-tempered wares and distinctive St. Johns sponge-spicule-tempered ceramics. The recovery of St. Johns pottery actually begins well within the eastern boundary of the Alachua area and increases in frequency the closer sites lie to the river. Although at times the Alachua may have shared access to abundant riverine resources with their eastern neighbors, in the early historic period the Potano (Alachua) and Outina (St. Johns) were at war (Worth, chapter 7, this volume). Alachua's western boundary also is vague and seemingly based more on the paucity of Safety Harbor settlements located away from the coastal strand (Mitchem, chapter 8, this volume). This region is either extremely swampy or extremely dry and offered Alachua and Safety

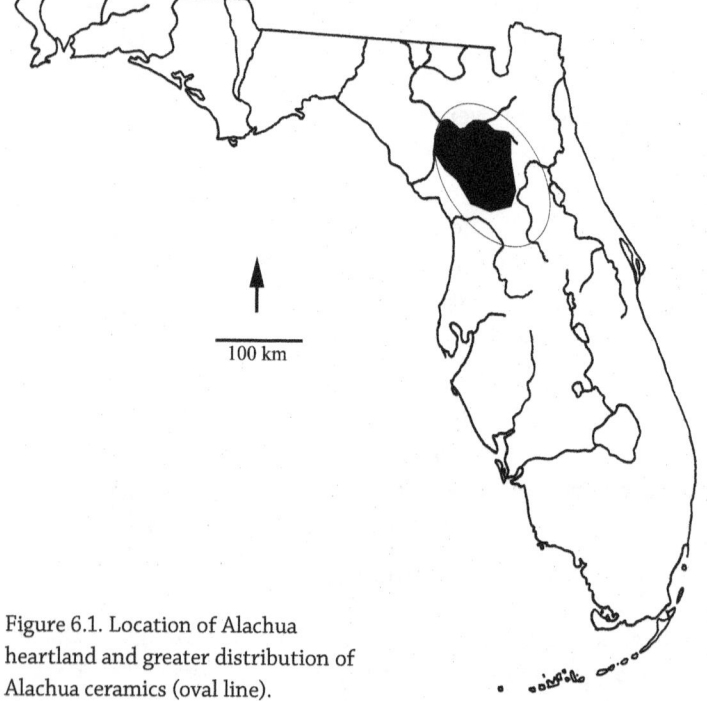

Figure 6.1. Location of Alachua heartland and greater distribution of Alachua ceramics (oval line).

Harbor peoples fewer of the resources so plentiful within their respective heartlands. It is an area sparsely populated even today.

The Alachua territory contained a unique set of land and surface-water formations that distinguished it from neighboring culture areas (Milanich 1994: 331–33). North-central Florida is dominated by an exposed, raised ridge of fractured limestone and weathered clay formations interspersed among chains of sinkholes and spring-fed lakes and streams. This linear geological structure runs from the northwest in Union and Columbia counties southeast into Marion and northern Lake counties and is known as the Northern Highlands. The majority of Alachua sites lie on or east and north of the ridge, which contains fertile, well-drained soils and rolling hills where temperate hardwood and pine forests flourish (Platt and Schwartz 1990). To the west, the terrain contains a mixture of shallow, poorly drained spodic soils and well-drained sand hills that provide little surface water (Austin 2001; Brown, Stone, and Carlisle 1990).

The Northern Highlands plateau does not continue east or south of Gainesville, where gently sloping sand hills and plains have been sculpted by flat-bottomed shallow lakes, highland marshes, and wet prairies (Austin 2001; Bullen 1949a; Loucks 1976). Still-active geological processes produced by interaction of subsurface water and highly soluble limestone present a decidedly unstable landscape. The porous karstic bedrock that underlies this whole region contains solution holes that allow the Florida Aquifer to rise to the surface in the form of springs or ponds. Springheads are often connected by a system of slow-moving navigable streams. However, Alachua surface-water accumulations are by no means dependable resources for humans or wildlife. At times underlying fractured limestone formations are plugged, allowing surface water to collect and create a habitat for fish, shellfish, reptiles, mammals, and local and migrating birds. But if large enough solution holes develop, significant volumes of surface water can drain away in only a few days. In 1791 when Bartram (1955) came upon a dry Paynes Prairie he referred to the area as the Alachua Savannah (figure 6.2). Although Paynes Prairie is a wetland once again, environmental conditions might have been very different during the Woodland and Mississippi periods. Those Alachua sites located on the crests or slopes of the

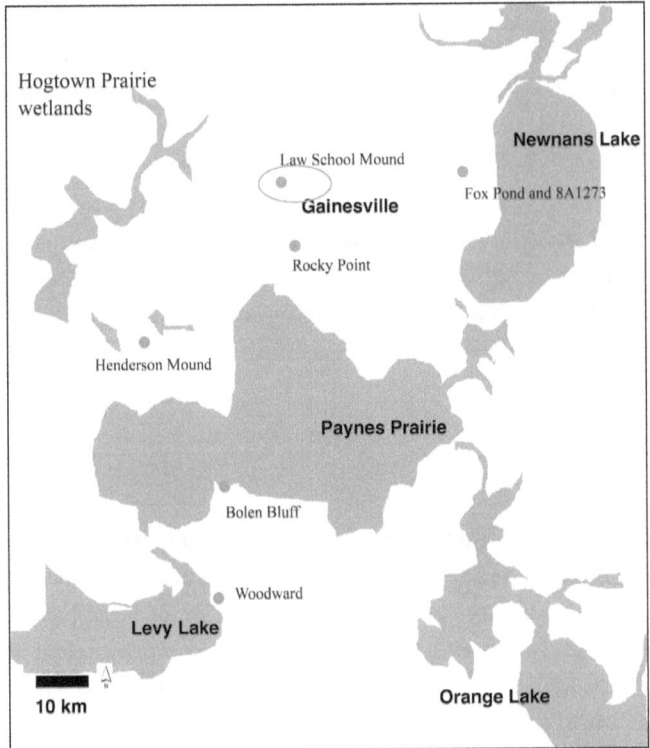

Figure 6.2. Gainesville-area sites: Law School Mound within Gainesville city limits; Henderson Mound; Bolen Bluff; Rocky Point; Woodward Mound and Village; Fox Pond and 8Al273. Gray areas represent wetlands.

Table 6.1. Commonly accepted Alachua chronology and associated pottery types

Phase	Dates	Pottery Types
Hickory Pond	A.D. 600/800–1250	Prairie Cord Marked and Lochloosa Punctated
Alachua	A.D. 1250–precontact	Alachua Cob Marked
Potano	Postcontact (A.D. 1539)	Alachua Cob Marked, occasional Prairie Cord Marked, Colonoware, and Spanish wares

Source: Milanich 1994.

sand hills may have once overlooked old lakebeds, relict lake terraces, or shallow or deepwater lakes (Austin 2001; Bullen 1949a; Loucks 1976).

Temporal Considerations

Building on Goggin's (1948b) seminal work in the region, Milanich (1971, 1994) established the basic chronology for north-central Florida by dividing the Late Woodland– through Mission-period Alachua culture into three phases on the sole basis of ceramic changes: Hickory Pond, Alachua, and Potano (table 6.1). Dates for the end of Middle Woodland Cades Pond culture, the beginning of Hickory Pond and Alachua phases, and the development of broad-scale maize horticulture are arbitrary because few Alachua (or Cades Pond) sites have been firmly dated. Consequently, our current perception of Alachua culture history is based on ceramic seriations from only five sites, each excavated more than 30 years ago (Bullen 1958a; Kohler 1991; Milanich 1971, 1972, 1994). Little has been done in recent years to fine-tune the Alachua chronology.

Ceramics

The emergence of Alachua culture is defined by the introduction of new ceramic types (Milanich 1994: 335; Kohler 1991: 95). Early Alachua- or Hickory Pond–phase pottery assemblages contain Prairie Cord and Fabric Marked, Lochloosa Punctated, and Punctated-over-Cord Marked (figure 6.3). Stratigraphic frequencies reveal that Alachua Cob Marked, Alachua Plaited or Twined Impressed, and Alachua Net Marked sherds were produced at a later time (Alachua phase), although exactly when they first appear in Alachua ceramic assemblages is unclear (figure 6.4). Production of the most resilient pottery type, Lochloosa Punctated, seems to have

Figure 6.3. Examples of Prairie Cord Marked rim treatments: *left* and *center* mimic appliqué strip. Sherds are part of the Ceramics Lab type collection, Florida Museum of Natural History, Gainesville. Sherds used with the same museum's permission.

Figure 6.4. Alachua period pottery. *Top row*: variations of Lochloosa Punctated; *left*, surface obliteration with cob-marked and punctated impressions. *Bottom row*: *left*, St. Johns; *right*, Alachua Cob Marked. Sherds used with the kind permission of the Florida Museum of Natural History: FLMNH Catalogue numbers A-1684 (AL331, the Thorpe site), A-1479 (8Al188, George Simmons Place A).

continued even as cord marking was fading from the repertoire (Bullen 1958a: 23; Milanich 1971: 39, 40, Milanich 1994: 344–45; Worth, chapter 7, this volume). Prairie Fabric Marked, Alachua Plaited, and Alachua Net Impressed are minority types within Alachua assemblages. Plain sand- or grit-tempered wares often dominate in village assemblages. Alachua and earlier Cades Pond plainwares (sand tempered and grit tempered), however, are virtually indistinguishable and difficult to separate on multicomponent sites. Vessel forms associated with all Alachua types are limited and contrast markedly with those of contemporaneous Mississippian sites.

It does not appear that Alachua Cob Marked vessels completely replaced Prairie Cord Marked pottery, but the former clearly dominates in late Alachua assemblages (see table 6.1), as evidenced at 8Al273 (Milanich 1971: 8). There, Alachua Cob Marked pottery constituted 96 percent of the decorated pottery recovered from levels 1 and 2. Combined, Prairie Cord Marked, Lochloosa Punctated, and Punctated-over-Cord Marked made up only 4 percent of the sample. During her more recent excavations at the same site, Stokes (1997: 29) reported similar findings: Alachua Cob Marked at 45 percent, Lochloosa Punctated at 10 percent, and Prairie Cord Marked at 5 percent. No maize or Spanish artifacts were recovered from 8Al273, although the site lies only 500 m from the Spanish mission at Fox Pond (8Al272).

A particular surface finish is documented for some Alachua Cob Marked and Lochloosa Punctated vessels (figure 6.4, top left, bottom right). After a textured surface was created, some potters chose to continue with a series of finishing strokes that actually smoothed over and obliterated the initial surface treatment. Obliteration was performed with different levels of intensity (some to the point of burnishing) and surface coverage (some just a few strokes and others over a broader area). During an inspection of the Hickory Pond– and Alachua-phase sherds curated at the Florida Museum of Natural History, I observed no obliterating strokes on cord-marked surfaces. This haphazard finishing has been recorded on contact-era San Pedro–series pottery from sites along the Atlantic coast from Cumberland Island, Georgia, south to St. Augustine, Florida (Ashley 2001, 2009). San Pedro surface treatments also include cob-marking.

Gulf coast ceramics, such as Pasco Plain, Fort Walton, Carrabelle Incised and Punctated, and Safety Harbor, are recovered from some Alachua sites, but in very low numbers (Milanich 1971). Originating from the east, St. Johns Plain and Check Stamped sherds occur in varying frequencies but tend to be more prevalent on eastern Alachua sites. It is not unusual to recover St. Johns pottery within multiple test unit levels. St. Johns interaction with north-central Florida cultures can be traced back to the Cades Pond era.

Radiocarbon Dates

Radiocarbon dates have been secured from four Alachua-phase sites (table 6.2). These sites are referenced throughout the chapter; the following provides a brief overview of the location and artifact assemblages associated with dated samples.

Rocky Point (8Al127; figure 6.2), excavated in 1968, lies 25 m above a steep bluff near Paynes Prairie (Milanich 1971; Schofield 2003). Table 6.3 illustrates the frequencies of Alachua pottery recovered from Rocky Point Group B units (adapted from Milanich 1971: 23). Plain sherds ($n=478$) were well distributed throughout the units, and because Alachua Plain is difficult to distinguish from Cades Pond Plain, they and sherd categories classified as "Other" were not included in this table. The earlier Prairie Cord Marked sherds ($n=928$) were deposited in high frequencies in the upper zones, while Alachua Cob Marked sherds ($n=365$) were mixed in the deepest levels. This inverted ceramic stratigraphy of Rocky Point suggests disturbance to some areas of the site. Woodland-period sherds from both the Atlantic and Gulf coasts were recovered in each level. Pinellas points were found in all stratigraphic zones, and both aquatic and terrestrial faunal remains were collected. An AMS assay of soot on a plain sherd yielded a two sigma calibrated date range of A.D. 660–790, which would suggest an early Alachua- or Hickory Pond–phase component. Based on the multicomponent nature of the site, the possibility exists that the dated plain sherd is not Alachua but relates to Cades Pond or an unidentified Late Woodland component.

Henderson Mound (8Al463) was excavated in 1975 (Loucks 1976). It lies on a low bluff, 25 m high, overlooking Hogtown Creek and Hogtown Prairie (figure 6.2). Radiocarbon samples were collected from the charcoal associated with three of 41 burials. No pottery or lithic artifacts were associated with the burials, although Late Archaic through Mississippi-period sherds and stone points were recovered throughout mound fill. Combined, the three dates represent a possible span of 700 years (A.D. 550–1230) during which Henderson Mound was revisited for mortuary purposes. No botanical evidence of corn was recovered in the mound or in Loucks's shovel tests placed outside the mound.

Table 6.2. Calibrated radiocarbon dates from Alachua sites

Site	Beta Lab#	Measured Radiocarbon Material	Age (BP)	$^{13}C/^{12}C$ Ratio	Conventional Radiocarbon Age (BP)	Calibrated Date Range A.D. (1 sigma)	Calibrated Date Range A.D. (2 sigma)	Intercept Date (A.D.)	Reference
8Al127	174323	Soot	1220±40	-20.9/0.00	1290±40	680–770	660–790	700	Schofield 2003
8A1463	UM1788	Charcoal	1360±80	-25/0.00	1360±80	630–710	550–860	660	Loucks 1976
8A1463	UM1789	Charcoal	1210±65	-25/0.00	1210±60	720–890	680–980	790	Loucks 1976
8A1463	UM1790	Charcoal	1015±95	-25/0.00	1020±100	910–1150	790–1230	1010	Loucks 1976
8A148	UM1784	Charcoal	590±75	-25/0.00	590±80	1290–1420	1270–1450	1330, 1340, 1400	Milanich pers. comm. 2002
8A148	UM1785	Charcoal	520±70	-24/0.00	520±70	1330–1440	1300–1470	1420	Milanich pers. comm. 2002
8Mr2722	169406	Charcoal	340±50	-25/0.00	340±50	1460–1640	1440–1660	1520, 1590, 1620	Wayne and Dickinson 2002
8Mr2722	169407	Charcoal	400±50	-25/0.00	400±50	1440–1620	1420–1640	1460	Wayne and Dickinson 2002
8Mr2722	169408	Charcoal	340±60	-25/0.00	340±60	1460–1640	1440–1660	1520, 1590, 1620	Wayne and Dickinson 2002
8Mr2722	260777	Corn	370±40	-26.4/0.00	350±40	1460–1630	1450–1650	1500, 1600, 1610	Chap. 6, this volume

Table 6.3. Frequency of Alachua surface treatments from Rocky Point

Pottery Type	Zone I	Zone II	Zone III	Zone IV
Prairie Cord Marked	48%	61.50%	70.10%	73.80%
Alachua Cob Marked	45%	31.50%	20.40%	9.50%
Lochloosa Punctated	7%	1.90%	3.90%	4.80%
Punctated-over-Cord Marked	0%	1.00%	0.50%	2.40%
Plaited, Twine, and Net Impressed	0%	4.10%	5.10%	9.50%

Source: Milanich 1976: 23.

Woodward Village (8Al48) and Mound (8Al47), excavated in 1949 (Bullen 1949a), lie on a steep bluff 12 m above Levy Lake (figure 6.2). Radiocarbon samples were taken from village contexts, but the antiquity of the mound is unknown (table 6.2). Middle Woodland Cades Pond through Mississippi-period ceramic types were recovered in the mound fill, but none was associated directly with burials. Prairie Cord Marked pottery was more numerous than Alachua Cob Marked, and one cord-marked sherd was recovered deep within the mound (Bullen 1949a: 60). Paleoindian through Mississippi-period lithic points and a greenstone celt (7 cm in length) also were recovered from the fill. The celt was not associated with a burial. Despite the dates, which indicate a late Alachua occupation of the village, no corn was recovered from either context.

The Ardisia site (8Mr2722), which lies within the urban setting of the city of Ocala, was excavated by Wayne and Dickinson (2002). Alachua Cob Marked pottery dominated the ceramic assemblage, and very few Woodland-period or Prairie Cord Marked sherds were recovered. Lochloosa Punctated and Prairie Cord Marked types each made up just 2 percent of the assemblage. Lithic artifacts were again seriated from the Archaic through Mississippi periods. One charred corncob was recovered, but no Spanish artifacts were found at the site. Four radiocarbon dates, including one from the cob, place the Alachua occupation of the Ardisia site between A.D. 1430 and 1660.

Origins and Cord-Marked Pottery

In north-central Florida it is against the Cades Pond cultural backdrop that Hickory Pond ceramics, site locations, subsistence patterns, and burial practices are distinguished (Kohler 1991; Loucks 1976: 50; Milanich 1994: 227–41; Steinen 1971). Cades Pond domestic ceramic assemblages are dominated by roughly finished plain sand- and grit-tempered sherds (Milanich 1971; Sears 1956). The frequency of plain sherds in Cades Pond domestic assemblages at times reaches 90 percent. In contrast to domestic assemblages, Cades Pond mounds contain Weeden Island Incised along with fewer numbers of St. Johns, Dunns Creek Red, and even earlier Deptford sherds. Based on the recovery of St. Johns Check Stamped pottery (common after A.D. 750 in eastern Florida) and Mississippi-period Pinellas-like points in Cades Pond deposits, some researchers have suggested that Cades Pond may have continued into the ninth century or perhaps as late as A.D. 1200 (Steinen 1971: 12–13). The sacred-secular ceramic dichotomy evident in Cades Pond culture is completely lacking in the Alachua culture.

Cades Pond burial mounds were placed near clustered village sites and were more elaborate in construction (layered colored soils and beds of broken pottery) than later Alachua earthworks. Continuous-use mounds with mass burials were the norm, and burials were concentrated away from the eastern portion of the mounds. These mortuary tumuli contain whole vessels, some of which were basally punctured or "killed." Exotic items such as celts, mica, and copper also occur in these burial mounds. These characteristics along with the presence of nonlocal ceramics strongly reflect the ceremonial and interaction sphere referred to as Weeden Island (Milanich 2002). Kohler (1991: 100–101, 106) suggested that the social and ritual ties that the Cades Pond culture once held with Weeden Island were weakened by A.D. 500.

Although the fate of the Cades Pond people is unknown, at least three scenarios may be put forward. First, Woodland-period Cades Pond people remained in the area, eventually adopting simplified ceremonial activities and mound constructions. This in situ population is the one that developed into the Alachua culture. Second, Cades Pond peoples along with a newly resettled Alachua population coexisted for a period in the region, but eventually the former merged with the latter (Milanich et al. 1976). *If* Cades Pond and early Alachua (Hickory Pond) peoples represent two distinct yet contemporaneous populations who were exploiting separate environments (uplands vs. wetlands), then there may have been little competition between the two groups for a period of time. Third, the Cades Pond populace abandoned the region and Alachua migrants moved in.

The search for the identity of the Alachua people has long rested on the sudden appearance of cord-marked pottery in north-central Florida (Ashley 2005d; Milanich 1971, 1994: 333; Milanich et al. 1976; Minar 2001; Schofield 2003). Cord-marked pottery was produced in many other areas including north below the fall line in southern Georgia and up the Atlantic coast from Florida to South Carolina. The wide distribution of cord-marked pottery during the tenth through fourteenth centuries has been linked to populations who persistently maintained a hunting-gathering way of life rather than adopting a sedentary agricultural lifestyle (Ashley 2005d; Minar 2001; Stephenson 1990).

Exploring the possibility that Hickory Pond–Alachua represented the immigration of an outside population, Milanich and others first turned to the Wilmington-Savannah cultures of the lower Georgia coast. Because of similarities in plain, cord-marked, and other fabric-marked pottery surfaces, Milanich (1971) initially posited that the Alachua migration originated in that region, but he pushed the Alachua date forward from A.D. 600 to A.D. 800 to fit better with the Wilmington chronology as it was then interpreted. Available evidence now casts doubt on this interpretation. As Milanich (1994) later realized, nonagricultural coastal fisher-hunter-gatherers are unlikely to have traveled to inland Florida, redirected their economic base, and confronted the huge learning curve involved in adopting farming—that is, dropping the net and picking up the hoe. Recent radiocarbon dates taken from the intervening hinterlands of Georgia along the Altamaha River show that Swift Creek occupations continued in southeastern Georgia until the early A.D. 800s (Ashley et al. 2007; Stephenson and Snow 2004). A coastal migration west would have necessitated negotiating passage through Swift Creek territory.

As a consequence, another Alachua homeland candidate arose. This time Milanich (1994: 336) looked to the people who lived in the Ocmulgee Big Bend area in south-central Georgia. In addition to sharing a social organization and subsistence lifestyle, potters living along the lower Ocmulgee River and nearby Satilla River produced sand- and grit-tempered cord-marked wares (Snow 1977). Some Ocmulgee vessels were constructed with a final appliqué strip (sometimes referred to as a folded rim) that also was cord-marked, but at a different angle from that of the body of the pot. Prairie Cord Marked rims do not bear the appliqué strip, but some of those rims were finished with a narrow band of oblique cord-marking that mimics a three-dimensional appliqué (figure 6.3, left and middle). Once again, recent radiocarbon assays clarified the ceramic time frame but complicated the commonly accepted chronology. Secure radiometric dates from the Ocmulgee homeland and northeastern Florida (on St. Johns II sites containing Ocmulgee Cord Marked pottery) reveal that Ocmulgee vessels were not produced until ca. A.D. 900/950. If the Alachua migration began in south-central Georgia, then the date for early Alachua must again be pushed forward, yet another one hundred years. At this time, the precise date for the onset of the Hickory Pond phase is still not known.

Minar's (2001: 101) study of cord-marked pottery traditions within different regions of the Southeast has potential relevance to Alachua origins. Through a series of detailed measurements, she reported a correspondence between Alachua and Ocmulgee cordage traits. In both Alachua and Ocmulgee samples she identified high frequencies of Z-twisted cordage and similar correlations in cordage width and tightness of the cord wrapping around the paddle. These correlations, she suggested, were the result of generational instruction and motor-memory skills. On the basis of her data she saw a relationship between Alachua and Ocmulgee cordage technology and ceramic tradition (Minar 2001: 100–103). She also discovered Z-twist cordage impressions on sherds from Georgia and Carolina coastal samples, but in those samples, cordage diameters and tightness of the wrap were more variable. Minar also included a sample of West Florida Cord Marked sherds in her study and found a much lower percentage of Z-twisted cordage impressions from that region.

Schofield (2003) took a different approach in reconciling Prairie Cord Marked pottery with the A.D. 900/950 date and the emergence of cord-marking in the Ocmulgee region. Her interpretation turned on a calibrated two sigma date of A.D. 660–790 from the Rocky Point site (discussed previously), which she used to propose that cord-marking had actually originated in north-central Florida (as early as A.D. 660). From there, according to her model, Alachua populations moved north carrying the cord-marking tradition into the Ocmulgee area around A.D. 900. The snag with the Schofield AMS date is that it came from soot on the surface of a plain sherd recovered from a chronologically mixed context. All four soil zones of the excavation units at the Rocky Point site contained Alachua- and Woodland-period pottery types (e.g., Pasco, Deptford, Swift Creek, and a variety of Weeden Island). Her migration hypothesis also cannot be reconciled with current data that suggest Ocmulgee pottery developed out of Swift Creek in southern Georgia around A.D. 900 (Stephenson 1990; Stephenson et al. 1996; Stephenson and Snow 2004).

An alternative to the migration explanations for the appearance of cord-marked pottery in north-central Florida involves no population movements. In this version, Prairie Cord Marked pottery may in fact have been an in situ development adopted by the local populace, who routinely interacted with other hunting and gathering groups inhabiting eastern Florida and southern Georgia, who themselves made cord-marked pottery. Until there is independent evidence for wholesale migration, mate exchange, or some other process, the adoption of cordage-wrapped paddle-impressed surface designs as an outcome of contact and diffusion might be the most prudent explanation. Thus, at this time, we should not dismiss the idea of an in situ Alachua development from Late Woodland to Mississippian times.

Upland Settlement, Resources, and Subsistence

Austin's (2001) comprehensive survey of Alachua County sites revealed that 70 percent of Alachua sites are found on hills and ridge crests or slopes (also see Milanich 1971: 16–22). Although these locales are reported as upland occupations, in some cases "upland" is a relative designation. For instance, Woodward Mound and Village sites are situated 12 m above a relict lake terrace that was once part of Lake Levy (Bullen 1949a). In fact, most upland Alachua site locations are adjacent to landforms today described as relict wetlands. Goggin (1949a) and Milanich (1994: 335) offer two reasons why the Alachua preferred upland locales. First, northern-northeastern Alachua County contains loamier soils better suited for agriculture. When crops depleted soil nutrients, fields could be simply moved to adjacent areas. Second, as established hunters and gatherers, the Alachua found deer and other terrestrial animals plentiful in the uplands, while hickory nuts and acorns also abounded in the same locales. Milanich (1994: 335) speculated that Alachua hunters focused on fewer terrestrial species because wild game had become supplemental to a subsistence routine primarily focused on maize.

To an extent, the zooarchaeological record supports this explanation. Fewer numbers of wild species are reported from Alachua middens, and although fish flourish in nearby streams and ponds, they appear to be minor dietary components. Milanich (1971: 21) reported that 80 percent of the faunal remains from Feature 2 at Rocky Point were made up of "deer, turtle, and terrapin bone" (densely structured skeletal elements) but that remains of aquatic species such as mud eels, bowfin, sunfish, and bluegill also were present. Rabbit and turkey bone also were deposited in the feature. Unfortunately, subsistence research in this area is hampered by problems of organic preservation and, perhaps, excavation biases that do not connect off-site aboriginal catching and processing areas with upland habitation locales. Thus, we lack a comprehensive understanding of the Alachua subsistence regimen.

Preservation is certainly a factor in the recovery of fine-sized fish bone and plant remains. Freshwater shellfish, a nutritional resource seemingly ignored by the Alachua, would have counteracted the acidity of sandy and clayey midden soils and aided in preservation. However, freshwater mollusks such as mussels, clams, and snails are rarely reported in Alachua middens. Alternatively, the paucity of fish bone recovered in upland sites might reflect a different discard pattern: fish bones might have been left at the capture site, or small fingerlings might have been swallowed whole. When describing the range of bone tools recovered from Alachua middens, Milanich (1994: 338–39) noted that fishing hooks and gigs, common in Cades Pond assemblages, were absent in Alachua middens. Nevertheless, indirect evidence suggestive of fishing gear (and small animal snares) is present in the impressions of woven or tied netting, which is occasionally observed on Alachua pottery.

Perhaps as important as the fertility of upland soils were the scattered surface limestone outcroppings of chert (Austin 2001: 10–29; Estabrook 2002: 11–14; Loucks 1976: 83). This highly accessible and valuable resource allowed the Alachua people to engage in lithic tool production on a regular basis and provided a locally available trade item to offer groups to the east in the chert-poor St. Johns region. Milanich (1971: 37, 1994: 340–43) observed that Alachua-phase stone tools exhibit a certain expedient and unfinished quality. Small triangular Pinellas, Tampa, and Ichetucknee points, all associated with the Late Woodland and Mississippi periods, are recovered in mound fill, domestic middens, and extraction sites.

Austin (2001: 29) reported that lithic scatters and stone extraction sites abound in north-central Florida, but because of either the absence of diagnostic artifacts or the multicomponent nature of these sites, they are difficult to date. It is worth noting that some sand mounds were constructed in close proximity to chert outcroppings, although mound burials lacked lithic grave goods (Loucks 1976; Austin 2001: 30–42). In his discussion on the distribution of lithic artifacts from Woodward Village, Milanich (1971: 13) noted that 50 percent of the material was recovered from Archaic-period zones. Clearly, favored lithic extraction sites were well known and revisited throughout the centuries. Social or political access to these resources may have been controlled or inherited within particular extended families, as were the rights to exchange the material to groups outside the Alachua region. In addition to chert nodules, limestone outcrops also produce chunks of iron oxide. As discussed in the following section, this material played an important role in Alachua burial ritual, again, some of which took place in the vicinity of such outcroppings.

Alachua Burial Mounds

Repeated patterns of burial-ground preparation, interment ritual, and mound refurbishment provide a picture of Alachua ceremonial practices. Even though the following comparison is based on extremely limited data gathered from the Woodward (Bullen 1949a), Henderson (Loucks 1976), and Law School (Fradkin 1976) mounds, similarities suggest continuity in burial practices through time (A.D. 550–1230). Radiocarbon dates are available only for the Henderson Mound, and two of the dates appear to be too early for Alachua. The three mounds share a series of attributes: premound preparation for the initial mortuary event; continued placement of burials to the east, resulting in horizontal rather than vertical accretion; mostly primary burials with head toward mound center; and an overall lack of burial goods directly associated with the deceased.

Excavations indicate that the initial Alachua ritual for mound construction began with the removal of the ground surface and replacement with soils infused with crushed charcoal. This lens was 45-cm deep beneath Woodward Mound (Bullen 1949a: 50). In anticipation of future use, the prepared surface was broader than the area covered by the initiatory burials, which might have involved multiple interments. Burial pits were shallow depressions placed in the southeastern quadrant of the mound. In addition to the basal charcoal-mixed sand lens, some burial pits contained remnants of burnt wood on or near the body. Thirteen (32 percent) of the Henderson burial pits contained burnt wood inclusions beneath, along, or covering the deceased. Two of the Henderson burials may have been placed in wood-lined pits that were then burned (although the bones themselves were not burnt or calcined). Bullen (1949a) reported that a burial in the Woodward Mound had been placed between a burnt log and a fire pit. Because various oaks, gums, and magnolia charcoal fragments have been identified, it seems that burial ritual was not strictly associated with a single wood species.

Another similarity is found in the restricted positioning of the bodies within the mound. Loucks suggested that all bodies in the Henderson Mound were laid in shallow pits dug into the mound surface and covered with a thin layer of sand. She thought the undulating outline of previous burials was likely visible and that subsequent interments involved digging a shallow grave pit to avoid disturbing existing graves. The maintenance of the circular shape of the mound required the addition of soils around the peripheries of the other three quadrants. In this way the Henderson Mound was recentered after each burial event. In his countywide survey, Austin (2001) documented that some mounds (of undocumented cultural affiliation) were slightly rectangular; thus, recentering may not have always occurred. Over time, burial placement eventually extended beyond the limits of the initial charcoal-laden mound footprint, but the ceremony was not repeated to enlarge the mound base. Mound fill consisted of soils taken from locations near the mound that in some cases included midden deposits.

Unlike Mississippian conical and platform mounds, Alachua mounds maintained a low profile because they grew horizontally toward the east. Mound sizes are similar in height and diameter. Based on previous descriptions, Fradkin (1976: 21) reported that the original dimensions of the Law School Mound were over 2 m high and 27 m in diameter. At the time of her excavation, however, it was 1 m high and 18 m across. Henderson and Woodward Mounds were both 1 m high at the time of excavation. Henderson was somewhat oval (8-x-10 m), and Woodward Mound was roughly 12 m in diameter. Austin (2001: 38–41) reported six other mounds in Alachua County with a height of 1 m or slightly higher. However, many of the other mounds he relocated had been so impacted by agricultural activities, urban development, or looting that their original sizes and cultural affiliations could not be determined.

The majority of Alachua deceased were primary burials, placed on their backs, body extended, and heads positioned toward the center of the mound. Burial orientation at Henderson was northwest (crania) to southeast. Woodward Mound burials were similarly placed with a small number of pits oriented slightly more to the west-northwest (crania). No intentionally pigmented sand lenses denoted or capped burial pits, as recorded for Middle Woodland Cades Pond mounds in the area and St. Johns II mounds to the east. However, finely ground iron oxide was employed during ritual preparation of some interments. Twelve (30 percent) of the Henderson Mound burials were either lightly dusted or heavily covered with this powder, which was placed most prevalently around the skulls, upper torso, humeri, and upper femora (Loucks 1976: 74). At Woodward, ground ochre was associated with six (21 percent) of excavated burials. Use was not restricted by gender or age, as males, females, and one child were treated in this manner. In the Woodward Mound the powder was placed around the skulls and shoulders, one forearm, and upper legs.

Because of the looted condition of the Law School Mound, only one nearly complete bundle burial was recovered. Ripley Bullen (1949a) also recovered bundle burials in the Woodward Mound (see below) but felt those were intrusive from a later date. Teeth from the Law School Mound bundle burial showed extensive wear. Other human teeth and fragmented skulls and long bones were scattered throughout mound fill (possibly the result of looting). Fradkin (1976: 30) reported in detail on the detrimental effects caused by soil acidity and burrowing animals that she and her crew encountered during excavation.

Henderson Mound contained forty-one whole or partial burials, of which 61 percent were extended and supine. Eight (20 percent) adult individuals were represented only by skulls. An additional four (of five) child burials and three (of six) subadult burials were represented by skulls. This situation may be the result of soil chemistry and preservation biases. Sixteen (39 percent) burials were sexed as female. One adult male was identified. Although the majority of burials were female, preservation problems preclude offering assessments of a matrilineal nature of Alachua culture. One of the Henderson Mound burials was accompanied by freshwater mussel shells (lacking in domestic middens) along with one unmodified and two modified deer phalanges. A bone pin or awl also was recovered beneath the head. In contrast to a negligible ceramic inventory ($n=31$), Henderson mound fill held over 12,000 lithic artifacts. Eighty-three percent of the sherds were plain and could not be assigned to a cultural period.

Woodward Mound had been partially disturbed by the property owners; therefore, the original number of burials is unknown. Twenty-nine were recovered during Bullen's (1949a) excavation, but bone preservation was very poor. In situ burials were found beneath the disturbed areas (Bullen 1949a: 50–54). Sixty-two percent of the Woodward burials were supine and extended. Three bundle burials probably represent later use of the mound. Six children, one isolated cranium, and another partial burial were recovered. Bullen reported that all age groups were represented in the mound. Because of the extremely poor condition of the bone, just nine burials were identified with some certainty as to sex: seven were male and two were female. While no burial goods were associated with adult male or female burials, a handful of shell beads were found near at least one child. Bullen (1949a: 59) also recovered tool fragments and stone points (the oldest being a Folsom-like point) that represent a wide span of cultural periods.

As this summary shows, Alachua mounds—in significant contrast to Cades Pond burial practices—lack burial goods or other funerary offerings placed in direct association with the deceased. The majority of artifacts were recovered in mound fill, and with the exception of one small celt recovered in Woodward Mound, no other nonlocal stone, exotic minerals or artifacts, pottery caches, or ritual pottery styles have been documented. Bullen, as well as Loucks, believed that all the cultural materials recovered from mound fill had been inadvertently deposited.

Lack of Village Data

In other parts of the Mississippian world, hierarchical village settlements and mound centers appear, complete with central plazas banked by temple mounds (Smith 1978; Lewis and Stout 1998). Such prestigious centers and community-built architecture have not been located in the Alachua region. The only village associated with any of these mounds was found immediately west of the Woodward Mound (Milanich 1971: 9–15). The early A.D. 1400 dates from this site may provide evidence that the Alachua were becoming more sedentary, but again, no maize was recovered. Mitchem (chapter 8, this volume) reports that, beyond the nucleated Safety Harbor coastal centers, mounds are isolated and not associated with particular villages. This may be a pattern shared by the Alachua culture.

Loucks (1976) thought that the dense lithic scatters found near Henderson Mound implied that a village was located nearby. She was unable to locate evidence of a permanent occupation near the mound and speculated that perhaps road construction had destroyed it. If that is the case, the associated village population was very small. Recently, Nodine (2006: 21–25) returned to Henderson, but those excavations also failed to locate evidence of a village (either by artifact density or by soil colors).

Henderson Mound, which was in use between A.D. 550 and 1250, may demonstrate the practice of mobile hunters and gatherers placing mounds near historically significant landmarks, such as exposed lithic outcroppings. The specific location or antiquity of the revisited outcrop may have held a greater significance, rather than the quality of the iron oxide or chert quarried in that immediate area. Fradkin (1976), whose excavations took place within the city of Gainesville, also failed to find evidence of a village near the Law School Mound but believed that it may have been situated near Lake Alice. As is a common situation, any evidence of such a settlement would have been destroyed by residential development. Bullen (1958a) did not refer to his Bolen Bluff sites as villages. Instead he interpreted the deep and widespread accumulations of pottery and stone as extraction sites that were revisited by many generations.

What about Maize Agriculture?

A long-standing label applied to Alachua is that of a farming society. Though this is technically not incorrect, we have yet to pin down exactly when maize agriculture became part of the Alachua domestic economy. De Soto in 1539 reported an "abundance of maize" from the town of Cholupaha, now believed to have been located in northwestern Alachua County, south of the Santa Fe River (Johnson 1991: 252–60; Milanich and Hudson 1993: 144), so it was definitely being grown at the time of first contact. Conventional thinking among Florida archaeologists is that the transition to maize farming occurred with the arrival of Alachua people to the region, which witnessed a settlement shift from Cades Pond sites in lowlands to Alachua villages in uplands (Milanich 1994: 332). Interestingly, evidence for horticulture is lacking during the Hickory Pond phase, leading Milanich to suggest that perhaps farming was employed as an adjunct to hunting and gathering. The possibility exists that the initial settlement pattern change to the uplands was unrelated to agriculture but instead linked to ecological changes on the prairie floor.

Alachua Cob Marked, which was possibly a minor type during the Hickory Pond phase, is thought to have emerged as the dominant ware around A.D. 1250, and its occurrence is taken as evidence of a more intensive focus on maize farming. Presumably so clear are cob impressions on Alachua pottery that Kohler (1979) was able to measure kernel widths and depths and ascertain that kernel size evolved through time. His study suggested that after an initial increase in kernel size during the prehistoric era, little change occurred until the Spanish period, when a larger Mexican species (or hybrid) was introduced to the area (Kohler 1979: 4). While cob impressions on ceramic vessels are undeniable, the date of A.D. 1250 for the ware's emergence is not. As the chief architect of the Alachua chronology admitted, the mid-thirteenth-century date for cob-marked pottery is "little more than a guess" (Milanich 1994: 338).

At this time there is no physical botanical evidence (carbonized cobs or kernels) to support a thirteenth- or fourteenth-century date for maize production in the Alachua region. In terms of maize consumption archaeologists have turned to the study of human bone (Hutchinson et al. 2000; Larsen 2001; Larsen et al. 2001; Price and Tucker 2003; Tucker 2007). In fact, bioarchaeological analyses have begun to shed light on aspects of Native American diet and health, including precolumbian corn consumption in Florida. Four burials from Henderson Mound were included in bone isotopic studies that analyzed precolumbian coastal and inland diets through time (Hutchinson et al. 2000; Larsen et al. 2001). The Henderson samples indicated a diet focused on traditional terrestrial fauna and flora with little evidence of maize consumption. Moreover, as Larsen (et al. 2001: 73) noted, "archaeobotanical remains recovered from various sites in northern Florida contain no evidence of maize prior to the contact era." The only precolumbian burials in that study indicating a maize-based diet came from Waddell's Mill Pond and Lake Jackson, both of which are located in northwest Florida, a region more actively engaged in Mississippian culture (Larsen et al. 2001: 66–67; Marrinan, chapter 9, and White et al., chapter 10, this volume).

Dental health has long been used to identify corn in the aboriginal diet. Specifically, archaeologists often associate dental caries with a high carbohydrate/sugar diet that included maize. Loucks (1976) reported that 13 individuals interred in Henderson exhibited caries, but such evidence from one small and somewhat circumscribed population does not necessarily prove maize consumption by Alachua groups in general. In a related study of seven adult burials from the Cannon (9Cp52) and Telfair (9Tf2) sites in inland Georgia, Tucker (2007: 128–29) discovered that even though his sample displayed a high rate of caries and antemortem tooth loss (comparable to numbers recorded in Mission-period cemeteries), bone isotopic levels revealed that those individuals, like their Alachua counterparts to the south, lived on a diet of terrestrial fauna and freshwater fish, with little to no maize consumption. Both sites are located in the south-central Ocmulgee region and temporally fall within a date range of A.D. 885–1300 (Tucker 2007: 126). Although Tucker's sample is extremely small, his results offer alternative evidence regarding dental caries and tooth loss in a Native American population living on a nonmaize diet.

From a broader behavioral perspective, we lack information on populations transitioning from a subsistence regimen based on wild resources to one involving cultivated plants. Did the transition take 50 years, 100 years, or even longer? Did the entire Alachua populace abandon mobile hunting and gathering for sedentary or semisedentary agriculture? Perhaps initially only a portion of the late Alachua population engaged in farming, and these intermittent pockets of fields were what the Spanish reported. The only thing evident from this review is that current archaeological evidence and assumptions cannot yet resolve this problem.

Discussion

With respect to the Alachua culture, Kohler (1991: 103) asks an important question: "How can such a society be so invisible in the archaeological record?" In lieu of "visible" or defining data, and despite continuous archaeological evidence to the contrary, Hickory Pond–Alachua sites continue to be pressed into a mold of immigration and Mississippian socioeconomics. But why should we expect the Alachua to manifest the material and political characteristics of a Mississippian culture? For most of their history, they appear to have been content leading a hunting and gathering lifestyle and, as a whole, were unimpressed by or uninterested in the social strictures and material trappings of the greater Mississippian world. Far from being isolationists, however, they appear to have been in regular contact with their immediate neighbors, Safety Harbor and St. Johns peoples, both of whom were actively engaged in broader interaction spheres.

As for ceramics, although ratios of types changed, Alachua wares reveal little diversity through time and space. The recurring evidence of the co-production of cob- and cord-marked pottery allows for seriation at only the broadest level. In contrast, Mississippi-period Pensacola, Fort Walton, and Safety Harbor ceramic assemblages (Harris, chapter 11, Marrinan, chapter 9, Mitchem, chapter 8, White et al., chapter 10, this volume) include vessels with abstract and geometric heartland Mississippi Valley iconography as well as bottle and plate forms. The Alachua did not develop funerary ceramic styles (as did the region's earlier Weeden Island–Cades Pond culture). Alachua vessels were not finished with special attributes, such as *adornos* or burnishing, which might imply that they were produced for anything other than generalized utilitarian wares. Not even simple domestic pots accompanied the final burial ritual.

Alachua burial practices, compared to those in the broader Mississippian world, might best be described as unassuming. Because the burning of wood played an important role at multiple stages of burial practices, perhaps the Alachua created specific styles of wooden objects or bowls, or woven or plaited basketry that were more highly regarded than pottery for this purpose. And it is the charred remains of those types of organic items that were included in individual graves. Their mounds were not high earthworks carefully constructed with lenses and caps of specially chosen or manipulated soils. At this time we cannot even be sure whether all Alachua mounds represent burial constructions.

Other material or symbolic Mississippian traits are absent. Exotic minerals, stones, or copper objects associated with Mississippian social and political interactions were not included in Alachua domestic middens or ritual life. Incised shell or bone expressing the artistry and symbols of their culture has not been recovered. Worked bone and modified shell are recovered, but I suggest they are utilitarian tools. Alachua middens appear to contain subsistence remains that lack representation of predatory species of mammals or birds often associated with other Mississippian ceremonial contexts.

The lack of a "Mississippian" material culture or ideological system should not suggest that the Alachua were unsophisticated in dealing with internal and external interactions. Perhaps the complex balance of diplomatic and economic consensus that they seem to have achieved during most of the Mississippi period is what has contributed to their "invisibility" in the archaeological record of north-central Florida (see Worth, chapter 7, this volume). Moreover, agriculture intensification, raiding, and chiefdom-level politics, all hallmarks of the historic Potano Timucua of north-central Florida, may quite possibly have developed late in the Mississippi period, when long-distance exchange across the Southeast was actually waning. As more research is done in the region, a more accurate portrait of their culture and their place in time is expected to become clearer, and we will better understand the variety of lifestyles that thrived during the Mississippi period.

7

An Overview of the Suwannee Valley Culture

JOHN E. WORTH

During the Mississippi period the interior riverine region of northern Florida was characterized by an archaeological culture that, by almost any measure, seems to have lacked any of the more obvious and visible trappings of the otherwise widespread Mississippian cultural phenomenon, including platform mounds, Mississippian iconography, and unequivocal evidence for intensive maize cultivation. This northern Florida culture, now known as Suwannee Valley, was so indistinctive from the standpoint of material culture and public architecture that it remained virtually unrecognized by archaeologists for decades, sandwiched neatly between the more well-known Weeden Island and Leon-Jefferson cultures of the Woodland and Mission periods, respectively. Only in the 1980s did the post–Weeden Island ceramic assemblage indigenous to northern Florida begin to be distinguished, and the formal definition of Suwannee Valley crystallized only in the early 1990s.

Despite its relatively recent emergence as a distinct archaeological horizon, the Suwannee Valley culture of northern Florida can now be claimed to represent one of the few Mississippi-period cultures across the southeastern United States for which there is a direct and essentially unequivocal identification with a thoroughly documented historic American Indian group—the Timucua—whose occupational history continued largely unbroken from the moment of first Spanish contact through the early eighteenth century. Though recent advances in ethnohistorical reconstructions of the social geography of the Southeast from the sixteenth through eighteenth centuries have permitted the identification of many ethnic and political correspondences between Mississippi-period archaeological cultures and named historic groups across much of the Southeast (Hudson 1987), this same body of research also has demonstrated convincingly the extent to which widespread sociopolitical and economic transformations and long-distance relocations during the colonial era affected many or most of those same Mississippian cultures, marking sometimes substantial discontinuities between pre- and post-European-contact data sets (Smith 1989). This does not appear to be the case with the Suwannee Valley culture, which demonstrates at minimum considerable geographic and biological continuity with postcontact Timucuan populations in the same region, as is also the case with a number of groups across much of Florida. Though internal transformations in material culture during the early historic era are clearly evident in the archaeological record of the Suwannee Valley region, available evidence nonetheless suggests that the Mississippi-period populations are largely continuous with missionized Timucuan populations in the same region, allowing a remarkable opportunity to examine the same group using extensive ethnohistorical information as a direct complement to archaeological data.

Definition

The archaeological culture now known as Suwannee Valley was initially defined during 1989 and 1990 excavations at the Fig Springs archaeological site in Columbia County, Florida (Weisman 1992; Worth 1990, 1992a). It should be noted here that, like most other cultures delineated in this volume for Mississippi-period Florida, Suwannee Valley is defined principally by archaeological evidence for material culture. Most particularly, it is recognized by a distinctive domestic ceramic assemblage comprising a suite of types that can be demonstrated to have been in use within a restricted geographic area over a specific length of time. Far from being a simplistic culture-historical equation of pots with people, the cultural unit described here as Suwannee Valley is viewed by this author more as a social interaction zone within which people and communities were connected far more extensively on a day-to-day basis with each other than with other individuals and groups outside this zone (see Rolland, chapter 6, this volume). The assortment of ceramic decorations and styles within Suwannee Valley was not so much a conscious and intentional communication of cultural identity as a simple secondary by-product of a shared aesthetic of household craft production among people whose lives were intertwined on a daily basis. Similarly, the ceramic style zone defined as the Suwannee Valley culture almost certainly does not delineate a neatly bounded political or ethnic or even linguistic unit (for a more detailed explanation of this perspective, see Worth 2009: 203–7).

Archaeological definitions of material culture "style zones" are perhaps best characterized less by their internal homogeneity and more by their external dissimilarity to other such zones. In this sense, what probably requires anthropological explanation are the reasons for long-term barriers to social interaction between geographic areas, as opposed to the reasons why relatives and neighbors in close geographic proximity would naturally have shared a collective sense of how to decorate utilitarian household pottery. Though this discussion is best left for other venues, it is important to acknowledge that the Suwannee Valley culture most likely does not equate with a precisely bounded political or ethnic group with a common identity as such but instead reflects an area of open social boundaries within which residents interacted and shared ideas regularly.

Early syntheses of Florida archaeology had incorporated what is now known as the Suwannee Valley culture area ("north Florida") into a much broader region then called "central Florida," which incorporated the more well-defined (at the time) Alachua Tradition as a broad chronological framework (Willey 1949a). When the Alachua culture was subsequently explored in greater depth by Jerald Milanich (1971), its extent was recognized to be limited to the southern portion of this broader regional designation and then named "north-central Florida." As late as 1980, however, what would later be known as "north Florida" still remained a void on the archaeological landscape between the Fort Walton culture to the west and the Alachua culture to the south (Milanich and Fairbanks 1980). Only in the context of the McKeithen Mound project and the definition of the McKeithen Weeden Island culture would a regional distinction begin to emerge and become formalized for "north-central Florida" and "north Florida" during the Woodland period, corresponding to the Cades Pond and McKeithen cultures, respectively (Milanich et al. 1984).

At that time, survey and testing by Brenda Sigler-Lavelle at other nearby sites suggested the persistence of a late Weeden Island II culture in north Florida that temporally overlapped with the neighboring Alachua culture of north-central Florida (Milanich et al. 1984: 196, 198, 201–8). The material culture and settlement distribution of this post-McKeithen culture was explored in greater depth during the late 1980s by Kenneth Johnson (1991; Johnson and Nelson 1990). Johnson's "Indian Pond complex" and "Northern Utina" designations roughly correspond to the "Suwannee Valley culture" and "Timucua province" as employed in this chapter. Both nomenclatures were in use simultaneously during their initial development in 1989–90. However, it was in the context of a concurrent revision of the existing ceramic typologies for northern Florida (e.g., Milanich 1971; Scarry 1985; Willey 1949a) for purposes of the Fig Springs excavation directed by Brent Weisman that the ceramic assemblage denoted Suwannee Valley was first named and described, and subsequently published in 1992 (Weisman 1992; Worth 1990, 1992a).

Considerable previous archaeological work had of course already been carried out by a number of other researchers on sites now recognized as belonging to the Suwannee Valley culture (e.g., Deagan 1972; Goggin 1953; Johnson 1991; Johnson and Nelson 1991; Loucks 1979; Milanich et al. 1984; Weisman 1992). But it was not until the 1990 implementation of intensive block excavations by this author in the precolumbian portion of the Fig Springs site that a detailed exploration of Suwannee Valley material culture, subsistence, and architecture resulted in a more comprehensive portrait of this recently defined culture, explicitly distinguishing it from preceding and subsequent cultures in the same area (Worth 1990, n.d.). In the years following this project, a number of synthetic volumes relative to the Timucuan Indians of the late prehistoric and early historic period adopted the Suwannee Valley cultural designation, and the Suwannee Valley ceramic series has similarly been employed in a number of contexts, including outside the state of Florida in southernmost Georgia (Ashley and Rolland 1997; Hann 1996: 15; Milanich 1994: 348–53, 1995: 90–93, 1996: 34–37; Milanich and Hudson 1992: 151, 156; Smith and Marks 2003; Weisman et al. 1998; Williams and Thompson 1999; Worth 1992b: 11–18; Worth 1998a, 1998b).

Geographic Extent and Neighbors

The geographic extent of the Suwannee Valley culture is at present poorly defined, though at minimum it can be said to encompass the interior region drained by the Santa Fe and lower Suwannee River drainages (figure 7.1). To date, the clearest portrait of the core area of what corresponds to the Suwannee Valley culture was provided in Kenneth Johnson's 1991 dissertation, in which the distribution of late prehistoric archaeological sites in this region was characterized as a settlement network of spatially discrete "site clusters" focusing on specific riverine and lacustrine resources near and between these two major waterways (Johnson 1991; see also

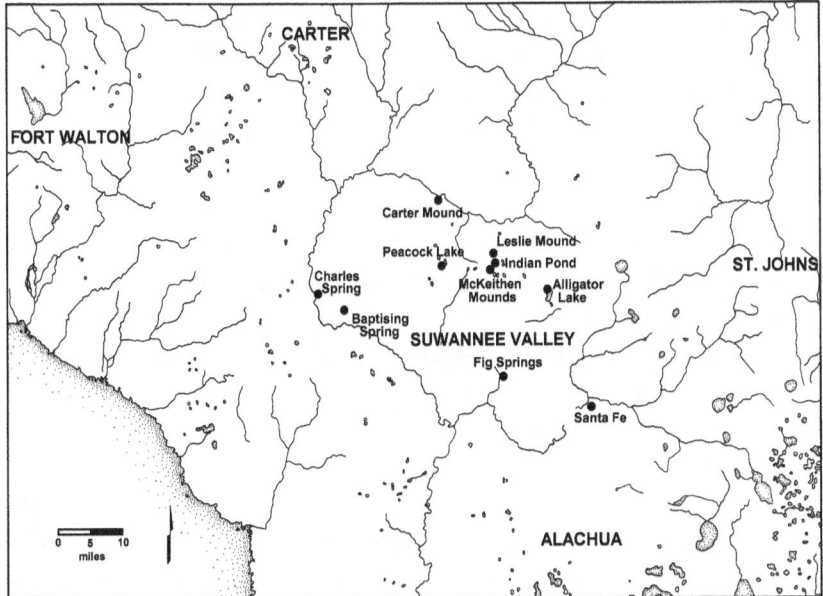

Figure 7.1. Map showing major Suwannee Valley and Suwannee Valley–related sites and site clusters, as discussed in this chapter (and in Milanich et al. 1984: 196, 198, 201–8; Johnson and Nelson 1990; Johnson 1991; Milanich 1994: 331–53). Major adjacent archaeological cultures are also indicated. Base map by Julie Barnes Smith.

Johnson and Nelson 1990). The extent to which the Suwannee Valley culture extends beyond this core area into adjacent cultural zones is unclear, but an overview of neighboring cultures is instructive in this regard.

To the south, the Suwannee Valley culture borders the more widely recognized Alachua culture, which bears clear affinities to the Suwannee Valley culture not only in its characteristic material culture and lack of platform mounds but also in its documented correspondence to the closely related Potano regional subdivision of the broader Timucuan cultural area (Goggin 1949a; Milanich 1971, 1994: 333–48; Rolland, chapter 6, this volume). The boundary between these two cultures has been interpreted to fall somewhere between the site clusters in and around the lake district surrounding present-day Gainesville and the site clusters on the south side of the Santa Fe River to the north (Johnson 1991: 84–91). Whether or not the Suwannee Valley culture extended downriver toward the mouth of the Suwannee River is presently unknown, though ceramics there appear to differ at least from the Alachua culture farther east (Milanich 1994:

336–37). Nevertheless, the overall similarity of rosters of ceramic types present in Suwannee Valley and Alachua (though in substantially different proportions) makes any attempt to establish unequivocal boundaries between the two regions difficult, especially in the absence of fine-grained chronological data.

The distinction between the Suwannee Valley and Alachua cultures may indeed be largely environmental; I have previously characterized this distinction as a difference between predominantly riverine and lacustrine Timucuan adaptations, given that the Alachua culture, unlike Suwannee Valley, is situated in a karstic, inter-riverine lake district without major surface waterways (Worth 1998a: 26–32). While this might seem to imply an ecological determinism that clearly is not warranted (and certainly not based solely on data in hand), the difference between the mechanisms and extent of daily transport, trade, and communication in predominantly riverine and lacustrine landscapes might well have contributed to differences in social interaction patterns between two such regions, accounting at least in part for the observed distinction in regional material culture between Suwannee Valley and Alachua and perhaps even other regional cultures as well, as noted below.

To the east, the Suwannee Valley culture borders the St. Johns culture area of northeastern and eastern Florida, specifically during St. Johns II times, roughly corresponding to the Mississippi period (e.g., Ashley 2002, 2005b; Goggin 1949a, 1952; Milanich 1994: 243–74, 1992a). While the St. Johns culture appears to be largely centered on the St. Johns River and its tributaries along the eastern margin of the Suwannee Valley distribution, limited archaeological survey in the inter-riverine lake zone between these two areas has produced some evidence for the presence of possible Suwannee Valley ceramic types (specifically, cord-marked pottery), though this might instead relate to other cultural traditions to the north and northeast (Johnson 1991: 84–91). Regardless, the presence of St. Johns ceramics as minority types within the Suwannee Valley assemblage (Worth 1990, n.d.) bears witness to a certain amount of interregional interaction, which is not surprising given ethnohistorical evidence for a common language (Timucuan). However, the existence of a state of war between the sixteenth-century Outina chiefdom along the middle St. Johns River and the Potano chiefdom of the Alachua region tends to confirm what appears to be a long-term barrier to social interaction along the prehistoric frontier between the St. Johns culture and its immediate neighbors to the west in the Alachua and Suwannee Valley areas. In addition, the presence of several "classic" Mississippian characteristics in the St. Johns region, including platform mounds and Mississippian-style iconography, may provide further evidence for this cultural boundary.

The extent to which the post–St. Johns II cultures of far northeastern Florida, characterized by St. Marys– and San Pedro–series ceramics, may have constituted yet another adjacent cultural region bordering the Suwannee Valley heartland at the end of the Mississippi period has not yet been explored, though this question clearly begs examination (Ashley 2005b, chapter 5, this volume; Ashley and Rolland 1997, 2002; Rolland 2005, chapter 6, this volume).

To the west and northwest, geographic distributional data become even more ambiguous for the Suwannee Valley culture. While it seems to have encompassed much of the inter-riverine landscape inside the long westward curve of the Suwannee River, the region immediately west and north of the river has not received as much comparable attention in terms of regional archaeological survey focusing on the Mississippi period (Worth 1998a: 32). Ethnohistorical data from the Spanish mission era confirm that this more-western region was known as Yustaga and was distinct from, if nonetheless affiliated with, the Timucua/Suwannee Valley province to the east (Worth 1998a: 94–102).

Recent archaeological work in the immediate vicinity of one of the northernmost Timucuan regions in this area—Mission Santa Cruz de Cachipile, located just over the Georgia state line in the lake district surrounding the Withlacoochee River—has resulted in the identification of a mission-era (and possibly also earlier) ceramic complex that appears considerably different from the Suwannee Valley series in both paste and decoration. The principal type of this complex has been named Carter Complicated Stamped (Smith and Marks 2003). Nevertheless, minority ceramic types and attributes are present from both the Suwannee Valley region to the southwest and the Fort Walton region to the west. In this connection the Fort Walton culture itself forms a well-defined ceramic assemblage west of the more ambiguous Yustaga region (Marrinan, chapter 9, this volume; Marrinan and White 2007; Scarry 1985; Willey 1949a), and extremely small quantities of Fort Walton ceramic types do appear within Suwannee Valley contexts (Worth 1990, n.d.). Whether or not the Suwannee Valley culture (as originally defined) will ultimately be found to extend as far west as the Fort Walton culture area at the Aucilla River, or whether it is instead bordered exclusively along its western and northern margin by an as-yet undefined regional culture, is not presently known.

Chronological Parameters

Based on available radiocarbon dates combined with regional survey data, the Suwannee Valley culture appears to span the entire temporal gap between the Late Woodland Weeden Island II culture (in the McKeithen regional subdivision of the broader Weeden Island culture area) and the early historic Jefferson culture of the mid-seventeenth-century Spanish Mission period. As such, Suwannee Valley corresponds directly to the Mississippi period, providing apparent cultural continuity in northern Florida for many centuries prior to European contact. A series of four radiocarbon dates were processed in the South End village portion of the Fig Springs archaeological site during 1989 and 1990 (table 7.1), where ceramic distributional data from Weisman's (1992) detailed auger survey revealed no spatial overlap with seventeenth-century mission-era occupation relating to the Jefferson culture (Worth 1990, n.d.). These dates range from the late tenth through sixteenth centuries A.D. and are directly associated with archaeological proveniences (all features) containing the ceramic assemblage originally identified as Suwannee Valley.

Moreover, the lack of virtually any material evidence for preceding Weeden Island or subsequent Jefferson occupation in this specific section of the Fig Springs site makes it unlikely that these radiocarbon dates are associated with cultures or occupations unrelated to Suwannee Valley. Weeden Island is almost wholly absent from the entire Fig Springs site inventory (save three possible sherds that might be contemporaneous with early Suwannee Valley assemblages), and only 39 of the total 5,590 identifiable sherds recovered at Fig Springs and an adjacent site tested during 1990 excavations could clearly be associated with the Jefferson complex (Worth n.d.). Furthermore, the stratigraphic distribution of these few sherds reveals that they are strongly associated with the uppermost cultural strata (in comparison to the total assemblage) and that the only deeply buried sherds were recovered from positively identified "sherd clusters" within rodent burrows. None was recovered in feature context. In addition, no Spanish artifacts were recovered in direct association with Suwannee Valley ceramics in the Fig Springs South End village.

In sum, the South End component at the Fig Springs site appears to represent an essentially "pure" Suwannee Valley occupation, with framing radiocarbon dates spanning at least six centuries of site occupation. This is actually a relatively uncommon circumstance, given that Johnson's regional surface-survey data from other site clusters in the Suwannee Valley

Table 7.1. Calibrated radiocarbon dates for Fig Springs, South End Village (8Co1)

Site	Beta Lab#	Measured Radiocarbon Material	Age (BP)	$^{13}C/^{12}C$ Ratio	Conventional Radiocarbon Age (BP)	Calibrated Date Range A.D. (1 sigma)	Calibrated Date Range A.D. (2 sigma)	Intercept Date (A.D.)	Reference
8Co1	322577	Charcoal	110±60	-10.1/0.00	360±60	1450–1640	1420–1660	1490	Weisman 1992
8Co1	38509	Charcoal	820±50	-26.8/0.00	790±50	1210–1270	1160–1290	1260	Worth 1990, n.d.
8Co1	41053	Charcoal	700±70	-26.1/0.00	680±70	1270–1390	1220–1410	1290	Worth 1990, n.d.
8Co1	41054	Charcoal	1000±50	-26.4/0.00	980±50	1010–1140	980–1170	1030	Worth 1990, n.d.

region demonstrate that multicomponent sites are clearly the norm (Johnson 1991; Johnson and Nelson 1990). Nevertheless, detailed ceramic seriations from these site clusters provide substantial confirmation that ceramic types associated with Suwannee Valley do indeed occupy the chronological "window" between Weeden Island and Jefferson assemblages. However, there is some stratigraphic evidence for chronological variation in the relative proportions of specific ceramic types within the Suwannee Valley assemblage, as discussed below.

Material Culture

Apart from the decorative characteristics of the ceramic assemblage, the material culture of the Suwannee Valley culture appears to resemble that of the Alachua culture to the south in many respects (e.g., Milanich 1971, 1972; Rolland, chapter 6, this volume; Willey 1949a). Moreover, in a general sense, the ceramic assemblage of the Suwannee Valley and Alachua cultures are together more similar to each other than to any of the more well-defined neighboring cultures to the west-northwest (Fort Walton) and east-northeast (St. Johns). Not only is there overlap in the basic roster of major ceramic types, but the overall appearance of vessel morphology and surface decoration for the two ceramic series also is generally similar. Nevertheless, sufficient differences exist, most notably in terms of the relative proportions of important ceramic types, to characterize the Suwannee Valley assemblage as distinct (see Worth n.d.).

Apart from the three more well-known major decorative types of the Alachua tradition (Alachua Cob Marked, Prairie Cord Marked, and Lochloosa Punctated), the Suwannee Valley series incorporates a fourth major type, named Fig Springs Roughened (table 7.2). Created by scraping either the fluted edge of a scallop shell (presumably imported from the coast) or a bundle of straw or small sticks on the exterior of the vessel, this type consistently forms one of the most frequent features of the Suwannee Valley ceramic assemblage and serves as an effective "marker" for the distinction between Suwannee Valley and Alachua. The type has since been recognized by the author in Florida and Georgia ceramic collections from far beyond the Suwannee Valley core area and may include earlier classifications such as scored or scraped (e.g., Goggin 1952). In many instances in the past it also has almost certainly been erroneously classified as "simple stamped," and thus commonly dismissed as a pre-Mississippi-period type. Apart from these four primary decorative types (together with the ubiquitous

Table 7.2. Ceramic types identified within the Suwannee Valley series at Fig Springs, 1990

Local Types	Extralocal Types
Fig Springs Roughened (31%)	St. Johns Check Stamped (<1%)
Prairie Cord Marked (19%)	St. Johns Plain (<1%)
Lochloosa Punctated (17%)	Pasco Roughened (<1%)
Alachua Cob Marked (7%)	Pasco Plain (<1%)
Fig Springs Incised (<1%)	Fort Walton Incised (<1%)
Trestle Point Shell Impressed (<1%)	Lake Jackson Incised (<1%)
Grassy Hole Pinched (<1%)	
Alachua Plain (9%)	

Note: Percentages out of 5,590 sherds total.

Alachua Plain), Suwannee Valley also is characterized by the appearance of several minority decorative types including Fig Springs Incised, Trestle Point Shell Impressed, and Grassy Hole Pinched, all of which display affinities to earlier Weeden Island II ceramic types, as discussed below. Figure 7.2 provides images of various pottery types associated with the Suwannee Valley culture.

While the Suwannee Valley ceramic series is normally characterized by sand and grit temper, small numbers of sherds with radically distinct temper and paste characteristics also appear as minority wares, including several St. Johns, Pasco, and Fort Walton ceramic types. Though most of these also display extralocal decorations and are likely trade wares reflecting limited interaction with external groups, the presence of Fig Springs–style roughening on the surface of vessels with limestone-tempered Pasco paste implies that at least some of these minority wares were produced locally. Only more detailed ceramic analysis will allow exploration of this possibility.

Overall, the Suwannee Valley ceramic series appears to represent a decorative tradition that emphasized the creation of a "rough" exterior on domestic pottery vessels. There seems to have been little or no attempt to create formalized designs on pots, and the resultant roster of ceramic types might easily be explained as an attempt simply to vary the tools, methods, and final appearance of the "roughened" exterior. In a general sense, the Suwannee Valley ceramic series displays a range of surface treatments, though characterized here as decorations, that may have had more to do with increasing heat absorption efficiency (by increasing the surface

Figure 7.2. Ceramic types associated with the Suwannee Valley culture; specimens all excavated at Fig Springs, South End Village, 1990. *Top, l–r*, Fig Springs Roughened, var. Ichetucknee; Fig Springs Roughened, var. Santa Fe; Prairie Cord Marked. *Middle, l–r*, Alachua Cob Marked; Lochloosa Punctated, var. Lochloosa; Lochloosa Punctated, var. Devil's Eye. *Bottom, l–r*, Fig Springs Incised; Trestle Point Shell Impressed; Grassy Hole Pinched.

area) and making pots easier to grip than with a conscious attempt to increase the aesthetic appeal of a vessel. The great majority of vessels were decorated in this fashion, and indeed the low percentage of plain sherds is one of the more unusual features of the Suwannee Valley series. Tools employed in the modification of vessel surfaces included fluted shells (scallops), sticks, straw, cordage (wrapped around paddles or sticks or possibly woven into fabric), corncobs, and fingers and fingernails. These items were either impressed into the wet clay surface of completed vessels or dragged or scraped across the surface. All of the tools used to decorate Suwannee Valley vessels seem to have been items commonly available in a domestic context.

While each ceramic type described above for the Suwannee Valley series was typically created using only one of these tools, certain decorations may have been the result of two or more tools applied in a similar fashion.

Table 7.3. Decorative overtreatments identified within the Suwannee Valley series at Fig Springs, 1990

Primary Treatment	Overtreatment								
	FSR	PCM	LP	ACM	TPSI	GHP	ACM/LP	FSR/LP	Total
Fig Springs Roughened	7	7	222	2	16	2	1	1	258
Prairie Cord Marked	45	—	56	5	3	—	—	7	116
Lochloosa Punctated	11	—	—	1	—	—	—	—	12
Alachua Cob Marked	6	—	1	—	2	—	—	—	9
Total	69	7	279	8	21	2	1	8	395

Abbreviations: FSR (Fig Springs Roughened), PCM (Prairie Cord Marked), LP (Lochloosa Punctated), ACM (Alachua Cob Marked), TPSI (Trestle Point Shell Impressed), GHP (Grassy Hole Pinched).

For example, although Fig Springs Roughened, *variety* Santa Fe was most commonly created by brushing bundles of straw or tiny sticks across the surface, some examples could have been created by scraping small shells (with narrow flutes) or even corncobs over the clay. Similarly, Fig Springs Roughened, *variety* Ichetucknee was sometimes created by brushing larger sticks or straw over the surface, and perhaps even cord-wrapped sticks or paddles, although the most common tool used in its creation was a scallop shell. The ceramic types and varieties noted above were created based on the ultimate visual appearance of the surface treatment, and thus in some cases the tools used may overlap between various types and varieties. The typology was intended for effective and practical ceramic analysis by modern researchers and thus focused on characteristics that may be visually discerned from sherds.

Additionally, while the above discussion focuses on what here is termed the primary surface treatment, there is ample evidence that secondary surface treatments, or overtreatments, were occasionally applied on top of the primary treatment (table 7.3). For example, 11 percent of all Prairie Cord Marked sherds exhibit overtreatments, most commonly with Lochloosa Punctated or Fig Springs Roughened decorations. Fig Springs Roughened displays a higher overtreatment rate (15 percent), but the great majority of these are Lochloosa Punctated. While these three combinations are by far the most common, the fact that such a diversity of overtreatments is present, including both single and double overtreatments, precludes the definition of new ceramic types or varieties based on such overlapping decoration. Although in the Alachua series, Prairie Punctated-over-Cord Marked was originally set apart as a distinct type (Milanich 1971: 34–35), the many and diverse overtreatments within the Suwannee Valley series are not distinguished here at a typological level. Instead, overtreatments are considered a variation of the primary surface treatment and are examined within the existing typological framework. This decision is further justified by the fact that many overtreatments are not uniform across the entire vessel surface and indeed may occur only on isolated portions of the vessel (e.g., the single swipe of a scallop shell over the shoulder of a reconstructed portion of an Alachua Cob Marked vessel). This appears similar to the obliteration noted on Alachua-series sherds in north-central Florida (Rolland, chapter 6, this volume).

In addition to its decorative characteristics, the Suwannee Valley ceramic series displays other distinguishing features, specifically from the perspective of vessel form and function (table 7.4). In a general sense the range of vessel forms commonly represented in the Suwannee Valley assemblage at the Fig Springs site suggests a rather simple and unelaborate utilitarian ceramic tradition. Following the form-and-function analysis outlined by Hally (1986), within an apparently domestic context, Suwannee Valley vessels were created to solve only the most basic, pragmatic considerations of function. Cooking and manipulation of either large or small quantities of liquid foods and relatively small amounts of solid or viscous food could have been carried out using a limited range of jar and bowl forms, and these foods could have been served in several different bowl forms. Storage of liquids or fine-grained dry foods could have been accomplished using several jar forms. One vessel form is conspicuously absent from the Fig Springs collections so far: a bottle used for storing drinking liquids such as water. This suggests that other materials, such as gourds, may have been used in place of ceramic bottles.

Overall, the Suwannee Valley vessel assemblage displays little technical elaboration, as evidenced by the general lack of sharp breaks in vessel profiles, save the typically gentle rim flare on flaring-rim jars. No appendages, such as lugs, handles, legs, nodes, or adornos, are present. Rim modification, when present, is typically limited to narrow, irregular folds and rolled lips. Vessel walls were occasionally drilled, either for suspension or repair, but this practice seems to have been relatively uncommon. Even the few fragments of ceramic pipes display a plain, unfinished surface and uneven profile.

That the Suwannee Valley ceramic series went largely unrecognized for decades may be in part due to its unusual character for a Mississippi-period assemblage. As late as the spring of 1989, the denotation "crudware" was

Table 7.4. Rim profile distribution as percentage of ceramic type at Fig Springs, 1990

Ceramic Type	Incurvate	Straight-Walled	Open	Flaring Rim	Straight Neck	Total
Fig Springs Roughened	52	34	37	17	2	142
Prairie Cord Marked	46	39	22	9	—	116
Lochloosa Punctated	19	21	20	13	1	74
Alachua Cob Marked	5	11	3	28	2	49
Alachua Plain	9	7	12	20	1	49
Total	131	112	94	87	6	430

occasionally applied in the field to these ceramics. Only with the detailed description and formalization of this ceramic series has making an effective comparison between the Suwannee Valley series and other regional cultures become possible. In this connection, the Suwannee Valley vessel assemblage contrasts markedly with that of contemporaneous Mississippian cultures across a wide region to the west and north. The range of nearby Fort Walton vessel forms (e.g., Marrinan, chapter 9, this volume; Marrinan and White 2007; Scarry 1985; Willey 1949a) is considerably larger than that of the Suwannee Valley series and includes elaborate and technically complex vessel shapes with sharp profile breaks and diverse appendages, as well as more deliberate incised and punctated decorations with sometimes elaborate designs. The typical Lamar vessel assemblage (e.g., Hally 1986) also includes a greater range of more-complex vessel forms, as does the Lamar-related Jefferson series of the subsequent Mission period, which characterized the Suwannee Valley region (and several others) after the first quarter of the seventeenth century (e.g., Weisman 1992; Worth 1992a). In general the Suwannee Valley series stands out as a remarkably unelaborate and simplistic assemblage of vessel forms when compared with virtually every other late prehistoric culture surrounding it (excluding the related Alachua series), as well as that which specifically preceded it prior to the Mississippi period.

From a chronological perspective, within the apparent six-century duration of the Suwannee Valley culture, some temporal trends in ceramic material culture can be posited based on available data. Despite considerable geographic variation in seriation data based on surface collections across the Suwannee Valley region (Johnson 1991; Johnson and Nelson 1990), stratigraphic data from the 1990 excavations at the Fig Springs site provide some evidence for temporal variation at least within the Fig Springs cluster (Worth n.d.). Although the following comments are largely impressionistic, they are based on extensive examination of ceramic data from excavated context.

The type Fig Springs Roughened, the primary decorated type of the Suwannee Valley series, consistently exhibits a stratigraphic decrease in frequency over time. The drop is probably on the order of only 20 percent (from roughly 40 percent to perhaps 20 percent), but it seems to indicate that other types increased in popularity over the course of the Suwannee Valley phase. Prairie Cord Marked seems to display a similar decrease over time but may actually decrease only after an earlier increase. Lochloosa Punctated may increase slightly over time, and Alachua Cob Marked almost certainly does. Indeed, the appearance of Alachua Cob Marked in percentages up to roughly 20 percent in certain proveniences may reflect the late florescence of that type in nearby Alachua culture assemblages to the south, though this must be considered speculative at this point. There seems to be little change in the comparatively low percentage of plain ceramics over time. All minority types within the Suwannee Valley series may be predominantly early, although only Trestle Point Shell Impressed displays fairly good stratigraphic evidence for this. In addition to the fact that none of these types has been recognized in any Mission-period contexts, their earlier date also is suggested by the similarity of several of these minority types to Weeden Island ceramic types, as discussed below.

Probably not insignificantly, the Mississippi-period Suwannee Valley and Alachua cultures both appear to correspond geographically to similarly distinctive cultural areas of the preceding Weeden Island period (Milanich 1994: 159–63). Suwannee Valley corresponds to the earlier McKeithen Weeden Island culture area, while Alachua is roughly contiguous with the earlier Cades Pond culture (Milanich 1994: 164–94, 227–41; Milanich et al. 1984). Though evident cultural discontinuities between Cades Pond and Alachua have been argued to represent a possible prehistoric in-migration of extralocal populations into north-central Florida (e.g., Milanich 1971, 1994: 333–36), the ceramic assemblage of the Suwannee Valley culture bears a number of striking resemblances to that of the earlier Weeden Island II culture in this same region, implying at least some degree of population continuity and in situ cultural evolution across the transition to the Mississippi period.

A comparison of the Suwannee Valley series with ceramics of the preceding McKeithen Weeden Island period (Milanich et al. 1984; Willey 1949a) provides some indication of a cultural connection between the two traditions. The roster of tools used for surface treatment is quite similar, although the manner in which these tools were employed differs in one major respect. Whereas Weeden Island ceramic decorations were typically applied in a neat and ordered fashion, Suwannee Valley decorations were applied randomly, with no real attempt at order. Most of the Suwannee Valley types may be derived from Weeden Island forms, and a comparison between several types is striking. The Suwannee Valley type Lochloosa Punctated may relate to the Weeden Island type Carrabelle Punctated (and perhaps other punctated types), as both display punctations with sticks or dowels and fingernails. Carrabelle Punctated decorations are simply placed within a band below the lip of the vessel, and the punctations are typically neat instead of random. The type Grassy Hole Pinched may relate to the earlier type Tucker Ridge Pinched, and once again, the difference seems to be that the Weeden Island form displays neat and ordered rows within a band below the lip, whereas the Suwannee Valley form is randomized. In addition, the type Fig Springs Incised displays clear similarities to the Weeden Island type Keith Incised. The difference once again is related to the degree of neatness and order and to the restriction of the Weeden Island decoration to a band below the lip. Additionally, the use of scallop shells in decoration also is common to both the Weeden Island and Suwannee Valley series, although the application of the shell does vary.

In general much of the Suwannee Valley ceramic series may be characterized as a randomized, almost degenerate, form of a number of Weeden Island decorations (see Mitchem, chapter 8, this volume, for a similar comment regarding Weeden Island and Safety Harbor ceramics). Although considerable differences do of course exist between the two assemblages, there seems to be evidence for a cultural or historical connection between them. If this interpretation can be confirmed, it would provide support for the conclusion that the Suwannee Valley culture represented an intermediate step between northern Florida's McKeithen Weeden Island culture and that of the Timucuan Indians of the seventeenth and eighteenth centuries, establishing at least some degree of long-term cultural continuity in this region.

In situ cultural continuity does not necessarily mean that local populations were not augmented or even in part replaced by immigrants from other regions, no more than a lack of such continuity would necessarily mean that indigenous populations were wholly replaced by outsiders. Given that household ceramic traditions in the Southeast can be demonstrated to change radically both in situ as a result of shifts in broader social interaction networks, and also as a result of the wholesale adoption of local styles by immigrant populations (e.g., Worth 2009), observed transformations in archaeological pottery styles obviously cannot be presumed a priori to represent either the presence or the absence of immigration. Nevertheless, the evident persistence of earlier decorative styles even after such a transformation (such as from McKeithen Weeden Island to Suwannee Valley) does suggest that living local populations most likely remained present throughout the transitional period at least, even if immigration can be independently posited using other data.

Posts and Pits

Despite intensive and lengthy block excavations at the Fig Springs site, resulting in the discovery of many postmolds, postholes, and other pit features, no clear and unequivocal structural patterns were identified during the 1990 season. Nevertheless, apart from a range of more ordinary postmolds identified, at least one clear example of a substantial and deep post with an immense asymmetrical entry trench was found, remarkably similar to several other unusual posts of this kind identified on the summit of the Weeden Island platform mound at the McKeithen site (Milanich et al. 1984: 98, 101–2). At Fig Springs, as at McKeithen, the entry trench was long (nearly 2.5 m in length and nearly 1 m wide), and the post itself plunged to the considerable depth of over a meter below the presumed ground surface at the time (Worth n.d.). The post itself, apparently charred and deteriorated in place, was probably only 20–30 cm in diameter; it was radiocarbon dated to cal A.D. 1210–70 (one sigma; see table 7.1) and was clearly associated with a Suwannee Valley ceramic assemblage. While the function of this post, like those at nearby McKeithen, is not clear, its unique entry trench among all others at Fig Springs might hint at yet another possible cultural connection between Suwannee Valley and Weeden Island.

Also identified in association with Suwannee Valley deposits at Fig Springs were various other pit features, including several basin-shaped storage or trash pits and a large bell-shaped pit, all containing an array of debris. Originating from the uppermost layers of the excavation was the only cob pit found, located in the South End portion of the Fig Springs site (Weisman 1992: 107–8). This small, round-bottomed pit, filled with intact and fragmentary charred corncobs, was radiocarbon dated to cal A.D. 1450–1640 (one sigma; table 7.1), suggesting that it may date to the initial phase of the Franciscan mission era and definitely at the later end of the Suwannee Valley sequence.

Subsistence

Specialized analysis of subsistence remains specifically associated with prehistoric Suwannee Valley deposits has been carried out only in a limited fashion, especially when compared with more-extensive work undertaken for the Mission-period component at the Fig Springs site (Newsom and Quitmyer 1992). Some samples were analyzed as part of the South End Village excavations at Fig Springs. They provide at least some precontact basis for comparison with mission-era subsistence patterns observed at the same site, which were described as "a well-developed hunting, fishing, and gathering economy integrated with the horticultural system," and including "terrestrial plants and animals from forested and open brushy areas" as well as "a variety of aquatic resources" (Newsom and Quitmyer 1992: 233).

Faunal material from a single Suwannee Valley trash-pit feature was examined by Irv Quitmyer. While the sample was limited to only 174 g of bone and 553 fragments, with a minimum number of individuals (MNI) of only 4, the species represented are perhaps emblematic of the presumably far more diverse faunal component of the Suwannee Valley diet (table 7.5). Among a large number of unidentifiable vertebrate and mammal bones, several examples of fish, deer, and gopher tortoise elements were identified (Quitmyer 1991). This small sample corresponds well to the range of indigenous species identified for the mission component at Fig Springs, including a variety of terrestrial mammals (deer, fox, opossum, skunk), birds (turkey), several varieties of turtle, and a diversity of fish, including catfish, bass, sunfish, gar, and bowfin (Newsom and Quitmyer 1992: 211).

Archaeobotanical analysis of charred plant remains from three Suwannee Valley pit features was carried out by Lee Newsom, and the results are similarly sparse, though informative (table 7.5). Among the food plants identified were abundant hickory nut and acorn shell fragments, single examples of pecan and walnut shell fragments, honey locust and cabbage palm seed fragments, and a small number of maize fragments, including a kernel and cupules from two features (Newsom 1991). One of these features has yet to be dated, but the other, principally composed of hickory nut shell fragments, resulted in the earliest date yet for the Suwannee Valley culture, cal A.D. 1010–1140 (one sigma; see table 7.1). Though introduced chinaberry seed fragments were also found in this sample, suggesting

Table 7.5. Indigenous food taxa identified from all Suwannee Valley contexts, including mission-era Jefferson components, Fig Springs, 1988–1990

Fauna (Quitmyer 1991)	Flora (Newsom 1991)
white-tailed deer*	hickory*
opossum	acorn*
gray fox	pecan*
skunk	walnut*
hispid cotton rat	persimmon
duck	hackberry
wild turkey	maypop
musk turtle	honey locust*
cooter	cabbage palm*
gopher tortoise*	saw palmetto
Florida gar	maize*
bowfin	common bean
bullhead catfish	
channel catfish	
sunfish	
redbreast	
freshwater bass	
largemouth bass	
ambersnail	
clams	
freshwater mussel	

Note: Taxa from pure Suwannee Valley pre-mission contexts marked by asterisk.

potential mixing with later deposits, the possibility remains that these maize fragments are the earliest yet dated from peninsular Florida.

Nevertheless, the only direct date from charred maize in a Suwannee Valley context is A.D. 1450–1640, as noted above. Given that sixteenth-century maize is therefore known to be present within the area encompassed by the 1990 excavations, bioturbation might account for some component mixing in both features containing maize fragments. However, whether or not these specimens of Suwannee Valley maize are early or late in the chronological sequence for this culture, their presence at the Fig Springs South End Village still provides substantial confirmation for the existing ceramic evidence (i.e., Alachua Cob-Marked pottery) for maize cultivation at some point prior to the changes in material culture that occurred with the advent of the Jefferson ceramic series in this area during the Mission period. Whether the adoption occurred shortly after sustained Spanish contact in the late sixteenth century, or shortly prior to contact in the late prehistoric period, or as many as six centuries before European contact, the Suwannee Valley culture did adopt maize as a component of its overall mixed subsistence strategy. This observation squares well with later ethnohistorical analysis of seventeenth-century Timucuan corn production within the context of a preexisting chiefly political economy, noted below.

Sociopolitical Structure

One of the most intriguing and important spatial dimensions of the Suwannee Valley culture is the fact that its early historic-era equivalent—the Timucua mission province—possesses such a rich and detailed ethnohistorical record, particularly with regard to the sociopolitical structure of local and regional Timucuan chiefdoms (Worth 1998a, 1998b). To this extent, any discernible archaeological evidence (or lack thereof) for sociopolitical complexity, particularly in the form of chiefdoms, takes on even greater significance from a methodological standpoint, given that the availability of two alternative but complementary sources of evidence (documentary and archaeological) are available regarding the Suwannee Valley culture.

Of considerable import, there is presently no clear and unambiguous archaeological evidence for what would normally be interpreted as chiefly social organization at any scale within the Suwannee Valley culture. Though survey and excavations in pre-mission-period Suwannee Valley sites have of course been limited to date, as yet there is a general absence of any commonly accepted and obvious markers for chiefly social organization, such as platform-mound construction and use, clear site-size hierarchies, or any other evidence for status markers or craft specialization (e.g., Milanich 1996: 150–66). This, combined with the overall lack of any other visible trappings of the more widespread Mississippian culture (ranging from ceramics to artistic iconography), would tend to make any archaeological interpretation of Suwannee Valley chiefdoms tenuous at best. Indeed, in the absence of ethnohistorical documentation, it seems unlikely that any archaeologist would ever independently posit the existence of chiefly social organization during the late prehistoric period in northern Florida, and certainly not of the complexity and intricacy known to have existed well into the seventeenth century among Suwannee Valley populations.

What has nevertheless become abundantly clear based on detailed recent analysis of a range of pertinent Spanish archival sources is that the Suwannee Valley region was unquestionably characterized by chiefly social organization at the time of first European contact and that intricate local and regional chiefly social structures were still operating more than a century later (Worth 2002), even as demographic collapse and slave raiding ultimately resulted in the withdrawal of remaining Timucuan populations to St. Augustine and eventually to Cuba (e.g., Hann 1996: 296–325; Milanich 1996: 204–16; Worth 1998b: 140–58). Documentary evidence for these conclusions comes from a range of primary archival sources, including not just the standard range of commonly used mid-sixteenth-century narratives of exploration by early Spanish and French expeditions to Florida from the 1520s through the 1560s but also a rich diversity of data from the Franciscan mission era (1587–1706). The latter includes detailed information on indigenous demographic, political, and economic structures at various scales, such as the multidecade dispute over chiefly inheritance in the Timucuan chiefdom of Machava that culminated in a 1670 chiefly council resolved in view of Spanish witnesses (Worth 1998a: 96–102, 1998b: 122–24, 192–97). While the full details of this research are beyond the scope of this paper, it suffices to note that the small-scale chiefdoms apparently characteristic of the interior Timucua living within the Suwannee Valley region were marked by hereditary administration of multicommunity political units normally ranging between 750 and 1,500 individuals distributed in some four to six communities and that these spatially disparate local chiefdoms were also integrated into regional political units, all administered by hierarchically ranked chiefly councils on both a local and a regional scale (Worth 1998a: 81–102, 162–68, 1998b: 2–8).

Chiefly social organization was embedded in a centralized system of public finance characterized by chiefly management of land and labor. The production of surplus staple foods on chiefly lands using labor from subordinate Timucuan lineages formed the economic basis for traditional chiefly power. Social rank for chiefly and other noble lineages (including warriors and ball players with achieved ranks) was expressed in a variety of means, ranging from the relative elevation of the seat on which each person sat during chiefly councils to the exclusion of such individuals from manual labor, including the construction of chiefly houses and other public structures using public labor. Chiefs also acted as intermediaries in exchange relationships with foreign (i.e., Spanish) officials, managing the sale of surplus corn or administering the distribution of cloth, beads, and other wage goods to subordinates (Worth 1998a: 177–84, 190–96).

All these well-documented facets of Timucuan sociopolitical organization during the late sixteenth and seventeenth centuries may be inferred to have corresponding roots within the Suwannee Valley culture of the

Mississippi period in northern Florida. Indeed, to some extent, the rich detail with which the Timucuan chiefly social system can be described is comparable in many ways to existing archaeological interpretations of Mississippian chiefly social structure in a variety of geographic locations across the southeastern United States, where platform mound construction and clear evidence for status differentiation and settlement hierarchies are beyond all doubt. The fact that the Timucuan heirs of the Suwannee Valley sociopolitical structure possessed such an intricate and complex chiefly system, in the total absence of all commonly accepted archaeological indicators, provides considerable food for thought, especially as regards the extent to which such social systems may be largely "invisible" to archaeological observation.

Nevertheless, the fact that we are blessed with archaeological *and* documentary data regarding the Suwannee Valley culture and their lineal descendants in the Timucua province allows this intriguing culture of the Florida Mississippi period to be explored in far greater depth (and perhaps with far greater accuracy) than might be possible using archaeological evidence alone. While I readily admit that the present chapter is largely descriptive in nature (in part due to the fact that Suwannee Valley was only defined in the past quarter century), my hope is that it will nonetheless provide a basis for more sophisticated and synthetic analyses to be carried out in the future. Although the Suwannee Valley culture largely escaped the notice of archaeologists for many decades, further investigation is almost certain to provide important new clues as to the nature of Florida's indigenous societies during the Mississippi period.

8

◄◆◆◆►

Safety Harbor

Mississippian Influence in the Circum–Tampa Bay Region

JEFFREY M. MITCHEM

The Mississippi-period occupation in the central peninsular Gulf coast Florida region (figure 8.1) has been termed Safety Harbor by archaeologists (Milanich 1994: 389–412; Mitchem 1989: 556). Gordon Willey (1949a: 475–88) was the first to define formally what he termed the Safety Harbor period, and he called attention to its attenuated Mississippian influences (Willey 1949a: 569). In this chapter I examine the Mississippian traits in Safety Harbor culture and factors that may have affected the movement (or lack thereof) of Mississippian influences into the central peninsular Gulf coast.

A few comments about theoretical perspective are in order. The environment and climate of Florida are substantially different from that of the rest of the Southeast and the continental United States, and it is my contention that these characteristics had profound effects on the establishment and development of Safety Harbor culture (as well as earlier cultural manifestations in the region). My general approach therefore falls within the cultural-ecological realm of theory. I believe that this strategy offers the best perspective from which to make well-reasoned, testable interpretations. Much of this chapter is descriptive, without concrete interpretations, but this is largely because of the incomplete and biased nature of the archaeological data currently available for Safety Harbor. Interpretations are offered when possible and appropriate.

Mississippian Influence

The term *Mississippian* has been used in many ways over the years (Anderson 1994: 108–11; Ashley and White, chapter 1, this volume; Caldwell 1958:

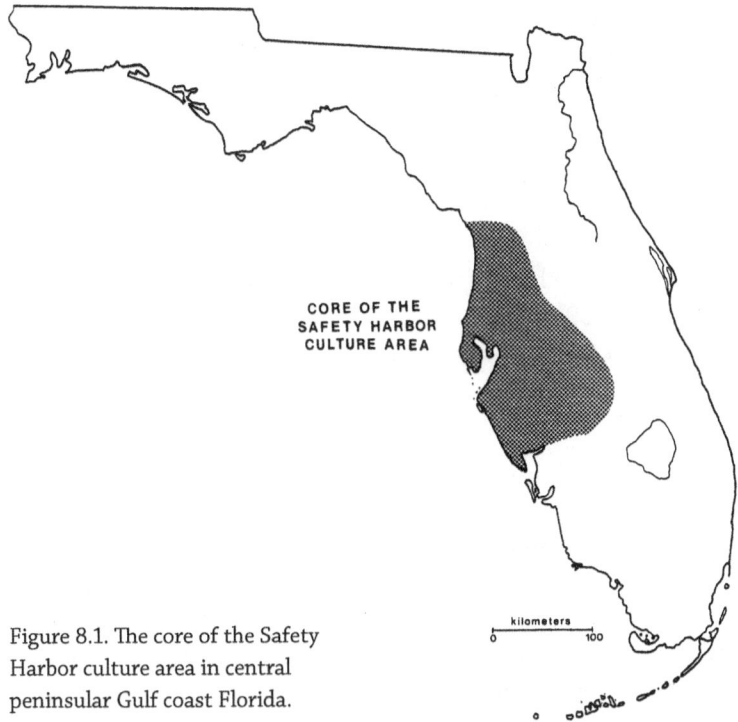

Figure 8.1. The core of the Safety Harbor culture area in central peninsular Gulf coast Florida.

59; Griffin 1985; Pauketat 2007: ch. 4; Stoltman 1978: 723–28). The combined definition provided by Adam King and Maureen Meyers (2002: 113) is probably the most widely accepted among contemporary archaeologists: "[L]ate prehistoric societies of the Southeast and Midwest that were organized as chiefdoms and whose members practiced maize agriculture and constructed earthen platform mounds." Most Mississippian groups were located in the interior Southeast and greater Mississippi Valley. The focus on maize agriculture meant that alluvial river valleys were the preferred environments for settlement.

It is difficult to pinpoint when researchers first referred to Mississippian characteristics along the central peninsular Gulf coast, but connections and similarities were recognized in the early twentieth century. Matthew Stirling (1936: 354) hinted that some pottery types found in association with what he called Safety Harbor pottery were related to contemporaneous types in the interior Southeast and the Mississippi Valley, but he stopped short of actually suggesting Mississippian connections. A few years later, Willey and Woodbury (1942: 245) cited Stirling when they explicitly stated that the Fort Walton and Safety Harbor pottery complexes were the result of Mississippian influences upon the indigenous Weeden Island types. John Goggin (1947: 118, 1949a: 39) noted significant middle Mississippian attributes in Safety Harbor pottery, while pointing out that many other classes of material culture remained unchanged from the earlier Weeden Island cultures in the region. When Willey (1948: 213–14) was devising his culture sequence for the greater Tampa Bay region, he likewise noted the Mississippian influences evident in both Englewood and Safety Harbor pottery types. When he published his formal definitions in 1949, Willey (1949a: 470–88) made no mention of Mississippian influence in his Englewood period, but he stressed its importance in his Safety Harbor period.

Chronological and Geographical Variation

In 1989, after summarizing all of the archaeological evidence for Safety Harbor and Englewood as of that time, I updated Willey's definition, proposed a phase sequence (Englewood, Pinellas, Tatham, and Bayview), and identified four regional variants (Northern, Circum–Tampa Bay, South-Central, and Inland; Mitchem 1989: ch. 4). I originally proposed five regional variants (Mitchem 1989: 567–79) but later withdrew the South Florida variant (Milanich 1994: 392). The Mississippi-period cultural affiliations in the region south of Charlotte Harbor are unclear and apparently changed through time (see further discussion below). Therefore, the map in figure 8.1 depicts the core area of Safety Harbor culture, but it probably extended farther south at various times.

I also proposed considering Willey's (1949a: 470–75) Englewood "period" as the earliest emergence of Safety Harbor rather than a separate cultural entity. Based on radiocarbon dates and archaeological data, I suggested that the Englewood "phase" may have begun as early as A.D. 900 and that Safety Harbor continued to exist well after European contact, perhaps as late as A.D. 1725 (Milanich 1994: 389; Mitchem 1989: 557–67). The early date for the appearance of Englewood would indicate very early contact with or influence from Mississippian people, although it must be stressed that the paucity of data demands that the proposed beginning date be regarded as tentative. Willey's Englewood period was defined almost exclusively on the basis of materials excavated by WPA labor in 1934 from the Englewood site (8So1), a burial mound in Sarasota County (Willey 1949a: 126–35). Although Willey (1949a: 470) claimed to use additional data from the Clearwater site (8Pi5) in Pinellas County and the Osprey site

(8So1) in Sarasota County in the formulation of his Englewood period, tables elsewhere in his book (Willey 1949a: 332, 342) reveal that only one Englewood sherd was in the Clearwater collection and four were in the Osprey collection. As with the later phases of Safety Harbor, most information about the Englewood phase comes from burial contexts and is based solely on pottery types.

For the several centuries prior to A.D. 900, the cultures that inhabited the region around Tampa Bay were well adapted to the coastal environment (Milanich 1994: 227). Archaeologists have bestowed the name Manasota upon this archaeological manifestation, a regional variant of the more widespread Weeden Island cultures. Distinctive, elaborate mortuary pottery and well-made utilitarian wares characterize Manasota archaeological sites. Most of the Safety Harbor sites in central peninsular Florida overlie Manasota components (although it is unclear whether the Weeden Island cultures in the northern part of the region should be characterized as Manasota or some other variant of Weeden Island [Kohler 1991: 96–99]), and there is nothing to indicate a break in the cultural continuum, such as intrusion of new populations or a hiatus in site occupation. All indications are that Safety Harbor evolved directly from the preceding Weeden Island/Manasota "culture" (Luer and Almy 1982) or archaeological tradition (Goggin 1949a: 17; Willey and Phillips 1958: 34–37).

Recent research at the Bayshore Homes site (8Pi41) has revealed that in some locations Manasota apparently continued later than previously thought and that in several areas Englewood may not have occurred at all (Austin and Mitchem 2008; Austin et al. 2008: 167–68). The lack of diagnostic Englewood pottery at many Safety Harbor sites clearly underlain by Manasota occupation indicates that at times the Englewood phase was skipped in the developmental sequence from Manasota to Safety Harbor. This may have been the norm rather than the exception.

Distribution of Safety Harbor sites indicates that the culture did not extend any farther north than the Withlacoochee River in Citrus County. As mentioned earlier, the southern boundary was more fluid, probably fluctuating through time because of shifting sociopolitical frontiers with the Calusa and their predecessors. In general, Charlotte Harbor can be considered the southernmost extent of the Safety Harbor culture area. The inland extent is unclear, but there are sites in Polk, Hardee, and DeSoto counties that were occupied either by Safety Harbor people or by unrelated groups whose residents interacted frequently with coastal Safety Harbor peoples (Claggett 1996; Mitchem 1989: 576–77). It is clear that the Safety Harbor culture was primarily a coastal phenomenon, with the largest settlements along the Gulf coast and around Tampa Bay. The majority of sites with Safety Harbor components are in the coastal sector.

Variations in settlement patterns and site types have been noted, with Mississippian-like nucleated villages generally restricted to the coastal region around Tampa Bay (Luer and Almy 1981). Away from the coastal plain and in the regions north and south of Tampa Bay, a more dispersed pattern of smaller settlements was the norm (Mitchem 1989: 583–86). The nucleated villages typically include platform mounds, presumed plaza areas, extensive habitation/midden areas, and at least one burial mound (Luer and Almy 1981). In the outlying regions, not only are settlements much smaller, but burial mounds appear to have been located intentionally away from habitation areas (Mitchem 1988).

Safety Harbor Pottery

The majority of excavated Safety Harbor sites are burial mounds, which are, of course, specialized localities, and most examples of decorated Safety Harbor pottery types have come from these mounds. Our knowledge of Safety Harbor habitation sites, in contrast, is limited. The best single-component Safety Harbor habitation site from which we have controlled excavation data is the Anderson site (8Pi54) in Pinellas County, also known as the Narvaez or Jungle Prada site (Austin 2000; Simpson 1998). The data on material culture from there and a few other sites indicate that many utilitarian pottery types and other classes of tools, as well as subsistence patterns, changed little from the preceding Manasota/Weeden Island period to Safety Harbor.

Typical Safety Harbor utilitarian wares, like those from Manasota/Weeden Island–period sites, tend to be the limestone-tempered Pasco Plain in the north and sand-tempered plain in the south, with some admixture of Belle Glade Plain in parts of the area from Tampa Bay south (Mitchem 1989: ch. 4). In the immediate Tampa Bay area, the distinctive, laminated Pinellas Plain predominates in Safety Harbor habitation sites. This type first appeared in late Manasota times. St. Johns Plain and St. Johns Check Stamped vessels also were present in both Manasota/Weeden Island and Safety Harbor sites. Clearly the Safety Harbor culture was primarily an in situ development out of the earlier Weeden Island and Manasota cultures around Tampa Bay (Mitchem 2008), similar to the in-place development

Safety Harbor: Mississippian Influence in the Circum–Tampa Bay Region · 177

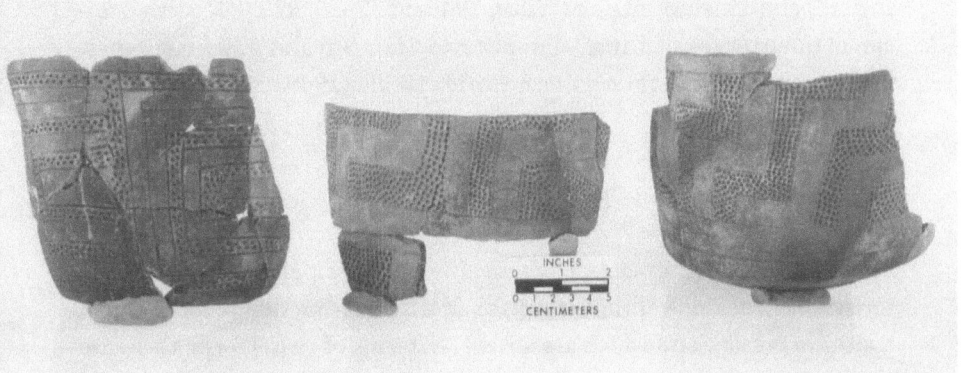

Figure 8.2. Englewood Incised pottery from Tatham Mound. Photograph by Bunny Ingles.

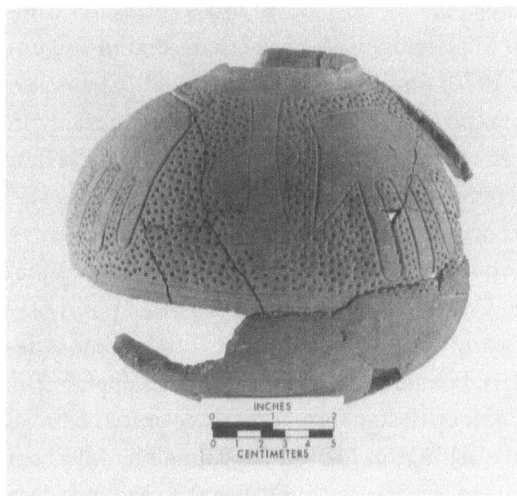

Figure 8.3. Partial Safety Harbor Incised vessel from Tatham Mound. Photograph by Bunny Ingles.

of Fort Walton farther northwest along the Gulf (White et al., chapter 10, this volume).

The *decorated* pottery types from Safety Harbor sites (figures 8.2 and 8.3) have been found primarily in burial mound contexts, but they also have been recovered in smaller quantities from domestic sites. Although the differentiation of Safety Harbor mortuary and utilitarian wares is not as well-defined as Sears's (1973) proposed "sacred-secular" dichotomy of Weeden Island ceramics, decorated pottery does appear to have been produced primarily for mortuary purposes by Safety Harbor peoples. Typical Safety Harbor decorated types include Englewood Incised, Sarasota Incised, Lemon Bay Incised, St. Johns Check Stamped, Safety Harbor

Incised, and Pinellas Incised (Willey 1949a: 472–75, 479–84), with occasional occurrences of Lamar Complicated Stamped and other late types, probably imported from northern Florida (Willey 1949a: 486).

Mississippian Ceramic Traits

Several Safety Harbor pottery types exhibit Mississippian ceramic characteristics. A brief look at these reveals some interesting things about which traits are present and which are absent. In terms of vessel form, there are clear differences from the earlier Manasota/Weeden Island period. This is most evident in the predominance of jars and the appearance of bottle forms, especially in the types Pinellas Incised and Safety Harbor Incised, respectively (Willey 1949a: figs. 63, 65, 66). These vessel forms are common in the central and lower Mississippi Valley in both decorated and undecorated varieties (Phillips 1970; Phillips et al. 1951: 105–6). There also are holdovers from Manasota/Weeden Island, however, most notably in the cylindrical beaker forms so common in Englewood Incised and the flattened-globular bowls typical of Sarasota Incised (Willey 1949a: 472–74).

Examination of the motifs of decoration is most instructive. Decorative techniques on Safety Harbor pottery consist primarily of incised or punctated designs on wet or leather-hard paste, and these are often poorly executed (Willey 1949a: 481). Many of these designs appear to be almost degenerate Weeden Island motifs, but some are definitely Mississippian. The best example is the guilloche or loop design formed by three or four parallel lines below the rim in Point Washington Incised (as defined by Mitchem 1989: 4–5), which is analogous to the Mississippi Valley type Mound Place Incised (Phillips 1970: 135–36). This design is widespread over the entire Southeast during Mississippian times. Variations also frequently occur on Safety Harbor Incised vessels (Luer 1993: fig. 2, 2002b: figs. 38, 39; Willey 1949a: fig. 63).

Some bottle forms from Safety Harbor mortuary contexts (figure 8.3) also depict human hands and maces in association (Luer 1993, 2002b: figs. 12 and 13, 2002b: figs. 4 and 5), reminiscent of some of the motifs from Spiro (Phillips and Brown 1978: 152–53; Waring and Holder 1945: figs. I, II). Hands are likewise a frequent motif at Moundville (Steponaitis 1983: 60–61). It should be noted, however, that the many additional Mississippian motifs typical of these large, famous sites are *not* present on Safety Harbor pottery.

Rather than continuing to point out the occasional bits and pieces of Mississippian art styles that show up in Safety Harbor pottery, looking at some of the things that are missing is interesting. Red-and-white painted pottery (Nodena Red and White), hooded bottles, spiral incised vessels (Rhodes Incised), and the nearly ubiquitous types Parkin Punctated and Barton Incised are totally absent from the Safety Harbor region. Only one Safety Harbor Incised effigy vessel is known (Luer 2002a), and red-on-buff painted pottery analogous to the Mississippian type Carson Red on Buff is present only in rare vessels of St. Johns Red on Buff. That the most common central and lower Mississippi Valley types are not found in the Safety Harbor area argues against any sustained direct interaction between the Mississippi Valley and the Safety Harbor region during Mississippian times. Locally made copies of these types also are lacking.

Taken together, the overall impression is that the Mississippian traits in Safety Harbor pottery are from the Early to Middle Mississippi period (A.D. 1000–1350) rather than the Late Mississippi period (post–A.D. 1350). This argues for contact or introduction of influences rather early into a conservative Safety Harbor pottery tradition that changed little through time. The curious lack of Late Mississippi–period types could be due to several different factors. It is possible that the Safety Harbor peoples decided that their existing lifestyle was sufficient, so they resisted later Mississippian influences after their initial introduction in the Early or Middle Mississippi period. The lack also could be due to a shift in the interior Mississippian groups or regions with which the Safety Harbor populations were in contact. A less likely scenario is that interaction with interior Mississippian groups stopped altogether in later times. It also is possible that the Mississippian pottery traits were incorporated primarily into mortuary or religious vessels (rather than utilitarian wares) and that these changes, once adopted, were not altered (this subject is addressed in additional detail below). These hypotheses can be addressed by future work on Safety Harbor sites.

A striking difference between Safety Harbor pottery and contemporaneous pottery in the Mississippi Valley is in the paste, specifically, aplastics (or temper). Safety Harbor potters continued the tradition of tempers used by the Manasota/Weeden Island potters. Most decorated pottery is sand tempered, and the majority of plain pottery is either tempered with sand or limestone (or similar material), or made from spiculate clay (St. Johns wares) (Mitchem 1986). Some Pinellas Plain may be temperless, where no aplastics were added to the clay. In contrast, Mississippi-period pottery from the Mississippi Valley area is tempered with crushed mussel shell, often in large quantities (Phillips 1970: sec. I; Phillips et al. 1951: sec. III).

Based on remarkable pottery similarities, some researchers have suggested possible connections between Safety Harbor peoples and residents of the Cemochechobee site (A.D. 900–1400) on the Chattahoochee River in southwestern Georgia. Schnell et al. (1981: 159–71) noted the similarities in their report on the site, as did Luer (1985, 1993: 240, 2002b) in later writings on Safety Harbor pottery. But the evidence against direct association is the lack of negative-painted wares, hooded bottles, and effigies of dogs and humans in Safety Harbor (Schnell 1998: 114–15). Numerous nonceramic differences also argue against any sort of direct contact, but the similarity of much of the pottery is compelling. Even if there was a direct connection, however, other researchers have proposed that much of the Mississippian occupation (especially the A.D. 1100–1400 Rood phase) in the lower Chattahoochee River valley above the Fort Walton area was itself the result of immigrants from elsewhere (Blitz and Lorenz 2006: ch. 5; Jenkins 1978: 84–85; Sheldon 2001).

At present, it appears likely that the Mississippian influences in Safety Harbor pottery probably originated from the western Georgia and eastern Alabama region rather than farther west. And it is almost certain that some Fort Walton influence was included, as the Fort Walton culture area lies between the lower Chattahoochee basin and the central peninsular Gulf coast. If this hypothesis is correct, the Safety Harbor culture (at least in terms of pottery) resulted from broad Rood-phase, Fort Walton, and possible Lamar influences on a local Manasota/Weeden Island template. This is a hypothesis that can be tested in the future.

Factors Affecting Mississippian Influence

One question that comes to mind is, why was the Mississippian influence so attenuated—in other words, why did the Safety Harbor culture not become a full-fledged Mississippian manifestation? The answer to this may be relatively simple. The Manasota and Weeden Island peoples who inhabited the region from about A.D. 300 through 900 were well adapted to their diverse environment of coastal marshes, inland wetlands, rivers, and estuaries (Luer and Almy 1982; Milanich 1994: 205–27). The first Mississippian influences showed up around A.D. 900, but there was not a major shift to new ecological areas. Most Safety Harbor sites are near or on top of Manasota and Weeden Island sites (Mitchem 1989: 583–86).

Because of the nature of rivers in peninsular Florida, it was ecologically impossible for the late Manasota/Weeden Island or early Safety Harbor peoples to adopt intensive maize agriculture (Mitchem 1996b: 234–35). Rivers in peninsular Florida are spring-fed or blackwater streams, which do not flood and deposit alluvium (Estevez et al. 1984; Shapiro 1986). Without the broad alluvial valleys found in the greater Mississippi Valley and other areas of the interior Southeast, intensive maize agriculture was simply not an option for the Safety Harbor people. In addition, the sandy soils, salinity, and scarcity of fresh water along the coast would have made large-scale maize farming exceedingly difficult in the region. Limited stable isotope data from the Tatham Mound (8Ci203) support the argument that maize was not a major food source of Safety Harbor people (Hutchinson et al. 1998). In effect, they continued a Weeden Island subsistence pattern but changed in terms of material culture, sociopolitical organization, and possibly religious practices.

Mechanisms of Mississippian Interaction

A logical question that then arises is, why did they adopt any Mississippian traits at all? There were probably many factors, but evidence points to the likelihood that the Safety Harbor people were involved in the shell trade, specifically, marine whelk (*Busycon* sp.) and conch (*Pleuroploca* sp.) shells (Mitchem 2008). These shells were in great demand in the interior Southeast and the Midwest (Kozuch 1998; Prentice 1987; Trubitt 2003, 2005), and their abundance along the coasts of Florida made the state a likely source (see also Ashley, chapter 5, Marquardt and Walker, chapter 2, and White et al., chapter 10, this volume). While some may have been processed into beads, dippers, and other finished products before being shipped out, most shells are likely to have been exchanged in unmodified form.

Shell chemistry studies by Cheryl Claassen (1989; Claassen and Sigmann 1993) revealed that *Busycon* shells collected from different localities have distinctive chemical signatures, and her tests of archaeological specimens included parts of shell dippers from the Safety Harbor culture Tatham Mound. A number of her control specimens were from the western and southwestern coast of Florida, and the results showed promise for getting at least a rough idea of the origin of individual whelks. As would be expected, composition of the Tatham artifacts matched what was typical in whelks from the nearby eastern Gulf (Claassen and Sigmann 1993:

344–45). Expansion of her research would be a boon to archaeologists interested in long-distance exchange, and a broadened project is under way (Cheryl P. Claassen, personal communication 2010).

Abundant archaeological research in the greater Mississippi Valley has shown that beads and other marine shell ornaments were being manufactured in many places. Cahokia in Illinois is probably the best known (Trubitt 2003, 2005), but a number of other sites in Illinois and surrounding states also have been noted. Although there is debate about whether the evidence at these sites represents craft specialization (Pauketat 1987, 1997), clearly raw material in the form of *Busycon* shells was being imported into the region.

Recent research in Arkansas has turned up additional evidence of large quantities of marine shell being imported and fashioned into beads, gorgets, dippers, and other implements. At the Parkin site (3Cs29), excavations in 1996 uncovered a marine shell gorget with an unfinished spider design engraved on it (Mitchem 1996a). This was apparently broken during the engraving process. More recently, surface collections recorded from other parts of northeastern Arkansas have included large numbers of marine shell beads in various stages of manufacture. Some of these collections number in the thousands, and they are just surface collections. Substantial amounts of raw shell were clearly being brought into the region. I cannot say for certain that these shells were coming from the Safety Harbor region, but the market definitely existed.

The vast numbers of *Busycon* shells found by Clarence B. Moore (1894a: 20–21) at Mt. Royal (8Pu35) in Putnam County, Florida, were most likely commodities intended to be shipped north (Ashley 2002: 167–68, chapter 5, this volume; Mitchem 1996b: 234–35). In one trench, Moore (1894a: 20) recovered 1,307 shells. Mt. Royal probably served as a major transshipment point, a supposition that is supported by the great quantities of native copper and exotic ground stone artifacts that Moore (1894a) excavated there. Whether or not the Safety Harbor people were transporting or exchanging shells to Mt. Royal is unclear. Even though Mt. Royal is closer, transporting shells up the Gulf coast or even overland to some point farther north would seem more logical. It is possible that they were being shipped north on the Apalachicola and Chattahoochee rivers, either from the coast or through Fort Walton entrepreneurs.

What were Safety Harbor people getting in return? Certainly some exotic goods were making it into the region. The Tatham Mound yielded ground stone celts and a ground stone plummet of non-Florida metamorphic rock, plus quartz-crystal pendants and galena fragments (Mitchem 1989: ch. 3). Excavations at other Safety Harbor burial mounds have produced a fair number of ground stone plummets, some of which were elaborately carved (Bullen 1952: fig. 15, 16, and 17).

Native copper artifacts were undoubtedly sought after, but few made it as far south as the domain of the Safety Harbor culture (Goodman 1984: 44). The lower stratum of the Tatham Mound in Citrus County contained several copper objects with primary burials near its center: a copper-covered cypress wood baton with a hair or fiber tassel was with an adult female; a circular copper plate (23 cm in diameter) covered an infant burial; and an adult of indeterminate sex next to that plate was wearing one copper ear spool and had an elaborate repoussé copper plume ornament in the shoulder area that was probably attached to the person's hair (Hutchinson 2006: appendix A; Mitchem 1989: 419–33). Only 28 individuals were buried in this lower stratum, which was estimated to date to approximately A.D. 900–1150 based on three calibrated radiocarbon dates on wood, one uncorrected date on marine shell, and one ceramic thermoluminescence date (Mitchem 1989: 519–27, 1996b: 231).

Other than the few Tatham objects, only two copper plate fragments are known from the general region: one at the Old Okahumpka site (8La57) in Lake County (Mitchem 1996b) and another from an unrecorded site 32 km southeast of Cedar Key (Mitchem 2001). These two are not Safety Harbor sites. Old Okahumpka was apparently a St. Johns II site (Mitchem 1996b, 1999: 5) but showed evidence of Safety Harbor contact (Mitchem 1999: 17). The exact location of the site near Cedar Key is unknown, but Mississippi-period sites in that area are probably Alachua Tradition or some as-yet-undescribed cultural affiliation (Johnson and Kohler 1987: 282–83; Rolland, chapter 6, this volume).

The great quantities of copper recovered from Mound 3 at the Lake Jackson site (8Le1) (Jones 1982) obviously reveal that Fort Walton people in the Tallahassee Red Hills region were involved in extensive Mississippian exchange networks. Their primary export commodity may have been shell, some of which they may have been getting from groups in peninsular Florida, including Safety Harbor peoples (but of course, shells were available from the nearby Gulf coast as well). If that was the case, and they were getting copper in return, most of it was staying in the region rather than being exchanged to the south.

B. Calvin Jones (1982: 19–20), the excavator of Mound 3, noted the similarity of the ceramics in that mound to the Rood-phase ceramics from the Cemochechobee site. Although it is not conclusive, this similarity does add some credence to the hypothesis that the Mississippian influence evident in the central peninsular Gulf coast region may have come from the lower Chattahoochee Valley via Fort Walton peoples.

It is impossible to know with certainty whether the Safety Harbor people were involved in the shell trade, but shell would seem to be the most valuable material they would have possessed to exchange for copper and other exotic goods. One can only speculate about what other things they were getting in return for shell. Perhaps food or even slaves were being exchanged. The key to testing this hypothesis will be continued sourcing of shell from securely dated contexts at interior Mississippi-period sites. Mississippian (Southeastern Ceremonial Complex) copper probably only dates from earlier Mississippian times (unless curated), so those items may represent only the beginning phases of the shell trade.

The exotic goods found in some Safety Harbor sites are not necessarily the result of trade. There could be many other explanations for the presence of these items: bride wealth, gifting, alliance building (Mitchem 2006), pilgrimage, and so forth. Also, small items can be carried far, and their recovery from a burial context may not reflect where they were housed or used in life. Even so, based on the evidence available at this time, I believe that the shell trade is the best mechanism to explain their presence.

While there is no evidence to support any large-scale movement of people into the central peninsular Gulf coast area in early Mississippian times, changes in pottery styles occurred abruptly in the region. On sites where they occur, the Englewood pottery types represent a sudden and very noticeable change in decorative styles from the earlier Manasota/Weeden Island cultures, as well as the beginning of a substantial, continuing decline in the quality of decorated pottery. Even the importation of some new pottery types copied by local potters would not offer a satisfying explanation for the sudden shift. Although it may be impossible to prove, Mississippian religious beliefs may have been introduced to the late Manasota/Weeden Island peoples' lives, causing them to change their belief systems and possibly even their sociopolitical structures. These elements were possibly introduced by the same local people involved in the shell trade.

If this was the case, the introduction of new religious beliefs would support Sears's (1973) hypothesis of a sacred/secular dichotomy in Weeden Island ceramics. Although there is not a clear dichotomy between decorated and undecorated pottery in the Safety Harbor culture, most decorated pottery does appear to have been made specifically for mortuary use. The decline in quality from Weeden Island to Englewood to Safety Harbor decorated pottery types may be a material reflection of the demise of Manasota/Weeden Island religious beliefs and the adoption of new Mississippian ideas. Whether or not this was what happened, the changes in pottery styles occurred early in Safety Harbor times, during the Englewood and early Pinellas phases. As noted earlier, there is no evidence of major changes later in the sequence.

Conclusion

While the Safety Harbor peoples were not a Mississippian culture in the strictest sense, they were most certainly in direct contact with Mississippian groups in the interior Southeast. It appears likely from Spanish accounts (Bullen 1978; Milanich 1995: 72–78; Solís de Merás 1964: 224–28) that the Safety Harbor societies were organized into chiefdoms (at least in the immediate Tampa Bay area in the early to mid-1500s), but there is no evidence that they were involved in maize agriculture on a large scale. Isotope and bioarchaeological studies by Hutchinson and colleagues have revealed that maize consumption in peninsular Florida was rare before sustained European contact in the 1600s (Ashley and White, chapter 1, this volume; Hutchinson 2004: 40, 132–33; Hutchinson et al. 1998). The failure to adopt a totally Mississippian lifestyle was due to environmental factors (Mitchem 1996b: 234–35) as well as the fact that the local populations were well adapted to the regional subsistence base, which had remained largely unchanged for centuries. Although contact with Mississippian peoples may have led to religious and political change, there was simply no compelling reason for them to change their lifestyle completely.

Acknowledgments

I am grateful to Nancy White and Keith Ashley for inviting me to participate in the Mississippian in Florida symposium. Many of the thoughts herein were clarified through discussions over the years with Bob Austin and George Luer. This paper was improved by thoughtful comments provided by the volume editors and two anonymous reviewers.

9

Fort Walton Culture in the Tallahassee Hills

ROCHELLE A. MARRINAN

Mississippi-period archaeology in the Tallahassee Hills region suffers from a surfeit of interpretation by proxy. We have the illusion of interpretation but the reality of a database representing very few local sites. *Local* culture history is woefully underdeveloped from *local* archaeological evidence. This is all the more problematic as urban development escalates and sites are lost. The illusion that we "know" or "understand" the late prehistoric culture, called Fort Walton (or Mississippian) in the area, has contributed to a malaise regarding the promotion of new research. Unless this situation changes, the archaeological literature will continue to be derived from the extant, meager database. These statements might seem naive or even heretical to some, but in the following discussion, the available data are presented and their significance explored.

Archaeological investigation usually begins in a "top down" manner. Large and complex sites receive attention because they are easily identified. Their investigation and interpretation significantly affect our understanding of other sites in a region because, as the first sites identified and investigated, they often anchor chronology or are the type sites for archaeological cultures. Subsequent research conducted at the smaller, less-remarkable sites may result in a wholesale rethinking of the prevailing archaeological paradigm. Recently, Berle Clay (2006) has reminded us that our understanding of Mississippian development has been affected in just this manner and that many assumptions about polities, status and ranking, complexity, settlement organization, redistributive economies, mortuary behavior, and alliances have been imposed on smaller, often uninvestigated sites as well as sites on the periphery of the Mississippian world. In many instances, if we examine available evidence, that is, go back to original source materials, we learn that there is little support for earlier attributions that have gained the status of received wisdom. We can, however, gain an understanding of how such social and material elements are incorporated and possibly modified, as well as how they changed local cultural trajectories.

My task in this chapter is to discuss the Mississippi-period cultural expression in the Tallahassee Hills area. This involves taking a critical look at the Lake Jackson site (8Le1), one of two large, complex sites in the region, and the body of interpretation that has secured its place in the Mississippian "club" as the seat of a "paramount chiefdom" that controlled the people affiliated with all other platform mound sites in the area. The second large and complex site is the Letchworth site (8Je337), where testing around the mounds has not settled the question of cultural affiliation(s). Just as Clay (2006) has warned, most of this interpretive accretion has occurred in the absence of substantive local data and without an understanding of local cultural elaboration and relationships to developments elsewhere, both inside and outside of Florida. So I explore the characteristics of Fort Walton culture in the Tallahassee Hills and its Mississippian affiliation by examining the primary, albeit often hastily recovered, archaeological evidence of this late prehistoric society. In this region, we are hampered by a lack of field investigations and reporting, not only at Lake Jackson but also particularly at outlying sites identified as affiliates.

Background

Lake Jackson, as the "big fish" in the local pond, is clearly a geographic outlier in the larger arena of Mississippian cultural development. The conventional interpretation of Lake Jackson, however, has been developed largely by proxy, that is, borrowed from sites outside the Fort Walton region. It gives the impression that we know a lot about Lake Jackson and other sites in the region, but I contend that we know relatively little about local sites. We have a presentation of Fort Walton culture that ascribes behaviors, motivations, and material culture to local peoples based on similar features in other regions, some quite distant. As a result, we do not know the extent to which the people who built Lake Jackson and other mound sites in the Tallahassee Hills are like those in the interior Southeast or whether they differ in significant ways. In fact, the more we learn about regional expressions of Mississippian culture, the more variable they seem.

Since the 1940s, the Mississippian cultural expression in the Tallahassee

Hills has been subsumed under the Fort Walton cultural nomen (Willey 1949a; Willey and Woodbury 1942). "Fort Walton" actually is a misnomer, because the type site (8Ok6) is now subsumed in the Pensacola culture of western Florida. As a consequence, we now discriminate between Tallahassee Fort Walton (sometimes called Apalachee Fort Walton; see Tesar 1980) and the contemporaneous late prehistoric Pensacola and Apalachicola Fort Walton manifestations to the west (see Harris, chapter 11, and White et al., chapter 10, this volume).

The interpretation of the Mississippi period in the Tallahassee Hills also is complicated by the direct historical approach, the attribution of tribal identity to prehistoric, nonliterate peoples using ethnohistorical data and material culture to link them to groups of the historic period. The Fort Walton people thus become the Historic Apalachees,[1] with little concern for how their culture may have changed after Columbus's first voyage of discovery in 1492 and before the first recorded contact in 1528. We have meager descriptions of the area in 1528 from Cabeza de Vaca and in 1539–40 from chroniclers of the De Soto *entrada* but no record of events or cultural changes in the area afterward. Almost a century passed between the time De Soto left the area in 1540 and before missions were established in 1633. Thus, we have little understanding of cultural change for several generations of indigenous people in the Tallahassee Hills before the first recorded direct contact or in its aftermath as European activity increased in the Gulf of Mexico and northeastern Florida. The "Mission Indians" of the seventeenth-century Tallahassee Hills region, the Apalachees (Hann 1988a; McEwan 2004), may have differed significantly from their late prehistoric antecedents (Brose 1990).

In general, Fort Walton culture in the Tallahassee Hills has these agreed-upon characteristics:

- radiocarbon dates that place the culture in a time range from approximately A.D. 900 to at least A.D. 1500, perhaps as late as 1550; research on Franciscan-Apalachee mission sites suggests that Fort Walton–style ceramics continued to be made in the early Mission period, possibly at least as late as 1650;
- a subsistence base that evidences increasing dependence on maize agriculture;
- a change from conical and rounded sand mounds with a mortuary style featuring group interment and "corporate" caches of

mortuary ceramics and gifts to truncated pyramidal mounds containing evidence of multiple building stages and a mortuary pattern of individual interments directly associated with exotic goods, gender indicators, and special treatment;
- a change in sociopolitical organization that indicates unequal social rank and ascribes authority and leadership roles to superordinate individuals and possibly to their kindred, as evidenced primarily in mortuary contexts;
- construction of large platform mounds with an apparent symmetry or site organization (at the Lake Jackson site primarily) indicating the ability of the leadership group to mobilize assistance for construction and have a conceptual plan that was carried forward into succeeding generations, a continuing cultural commitment to the worldview in which these activities were normative, and abilities requisite to the execution of the architectural plan;
- creation of a true ceremonial center at Lake Jackson;
- contact with contemporaneous peoples north and west of the Tallahassee Hills region who shared these cultural traits and from whom they received, through trade, gifting, or other exchange, exotic objects of ritual significance, as attested by their inclusion at death with individuals important enough to be buried separately in mound stages;
- a settlement pattern that featured dispersed farmsteads and larger population aggregates that might be termed villages or towns; and
- given the widespread presence of matrilineality among historic Southeastern native peoples, an assumed matrilineal kinship system.

Each of these characteristics, except matrilineality, is directly supported by archaeological evidence from the Tallahassee Hills region, principally from the Lake Jackson site, and within the site, from the excavation of Mound 3 in 1975 and 1976 (Jones 1982). This is a rather restricted view of Fort Walton culture because it is based on the evidence at hand, not on findings from other areas. Other interpretations, such as the Lake Jackson site as the seat of a paramount chiefdom (Payne 1981, 1994, 2006; Payne and Scarry 1982, 1998; Scarry 1984, 1994, 1996), cannot be confirmed unless and until other mound sites in the region are demonstrated to be precisely contemporaneous.

The Tallahassee Hills

The Tallahassee Hills region, also called the Tallahassee Tertiary Highlands (Hendry and Sproul 1966: 22–26) or Tallahassee Red Hills of northwest Florida, is part of the Northern Highlands Formation, a long elevated ridge composed of ancient deltaic sediments (figure 9.1). This feature is approximately 40 km wide north–south. The soils of this area, principally sandy loams, support an extensive hardwood community. They are underlain by the Hawthorn and Miccosukee Formations, geologically characterized by limestone and clastics, respectively. Elevations reach over 85 m above sea level. The Cody Scarp, a low escarpment, marks the geological boundary between the Tallahassee Hills and the relict dune fields and low marshy areas of the Gulf Coastal Lowlands that extend to the coast. This geological break has a slope of 5 to 12 percent and an average change in elevation from 70 m in the Tallahassee Hills to 15 to 24 m in the lowlands. The red clay substrate of the hills is underlain by karst topography that becomes a prominent feature of the lowlands landscape south of the escarpment, where it is closer to the surface.

In some areas the Northern Highlands Formation is cut by lowlands. It is in just this kind of feature that the Lake Jackson site is located, at approximately 31 m elevation. Below the escarpment, soils are very sandy and karst features are frequent. In the Woodville Karst Plain, water is available in small sinkholes. Site density for the Fort Walton period is much lower south of the escarpment, suggesting that primary settlement was located in the Tallahassee Hills, while the area between Cody Scarp and the Gulf of Mexico was used less during this time. Coastal sites may represent the seasonal encampments of inland people or groups allied for trade of local products, but this is a question that must be addressed by more than ceramic comparisons. Until radiocarbon dates and seasonality data are available from coastal middens and DNA studies have been performed on coastal and inland skeletal populations, relationships between these groups will remain unconfirmed.

The Fort Walton culture area of the Tallahassee Hills is generally bounded on the east by the Aucilla River and on the west by the Ochlockonee River, a span of approximately 48 km. Although these are also the boundaries of historic Apalache, whether they are an accurate representation of the late prehistoric territorial situation is not clear. The Tallahassee Hills includes northern Leon and Jefferson counties, but for the purposes of this discussion, I also include southern Leon and Jefferson counties, and Wakulla

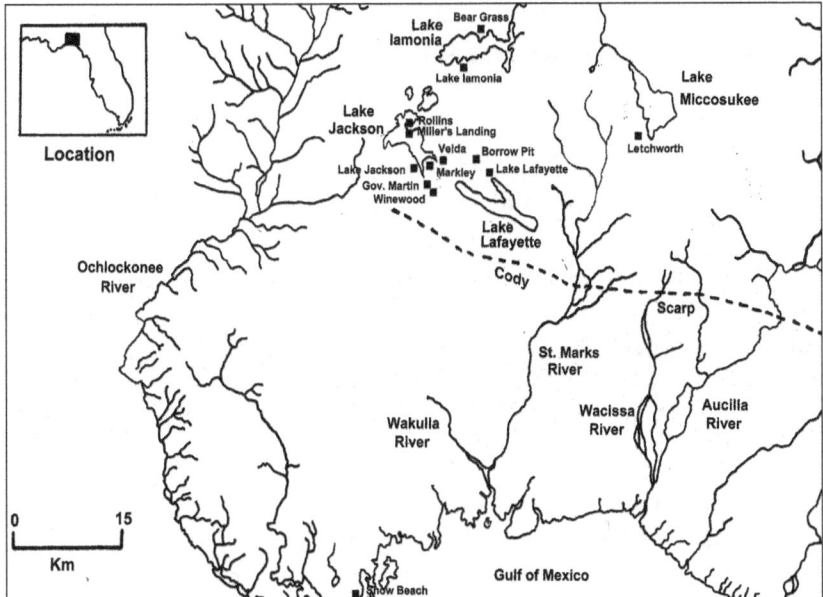

Figure 9.1. The Tallahassee Hills region and immediately adjacent territory. The locations of sites mentioned in this chapter are indicated.

County and part of Franklin County, both to the south (see figure 9.1). This area stretches from the Gulf of Mexico into present-day southern Georgia, with evidence of sustained indigenous occupation from 11,000 B.P. (Sloth Hole, 8Je121) through the early sixteenth-century arrival of the Spaniards (Martin–De Soto site, 8Le853b) to the end of the Mission period in 1704.

Although there are no rivers within the Tallahassee Hills, lakes, both large and small, are a significant feature. Several large lakes—Iamonia, Jackson, Lafayette, and Miccosukee—are classified as "prairie lakes" because they are contained within broad, relatively shallow basins. They represent the Floridan aquifer at the surface, and their discharge through sinkholes into the aquifer is critical in its recharge. Lacking records earlier than 1950 (Hughes 1967: 1), we are uncertain of the prehistoric frequency of lake draining, as well as the relative level of Lake Jackson. In years of high rainfall, it may have communicated directly with the Ochlockonee River as Lake Iamonia does in periods of high water. If the pattern of natural lake draining and refilling was a feature of prehistoric periods, the social and economic adaptations and magico-religious practices required to succeed in the Tallahassee Hills might have been substantively different than for river-dwelling peoples. Rapid, catastrophic water loss might undermine the existing leadership structure and result in population movements or shifts to more-sustainable areas. Lakes may refill in a year's time or require several years.

Climatological data suggest that periods of greater warmth and cooler temperatures occurred during the late prehistoric and postcontact periods, ca. A.D. 900 to 1633 (see Marquardt and Walker, chapter 2, this volume). The Medieval Warm, which lasted from A.D. 900 to A.D. 1580 (Broecker 2001), was a period during which maize agriculture became a dominating subsistence pursuit in eastern North America, including the Tallahassee Hills. To what degree climatic oscillations and lake-draining episodes can be correlated remains to be determined. Coring of local lake bottoms might reveal a record of wetness and dryness akin to glacial varves in Scandinavia.

The location of archaeological sites provides some indication of water levels, assuming that they would have been located above the water's edge, though during a period of low or absent water, settlement might have occurred within the lake basin itself. Tesar's (1980) survey data indicate that the elevation of sites dating from the Archaic to the Mission period (ca. 8000 B.C. to A.D. 1704) ranged from 28 to 77 m. Bryne's (1986; Marrinan and Bryne 1986) survey for late prehistoric and Mission-period-related sites indicated two elevation clusters, one at 18–58 m and the second at 62–68 m. Both surveys found a strong relationship between late prehistoric and Mission-period site location and the Orangeburg Fine Sandy Loam soil types. Dothan-Orangeburg Series soils are excellent for maize agriculture.

The Woodland-Period Base

Was the development of Fort Walton culture in the Tallahassee Hills the result of migration of people from other areas or in-place cultural evolution? Migration has been an early and persistent view (Knight 1991; Tesar 1980; Willey 1949a), but other researchers (e.g., Percy and Brose 1978: 89) have suggested that population growth may have been a critical factor. White (1982) suggested that the Fort Walton culture developed from the local Woodland base but incorporated exotic material culture, settlement organization, architectural elements, and magico-political and ideological changes to become a hierarchically organized society. The mechanism for this influx of materials and ideas, if not migration, may well have been through trading contacts and alliances.

What we know is that the preceding culture in the area is Weeden Island, a Middle to Late Woodland–period (A.D. 600–1000) manifestation spread along the Gulf coast from southwest Florida into lower Alabama and Georgia (Milanich 1994; Milanich and Fairbanks 1980; Sears 1971; Willey 1949a). It was a culture known principally for its well-crafted ceramics and mortuary traditions. Archaeologists have identified both coastal (more common) and inland sites where residential middens were frequently paired with sand burial mounds (Fairbanks 1965a: 59–60). Mound configuration was generally conical or rounded, although a few platform mounds are known, namely, McKeithen (Milanich et al. 1997) and Kolomoki (Sears 1992). Village areas have been identified, but little is known of residential structures. Subsistence data indicate that hunting and gathering were critical for Weeden Island populations, but there have been findings that also suggest maize agriculture figured to some degree in the Late Woodland–period diet.

Although there is no direct evidence of Late Woodland maize in the Tallahassee Hills, there are such findings from the Apalachicola River to the west (Brose and Percy 1978; Milanich 1974; Percy and Jones 1976) and possibly in the coastal strand to the south (Penton 1970; Smith 1956). Milanich's (1974) investigations at the Sycamore site (8Gd13), though not located in the Tallahassee Hills, provide direct evidence of residential structures and subsistence. Milanich (1974: 13, 35) dated the footprint of an oval house to A.D. 860, but the two sigma calibrated date range is A.D. 713–1154 (table 9.1). Evidence of maize in this Late Woodland context is both direct (kernels from an interior storage pit) and indirect (Northwest Florida Cob Marked sherds). The subsistence base, as evidenced by discarded animal bone and plant remains, indicated an intensive hunting and foraging economy. Acorns (*Quercus* sp.) were the most significant plant foods as indicated by weight.

The presence of pre–Fort Walton maize east of the Apalachicola River is less clear. Smith (1956: 122) reported it in features exposed when the hotel at Wakulla Springs was constructed in 1937, but the dating is not secure and there is no extant collection for study. Penton (1970: 43) notes the recovery of a "possible maize cob" at the Bird Hammock site (8Wa30). Both sites lie below the escarpment south of the Tallahassee Hills. Farther east, in Columbia County, the Weeden Island–period McKeithen site (8Co17) population does not evidence maize consumption, based on isotopic studies (Turner et al. 2005). One individual, however, is an exception. She is the single burial within a structure on the low platform Mound B. Her

Table 9.1. Radiocarbon dates cited in text

Site	Lab#	Material	Measured Radiocarbon Age	Calibrated Date Range A.D (1 sigma)	Calibrated Date Range A.D. (2 sigma)	Reference
Sycamore (8Gd13)	I-7252	Charred wood	1090±85 BP	784–787	713–745	Milanich 1974: 15, 35
				825–841	767–1057	
				862–1025	1076–1154	
Lake Jackson (8Le1), Mound 3 (upper)	I-9919	Charcoal	365±80 BP	1451–1526	1416–1666	Jones 1982; Radiocarbon Files, DOS Collections[a]
				1556–1632	1783–1796	
Lake Jackson (8Le1), Mound 3 (lower)	I-9918	Charred wood	1025±0 BP	897–921	784–787	Jones 1982; Radiocarbon Files, DOS Collections[a]
				943–1049	822–842	
				1084–1124	861–1210	
				1137–1151		
Lake Jackson (8Le1), Mound 3 (premound)	I-9920	Charcoal	715±80 BP	1222–1312	1162–1410	Jones 1982; Radiocarbon Files, DOS Collections[a]
				1358–1387		
Lake Jackson (8Le1), Mound 5 (base)	Beta-44592	Charcoal	670±90 BP	1267–1329	1187–1199	Payne 1994: 258
				1339–1396	1206–1434	
Lake Jackson (8Le1), Mound 5 (base)	Beta-47654	Charcoal	910±10 BP	1026–1216	896–923	Payne 1994: 258
					939–1284	
Velda (8Le44)	I-6583	Charcoal	445±90 BP	1405–1522	1309–1361	Radiocarbon Files, DOS Collections[a]
				1574–1626	1386–1646	
Velda (8Le44)	I-13613	Charcoal	430±80 BP	1415–1521	1323–1346	Radiocarbon Files, DOS Collections[a]
				1575–1583	1393–1646	

Notes: Calibration by Calib6.
a. Radiocarbon files of the Division of Historical Resources, Florida Department of State Collections, Tallahassee.

isotopic values suggest that she was an outsider, perhaps a bride acquired to cement trade or political alliances. Her burial location and grave goods suggest that she filled a superordinate social status and role (Milanich et al. 1997). The ceramic vessels (13 reconstructed) interred with her on the mound platform floor and within the structure suggest elite status rather than funerary *sacra* (Knight 1986). The individuals buried in Mound C, the major burial area at the site, do not exhibit evidence for maize consumption, and the accompanying ceramic cache contains funerary sacra.

At this time, the question of migration or in-place development cannot be settled. We do not know unequivocally whether Weeden Island populations are genetically related to later Fort Walton people or to groups from more distant places. There are stylistic similarities in the local ceramics (incised decorative motifs and a new type or continued use of check stamping) and a continued tradition of mound construction. The change in subsistence base is perhaps the most dramatic difference between Weeden Island and Fort Walton cultures. Percy and Brose (1978) suggest a model wherein by ca. A.D. 900 or so, plant domesticates became critical to maintaining a population increased by generations of hunting and gathering.

In the Tallahassee Hills we lack evidence of early Fort Walton culture. This may be a consequence of the direction and kinds of archaeological investigations conducted in the area, or it may indicate that migration from another area occurred. Tesar's (1980) data included 125 "Apalachee Fort Walton" sites in Leon County. Of these, only 29 were listed as early Fort Walton (Tesar 1980: 609–14). Tesar's study of the ceramics, most recovered from surface survey, suggested that there was a distinct, abrupt change from Weeden Island to Fort Walton types, although he noted evidence of "continuity at several sites from Weeden Island 5 through Early Apalachee Fort Walton" (Tesar 1980: 607). He concluded that Weeden Island ceramics differ sufficiently from Fort Walton ceramics to indicate an "immediate replacement," and he proposed that "invasion of Weeden Island territory by Mississippian peoples coming from the Apalachicola–Flint River drainage area" (Tesar 1980: 607–8) was responsible for the replacement of ceramic types.

Willey (1949a: 452) initially stated that he could see no continuity from Weeden Island to Fort Walton ceramic types. Yet he also noted some resemblances between Weeden Island incised and punctated types and Fort Walton types. Wakulla Check Stamped, he believed, persisted and provided the source for the later Leon Check Stamped type. Without radiocarbon dates and stratigraphic control for most ceramic assemblages, it is truly unclear whether changes in ceramic styles are abrupt or gradual.

The Lake Jackson Site (8Le1)

The Lake Jackson group of seven mounds is the most complex site in the Tallahassee Hills and has a well-developed archaeological literature (figure 9.2). The publications of John Griffin (1950), B. Calvin Jones (1982, 1994), John Scarry (1984, 1990, 1994, 1996, 1999), and Claudine Payne (1994, 2002, 2006, 2010) account for most of the contributions concerning the site and the region. For years, the Lake Jackson site has been presented as a paramount chiefdom with single-mound tributary affiliates (Payne 1994; Payne and Scarry 1982; Scarry 1990). This representation has promoted the sense that we understand the Lake Jackson site as being like many other distant Mississippian sites, including their attendant cultural attributions. Archaeological investigation there, however, has been intermittent, piecemeal, and rarely problem-oriented. Table 9.2 traces the history of archaeological work at the Lake Jackson site, and table 9.3 summarizes the work that has been done in each mound.

Mounds 1, 2, 4, 6, and 7 have yet to be radiocarbon-dated. Mound 7 remains unexplored, its structure is unknown, and its mound status is unverified. Willey (1949a: 97) represented it as a rounded rise. Although the Lake Jackson site has been called "palisaded" (Tesar 1980: 163), there is no archaeological evidence to support such a claim. Fryman's (1969) "wall trench" is the most unambiguous structural evidence, but whether this feature relates to a dwelling, a screen, or some other type of enclosure is not clear. Its location adjacent to the "plaza" (Payne 1994) and orientation do not suggest that it is part of a palisade in the sense of a site or mound precinct–encircling structure.

Too often we use terms such as *plaza* and *farmstead* without considering their implications. I think it is important to discuss the criteria for a "plaza" designation. We use this word to connote an empty space or a space among mounds with public or ritual functions. In essence, we mean a space relatively clear of cultural debris or one perhaps having a prepared surface. The 1989 auger survey conducted by Payne (1994) indicated a substantial spread of material culture across the intervening space between Mounds 2 and 4. The area tested overlaps the area Griffin (1950) called a "village" and where Willey, Griffin, and Penton noted heavy concentrations of cultural materials. If a plaza is kept clean of midden deposits, then this space does

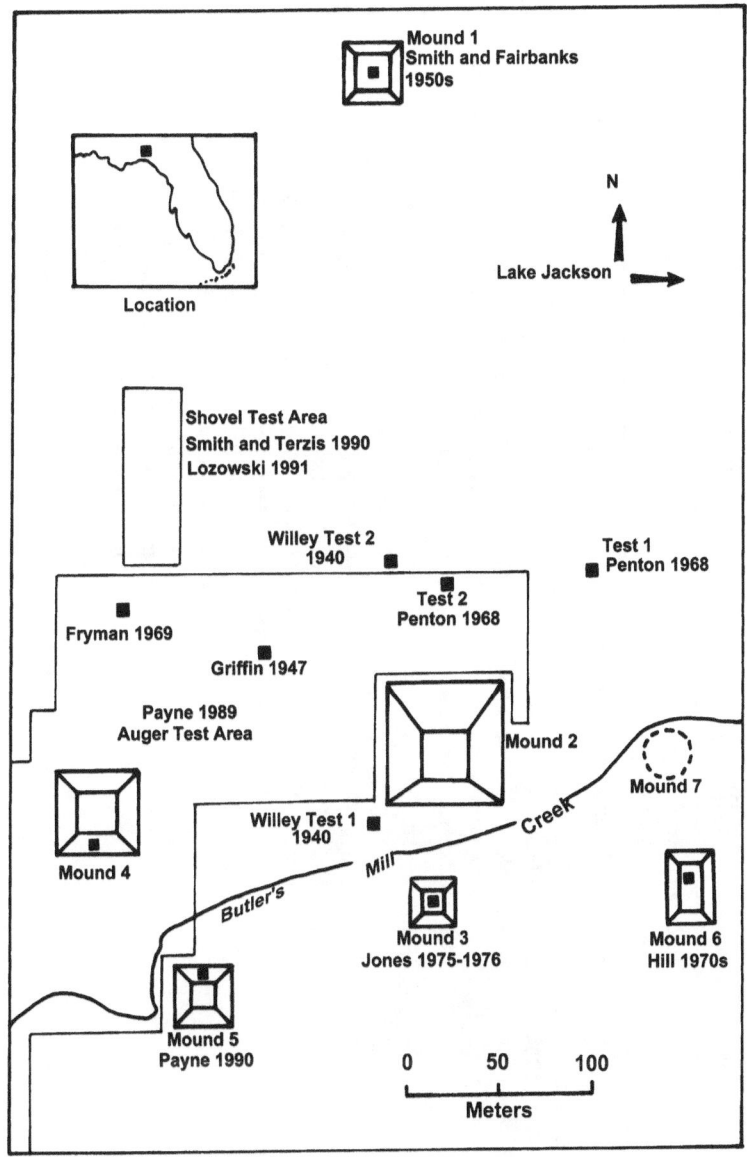

Figure 9.2. A diagrammatic representation of the Lake Jackson site (8Le1); approximate areas of excavation and testing are indicated (adapted from Payne 1994: 245).

Table 9.2. Archaeological history of the Lake Jackson site (8Le1)

Archaeologist/Observer	Year	Observations	Material Culture	Reference
A. M. Randolph	1852	Surveyor; 3 mounds noted		Randolph 1852
Nels Nelson	1918	Included mention in chronological overview of Florida		Nelson 1918
Mark F. Boyd	1939	Historian; listed as significant archaeological site		Boyd 1939
Gordon R. Willey, Richard B. Woodbury	1940	Excavated two 3-x-3-m tests: Test 1, south of Mound 2 (little cultural material); Test 2, 60 m north of Mound 2 (dense midden accumulation)	Test 1: not enumerated Test 2 (n=708 sherds): Fort Walton Incised (51); Lake Jackson Plain (24); Safety Harbor Incised (6); Lamar Comp. Stmp. (3); Plain Red (1); Residual Plain (614); Unclassified (9)	Willey and Woodbury 1942; Willey 1949: 98–99
John W. Griffin	1947	Excavated approx. 725 m² area 30 m west of Mound 2; "village area"; reported profile of Mound 2 from looter's trench on south flank; removed topsoil from Mounds 4 and 5	n=7,771 sherds: Fort Walton Incised (224); Safety Harbor Incised (21); Pinellas Incised (286); Lake Jackson Plain (192); L. J. Fingernail Impressed (6); Marsh Island Incised (102); Alachua Cob Marked (10); check-stamped pottery (9); Jefferson Stamped (3); brushed pottery (6); shell-tempered pottery (12); Residual Plain (unreported); miscellaneous decorated (150)	Griffin 1950: 104–7
Daniel T. Penton	1968	Excavated two 2-x-2-m tests for drainage ditch: Test 1 near Mound 2 had low artifact frequency and no structural evidence; Test 2, 72 m west of the first test, had a denser deposit of cultural materials and a 20 cm postmold	Not mentioned in project summary; collection not located	Penton 1968; Accession #72.4, DHR Collections

Archaeologist/Observer	Year	Observations	Material Culture	Reference
Frank Fryman	1969	Excavated site of proposed restroom, ranger's residence, and workshop; excavated seven 2-×-2-m units northwest of Mound 2, yielding dense midden accumulation and short wall-trench segment	Collection unanalyzed; project summary mentions pottery, flint, sandstone, and bone	Fryman 1969; Accession #72.4, DHR Collections
Louis Hill	1970s	Excavated trench in north side of Mound 6; no burials encountered; series of packed clay floors and flat-topped mound form reported	Stone disk with cross-type decoration; Fort Walton Incised vessel fragments with handles, daub, effigy handles; pipe fragment	Hill n.d.; Accession #93A.383; Scarry 2007b
B. Calvin Jones	1975–76	Excavated Mound 3; salvage excavation	See table 9.5	Jones 1982, 1994
Henry Baker	1980s	Posthole tests on Mound 2 for replacement of stairs	None mentioned	Payne 1994: 252
Claudine Payne	1989–90	Auger survey around mounds; flanking excavations of Mounds 4 and 5	See table 9.4 for best summary possible of ceramics	Payne 1994
B. Calvin Jones	1990	Auger survey for fencing along park boundary; 150+ tests at 3-m intervals	Potsherds, daub, charcoal	Payne 1994: 259–60
KC Smith, Museum of Florida History Day Camp	1990–91	Shovel-testing of area north of park boundary	Lake Jackson Plain; Lake Jackson Incised; Wakulla Check Stamped; San Luis B-o-W majolica; grog-tempered plain sherds	Terzis and Smith 1990; Lozowski 1991
B. Calvin Jones	1992	Monitoring of septic tank drainfield at ranger's residence	Fort Walton Incised; L. J. Fingernail Imp.; L. J. Plain types; untyped majolica sherd	Jones 1992
Florida Park Service	2007	Clearing for an artifact storage facility	Potsherds, chert, bone	Archaeological Research Monitoring Program; Accession # 07.140, DHR Collections

Table 9.3. Overview of the Lake Jackson mounds

Site	Description	Radiocarbon Dates (cal)	Comments	References
Lake Jackson (8Le1)	6 verified mounds; 1 unverified mound			
Lake Jackson 1	Low platform mound	Undated	Located near lake edge, ca. 300 m distant; 21×20×2 m	
Lake Jackson 2	Largest mound of group	Undated	65×48×8 m; northeast side ramp possible	Griffin 1950
Lake Jackson 3	Platform mound; most extensively excavated; virtually destroyed	Mound cap: A.D. 1540±75; premound: A.D. 1293±71	See table 9.5 for mortuary data summary; dog burial; 22×26×3 m	Jones 1982, 1994
Lake Jackson 4	Platform mound	Undated	34×43×3.5 m; 2-×-2-m excavation unit, south flank; ash layer in northwest corner, possible living surface	Griffin 1950; Payne 1994
Lake Jackson 5	Platform mound	A.D. 1370±62; A.D. 1114±94	30×28×3 m; 1-×-2-m excavation unit, north flank; Wakulla Check Stamped; Fort Walton Incised	Payne 1994
Lake Jackson 6	Platform mound; tested seven excavation units	Undated	38×25×3 m; ceramics for purification rituals proposed	Hill n.d.; Scarry 2007b
Lake Jackson 7	Unclear type	Undated	1-m height	
Circum-mound area	Auger testing	None	See table 9.4 for ceramic types recovered	Payne 1994

not meet the criterion. If this area is a plaza, then we must accept the presence of a substantial sheet midden. The midden in this area may have been deposited by adjacent "village" dwellers, as proposed by Griffin (1950), or it may represent an accumulation from activities that occurred in the area.

The terms *farmstead* and *village* also require criteria for recognition. In her discussion of testing for the placement of a park boundary fence, Payne

(1994: 259–60) suggests that several concentrations of higher artifact density encountered during the project indicated the location of farmsteads. My understanding of this term, as applied to late prehistoric people in the Tallahassee Hills, is that it is a discrete dwelling area of a family or extended family surrounded by their maize fields and gardens. What criteria should we use for a "farmstead," and how close to a town or center should a farmstead be? These questions are rarely asked. One local study offers data that may be useful: Stephen Bryne's (1986) survey for late prehistoric and Mission-period sites.

Bryne's (1986; Marrinan and Bryne 1986) study was centered on the Mission Patale site in eastern Leon County. Bryne used grid-based shovel testing to delimit site size. Shovel tests were screened. In total, 139 sites were identified in the following culture groups: Fort Walton ($n=33$), Leon-Jefferson ($n=36$), Fort Walton and Leon-Jefferson ($n=52$), and undetermined (n=18). Bryne (1986: 57) proposed a four-tier settlement pattern based on site size: farmsteads, hamlets, villages, and towns. Farmsteads ($n=33$) were areas of material culture, mostly ceramic, that had an average diameter of 30 m and an average area of 700 m². Villages ($n=8$) clustered in the size range of 4 to 5 ha. A farmstead, Bryne (1986: 57) suggested, had a single structure; villages as many as 25. Because of the type of survey methods used for site identification, sampling, and boundary justification, Bryne did not expose structures. Thus, the true size of a farmstead and the number of structures that a family or extended family occupying a farmstead might have remain unknown. If we use the midden deposit as a proxy for a farmstead, we understand this settlement component as discrete, relatively small, and located on or adjacent to arable land and available water. We expect them to be outliers. Early Spanish chroniclers made note of dwellings located among the fields in sheltered places (Covey 1961: 40).

Chronology at Lake Jackson is incompletely represented. Reported calibrated dates (Jones 1982) from Mound 3 indicate a construction time range for the lower mound from A.D. 784 to 1210 (table 9.1). For the upper mound, calibrated dates are A.D. 1416 to 1796. A basal date for Mound 5 (Payne 1994), after calibration, ranges from A.D. 1187 to 1434. None of the other mounds or cultural materials recovered in the "village" or "plaza" has been dated. Consequently, we have dates that indicate at least middle to late Fort Walton development. We do not know if this is the situation for other mounds at Lake Jackson or at any other mound site in the Tallahassee Hills.

On the basis of ceramics recovered during auger testing and flanking tests in Mounds 4 and 5, Payne has proposed a ceramic chronology and developmental scheme for the Lake Jackson site. Table 9.4 summarizes data from Payne's (1994) dissertation. This developmental overview also includes her reexamination of Griffin's (1950) and Penton's (1968) collections. The recovery of a single glass bead and majolica sherds suggests seventeenth-century activity in the area, but its nature and locus remain undetermined. Payne (1994: 232) estimated that, before the purchase of additional land, the Lake Jackson site was at least 24 ha in extent, but less than 1 percent had been investigated. A general lack of information about most of the Lake Jackson mounds and other sites in the Tallahassee Hills promotes ideas about migration to the area and leaves the question of in situ early Fort Walton development unanswered.

What is not discussed by Payne (1994) is the tempering material of recovered ceramics. It is clear that the Fort Walton people of the Tallahassee Hills area did not adopt shell tempering, as did western Fort Walton groups whom we call Pensacola (Harris, chapter 11, this volume). Clearly the resources for shell tempering were available, but grit, sand, and grog temper (and combinations of these) are the norm in the area. Griffin's (1950: 104) excavations produced a total of 7,771 sherds from the "village area." Only 12 sherds (0.002 percent) were shell tempered, and Griffin (1950: 107) believed these were probably Pensacola Plain and Pensacola Incised. Tesar (1980: 167–68) notes that early Fort Walton Apalachee ceramics are characterized by grog-tempered pastes with particles that decrease in size by late Fort Walton–Apalachee times. Grog tempering persists into the Mission period. White and colleagues (chapter 10, this volume) suggest that retention of traditional tempering practices was a factor in the maintenance of social identity for Fort Walton people.

Subsistence data from Lake Jackson contexts are meager. Griffin (1950) reported that deer remains predominated, with minor amounts of bird and turtle. He did not report the recovery of maize. Fryman's excavations produced 35 charcoal samples, but these were all of wood: pine and hickory (Alexander 1984: 105). Jones's excavations in Mound 3 produced the only maize reported from the site. Alexander (1984: 106, 178) examined 17 samples and reported Eastern Flint maize from Burial 6, Structure 1 (a charcoal lens in association with Burial 6), and Zones 12, 13, and 14. Thus, all maize was recovered from Mound 3 and most from the lowest levels. Jones (1982: 20) reported a total of 22 individuals from the vertebrate faunal sample from the Mound 3 excavation. Deer dominated the small

Table 9.4. Summary of site development and ceramic chronology at the Lake Jackson site

Suggested Dates	Site Phase	Ceramic Types and Characteristics	Site Development
A.D. 1050 or 1100 to 1150	Lake Jackson I	Wakulla Check Stamped; Fort Walton Incised; mica inclusions; unaltered rim forms	Site was small; earliest component is below Mound 5; area about 30 m in diameter; small occupation areas north of Mound 4 and between Mounds 2 and 4 possible
A.D. 1150 to 1250	Early Lake Jackson II	Wakulla Check Stamped; Carabelle Punctated; Fort Walton Incised; Cool Branch Incised; Marsh Island Incised; Lake Jackson Incised; cob-marked pottery; red-filmed pottery; occasional mica inclusions; unaltered or folded rims; loop and strap handles	Considerable expansion of site; Mound 5 begun and may have been completed during this phase; Mound 2 probably under construction; cultural debris at sites of Mounds 3, 4, and 6; cultural debris northeast of Mound 4; cultural debris around Mound 5 continues; dense cultural debris north of Mound 4 and between Mounds 2 and 4
A.D. 1250 to 1400	Late Lake Jackson II	Fort Walton Incised; Cool Branch Incised; Marsh Island Incised; Lake Jackson Incised; red-filmed pottery; occasional mica inclusions; altered rims (notched, ticked, scalloped); loop and strap handles	All platform mounds under construction; Mound 5 probably completed; Mound 6 begun and possibly completed during this phase; Mounds 2 and 3 in use but not completed; Mound 4 in use and possibly completed; no cultural debris around Mound 5; cultural debris north of Mound 4 decreased
A.D. 1400 to 1500	Lake Jackson III	Fort Walton Incised; Lake Jackson Incised; red-filmed pottery; altered rims (notched, ticked, scalloped, fluted); fluted rims characteristic of period; carinated bowls absent	Cultural debris heaviest in central part of site; Mounds 4, 5, and 6 probably completed before beginning of this phase; Mounds 2 and 3 completed during phase; cultural debris between Mounds 2 and 4
After A.D. 1500	Protohistoric	Complicated-stamped sherds; blue glass bead; seventeenth-century majolica sherds	Indications of residents or occasional visitors

Source: Payne 1994.

collection, but other mammals, birds, and reptiles also were present. Griffin (1950: 103) reported a small amount of badly preserved shell that he thought might be a freshwater type.

Faunal remains from the auger testing survey (Division of Historical Resources Collections; Payne 1994) were distributed widely among the 377 tests dug (75 or 20 percent of all tests contained vertebrate fauna). Deer remains were dominant, but rabbit, turtle, snake, and fish (mullet and bowfin) also were present. Excavation of postholes on Mound 2 in 1989 (Payne 1994) resulted in a stratified sample that included deer, rabbit, fishes (mullet), and unionid mussel shells. Mussel shell was recovered from the upper four levels and absent in the basal fifth level.

Table 9.5 compiles the available mortuary data for the Lake Jackson site (Jones 1982, 1994; Larsen 2001; Storey 1993). Mortuary evidence indicates that some individuals were more important than others, a requisite for a ranked society. Thus, we can say that the sociopolitical organization of Fort Walton culture involved ranking and probably stratification, most likely based on lineage membership. The impetus for the development of ranking, whether from migration of people or ideas or a local development from other kinds of cultural change, is not clear. Trade with distant areas is apparent. Both lithic and metal artifacts indicate an origin above the Fall Line to the north. Iconography on copper repoussé plates has been interpreted as suggesting a relationship with Etowah in northwestern Georgia and Spiro in eastern Oklahoma (Jones 1982), but whether these items came to Lake Jackson through a common trade source or whether the sites were linked directly is not clear. Although migration may account for the appearance of Mississippian-style culture in some areas, the presumption that we must look to population movement for an answer in the Tallahassee Hills is not supported.

In summary, the data clearly leave a lot to be desired. From limited radiocarbon dating at Lake Jackson, we have some idea about the time range for Mound 3 as around A.D. 1200 and a basal date for Mound 5 possibly around A.D. 1100. We have a very limited view of mound contents. Whether Mound 3 is the only burial mound is not clear, but it is the only one that has produced mortuary evidence thus far. Testing or excavation in other mounds (4, 5, and 6) has not revealed additional burials. Documentation of artifacts recovered is not comprehensive; to help fill in this gap, figures 9.3, 9.4, and 9.5 are previously unpublished photos of notable materials. Until structural evidence is exposed through excavation, there is no direct evidence of a village in association with these mounds. Midden

Table 9.5. Summary of mortuary data from Lake Jackson Mound 3

Burial #	Associated Floor	Burial Orientation	Associated Material Culture	Sex	Age
1K	1	Extended, on back; head southwest	Flat, flared copper axe; wooden axe handles; plain oval copper plate; arrowhead-shaped symbol badges; human hair; shell beads; pearl beads; univalve shell pendant; yellow ochre pigment; red ochre pigment; mica; small mammal fauna; clay lumps with depressions; cloth; split cane or wood plate backing. Uncertain: other decorated forms of spangles, pendants, or hair ornaments of copper; other plain forms of spangles, pendants, or hair ornaments of copper; sack.	Male	35–39
2K	1	Flexed, on back; head southwest	Flat, flared copper axe; plain round copper plate; plain cutout copper falcon plate; triforked eye copper plate fragment; decorated copper plate fragments; plain copper plate fragments; small stone cups; cloth; small sandstone pebbles; arrowhead-shaped symbol badges; featherlike copper plumes; other decorated forms of spangles, pendants, or hair ornaments of copper; impressions of feathers; human hair; human teeth spangles (?); shell beads; pearl beads; shell gorgets; univalve shell pendant. Uncertain: wooden boards, split log.	Male	50+

(continued)

Table 9.5—*Continued*

Burial #	Associated Floor	Burial Orientation	Associated Material Culture	Sex	Age
3K	1	Undetermined; head southwest	Flat, flared copper axe; cloth, shell cups. Uncertain: decorated arrowhead-shaped head-dress symbol badges; other decorated forms of spangles, pendants, or hair ornaments of copper; other plain forms of spangles, pendants, or hair ornaments of copper; shell beads; pearl beads.	No data	No data
4K	1	Knees flexed to right side; head southwest	Flat, flared copper axe; plain oval copper breastplate; clay elbow pipe; shell cups; shell beads; pearl beads; shell gorget.	Male	Adult
5K	1	Semi-flexed; on left side; head southwest	Shell gorget; pottery vessels (?). Uncertain: shell beads.	Mixed remains	Mixed remains
6K	1	Extended on back; head southwest	Flat, flared copper axe; cane matting; leather; anthracite (?) hones; small triangular projectile points; univalve shell pendant. Uncertain: shell cups; shell beads.	Male	Young to middle age
1	1	Semiflexed on left side; head 88E (northeast)	Flat, flared copper axe; perforated flat, flared copper axe; wooden axe handles; copper hawk plate; red ochre pigment; steatite Chandler-style T pipe; clay elbow pipe; shell beads; carved limestone bowl; cloth; cane matting; wooden boards (split log); polished gravel stone; irregular-shaped clay lumps; stone celt. Uncertain: wooden litter poles.	Male	50+

Burial #	Associated Floor	Burial Orientation	Associated Material Culture	Sex	Age
3	1	Semiflexed on back; head west of south (southwest) 64E	Flat, flared copper axe; wooden axe handle; chert scrapers; polished gravel stone; irregular-shaped clay lumps; clay lizard pipe; shell beads; pearl beads; galena fasteners; copper-inlaid bone hair pins; shell hair pin; shell pendant; univalve shell pendant; discoidal; mica.	Male	30–34
4	1	Semiflexed on left side; head north of west (northwest) 5E	Flat, flared copper axe; wooden copper axe handle; cloth; cane sheath or wrapping. Uncertain: shell beads; discoidal (one concave side).	No skeletal remains	No skeletal remains
10	2	Semiflexed on left side; head west of south (southwest) 27E	"Elder hawkman" copper plate with reed backing frame (15×57 cm); copper hawk plate; cloth, split cane or wood plate backing; wooden boards (split log); sack; shell beads; pearl beads; shell hair pin; 2–3 copper spangles present between plates. Uncertain: other plain forms of spangles, pendants, or hair ornaments of copper; leather.	Male (Storey 1993) or female (Larsen et al. 2001)	45–49
9K	3	Extended on back (?); head north of west (northwest) 6E	Antler projectile points; impressions of feathers; shell beads; pearl beads. Uncertain: stone celt.	No data	No data
16	4–7(?)	Extended on back; head west of south (southwest) 97E	Copper hawk dancer plate similar to Etowah; cloth; cane matting; wooden litter poles; pearl beads; discoidal (flat or convex). Uncertain: wooden boards, split log, leather, shell pendant. East slope of mound.	Female	50+

(continued)

Table 9.5—*Continued*

Burial #	Associated Floor	Burial Orientation	Associated Material Culture	Sex	Age
5	8	Extended on back; head south of west (southwest) 0E	Stone celt. Uncertain: leather.	Male	50+
13	8	Extended on back; head east of north (northeast) 6E	Cloth; leather; shell beads; pearl beads; copper hawk plates.	Male	11–12
14	8	Flexed on left side; head south of east (southeast) 16E	Shell beads.	Male	7–8
11	9	Extended on back; head north of west (northwest) 19E	Mantle (cloak); shell beads.	Male	35–39
15	9	Flexed on right side; head north of west (northwest) 15E	No grave goods indicated. Excavator's notes state that this is the only burial without grave goods (Jones 1982).	Male	35–39
7	9	Extended on back; head north of west (northwest) 7E	Hawk dancer copper plate similar to Etowah Rogan plates (oldest or earliest plate, 23×54 cm); cloth; wooden boards (split log); leather; shell beads; pearl beads. Uncertain: split cane or wood plate backings.	Female	50+
8	10	Undetermined; head north of west (northwest) 0E?	No grave goods indicated.	Male	Adult

Burial #	Associated Floor	Burial Orientation	Associated Material Culture	Sex	Age
2	10	Semiflexed on right side; head east of north (northeast) 87E	Spatulate-form stone axes; cloth; shell cups; wooden boards (split log); chert scrapers; chert spall cache; chert core; small triangular projectile point; shark jaw knife (?); red ochre pigment; paint palette with red ochre pigment; mica; lumps of graphite pigment; galena-backed mirror frame (for mica mirror)(?); red ochre rubbed on forehead. Jones (1982: 13) indicates shark's-tooth spangles on clothing and a cloak with beaded fringe. Uncertain: mantle or shirt.	Male	40–44
6	11	Extended on back; head north of west (northwest) 16E	Wooden boards (split log); pearl beads.	Male	45–49
17	Undet.	Extended on back; west of south (southwest) 97E	Pottery vessels? Uncertain: wooden boards (split logs).	No skeletal remains	No skeletal remains
18	Undet.	Undetermined; south of east (southeast) 0E	No grave goods indicated.	Male	25–29
12	10	Cremation in pit	No grave goods associated with cremation.	Male	35–39

Sources: Jones 1982, 1994; Larsen 2001; Storey 1993.
Note: The "K" burials are those recovered by Mr. Joby Kidd, a volunteer assistant to Jones who was present in Jones's absence.

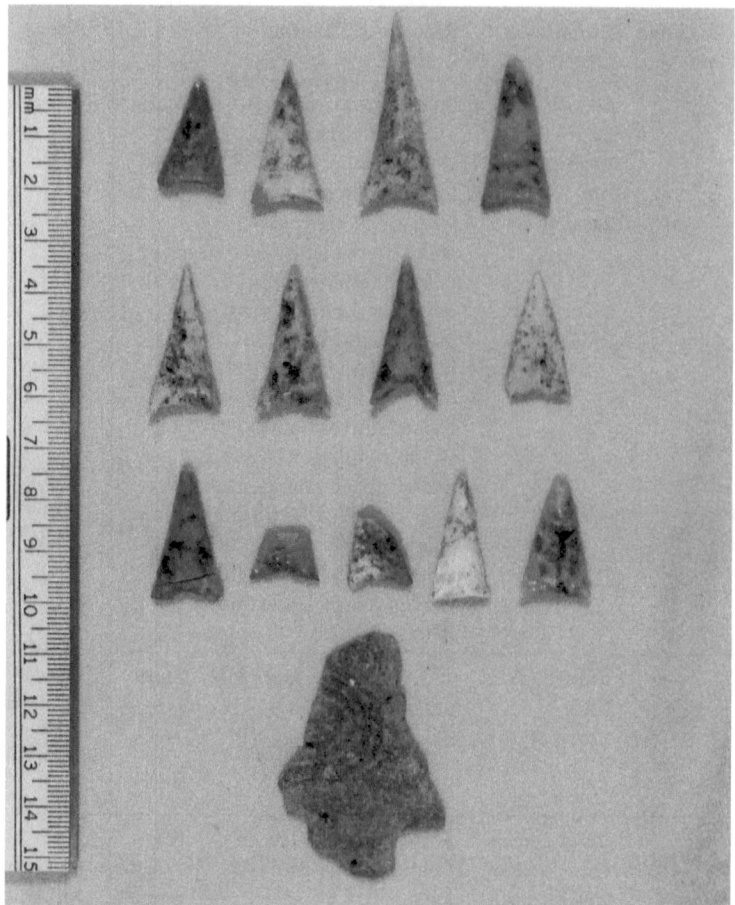

Figure 9.3. Chert projectile points excavated from Mound 3, Lake Jackson. Provenience of individual specimens is not indicated. The lower projectile point–like object is a copper repoussé fragment. Courtesy of David N. Dickel, Collections Manager, Division of Historical Resources, Florida Department of State.

accumulation, such as that clearly present to the north and west of the mounds, can result from other kinds of activities. There is some indication of a mixed subsistence base—maize agriculture and hunting and gathering of local resources—but the intensity of agriculture is difficult to assess from the data currently available. Poor preservation conditions, common to the Tallahassee Hills, make evaluation of the relative dependence on wild and domesticated foods difficult.

Figure 9.4. Fort Walton Incised ceramic rim sherds from Mound 3, Lake Jackson. Specific provenience is not indicated. Courtesy of David N. Dickel, Collections Manager, Division of Historical Resources, Florida Department of State.

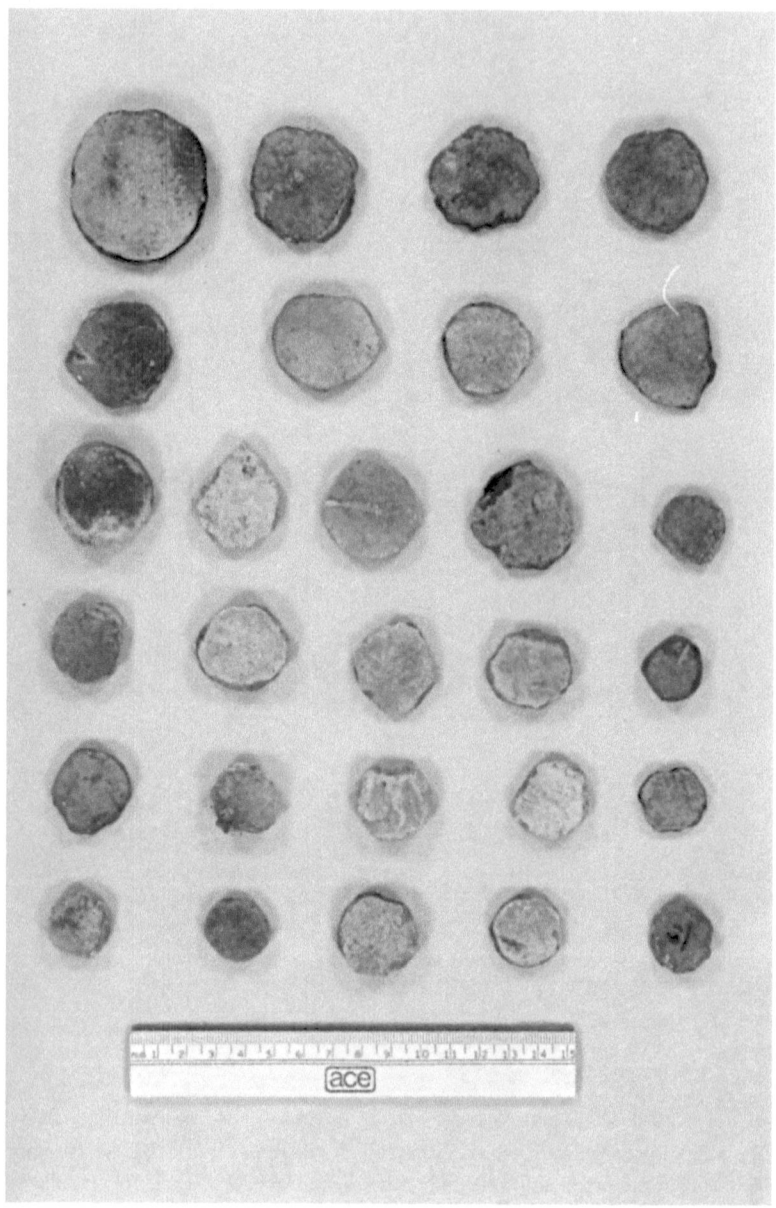

Figure 9.5. Ceramic disks excavated from Mound 3, Lake Jackson. Provenience is not indicated. Courtesy of David N. Dickel, Collections Manager, Division of Historical Resources, Florida Department of State.

Other Mound Sites in the Tallahassee Hills

Single mound sites in the Tallahassee Hills have received some professional investigation through the years, but the findings are known only from occasional references. Table 9.6 summarizes what is known for the Rollins, Miller's Landing, Velda, and Lafayette mounds. I also include the Letchworth Mounds site in this discussion because it contains the tallest earthen platform-style mound in the state, but its chronology is poorly understood.

Table 9.6. Mound sites in the Tallahassee Red Hills area

Site	Description	Radiocarbon Dates	Material Culture	References
Lake Lafayette (8Le2)	"Flat-topped pyramidal" mound; "temple mound"; survey around mound in anticipation of Fallschase development	Undated	20 Fort Walton Complex; Fort Walton Incised; Lake Jackson Plain; Pensacola Plain; Leon Check Stamped; Lamar Complicated Stamped; 2 Weeden Island Complex; Carrabelle Punctated; Wakulla Check Stamped; Fort Walton, Lake Jackson, and Leon-Jefferson	Willey 1949: 284; Smith 1956: 123; Causey 2000; Austin 2006; Stickler 2006
Rollins Mound (8Le3)	Platform mound; eastern shore Lake Jackson	Undated	5 Fort Walton	Willey 1949: 285
Lake Iamonia (8Le5)	"Temple mound"; south margin of Lake Iamonia	Undated	17 Fort Walton; 12 Lake Jackson (1 sherd disk)	Willey 1949: 286; Tesar 1980: 481–84
Velda (8Le44)	Platform mound and associated village (62 m south of mound)	Mound undated; A.D. 1499±92, postmold 84; A.D. 1510±84, no provenience indicated; 5380 BC±292, charcoal in irregular oval feature	Unknown—looting for pottery; no ceramic inventory provided	Fairbanks 1950s; Division of Historical Resources Files
Miller's Landing (8Le70)	9 m in diameter; 1 m high	Undated	38 plain (28 grog, 11 sand/grit); 1 incised carinated sherd (grog); 1 Ichetucknee point	Florida Master Site File; Fairbanks 1961
Letchworth Mounds (8Je337)	1 platformlike mound; 5 (at least) smaller mounds	Undated	Swift Creek; Weeden Island; Leon-Jefferson	Tesar et al. 2003: 51

Willey (1949a: 285) reported the Rollins Mound (8Le3), a platform mound located on a small peninsula (Rollins Point) on the eastern shore of Lake Jackson. There has been no further professional investigation of this site, and it is undated. Nearby on the same peninsula, Charles Fairbanks (Florida Master Site File record) reported the Miller's Landing mound (8Le70) in 1961. Ceramic and lithic materials, curated by Florida State University, are reported in table 9.6. The lone lithic specimen is a small projectile point (26 mm in length by 12.5 mm at its widest) that appears more like later Ichetucknee points than the triangular type recovered from Lake Jackson (figure 9.3). The Lake Jackson points represent the Pinellas type (Bullen 1975: 8), the local Mississippian variant. The site file form suggests that the Miller's Landing mound collection may have been from the roadbed and plowed field adjacent to the mound. Fairbanks did not comment on the shape of the mound (truncated or rounded). The site is reported as Fort Walton, although it is undated. Both Rollins and Miller's Landing lie approximately 5.5 km northeast of the Lake Jackson site (straight-line distance).

Willey (1949a: 286) also listed a mound on Lake Iamonia (8Le5), 18.5 km northeast of Lake Jackson, as a Fort Walton site. He did not visit it but studied collections curated by the Peabody Museum at Harvard. The site file form lists the site as a "temple mound," and there is a notation that it was measured, mapped, and trenched by Hale G. Smith. To date, neither field notes nor a reference to a report has been located. The site was visited by Joe Hutto during the Bicentennial Survey (Tesar 1980). The site file form locates it on Horseshoe Plantation on the southern margin of the lake. This site is undated.

The Velda Mound site (8Le44) has a single platform mound and a residential component, located 10 km east of the Lake Jackson site. It was originally reported by Fairbanks in the 1950s and has since been virtually destroyed by looting. There is little knowledge of the kinds of material carried away, and the mound is undated. A residential area excavated by Ross Morrell in 1968 lies approximately 62 m south of the mound. John Scarry (1995; Scarry and McEwan 1995) has studied the ceramic assemblage and site features and interprets the area as a farmstead. Although a site report has not been published, Scarry (1995) reported the prehistoric structural evidence. Two round structures, 5.5 m and 7.5 m in diameter, were single-post constructions, and neither had subfloor burials. Refuse-bearing features, some with maize, were identified outside the structures, and a possible elevated storage structure was located nearby (Scarry 1995).

Radiocarbon dates indicate a late fifteenth- to early sixteenth-century occupation (table 9.1), but European-derived cultural materials were not recovered (Radiocarbon Files, Department of State).

Willey (1949a: 284) visited the Lake Lafayette site (8Le2), 13 km east of the Lake Jackson site, and described a "flat-topped pyramidal mound of clay surrounded by fields which bear evidence of having been an old village site." Smith (1956: 123) excavated there in the 1950s and reported Jefferson Complicated Stamped sherds associated with Lake Jackson and Fort Walton ceramic types. Recent road projects and commercial development have required assessment of the Lafayette mound locality (Austin 2006; Causey 2000; Stickler 2006). Fort Walton and Leon-Jefferson ceramics were recovered in shovel tests around the mound. Artifact density is greatest east and west of the mound. The mound is now protected by a 0.3-ha buffer, but the nature of the deposits around the mound—a village, perhaps—has not been determined by these projects (Stickler 2006: 22). The small size of the buffer also means that the area beyond will be developed without any lateral excavation that might identify structures, a task for which shovel tests are inadequate.

The Letchworth Mounds site was initially listed as the Miccosukee Mound by Boyd (1939), and Payne and Scarry (1990) include it in their Lake Jackson Mississippian polity. It is located 29 km east of the Lake Jackson site. Composed of one large, platformlike mound and at least five smaller mounds, it was initially reported as a Swift Creek/Weeden Island site based on surface collections. At over 13 m, its principal mound is the highest in Florida. Auger- and shovel-testing programs and limited test excavations around the mounds have been undertaken, but none of the mounds has been dated (Tesar et al. 2003: 51). It is possible that this site has more in common with earlier Weeden Island sites such as Kolomoki and McKeithen than with Fort Walton culture.

Nonmound Sites

Several nonmound sites should also be discussed because they appear frequently in the literature. The Bear Grass site (8Le473) was located and tested during the Bicentennial Survey (Tesar 1980: 782). It is a multicomponent site with structural evidence. Excavation revealed a curving postmold line that suggested a round structure with a 12-m diameter. No burial features were identified in the "interior" of the structure. The feature was not completely exposed in the area excavated, and we are left to wonder whether it represents a residential building. Its projected diameter is similar to that of Structure 3 at the Borrow Pit site discussed below. A small amount of maize was recovered among a variety of plant remains (Tesar 1980: 789).

The Borrow Pit site (8Le170) was investigated by B. Calvin Jones (1990: 83) in 1970. He identified five round structures but excavated only two. Structure 3, the largest at about 12 m in diameter, contained eight flexed and semiflexed burials beneath a hardened red clay floor. Osteological analysis of these burials was not undertaken, but Jones noted that men, women, and children were present. He believed that these individuals were elite members of a Fort Walton–period hamlet. On the basis of the ceramics recovered, Jones (1990: 83) dated the site between A.D. 1400 and 1500. He reported large quantities of potsherds, most of which he identified as Lake Jackson Plain (some with loop handles), Lake Jackson Incised, and other Fort Walton Incised types (Jones 1990: 85). Jones (1990: 84) noted ceramic similarities between the Borrow Pit and Winewood sites. It is possible that the Borrow Pit site represents a hamlet or small village. In that interpretation, the burials may be family members buried beneath a house floor. Whether this represents "elite status" remains in question.

The Winewood site (8Le164) was identified by Jones in 1971. I have been skeptical of its being a purely Fort Walton–period site, as reported by Jones and Penman (1973). If the Borrow Pit site burial pattern is truly a Fort Walton–period pattern, it may indicate a more typical domestic type of interment—subfloor burial. The Lake Jackson burials in Mound 3 exhibited a variety of burial styles from fully extended ($n=9$) to flexed and semiflexed ($n=12$). The Winewood burials, in parallel arrangement and all fully extended, are more similar to those seen at the early Franciscan-Apalachee mission, San Pedro y San Pablo de Patale (8Le152), also excavated by Jones in 1971 (Jones et al. 1991: 39). The ceramics at Winewood and in the church area at Mission Patale are similar (Jones et al. 1991: 61–62; Jones and Penman 1973: 73). Maize cob fragments were recovered from Feature 1, identified as an "oval shaped fire and trash pit" (Jones and Penman 1973: 67, 84).

The High Ridge site (8Le117) was investigated by Fryman (1970, 1971) as part of the Interstate 10 project in the Tallahassee area. Fryman (1970: 5–6) reported a small pre-Spanish village site with two circular structures of single-post construction approximately 6 m in diameter. Ethnobotanical materials from two "storage pits" and small, shallow pits were analyzed by Alexander (1984). Of 50 samples, 17 were food remains and the rest were only wood charcoal (pine, sweetgum, and oak; Alexander 1984: 95). Northern Flint corn, beans, sunflower, and saw palmetto were most dominant in the samples. Fryman (1970) likened the site to Velda.

The Markley–Sharer Road site (8Le213) is of relatively unknown significance. It was brought to Jones's attention by Mark Markley, a 12-year-old Tallahasseean (Anonymous 1974: 2). This site was identified from a scraped road right-of-way. Jones observed three to five structural mounds and assigned a Fort Walton–period date based on the ceramics. The site file form indicates that the structures were single-post constructions and that several were round with clay-lined hearths. The condition of the site permitted Jones to observe the floors of two structures, and he noted that they "had been renewed or rebuilt eight and nine times, as evidenced by baked clay floors layered on top of each other" (Anonymous 1974: 2). Jones's (n.d.) papers make clear that he considered the ceramic assemblage to be similar to those of the Borrow Pit and Winewood sites.

The End of Fort Walton Culture

When and how did Fort Walton culture end? The processes of decline in Fort Walton culture or of the "Lake Jackson chiefdom," as it is often called, are not well understood. In the 1980s, the prevailing explanation for the "abandonment" of the Lake Jackson site and the end of Fort Walton culture was attributed to an influx of middle-Georgia Lamar peoples in the late prehistoric period. In this scenario, the arrival of new people destabilized the Lake Jackson chiefdom and resulted in the cessation of mound building in the area. Three arguments along this line of reasoning have been advanced (Shapiro 1987: 2–5; Tesar 1980: 161–63).

First, the presence of Lamar-like ceramics in Apalache was believed to represent an influx of people from central Georgia. The Lamar type was defined by Jennings and Fairbanks (1939) from their collections on the Macon Plateau as grit tempered with complicated-stamped and incised surface decorations. Georgia sites have produced a wide variety of stamping patterns, such as those reported by Hally (1994: 153) for central Georgia and Wauchope (1950, 1966: 31, 82) for northern Georgia. In the Tallahassee Hills, late complicated-stamped ceramics were given a different type name, Leon-Jefferson (Smith 1948; Willey 1949a). They are predominately grog tempered, but sand, grit, and grit and grog tempering also are present. Complicated-stamped patterns are a relatively few simple motifs of parallel curvilinear and/or rectilinear lines sometimes enclosing a central boss, herringbone elements, or combined circular and triangular elements (Scarry 1985: 223).

When do Lamar-like complicated-stamped ceramics occur in the Tallahassee Hills? They are present on the Macon Plateau in Georgia as early as A.D. 1350 (Hally 1994: 147). Data from the Governor Martin–De Soto site (8Le853b), identified in 1987, strongly indicate that these ceramics postdate the De Soto *entrada*. This site, believed to be Anhaica, the principal town of Apalache, contains several features that appear to be directly associated with De Soto's winter encampment (Ewen and Hann 1998). No complicated-stamped ceramics are reported from early sixteenth-century contexts. At this time, it seems that these ceramics appear after De Soto, a conclusion supported by findings in the Apalachicola River valley region (White et al., chapter 10, this volume).

With regard to the presence of Lamar ceramics, there is one other issue that I must consider briefly: trading and social relationships between Apalachees and other cultural groups, some of which may have been in northwestern or central Georgia. Recent data noted above from the Weeden Island–period McKeithen site near Lake City, Florida, suggest the possibility of bride exchange for at least one high-status female, buried alone in a low platform mound (Milanich et al. 1997; Turner et al. 2005). In matrilineal societies, land use-rights and chiefly entitlement are vested in the matrilineage. If there were spousal exchange, either male or female, could a distant high-status individual have a claim on a leadership position in Apalache? Who made the decisions about the suitability of such an exchange? Late prehistoric kinship and trading relationships may have provided the impetus for movement or changes in ceramic decorative styles. It is also possible that social instability in the period between the De Soto entrada and the establishment of missions in Apalache, almost a century later, prompted resettlement of people with a Lamar ceramic repertoire.

The second argument is based on the observation that chroniclers of the De Soto entrada do not mention mounds in the Tallahassee Hills region or in most of the Southeast. Thus, the demise of prehistoric cultures and the cessation of mound building and mound use are inferred. The chroniclers may not have seen these constructions or may not have found them worth mentioning. Later French explorers observed mortuary ritual and reported mounds (Le Page Du Pratz 1774). Whether mound building or mound use had ceased in the Tallahassee Hills by the time of De Soto's arrival is not clear, because the radiocarbon dates from Lake Jackson and Velda suggest that both sites may have been active in the early sixteenth century. What relationship, if any, may have existed between Anhaica and Lake Jackson some 8 km distant also is unknown. We do not know if there was an Anhaica in 1528, when Narváez and his company entered the eastern periphery of Apalache, but eleven years later, it was the principal town of the region. No indigenous mortuary pattern has been discovered at the Martin–De Soto site.

Significantly, however, mound building did continue. The mound at Snow Beach (8Wa52) is dated to the late Fort Walton or "protohistoric" Fort Walton period (Magoon et al. 2001). It contained earlier Swift Creek midden fill overlain by a white sand cap from which seven burials were excavated by David Phelps in the late 1960s. Six primary burials of single individuals were reported, all in recumbent extended style with few burial goods. Burial 7 was a "multiple burial," an adult associated with dispersed subadult remains. Seventeenth-century glass beads ($n=212$) were recovered with Burial 7 (Magoon et al. 2001: 19) and two Ichetucknee points from Feature 12. The Snow Beach site lies within a coastal embayment some 48 km from the Tallahassee area.

The third argument involves the absence of sixteenth-century cultural materials at the Lake Jackson site. To date no sixteenth-century Spanish materials have been recovered, but seventeenth-century material culture has been produced by subsurface testing (Jones 1992; Payne 1994; Terzis and Smith 1990). It seems prudent to maintain that the issue of contact-period materials at this site is not settled, given the limitations of previous investigations as well as the conditions under which the Mound 3 salvage was conducted.

Fort Walton Culture and Archaeological Interpretation

I began this overview by asserting that the theoretical or interpretive literature relative to the Mississippi period in the Tallahassee Hills has outstripped the available hard data, then reviewed the available data and discussed the inherent problems. When one is not arguing from hard data, being proven wrong is impossible. Conversely, and more significantly, being proven right also is impossible. Given the data we do have, I believe it is possible to explore a number of directions relating to Fort Walton culture in the Tallahassee Hills, particularly mortuary customs, social memory, and settlement patterns. Because most of the available data originate from the Lake Jackson site, I concentrate on it in particular.

Mortuary Customs

Clearly one function of the Lake Jackson site was as a place of burial, a resting place of the ancestors. Only Mound 3 has been demonstrated to contain burials; Mounds 4, 5, and 6 have not. The investigations in Mounds 4 and 5 were flanking excavations, so burials may be located more centrally. If we accept Mounds 4, 5, and 6 as substructural mounds, however, we can hypothesize that they represent the location of structures, venerated places where celebrations of social ritual, clan or group deliberations, repositories of ancestral bones or sacred artifacts, or all of these activities may have taken place. But Mississippian mortuary customs include a number of different burial locations other than mounds: beneath house floors in residential areas and in discrete cemeteries near or among mounds (e.g., Peebles 1974; Goldstein 1980; Larson 1971; Sullivan 2006). There may be cemeteries located near or among the mounds, but none has been identified at Lake Jackson or elsewhere in the Tallahassee Hills.

There are many ways to determine origin and distribution of mortuary goods, such as stylistic similarity and trace element analysis. Similarly, there are various approaches to interpreting their meaning. Some scholars have looked for correspondence with surviving ethnohistorical data such as origin myths or culture heroes (e.g., Prentice 1986) or cosmological meaning (Brown 2010). Energy expenditure has been investigated by Saxe (1971) and others. The amount of energy expended on an individual, as measured by quantity, quality, and goods of exotic origin, is taken as a measure of his or her significance in a social group. Others have seen linkages between or among Mississippian sites based on the presence of ritual goods and iconography (Scarry 2007a). I believe there are some fundamental questions that must be asked and different approaches that can be used to think about what Lake Jackson and other Mississippian sites represent.

We must ask—what do the living owe the dead, and by contrast, what do the dead owe the living? A number of archaeologists and other anthropologists have considered these questions (Binford 1971; Goldstein 1980; Goody 1962; Hertz 1907; Kroeber 1927; Miles 1965; most recently for Mississippian sites, Sullivan and Mainfort 2010). The answers depend on several variables: status, role, age, memorialization, and circumstances at death. In hierarchically arranged societies, status may be a significant determinant of the duties that survivors owe to the deceased. Role may be dependent on birth, sex or gender, life accomplishment, and age. Each variable may affect what is "owed" to the deceased. Age also may be a factor, dependent on whether the individual has reached old age or only a few years. In the case of the former, societal roles, ascribed status, and life accomplishments may dictate what is "owed," and a significant "mortuary capital" may have accumulated over a lifetime. In the case of an infant or very young individual, who has not lived long enough to accrue a "mortuary debt," there may be few grave goods. However, here too, ascribed status may be a mitigating factor in the ritual attendant at the death of an elite infant or young individual or familial attachment in the case of non-elite children. Circumstances at death also may be factors in the treatment of the deceased. If the individual died at a distance from home, during a visit, raid, war, or perhaps during a trading venture, social memorialization may differ significantly. If the individual died under questionable circumstances, conditions that might portend ill for a group, mortuary treatment may deviate from the norm.

We also must ask—what are the functions of grave goods? In contemporary American culture, we hear the adage, "You can't take it with you." It is at once an admonition against greed and a reminder of the inevitability of death. But the quantities of grave goods often seen with Mississippian burials suggest that the deceased of this culture did take it with them. Is what we witness in Mississippian mortuary rites "taking it with you," or are there other ways to explain this behavior? Grave goods may function in several realms: that of the survivors, the "living"; in an envisioned existence for the deceased beyond their life among the "living"; or perhaps in a realm of societal testimony in which the "worth" of the deceased or the "worth" of a society, before a pantheon of deities, is demonstrated by the materials interred. Grave goods may be used to attest to the importance of the individual in some next life. One may need material affirmation of "worth" or "value" when entering a new realm, one beyond the living. Grave goods may attest that the living send someone into an afterlife asserting that this individual is worthy of an exalted or special place. The accompanying goods serve notice that the deceased was significant among the living, perhaps even indicating his or her societal role. Grave goods may assist the deceased in "living" in the next life. Thus, gifts of food, weapons, and commodities to "live the next life" represent a kind of capital that the deceased brings into the next life (Reber et al. 2010).

Grave goods may be bestowed by individuals, families, and societal groups. They may be simply the possessions of the deceased or tokens placed with the deceased by friends, family, and societal entities such as warrior or curing sodalities. Grave goods may represent gifts from loved ones of materials significant in life—heirloom items, much-loved objects—from the life of the deceased that the living think the deceased valued and would "want" in death. They may represent a testimonial by the living to the "worth" of the individual. Amassing goods of importance by the deceased is an attestation from those who survive, demonstrating the significance that the deceased had in their lives. Grave goods and attendant rituals may represent a patterned or prescribed way of "paying off" the dead—perhaps to appease the spirit of the dead—to prevent malicious acts or malingering on the part of the deceased's spirit, thereby ensuring community safety.

The inclusion of grave goods with a society's dead is essentially alienation of material wealth from the living. The interring of grave goods decreases the collective wealth of a society. Another aspect of mortuary goods is the matter of ownership. Were the grave goods societal, clan/lineage, or personal items? Proper treatment of deceased members of society represents a means of ensuring that the disharmony of death and decay is ameliorated (Douglas 1966). The mound precinct, as the sacred space where the dead and the sumptuous goods buried with them are remembered, represents a constructed identity that ties the members of a society to a specific place.

What do the dead owe the living? In death, they may become intercessors with the gods on behalf of their people. They also become ancestral role models who are physically present in the mound precinct, although not visible to the living. In nonliterate societies, the duty of remembering social history, of relating that history as stories or parables, is significant. In many societies, the dead as ghosts or spirits are believed to owe their surviving relatives a harmonious life. They must be appeased, however, to insure that they do not linger. If the proper ceremonies are performed, appropriate treatment is accorded the deceased's body, and suitable grave goods are included, the deceased is "paid off" and encouraged not to loiter among the living nor to interfere in their affairs.

A close examination of the data produced by Jones's (1982) salvage excavations in Mound 3 provides insights about the Tallahassee Hills Fort Walton burial pattern. Compared to Mississippian sites elsewhere, it is not typical. In the Lake Jackson population, copper repoussé plates with raptor iconography were buried with the remains of mature women (estimated 49+ years; Storey 1993). Osteological analysis clearly identifies Burials 7 and 16 as females, but Burial 10 is equivocal. Storey (1993) identified the individual as a male, but Larsen and colleagues (2001: 61) list the person as female. If this third individual is female, all of the plates with complex raptor iconography recovered in Mound 3 are associated with mature women. We could assert that these women were chiefs (Trocolli 2002: 178), but their importance may have been vested in their role as matriclan leaders. Sullivan (2001: 122–23) has shown that males and females at the Mississippi-period Toqua site in Tennessee had different grave goods and burial locations and argued that these reflected their role in society.

Ethnohistoric accounts of the treatment of copper plates indicate veneration and segregation of males who carried them during the Tukabatchee removal to Arkansas in 1826 (C. Brown 1982: 3). All of the Lake Jackson iconographic plates are believed to be "heirloom" items, as evidenced by mends and joining of unrelated fragments. Leader (1988) has noted the frequency of breaks and mends and attributes breakage to repetitious polishing. Polished copper gleams and may have represented the sun on earth, a sacred capturing of the essence of the sun and sky world. Miller and Hammel (1986) stress the importance of copper to precontact native societies and emphasize the continued preference for copper by indigenous people over gold and silver, something that Europeans never understood but used to their advantage.

The locus of manufacture of iconographic plates is unknown. Some have seen Etowah as a workshop (Leader 1988), and there are stylistic resemblances to copper from Etowah. A workshop, however, must have evidence of tools, raw materials, and waste. Although there are tools that might have been used to work copper (antler tines, shark's teeth, and stone), to date, no raw copper has been recovered there (Leader 1988: 137–39). Etowah is closer to naturally occurring copper sources, but copper nuggets have not been recovered. A case for Etowah as a source for these plates is not as strong as the Cahokia evidence around Mound 72. Thus the origins, length of time at Lake Jackson, and role of copper plates in Fort Walton society are not well understood. These important cultural items do seem to have been "retired" upon the death of a senior woman of an elite matrilineage, but they were retained within a sacred place that manifests group identity.

Male gender is usually assigned to the figures on these repoussé plates, but Catherine Brown (1982) and Nancy White (1999) have questioned this representation. Brown (1982) specifically questions the male attribution to figures with shell pendants and the suggestion of breasts in the iconography. Two of the plates from Lake Jackson, with Burials 7 and 16, have shell pendants, and the suggestion of breasts is stronger on the plate with Burial 16. The plates with Burial 10, the "elder hawkman" (Jones 1982) and the attached falcon fragment, differ significantly in style. Although the "elder hawkman" does appear to be male, the falcon has no anthropomorphic elements. This elder hawkman specimen is comparable to several plates from the Spiro site (Hamilton et al. 1974).

Males do have associated copper artifacts. Flared copper axes were buried with six males and with two others lacking a sex assignment (Jones 1982; Storey 1993). Burial 10, the equivocal burial, does not have an associated copper axe, suggesting that copper axes may be a dependable male marker and that this individual is indeed female, as Larsen and colleagues (2000) contend. Four males were buried with copper plates cut in the shape of a raptor or with plate fragments, but not the stylized iconographic repoussé plates. Two of these males were estimated to be in excess of 50 years old, one is in the 35–39-year-old range, and the fourth is in the 11–12-year-old range (the last suggests ascribed status). Outside of Mound 3, no other burial areas have been identified at Lake Jackson. At other Mississippi-period sites, discrete cemeteries and burial beneath house floors in residential areas have been identified. The burial evidence at Lake Jackson supports contentions of ranking and elite status. Unlike Mississippian centers elsewhere (Goldstein 1980), however, there is no clear evidence of retainer sacrifice. The burials appear to be individual interments, nearly all buried with significant grave goods.

Annette Weiner (1992) has written about inalienable possessions. Some possessions, Weiner says, embody a society and are critical to their socially constructed identity. They are too integral to that identity to be "given." Thus, a means of "keeping" the possessions while ostensibly giving them away is needed. We can regard Southeastern Ceremonial Complex objects in this way. They have been seen as sacra related to an overarching participation in a pan-areal mortuary cult (Waring and Holder 1945; Waring 1968) or at least as evidence of association through trade networks. Copper was revered in native North America and fashioned into a variety of forms. How copper plates, axes, symbol badges, and exotic stone came to northwest Florida is not known, but they become "social capital" consistently interred with the elite dead at Lake Jackson. The earliest copper, a hawk dancer iconographic plate from floor 9, is associated with older female Burial 7. The latest interments, associated with floor 1, have considerably more copper artifacts. The nine burials that represent the final stage of interments include males and females as well as young children (see table 9.4).

Southeastern Ceremonial Complex goods are present at Lake Jackson but have limited associations. Two copper plates with Braden-style raptor iconography are associated directly with mature females, and a third, with Spiro-style "elder" iconography (Hamilton et al. 1974), is associated with a mature female. To return to Weiner's point, by giving these precious goods to the elite dead of Lake Jackson society, the society was, in my opinion, essentially keeping the materials within a landscape constructed for social identity and remembering.

Social Memory

Several scholars (e.g., Bradley 1993; Connerton 1989) stress the power of place in social memory. The Lake Jackson site and the other mound sites of the Tallahassee Hills represent constructed landscapes that persisted for at least several centuries and an unknown number of generations. As Connerton (1989) has said, the meaning of such a place begins with the first construction and varies through time. Beside its mortuary function, we have little understanding of how the Lake Jackson site functioned, because we have no substantial excavations of areas that can be called residential (on or off mounds). Willey, Griffin, Penton, Fryman, and Payne all encountered dense midden accumulations west of Mound 2. Were these deposits made by village dwellers, as nearly everyone has assumed, or was this a discard area that resulted from other kinds of activities such as ceremonies or mound construction? Given the lack of structural evidence, the question is reasonable.

We do not know whether Lake Jackson represents a political center with residence limited to the elite of society and their retainers. We do not know whether there was an associated village or whether the population was spread around the locality in hamlets or farmsteads. We do not know whether the Lake Jackson site was a ritual precinct—home to religious functionaries who cared for the dead and oversaw the site. We also do not know how function may have changed over time. Fryman's excavation revealed a wall segment, but the feature was not pursued laterally to determine its extent and function. Researchers have difficulty evaluating whether these food remains, broken vessels, and lithic debris are evidence of rites of intensification that required the presence of large numbers of people for ritual, refurbishment, or building, or whether they represent an established village, seasonal occupations, or episodic use. The presence of a stream running through the site also is unusual and its significance, if any, unappreciated.

Recently, Payne (2010) has used the vehicle of memory studies (e.g., Crawford 2007; Lillios 1999; Mills 2008; Rowlands 1993) to interpret the disposal of heirloom items with the last interments at Lake Jackson Mound 3. Payne (2010) and Scarry (2006) suggest that the copper plates were old, possibly even antiques when they arrived at Lake Jackson, based on the presence of mends, repair patches and rivets, and the quality of the repair. If Leader (1988) is correct about the effects of repeated polishing, a plate could become thinned and not be particularly old. Whether artisans at the Lake Jackson site had the skill and could obtain copper scrap to make the repairs locally is not known. Payne (2010: 4) suggests that the final burials in Mound 3, and the disposal of so many high-quality grave goods, represent "an attempt by the Lake Jackson chiefs to reinvent themselves, to dispose of their identity as Mississippians, an identity which no longer had advantages." Payne points out that just as memory is a tool for constructing identity, it also could be a means of forgetting in a changing social and political milieu. These are interesting ideas, and given the date of the final stage of Mound 3, substantial cultural change could possibly have been under way.

Settlement Pattern

We often have been so focused on the Lake Jackson site that we have failed to consider how land was apportioned and used during the Fort Walton period. This was the time during which true agriculture was established in the Tallahassee Hills, but what are the constituent parts of the Mississippian settlement pattern here? If we accept the hypothesis that Lake Jackson was a central place and the outlying single mounds do represent contemporaneous affiliates, we also must accept that the number of mounds in the Lake Jackson/Lake Iamonia locality would represent a dense population and, most likely, overlapping catchment areas (Vita-Finzi and Higgs 1970). The lake is a resource-rich area, but how were hunting/gathering/fishing territories decided? The proximity of the Rollins and Miller's Landing mound sites, both of which lie within 6 km of the Lake Jackson site, might indicate others' claims on the resources of the lake. If these represent concentrations of population affiliated with Lake Jackson, their catchment areas must lie inland of the lake itself, but that might also infringe on the catchment area of the Lake Iamonia site, lying some 18 km distant from Lake Jackson and 12 km from Rollins and Miller's Landing.

The Rollins and Miller's Landing mound sites, about 1.3 km apart, might represent another complex site in the making or earlier and later mounds in a locality. Without radiocarbon dates from any of these outlying mounds, it is impossible to propose a theoretical model of a paramount chiefdom or to understand how the people of these localities interacted with Lake Jackson. Paramountcy remains a hypothesis that must be tested.

Concluding Remarks and Recommendations

This presentation of the archaeological data from the Tallahassee Hills has shown that there are substantive problems in our understanding of Fort Walton culture generally and in this region of Florida specifically. This overview should not be viewed as negative or pessimistic; rather, it is simply realistic. When the available data are examined, they clearly are relatively meager. The problems inherent in the current database provide, I believe, the basis for future archaeological investigations. The pace of urbanization in the Tallahassee Hills confers immediacy to the need for archaeological research in a number of directions.

One critical need is a comprehensive report of Jones's excavation of Mound 3 at Lake Jackson. Examination of Jones's field notes, maps, photographs, and artifacts suggests that a detailed presentation of context and artifact assemblage is badly needed. Neither of Jones's (1982, 1994) articles on Lake Jackson adequately illustrates the variety of material culture present (see figures 9.3, 9.4, and 9.5).

We must understand what kinds of activities occurred at Lake Jackson. Is the site ceremonial *and* residential, a town or large village with a settled population? If so, there are approaches we can use to answer this question. We need to understand whether the substantial refuse deposit on the north and west sides of Mound 2 is residential debris from individuals residing on or very near the mounds and whether it relates to higher- or lower-status individuals. We need to expose clear structural evidence; we simply must *verify* the presence of a village. Delimiting the boundaries of the refuse deposit noted by Willey, Griffin, and Penton would provide insight into its size and extent relative to the mounds. Structural evidence may lie in areas where residential refuse is absent (Binford et al. 1970). It is important to consider whether the ceramic component includes large or special-use vessels that might indicate feasting (Blitz 1993b: 84–90; Rolland 2005: 222–27).

At Lake Jackson, Mounds 1, 2, 4, 6, and 7 must be dated and their function(s) evaluated. Payne (1994) did not include the ceramic inventory from her auger tests in her dissertation, but these data would be helpful as a guide to identifying areas of high and low artifact frequency. The flat areas (Payne's [1994] plaza) around the mounds need to be explored to insure that we have not missed features because of the restrictions imposed by project-limiting excavation and auger-testing protocols. For example, there might be structures or discrete cemetery areas. In the Tallahassee Hills, preservation of human and faunal remains is so poor that only a burial pit with a few surviving teeth may remain to indicate their location. We must determine whether Mound 7 is a mound, and if so, its type and period of construction. Although Mound 3 was destroyed in the mid-1970s, submound features may remain. The area where Mound 3 once stood is now part of the park, and this possibility must not be overlooked.

There is not yet any evidence of palisades in late prehistoric sites in the Tallahassee Hills. I do not rule out the possibility that a palisade existed at Lake Jackson, but we have not demonstrated its presence or location; an extensive remote sensing program might reveal such evidence. Each of the mound sites in the Tallahassee Hills—Rollins, Miller's Landing, Iamonia, Lafayette, Velda, and Letchworth—must be radiocarbon-dated. This is the only viable means of determining contemporaneity and the reasonableness of a designation of a mound site as a Lake Jackson affiliate. This will require excavation rather than less-invasive techniques such as coring. I personally have reservations about how clearly we can understand what a core has intersected, and how relevant the material produced is to our questions (mound fill can date earlier than the mound in question). We will be able to grasp the level of complexity of Fort Walton culture in the Tallahassee Hills only when we understand the number of components and their temporal relationships. Once we have secured those data, we can speak more confidently about polities, power relationships, and affiliation.

Early Fort Walton culture is not well developed in the Tallahassee Hills. We must seek sites of this period for investigation to gain insights relating to the change from Weeden Island culture, the increasing dependence on maize agriculture, and development of social complexity. We need to rule out migration and/or local development and where possible, use trace-element analysis and other techniques to reveal the points of origin of artifacts or contacts with outside groups. The land changes required for extensive maize agriculture must have been significant. Are there techniques with which we can model extensive land clearing and its environmental impact? I return to the question of water availability and whether coring of lake bottoms would produce stratigraphic evidence of past lake drainage or carbon or pollen indicating field clearing.

Some contend that Fort Walton culture bearers originated in the Chattahoochee and Apalachicola River valley and that migration accounts for the establishment of Fort Walton culture in the Tallahassee Hills. At present, very few sites have been reported to the Florida Master Site File for the intervening area. Site survey in the area between the Tallahassee Hills and the Apalachicola River bluffs, in Leon and Gadsden counties, is needed to investigate the proposition that it was underutilized or passed by in late prehistoric times as people made their way to the Tallahassee area. Marrinan and White (2007: 301) briefly considered this problem and found sites in the Interstate 10 corridor, suggesting that a lack of site survey projects in this area may account for the current low density.

These suggestions address what I believe are the most fundamental weaknesses in our understanding of Fort Walton culture in the Tallahassee Hills; gaining this information will require long-term research. If we do not make this commitment, the local evidence will be substantively compromised by encroaching urban development. Then we truly will have to depend even more on proxies for our presentation of late prehistoric lifeways.

Since 1983, a sustained program of archaeological research has targeted the Mission period (1633–1704) in this region, demonstrating the value of a collaborative effort and a problem-oriented approach. The same kind of approach is needed to develop a *local* understanding of the development, florescence, and decline of Fort Walton culture in the Tallahassee Hills. It is incumbent on us to develop interpretations based on hard evidence, not appealing narratives.

Acknowledgments

I owe a number of individuals a great deal of thanks for assistance with collections, archived manuscripts, and maps. David N. Dickel and Marie Prentice made the Department of State collections available and gave good advice about other things I might want to examine. They led me to collections and manuscripts that have made this overview stronger. The late Charley Branham was always helpful with maps and queries about site locations, distributions, and density. His quiet, cheerful professionalism is missed by all, as is his friendship. I also commend the members of the Florida Master Site File staff. The availability of digital copies of site reports and manuscripts is of very real assistance to researchers. Claudine Payne made a copy of her most recent paper available, and I thank her for her promptness. Last, I thank David Hurst Thomas for recent conversations about the nature of archaeological evidence. I have paraphrased him unashamedly.

Note

1. In this chapter, the place-name Apalache refers to the Tallahassee Hills area from late prehistory to the time that missions were founded in Apalachee Province. The name Apalachees is used to refer to the indigenous people inhabiting the Tallahassee Hills at the time of European contact and thereafter. Apalachee is used as a modifier, as in Apalachee culture.

10

Fort Walton Culture in the Apalachicola Valley, Northwest Florida

NANCY MARIE WHITE, JEFFREY P. DU VERNAY, AND AMBER J. YUELLIG

Fort Walton is the Mississippian variant in northwest Florida–south Alabama–southwest Georgia, defined 60 years ago by Gordon Willey (1949a), and characterized by agricultural villages, temple mounds, and Mississippian forms of ceramics that are, however, *not* shell tempered like most other Mississippian pottery, as well as other distinguishing elements. This chapter expands on our current knowledge and interpretation of Fort Walton in the Apalachicola–lower Chattahoochee Valley region with some new information (Marrinan and White 2007). Fort Walton societies were indeed complex, ranked, possibly stratified chiefdoms (to use a convenient, though ambiguous and debatable term) participating in the wider Mississippian world. But they had a traditional and distinctive material culture that mostly evolved in place and may reflect some degree of isolation or maintenance of some ethnic or geographic identity.

Geography, Sites, and Types of Evidence

The Apalachicola River forms at the confluence of the Chattahoochee and Flint rivers and flows some 177 km (110 river or navigation miles) south to the Gulf of Mexico. The only Florida river with snowmelt, the Apalachicola is the lowest part of the great Chattahoochee basin, which originates 870 km inland in the Blue Ridge Mountains. The Chattahoochee-Flint confluence marks the border between Georgia, on the east bank, and Florida, on the west bank of the Chattahoochee for its lowest 25 river miles (figure 10.1). Above that the river marks the Alabama-Georgia border, and Fort Walton culture extends about another 40 km upstream. This rich environment had abundant resources and fertile alluvial bottomland good for

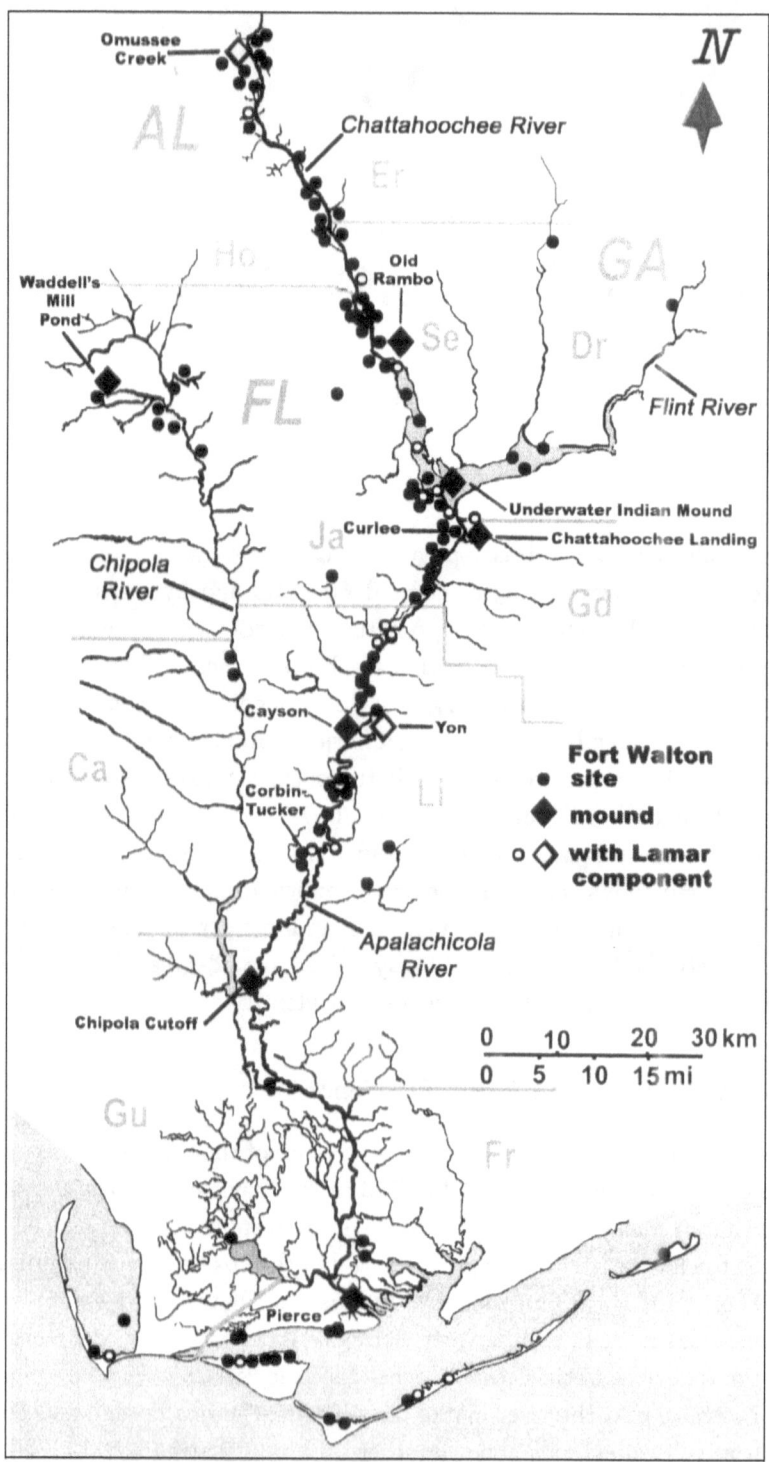

Figure 10.1. Map of Fort Walton sites, including those with Lamar components, in the Apalachicola/lower Chattahoochee Valley.

agriculture. The lower delta is low-lying and swampy but full of aquatic resources that made for a different (nonagricultural) late prehistoric adaptation. The same is true for the coast, sheltered by white-sand barrier islands and shallow bays with abundant fish, crustaceans, and shellfish.

Fort Walton sites range from small probable farmsteads to large villages with temple mounds in typical Mississippian layout (Lewis and Stout 1998; Lewis et al. 1998; Payne 2002). On the coast and lowest part of the delta, sites are usually shell middens. Mounds are interestingly distributed and enigmatic (detailed in Marrinan and White 2007: table 1); figure 10.2 shows them schematically. It is still unclear how contemporaneous or sequential they are.

The Apalachicola Valley proper has four known temple (platform) mound centers (Moore 1902, 1903): Pierce (8Fr14) on the west bank at the river mouth, Yon (8Li2) and Cayson (8Ca2) in the middle valley on opposite sides of the river, and Chattahoochee Landing (8Gd4) at the upper, east side right below the confluence. Across the river from Chattahoochee Landing, the Curlee site (8Ja7, now washed away) was probably a riverbank cemetery, not a mound (White 1982). A platform mound of possible Woodland origin with later Fort Walton burials and expansion (near another, conical probable Woodland mound) is Waddell's Mill Pond (8Ja65) in the upper drainage of the Chipola River, the biggest tributary of the Apalachicola (Tesar 2006; Tesar and Jones 2009). A conical burial mound with a Fort Walton (and a Middle Woodland) component was Chipola Cutoff (8Gu5, now washed away), near the upper confluence of the Apalachicola and Chipola rivers (Moore 1903; White 2011). Two mounds along the lower Chattahoochee are Old Rambo (9Se15) on the east bank in Georgia, possibly conical, tentatively assigned to Fort Walton (Moore 1907: 437; White 1981); and Seaborn (or Mound below Columbia or Omussee Creek mound, 1Ho27), a platform mound at the northernmost extent of Fort Walton culture, 240 km (150 navigation miles) upstream from the Gulf on the west bank in Alabama (Belovich et al. 1982; Blitz and Lorenz 2006; Moore 1907: 444–46). A possible additional Fort Walton mound (with Middle Woodland materials) at the now-drowned mouth of the Flint River was the Underwater Indian Mound (9Se27; White 1981). None of these mound centers has had enough research to permit the kind of interpretation possible for better-known Mississippian sites elsewhere in the Southeast. However, recent field, archival, and collections work has produced interesting new data and insights.

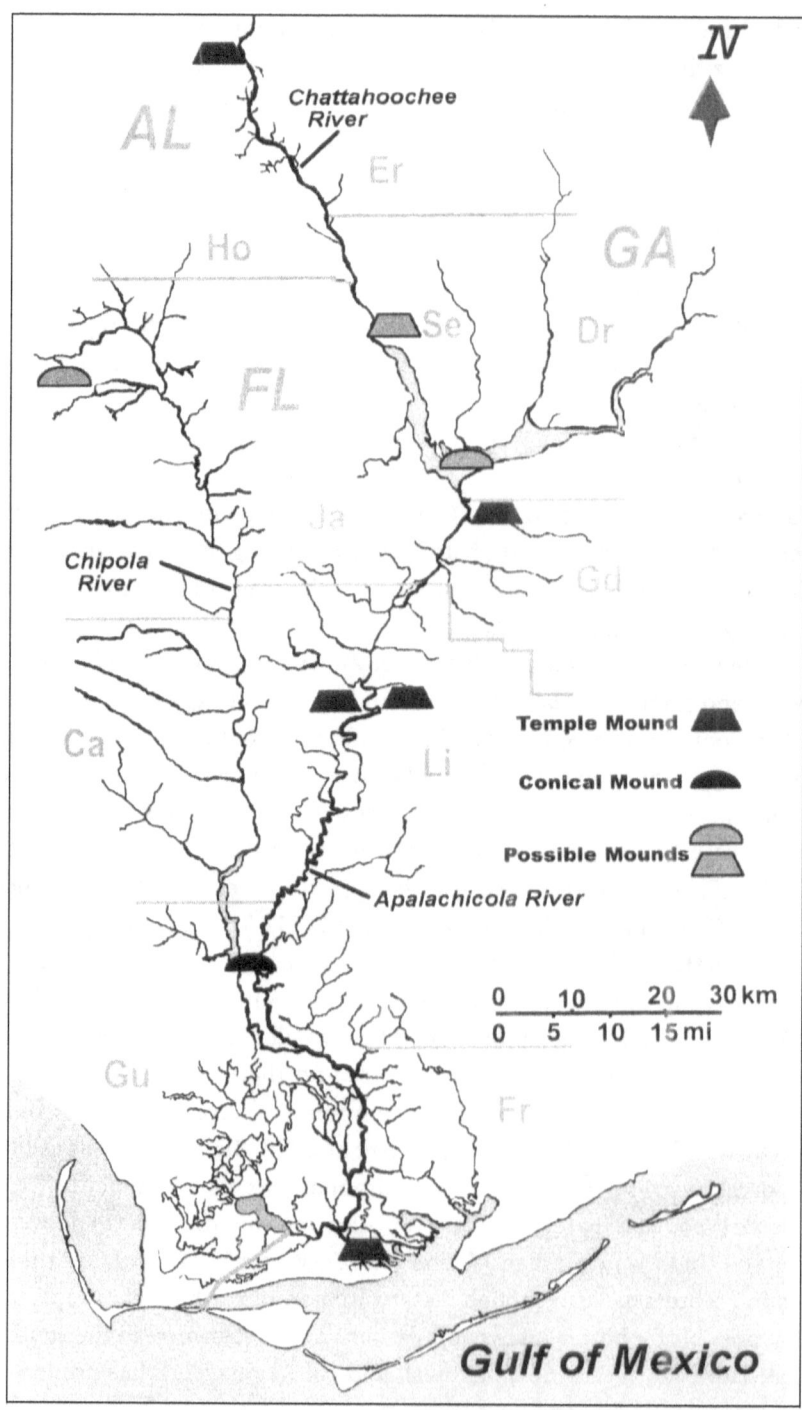

Figure 10.2. Schematic map of Fort Walton mound sites in the Apalachicola/lower Chattahoochee Valley.

Structural evidence, while limited, includes remains of at least one plaza, daub buildings, occasional wall trenches, postmolds, hearths, storage and refuse pits, and darkened or burned-clay areas that might be floors. At Waddell's Mill Pond, a rectangular postmold pattern (7×14 m) near the western edge of the platform mound was labeled a townhouse (Tesar and Jones 2009). Bullen (1958b) uncovered 30 postmolds at the Chattahoochee River #1 village site (famously J-5, now 8Ja8) but could not determine any structure outline; his map shows at least one straight line of posts and one or two short segments of possibly curved lines. Four pits filled with charred maize aligned in the cardinal directions in a square may relate to a structure (they may also represent ceremonial activity or just insect control). At the Curlee site, White (1982) documented an apparent wall trench and large postmolds in a possible arc. A wall-trench feature was excavated at the Cayson site (Brose 1975).

There is so far no unquestionable evidence for Mississippian-type palisades, embankments, or ditches at any Fort Walton sites. The only possibility is at Waddell's Mill Pond, where Gardner (1966) reported an artificial embankment he called a stockade ridge curving around the hilltop occupation (on top of the occupied caves). It was between a few centimeters and over a meter high and a meter or more wide. Of his four trenches across this ridge, only one exposed postmolds ($n=5$). Jones's 1973 investigations included one 2-×-2-m unit into the ridge, described only as "reveal[ing] part of the palisade wall" (Tesar and Jones 2009: 69). Because the site was occupied from the Early Archaic onward, with a large Middle Woodland component and two mounds, which cultural component this ridge/possible fence line is associated with is unclear. Furthermore, the mounds and heavy occupation areas are outside of it. If it really was a wall of posts in an earthen ridge, its hilltop location may mean it was not for defense but for delimitation or concealment of some ritual or elite area (Cobb 2003: 69). More evidence is needed before it can be called a "defensive palisade protecting [the] occupants" (Tesar and Jones 2006: 790).

Subsistence remains from several Fort Walton sites include maize, wild plants, and typical terrestrial and aquatic fauna. Coastal and estuarine sites are smaller but provide more evidence (because of the preservative properties of shell): mollusks, fish, and turtles, but so far no maize. Extremely curious is the fact that, for unknown reasons, Fort Walton sites produce far less chipped stone than do sites of earlier and later time periods in the same region and also less than in contemporaneous Mississippian settlements elsewhere in the Southeast. This has been known for a long while

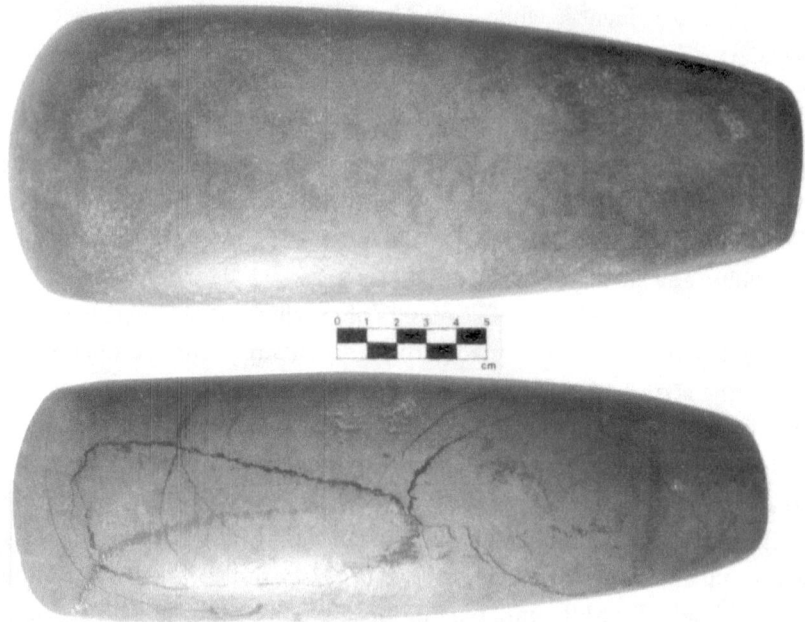

Figure 10.3. Celts from Fort Walton burials at the Corbin-Tucker site (in collection of landowner): *top*, from Test Unit E; *bottom*, from Test Unit G (note more serpentine raw material and vertical stain on butt from hafting).

(Bullen 1950: 124), though never explained. But imported greenstone is significant, mostly as celts (figure 10.3) with, near, and apart from burials. There are also marine shell artifacts, commonly of lightning whelk (*Busycon sinistrum*).

Burials occur in cemeteries, in temple mounds, in burial mounds, and isolated in middens. At least two platform mound centers (Pierce and Chattahoochee Landing) were built near existing Middle Woodland mounds, and there are several cases of Fort Walton burials intrusive into older Woodland mounds. Besides the examples noted above, the Middle Woodland burial mound at Richardson's Hammock (8Gu10) on St. Joseph Bay had at least one Fort Walton burial (White et al. 2002: 5). Fort Walton burials are primary and secondary, and grave goods are diverse but occasionally include Southeastern Ceremonial Complex (SECC; e.g., Galloway 1989; King 2007; Reilly and Garber 2007) items such as copper, a sherd engraved with a "sun circle" motif (White 1982: plate 18), and a Williams Island or "spaghetti-style" engraved shell gorget (Wheeler 2001; White 2011). Fort Walton burial practices are quite variable (Shahramfar 2008; Willey 1949a: 456–57), complicating efforts to extract social data (though mortuary practices throughout the greater Mississippian world do demonstrate a rich diversity; Sullivan and Mainfort 2010).

Lacking extensive mound-village excavations, we have few data on site layout and sociopolitical organization to compare with Mississippian elsewhere. Fort Walton societies may have been hierarchical and economically stratified, with elites and commoners, labor specialization, and hereditary leaders, or they may have been merely socially ranked, kin-based entities with differential treatment according to status, but no real economic inequality. So far we have no adequate means to evaluate either scenario (or numerous variations thereof), but this is the case for most Mississippi-period archaeological cultures (Butler and Welch 2006; Cobb 2003; Muller 1997). However, given the existence of hereditary chiefdoms in the Suwannee Valley, with far less material evidence but ethnographic documentation (see Worth, chapter 7, this volume), as well as in other places once considered to have more simply organized societies (such as Amazonia; Heckenberger 2005: 325), it is probably safe to say that Fort Walton societies were complex and economically stratified to some degree. As Blitz (2010: 3) has noted, all-inclusive, broad definitions of what is Mississippian, even when widely accepted, do not work when applied in many specific regions in different environments that shared some but not all of the same cultural practices.

We do have a growing database of Apalachicola Valley radiocarbon dates associated with diagnostic ceramics (Marrinan and White 2007: table 2), showing Fort Walton emerging soon after A.D. 900 and continuing, at least in some places, well into postcontact times, perhaps as late as 1700. We think the nature of Fort Walton sociopolitical systems in individual societies or at specific sites probably changed a lot through time. Whether they conformed to models of political cycling (Anderson 1994, 1996a); fusion-fission (Blitz 1999; Blitz and Lorenz 2006); growth and dominance through warfare, migration, and/or ideological power (O'Brien 2009; Pauketat 2007); or other processes of change, growth, and/or decline is still far from being demonstrated archaeologically.

Ceramics

Assemblage Composition

Most diagnostic Fort Walton vessel forms and types are easily recognizable as classical Mississippian styles (figures 10.4–10.8). Lake Jackson Plain/Incised (figure 10.6) is similar to Mississippi Plain jars. Cool Branch

Figure 10.4. Fort Walton ceramic types (with catalog numbers): *a–c*, Marsh Island Incised rims: *a*, with loop handle, rim point, grit temper (Feat. 07-4 at Yon, 8Li2-07-284); *b*, with grit and grog temper (Curlee site Perry collection MI33); *c*, with broken lug, grog temper (Curlee site Perry collection MI35); *d*, body of grit- and grog-tempered Point Washington Incised bowl or bottle (burial at Corbin-Tucker site, 8Ca142-91, 244, 315, 316); *e–g*, Cool Branch Incised rims (all Curlee site Perry collection): *e*, with strap handle, grog temper, double-arc punctations (CB7); *f*, with notched strap handle, "eyelash" punctations (short incisions), grit and grog temper (CB3); *g*, with B-lug, ticks, 3 incisions on neck, double arc incisions, grit and grog temper (CB6).

Incised jars with incised arcs on the body and often punctations (like eyelashes) over them (figure 10.4e–g) are sand-/grit-/grog-tempered versions of Moundville or Dallas Incised. (Cool Branch Incised may have originated outside the Fort Walton area, farther up the Chattahoochee [Du Vernay 2011].) Fort Walton Incised is more distinctive, with incisions and punctations on typical Mississippian carinated bowls (figure 10.5 bottom, figure 10.8a–d), but also other shapes. The most unusual form in this type is the six-pointed open bowl (figure 10.5 top, figure 10.8i), which may be exclusive to Fort Walton (though it occurs in shell-tempered form in Pensacola ceramics to the west [Harris, chapter 11, this volume]). Other important types are Point Washington Incised (figure 10.4d), with scrolls or other incisions but no punctations, and Marsh Island Incised (figure 10.4a–c), with

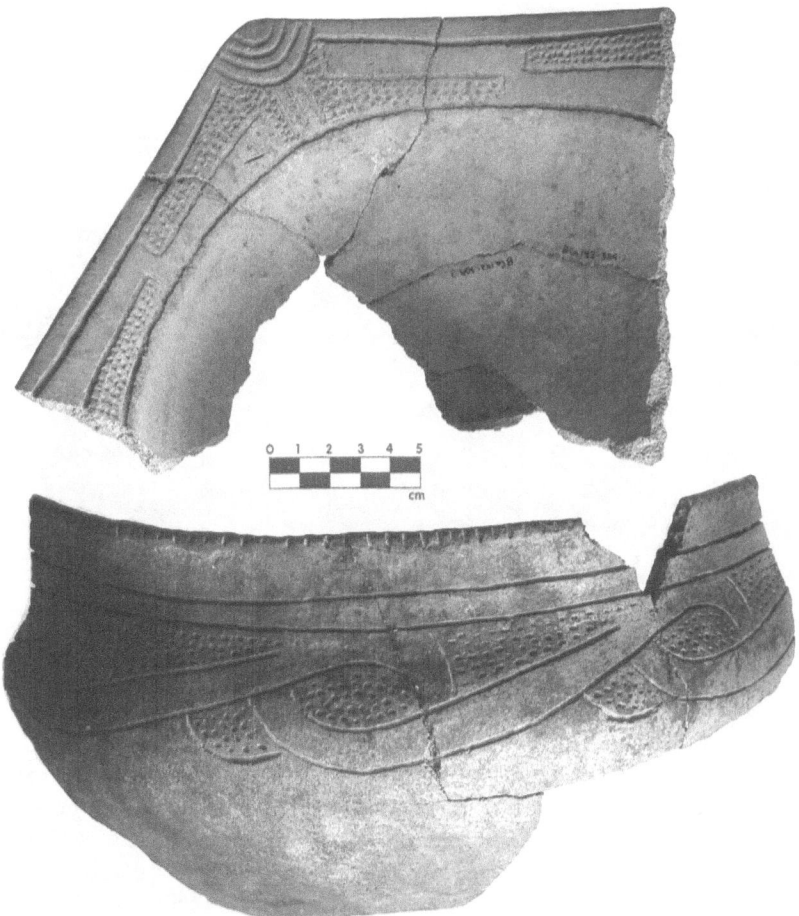

Figure 10.5. Fort Walton Incised partial vessels: *top*, six-pointed open bowl (grit temper, ticked on exterior lip) from burial at Corbin-Tucker site (cat. no. 8Ca142-304); *bottom*, casuela bowl (grit temper, ticked lip) from Perry collection, Curlee site (FW41).

parallel diagonal incised lines on the vessel neck only. In early Fort Walton, check-stamped pottery is abundant, holding over from Late Woodland (late Weeden Island) times.

Fort Walton pottery is predominantly tempered with grit, with lesser amounts of sand and/or grog (crushed hardened or fired clay). Shell-tempered sherds are rare, typically only about 2 to 5 percent of an assemblage, with more of them earlier than later in time. Willey's (1949a) original typology works well for sorting sherds in the lab, unlike later revisions using

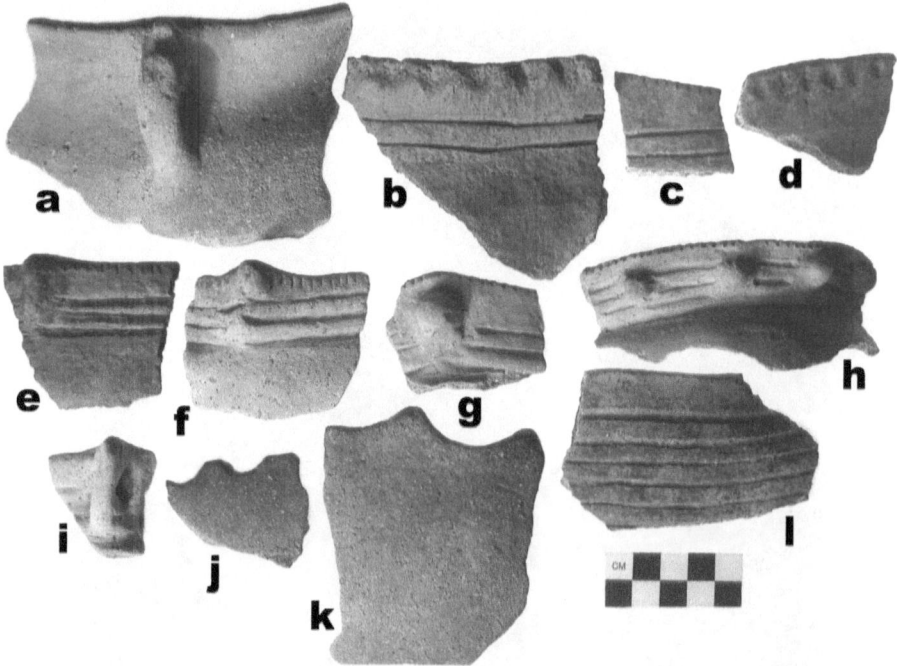

Figure 10.6. Lake Jackson rims showing attributes, all from Curlee site Perry collection: *a*, strap handle with nodes, grog temper (LJ100); *b*, notched, 2 incisions, grit temper (LJ16); *c*, ticked, 3 incisions, grit temper (LJ285); *d*, notched, grit and grog temper (LJ31); *e*, D-lug, ticks, 3 incisions, grit and grog temper (LJ388); *f*, B-lug, ticks, 3 incisions, grit and grog temper (LJ468); *g*, node, ticks, 3 incisions, slight rim point, grit temper (LJ462); *h*, many nodes, ticks, 4 incisions, grit and grog temper (LJ442); *i*, loop handle, rim point, 3 incisions, grit and grog temper (LJ102); *j*, scalloped, grog temper (LJ616); *k*, scalloped, grit and grog temper (LJ612); *l*, 5 incisions, grit temper (LJ60).

subtypes (Bullen 1958b; Griffin 1950) or the type-variety system (Scarry 1985), which have countless problems (Blitz and Lorenz 2006: 237; Marrinan and White 2007; Tesar and Jones 2006; White 1982: 85). A sorting guide developed out of Willey's typology and including later-named types (e.g., Cool Branch Incised [Sears 1967]) has been used in our labs and elsewhere in the panhandle for more than 20 years (White 2009). For sherds not fitting clearly into named types, we use generic terms based on temper, surface treatment, and other less-diagnostic attributes, rather than importing inappropriate type names from other regions. Fort Walton assemblages include some cob-marked, red-painted, black-painted, and engraved ceramics made on the typical local paste.

Yuellig (2007) documented the Perry collection, over 10,300 sherds obtained by a collector from the Curlee site (White 1982). This site was a large Fort Walton village and cemetery (or less likely, a mound) with high-status grave goods, right on the riverbank, now all washed away after construction of a dam just below the Flint-Chattahoochee confluence in 1950. The ceramics appeared to date to early Fort Walton because of the high frequency of check-stamped sherds. Testing had uncovered a deeply buried, earlier dark midden zone, up to a meter thick, under a thinner (20 cm thick), later midden zone. The two midden strata were separated by pale, mostly culturally sterile sand. The one radiocarbon date, from the top of the earlier midden, originally reported as A.D. 1190 (White 1982: 63), is now calibrated at closer to 1250 (table 10.1). Maize cobs indicated an agricultural village; the site is directly across the river from the Chattahoochee Landing temple mound.

The Perry materials were all from the eroding riverbank; we assume the majority would have been from the earlier, thicker midden. The Perry collection type frequencies correspond well with those from excavated levels from this earlier midden (though surface collections may be biased in favor of decorated sherds). Diagnostic types such as Fort Walton Incised and Lake Jackson (Plain and Incised) constitute over 10 percent of the collection. Check-stamped sherds make up about 20 percent, and the nearly 6,800 plain sherds are 66 percent by count and 59 percent by weight (Yuellig 2007: table 2).

What we now call the ceramic type Lake Jackson has been traditionally divided into Lake Jackson Plain and Lake Jackson Incised, recognizable only from rim sherds, as the rest of the vessel is plain-surfaced. The original definitions of the two types overlap (Sears 1967: 37; Willey 1949a: 458–60, plate 44). Plain has one horizontal incision below the rim or no incision, and Incised has one, two, or more incisions, while the rest of the vessel attributes, including rim treatments, are the same. We continue (Yuellig 2007) the unpublished work of the late B. Calvin Jones of the Florida Division of Historical Resources, who noted individual rim treatments for Lake Jackson sherds (and 20 years ago gave White copies of his sketches). Rims (figure 10.6) may be plain, ticked (tiny incised lines or fingernail punctations on the lip edge), notched or pinched, scalloped (rare), or incised with short, wide, vertical, parallel lines; they may also have handles, lugs (like

Table 10.1. Details of Fort Walton radiocarbon dates discussed in this chapter

Site	Lab #	Material	Measured Radiocarbon Age	$^{13}C/^{12}C$ Ratio	Conventional Radiocarbon Age	Calibrated Date Range A.D. (1 sigma)	Calibrated Date Range A.D. (2 sigma)	Intercept Date A.D.	Reference
Curlee, 8Ja7	DIC 1048	Charcoal from TU4-6S, L2-3, -70-80 cm, stratum IIId	760±50	*	*	1224-1280	1168-1380	*	White 1982: 63; Yuellig 2007
Yon, 8Li2	Beta 91164	Charcoal next to mound burial	1020±60	-26.8	990±60	1000-1055; 1090-1150	970-1195	1025	White 1996; Du Vernay 2011
	Beta 91165	More charcoal next to mound burial	970±50	-27.1	930±50	1030-1180	1010-1225	1055; 1090; 1150	
	Beta 91844	Charcoal from earliest mound construction	870±50	-28.1	820±50	1195-1270	1065-1075; 1155-1285	1235	
	Beta 110362	Charcoal from TU D Feature 17	870±60	-29.6	800±60	1205-1280	1065-1075; 1155-1295	1250	
	Beta 235137	Charcoal from TU I Feature 07-4	850±40	-24.4	860±40	1160-1220	1040-1100; 1120-1260	1200	

	Beta 239749	Charcoal from TU E L7, with Lamar ceramics only	140±40	-25.5	130±40	1680–1770; 1800–1890; 1910–1940; 1950–1950	1660–1960	1690; 1730; 1810; 1920; 1950	
Corbin-Tucker, 8Ca142	Beta 30633	Pine charcoal from Stratum II of Feature 1	1080±90	-25	1080±90	880–1030	770–1170	990	White 1994; Marsh 2006
	Beta 68757	Pine charcoal from Stratum I of Feature 1	1060±80	-25	1060±80	900–1030	800–1170	1000	
	Beta 40905	Charcoal near burials, under copper disk	1840±110	-25	1840±110	70–340	50–430	210	
	Beta 213055	Bone, burial E1(?)	70±40	-18.3	180±40	1660–1680; 1730–1810; 1910–1950	1650–1710; 1720–1880; 1930–1950	1670; 1770; 1800; 1940; 1950	
	Beta 217850	Bone, burial G4	230±40	-16.1	380±40	1450–1520; 1590–1620	1440–1640	1480	
Pierce, 8Fr14	Beta 221908	Charcoal, core 1, -100 cm, 200 m SE of platform mound	780±40	-27.1	750±40	1260–1290	1220–1300	1270	White 2007; USF archaeology lab

(continued)

Table 10.1—Continued

Site	Lab #	Material	Measured Radiocarbon Age	$^{13}C/^{12}C$ Ratio	Conventional Radiocarbon Age	Calibrated Date Range A.D. (1 sigma)	Calibrated Date Range A.D. (2 sigma)	Intercept Date A.D.	Reference
Lighthouse Bayou, 8Gu114	Beta 165601	Shell Pile 2, Lamar ceramics only	120±50	-25.0	120±50	1680–1770; 1800–1940; 1950–1950	1660–1950	1690; 1730; 1810; 1920; 1950	White 2005
	Beta 193568	Shell Pile 3 (near Pile 2), Lamar ceramics only	150±50	-26.4	120±50	1680–1770; 1800–1940; 1950–1950	1660–1950	1690; 1730; 1810; 1920; 1950	
	Beta 177996	Shell Pile 12, Fort Walton ceramics	380±60	-25.0	380±60	1440–1530; 1560–1630	1420–1650	1480	

Note: Asterisk (*) marks unreported data.

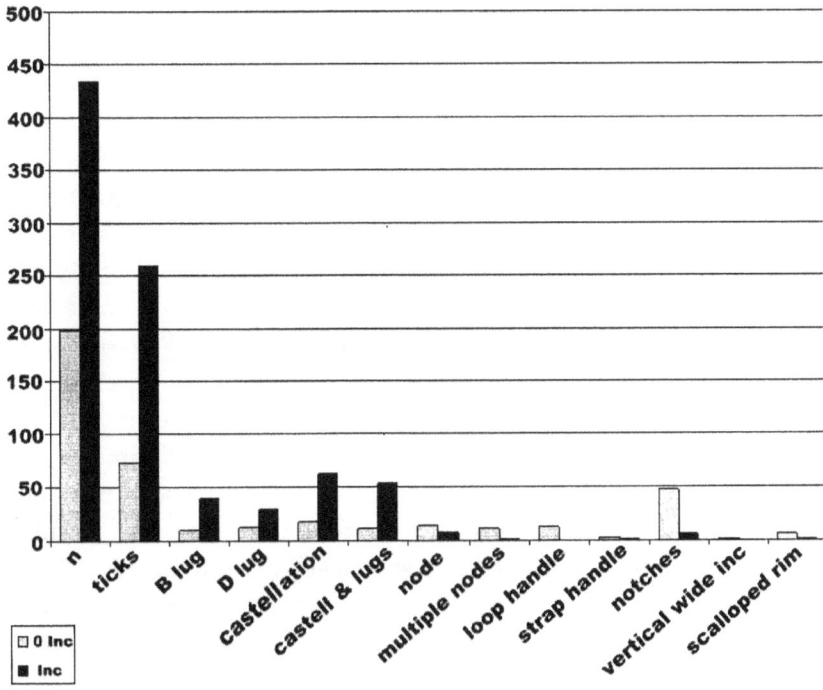

Figure 10.7. Frequencies of the different Lake Jackson rim attributes, also comparing sherds with incisions and no incisions Perry collection, Curlee site.

filled-in small handles in D or B shapes), nodes (rounded protrusions lower down the neck), and/or castellations (rim points). Such rim treatments are similar to those seen on the basic (and shell-tempered) Mississippian jar forms (e.g., Phillips et al. 1951).

Data on rim attributes of 631 Lake Jackson sherds in the Perry collection (figure 10.7) demonstrate that there were more jars with incisions below the rim than no incisions, and more ticks and lugs than other attributes such as handles or notches. Notched rims most often had no incisions below the lip, as did the scalloped rims and those with nodes or handles. The same rim treatments are seen on the types Marsh Island Incised and Cool Branch Incised (Sears 1967: 32, 37). What significance these attribute frequencies and co-occurrences may have is still unknown, but at least the quantification makes possible real comparison with assemblages at other sites. Further, we demonstrate the ambiguity and lack of utility in separating Lake Jackson into more than one type.

Temper

Grit is the predominant temper that distinguishes Fort Walton ceramics (Willey 1949a: 458), but there are lesser amounts of sand and grog and combinations of tempers. Grit temper is distinguishable from sand in that the quartz particles are bigger and more angular, because they are from crushed rock. Grit is white, clear, brown, or a distinctive red. Admittedly, distinguishing between big sand grains and grit particles can be difficult (e.g., Blitz and Lorenz 2006: 227), because they may appear to be on a size continuum. Sand is usually smaller and smoother as a result of its water travel as alluvium. Other workers have reinterpreted the characterization of typical Fort Walton ceramic pastes. In a study of ceramics from a mound in south peninsular Florida dating to the Safety Harbor period (see Mitchem 1989 and chapter 8, this volume), Cordell (2005) never mentions grit temper. She defines Lake Jackson paste as sherd tempered, meaning tempered with clay bits made by crushing old potsherds, distinguishable probably by the straight edges of the vessel surface remaining on the temper particles. There are some important issues here, the first being how to tell most sherd particles, which would not manifest straight edges, from other grog particles. Second, Lake Jackson paste has long been recognized as having a lot of grit temper as well (e.g., Willey 1949a: 458–59). The third issue is whether Fort Walton ceramics in the Tallahassee region, home of the Lake Jackson site, actually have a much higher instance of grog temper (and see Marrinan, chapter 9, this volume), and whether it can be quantified. Hardly any of the literature on Fort Walton sites reports temper in detail, but Griffin (1950: 104) noted that although the "vast majority of the sherds" he recovered from the Lake Jackson site had coarse grit, there was also some sand tempering.

In the Apalachicola Valley, temper seems to be whatever is handy, except for shell. The sherds of a Point Washington Incised vessel shown in figure 10.4d demonstrate this. They clearly fit together but must have had different life histories after the pot broke. The upper-left sherd is more worn and its grog temper more exposed, while the lower-right sherd looks sand tempered and the lower-left looks grit tempered, with an unsmoothed coil mark on the inside. Temper is thus not spread evenly throughout. If temper indicates even the least bit of meaningful tradition, it may be due to geography, with quartzite cobbles available on the Chattahoochee-Apalachicola river system to grind up for grit and perhaps fewer such rocks in the Tallahassee Red Hills. But none of this explains the reluctance of these

Mississippi-period potters to use crushed shell temper as most of their contemporaries across the Southeast were doing.

There is potential for great confusion if we do not describe temper clearly. The type definitions often depend upon the presence of a specified paste, and then the types are used as proxies for some phase or other tradition, at which point the discussion gets many degrees removed from the original data. The shorthand of "phases" and other derived terms may mask real differences or similarities among assemblages. We must go back to the original data and agree on terminology; ceramic paste is a good place to start.

Occasionally Fort Walton ceramics have crushed limestone temper, especially in the lowest portion of the Chattahoochee Valley, including the upper Chipola, where there are chert and limestone outcrops and caves (Blitz and Lorenz 2006: 227; Bullen 1949b; Gardner 1966; White 1981). A little limestone-tempered pottery also appears in the shell middens of the lower valley (White 1994). Also important is the distinctive micaceous paste of Apalachicola–lower Chattahoochee basin ceramics (of all time periods); glittery mica flecks are natural in the region's soils.

Yuellig (2007: table 3) tabulated ceramic tempers in the Perry collection. On the basis of that work, we quantify temper in table 10.2 for all 1,199 specimens of the two most diagnostic types, Fort Walton Incised (rim and body sherds) and Lake Jackson (by definition, only rims). Grit is the most common at over 70 percent. About 10 percent is grog tempered, 4 percent sand tempered, and then there are several temper combinations. Six sherds did have a tiny amount of shell in with the grit (not enough to classify them as shell tempered), and one had both shell and limestone and thus was listed as Lake Jackson instead of Pensacola ware. Of the nearly 7,000 plain sherds, 81 percent have grit temper; 7 percent, sand temper; 3 percent, grog temper; and 6 percent, combinations of two or three of these. Shell-tempered plain pottery, with or without other tempers, made up 3.4 percent; whether it was produced locally is unknown. Shell-tempered sherds were classified as either Pensacola Incised (if they had incisions or punctations) or shell-tempered plain (rather than distinguish between Pensacola Plain and any other of the many shell-tempered Mississippian plain types). With all the cautions necessary in basing interpretations upon a surface collection, long experience in this region leads us to see these relative frequencies of temper as typical in a Fort Walton assemblage.

Prehistoric people in the Apalachicola Valley used grit, sand, and grog

Table 10.2. Temper in two diagnostic Fort Walton ceramic types in the Perry collection, Curlee site (8Ja7)

Ceramic Type	Grit		Grog		Grit & Grog		Sand		Grit & Sand		Grog & Sand		Grit & Shell		Shell & Limestone		Total	
	N	%	N	%	N	%	N	%	N	%	N	%	N	%	N	%	N	%
Fort Walton Incised	423	74.5	59	10.4	38	6.7	23	4.0	15	2.6	6	1.1	4	0.7	0	0	568	100
Lake Jackson	453	71.8	60	9.5	61	9.7	28	4.4	20	3.2	6	1.0	2	0.3	1	0.2	631	100
Totals	876	73.1	119	9.9	99	8.2	51	4.2	35	2.9	12	0.6	6	0.5	1	0.1	1,199	100

tempers in their ceramics from Early Woodland onward. Retention of the traditional and, by Fort Walton times, distinctive local tempers instead of changing to the Mississippian crushed shell may reflect a strong Woodland pottery-making practice that smoothly transformed in place into Fort Walton. Even the incised/punctated Fort Walton designs (such as scrolls) are often similar to those on Woodland types. The lack of shell tempering is very interesting because there was certainly no lack of shell—marine, freshwater, or even fossil shell on sandbars along the river and in the subsoil. Perhaps there was a deliberate goal demonstrated in everyday craft production to maintain some kind of strong regional tradition, social memory, or identity within the Mississippian world. The Pensacola series of shell-tempered Mississippian ceramics, sometimes with Fort Walton elements (such as incised-punctated designs or the six-pointed bowls), centers on Pensacola and Mobile bays, 200–300 km west of the Fort Walton region (see Harris, chapter 11, this volume). The area in between, around Choctawhatchee Bay, has an interesting blend of both Pensacola and Fort Walton ceramics that might be expected in a border area.

Refining Chronology

Within the type Fort Walton Incised, Yuellig (2007) identified in the Perry collection nine variations in the incised designs (beyond the distinctive six-pointed bowl design), mostly of the classic running scroll or guilloche pattern. These were named curvilinear running scroll, rectilinear running scroll, stylized curvilinear running scroll, stylized rectilinear running scroll, unidentifiable scroll, unusual square pattern, unusual unknown pattern, and other unusual variations (figure 10.8). Reexamining all the sherds in the excavated ceramic assemblage at the Curlee site (White 1982b), she found that earlier levels in the lower midden contained only four of the nine variations, but later levels in the lower midden and the entire upper midden stratum had seven variations. This possible increase in ceramic design diversity through time is easily testable in future work at other sites.

Within the Perry collection and assemblages from other sites, check-stamped pottery has not yet been thoroughly investigated. We use the generic name because, though it is probably Wakulla Check Stamped holding over from late Weeden Island times, it has no features distinguishing it from several other check-stamped types in this region that occur in different time periods (Marrinan and White 2007: 295–96). This is true for check-stamped ceramics in neighboring regions as well (e.g., Brown

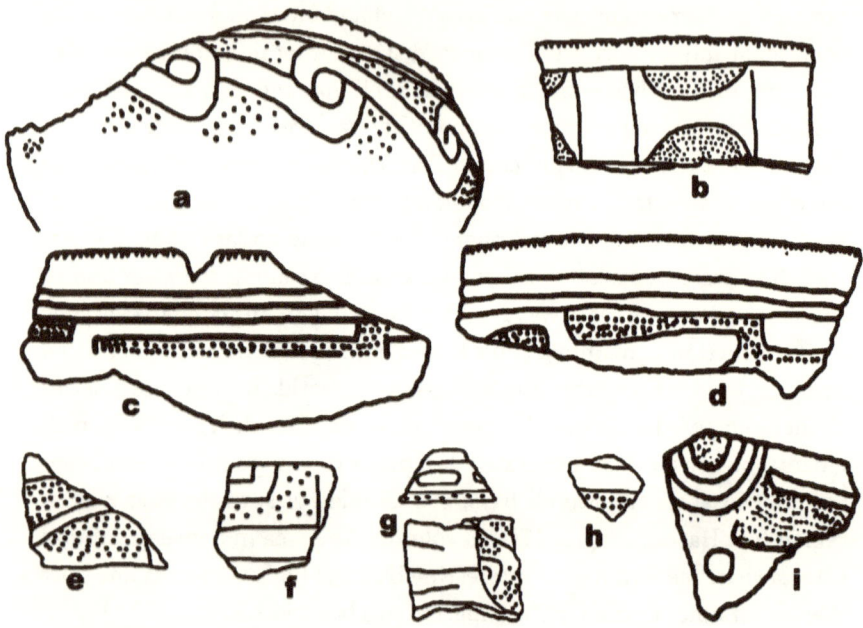

Figure 10.8. Fort Walton Incised design styles classified by Yuellig (2007): *a*, curvilinear running scroll; *b*, stylized rectilinear running scroll; *c*, rectilinear running scroll; *d*, stylized curvilinear running scroll; *e*, unidentifiable scroll; *f*, unusual square pattern; *g*, unusual unknown pattern (two); *h*, unidentifiable; *i*, rim point from six-pointed bowl. All are rims except *e*, *f*, lower *g*, and *h*.

2009). A small study (Rosenthal 2010) comparing Fort Walton check-stamped sherds from the Perry collection with others from late Weeden Island and Deptford sites in this valley found that those of Fort Walton age had slightly more rectangular checks, more grit temper, and more frequent slight linearity in the checkerboard pattern (the type Deptford Linear Check Stamped was not included in the study, only standard check-stamped from a dated Deptford component); the total sample size was under 200 sherds and may reflect site-specific idiosyncrasy.

Willey (1949a: 458) recognized long ago that check-stamped ceramics carry over from late Weeden Island into Fort Walton. They constitute perhaps half of a typical late Weeden Island assemblage, and their numbers diminish to something around 20 percent in early Fort Walton. By the time of the latest component at the Curlee site (the upper midden), they constituted 7 percent of the Fort Walton assemblage (White 1982). By later Fort Walton times, this type disappeared. Though Willey thought it served as the basis for Leon (Lamar) Check Stamped, this is probably not the case, as we now think Lamar is something intrusive and much later in the Apalachicola Valley. As detailed below, new analyses from the Yon and Corbin-Tucker sites show a localized distribution of check-stamped pottery in domestic areas, suggesting that it may be functionally as well as temporally distinct within Fort Walton assemblages.

A distinguishing characteristic indicating change through time within Fort Walton is this eventual disappearance of check-stamped pottery. Besides the possible increase through time in design variation on Fort Walton Incised vessels, we suggest a few other temporal markers. Cob-marked pottery appears very early. The six-pointed bowl form may appear by middle Fort Walton and last very late. The type Marsh Island Incised is now solidly dated to at least early to middle Fort Walton, around A.D. 1200 (see discussion below). At some point very late in or more probably after the Fort Walton ceramic sequence, complicated-stamped and other very different ceramics of the Lamar complex from Georgia begin to appear (Willey 1949a: 485–86). These are also not shell tempered, possibly indicating some important relationship within the larger Mississippian world. When or why Lamar ceramics first show up in the Apalachicola Valley has been unknown, though they are associated with the Mission period (seventeenth century) in Tallahassee, where they are called Jefferson ware (Willey 1949a: 488–93). Our new work (detailed below) shows that Lamar is later than, or possibly contemporaneous with but separate from, contact/Mission-period Fort Walton.

Pierce Mounds

Pierce (8Fr14; Moore 1902: 217–29), at the river mouth, commanded north–south river traffic and east–west travel along the Gulf and bays. It is a continuous *Rangia* and oyster shell midden with at least nine mounds that together made up a major center from Early Woodland onward. The Fort Walton portion surrounds the small flat-topped mound (of shell) on the east side. The Fort Walton artifact assemblage is mostly from disturbed surfaces; ceramic types are typical Fort Walton diagnostics. Focused research at Pierce has become possible only after recent clearing for planned development. The topographic map seemed to show several mounds arranged in an oval with a plaza in the middle. A core outside this oval, 200 m southeast of the platform mound, revealed a dark, meter-thick Fort Walton midden dated to about A.D. 1270 (table 10.1). Testing in 2007 in the middle of this possible plaza recovered no evidence of anything prehistoric.

We also tested the lower slope of one low, flat-topped rise that had only modern glass on top and nothing below, so it is still not demonstrated to be an aboriginal mound. Perhaps the Fort Walton component is smaller than originally thought, and the site was more important as a regional capital during the Middle Woodland. But Fort Walton people deliberately utilized what had been an earlier sacred center.

Pierce and Chattahoochee Landing are the only two multiple-mound Fort Walton centers in this valley. Cayson has a large temple mound and a probable small (burial?) mound; Waddell's Mill Pond has a platform and a conical (probably Woodland) mound, and the rest are single-mound sites. Both Pierce and Chattahoochee Landing have mounds dating one or two millennia before Fort Walton, but each clearly has at least one temple mound and a Fort Walton village. Furthermore, Pierce sits at an important geographic location at the bottom of the river, and Chattahoochee Landing is at the top of the Apalachicola, right below the Chattahoochee-Flint confluence. These two sites were long-standing mound complexes when Fort Walton people first used them. They are shown with an individual temple-mound symbol on figure 10.2 because we have not yet established how many of the other mounds date to Fort Walton.

If Fort Walton people built their own mound and/or village sites near Woodland mound centers and also used Woodland mounds for their own later burials, they may have been paying homage to the distinctive heritage of their Woodland ancestors while simultaneously establishing new Mississippian traditions. They may have used the earlier mounds as foundations for platform mounds too; there is evidence of this farther up the lower Chattahoochee beyond the Fort Walton area (Blitz and Lorenz 2006: 94–95) and elsewhere in the Southeast (e.g., Weinstein 2006: 148, 158). Woodland-period flat-topped platform mounds are now also known in small numbers throughout the Southeast (e.g., Mainfort 1988), including Florida (Milanich et al. 1984). Reuse and rebuilding of them by Mississippi-period peoples has been documented (Blitz and Lorenz 2006: 94); a possible example of this in the Fort Walton region is at Waddell's Mill Pond (Jones and Tesar 2006).

Corbin-Tucker Site

Corbin-Tucker (8Ca142) is a village and cemetery in the middle Apalachicola Valley recorded in the 1980s when plowing for pine plantation unearthed Fort Walton pottery. Testing in 1988 uncovered a habitation area on the south (downstream) side and a cemetery (White 1994). A refuse pit in the domestic area produced the only preserved fauna: freshwater mollusks, terrestrial snails, gar and other fish, turtle, and raccoon and other mammals. Ethnobotanical specimens from this feature consisted of pine, oak, unidentifiable woods, acorn and hickory nutshell, and seed fragments including a possible wax myrtle seed. Other botanical remains from the site were additional wood fragments, including *Prunus* (plum/cherry) in both the domestic and cemetery areas. Two charcoal samples from the refuse pit dated to about cal A.D. 990–1000 (table 10.1), and it contained check-stamped and plain ceramics. The village area around this feature constituted the southern two-thirds of the site and produced check-stamped and plain ceramics and a few diagnostics: a Lake Jackson and a shell-tempered plain sherd, plus a few indeterminate incised and punctated sherds. Since there were no recognizable sherds of any late Weeden Island types indicating a Late Woodland presence, the assemblage is considered early Fort Walton, not inconsistent with the date. The very few pieces of lithic debitage recovered from the whole site (10 flakes in total from five excavated units) also suggest that it is culturally Fort Walton, because late Weeden Island sites have much larger lithic assemblages.

At the north end of the site, 50 m from the dated feature, is the cemetery with elite burials. Remains exposed in a 1-×-1-m test unit (TU E) included a woman's skull with a copper disk (figure 10.9 top) on the forehead and a large greenstone celt (figure 10.3 top) under the chin (Marrinan and White 2007: fig. 8), as well as many long bone fragments and sets of teeth. Additional brief testing was conducted here in 1990 to obtain material for dating, because the ceramics interred with the dead were all Fort Walton (figures 10.4d, 10.5 top) but somewhat different from those in the occupation area. More burials were encountered (figure 10.10) in a 1-×-2-m unit (TU G), including skulls, long bones, teeth, another celt (figure 10.3, bottom), a *Busycon* shell cup and other marine shell artifacts, and a ceramic mushroom-shaped object. An additional copper disk came from the edge of the original unit; it was of wood with a thin copper cover and a central boss (figure 10.9 bottom). Charcoal from a few centimeters below this disk was radiocarbon-dated to cal A.D. 210 (table 10.1), obviously not a Fort Walton date and probably erroneous, because the site produced no Woodland material at all.

Preservation conditions were awful; most of the individuals buried were represented only by teeth and bone fragments, not enough to tell whether some were just trophy heads, whether all were bundles, or whether the

Figure 10.9. Copper disks from the Corbin-Tucker site cemetery (in collection of landowner).

smaller bones simply decayed. The remains were jumbled together such that it is impossible (without massive amounts of DNA analysis, perhaps) in many cases to tell which bones and teeth go together. There were no burial pits, just churned-up soil, evidence of many earlier and later interments. Study of the human remains by honors student Elan Marsh (2006) included a University of South Florida (USF) Undergraduate Research grant for AMS dates. With forensic anthropologist Erin Kimmerle and her students assisting, we identified between 10 and 19 individuals within the total three square meters of cemetery exposed.

Fort Walton Culture in the Apalachicola Valley, Northwest Florida · 255

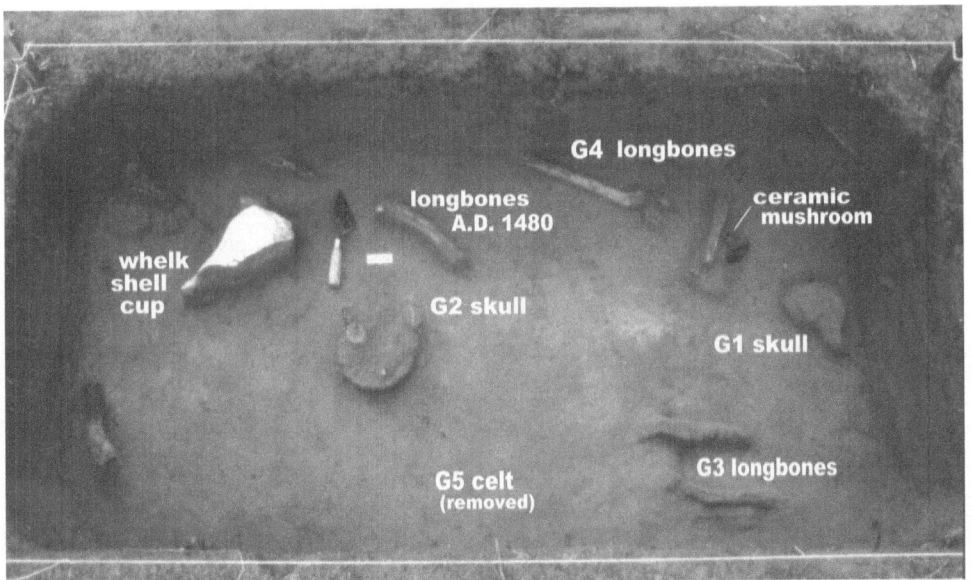

Figure 10.10. Test Unit G at the Corbin-Tucker site, showing elite burials of at least five individuals (celt shown in figure 10.3 [lower] had been removed at time of photo).

Long bone fragments from Individual G4, near the ceramic "mushroom," were dated to cal A.D. 1480 (table 10.1), late Fort Walton. Individual E1 was the first uncovered, the woman lying on her right side facing north, with the celt and the copper disk. Teeth of at least four other individuals, some articulated, lay around her, including near her skull a canine from a child between 3 and 10 years old. Bone fragments not far from her skull, thought to be from her legs (Marrinan and White 2007: 307) but possibly from another person (E6 or someone else), were dated to between A.D. 1670 and 1770 (table 10.1, ruling out the obviously too recent intercepts), much later than the usual Fort Walton, in historic Mission or post-Mission times. Though the earlier date has a two sigma range that includes early historic time, it does not overlap with this later date. No historic materials came from this cemetery, but the first copper disk, embossed with a raised center and small bumps around the circumference (figure 10.9 top), could be an early historic style (White 1994: 190). If this date is correct, the cemetery was apparently so important to late prehistoric Fort Walton people that their descendants continued to use it for a couple centuries well after contact, continuing maintenance of their distinctive heritage.

The ceramic assemblage from the cemetery gives a few clues. There is no Lamar; the types (Fort Walton Incised, Lake Jackson, Cool Branch Incised,

Point Washington Incised, and a few shell-tempered sherds) are similar to those at sites dating hundreds of years earlier within Fort Walton. Among the Fort Walton Incised sherds were at least two and possibly three six-pointed open bowls (figure 10.5 top), suggesting a late date and mortuary association for this vessel form. Check-stamped sherds were few (only five) and only from the surface and uppermost levels, not associated with any burials. Combined with the dates, the fact that the domestic area at Corbin-Tucker had different ceramics from those of the cemetery area suggests that it could be an earlier component or that the domestic assemblage was functionally different from the ritual materials in the cemetery. Alternatively, the ceramics could indicate that what had been a village very early in Fort Walton had changed over the (up to six) centuries to become an important (family?) burial place, a tradition that continued even while the rest of the culture was coming to an end. Perhaps the tradition was all the stronger because of the movement of new peoples and influences into the valley after contact and depopulation.

Yon Mound and Village

Upstream from Corbin-Tucker in the middle valley, Yon (8Li2) is a single mound and village site on the east bank. Recorded by Moore (1903), it has been sporadically investigated since (Brose 1975; Scarry 1984; White 1996). In 1995, 2000, and 2007, USF conducted test excavations, opening 10 units and over 100 cores (figure 10.11). The mountain of materials and data recovered (Du Vernay 2011) provide new information on occupational history, mound construction and use, and ceramic stratigraphy. Habitation was dense all around the platform mound and concentrated close to the river. Midden soils and artifacts did not occur beyond 100 m south or 200 m east or west of the mound. Village evidence includes daub, bone tools, a celt fragment and greenstone flakes, a few lithic tools and debitage, typical Fort Walton ceramics, and some pit and postmold features. A few late Weeden Island sherds (Keith Incised, Tucker Ridge Pinched) were recovered from TU D, west of the mound. Radiocarbon dates on charcoal from deep in this unit, as well as from a domestic feature in TU I on the east side of the mound, indicate occupation between cal A.D. 1200 and 1250 (table 10.1). A later Lamar component (described below) is present on and east of the mound.

The dated Feature 2007-4 provided valuable subsistence information. It was a large garbage pit with abundant pottery, antler, bone, shell,

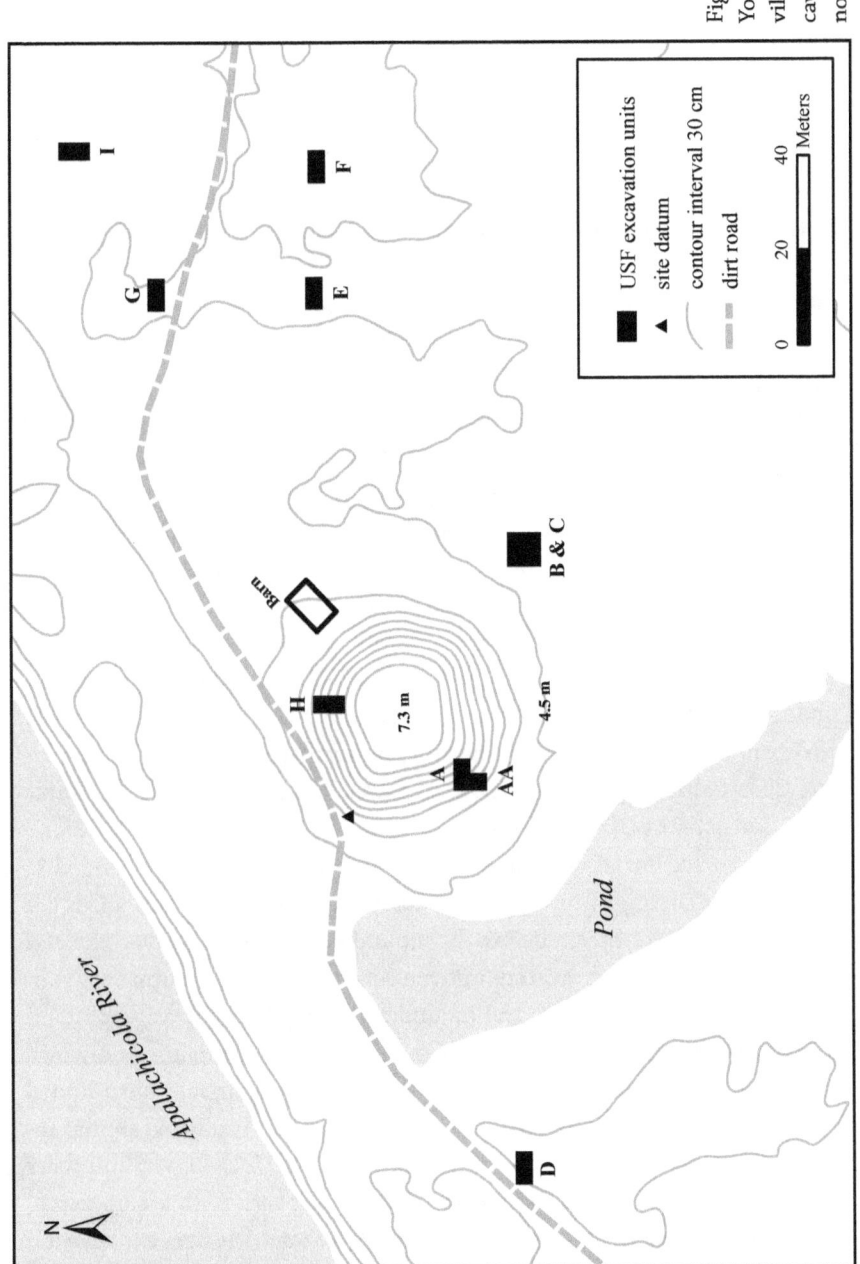

Figure 10.11. Yon mound and village site (excavation units not to scale).

a grinding stone, and two tiny bone (fish?) hooks, as well as numerous large Marsh Island Incised sherds (figure 10.4a), representing at least five vessels. Feature contents were studied by honors student Elicia Kimble (2008), who identified the faunal remains under the tutelage of Irv Quitmyer of the Florida Museum of Natural History. Quitmyer (1997) had earlier identified the few Yon faunal samples from 1995 as mammal, fish, and shellfish. The 2007 feature sample had greater diversity, probably because of its better preservation in the presence of the freshwater shells, which helped neutralize acidic soils. The fauna in this feature added seven taxa to the list for the site, including more fish, raccoon, snake, and rodents. Though clearly deer and other mammals were important, the role of fish in the subsistence system of these inland farmers was probably far greater than we realize. The high numbers, species diversity, and small sizes of the fish suggest they were netted.

Yon mound is 7.3 m high, flat topped, and close to square, with no discernible ramp. Extensive coring around it produced no evidence for a plaza. Excavation into the lower slope of the mound's southwest side in 1995 (TUs A and AA) produced Fort Walton and Lamar ceramics, a single red glass seed bead, small metal and glass fragments in the upper levels, and evidence of multiple construction stages and basket loading. Below the mound was the flat surface of pale, yellowish brown riverbank sand upon which construction had begun (and upon which the earliest Fort Walton midden was deposited). Over this alluvium was a thin (12 cm), flat layer of darker fine sand that may have been a prepared surface for mound building. Charcoal from an early basket load was dated to cal A.D. 1235 (table 10.1), consistent with village dates.

An intrusive burial of an adult was encountered in TU A, extended in a pit clearly cutting into the basket-loaded stratigraphy from an upper stratum only 20 to 66 cm below the mound surface. The decayed skeletal remains were left unexcavated, but the rest of the 1-x-2-m unit was continued next to it, higher up the mound slope, to obtain stratigraphic information. The bones (a skull, one arm, legs) were accompanied only by a greenstone celt inside the upper arm. The burial was partially surrounded by a curved line of charcoal, from which two samples produced similar radiocarbon dates in the mid-eleventh century (table 10.1)—up to 200 years earlier than the early mound date, but the ranges overlap. This is up to 600 years too early for what we think is the age of Lamar. The best explanation is that this was a Fort Walton burial and the charcoal was from a wooden artifact (a staff?) that may have been curated from an earlier time (possibly showing heritage maintenance again). In the upper part of the burial pit was another greenstone celt, small and worn, perhaps thrown in during the filling of the grave as a last offering. A second unit excavated into the lower slope of the mound on the east side in 2007 produced far fewer ceramics and only Lamar types. Under the base of the mound and above the culturally sterile pale riverbank sand here, the prepared-base layer was absent, and the deep stratigraphy in the 2-m-long profile showed the earliest construction sloping in the opposite direction from the mound slope. This could mean that an earlier low platform was constructed farther east of the present mound or that a trench had perhaps been dug around the earlier mound.

A significant research question at Yon is the temporal relationships of various ceramic types. While the Fort Walton component is securely dated to A.D. 1200–1250, the Lamar complex now appears to be protohistoric. In the six units dug on the south and east sides of the mound, the uppermost levels usually contained some Fort Walton ceramics but also Lamar Complicated Stamped and Plain types. Under this were levels dominated by common Fort Walton diagnostics. Cob-marked sherds were few but always in deep levels, suggesting they are early. The small amount of check-stamped pottery was all localized in the midden on the west (downriver) side of the mound. Because the date from the west side is contemporaneous with the dates for Fort Walton from elsewhere around the site, the localization of check-stamped ceramics may indicate a functional difference, an association with some domestic activity. The spatial limitation of check-stamped sherds to the domestic midden area is also the case at Corbin-Tucker (described above), and Bullen (1958b: 348–49) found a similar situation at J-5.

Unlike at Corbin-Tucker, there are no six-pointed Fort Walton Incised bowls at Yon. This may be because these fancy vessels were strictly for burial purposes or because they were temporally or ethnically different (or combinations of these reasons). Typical Fort Walton Incised vessels of casuela bowl and other shapes and Lake Jackson jars are abundant, however. One sherd of a beaker or bottle (recognizable by its small diameter of 4 cm) was recovered from the mound in TU A. Marsh Island Incised has been a poorly known minority type; Willey (1949a: 466) had "limited data" and provided only a very brief description, though Griffin's (1950: 105–6) excavations at the Lake Jackson site expanded the definition a bit. Marsh Island Incised is now solidly dated to around A.D. 1200 in Feature 2007-4 at Yon. Interestingly, this type is represented by only 35 of the 10,000 sherds in the Perry collection from the Curlee site (Yuellig 2007). If the date from Curlee is correct, that site should be roughly contemporaneous with Yon, though it may be a generation earlier or later.

The relationship of Fort Walton with Lamar is becoming clearer with a new date on the Lamar component at Yon. We isolated the clearest Lamar level, in TU E, east of the mound, with no Fort Walton ceramics. A charcoal sample here produced a date with five calibrated intercepts (table 10.1), the earliest (and only reasonable) two being A.D. 1690 and 1730. This compares favorably with the only other good Lamar date in the region, from the Lighthouse Bayou site (8Gu114), some 80 river miles downstream and around the west side of the delta on St. Joseph Bay. Lighthouse Bayou consists of scattered shell piles dating to both prehistoric and protohistoric times. Pile 12, with Fort Walton ceramics, was dated to cal A.D. 1480, while Piles 2 and 3, with Lamar ceramics but no Fort Walton types, produced two radiocarbon dates of between A.D. 1690 and 1730 (the two reasonable of five intercepts, again; White 2005a). While the earlier date's two sigma range does extend into early historic time, it does not overlap with that of the later date. Lamar thus appears to have been perhaps as early as a generation after the latest Fort Walton—from the late Mission or post-Mission period. If the radiocarbon dates from Yon and Lighthouse Bayou are correct, each could be a Fort Walton occupation site that later, foreign people returned to, possibly after the site was empty for generations or even centuries. X-ray fluorescence analysis of samples of Fort Walton and Lamar types of sherds from Yon (Du Vernay 2011) indicated clear differences in paste between the two, supporting the idea of different manufacturing techniques associated with ethnicity and/or time.

Old Rambo Landing Mound

We add this brief note about Moore's (1907: 437) Mound near Old Rambo Landing (9Se15), to which he devoted only a couple sentences and which has had little attention since. This mound was on the east bank of the Chattahoochee 19 river miles (31 km) up from the confluence (see figure 10.2). It was circular, 20 m in diameter and 2 m high, and looted when Moore got there; he judged it to be "domiciliary" and did not mention any artifacts. A. R. Kelly's 1948 site form at the University of Georgia (UGA) said he collected plain sherds near a circular mound 15 m in diameter and 1.5 m high. Joseph Caldwell did another site form in 1953 and included a map showing a village area on the north and south sides of the mound, with the larger, southern one labeled "Weeden Island II" and a "chipping area" identified to the southwest.

Visiting the site in 1980, White (1981a: 490–93) found huge agricultural fields, some with crops too high to see anything. The judgment then was that the mound had been plowed down but something might remain below the plow zone. A Fort Walton Incised rim and other, less-diagnostic sherds (two indeterminate incised, one fabric-impressed, many plain sand, grit, and grog tempered) were recovered, as well as six chert flakes. In 2005 we looked at the UGA artifact collection for 9Se15 and found it to contain chert, check-stamped and cob-marked pottery, and even one Chattahoochee Brushed sherd attributable to the Creeks of the late eighteenth to early nineteenth century. The materials other than this last-mentioned sherd might indicate a Late Woodland (late Weeden Island) site with typical check-stamped pottery (on the downriver side), lithic debitage, and a conical mound, either reused or kept in use by early Fort Walton people. Caution is required here not only because so little information is available but also because the confused site numbering in this part of Georgia in the 1940s and 1950s meant that different sites were often given the same number (White 1981: 24–27).

Discussion

Investigations of the sites described are still ongoing, but we have more knowledge than ever before of Apalachicola–lower Chattahoochee Valley Fort Walton and its place in the wider Mississippian sphere.

Spatial and Temporal Distinctions

The ceramic sequence is becoming clearer: check-stamped and cob-marked pottery is very early (perhaps A.D. 800–1000), holding over from late Weeden Island; both disappear in later Fort Walton. Marsh Island Incised is still a minority type but more common in middle Fort Walton; Bullen (1958b: 348) saw it decline in later levels at J-5. The Fort Walton Incised six-pointed open bowl seems unique to the region, associated with burials, and possibly appearing or lasting very late (though there are some 40 sherds of these bowls in the Perry collection from the Curlee site, which is thought to date to early–middle Fort Walton) or perhaps representing some subgroup affiliation or functional specialty. This shallow, flared-rim open soup bowl/plate shape is common in Mississippian times but with shell temper and a round rim. Farther upriver on the lower Chattahoochee, this Mississippian shallow bowl (still grit/sand tempered) is called Columbia Incised (Blitz and Lorenz 2006: 239–40). Its manifestation with the six-pointed rim shape is, however, apparently confined to the Fort Walton region, with a shell-tempered version (Pensacola Incised) also seen very late in the sequence, often postcontact, in the Pensacola area (Harris, chapter 11, this volume). A rare variant of this vessel form is the five-pointed open bowl (e.g., at the Chipola Cutoff mound [Moore 1903: 449–51]).

A very small number of sherds of bottles or beakers are known from Fort Walton sites; these are usually classified as Fort Walton Incised. These distinctive forms are important on the Chattahoochee above the Fort Walton area. They occur mostly in mound contexts, such as at Cemochechobee mounds near Fort Gaines, Georgia (Blitz and Lorenz 2006; Schnell et al. 1981), which also produced effigy bottles. Beakers and bottles also are important southward as far as the Safety Harbor area around Tampa (Mitchem, chapter 8, this volume). Apparently nowhere in Florida has anyone recovered Mississippian-style hooded water bottles or effigy bottles like those from farther up the Chattahoochee and elsewhere across the Mississippian Southeast. Bullen (1958b: 346) noted "one or two" bottle sherds from J-5, and Moore got a stirrup-spout bottle neck from Chipola Cutoff Mound. There are up to five sherds of beakers or bottle necks (all rims of vessel openings about 6 cm in diameter) from the Curlee site (three from midden contexts, one from the disturbed cemetery, one in the Perry collection) and one sherd from Yon, as noted above.

An artifact type of interest is the ceramic mushroom, described above from the Corbin-Tucker site (figure 10.10). Three similar specimens came from Chipola Cutoff Mound; Moore called them stopper-shaped objects. He illustrated only the one with a central depression on top and an encircling line of triangular punctations around the side edge of the top (Moore 1903: 382, 386); the other two were plain. The illustrated one might be a stamp rolled along a surface to make a pattern (on ceramics, cloth, or skin?). Gardner (1966:54, 63) excavated five ceramic mushrooms from the Waddell's Mill Pond site and noted that they had been called pottery trowels, bottle stoppers, and ear plugs. He illustrated three of them, including one with an incised and punctated design on the top face that would seem to rule out use as a pottery-smoothing trowel and make it more likely an ear decoration or body stamp. Another one from Waddell's Mill Pond had a nodelike projection. These artifacts possibly had many functions, given such a variety of shapes.

Fort Walton people were clearly agricultural; maize has been recovered at several inland sites (table 10.3). Coastal and inland sites have also produced charred acorns, hickory nuts, cane, palm, wood, and fruit bits, as well as a wide array of faunal remains, indicating hunting, fishing, and shellfish collection from fresh, brackish, and marine waters (White 1982, 1994, 2000, 2005a; White et al. 2002). Inland sites such as Curlee, Yon, and Corbin-Tucker have small piles of freshwater bivalves, suggesting deposition of food garbage from one household, perhaps one meal. Up to 40 percent of the Late Woodland (late Weeden Island) sites all over the valley have such piles of freshwater shell as well (White 1981). If the sea-level data presented by Marquardt and Walker (chapter 2, this volume) are correct, the transition from Woodland into Mississippian may be marked by lower water levels that may have exposed more shellfish beds. Or perhaps increasing use of riverbanks for agricultural fields meant more harvesting of easily available mollusks (possibly a task for children while adults planted crops).

The maize remains are all from inland sites. Cob-marked pottery at Yon, in the middle valley, is the farthest-downriver evidence for farming. Below that there is no evidence but also few plant remains in general, and even fewer known sites, so the sample is biased. The picture is one of probable intensive farming inland in the upper and middle valley, coupled with a wide collection of wild resources. In the lower delta wetlands and coastal areas, subsistence continued to emphasize aquatic resources, as in earlier times. Perhaps some maize may have been brought in when the in-laws upriver came down to visit. To the west, there are reports of maize from the Choctawhatchee basin (Harris, chapter 11, this volume; Mikell 1990) and the Bottle Creek site in the Mobile delta region of coastal Alabama (Brown 2003: 22). It may have been brought in, not grown there on the swampy, low, salty coast. The Bottle Creek maize is thought to have been brought there already processed, possibly as tribute (Scarry 2003).

Many mysteries remain within Fort Walton material culture, such as the paucity of chipped stone. The 10 chert flakes (in five units, totaling 11 m^2) at Corbin-Tucker amount to an average density of one flake every 1.1 m^2 for both village and cemetery. From his Fort Walton village at J-5, Bullen (1958b: 346) got only 289 chipped stone pieces from the 450 m^2 (estimated from his fig. 10.13 map) that he dug, a density of one piece every 1.5 m^2 (though he may not have used screens). All but three of these were debitage; among the three worked fragments was a side-notched point base that must have been from an earlier time period, picked up by

Table 10.3. Maize from Fort Walton sites in the Apalachicola/lower Chattahoochee Valley

Site	Evidence	Context/Date	Reference	Comments
Omussee Creek (or Seaborn, or Columbia) mound, 1Ho27	Cob fragments, 8- or 10-row, similar to northern flints	In a feature associated with first and possibly second platform mound stage	Neuman 1961; Blitz and Lorenz 2006	Analysis by Missouri Botanical Gardens; mound is just outside Florida in S. Alabama
J-5 (Chattahoochee River #1, 8Ja8)	Kernels, cob frags. of 10-row and poss. 8-row, looks like Caribbean flints	Charcoal from Fort Walton zone C14 dated to A.D. 400±200 (= cal 2-sigma 1317–1467)	Bullen 1958; White 1981	Examined by Mangelsdorf and Galinat at Harvard
Curlee, 8Ja7	Charred cobs, Eastern 8-row, one 12-row but no popcorn or small flints	Surface collection by many local residents; one fragment washing out of midden; site date is cal 2-sigma 1168–1380	White 1982	Analysis by Missouri Botanical Gardens
Waddell's Mill Pond, 8Ja65	6 charred cobs, fragments	24 inches deep in midden next to pond/stream/cave	Gardner 1966	Never analyzed
Thick Greenbriar, 8Ja417	Kernels, cupules, cob fragments, probably 8-row, probably flint	Good context in an earlier midden dated to cal 2-sigma 1270–1430	White 2000; Rodriguez 2004	Analysis by E. Sheldon of SITE, Inc, Montgomery, Ala.
Thick Greenbriar, 8Ja417	Possible cob fragment	Good context in later midden, all Fort Walton with Spanish items (glass beads, iron spike), dated 1485 (intercept), cal 2-sigma 1420–1660	White 2000; Rodriguez 2004	Analysis by E. Sheldon of SITE, Inc, Montgomery, Ala.

Fort Walton surface collectors. When projectile points are found at Fort Walton sites, they are most often small triangles, usually called Pinellas points, ubiquitous in late prehistory but appearing as early as Late Woodland. A reason for the lack of Fort Walton chipped stone tools that has been thrown around in conversation over the years is that these people used sharpened cane or bone arrow points instead of stone. If this is indeed the case, we must ask why, when the rest of the Mississippian peoples (not to mention previous and succeeding cultures) were happy with stone points and knives. One explanation could be that this, too, was part of asserting ethnic or geographic identity.

Relationship between Fort Walton and Lamar

Though still few, the data suggest that the Lamar ceramic complex resulted from something new appearing during or after late Fort Walton. As yet we have no subsistence or other distinctions for Lamar, and one seed bead from Yon plus three radiocarbon dates from Yon and Lighthouse Bayou hardly constitute adequate proof for a late seventeenth- to early eighteenth-century date. But preliminary tabulations of lithic materials at Yon suggest there are more in Lamar levels than in earlier Fort Walton levels (Du Vernay 2011), possibly suggesting ethnic or other cultural distinctions, and other differences may emerge as more data are processed. Meanwhile, the dates from Corbin-Tucker cemetery and other sites and the mixture of Fort Walton and early Spanish artifacts at places such as Chipola Cutoff Mound and Thick Greenbriar site (Moore 1903; White 2000, 2011) suggest that Fort Walton as a cultural tradition was able to hang on into historic times.

It is tempting to imagine indigenous Fort Walton people, already characterized by their non-shell-tempered pottery and other distinctions amid the wider Mississippian world, continuing their traditional practices as long as possible in the face of large-scale disruption. They may have been decimated from the impact of European diseases that filtered in even in the absence of direct Spanish contact. These original valley inhabitants could have continued their own material culture and burial rituals in small numbers and remote places. Such a situation is not uncommon. By the early 1800s, California's Yahi Indians numbered only a few hundred, but the last one, Ishi, practiced his traditional cultural ways until he came down out of the remote hills in 1911 (Kroeber 1961). Closer to home, the

Calusa of south Florida lasted two centuries after contact (Marquardt and Walker, chapter 2, this volume).

Historic pressures may have resulted in the native Fort Walton adaptation being either replaced by or absorbed into something new when Lamar appeared. Lamar pottery appears as early as A.D. 1350 in north and east-coastal Georgia, and then in South Carolina and eastern Alabama, as well as down the Chattahoochee into southwest Georgia. But it is associated with historic Indians of many different cultures and linguistic groups, including both Muskogean speakers and the Iroquoian-speaking Cherokee (Hally 1994), as well as the Apalachee Indians of the Tallahassee-area missions. In the Apalachicola Fort Walton region, Lamar ceramics may represent the ancestral Creeks later documented there (themselves ancestral to the first Seminoles). But such an ethnic affiliation is still difficult to see archaeologically, as well as to pinpoint in time, despite all we know about Creeks in Georgia (Knight 1994; Williams 2008; Worth 2000).

An important question is why these people or even just the Lamar ceramics did not appear in northwest Florida and the corner of southwest Georgia and southeast Alabama earlier. A strong Fort Walton presence may have prevented it. Blitz and Lorenz (2006) do see a mixture of Fort Walton and Lamar ceramic types farther up the lower Chattahoochee after 1400, so movement downriver may have started this early and accelerated later. In fact, the earliest historic Indians in the Tallahassee area, as encountered by Narváez and De Soto, were probably Fort Walton peoples, who began dying off immediately as a result of early contact and were quickly replaced by groups from the north, bringing their Lamar pottery. These Lamar groups then became the Apalachee of the early 1600s who were missionized and produced Jefferson ware, which is the same as Lamar pottery. Willey (1949a: 493) noted the relationship and suggested this answer to the puzzle a half century ago but did not have associated accurate dates.

Smith (1956: 123) and others after him (e.g., Payne and Scarry 1998; Scarry 1996) suggested that Fort Walton culture represented the prehistoric and early historic Apalachee, but Brose (1990) cautioned against using the Apalachee as a model for Fort Walton when there was at least a century of radical change between the two. Marrinan (chapter 9, this volume; Marrinan and White 2007) noted the mixture in the Tallahassee area of Fort Walton and Lamar-like ceramics at sites from both contact and Mission periods and the difficulty of teasing apart what may be separate components, possibly even separate ethnic groups (even if they were in the process of merging). In the Apalachicola Valley, we do not even know the ethnic identity of the pre-Mission- and Mission-period indigenes, not to mention the post-Mission groups, and associating ceramic series with ethnicity is always tricky (even if appealing).

Some 12 percent of the Fort Walton sites in the Apalachicola Valley have Lamar components. They are very interestingly distributed (see figure 10.1), with a cluster at the top of the river around the forks, a few in the middle valley, and a few on the barrier islands. The reason for this distribution is unknown; perhaps it relates to the quality of land for agriculture inland, the probable locations of briefly occupied mission sites around the forks, and the movement along the coast and barrier islands from European-Indian interaction during historic times. One Lamar question we continue to investigate is whether there are any pure Lamar sites, or whether Lamar materials always occur with Fort Walton. The dramatic picture of a dying people either being assisted by or taken over by their relatives from upriver can only be correct if the dates overlap. If they do not overlap, then we have an alternative scenario of natives from elsewhere moving into a completely depopulated area much later in time. We also have the question of why they waited so long to take over such rich lands or how closely they were even related to the Fort Walton people in the first place (though both made grit-tempered pots).

Fort Walton Development

At the other end of the temporal spectrum is the perennial question of Fort Walton origins. Since Willey's original description, models have been generated to characterize the emergence of Fort Walton sociopolitical systems (e.g., Brose 1984; Brose and Percy 1978; Knight 1991; Marrinan and White 2007; Milanich 1994; Scarry 1990; White 1982). Most now agree that there was no invasion of corn-carrying, temple mound–building peoples but instead a fairly seamless development from Late Woodland into the Fort Walton brand of Mississippian. The Middle and Late Woodland Weeden Island ceramics so prominent in this region are clearly ancestral in form, temper, and decoration to Fort Walton types. Maize was already being grown in Late Woodland times (Milanich 1974, 1997), so Fort Walton may represent an expansion of gardening with this productive crop into full-blown farming. Such agricultural intensification can be combined with factors ranging from population growth to influences from the wider Mississippian world to explain the emergence of more complex society here. Evidence for this was seen long ago (e.g., Bullen 1950: 124) in the settlement shift from a pattern of late Weeden Island sites in many different ecological zones to a pattern of larger, predominantly riverbank sites during Fort Walton times, better for agriculture as well as possibly intensified communication and transportation.

Upriver from the Fort Walton area, on the upper part of the lower Chattahoochee, from about 160 river miles inland northward, Blitz and Lorenz (2002, 2006) have documented the presence of a Mississippian cultural variant named Rood, manifested at the multiple-mound centers at Rood's Landing, Singer-Moye, and Cemochechobee, as well as at several single-mound sites. Early Rood is dominated by shell-tempered ceramics, like a more typical Mississippian adaptation and unlike the contemporaneous Fort Walton archaeological culture downriver, though some small proportion of Fort Walton ceramics show up after about A.D. 1400. These researchers explain the appearance of Rood in terms of an in-migration of Mississippian peoples. But this interpretation is less important for us here than their good documentation for something else going on at the edge of the Fort Walton region that may represent real ethnic differentiation within Mississippian. The existence of Rood only strengthens the picture of a vibrant Fort Walton people maintaining their own identity but fully participating in Mississippian ceremonialism and economic/subsistence reorganization. Rood, to the north of Fort Walton, and Pensacola, to the west, are more typical Mississippian manifestations in that they are dominated by shell-tempered pottery. Pensacola may share even more than just ceramic styles (such as six-pointed bowls) with Fort Walton, in that the coastal segment of this adaptation may not have been agricultural. If people with different but related cultural traditions lived to the north and west of them, the emerging Fort Walton groups seem to have been holding their own and culturally evolving in place. In fact, Blitz and Lorenz (2002: 130–31) even suggest that Fort Walton developed in place "as a regional defensive reaction to the real or perceived threat of intrusive Rood populations on their northern frontier."

Fort Walton Political Systems

Explanations of Fort Walton sociopolitical organization are numerous; many of the models have become more and more derived and unusable. Though proposed as hypothetical, many are taken as received wisdom by subsequent researchers, instead of being tested with new data (Marrinan and White 2007). This chapter being more of a descriptive summary of Fort Walton material culture and less of a theoretical treatise, we will not dwell on the beleaguered concept of the prehistoric "chiefdom" and whether or how Fort Walton exemplifies it in the wider Mississippian context. Blitz (2010) has recently noted how flexible, variable, and regionally diverse nearly all societies traditionally classified under the Mississippian rubric actually were. Our interpretive viewpoint is similar to what he documents for most current Mississippian studies: eclectic, emphasizing what can readily be inferred from the empirical evidence, combined with moderate use of more humanistic, less grounded speculation. We agree with Smith (1990), who called for good documentation of local Mississippian developmental sequences before we can compare them and explain culture change at a broader level.

More recently Smith (2007: xxii) suggested that the use of ideological innovations to explain Mississippian emergence might be inadequate to account for the broad range of variation across the Southeast and that little research has explored the transformation from Late Woodland to Mississippian or investigated the smaller, local chiefdoms as compared with the complex regional centers. We note throughout this chapter a great deal of continuity from Woodland to Fort Walton, in-place development out of the solid, at least horticultural late Weeden Island base. Perhaps the distinctive settlement pattern changes, from dispersed to more aggregated and concentrated along the riverbanks, reflect not only the intensification of maize agriculture but also the "corporate" organization (e.g., Smith 2007: xxviii) and community integration of the Fort Walton chiefdoms. There is so far no evidence for the development of Fort Walton out of conflict or warfare. Nor do any data support more-humanistic models attributing increasing sociopolitical complexity to the emergence of individual "agents" such as war leaders, economic leaders, "big-man" personalities, or religious specialists (e.g., Smith 2007), self-aggrandizers who are hard to discern in the archaeological record anyway.

Finally, no evidence indicates movements of people into the region or the supplanting of indigenous groups to account for Fort Walton origins, as hypothesized, for example, farther up the Chattahoochee (Blitz and Lorenz 2006) or at Etowah in north Georgia (Cobb and King 2005). Rather than new people intruding and reinventing old traditions to validate claims to power, perhaps Fort Walton politics and ceremony involved heirs of established groups strengthening leadership by continuing a long-hallowed local tradition and adding just a little new Mississippian flavor throughout Fort Walton. Near the end, when populations had become decimated or after they had died out completely, we think new people (Lamar) did move downriver and claim some Fort Walton sites, including at least one mound (Yon), but by this historic time all Mississippian societies had been transformed into something very different.

We have discussed mostly small, local centers; Fort Walton multimound centers in this valley are rare. At Chattahoochee Landing and Pierce, many of the mounds were made sometime during the Woodland period, but the locations of these two sites, at the two most strategic spots in the valley, must have contributed to their political importance. At Cayson, in the middle valley, there may be two mounds, but one may be a burial mound, and most of the site data remain unreported. Whether having multiple-mound centers makes for a "complex chiefdom," with single-mound centers indicating only "simple chiefdoms," is a topic still worth exploring. So is the concept of mound size relating to importance of a site and the amount of power it represented (Blitz and Livingood 2004). Those who think greater size and numbers in population, architecture, or other material evidence equals greater political power should consider Florida's capital today, the small city of Tallahassee, compared with Miami, Jacksonville, or Tampa (not to mention the same situation with other state capitals).

Also argued constantly in discussions of Mississippian organization is the concept of cycling, becoming more or less complex through time as complex chiefdoms emerge and collapse "amid a regional landscape of simple chiefdoms" (Anderson 1994: 323). It can also be interpreted as continual aggregation and dispersion through time or even moving from hierarchical and stratified to more egalitarian and ranked societies. Complexity is often taken to mean levels of hierarchy, as represented by mounds. But we still do not know how hierarchical or economically stratified any Mississippian societies were.

If fisher-foragers of south Florida such as the Calusa were organized in real, tributary, but nonagricultural chiefdoms (e.g., Marquardt and Walker, chapter 2, this volume) and historic north-central Florida peoples with nondescript archaeological evidence were historically documented as complex societies (Worth, chapter 7, this volume), certainly more-sedentary farmers far northwest of these groups and closer to Mississippian heartlands of the Southeast were complex chiefdoms. But how much of the hierarchy was due to social ranking and how much to real economic difference? These are tricky issues to test with material data. Possibly only skeletal analyses showing that some people were beaten, sacrificed, or starved and that others were not could demonstrate such stratification.

Coercion versus persuasive organization versus willing aggregation are not easy to distinguish in the archaeological record, and dominance can be achieved with radically different strategies (e.g., Beck 2003, 2006). Not all leadership is hierarchical, either, and political power can be held by many different kinds of leaders (Sullivan 2001, 2006). There is a huge Western bias at work in inferring that hierarchical and centralized organization was needed to accomplish mound building or other major works; and heterarchy or other kinds of horizontal, cross-cutting social divisions are now recognized as equally possible (Blitz 2010: 4–6). Whatever status was associated with Fort Walton elite grave goods, it seems to have been available to women as well as men, as seen at the Corbin-Tucker site, as well as at Lake Jackson and possibly other Fort Walton sites (Marrinan, chapter 9, this volume; Shahramfar 2008). Because at so many traditional Mississippian sites adult males are more often buried in mounds and with prestige goods than are adult females (Blitz 2010: 17), perhaps some kind of honored status for women is another distinguishing characteristic of Fort Walton (though what fancy perishables might have been placed in graves remains unknown). The existence of hereditary positions as indicated by wealth items buried with children is less easy to confirm, due to both a lack of evidence and some logical difficulty with this explanation.

Change through time in Mississippi-period chiefdoms has been related to environment, subsistence, politics, social evolution, mortuary practices, ideology, and a host of other factors. Issues of agency and political leadership are currently prominent, if difficult to document archaeologically (e.g., Butler and Welch 2006). But to infer cycling or any other diachronic picture, we need tightly dated sites (to see whether they are contemporaneous or sequential), clear inter- and intrasite settlement patterns, and a host of other information yet to be obtained. Plus we need to examine assumptions. While some rising and falling of Mississippian chiefdoms certainly seems to be prehistoric, there is far more evidence in historic times for this kind of sociopolitical fragmentation, traceable in large part to the disruption induced by the European invasion. Finally, concerning mound size and site complexity, we challenge the perceived wisdom to suggest that conflict and constant competition for resources and political limelight may not have been the most important things in Fort Walton daily life. If constructing new mounds or adding new stages to existing mounds, making them bigger, took place every time there was regime change (e.g., Anderson 1994; Hally 1996), then smaller/fewer mounds may mean not less complexity but more stability! Smaller or fewer mound centers might even have meant less competition and a more peaceful existence. In the rich Apalachicola/lower Chattahoochee Valley, there may have been little competition for the abundant resources. There is a decided lack of evidence for fortifications at Fort Walton sites. Though this might be due to the lack of large-scale excavations that might uncover such features, it might also be because the conflict or threats that characterized Mississippian elsewhere in the South were minimal here.

There has been in the literature the notion that late Fort Walton sites are absent from the Apalachicola Valley and early Fort Walton sites are absent from the Tallahassee Hills area to the east (see Marrinan, chapter 9, this volume). Coupled with the prominence of the Lake Jackson site in the latter area, this has led some (Brose 1984; Knight 1991; Payne and Scarry 1998; Scarry 1990, 1994; Tesar 1980) to hypothesize a late prehistoric "segmentation" of Fort Walton, with one segment then moving eastward and becoming more complex in Tallahassee. Knight (1991) suggested that the Apalachicola Valley was overpopulated but that this never led to developing more than simple chiefdoms, while Lake Jackson was a complex chiefdom that emerged when colonies of people migrated eastward from Apalachicola because of demographic pressure. Scarry (1994: 169) said that farmland was limited in the Apalachicola Valley but not in the Tallahassee area, where land was more productive and could support larger populations. Payne and Scarry (1998: 42–44) derive the historic Apalachee Indians from these hypothesized later prehistoric movements of people eastward and partly base their analysis upon numbers of sites, ignoring site sizes and what aggregation into chiefdoms might have meant. None of these scenarios has ever been supported by the data, nor have any means of testing them been determined. There is no documentation of demographic pressure or of any shortage of resources or good farmland in the rich Apalachicola Valley. Several late Fort Walton sites are now known, including some with postcontact and Mission-period dates, as noted above. The hypothesis of early postcontact depopulation here makes better sense than the explanation that late prehistoric natives were just moving eastward in droves for no demonstrated reason.

Meanwhile, the valley's abundant, yet differentially distributed, resources could make other areas of investigation more productive. For example, examining the relationship between inland riverine sites and their coastal/estuarine counterparts has the potential to show differing social organization and economic strategies on the part of societies producing the same material culture. For coastal people, the avoidance of sedentism and farming life need not have meant less complexity or any less economic interaction along waterways, but perhaps more mobility and seasonality.

In sum, the material record suggests that Fort Walton is clearly a Mississippian culture but with great regional distinctiveness. No techno-functional or environmental reasons can be postulated for preferring non-shell-tempered ceramics or using far fewer chipped stone tools than anyone else or having distinctive bowls or other aspects of material culture different from mainstream Mississippian (whatever that might be!). The explanation has to lie in the realm of regional identity, possibly long-standing participation in communal traditions established in Woodland times, even while they were being gradually transformed in the light of Mississippian influences from the outside. Meanwhile, although we would love to picture peaceful folks organized into sociopolitical entities headed by chiefs who were sisters and cousins, nicely and profitably interacting with friends in other cultures upriver and relatives downriver in the coastal wetlands and coordinating with other clan matriarchs the communal building of some mound centers that lasted for centuries, we are some distance from producing testable hypotheses for such speculation.

But coast-inland cultural differences and economic interaction are important research issues, not only within the region but also possibly to explain relationships with the wider Mississippian world. The Apalachicola delta coast and barrier islands, especially St. Joseph Bay, were prime locations for harvesting large gastropods, especially *Busycon sinistrum*, the left-handed or lightning whelk. While coastal Fort Walton people were apparently eating these and making expedient tools from the shells (White 2005a), the lack of evidence that they used them for fancier things may mean they were trading them far into the continent to be used for the elaborate Mississippian ceremonial items so famous in the SECC. This is what Mitchem (chapter 8, this volume) and others have suggested for Safety Harbor and other Florida Mississippi-period groups. The hypothesis of shell movement might be investigated relatively easily with some trace element analyses. Within the Apalachicola–lower Chattahoochee region, perhaps coastal people were sending up Gulf shell and yaupon holly for black drink in return for maize from Fort Walton groups in the interior, who themselves made a few shell tools but sent most of the big shells farther along. These prehistoric lifeways involving interregional interaction while keeping intraregional cohesion may have been so successful that they continued for a while in the face of massive depopulation and change. The demise of Fort Walton must have come a couple centuries after Old

World invaders arrived and began the disruptive processes that caused other aboriginal peoples to move southward into Fort Walton lands and change the landscape and the lifeways forever.

Acknowledgments

For comments on this chapter we thank other contributors and reviewers, especially Rochelle Marrinan. Du Vernay appreciates grants for the Yon mound and village research from the Florida Archaeological Council (Griffin Award) and Sigma Xi and thanks Steven Fernandez for assistance in producing the Yon site map.

11

Defining Pensacola and Fort Walton Cultures in the Western Panhandle

NORMA HARRIS

Pensacola culture is an archaeological construct first defined by Gordon Willey (1949a) based on a series of plain and decorated shell-tempered pottery found on the Gulf coast of the western Florida panhandle (figure 11.1). Although he recognized the distinctive pottery as somehow related to Moundville-influenced ceramics to the west in Mobile Bay, he also saw a relationship between Pensacola and Fort Walton ceramics to the east. He described the Pensacola series as a "regional or subregional variable" in assemblages from the extreme western reaches of the Fort Walton culture area (Willey 1949a: 452). This chapter presents an up-to-date perspective on the Pensacola culture and examines how it relates to and differs from the Fort Walton culture.

Geographic Overview

This chapter covers extreme northwest Florida, an area that lies within the East Gulf Coastal Plain physiographic province (Fenneman 1938; Hunt 1974) and the Coastal Lowlands physiographic subdivision of the coastal plain (Marsh 1966). The province is blanketed by sediments of the Citronelle Formation, deposited during the Plio-Pleistocene epoch some one million years ago. High-energy streams deposited upland sediments of sand, clays, and gravels in alluvial fans that have coalesced on most of this section of the coastal plain, east to interior Washington County. In contrast to most of Florida, the western panhandle counties are situated on loosely consolidated sandstone bedrock, with few outcroppings, especially near the coast. The limestone bedrock and its associated sinkholes and numerous springs characteristic of Florida karst topography begin in

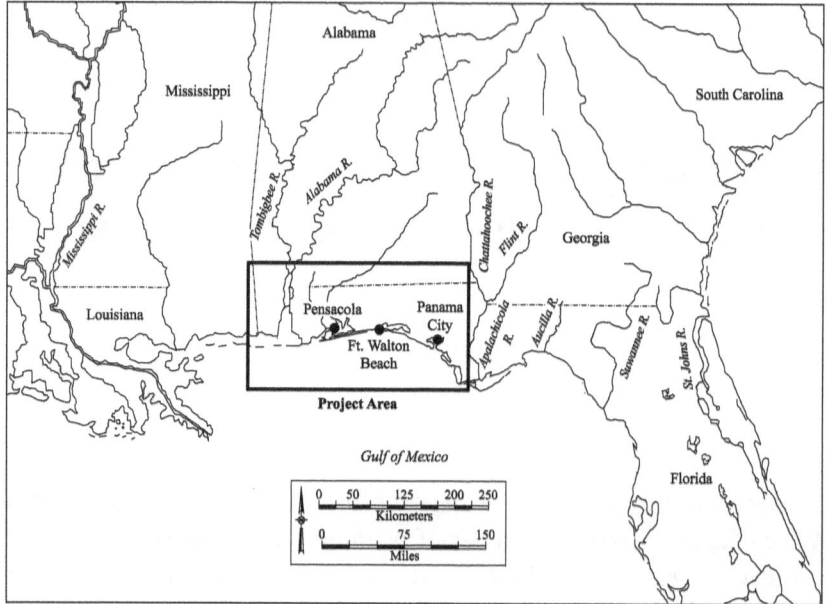

Figure 11.1. The western Florida panhandle. Courtesy of UWF Archaeology Institute.

interior Washington County, dipping into northern coastal Bay County, the easternmost county examined in this chapter (Puri and Vernon 1964).

Mississippi-Period Northwest Florida: Fort Walton and Pensacola Cultures

Among the 39 "Fort Walton" sites in the Florida panhandle reported by Willey (1949a: 452–53), 24 are located in the westernmost counties adjacent to the Alabama state line: Escambia, Santa Rosa, Okaloosa, Walton, and Bay (figure 11.2). These five counties encompass three large estuary systems along the central Gulf coast, which are the focus of this chapter: Pensacola, Choctawhatchee, and St. Andrew bays. Willey included the site of Bear Point (1Ba1) on the much smaller Perdido Bay system in Alabama in his list of Fort Walton sites, because of its obvious ceramic connection to his newly named Pensacola ceramic series, but he was apparently unaware of the much larger ceremonial center of the Pensacola culture to the north, Bottle Creek (1Ba2).

Until recently, Pensacola culture in southwestern Alabama was not viewed as a fully developed Mississippian society (Brose 1984, 2003;

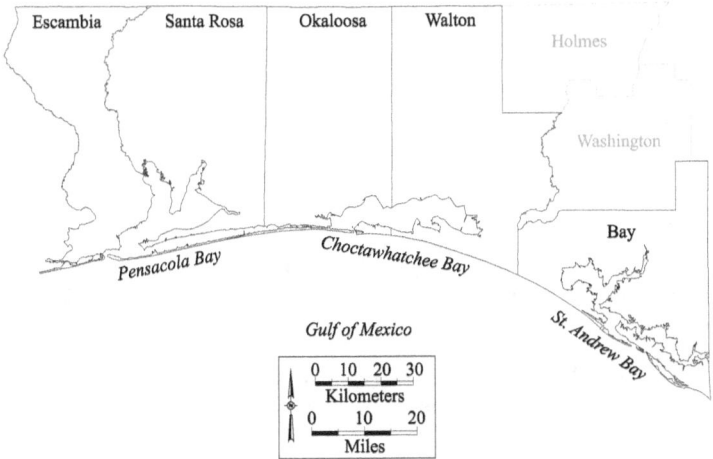

Figure 11.2. The counties of the western panhandle surrounding Pensacola, Choctawhatchee, and St. Andrew bays. Courtesy of UWF Archaeology Institute.

Brown 2003; Fuller 1985, 2003; Knight 1984; Milanich 1994; Stowe 1985). Rather, Pensacola was considered the "fringe" of the Mississippian world, lacking key Mississippian characteristics such as substantial agricultural production in its subsistence base, complex sociopolitical organization, and iconographic complexes traditionally associated with centers such as Moundville and Etowah (Knight 1989, 1990; Peebles and Kus 1977; Scarry 1996; Smith 1985). This view also was shared by archaeologists working in the core Fort Walton region, at least until a few decades ago (Brose 1984; Brose and Percy 1978; Jones 1982; Scarry, 1980, 1985, 1990; Tesar 1980). As it became evident that Pensacola may not be merely a Fort Walton variant, researchers began to question the relationship more deeply. Brose and Percy in 1978, for example, suggested that Pensacola culture "was a veneer, overlain on western Fort Walton coastal sites in Florida" (Brose 2003: xvii); whereas Louis Tesar defined five Fort Walton "subareas," calling the coastline from Mobile to Choctawhatchee Bay the Pensacola–Fort Walton subarea (Phillips 1995; Tesar 1980).

Excavations at Bottle Creek, led by Ian Brown (2003), have provided a substantially different view. His work has revealed preserved maize, at least 18 mounds, several plazas, habitation middens, and dates ranging between A.D. 1250 and 1550. The Bottle Creek complex is located on Mound Island in the upper Mobile-Tensaw Delta, just south of the confluence

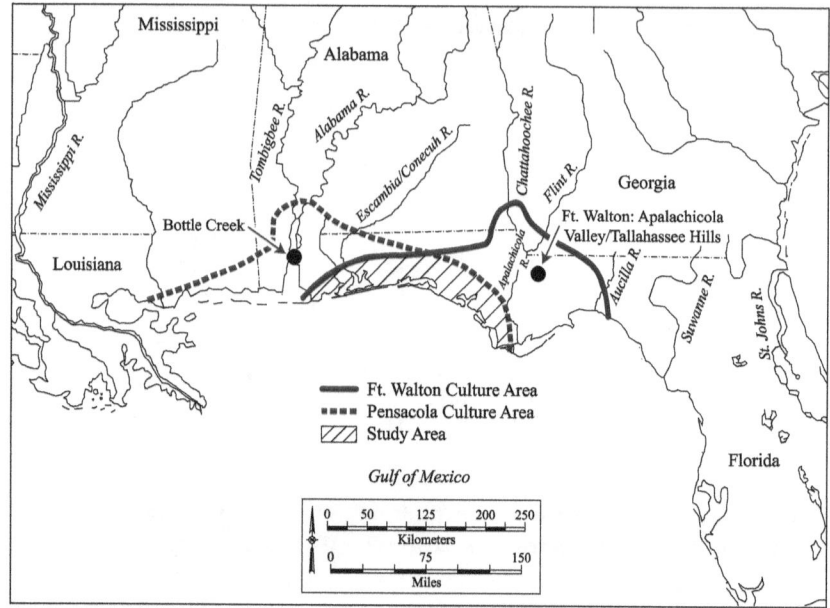

Figure 11.3. Geographic limits of Fort Walton and Pensacola pottery and coastal area with both types in the assemblages. Courtesy of UWF Archaeology Institute.

of the Tombigbee and Alabama rivers. The environmental setting is not that of a terrace overlooking a major drainage, as with most Mississippian mound centers, but a low natural levee surrounded by swamps at the head of Mobile Bay. Brown (2003: 9) states, "One reason for the unusual setting may be political and/or economic; its location in the heart of a major delta near the juncture of two major river valleys places Bottle Creek in the geographical center of the northern Gulf Coast." This location also was near the intersection of two major overland trails (Brown 2003; Higginbotham 1991).

Pensacola-series pottery is found from south-central Alabama west along the coast to southeastern Louisiana and east beyond Panama City in Florida (figure 11.3). Pensacola ceramics occur infrequently as far east as the Apalachicola River basin (Brose 1984; Marrinan and White 2007; White 1982, 1996; White et al., chapter 10, this volume). From east to west, shell-tempered wares increase steadily through time and space on sites west of the Apalachicola and regularly begin to dominate Middle Mississippi–period assemblages around Choctawhatchee Bay (Bense 1989a, 1989b; Brose and Percy 1978; Fuller and Stowe 1982; Lazarus 1971).

The core area of sand- and grit-tempered Fort Walton–series ceramics extends from east of Lake Jackson, the large mound center located in the Tallahassee Hills region, north into the Chattahoochee River valley and south to the Gulf coast (Marrinan, chapter 9, this volume; Marrinan and White 2007; Scarry 1985; White et al., chapter 10, this volume; Willey 1949a). The Aucilla River marks its approximate eastern boundary, while Fort Walton pottery can be found as far west as Mobile Bay (Thomas 1989; Waselkov and Gums 2000). Fort Walton types diminish in Mississippi-period ceramic assemblages moving westward along the coast; in these areas they co-occur on many sites with the Pensacola series.

The core regions of Pensacola and Fort Walton cultures and their Mississippian connections are now better understood, although settlement in the coastal estuaries between the population centers at Bottle Creek, the Apalachicola Valley, and the Tallahassee Hills remains enigmatic. Explanations for the overlapping mixture of Fort Walton and Pensacola ceramic series have been debated for decades and continue today, with little resolution (Bense 1989a, 1989b; Brose and Percy 1978; Brown 2003; Fuller and Stowe 1982; Lazarus 1971; Lazarus et al. 1976; Mikell 1990, 1992a, 1995a; Tesar 1973, 1980; Thomas and Campbell 1993; Willey 1949a). Many researchers hesitate to sever the connection between the two in the Florida coastal panhandle, and for good reason. The consistently mixed nature of the ceramic assemblages may be a reflection of vast differences between the communities in the core areas and those on the coastal periphery of the western panhandle. Nonetheless, Fort Walton and Pensacola connections to the broader Mississippian world are clear in iconography and many ritual practices, if not in other cultural patterns.

The frequency of Fort Walton–Pensacola sites recorded around the bay systems is fairly consistent (table 11.1). The lack of sites in the interior (away from the estuaries and major rivers) also is consistent. Once it was suspected to be a result of sampling error, but survey on Eglin Air Force Base by Prentice Thomas and Associates now suggests that these areas truly lack Pensacola (Mississippi-period) sites (Thomas and Campbell 1993). Eglin covers approximately 13,000 ha, encompassing parts of five counties, bordering Choctawhatchee Bay and the eastern side of Pensacola Bay. Limited Mississippi-period occupation of the interior also is indicated by data collected during a multiyear survey of the eastern Choctawhatchee River valley in Bay and Washington counties by the University of West Florida (White 2006). It is interesting to note that most interior Weeden Island sites were abandoned as settlement shifted to the coastline and

Table 11.1. Total Mississippi-period sites in five northwest Florida counties

Estuary System	Number of Mississippi-Period Sites
Pensacola Bay	160
Choctawhatchee Bay	151
St. Andrew Bay	112

Note: Data compiled from the Florida Master Site File.

some of the larger rivers during the succeeding Mississippi period (Mikell 1995a; Thomas and Campbell 1993; White 2006).

Debates over which culture, Fort Walton or Pensacola, dominates the area continue, and although there has been a large amount of data gathered in some areas, answers to these questions remain elusive. Over the past 20 years, the cord has been severed between Pensacola and Fort Walton in the core areas of Mobile Bay and the Apalachicola/Tallahassee Hills region. However, many Mississippian sites on the coast between these regions do not fit nicely into either category. Is there a *third* culture region along the Gulf coast, one that shares few characteristics with the core regions? What follows are a summary of recorded Pensacola sites and a general description of typical sites for each estuary. Sites in this region of the Gulf coast may be far more similar to one another than to the Mississippian centers that border them to the east and west. Where ceramic data are available, the ratio of Fort Walton (non-shell-tempered) and Pensacola (shell-tempered) ceramic types has been quantified to act as a baseline for what may prove to be yet another coastal Mississippian variant. At least one example from each bay has been selected for a more in-depth discussion.

Examples from St. Andrew, Choctawhatchee, and Pensacola Bays

The three estuary systems share similar environmental characteristics, with a few exceptions. Generally, they represent drowned river valleys with at least one major river and multiple second- and third-order streams feeding bayous that empty into the bays. The landscape is dominated by well-drained sands vegetated with live oak–magnolia maritime forests in the higher elevations; pine flatwoods and inundated soils occur in the lowlands. Sparsely vegetated barrier islands line the coast at bay entrances. One barrier island, Santa Rosa, spans approximately 31 km and shields both Pensacola and Choctawhatchee bays.

St. Andrew Bay

Within St. Andrew Bay, the smallest of the three systems, 112 sites are recorded in the Florida Master Site File with a Mississippi-period component; the vast majority of them lie adjacent to the bay and its bayous. Among these sites are 16 mounds and at least two Mississippian cemeteries, one of which was recorded by Gordon Willey (the cemetery at St. Andrew [8By9]). Many of the sites in St. Andrew Bay are composed of linear and/or individual circular shell middens, consisting primarily of oyster shell. Subsistence remains generally consist of large numbers of fish, shellfish, reptiles, deer, and a few small mammals. Lithic materials and shell tools are rare.

New World Research (NWR), in 1985, conducted a survey of Tyndall Air Force Base, which covers a peninsula on the west side of St. Andrew Bay, and recorded 14 sites with a Mississippian component (Thomas and Campbell 1985). During this survey, NWR collected both Fort Walton and Pensacola pottery, with a site average of 12 percent Pensacola and 88 percent Fort Walton types. NWR later tested several of those sites, including a small Mississippi-period village, the Sheephead Bayou site (Mikell 1990).

Sheephead Bayou (8By150) is a single-component site that consists of a relatively circular shell midden, encompassing 11 individual shell heaps. The faunal assemblage is dominated by fish and shellfish but also includes a small amount of turkey. Among the indigenous floral remains are persimmon, acorn, and hickory. Surprisingly, corn ($n=7$) and beans ($n=5$) also are present (Mikell 1990).

No radiocarbon dates are available for the specific context containing the corn and beans; however, a hearth or pit feature (Feature 1) underlying the shell midden yielded Lake Jackson Plain and Point Washington Incised pottery. As shown in table 11.2, a radiocarbon date range of cal A.D. 1280–1390 was obtained from the feature (Beta 12896). In addition, Feature 1 produced a date of cal A.D. 1290, whereas charred wood (Beta 12895) from the base of the midden produced a date of cal A.D. 1400 (Mikell 1990: 203).

Identifiable ceramics at Sheephead Bayou are dominated by Fort Walton types ($n=107$) at 84 percent but include Pensacola wares ($n=21$, or 16 percent) as well. Although Mikell interprets this site as "single component," protohistoric or historic Native American ceramic types also are present in the assemblage: Chattahoochee Brushed ($n=1$), Leon Check Stamped ($n=1$), and Jefferson Plain ($n=3$). Mikell (1990) correlates this site with the

Table 11.2. Calibrated radiocarbon date information for sites discussed in chapter

Site	Beta Lab#	Measured Radiocarbon Material	Age (BP)	$^{13}C/^{12}C$ Ratio	Conventional Radiocarbon Age (BP)	Calibrated Date Range A.D. (1 sigma)	Calibrated Date Range A.D. (2 sigma)	Intercept Date (A.D.)	Reference
8By150	12895	Charcoal	570±50	-25.0 o/oo	550±50	1280–1420	1290–1440	1400	Mikell 1995
8By150	12896	Charcoal	670±50	-25.0 o/oo	660±50	1280–1390	1260–1290	1290	Mikell 1995
8Es1280	30702	Charcoal	500±60	-25.0 o/oo	520±60	1400–1440	1310–1470	1430	Phillips 1995
8Ok19	64278	Charcoal	580±60	-25.0 o/oo	550±60	1300–1420	1280–1440	1400	Mikell 1995

"Sneads"-phase Fort Walton assemblages (Scarry 1980; cf. Marrinan and White 2007) of the Apalachicola River valley (A.D. 1200–1400).

Choctawhatchee Bay

To the west of St. Andrew Bay, Choctawhatchee Bay was densely occupied from the Late Archaic through the Late Mississippi period. While Woodland-period deposits appear to dominate the landscape, the most visible prehistoric feature today is the Fort Walton Temple Mound (8Ok6), a substantial platform mound located in downtown Fort Walton Beach. The Fort Walton Temple Mound was first reported in the late 1800s by S. T. Walker (1885), who observed large shell heaps south of the mound, along the shoreline of Santa Rosa Sound. C. B. Moore (1901) also reported the shell heaps. By the 1940s, when Willey revisited the site, all but one of the heaps was gone. Willey's excavations on the shoreline south of the mound uncovered very few Mississippi-period remains, but he found dense Early, Middle, and Late Woodland deposits (Willey 1949a). Willey suspected that the Mississippi-period component had been seriously disturbed, and recent excavations at Fort Walton Landing (8Ok1507) and the Indianola Mound (8Ok1012) near Willey's units have confirmed that historic landscaping and construction have scraped away much of the Mississippi-period component associated directly with the Temple Mound (Harris and Pokrant 2002, 2003; Lazarus 1986; Wood et al. 2004). Some Fort Walton and Pensacola deposits have been found on the extreme southeastern side of the Landing site, but again, the majority of the cultural materials recovered date to the Woodland period (Harris and Pokrant 2002, 2003).

Excavations within the Fort Walton Temple Mound itself revealed Mississippi-period burials and redeposited Woodland materials in the mound fill. Fairbanks (1965) speculated that the core of the mound (which has never been tested) might be Deptford. Willey classified Moore's (1901) illustrated wares, documenting 13 Fort Walton vessels, 8 Pensacola vessels, and 1 Moundville Engraved vessel (Lazarus and Fornaro 1986; Moore 1901; Willey 1949a).

Thomas and Campbell's Eglin Air Force Base Historic Preservation Plan of 1993 summarized each component found on the base and in the immediate area. Fort Walton–Pensacola habitation sites on Choctawhatchee Bay tend to cluster around a mound or cemetery. The Fort Walton Temple Mound is part of one of these clusters, which includes earlier mounds apparently not reused by Mississippi-period people, a few low mounds, and several cemeteries, including the Camp Walton site (8Ok780) and the Brooks Street Mound (8Ok74) (Harris and Pokrant 2002; Mikell 1995b, 2003; Prewitt and Heintzelman 1998; Thomas and Campbell 1993).

Data from Eglin and other sources hint at a general trend toward increasing frequencies of Pensacola-series pottery through time (Mikell 1992; Thomas and Campbell 1993). Thomas and Campbell (1993) documented 16 sites with 10 or more Fort Walton–Pensacola sherds ($n=703$ total) in their Eglin study; Pensacola outnumbered Fort Walton 13 to 7. However, a more in-depth look at each site reveals ceramic ratio ranges on suspected early Indian Bayou–phase sites (A.D. 1200–1400 [Mikell 1990]) from 100 percent Fort Walton (8Ok182) to 60 percent Pensacola (8Wl58). All sites assigned to the later Four Mile Point phase (A.D. 1400–1600) range from 60 percent Pensacola at 8Wl168 to 83 percent Pensacola at 8Wl119 (Thomas and Campbell 1993: 607–8; also see Mikell 1992, 1995a).

To date, maize has been found at two sites on Choctawhatchee Bay: the Bell site (8Ok19) in Destin and 8Wl119 on Eglin's Alaqua Bayou. Flotation samples from Greg Mikell's excavations at the Bell site yielded maize (12 cupule fragments) in a fire pit or hearth feature. A carbonized wood sample from this pit produced a radiocarbon date of cal A.D. 1280 to 1440 (two sigma; see table 11.2). A Jefferson Ware vessel also was recovered by Mikell from the same feature. Fort Walton ceramics totaled 85 percent of the assemblage when plain sand- and grit-tempered wares are included, or 72 percent without plainwares included. Among the shell-tempered wares recovered from the two sites are Pensacola Plain and Incised, Bell Plain, Mississippi Plain, D'Olive Incised, Moundville Incised, and Mound Place Incised; all occur in small quantities. Moreover, the Bell site produced a small number of protohistoric or historic sherds, including Lamar Complicated Stamped, Leon Check Stamped, and Jefferson Ware (Mikell 1995b: 114), suggesting a later component.

Site 8Wl119 is a large, essentially single-component habitation site found within one of the familiar clusters of Mississippi-period sites on Alaqua Bayou. Associated with this site are two other large villages, a mound-village complex, a cemetery, a burial site, and a camp. No radiocarbon dates are available from 8Wl119 (Campbell et al. 2007).

Maize found at 8Wl119 was directly associated with Pensacola Plain, Pensacola Incised, Fort Walton Incised, and Point Washington Incised ceramics. The shell-tempered wares constitute 37 percent of the assemblage, whereas the sand/grit-tempered Fort Walton types total 63 percent of the inventory. Bell Plain, a type found in significant numbers closer to Mobile Bay but very uncommon in this area, also was recovered. Moreover, Moundville Incised and Mound Place Incised, again rare in this part of the panhandle coast, were recovered from the site. Also found were a few protohistoric or historic sherds, including Lamar Complicated Stamped, Ocmulgee Fields Incised, Chattahoochee Brushed, and Leon Check Stamped. Most of the protohistoric or historic materials were surface finds, but two Leon sherds were found at depths between 50 cm and 80 cm below the surface (Campbell et al. 2007: 82).

There are some notable correlations in the Late Mississippi–period component and the later protohistoric shell middens at 8Wl119. Oyster shell midden deposits were associated with Fort Walton and Pensacola ceramics, while protohistoric sherds were found in direct association with a large concentration of *Rangia*, or marsh clam, shells. During the Middle Woodland in Choctawhatchee Bay, the salinity apparently greatly decreased, and previously abundant oysters were replaced by *Rangia*. The narrow pass into the extreme eastern part of the bay at Destin may have been closed, causing serious changes in the local environment. This stark transition can be seen in the archaeological record at Santa Rosa–Swift Creek sites. Perhaps a brief change in salinity also occurred in the sixteenth or seventeenth century, resulting in a temporary shortage of oysters (Campbell et al. 2007; Harris and Pokrant 2003; Thomas and Campbell 1993).

Pensacola Bay

As he did elsewhere, Gordon Willey followed C. B. Moore into Pensacola Bay. Few studies in the Pensacola estuary system have focused on the Mississippi period, although there are some limited data from different areas around the bay. Pensacola Bay is the largest estuary in the central part of the northern Gulf coast, with three rivers feeding it from the north: the Escambia, Yellow, and Blackwater rivers. The Escambia River has more sites along its margins than any other drainage in the study area (the larger number of sites could possibly be due to sampling bias). Although the bay has been the subject of reconnaissance surveys over the years, no comprehensive surveys have been undertaken. Reconnaissance survey also has been conducted along the rivers and in some areas adjacent to the bay and bayous, but there is no synthesis of any chronological period (Bense 1989a, 1989b; Little et al. 1988; Phillips 1989, 1995; Phillips and Bense

1990; Phillips and McKenzie 1992). Florida Master Site File data indicate that mounds, villages, short-term camps, and a number of cemeteries are present within the bay system

In the late 1980s, UWF's John Phillips (1989, 1995) excavated a Mississippi-period cemetery site, Hickory Ridge (8Es1280), near a large estuary just west of Pensacola. A Mississippi-period village site (8Es1052) was recorded about 50 m west of the cemetery. Survey and limited excavation of the cemetery identified an area of approximately 15 m by 18 m where burials were capped with many partially reconstructable vessels. Among the ceramics recovered was a Pensacola Incised, *variety* Gasque vessel; the Gasque motif seems to have been derived from Moundville Engraved, *variety* Hemphill, combining reptilian and avian elements. Hickory Ridge yielded other Moundville imports as well (Sommerkamp 2008). Three burials were documented with exotic grave goods, including mica and greenstone celts (Phillips 1989, 1995).

Ceramic vessels recovered from Hickory Ridge include Bottle Creek– and Bear Point–phase Pensacola pottery, as well as several Moundville types (Fuller and Stowe 1982; Phillips 1995). Over 99 percent of the vessels were shell tempered, with the final count totaling 3,202 sherds. More than 2,300 sherds were Mississippi Plain, *variety* Warrior (table 11.3). A radiocarbon date of cal A.D. 1310–1470 was obtained from Burial 1 (table 11.2). This burial contained 7 vessels, including 4 Pensacola Incised, *variety* Bear Point vessels, 1 Moundville Incised, *variety* Snow's Bend, and 1 D'Olive Incised, *variety* Arnica, as well as mica and a nonlocal chert (either Citronelle or Tuscaloosa gravel from the interior) projectile point (Phillips 1995:80).

On the eastern side of Pensacola Bay, the Aden Bayou site (8SR17) yielded an assemblage with more than 85 percent Pensacola-series pottery (Thomas and Campbell 1993). Prentice Thomas and Associates' recent return to 8SR17 for Eglin Air Force Base has produced more Pensacola ceramics, including a bird effigy. This work suggests that the site is probably a large village with one or more structures. Erosion has taken a substantial part of the site already, a trend that continues today. Several unusual features occur at Aden Bayou, including a clay-lined pit and a very large pit of unknown function, partly exposed and damaged by Hurricane Dennis in 2005. This site was originally assigned to the Four Mile Point phase (A.D. 1400–1600), and subsequent work there supports this designation (L. Janice Campbell, personal communication 2008).

Table 11.3. Sherds recovered from the Hickory Ridge site

Ceramic Type	Count
Mississippi Plain, *variety* Warrior	2,391
Bell Plain, *variety* Hale	144
Moundville Incised, *variety* Moundville	13
Moundville Incised, *variety* Snow's Bend	15
Moundville Incised, *variety* unspecified	10
D'Olive Incised, *variety* Arnica	27
Pensacola Incised, *variety* Gasque	35
Pensacola Incised, *variety* Bear Point	188
Pensacola Incised, *variety* Moore	21
Pensacola Incised, *variety* unspecified	15
Moundville Engraved, *variety* unspecified	24
Shell-tempered indeterminate	313
Sand-tempered plain	6
Total	3,202

Source: Phillips 1995: 86–93.

In 1942, Willey visited a tract of land that is now part of the National Park Service Naval Live Oaks Reservation on Gulf Breeze peninsula in Pensacola Bay (Willey 1949a). Of the many sites on the reservation, 15 have Mississippi-period components. Two of the largest sites on the reservation are the Butcherpen Mound Complex (8SR29) and the Third Gulf Breeze site (8SR8). In addition to these, the reservation contains accretionary middens, shell midden ridges, individual shell middens, and a large Late Mississippi–period and/or protohistoric cemetery (Doran and Piatek 1985; Harris 1998; Lazarus 1961; Lazarus et al. 1976; Tesar 1973).

The Naval Live Oaks Cemetery (8SR36) was the subject of investigation in the 1960s, initially by a high school student (Randy Head) from Pensacola, who excavated the cemetery for a science fair project. Subsequently, the site was vandalized, and William Lazarus of the Fort Walton Temple Mound Museum led a salvage operation to rescue information (Harris 1998; Lazarus et al. 1976; Tesar 1973).

Collected by Lazarus, the only quantified sample we have from this cemetery is now curated at the National Park Service Southeastern Archaeological Center (SEAC). Ninety-eight percent of the 8,000-sherd assemblage is shell tempered; the most common types include Mississippi Plain and a larger number of unusual Pensacola Incised vessels (table 11.4). SEAC's collection may not be representative of the entire site because of the salvage nature of the project and because that collection was separated in two

Table 11.4. Naval Live Oaks Cemetery Lazarus Collection, National Park Service, Southeastern Archeological Center

Ceramic Type	Count	Weight (g)
Bell Plain	404	3,329.1
D'Olive Incised, *variety* Mary Ann	1	12.3
Fort Walton Incised	4	36.5
Fort Walton Plain	2	22.8
Lake Jackson Plain	1	3.3
Leon Check-Stamped	1	28.0
Mississippi Plain	4,006	32,313.1
Mound Place Incised, *variety* Walton's Camp	19	519.3
Moundville Incised	17	101.0
Parkin Punctated	3	28.3
Pensacola Incised	3,400	42,251.6
Pensacola Plain, *variety* unspecified	3	42.6
Point Washington Incised	8	134.0
Untyped	132	1,000.5
Untyped	29	439.9
Untyped	22	190.9
Total	8,052	80,453.2

Source: Compiled from NPS, SEAC Naval Live Oaks Cemetery 8SR36 database.

parts after excavations (Gail Meyer, Ft. Walton Temple Mound Museum, personal communication, 1999). Lazarus interpreted the large number of vessels from this cemetery as ritual breakage on a large scale (Lazarus et al. 1976). Most of the private collection of Randy Head, encompassing more than 100 boxes, is now curated at the University of West Florida. The Head Collection contains many whole vessels that do not necessarily fit nicely into Bottle Creek or Bear Point types, including many with Southeastern Ceremonial Complex–type motifs such as Pensacola Incised bird effigies and Fort Walton Incised, *variety* Choctawhatchee, six-sided bowls. Other artifacts in the Head Collection include engraved copper birds and gorgets, shell beads, chunky stones, and other worked shell objects.

One of the more unusual ceramic vessels from Naval Live Oaks Cemetery has incised, stylized waves over the entire small bowl. Interestingly, a virtually identical vessel was found at the Johnson site (8Wl50) on Choctawhatchee Bay, which Lazarus (1971) described as having a thick layer of pots that were ritually broken (figure 11.4). The Johnson site vessel was retrieved in 1961 by a local collector and is on loan to the Fort Walton Museum, where it is perhaps erroneously classified as Fort Walton Incised.

The Naval Live Oaks Cemetery was apparently used for a long period of time, but unfortunately we have no radiocarbon dates or good stratigraphic

Figure 11.4. Bowls with similar incised decorations from Pensacola and Choctawhatchee bays: *top*, Naval Live Oaks Cemetery site, Pensacola Bay (courtesy of UWF Archaeology Institute); *bottom*, the Johnson site, Choctawhatchee Bay (courtesy of Fort Walton Beach Indian Temple Mound Museum).

evidence from the site. Although the date for the earliest use of the site is unclear, we have chronological data from artifacts interred with several burials. Early Spanish contact-period artifacts including Nueva Cadiz and Chevron glass beads and lead shot also were found (Harris 1998).

A comparison of the assemblages from the Naval Live Oaks Cemetery, the Aden Bayou site, and the earlier Hickory Ridge site suggests an increasing frequency of Fort Walton ceramics in the Pensacola Bay system through time. A radiocarbon date from Hickory Ridge ranged from A.D. 1310 to 1470 (cal two sigma; see table 11.2), and shell-tempered ceramics (including Pensacola Incised, Mississippi Plain, Moundville Incised, and D'Olive Incised) made up 99 percent of the assemblage (Phillips 1989, 1995). The Aden Bayou site, assigned to the Four Mile Point phase (A.D. 1400–1600), yielded a lower percentage of Pensacola and related shell-tempered wares at 85 percent, with 15 percent Fort Walton ceramic types. Including the Naval Live Oaks Cemetery in this comparison is problematic because the quantified SEAC sample may not be representative of the assemblage as a whole. Ninety-eight percent of the salvaged sherds are shell tempered, which is consistent with the earlier Hickory Ridge assemblage. However, preliminary observation of the Head Collection from Naval Live Oaks seems to indicate a larger number of sand- or grit-tempered vessels. The presence of sixteenth-century Spanish artifacts from the cemetery confirms a late date for some portion of it, but the context of many Spanish artifacts and their relationship to the native ceramics is unclear.

Discussion

The Mississippi-period people of the Gulf coast estuaries of Pensacola, Choctawhatchee, and St. Andrew bays share some characteristics with their neighbors to the east and west, but generally the area exhibits less dependence on agriculture, fewer mounds, and probably smaller populations. The most convincing evidence for a consistent connection to the broader Mississippian world is iconography, with some ceramics displaying motifs similar to those seen at large Mississippian centers such as Moundville. Changes in settlement patterns following late Weeden Island times might also relate to circumstances beyond the local area. Choosing not to reoccupy sites in the interior may reflect a move closer to the bays, bayous, and major rivers, perhaps to facilitate trade with the core regions of Fort Walton and Pensacola cultures. Travel from one estuary to the other was made easier by the presence of barrier islands that shield the bays, and in the case of Pensacola and Choctawhatchee, the two are actually connected.

One geographic characteristic shared by these bays is the lack of major rivers that extend deep into the interior reaches of Georgia, Alabama, and Mississippi. With the exception of the Escambia River in Pensacola, the interiors north of the bays are almost devoid of Mississippi-period settlement. The larger number of Escambia sites may be explained because the river travels farther into the interior than the others (and for part of its course, in the general direction of the Bottle Creek site in the upper Mobile delta). Although there are pockets of marginally arable soils along the rivers, the region as a whole is not well suited for agriculture.

The three sites discussed at which maize was recovered may be very late, perhaps even protohistoric. Each site assemblage included late ceramic types from various contexts, even though some of the radiocarbon dates seem to be earlier. Work at the Mulatto Oaks site (8SR393) on Pensacola Bay also produced maize, but, as with the sites with maize from the other two estuaries discussed above, there is a protohistoric or historic occupation (Lee and Joy 1989). Excavations at eighteenth-century sites in Pensacola have shown that protohistoric types continue to be part of assemblages much later than previously thought. In fact, types such as Chattahoochee Brushed, Walnut Roughened (formerly Pensacola Brushed), and Lamar and Jefferson wares do not appear with any regularity until after 1722 in Pensacola (Harris and Eschbach 2006).

Current UWF ceramic classifications are not necessarily compatible with earlier Pensacola Bay investigations or with analysis by other researchers discussed above, so a one-to-one comparison cannot be made. Excavations at Pensacola's presidios have led to a finer-grained classification of protohistoric and historic Indian ceramics. Temper types are noted in all pottery sorting to avoid confusion regarding the relationship between shell-tempered prehistoric ceramics (usually classified as Pensacola, Bell, or Mississippi types) and purely historic types (Walnut Roughened, for example) seen at the eighteenth-century Spanish sites of Santa Maria and Santa Rosa. Lamar (sand- and/or grit-tempered) and Jefferson (grog-tempered) wares are distinguished using Worth's (1992) classification system developed at Fig Springs. Because there was no prehistoric tradition of grog tempering in Pensacola (with the exception of a minor amount in Fort Walton ceramics), the rather sudden introduction of grog tempering in the historic period is seen as a significant marker (Harris and Eschbach 2006).

There are no good ethnohistoric records for the three bay systems, so it is not possible to take a direct historical approach to establish cultural connections with the late prehistoric period along this part of the Gulf coast. Tristan de Luna observed corn growing somewhere north of Pensacola in 1559, but exactly where is not clear (Priestly 1928). The next known primary account of any named historic group comes from the late 1600s when scouts from New Spain and Apalache mention that some villages were home to the Panzacola Indians, a native population forced to flee because of wars (Andrez de Pez 1689; Hann 1988b, 2006; Leonard 1936; Sigüenza y Góngora 1693; Torres y Ayala 1693). Thus far we have not been able to establish a direct connection between the shell-tempered Pensacola ceramic series and the historic Panzacola (Harris 1999, 2003). Mikell (1992a: 61) states, "Perhaps concomitant with the Pensacola Bear Point Phase the Four Mile Point Phase witnessed a kind of Pensacola florescence around Choctawhatchee Bay that may have been related to the growing power of chiefdoms that eventually became the historic Pensacola and perhaps the Chatot." There is recent evidence that, at least by the eighteenth century, the Chatot assemblage was dominated by sand-tempered pottery (Waselkov and Gums 2000). There does seem to be a link historically between the Panzacola and the Chatot (also known as Chacato), but the Panzacola emigrated to Mississippi in the early 1700s (Coker 1997; Harris 1999).

Increasingly clearer direct connections exist between the bays of the western panhandle Gulf coast, particularly Pensacola and Choctawhatchee. Similar ritual practices in cemeteries and almost identical and unusual pottery designs suggest close communication. Thomas and Campbell (1993) consider the ritual breaking of large numbers of pots reflective of indirect evidence of agriculture. Citing Wright (1986), they further suggest that the presence of "sherd caps" on ceremonial Fort Walton–Pensacola sites may be evidence of the busk ceremony, a harvest ritual that commonly involved the breaking of pottery (Thomas and Campbell 1993: 615). This hypothesis is worthy of future investigation.

Mound construction in the Mississippi period decreased in northwest Florida, significantly reduced from the large number built by Weeden Island groups in the area. Complex social organization may be reflected more in the clustering of sites around mounds and cemeteries than in typical characteristics common at larger Mississippian sites. Evidence of palisade constructions has not been identified from the western panhandle region. Certainly, trade networks along the coast and into the core areas required coordination, and their existence suggests some level of complex social organization.

No doubt, the most obvious connection with the rest of the Mississippian Southeast is seen in iconography, particularly as it is associated with burial furniture and rituals. The presence of engraved copper and other exotic artifacts in Gulf coast cemeteries reflects a clear influence from other, more traditional Mississippian centers, especially on very late sites where Pensacola ceramics have been observed to increase in frequency through time to the east, as Fort Walton ceramics increase to the west. Traditional Mississippian influence can be seen in cranial deformation practices in late prehistoric cemeteries. Organic preservation in the area is normally poor, but some remains (such as those from the Naval Live Oaks Cemetery and the Fort Walton Temple Mound) clearly show evidence of this common Mississippian practice.

Mississippian settlement seems to have been concentrated very near the shores of estuaries in this region, with a few exceptions. Subsistence practices focused on estuary resources, with little arable soil suitable for cultivation of domesticates. If there was an increased dependency on domesticated plants in the region during the late prehistoric period, perhaps exchange facilitated that increase. Unlike in the core regions of Pensacola and Fort Walton, coastal populations were probably somewhat more dispersed.

Summary

Mississippi-period populations along the far western Florida and Alabama Gulf coast practiced many rituals familiar to the larger centers in the Southeast. Although there is little evidence of agriculture, some maize and beans have been found, but these may be associated with protohistoric or historic Indian components rather than the Mississippi period. And if the few domesticates found in the region are indeed prehistoric, they could have been traded into the area, rather than grown locally in any appreciable amount. Mounds are few, but sites tend to be clustered around mounds or cemeteries, at least in the larger two systems, Pensacola and Choctawhatchee bays. Palisades have not been identified, and known sites are virtually restricted to the shores of the estuaries. With the possible exception of the Escambia River valley, the interior was almost completely abandoned. The strongest evidence of broader Mississippian connections is reflected in symbolism represented in the ceramic arts, suggesting shared aspects of basic cosmology (Sommerkamp 2008).

Confusion over nomenclature continues: is it Pensacola, or is it Fort Walton? Gordon Willey set researchers up for confusion when he named these two assemblages. Pensacola is not the core area of Pensacola pottery production, and Fort Walton is not the core area of Fort Walton pottery production. Clearly the people of these three large estuaries borrowed ceramic traditions from the Pensacola and Fort Walton core regions, but they might have shared few other cultural traits. Fifty years after Willey visited the area, the relationship between these two ceramic traditions is still poorly understood. Pensacola, Choctawhatchee, and St. Andrew bays have more in common with each other than with the core regions, so maybe they have a separate culture history. It is possibly a mistake to continue trying to separate "Fort Walton" from "Pensacola" along the central Gulf coast; instead we should perhaps accept the existence of another coastal Mississippian variant.

Answering more complex (and relevant) questions regarding Gulf coast Mississippian people first requires recognition that the lifeways of those people may have been very different from those of the riverine centers that influenced their pottery designs. Current models of late Mississippian culture in the three estuaries still often begin with a description of the large ceremonial centers to the east and west, then move to the largest mound on this part of the Gulf coast, the Fort Walton Temple Mound, as an example of coastal culture. Fifty years after Gordon Willey described Pensacola pottery, we still know very little about coastal Mississippi-period culture in the bay system that inspired its name. Some sites have been investigated (primarily by cultural resource management projects with limited long-term research designs), but few questions have focused solely on Mississippian culture around Pensacola Bay. Research in all three estuary systems could benefit greatly from different perspectives that go beyond descriptive culture history, a necessary step in interpreting data but, it is hoped, only the very beginning. One small piece at a time, aspects of Mississippi-period lifeways in the northwest Florida panhandle are emerging as significantly different from Pensacola culture at Bottle Creek in the Mobile-Tensaw Delta and Fort Walton culture in the Apalachicola River valley and Tallahassee Hills.

Acknowledgments

Thanks to the staff and students at the UWF Archaeology Institute for graphics and support. Special thanks to John Phillips of UWF for sharing his ideas of 20 years regarding Pensacola's Mississippi period. I would also like to acknowledge Jan Campbell and the others at Prentice Thomas and Associates for providing data and ideas. The employees of the Fort Walton Beach Heritage Park and Cultural Center have been a great help with images and in their continued interest in the archaeological resources of the Choctawhatchee Bay area. And big thanks to Keith and Nancy for putting all of these articles together and for providing us with a platform from which to examine Florida's Mississippi cultures anew.

12

The Mississippi Period in Florida

A View from the Mississippian World of Cahokia

JOHN E. KELLY

In this closing chapter I attempt to place the Mississippi-period societies of Florida within a much broader temporal and spatial context of the larger Mississippian world, from the perspective that reflects my area of expertise, Cahokia, located within the central Mississippi River valley. As discussed in the introductory chapter, Mississippian culture is an archaeological construct that covers virtually the entire southeastern North American continent and beyond, especially to the north and west (see figure 1.3). It encompasses societies that created large residential communities with platform mounds that surround large plazas (Lewis and Stout 1998). Domesticated crops, in particular maize, dominate most Mississippian subsistence economies, especially after the twelfth century A.D. A majority of these societies exhibit material culture that includes a diverse ceramic assemblage. Except for many groups living along the coast and much of the lower Mississippi River valley, lithic assemblages were dominated by chert arrow points and hoes, especially in the core area centered on the Ohio-Mississippi river confluence (Brown et al. 1990; Cobb 2000). An exchange network that involved exotic materials such as copper, greenstone, basalt, fireclay, mica, fluorite, and marine shell used in the creation of ritual and status items important in their world was critical to the interaction of elites and religious specialists. The artisans responsible for these ritually important items were craft specialists embedded in the religious system of each society.

As evinced by the tribal groups at the time of contact, the diversity of languages reflects the cultural mosaic of their ancestors, these numerous precolumbian Mississippian peoples and their societies. The five centuries

(A.D. 1000–1500) of what we archaeologists term "Mississippian" represent a series of parallel histories for each of the various regions that constitute the geographic diversity of the Southeast and lower Midwest. Mississippian societies were linked through interactions that involved the procurement and movement of raw materials and finished products, not so much for what we as Western scholars perceive as trade but through complex relationships between individuals and groups embedded in ritual and an overarching worldview that still exists today throughout much of the native world. The roots of modern Indian societies are firmly set in the matrix of those precolumbian societies called Mississippian, although the directions they took after European contact were multiple and divergent.

In discussing the broader context of the societies inhabiting Florida, it is important to recognize the five centuries of interaction between the Mississippian world to the north and the natives of the panhandle state. A few assumptions underlie this discussion. First, we are dealing with a complex and dynamic set of natural settings where people lived for at least the past 12,000 years. Second, the chapters in this volume show how the various regions have distinct histories that themselves changed at various rates. In some instances the histories are not necessarily continuous through time, and their distribution in space is equally discontinuous. Given this dynamism, both the underlying natural components and the cultural landscape provide a unique opportunity to examine a complex set of interwoven relationships that extend northward into the interior of the Southeast as well as south and west into the Caribbean (White 2005b). The manner in which those Florida peoples and societies were interacting with the interior is the focus of this chapter.

Mississippian: The Concept

In general the preceding chapters accentuate the strides being made in Florida's Mississippi-period research. This is timely work, and Ashley and White's introductory chapter sets the stage for what is taking place. Although the term *Mississippian* can refer to a culture and a cultural tradition, Ashley and White make an important point at the outset when they use "Mississippi period" to characterize the time frame from A.D. 1000 through 1500, because many of the state's late precolumbian complexes are not Mississippian in their content.

The term has a lot of baggage associated with it, extending back to William Holmes (1903), who originally used "Middle Mississippi" to define a ceramic province in the central Mississippi River valley extending from Peoria to Memphis. The Midwestern Taxonomic System of the 1930s and 1940s (McKern 1934) and its trait list format brought order to the archaeological world of the Midwest at that time. Much of the systematic study of Middle Mississippi culture, especially its origins and development, was carried out by Phillips, Ford, and Griffin (1951) as part of their joint archaeological survey of the lower Mississippi alluvial valley between 1940 and 1947. Later Willey and Phillips (1958) modified this approach into a somewhat more useful system still used today. Griffin's (1968) seminal article in *Science* did not merely highlight what defined Mississippian; his map said it all. Griffin's paper emphasized the geographic diversity of Mississippian, with a number of specific macroregional complexes.

The WPA work of the late 1930s and early 1940s resulted in important and large-scale excavations that provided insight into the nature of Mississippian settlements, especially mound centers, such as Angel, Jonathan Creek, Macon Plateau, and Hiwassee Island, to a name a few. With the more recent cultural resource management work of the past half century, our understanding of Mississippian societies has accelerated dramatically, especially in the past three decades. Nonetheless, smaller, focused research still continues to contribute to various topics, and this is particularly true of many of the chapters herein.

Because we are dealing with 500 years of history, tradition, and an array of Mississippian complexes, the approach I employ involves the delineation of a sequence of horizons (Willey and Phillips 1958) that can be used to integrate regional differences within the Mississippian world. As discussed by Willey and Phillips (1958: 33), a "horizon . . . may be defined as *a primarily spatial continuity represented by cultural traits and assemblages whose nature and mode of occurrence permit the assumption of broad and rapid spread*" (italics in the original). Like its temporal counterpart "tradition," a horizon is the unit that serves to integrate spatial differences. There are certain horizon styles that in my opinion are the elements within the horizon that link numerous different societies geographically within a relatively short period of time. Whereas one may use the term *period* (thereby emphasizing the temporal aspect), I want to accentuate the spatial aspect.

Discussion

Formative or Pre-Mississippian

The *Formative* or *pre-Mississippian horizon* refers to a period that covers the tenth and first part of the eleventh century. This includes a diversity of cultural entities, such as Coles Creek, Emergent Mississippian, and a variety of other regional Late Woodland cultures, such as West Jefferson, Dillenger, Woodstock, Yankeetown, and McKelvey, contemporaneous yet very distinct complexes that interacted with one another. This would include the early St. Johns II Mill Cove Complex of northeastern Florida along the lower St. Johns River (Ashley, chapter 5, this volume) and the early Fort Walton components in the Apalachicola Valley (White et al., chapter 10, this volume).

The construction of earthen (and, in some areas such as Florida, shell) mounds has a long history in the Eastern Woodlands, with some of the earliest mounds built in Florida and Louisiana. Given this history, mound building represents an integral component of many pre-Mississippian communities throughout the Southeast, and some, such as Poverty Point, were massive areas of monumental construction and the focus of ritual activity. The construction of large rectangular platform mounds around large plazas was a major component of Coles Creek societies in the lower Mississippi River valley area and some Weeden Island societies of southern Georgia (e.g., Kolomoki) and Florida (e.g., McKeithen). Unlike later Mississippian societies where mounds and plazas were at the core of relatively large populations numbering in the hundreds and some instances a few thousand, most pre-Mississippian mound centers generally lacked much of a residential population. To the north in the American Bottom of the central Mississippi River valley, small villages have been defined, with larger nucleated villages evident by the latter half of the tenth century (Kelly 1990b; Kelly et al. 2007). Many of these widely dispersed agricultural villages were organized around small community squares or plazas with symbolically significant central features (Kelly 1990a; Kelly et al. 2007). In some instances by the beginning of the eleventh century, earthen architecture in the form of small rectangular platform mounds was present.

For many of the interior societies, corn was being integrated into an existing suite of native crops that included starchy seeds (*Chenopodium* sp., *Polygonum* sp., maygrass, and little barley grass), oily seeds (sunflower and marshelder), squash, and tobacco. While corn, squash, and beans were the dominant crops at the time of European contact, as discussed by Fritz and Lopinot (2007), there has been a tendency to see corn as the primary crop based upon its ubiquity in the archaeological record. Certainly maize was seemingly ubiquitous by the beginning of the ninth century in the lower Midwest (Johannessen 1984); however, $^{13}C/^{12}C$ ratios from human remains suggest that this was not the case even in early Mississippian Cahokia (Ambrose et al. 2003).

What seems to tie the pre-Mississippian societies to the north with those to the south is a duo of diametrically opposed materials. One, a utilitarian item, is check-stamped pottery (I. Brown 1982); the second is the small rectilinear copper plate. When the term *Emergent Mississippian* was coming into vogue in the mid-1980s (Kelly et al. 1984; Kelly 1987, 1990b) I tried to plot the distribution of different traits and materials. For example, shell-tempered ceramics, which initially occurred in the southern Ozarks (Price and Price 1984) and presumably spread into the upper part of the embayment area of the lower Mississippi alluvial valley, had a limited distribution at this time (Lafferty 2008). Even though cord-marked pottery is ubiquitous throughout the Eastern Woodlands, the presence of check-stamped pottery and its distribution are more intriguing. This connection is alluded to in several of the preceding chapters.

The small rectangular copper plate from northeastern Florida is the other item of interest (Ashley, chapter 5, this volume). Sorting out the specific contexts of such plates from Moore's (1894a, 1894b, 1895) excavations is difficult because some plates are similar to those that date to the eleventh century and the next horizon, the Pre-Classic Mississippian. Similar small square plates have been recovered from tenth-century contexts in the American Bottom and lower Illinois River valley (Sampson and Esarey 1993). Their presence is suggestive of a potential horizon style that is pre-SECC (Southeastern Ceremonial Complex). Unfortunately, we lack sufficient contextual data from southwestern Illinois and northeastern Florida that would provide a much better dating of these unique pieces. Likewise, the source of the copper also is an issue. Presumably the copper came from the southern Appalachians or the western Great Lakes or the glacial drift area to the south of the Great Lakes source (Halsey 2008).

One of the more attractive and symbolically significant raw materials from Florida is marine shell, especially whelk (*Busycon* spp.). The distribution of these items from pre-Mississippian contexts has yet to be studied fully. Some insight into the possible significance of marine shell at interior sites is evident in the "Cahokia" microlithic industry at the Zebree site in northeastern Arkansas during the mid-tenth century (Morse and Morse 1980, 1983). This craft industry was initially attributed to Cahokia (Morse and Morse 1983) and in some of the recent literature continues to be portrayed as being derived from Cahokia at the outset of the "Big Bang" (the florescence and sudden spread of Mississippian culture [Pauketat 2004: 11]). Instead we see the beginning of marine-bead manufacture occurring some 300 km to the south just before the amalgamation of sites into a single large (17–34 ha) community at Cahokia (Kelly 2008). It should be noted that Morse did correctly observe that the raw materials for the lithic industry were derived from the Crescent Hills quarry area, 275 km to the north and 30 km to the southwest of Cahokia. The route suggested by Morse involved going along the St. Francois River north to the St. Francois Mountains and into the Big River drainage, where the quarry was located at the junction of the Big and Meramec rivers. In addition to the chert raw materials, "basaltic" rocks were recovered from dikes and streams around the St. Francois Mountains. These materials became a major part of the megalithic-axe manufacture in the Cahokia area that appears to have begun as one of the first craft activities at the onset of the eleventh century prior to the Big Bang (Pauketat and Alt 2004). A similar lithic material, greenstone, from Alabama (Welch 1991; Wilson 2001), was presumably being used in the production of large spatulate celts present at sites in northeastern Florida. Whether these are from the next horizon is unclear at this time.

Villages in the American Bottom were part of the transformation of Woodland agricultural societies, which we have characterized as a stage of cultural evolution within the regions between St. Louis and Memphis called Emergent Mississippian. Because of the tautology associated with the term (Fortier and McElrath 2002; Muller 1997), we use it as a cultural complex on a taxonomic level comparable with Coles Creek. Part of the late Emergent Mississippian is the symbolic role of fertility and its material expression, in this instance, the red-filmed bowls, hooded bottles, and seed jars. The initial appearance of both these forms and red filming can be traced to the lower Mississippi valley (Kelly 1980). This fertility "cult" climaxes in the Cahokia area with the fireclay figurines of the twelfth century (Emerson 1982, 1997; Fortier 1992).

Pre-Classic Mississippian

The term *Pre-Classic Mississippian*, A.D. 1000–1200, refers to the beginnings of Mississippian at places such as Cahokia, Macon Plateau, and Obion. Again, Grant Mound along the St. Johns River in northeastern Florida, while not Mississippian, does exhibit continued interaction with early Mississippian societies to the north (Ashley, chapter 5, this volume). And Late Woodland societies continued to be interspersed throughout this area during the course of their transformation into Mississippian. With Cahokia well in place, the emergence of Mississippian throughout the numerous regions of the Southeast and lower Midwest as a phenomenon perhaps best lends itself to Stephen Williams's (1990) use of chaos theory.

One of the most important horizon markers is the long-nosed god (LNG) maskette ear ornament originally described by Williams and Goggin (1954) and discussed by Griffin (1968), Hall (1989, 1991, 1997), Kelly (1980, 1991), and Duncan and Diaz-Granados (2000). As noted originally by Hall (1989), these maskettes are linked to an individual in central Siouan myths known as Red-horn or "He-who-wears-human-heads-as-earrings." The story, originally recorded by Radin (1923) for the Ho-Chunk (Winnebago) and by Skinner (1925) for their tribal cognate, the Ioway, provides an important mythological bridge between pre-Mississippian societies in the midcontinent and their present-day descendants. The earliest clear representation of this individual occurs in the rock art of Picture Cave in east-central Missouri (Diaz Granados et al. 2001; Diaz Granados 2004) and the Gottschall rock shelter in southwestern Wisconsin (Salzer 1987). The art depicted highlights the Braden style of the SECC (Phillips and Brown 1978). In examining the onset of this style, Brown and Kelly (2000) pose that it emerged at Cahokia and the surrounding area by the onset of the Mississippi period, ca. A.D. 1050. The SECC crystallized in a formal manner by ca. A.D. 1200, when Mississippian societies were fully in place across much of the landscape of the Southeast and the lower Midwest.

Several aspects of these maskettes are important and have been noted by others. First, they are created from either marine shell or copper; the former are more common. Second, they are distributed throughout the Midwest and Southeast and, where evident, were in association with burials. Third, Hall (1991, 1997) has proposed that they reflect a form of gift associated with adoption and fictive kin relations—in effect, the tie that binds. Finally, several elements in the overall motif of this item include the bifurcated crown and the dot-in-circle eye. Hall (1991) has discussed the significance of the former. The latter I believe is symbolically important, and research on its distribution should be pursued. The eye can be viewed as a portal into the soul of an individual. As a rather simple but distinct motif, it appeared on other crafted items over two centuries prior to the SECC. Examples include a limestone bittern-effigy chisel at the Range site from a late tenth-century context (Williams 2007), two kingfisher bone pins from the region (Farnsworth and Koldehoff 2007), and a two-headed bird head from ninth- or tenth-century contexts (Sank and Sampson 1994). All are birds, that is, upper-world creatures, and two are birds with long beaks.

While it is not possible to speculate on its relationship to the long-nosed god maskettes, I believe the eye motif was important beginning in the late tenth century and persisting into the twelfth century. The copper long-nosed god maskettes from Grant Mound link this area of Florida to the rest of the native world to the north and thus highlight the importance of these items to societies over a large geographic area that includes much of the Mississippi Valley. In addition to the LNG maskettes, numerous other copper objects are present from the various mounds excavated by Moore (1894a, 1894b, 1895) in northeastern Florida. Unfortunately, as discussed earlier, we do not know the specific source of the copper.

For those societies in the interior, especially Cahokia, marine shell was an extremely important commodity. While some marine shell was present before A.D. 1050, its presence at Cahokia exploded into ubiquity with the onset of the "Big Bang." The most prevalent marine shell taxon in terms of number is the common Atlantic marginella, followed by the lightning whelk, a sinistral (left-handed spiral) species. Both species are prevalent along the Gulf of Mexico and south Atlantic (Kozuch 1998). The large whelks were converted into a variety of shell bead types and later shell pendants, gorgets, and cups.

Early Cahokia was at the center of a universe of agricultural communities within the central Mississippi River valley. Given its scale and ritual configuration within a region of highly differentiated settlements, it is considered to have been an ancient city (Kelly and Brown 2011), composed of a large (150 ha) epicenter of four quadrilateral plazas with Monks Mound, the largest earthen monument north of Mexico, at the center. Its origins are well rooted in the Emergent Mississippian societies of the region. There was undoubtedly some immigration, especially from down-valley in the area of the Ohio and Mississippi rivers' confluence; however, this was preceded by interaction with communities throughout this area until

Cahokia's abandonment in the latter part of the fourteenth century. Certainly Cahokia was dominant, reaching its apogee in the twelfth century; however, it did not dominate other societies politically in the manner some have suggested (Emerson 1997). The landscape of the midcontinent during this period was a mosaic of societies with distinct regional histories. In trying to grapple with some understanding of what was taking place, Robert Hall has best expressed it in his writings:

> There are some things that can be learned of Mississippian customs and beliefs directly from archaeology. There are other things that may be inferred from ethnographic knowledge of historic societies whose ancestors lived within the orbit of influence of Mississippian level cultures or were actually Mississippian town dwellers themselves. For an example of a tribe descended from Cahokia I would first look to the Siouan-speaking Osage. (Hall 2006: 8)

> If there is a role for Mesoamerican contacts in accounting for the Big Bang at Cahokia it minimally involved the receipt of new ritual practices that added a Mexican flavor to a *down-home menu of fertility, adoption, and world renewal rites*. To some extent it may also have involved new ways to personify aspects of nature that provided mantles of authority for religious and political leaders. In any case, the first evidence of suspected Mesoamerican contacts within the Cahokia Mississippian tradition coincides with the Big Bang itself, around A.D. 1050, although by that time there had already been two thousand years of interaction with tropical America whose effects were less dramatic and more unexpected. (Hall 2006: 14; italics added)

The fertility component was rooted initially in the Emergent Mississippian community plans and the ceramic vessels (red-filmed bowls, seed jars, and hooded bottles) of the late tenth century (Kelly 2007). The importance of fertility was enhanced, incorporating these themes of reproduction into the carefully crafted red fireclay earth-mother figurines (Emerson 1982, 1997; Fortier 1992) of the Cahokia apogee a century later. The world renewal rites that also have fertility as a major component were re-created at Cahokia and expressed in the design motifs seen on the surface of Ramey Incised jars. As discussed by Pauketat and Emerson (1991), these vessels epitomize containers used in rites of intensification. They, along with local copies, are widely distributed across much of the Midwest and out onto the Plains (Hall 1991; Kelly 1980, 1991). Although Pauketat (2004: fig. 6.1) attempts to portray these as having a comparable distribution south of Cahokia, this is not the case. Regardless, Ramey Incised jars are a palimpsest of several production traditions and do represent containers with a distinct symbolic message emblazoned on their shoulders. The design layout emphasizes the quartered circle and in other instances the hawk. The individual motifs that make up the design accentuate other meanings, such as the scroll reflecting the whelk spiral (see Emerson 1989).

Adoption was the mechanism for these ideas and material elements to move readily across the landscape of the midcontinent. The clan structure of historic groups was the social matrix in which all of this occurred, regardless of the material expression and subsistence economies.

The connection between Florida and the emerging Mississippian world at this time continued to be through the export of marine shell. This was not simply an economic transaction but one involving symbolically charged materials that involved pilgrimages to faraway places (see Helms 1988). This would include the Atlantic coast at the mouth of the St. Johns River and the Gulf coast from Tampa Bay north and west to Mobile Bay. While one would not classify St. Johns and the Mill Cove Complex of northeastern Florida as Mississippian, the early Fort Walton occupation of the Apalachicola region is generally seen as a continuation of Weeden Island, eventually exhibiting some of the trappings of Mississippian. While these societies may have been participating in the interactions to the north, they were uniquely independent except for the maize agriculture and mound centers with rectangular platform mounds in the Fort Walton culture. The only other links to this interaction are the numerous copper plates and long-nosed god maskettes from the Mill Cove Complex and the embossed copper plates in Fort Walton at Lake Jackson in Tallahassee, although the latter have been placed late in the sequence.

Classic Mississippian

The *Classic horizon* revolves around Holmes's (1903) concept of the Mississippian ceramic province. At the time, there was no real sense of the temporality of this province, and the overall purpose of his study was the observable geographic differences in the ceramic collections at repositories such as the Smithsonian Institution, where he worked. It was later that others began to expand the use of this concept, even before there was chronological control. The Mississippian ceramic assemblages studied were for the most part derived from cemeteries and mounds in an area along the Mississippi River that stretched from Memphis to Peoria. The stylistic similarities of effigy bowls and other forms from these cemeteries seem to indicate that many date to ca. A.D. 1200–1400. These two centuries also correspond to the rapid spread of the SECC, which we believe has its origins in the central Mississippi River valley around Cahokia during the preceding two centuries (Brown and Kelly 2000). In many respects this is the apogee of the SECC, as originally envisioned. By the beginning of this horizon the Mississippian world had crystallized. Large walled towns with mounds and plazas were spread throughout the greater Southeast (Lewis and Stout 1998) as part of what might be considered the incipient stages of urbanism (Kelly and Brown 2011). The cosmology of the SECC, while often associated with marine whelk shells and copper, was exhibited on other materials. For example, designs and motifs were often transferred to specific ceramic forms employed in ceremonies.

Negative-painted plates at the Angel site (Hilgeman 2000) and the negative-painted bottles from the Nashville basin and southeastern Missouri (Phillips 1970) accentuate some of the primary motifs and themes of the SECC. These vessels are not as well represented at Cahokia, although some unique forms with distinct designs tied to the SECC are present (Brown and Kelly 2000). The incised plates at Cahokia and other Mississippian sites throughout much of the Southeast accentuate a sunburst motif. The plates are an important form that evolves from an early, everted-rim bowl to a later wide-rimmed vessel with elaborate designs (Kelly 1984, 2001). They represent a horizon marker and, as serving vessels, were undoubtedly used in feasts that were an integral part of the ceremonies associated with the SECC. The six-pointed plates of Fort Walton culture are part of this horizon (White et al., chapter 10, this volume), and their massive size suggests their importance in a much larger social and ceremonial setting. These plates serve to identify the distinctiveness of these societies.

Another major horizon marker is the "block-lined" motif represented at Cahokia on Tippets Incised vessels (Hamlin 2004) and expressed in similar motifs such as the Davis Rectangle on the ceramics of the Caddo area (Newell and Krieger 1949); the engraved shell from Spiro (Phillips and Brown 1978); L'Eau Noire Incised, *variety* Shell Bluff vessels of the lower Mississippi River valley (Phillips 1970); and the painted bowls of other forms of Hiwassee Island Red-on-Buff from East Tennessee (Lewis and

Kneberg 1946; Moore 1915). At Moundville, some of the scrolls associated with Moundville Engraved, *variety* Elliot's Creek provide only some rather inexact similarities without the block-line (see Steponaitis 1983). Despite the variability in details it is part of a shared style that has yet to be identified in Florida (Brown and Kelly 1997; Kelly and Brown 2004).

Florida coastal areas continued to be a major source of shell, as well as shark teeth, especially for Cahokia. At this time, determining whether there was any change in the amount of marine shell coming to Cahokia or other Mississippian sites is difficult. Presumably there would have been an increase within the larger Mississippian world. For Cahokia, Trubitt (2000) has discussed the changes in status-related items and the temporal dichotomy of dual-process strategies employed, from the earlier corporate strategy to the later network strategy (see Saitta 1994). Such a shift relates to the crystallization of the Mississippian world in which the success of elites rested on their ability to interact with their social peers across the Southeast. Their positions of authority were underwritten by the ideology of the SECC (see Payne 2002).

For Florida, two areas stand out with regard to this horizon: the Pensacola culture of the Florida panhandle; and the interior, lacustrine-oriented variant of Fort Walton, centered on Lake Jackson near Tallahassee. The Mill Cove Complex of northeastern Florida does not appear to have lasted this long. Other SECC images have been found from Safety Harbor contexts around Tampa Bay. South of Safety Harbor, the pre-Calusa societies of Charlotte Harbor continued to thrive and develop, and they illustrate the ability of coastal societies focused on marine resources to construct elaborate monumental architecture and other public works. Presumably much of their interaction was with island societies of the Caribbean, with little evidence of their direct interaction with Mississippian societies farther north and inland.

The primary areas of direct contact were along the major rivers draining into the Gulf. The Bottle Creek site (Brown 2003) to the west and north of Pensacola was a conduit to Moundville and the Mississippian world farther north and west, while the chiefdoms along the lower Chattahoochee River (Blitz and Lorenz 2006) provided a connection to the Mississippian polities of the Piedmont and Appalachians, such as Etowah. An exception to the aforementioned connection is seen in the recent report of a fluorite bead from the area near the mouth of the Apalachicola River (Morse and Morse 2010). Although not directly tied to a drainage, the lacustrine polity of Lake Jackson was in relatively close proximity to the Apalachicola River and its upstream sources. The interaction is evident, yet these Florida societies maintained their own identity throughout this time.

Post-Classic Mississippian

The *Post-Classic horizon* corresponds to a period from ca. A.D. 1400 to the time of European and African contact with peoples and cultural traditions throughout the Southeast. A major reorganization of the Mississippian landscape is evident in this horizon. Stephen Williams's (1990, 2001) vacant quarter hypothesis highlights an area of major change where many of the mound centers between Peoria and Memphis were abandoned. The recent work of Milner (1996, 1998), Anderson (1996a), and Smith (2001) shows that the area of the vacant quarter extends north into much of the Midwest, with a significant depopulation and redistribution of Mississippian and Oneota peoples. In a recent study Kelly and others (2004) referred to this as the "Black Hole."

In other parts of the Mississippian world, a similar reorganization is evident. The various polities established by the end of the twelfth century were, at varying points in their history, going through processes of cycling that entailed abandonment and resettlement at some later point in their history. In some instances, such as the Savannah River valley, abandonment is evident. Blitz (1999) has expanded on Anderson's (1994, 1996a, 1996b) original work of cycling to discuss the fragile political nature of these polities. During this horizon, the paramount chiefdom or alliance of Coosa, encountered by De Soto during the early sixteenth century, was established. One can readily plot the major chiefdoms along his path across the Southeast. As De Soto crossed northern Florida west to the area of Tallahassee, he encountered Mississippian peoples. The question is how much continuity existed in the Tallahassee area between the early polity at Lake Jackson and the occupation at the time of De Soto. Much of the broader Fort Walton culture appears to have diminished in size.

The interaction evident in preceding centuries does not appear as strong during the Post-Classic horizon, although marine shell continued to make its way into the interior in the form of shell gorgets, engraved whelk cups with an artistic style known as Craig, and shell face-masks extending from the eastern part of the Midwest out onto the Plains.

Summary

The Mississippi period in Florida is characterized by a diversity of regional cultures with their own unique histories. Those to the north such as Fort Walton can be readily classified as Mississippian but also are unique. Others to the east such as the St. Johns II Mill Cove Complex are involved in the early beginnings of Mississippian to the north, while those along the Gulf Coast such as Safety Harbor are somewhat Mississippian in character. However, by the time one reaches Charlotte Harbor, where the ancestors of the Calusa resided, one can see a complex society that is on par with Mississippian but is part of a different world that stretches out into the Gulf.

Each spring thousands of young people make an annual pilgrimage to the white sandy beaches of this place we call Florida to bask in the sun. One can only speculate that similar pilgrimages were made by peoples to the north, not necessarily to enjoy the sun but to acquire a special material, marine shell, symbolically important to their cosmology. Except for copper, greenstone, and a few items of galena and fluorite, it was the Mississippian societies to the north that needed Florida, not the other way around.

References Cited

Abbott, R. Tucker
1974   *American Seashells: The Marine Mollusca of the Atlantic and Pacific Coasts of North America*. Van Nostrand Reinhold, New York.

Alexander, Michelle M.
1984   Paleoethnobotany of the Fort Walton Indians: High Ridge, Velda, and Lake Jackson Sites. M.A. thesis, Department of Anthropology, Florida State University, Tallahassee.

Allerton, David, George M. Luer, and Robert S. Carr
1984   Ceremonial Tablets and Related Objects from Florida. *Florida Anthropologist* 37: 5–54.

Alley, R. B., J. Marotzke, W. D. Nordhaus, J. T. Overpeck, D. M. Peteet, R. A. Pielke Jr., R. T. Pierrehumbert, P. B. Rhines, T. F. Stocker, L. D. Talley, and J. M. Wallace
2003   Abrupt Climate Change. *Science* 299: 2005–2010.

Ambrose, Stanley H., Jane Buikstra, and Harold W. Krueger
2003   Status and Gender Differences in Diet at Mound 72, Cahokia, Revealed by Isotopic Analysis of Bone. *Journal of Anthropological Archaeology* 22: 217–26.

Anderson, David G.
1994   *The Savannah River Chiefdoms: Political Change in the Late Prehistoric Southeast*. University of Alabama Press, Tuscaloosa.
1996a Chiefly Cycling and Large-Scale Abandonments as Viewed from the Savannah River Basin. In *Political Structure and Change in the Prehistoric Southeastern United States*, edited by John F. Scarry, 150–91. University Press of Florida, Gainesville.
1996b Fluctuations between Simple and Complex Chiefdoms: Cycling in the Late Prehistoric Southeast. In *Political Structure and Change in the Prehistoric Southeastern United States*, edited by John F. Scarry, 231–52. University Press of Florida, Gainesville.

Anderson, David G., and Robert M. Mainfort Jr.
2002   An Introduction to Woodland Archaeology in the Southeast. In *The Woodland Southeast*, edited by David G. Anderson and Robert M. Mainfort Jr., 1–19. University of Alabama Press, Tuscaloosa.

Anderson, David G., David W. Stahle, and Malcolm K. Cleaveland
1995   Paleoclimate and the Potential Food Reserves of Mississippian Societies: A Case Study from the Savannah River Valley. *American Antiquity* 60: 258–86.

Andrews, Evangeline Walker, and Charles McLean Andrews (editors)
1981   *Jonathan Dickinson's Journal*. Southern Printing Company, Stuart, Fla.

Andrez de Pez
1689   The Memorial of Andrez de Pez. In *Spanish Approach to Pensacola, 1689–1693*, 77–99. Translated by Irving Leonard. Quivira Society Publications, Albuquerque, N.Mex.

Anonymous
1974   12-Year Old Leads Archaeologist to Significant Find in Tallahassee. *Archives and History News* 5: 2.

Ashley, Keith H.
2002   On the Periphery of the Early Mississippian World: Looking Within and Beyond Northeastern Florida. *Southeastern Archaeology* 21: 162–77.
2003   Interaction, Population Movement, and Political Economy: The Changing Social Landscape of Northeastern Florida (A.D. 900–1500). Ph.D. dissertation, Department of Anthropology, University of Florida, Gainesville.
2005a An Archeological Overview of Mt. Royal. *Florida Anthropologist* 58: 265–87.
2005b Introducing Shields Mound (8DU12) and the Mill Cove Complex. *Florida Anthropologist* 58: 151–73.
2005c Toward an Interpretation of Shields Mound (8DU12) and the Mill Cove Complex. *Florida Anthropologist* 58: 287–301.
2005d Comments on the Broad-scale Distribution of Cordmarked Pottery across the Coastal Plain of Northern Florida and Southern Georgia during the Mississippian Period. Paper presented at the 2005 Symposium of Coastal Plain Archaeology, Southern Georgia Archaeological Research Team, South Georgia College, Douglas.
2006   Colorinda and Its Place in Northeastern Florida History. *Florida Anthropologist* 59: 91–100.
2008   Betz-Tiger Point Preserve Archaeological Project: The 2008 UNF Field School. Report on file, Florida Division of Historical Resources, Tallahassee.
2009   Straddling the Florida-Georgia State Line: Ceramic Chronology of the St. Marys Region (A.D. 1400–1700). In *From Santa Elena to St. Augustine: Indigenous Ceramic Variability (A.D. 1400–1700)*, edited by Kathleen Deagan and David H. Thomas, 125–39. Anthropological Papers of the American Museum of Natural History no. 90. New York.

Ashley, Keith H., and Greg S. Hendryx
2008   Archaeological Site Testing and Data Recovery and Mitigation at the Dolphin Reef Site (8DU276), Duval County, Florida. Report on file, Florida Division of Historical Resources, Tallahassee.

Ashley, Keith, and Vicki L. Rolland
1997   Grog-Tempered Pottery in the Mocama Province. *Florida Anthropologist* 50: 51–65.
2002   St. Marys Cordmarked Pottery (Formerly Savannah Fine Cord Marked of Northeastern Florida and Southeastern Georgia): A Type Description. *Florida Anthropologist* 55: 25–36.

Ashley, Keith, Vicki Rolland, and Rochelle Marrinan
2007   A Grand Site: Testing of the Grand Shell Ring. Report on file, Florida Division of Historic Resources, Tallahassee.

Ashley, Keith H., Keith Stephenson, and Frankie Snow
2007   Teardrops, Ladders, and Bull's Eyes: Swift Creek on the Georgia Coast. *Early Georgia* 35: 3–29.

Ashley, Keith, and Robert L. Thunen
2008   Reexamining an Archaeological Survey of Big Talbot Island. *Florida Anthropologist* 61: 133–48.

Austin, Robert J.
1993   The Royce Mound: Middle Woodland Exchange and Mortuary Customs in South Florida. *Florida Anthropologist* 46: 291–309.

2000   Microlithic Drills from the Anderson Mound at Jungle Prado: Possible Evidence for Late Prehistoric Craft Production on the Gulf Coast of Florida. *North American Archaeologist* 21: 291–321.
2001   An Archaeological Survey of Unincorporated Alachua County, Florida (Phases 1 and 2). Report on file, Florida Division of Historical Resources, Tallahassee.
2006   A Phase 1 Cultural Resource Assessment Survey of the Fallschase Property, Leon County, Florida. Report on File, Division of Historic Resources, Tallahassee.

Austin, Robert J., Ronald M. Farquhar, and Karen J. Walker
2000   Isotope Analysis of Galena from Prehistoric Archaeological Sites in South Florida. *Florida Scientist* 63: 123–31.

Austin, Robert J., and Jeffrey M. Mitchem
2008   Site Formation and Chronology at Bayshore Homes: A Late Weeden Island Mound Complex on the Gulf Coast of Florida. Paper presented at the Sixty-fifth Annual Meeting of the Southeastern Archaeological Conference, Charlotte, N.C.

Austin, Robert J., Jeffrey M. Mitchem, Arlene Fradkin, John E. Foss, Shanna Drwiega, and Linda Allred
2008   *Bayshore Homes Archaeological Survey and National Register Evaluation.* Report submitted to Bureau of Historic Preservation, Division of Historical Resources, Florida Department of State, DHR Grant No. S0819. Central Gulf Coast Archaeological Society, Pinellas Park, Fla.

Baker, Henry A.
1993   Spanish Ranching and the Alachua Sink: A Preliminary Report. *Florida Anthropologist* 46: 82–100.

Balée, William
1998   Introduction. In *Advances in Historical Ecology*, edited by William Balée, 1–10. Columbia University Press, New York.

Barker, Alex W.
2002   Myths and Monsters: Decoding Ritual Images of a Mysterious Ancient American Religion. *Archaeology* (July/August): 40–45.

Bartram, William
1955   *The Travels of William Bartram* (1791). Edited by Mark Van Doren. Dover Press, New York.

Beck, Robin A., Jr.
2003   Consolidation and Hierarchy: Chiefdom Variability in the Mississippian Southeast. *American Antiquity* 68: 641–61.
2006   Persuasive Politics and Domination at Cahokia and Moundville. In *Leadership and Polity in Mississippian Society*, edited by Brian M. Butler and Paul D. Welch, 19–42. Center for Archaeological Investigations, Occasional Paper no. 33. Southern Illinois University, Carbondale.

Bellomo, Randy V.
1996   Archaeological Investigations within Florida Power & Light Company's 115-kV Transmission Line Right-of-Way, Cape Canaveral Air Force Station, Brevard County, Florida. Report on file, Florida Division of Historical Resources, Tallahassee.

Belovich, Stephanie J., David S. Brose, Russell M. Weisman, and Nancy Marie White
1982   *Archaeological Survey at George W. Andrews Lake and Chattahoochee River.* Cleveland Museum of Natural History Archaeological Report no. 37.

Bense, Judith A.
1989a *Pensacola Archaeological Survey and Summary of Archaeological Information in Pensacola to 1988 Technical Report.* Vol. 1. Pensacola Archaeological Society, Publication no. 2.
1989b *Pensacola Archaeological Survey and Summary of Archaeological Information from Each Site in the City of Pensacola, Florida Technical Report.* Vol. 2. Pensacola Archaeological Society, Publication no. 2.
1994 *Archaeology of the Southeastern United States: Paleoindian to World War I.* Academic Press, San Diego.

Bense, Judith A., and John Phillips
1990 Archaeological Assessment of Six Selected Areas in Brevard County: A First Generation Model. Report on file, Florida Division of Historical Resources, Tallahassee.

Beriault, John G., and Robert S. Carr
2000 An Archaeological and Historical Assessment of the 1016 Waverly Place, Ft. Lauderdale, Broward County, Florida. Archaeological and Historical Conservancy Technical Report 277. Davie, Fla.

Binford, Lewis
1971 Mortuary Practices: Their Study and Their Potential. In *Approaches to the Social Dimensions of Mortuary Practices*, edited by James A. Brown, 6–29. Memoirs of the Society for American Archaeology no. 25. Davie, Fla.
1980 Willow Smoke and Dogs' Tails: Hunter-Gatherer Settlement Systems and Archaeological Site Formation. *American Antiquity* 45: 4–20.

Binford, Lewis R., Sally R. Binford, Robert Whallon, and Margaret Ann Hardin
1970 *Archaeology at Hatchery West.* Memoirs of the Society for American Archaeology no. 24. Davie, Fla.

Blanchard, Charles E.
2002 Canoe Navigation in the Northern Reaches of Charlotte Harbor. In *The Archaeology of Upper Charlotte Harbor, Florida*, edited by George M. Luer, 35–48. Florida Anthropological Society, Special Publication 15. Tampa.
2008 Matlacha Pass: Perspectives of Aboriginal Canoe Navigation. *Florida Anthropologist* 61: 59–72.

Bland, Myles C. P.
2001 Moore to the Point. Paper presented at the Fifty-eighth Annual Meeting of the Southeastern Archaeological Conference, Chattanooga, Tenn.

Blanton, Dennis B., and David Hurst Thomas
2008 Paleoclimates and Human Responses along the Central Georgia Coast: A Tree-ring Perspective. In *Native American Landscapes of St. Catherines Island Georgia*, vol. 2, *The Data*, edited by David H. Thomas, 799–806. American Museum of Natural History, Anthropological Papers 88. New York.

Blanton, Richard E., Gary M. Feinman, Stephen A. Kowalewski, and Peter N. Peregrine
1996 A Dual-Processual Theory for the Evolution of Mesoamerican Civilization. *Current Anthropology* 37: 1–14.

Blitz, John H.
1993a *Ancient Chiefdoms of the Tombigbee.* University of Alabama Press, Tuscaloosa.
1993b Big Pots for Big Shots: Feasting and Storage in a Mississippian Community. *American Antiquity* 58: 80–96.

1999 Mississippian Chiefdoms and the Fission-Fusion Process. *American Antiquity* 64: 577–92.
2010 New Perspectives in Mississippian Archaeology. *Journal of Archaeological Research* 18: 1–39.

Blitz, John H., and Patrick Livingood
2004 Sociopolitical Implications of Mississippian Mound Volume. *American Antiquity* 69: 291–301.

Blitz, John H., and Karl G. Lorenz
2002 The Early Mississippian Frontier in the Lower Chattahoochee–Apalachicola River Valley. *Southeastern Archaeology* 21: 117–35.
2006 *The Chattahoochee Chiefdoms*. University of Alabama Press, Tuscaloosa.

Bourdieu, Pierre
1977 *Outline of a Theory of Practice*. Cambridge University Press, Cambridge, U.K.

Boyd, Mark F.
1939 Mission Sites in Florida. *Florida Historical Quarterly* 17: 255–80.

Bradley, Raymond S.
1993 *Altering the Earth: The Origins of Monuments in Britain and Continental Europe*. Society of Antiquaries of Scotland, Monograph Series no. 8. Edinburgh.
2000 1000 Years of Climate Change. *Science* 288: 1353–55.

Bradley, Raymond S., Malcom K. Hughes, and Henry F. Diaz
2003 Climate in Medieval Time. *Science* 302: 404–5.

Brech, Alan
2004 Neither Ocean nor Continent: Correlating the Archaeology and Geomorphology of the Barrier Islands of East Central Florida. M.A. thesis, Department of Anthropology, University of Florida, Gainesville.

Breininger, David R., Mary Jo Barkazi, Rebecca Smith, Donna M. Oddy, and Jane A. Provancha
1994 Endangered and Potentially Endangered Wildlife on John F. Kennedy Space Center and Faunal Integrity as a Goal for Maintaining Biological Diversity. Report on file, NASA Library, Kennedy Space Center.

Broecker, Wallace S.
2001 Was the Medieval Warm Period Global? *Science* 291: 1497–99.

Brooks, H. Kelly
1972 Geology of Cape Canaveral. In: *Space-Age Geology: Terrestrial Applications, Techniques and Training*, edited by T. E. Garner, 35–44. Southeastern Geology Society, Tallahassee, Fla.
1974 Lake Okeechobee. In *Environments of South Florida: Present and Past*, edited by Patrick J. Gleason, 256–86. Miami Geological Society Memoir 2.
1981 *Physiographic Divisions: State of Florida*. Institute of Food and Agricultural Sciences, University of Florida, Gainesville.

Brose, David S.
1975 Case Western Reserve University Contributions to the Archaeological Investigation of Two Early Fort Walton Sites in the Apalachicola River Valley, Northwest Florida, 1973. Paper on file. Cleveland Museum of Natural History and Case Western Reserve University.
1984 Mississippian Period Cultures in Northwestern Florida. In *Perspectives on Gulf Coast Prehistory*, edited by Dave D. Davis, 165–97. University of Florida Press, Gainesville.

1990   Apalachee Impostors. Paper presented at the Forty-seventh Annual Meeting of the Southeastern Archaeological Conference, Mobile, Ala.
2003   Foreword. In *Bottle Creek: A Pensacola Culture Site in South Alabama*, edited by Ian Brown, xvii–xxiii. University of Alabama Press, Tuscaloosa.

Brose, David S., and N'omi Greber (editors)
1979   *Hopewell Archaeology: The Chillicothe Conference*. Kent State University Press, Kent, Ohio.

Brose, David S., and George W. Percy
1978   Fort Walton Settlement Patterns. In *Mississippian Settlement Patterns*, edited by Bruce D. Smith, 81–114. Academic Press, New York.

Brown, Catherine
1982   On the Gender of the Winged Being on Mississippian Copper Plates. *Tennessee Anthropologist* 7: 1–8.

Brown, Ian W.
1982   The Southeastern Check Stamped Pottery Tradition. *Midcontinental Journal of Archaeology* Special Publication 4.

Brown, Ian W. (editor)
2003   *Bottle Creek: A Pensacola Culture Site in South Alabama*. University of Alabama, Tuscaloosa.

Brown, Ian W.
2009   *An Archaeological Survey in Clarke County, Alabama*. Bulletin 26, Alabama Museum of Natural History. University of Alabama, Tuscaloosa.

Brown, James A.
2010   Cosmological Layouts of Secondary Burials as Political Instruments. In *Mississippian Mortuary Practices: Beyond Hierarchy and the Representationalist Perspective*, edited by Lynne P. Sullivan and Robert C. Mainfort Jr., 30–53. University Press of Florida, Gainesville.

Brown, James, and John Kelly
1997   The Context of Davis Rectangle Motifs at Cahokia. Paper presented at the Fifty-fourth Annual Meeting of the Southeastern Archaeological Conference, Baton Rouge, La.
2000   Cahokia and the Southeastern Ceremonial Complex. In *Mounds, Modoc, and Mesoamerica: Papers in Honor of Melvin L. Fowler*, edited by Steven R. Ahler, 469–510. Illinois State Museum Scientific Papers vol. 28. Springfield.

Brown, James A., Richard A. Kerber, and Howard D. Winters
1990   Trade and the Evolution of Exchange Relations at the Beginning of the Mississippian Period. In *The Mississippian Emergence*, edited by Bruce Smith, 251–74. Smithsonian Institution Press, Washington, D.C.

Brown, Randall B., Earl Stone, and Victor Carlisle
1990   Soils. In *Ecosystems of Florida*, edited by Ronald L. Myers and John J. Ewel, 35–70. University of Central Florida Press, Orlando.

Bryne, Stephen C.
1986   Apalachee Settlement Patterns. M.A. thesis, Department of Anthropology, Florida State University, Tallahassee.

Buikstra, Jane E., and Douglas K. Charles
1999   Centering the Ancestors: Cemeteries, Mounds, and Sacred Landscapes of the Ancient North American Midcontinent. In *Archaeologies of Landscape: Contem-*

porary Perspectives, edited by Wendy Ashmore and A. Bernard Knapp, 201–28. Blackwell, Oxford, U.K.

Bullen, Adelaide K.
1963 Physical Anthropology of the Goodman Mound. In *Papers on the Jungerman and Goodman Sites, Florida*, edited by Douglas F. Jordan, Elizabeth S. Wing, and Adelaide K. Bullen, 61–70. Contributions of the Florida State Museum Social Sciences no. 10. Gainesville.

Bullen, Ripley P.
1949a The Woodward Site. *Florida Anthropologist* 2: 49–64.
1949b Indian Sites at Florida Caverns State Park. *Florida Anthropologist* 2: 1–9.
1950 An Archaeological Survey of the Chattahoochee River Valley in Florida. *Journal of the Washington Academy of Sciences* 40: 101–25.
1952 *Eleven Archaeological Sites in Hillsborough County, Florida*. Report of Investigations no. 8. Florida Geological Survey, Tallahassee.
1958a *The Bolen Bluff Site on Paynes Prairie, Florida*. Contributions of the Florida State Museum, Social Sciences 4. Gainesville.
1958b Six Sites near the Chattahoochee River in the Jim Woodruff Reservoir Area, Florida. In *River Basin Survey Papers*, edited by Frank H. Roberts Jr., 315–76. Bureau of American Ethnology Bulletin 169. Smithsonian Institution, Washington, D.C.
1975 *A Guide to the Identification of Florida Projectile Points*. Kendall Books, Gainesville, Fla.
1978 Tocobaga Indians and the Safety Harbor Culture. In *Tacachale: Essays on the Indians of Florida and Southeastern Georgia during the Historic Period*, edited by Jerald T. Milanich and Samuel Proctor, 50–58. University Press of Florida, Gainesville.

Butler, Brian M., and Paul D. Welch (editors)
2006 *Leadership and Polity in Mississippian Society*. Center for Archaeological Investigations, Occasional Paper no. 33. Southern Illinois University, Carbondale.

Caldwell, Joseph R.
1958 *Trend and Tradition in the Prehistory of the Eastern United States*. Memoir no. 88. American Anthropological Association, Washington, D.C.

Caldwell, Joseph R., and Robert L. Hall (editors)
1964 *Hopewellian Studies*. Illinois State Museum Scientific Papers vol. 12. Springfield.

Campbell, L. Janice, Phillip Bourgeois, James H. Mathews, James R. Morehead, and Lee C. Thomas
2007 Delineation of 8WL119. Report of Investigations no. 979. Draft report submitted to Eglin Air Force Base, contract no. FA4890-04-D-004DK02. Prentice Thomas and Associates, Walton County, Fla.

Campbell, L. Janice, J. A. Homburg, C. Weed, and P. Thomas Jr.
1984 Reconnaissance Survey in the Upper St. Johns River Flood Control Project, Osceola, Brevard and Indian River Counties, Florida. Report on file, Florida Division of Historical Resources, Tallahassee.

Cantley, Charles E., M. B. Reed, Leslie Raymer, and J. W. Joseph
1994 Historic Properties Survey, Cape Canaveral Air Force Station, Florida. Report on file, Florida Division of Historical Resources, Tallahassee.

Carr, Robert S.
1973 An Archaeological and Historical Survey of the Martin Plant Tract in Martin County, Florida. Bureau of Historic Sites and Properties, Miscellaneous Project Report 9. Tallahassee.

1975   An Archaeological and Historical Survey of Lake Okeechobee. Bureau of Historic Sites and Properties, Miscellaneous Project Report 22. Tallahassee.
1986   Prehistoric Circular Earthworks in South Florida. *Florida Anthropologist* 38: 288–301.
2002   The Archaeology of Everglades Tree Islands. In *Tree Islands of the Everglades*, edited by Fred H. Sklar, 187–206. Kluwer Academic Publishers, Netherlands.

Carr, Robert S., David Allerton, and Ivan Rodriguez
1988   An Assessment of the Archaeological and Historic Resources of the Florida Keys, Monroe County. Archaeological and Historical Conservancy Technical Report 4. Davie, Fla.

Carr, Robert S., and John Beriault
1984   Prehistoric Man in Southern Florida. In *Environments of South Florida, Present and Past*, edited by Patrick Gleason, 1–14. Miami Geological Society, Coral Gables.

Carr, Robert S., David Dickel, and Marilyn Masson
1995   Archaeological Investigations at the Ortona Earthworks and Mounds. *Florida Anthropologist* 48: 227–64.

Carr, Robert S., Amy Felmley, Richard Ferrer, Willard Steele, and Jorge Zamanillo
1991   An Archaeological Survey of Broward County, Florida: Phase One. Archaeological and Historical Conservancy Technical Report 34. Davie, Fla.

Carr, Robert S., and John Ricisak
2000   Preliminary Report on the Salvage Archaeological Investigations of the Brickell Point Site (8DA12), Including the Miami Circle. *Florida Anthropologist* 53: 260–85.

Carr, Robert S., William Schaffer, and Ashley Gelman
2008   Archaeological Investigations of the Icon-Brickell Parcel, Miami, Florida. Archaeological and Historical Conservancy Technical Report 830. Davie, Fla.

Carr, Robert S., Jorge Zamanillo, and James Pepe
2002   Archaeological Profiling and Radiocarbon Dating of the Ortona Canal (8GL4), Glades County, Florida. *Florida Anthropologist* 55: 3–22.

Causey, Philip D.
2000   A Cultural Resources Assessment Survey of a Section of Buck Lake Road (CR 158) from Mahan Drive (US 90) to Pedrick Road, Leon County. Report on file, Division of Historical Resources, Tallahassee.

Chen, Ellen, and John F. Gerber
1990   Climate. In *Ecosystems of Florida*, edited by Ronald L. Myers and John J. Ewel, 11–35. University of Central Florida Press, Orlando.

Claassen, Cheryl
1989   Sourcing Marine Shell Artifacts. In *Proceedings of the 1986 Shell Bead Conference: Selected Papers*, edited by Charles F. Hayes III, Lynn Ceci, and Connie Cox Bodner, 17–23. Research Records no. 20. Rochester Museum and Science Center, Rochester, N.Y.

Claassen, Cheryl, and Samuella Sigmann
1993   Sourcing *Busycon* Artifacts of the Eastern United States. *American Antiquity* 58: 333–47.

Claggett, Heather Lea
1996   Occupational Nexus Modeling in the Interior Central Gulf Coast of Florida. *Florida Anthropologist* 49: 239–47.

Clay, R. Berle
2006   Interpreting the Mississippian Hinterlands. *Southeastern Archaeology* 25: 48–64.
Cobb, Charles R.
1991   Social Reproduction and the *Longue Durée* in the Prehistory of the Midcontinental United States. In *Processual and Postprocessual Archaeologies*, edited by Robert W. Preucel, 168–82. Occasional Paper no. 10. Center for Archaeological Investigations, Southern Illinois University, Carbondale.
2000   *From Quarry to Cornfield: The Political Economy of Mississippian Hoe Production*. University of Alabama Press, Tuscaloosa.
2003   Mississippian Chiefdoms: How Complex? *Annual Review of Anthropology* 32: 63–84.
Cobb, Charles R., and Patrick H. Garrow
1996   Woodstock Culture and the Question of Mississippian Emergence. *American Antiquity* 61: 21–37.
Cobb, Charles R., and Adam King
2005   Re-inventing Mississippian Tradition at Etowah, Georgia. *Journal of Archaeological Method and Theory* 12: 167–92.
Cobb, Charles R., and Michael S. Nassaney
1995   Interaction and Integration in the Late Woodland Southeast. In *Native American Interactions: Multiscalar Analysis and Interpretations in the Eastern Woodlands*, edited by Michael S. Nassaney and Kenneth E. Sassaman, 205–26. University of Tennessee Press, Knoxville.
Coker, William S.
1997   The Name Panzacola (Pensacola) Keeps Getting Newer and Newer. *Pensacola History Illustrated* 5: 29–31.
Coleman, Wesley, James McCullin, and Jeanie McGuire
1983   A Carved Shell Pendant from Dade County, Florida. *Florida Anthropologist* 36: 140–41.
Cologne Radiocarbon
2006   CalPal (radiocarbon date calibration program). Cologne Radiocarbon Calibration and Paleoclimate Research Package. Online at http://www.calpal-online.de/ (accessed June 2010).
Colquhoun, Donald J., and Mark J. Brooks
1986   New Evidence from the Southeastern U.S. for Eustatic Components in the Late Holocene Sea Levels. *Geoarchaeology* 1: 275–91.
Connerton, Paul
1989   *How Societies Remember*. Cambridge University Press, Cambridge.
Cordell, Ann S.
1985   Pottery Variability and Site Chronology in the Upper St. Johns River Basin. In *Archaeological Site Types, Distribution, and Preservation within the Upper St. Johns River Basin, Florida*, edited by Brenda Sigler-Eisenberg, 114–34. Report on file, Florida Division of Historical Resources, Tallahassee.
1992   Technological Investigation of Pottery Variability in Southwest Florida. In *Culture and Environment in the Domain of the Calusa*, edited by William H. Marquardt, 105–89. Institute of Archaeology and Paleoenvironmental Studies, Monograph 1. University of Florida, Gainesville.
2005   Revisiting the Aqui Esta Mound (8Ch68): Paste Variability in the Pottery Assemblage. *Florida Anthropologist* 58: 105–20.

2012   Technological Investigation of Pottery Variability at the Pineland Site Complex. In *The Archaeology of Pineland: A Coastal Southwest Florida Site Complex, A.D. 50–1710*, edited by William H. Marquardt and Karen J. Walker, 383–543. Institute of Archaeology and Paleoenvironmental Studies, Monograph 4. University of Florida, Gainesville. In press.

Covey, Cyclone (translator)
1961   *Cabeza de Vaca's Adventures in the Unknown Interior of America*. University of New Mexico Press, Albuquerque.

Crawford, Catherine L.
2007   Collecting, Defacing, Reinscribing (and Otherwise Performing) Memory in the Ancient World. In *Negotiating the Past in the Past: Identity, Memory, and Landscape in Archaeological Research*, edited by Norman Yoffee, 10–41. University of Arizona Press, Tucson.

Cronin, T. M., G. S. Dwyer, T. Kamiya, S. Schwede, and D. A. Willard
2003   Medieval Warm Period, Little Ice Age and 20th Century Temperature Variability from Chesapeake Bay. *Global and Planetary Change* 36: 17–29.

Crook, Morgan R., Jr.
1986   *Mississippi Period Archaeology of the Georgia Coastal Zone*. Georgia Archaeological Research Design Paper no. 1. University of Georgia, Athens.

Crowley, Thomas J.
2000   Causes of Climate Change over the Past 1000 Years. *Science* 289: 270–77.

Crumley, Carole L. (editor)
1994   *Historical Ecology: Cultural Knowledge and Changing Landscapes*. School of American Research Press, Santa Fe, N.Mex.

Crumley, Carole L.
2007   Historical Ecology: Integrated Thinking at Multiple Temporal and Spatial Scales. In *The World System and the Earth System: Global Environmental Change and Sustainability since the Neolithic*, edited by Alf Hornborg and Carole L. Crumley, 15–28. Left Coast Press, Walnut Creek, Calif.

Curtis, Jason H., David A. Hodell, and Mark Brenner
1996   Climate Variability on the Yucatán Peninsula (Mexico) during the Past 3500 Years and Implications for Maya Cultural Evolution. *Quaternary Research* 46: 37–47.

Cushing, Frank H.
1897   Exploration of Ancient Key Dwellers' Remains on the Gulf Coast of Florida. *Proceedings of the American Philosophical Society* 35: 329–448.

Davenport, Christian, Greg Mount, and George "Boots" Boyer, Jr.
2011   The Boyer Survey: An Archaeological Investigation of Lake Okeechobee. Report on file, Division of Historical Resources, Tallahassee.

Davidsson, Robert I.
2001   *Indian River: A History of the Ais in Spanish Florida*. Florida Heritage Series. Ais Indian Project Publication, West Palm Beach.

Deagan, Kathleen A.
1972   Fig Springs: The Mid-Seventeenth Century in North-Central Florida. *Historical Archaeology* 6: 23–46.
1987   *Artifacts of the Spanish Colonies of Florida and the Caribbean, 1550–1800*, vol. 1, *Ceramics, Glassware, and Beads*. Smithsonian Institution Press, Washington, D.C.

deFrance, Susan D., and Karen J. Walker
2012   The Zooarchaeology of Pineland. In *The Archaeology of Pineland: A Coastal Southwest Florida Site Complex, A.D. 50–1710*, edited by William H. Marquardt and Karen J. Walker, 305–48. Institute of Archaeology and Paleoenvironmental Studies, Monograph 4. University of Florida, Gainesville. In press.

deMenocal, P., J. Ortiz, T. Guilderson, and M. Sarnthein
2000   Coherent High- and Low-Latitude Climate Variability during the Holocene Warm Period. *Science* 288: 2198–2202.

Deming, Joan, and Elizabeth A. Horvath
1999   Phase II Test Excavation Report, Sixteen Archeological Sites, Cape Canaveral Air Station, Brevard County. Report on file, Florida Division of Historical Resources, Tallahassee.

DePratter, Chester
1991   *Late Prehistoric and Early Historic Chiefdoms in the Southeastern United States*. Garland, New York.

Deuel, Thorne
1935   Basic Cultures of the Mississippi Valley. *American Anthropologist* 37: 429–45.

Diaz-Granados, Carol, Marvin W. Rowe, Marian Hyman, James R. Duncan, and John R. Southon
2001   AMS Radiocarbon Dates for Charcoal from Three Missouri Pictographs and Their Associated Iconography. *American Antiquity* 66: 481–92.

Dickel, David N.
1992   A Survey of Indian River County, Florida. Report on file, Florida Division of Historical Resources, Tallahassee.

Dickel, David, and Robert S. Carr
1991   Archaeological Investigations of the Oak Knoll Mound, 8LL729, Lee County, Florida. Archaeological and Historical Conservancy Technical Report 21. Davie, Fla.

Dickel, David, Robert S. Carr, and Willard S. Steele
1992   An Archaeological and Historical Survey of Bonita Springs Parcel Three, Lee County, Florida. Archaeological and Historic Conservancy Technical Report 43. Davie, Fla.

Dickel, David N., and Glen H. Doran
2002   An Environmental and Chronological Overview of the Region. In *Windover: Multidisciplinary Investigations of an Early Archaic Florida Cemetery*, edited by Glen H. Doran, 39–58. University Press of Florida, Gainesville.

Dickinson, Martin F., and Lucy B. Wayne
1997   Magnolia Hammock: "Such Aboundaunce of Fishe": Data Recovery Excavations at the Mabry Mound Site 8SJ14. Report on file, Florida Division of Historical Resources, Tallahassee.
1999   Island in the Marsh: An Archaeological Investigation of 8Na59 and 8Na709, the Crane Island Sites, Nassau County, Florida. Report on file, Division of Historical Resources, Tallahassee.

Dietler, John E.
2008   Craft Specialization and the Emergence of Political Complexity in Southwest Florida. Ph.D. dissertation, Department of Anthropology, University of California, Los Angeles.

Doran, Glen H., and Bruce J. Piatek
1985   Archaeological Investigations at Naval Live Oaks: Studies in Spatial Patterning and Chronology in the Gulf Coast of Florida. Report on file, Department of Anthropology, Florida State University, Tallahassee.

Douglas, Marjorie S.
1947   *Everglades River of Grass*. Rinehart, New York.

Douglas, Mary
1966   *Purity and Danger*. Routledge, London.

Douglass, Andrew E.
1885   Florida Diaries, 1881–1885. Typescript on file at P. K. Yonge Library of Florida History, Gainesville.

DuBois, Betsy W.
1957   Celt and pendant from Jupiter Inlet Mound. *Florida Anthropologist* 10: 15–16.

Duffield, Lathel
1964   *Engraved Shells from the Craig Mound at Spiro, Le Flore County, Oklahoma*. Oklahoma Anthropological Society, Memoir no. 1.

Dunbar, James S.
2001   Archaeological Implications of the Fauna Remains from Tests I, II, and III at the Shields Mound Site. Report on file, Department of Anthropology, Florida State University, Tallahassee.

Duncan, James R., and Carol Diaz-Granados
2000   Of Masks and Myths. *Midcontinental Journal of Archaeology* 25: 1–26.

Du Vernay, Jeffrey
2011   The Archaeology of Yon Mound and Village, Middle Apalachicola River Valley, Northwest Florida. Ph.D. dissertation, Department of Anthropology, University of South Florida, Tampa.

Eck, Christopher
2000   A Picturesque Settlement: The Diary of Dr. Jefferies Wyman's Visit to Miami and the First Archaeological Excavations in South Florida, 1869. *Florida Anthropologist* 53: 286–93.

Eddy, Jack A.
1994   Solar History and Human Affairs. *Human Ecology* 22: 23–35.

Emerson, Thomas E.
1982   *Mississippian Stone Images in Illinois*. Illinois Archaeological Survey, Circular 6. Urbana.
1997   *Cahokia and the Archaeology of Power*. University of Alabama Press, Tuscaloosa.

Espenshade, Christopher T.
1983   Ceramic Ecology and Aboriginal Household Pottery Production at the Gauthier Site, Florida. M.A. thesis on file, Department of Anthropology, University of Florida, Gainesville.

Estabrook, Richard W.
2002   Phase III Archaeological Excavations at the West Pasture Site (8SM128): An Archaic through Mississippian Period Site in Sumter Country, FL. Report on file, Florida Division of Historical Resources, Tallahassee.

Estevez, Ernest D., Bradley J. Hartman, Randy Kautz, and Elizabeth D. Purdum
1984   Ecosystems of Surface Waters. In *Water Resources Atlas of Florida*, edited by Edward A. Fernald and Donald J. Patton, 92–107. Institute of Science and Public Affairs, Florida State University, Tallahassee.

Ewel, John J.
1990   Introduction. In *Ecosystems of Florida*, edited by Ronald L. Myers and John J. Ewel, 3–10. University of Central Florida Press, Orlando.

Ewen, Charles R., and John H. Hann
1998   *Hernando De Soto among the Apalachee: The Archaeology of the First Winter Encampment.* University Press of Florida, Gainesville.

Fagan, Brian
2000   *The Little Ice Age: How Climate Made History, 1300–1850.* Basic Books, New York.

Fairbanks, Charles H.
1965a   Gulf Complex Subsistence Economy. *Southeastern Archaeological Conference Bulletin* 3: 57–62.
1965b   Excavations at the Fort Walton Temple Mound. *Florida Anthropologist* 18: 239–64.
1981   *Archaeology of the Funeral Mound, Ocmulgee National Monument, Georgia.* Mercer Press Services, Mercer University, Macon, Ga.

Fandrich, Judith E.
1988   *Revision: A New Look at St. Johns II Subsistence.* M.A. thesis, Department of Anthropology, Florida State University, Tallahassee.

Farnsworth, Kenneth B., and Brad Koldehoff
2007   Kingfisher-Effigy Bone Hairpins: Clues to Late Woodland Iconography and Social Complexity in West-Central Illinois. *Illinois Archaeology* 15–16: 30–57.

Feathers, James K.
2006   Explaining Shell Tempered Pottery in Prehistoric Eastern North America. *Journal of Archaeological Method and Theory* 13: 89–133.

Feathers, James K., and Evan Peacock
2008   Origins and Spread of Shell Tempered Ceramics in the Eastern Woodlands: Conceptual and Methodological Frameworks for Analysis. *Southeastern Archaeology* 27: 286–93.

Fenneman, N. W.
1938   *Physiography of the Eastern United States.* McGraw-Hill, New York.

Florida Museum of Natural History
2010   South Florida: People and Environments. Online exhibit at http://www.flmnh.ufl.edu/sflahall/funding.htm.

Florida Natural Areas Inventory (FNAI)
1990   *Guide to the Natural Communities of Florida.* Florida Natural Areas Inventory and Florida Department of Natural Resources, Tallahassee.

Fontaneda, Do. d'Escalante
1973 [ca. 1575]   *Memoir of Do. d'Escalante Fontaneda Respecting Florida.* Edited by D. O. True, translated by B. Smith. Historical Association of South Florida, Miami.

Ford, James A., and Gordon R. Willey
1941   An Interpretation of the Prehistory of the Eastern United States. *American Anthropologist* 43: 325–63.

Fortier, Andrew C.
1992   Stone Figurines. In *The Sponemann Site 2 (11-Ms-517): The Mississippian and Oneota Occupations,* by Douglas K. Jackson, Andrew C. Fortier, and Joyce A. Williams, 276–303. American Bottom Archaeology FAI-270 Site Reports 24. University of Illinois Press, Urbana.

Fortier, Andrew C., and Dale L. McElrath
2002 Deconstructing the Emergent Mississippian Concept: The Case for the Terminal Late Woodland in the American Bottom. *Midcontinental Journal of Archaeology* 27: 171–215.

Fradkin, Arlene
1976 Excavations at the Law School Mound (8AL297), Alachua County, Florida. Report on file, Florida Division of Historical Resources, Tallahassee.

Frankenstein, Susan, and Michael Rowlands
1978 The Internal Structure and Regional Context of Early Iron Age Society in South-Western Germany. *Bulletin of the Institute of Archeology of London* 15: 73–112.

Fritz, Gayle, and Neal Lopinot
2007 Native Crops at Early Cahokia: Comparing Domestic and Ceremonial Contexts. *Illinois Archaeology* 15–16: 90–111.

Fryman, Frank B., Jr.
1969 Lake Jackson Site (8LE1). Field notes on file, Florida Division of Historical Resources, Tallahassee.
1970 Interim Report on Completed Highway Archaeological Research and Expenditures. Report on file, Florida Division of Historical Resources, Tallahassee.
1971 Highway Salvage Archaeology in Florida. *Archives and History News* 2: 1–4.

Fuller, Richard S.
1985 The Bear Point Phase of the Pensacola Variant: The Protohistoric Period in Southwest Alabama. *Florida Anthropologist* 38: 150–55.
2003 Out of the Moundville Shadow: The Origin and Evolution of Pensacola Culture. In *Bottle Creek: A Pensacola Culture Site in South Alabama*, edited by Ian W. Brown, 27–62. University of Alabama Press, Tuscaloosa.

Fuller, Richard S., and Noel R. Stowe
1982 A Proposed Typology for Late Shell-Tempered Ceramics in the Mobile Bay/Mobile-Tensaw Delta Region. In *Archaeology in Southwest Alabama: A Collection of Papers*, edited by Calip B. Curren Jr., 45–93. Alabama Tombigbee Regional Commission, Camden.

Furey, John
1972 The Spanish River Complex: Archaeological Settlement Patterning in Eastern Okeechobee Sub-Area. M.A. thesis, Department of Anthropology, Florida Atlantic University, Boca Raton.

Gallay, Alan
2002 *The Indian Slave Trade: The Rise of the English Empire in the American South, 1670–1717*. Yale University Press, New Haven, Conn.

Galloway, Patricia (editor)
1989 *The Southeastern Ceremonial Complex: Artifacts and Analysis: The Cottonlandia Conference*. University of Nebraska Press, Lincoln.

Gardner, William M.
1966 The Waddell's Mill Pond Site. *Florida Anthropologist* 19: 43–64.

Garner, Michael S.
1992 *An Archaeological Survey of the Oelsner Mounds Site*. Report to the Florida Division of Historical Resources, Tallahassee.

Goad, Sharon I.
1978 Exchange Networks in the Prehistoric Southeastern United States. Ph.D. dissertation, Department of Anthropology, University of Georgia, Athens.

Goggin, John M.
1947   A Preliminary Definition of Archaeological Areas and Periods in Florida. *American Antiquity* 13: 114–27.
1948a   A Revised Temporal Chart of Florida Archaeology. *Florida Anthropologist* 1: 57–60.
1948b   *Some Pottery Types from Central Florida*. Gainesville Anthropological Association, Bulletin no. 1.
1949a   Cultural Traditions in Florida Prehistory. In *The Florida Indian and His Neighbors*, edited by John W. Griffin, 13–44. Rollins College, Winter Park, Fla.
1949b   The Archaeology of the Glades Area, Southern Florida. Manuscript on file, Yale Peabody Museum, New Haven, Conn., and University of Florida Library, Gainesville.
1949c   A Southern Cult Specimen from Florida. *Florida Anthropologist* 2: 36–38.
1952   *Space and Time Perspective in Northern St. Johns Archaeology, Florida*. Yale University Publications in Anthropology 47. Yale University Press, New Haven, Conn.
1953   Introductory Outline of Timucua Archaeology. *Southeastern Archaeological Conference Newsletter* 3: 4–17.

Goggin, John M., and Frank H. Sommer III
1949   *Excavations on Upper Matecumbe Key, Florida*. Yale University Publications in Anthropology no. 41. Yale University Press, New Haven, Conn.

Goggin, John M., and William T. Sturtevant
1964   The Calusa: A Stratified Non-agricultural Society (with Notes on Sibling Marriage). In *Explorations in Cultural Anthropology: Essays in Honor of George Peter Murdock*, edited by Ward Goodenough, 179–219. McGraw-Hill, New York.

Goldstein, Lynne G.
1980   *Mississippian Mortuary Practices: A Case Study of Two Cemeteries in the Lower Illinois Valley*. Northwestern University Archaeological Program, Scientific Papers no. 4. Evanston, Ill.

Goodman, Claire Garber
1984   *Copper Artifacts in Late Eastern Woodlands Prehistory*. Center for American Archeology, Evanston, Ill.

Goody, Jack
1962   *Death, Property, and the Ancestors: A Study of the Mortuary Customs of the Lodagaa of West Africa*. Stanford University Press, Stanford, Calif.

Griffin, James B.
1946   Cultural Change and Continuity in Eastern United States Archaeology. In *Man in Northeastern North America*, edited by Frederick Johnson, 37–95. Archaeology Paper 3. Robert S. Peabody Foundation, Andover, Mass.
1967   Eastern North American Archaeology: A Summary. *Science* 156: 175–91.
1985   Changing Concepts of the Prehistoric Mississippian Cultures of the Eastern United States. In *Alabama and Borderlands: From Prehistory to Statehood*, edited by Reid R. Badger and Lawrence A. Clayton, 40–63. University of Alabama Press, Tuscaloosa.

Griffin, John
1949   The Historic Archaeology of Florida. In *The Florida Indian and His Neighbors*, edited by John W. Griffin, 45–54. Rollins College, Winter Park, Fla.
1950   Test Excavations at the Lake Jackson Site. *American Antiquity* 16: 99–112.

1952a   Prehistoric Florida: A Review. In *Archaeology of Eastern United States*, edited by James B. Griffin, 322–34. University of Chicago Press, Chicago.
1952b   A Stone Spud from Florida. *Florida Anthropologist* 5: 36.
1988   *The Archaeology of Everglades National Park: A Synthesis*. National Park Service, Southeast Archaeological Center, Tallahassee.
2002   *Archaeology of the Everglades*. University Press of Florida, Gainesville.
Griffin, John W., Sue B. Richardson, Mary Pohl, Carl D. McMurray, C. Margaret Scarry, Suzanne K. Fish, Elizabeth S. Wing, L. Jill Loucks, and Marcia K. Welch
1982   Excavations at the Granada Site: Archaeology and History of the Granada Site. Report on file, Florida Division of Historical Resources, Tallahassee.
Gunn, Joel D.
1997   A Framework for the Middle–Late Holocene Transition: Astronomical and Geophysical Conditions. *Southeastern Archaeology* 16: 134–51.
Haeberli, Wilfried, and Hanspeter Holzhauser
2003   Alpine Glacier Mass Changes during the Past Two Millennia. *PAGES News* 11: 13–15.
Hale, H. Stephen
1976   Marine Shells in Midwestern Archaeological Sites and the Determination of Their Most Probable Source. M.A. thesis, Department of Anthropology, Florida Atlantic University, Boca Raton.
Hall, Joseph M., Jr.
2009   *Zamumo's Gifts: Indian-European Exchanges in the Colonial Southeast*. University of Pennsylvania Press, Philadelphia.
Hall, Robert L.
1989   The Cultural Background of Mississippian Symbolism. In *The Southeastern Ceremonial Complex: Artifacts and Analysis*, edited by Patricia Galloway, 239–78. University of Nebraska Press, Lincoln.
1991   Cahokia Identity and Interaction Models of Cahokia Mississippian. In *Cahokia and the Hinterlands: Middle Mississippian Cultures of the Midwest*, edited by Thomas E. Emerson and R. Barry Lewis, 3–34. University of Illinois Press, Chicago.
1996   American Indian Worlds, World Quarters, World Centers, and Their Shrines. In "The Ancient Skies and Sky Watchers of Cahokia: Woodhenges, Eclipses, and Cahokian Cosmology," edited by Melvin Fowler. *Wisconsin Archeologist* 77: 120–27.
1997   *An Archaeology of the South: North American Indian Belief and Ritual*. University of Illinois Press, Urbana.
2006   Exploring the Mississippian Big Bang at Cahokia. In *A Pre-Columbian World: Searching for a Unitary Vision of Ancient America*, edited by Jeffrey Quilter and Mary Miller, 187–229. Harvard University Press, Cambridge, Mass.
Hally, David J.
1986   The Identification of Vessel Function: A Case Study from Northwest Georgia. *American Antiquity* 51: 267–95.
1994   An Overview of Lamar Culture. In *Ocmulgee Archaeology, 1936–1986*, edited by David J. Hally, 144–74. University of Georgia Press, Athens.
1996   Platform-Mound Construction and the Instability of Mississippian Chiefdoms. In *Political Structure and Change in the Prehistoric Southeastern United States*, edited by J. Scarry, 92–127. University Press of Florida, Gainesville.

Halsey, John R.
2008   Mississippian Copper Sources, Usage, and Probabilities: A View from Up North. Paper presented at the Sixty-fifth Annual Meeting of the Southeastern Archaeological Conference, Charlotte, N.C.

Hamilton, Henry W., Jean T. Hamilton, and Eleanor F. Chapman
1974   *Spiro Mound Copper*. Memoir of the Missouri Archaeological Society, no. 11. Columbia.

Hamlin, Jenna M.
2004   Sociopolitical Significance of Moorehead Ceramic Assemblage Variation in the Cahokia Area. Ph.D. dissertation, Department of Anthropology, Washington University, St. Louis.

Handley, Brent M.
2001   The Blue Goose Midden (8IR15): A Malabar II Occupation on the Indian River Lagoon. *Florida Anthropologist* 54: 103–22.

Hann, John H.
1988a   *Apalachee: The Land between the Rivers*. University Press of Florida, Gainesville.
1988b   Florida's Terra Incognita: West Florida's Natives in the Sixteenth and Seventeenth Century. *Florida Anthropologist* 41: 61–107.
1991   *Missions to the Calusa*. Introduction by William H. Marquardt, translated by John H. Hann. University Press of Florida, Gainesville.
1996   *A History of the Timucua Indians and Missions*. University Press of Florida, Gainesville.
2003   *Indians of Central and South Florida, 1513–1763*. University Press of Florida, Gainesville.
2006   *The Native American World beyond Apalachee: West Florida and the Chattahoochee Valley*. University Press of Florida, Gainesville.

Harbor Branch Oceanographic Institution
2001   Indian River Lagoon Research Information. http://www.indianriverlagoon.org/ (accessed July 21, 2009).

Hardin, Kenneth, and Michael Russo
1987   Phase II Test Excavations at the Piney Point site, 8Na31, Amelia Island, Florida. Report on file, Florida Division of Historical Resources, Tallahassee.

Harris, Norma J.
1998   Prehistoric and Historic Archaeological Properties of the Naval Live Oaks Reservation, Gulf Breeze, Florida. National Register of Historic Places Multiple Properties Nomination prepared for Gulf Islands National Seashore, National Park Service, Southeastern Archaeological Center, Tallahassee.
1999   Native Americans of Presidio Santa Maria de Galve, 1689–1722. M.A. thesis, Department of Anthropology, University of West Florida, Pensacola.
2003   Native Americans. In *Presidio Santa Maria de Galve: A Struggle for Survival in Colonial Spanish Pensacola*, edited by Judith A. Bense, 257–314. University Press of Florida, Gainesville.

Harris, Norma J., and Krista E. Eschbach
2006   *Final Report: Archaeological Investigations at Presidio Isla de Santa Rosa*. University of West Florida Archaeology Institute Report of Investigations no. 133. Pensacola. Prepared for Gulf Islands National Seashore, National Park Service, Southeastern Archaeological Center, Tallahassee.

Harris, Norma J., and Marie E. Pokrant
2002   *Fort Walton Beach Landing and Brooks Street Renovations, City of Fort Walton Beach, Florida.* University of West Florida Archaeology Institute Report of Investigations no. 104. Pensacola.
2003   *Fort Walton Beach Archaeological Survey, Phase II.* University of West Florida Archaeology Institute Report of Investigations no. 111. Pensacola.

Heckenberger, Michael J.
2005   *The Ecology of Power: Culture, Place, and Personhood in the Southern Amazon, A.D. 1000–2000.* Routledge, New York.

Helms, Mary
1988   *Ulysses' Sail: An Ethnographic Odyssey of Power, Knowledge, and Geographical Distance.* Princeton University Press, Princeton, N.J.

Hendry, Charles W., Jr., and Charles R. Sproul
1966   *Geology and Ground-Water Resources of Leon County, Florida.* Florida Geological Survey Bulletin no. 47. Tallahassee.

Hendryx, Greg, Ryan Sipe, and Vicki Rolland
2008   Archaeological Data Recovery and Mitigation at a Portion of 8Du5599 (the St. Johns Bluff 3 Site), Duval County, Florida. Report on file, Florida Division of Historical Resources, Tallahassee.

Hendryx, Gregory S., and Greg C. Smith
2002   An Intensive Cultural Resource Assessment Survey of Windswept Point and Site Testing at 8DU5599, Duval County, Florida. Report on file, Florida Division of Historical Resources, Tallahassee.

Hertz, Robert
1907   The Collective Representation of Death. In *Death and the Right Hand*, translated by R. and C. Needham, 25–86. Free Press, New York.

Higginbotham, Jay
1991   *Old Mobile, Fort Louis de la Louisiane, 1702–1711.* Reprint, University of Alabama Press, Tuscaloosa. Originally published 1977, University of Alabama Press, Tuscaloosa.

Higgs, Charles D.
1942   Spanish Colonial Contacts with the Ais (Indian River). *Florida Historical Quarterly* 21: 25–39.
1951   Appendix A: The Derrotero of Alvaro Mexia, 1605. In *A Survey of Indian River Archeology, Florida*, by Irving Rouse, 265–74, Yale University Publications in Anthropology 44. Yale University Press, New Haven, Conn.

Hilgeman, Sherri L.
2000   *Pottery and Chronology at Angel.* University of Alabama Press, Tuscaloosa.

Hill, Louis
n.d.   Mound 6 Excavations at the Lake Jackson Site. Field notes on file, Florida Division of Historical Resources, Tallahassee.

Hodell, David A., Mark Brenner, Jason H. Curtis, Roger Medina-González, Enrique Ildefonso-Chan Can, Alma Albornaz-Pat, and Thomas P. Guilderson
2005   Climate Change on the Yucatan Peninsula during the Little Ice Age. *Quaternary Research* 63: 109–21.

Hodell, David A., Jason H. Curtis, and Mark Brenner
1995   Possible Role of Climate in the Collapse of Classic Maya Civilization. *Nature* 375: 391–94.

Hollister S. C.
1958   A Review of the Genus *Busycon* and Its Allies—Part I. *Paleontographica Americana* 4: 59–126.

Holmes, William H.
1903   Aboriginal Pottery of the Eastern United States. In *Twentieth Annual Report of the Bureau of American Ethnology*, 1–201. Smithsonian Institution, Washington, D.C.

Horvath, Elizabeth A.
1995   Final Report on the Archeological Investigations at the Seminole Rest Site (CANA-063/8VO124), Canaveral National Seashore, Volusia County, Florida. Report on file, Florida Division of Historical Resources, Tallahassee.

Huag, G. H., D. Günter, L. C. Peterson, D. M. Sigman, K. A. Hughen, and B. Aeschlimann
2003   Climate and the Collapse of Maya Civilization. *Science* 299: 1731–35.

Hudson, Charles
1987   An Unknown South: Spanish Explorers and Southeastern Chiefdoms. In *Visions and Revisions: Ethnohistoric Perspectives on Southern Cultures*, edited by George Sabo III and William M. Schneider, 6–24. University of Georgia Press, Athens.

Hughes, Gilbert H.
1967   *Analysis of the Water-Level Fluctuations of Lake Jackson near Tallahassee, Florida.* State Board of Conservation, Division of Geology, Report of Investigations no. 48. Tallahassee.

Humphreys, Jay, Shelley Franz, and Bill Seaman
1993   Florida's Estuaries: A Citizen's Guide to Coastal Living and Conservation. Sea Grant Extension Bulletin 23. Florida Department of Community Affairs, Tallahassee.

Hunt, Charles B.
1974   *Natural Regions of the United States and Canada.* W. H. Freeman and Company, San Francisco.

Hutchinson, Dale L.
2004   *Bioarchaeology of the Florida Gulf Coast: Adaptation, Conflict, and Change.* University Press of Florida, Gainesville.
2006   *Tatham Mound and the Bioarchaeology of European Contact.* University Press of Florida, Gainesville.

Hutchinson, Dale L., Clark Spenser Larsen, Lynette Norr, and Margaret Schoeninger
2000   Agricultural Melodies and Alternative Harmonies in Florida and Georgia. In *Bioarchaeological Studies of Life in the Age of Agriculture: A View from the Southeast*, edited by Patricia Lambert, 96–116. University of Alabama Press, Tuscaloosa.

Hutchinson, Dale L., Clark Spencer Larsen, Margaret J. Schoeninger, and Lynette Norr
1998   Regional Variation in the Pattern of Maize Adoption and Use in Florida and Georgia. *American Antiquity* 63: 397–416.

Jenkins, Ned J.
1978   Prehistoric Chronology of the Lower Chattahoochee Valley: A Preliminary Statement. *Journal of Alabama Archaeology* 24: 73–91.

Jenkins, Ned J., and Richard A. Krause
1986   *Tombigbee Watershed in Southeastern Prehistory.* University of Alabama Press, Tuscaloosa.
2009   The Woodland-Mississippian Interface in Alabama, ca. 1075–1200: An Adaptive Radiation? *Southeastern Archaeology* 28: 202–19.

Jennings, Jesse D., and Charles H. Fairbanks
1939   Type Descriptions of Pottery. *Southeastern Archaeological Conference Newsletter* 1(2).

Jennings, Jesse D., Gordon R. Willey, and Marshall T. Newman
1955   *The Ormond Beach Mound, East Central Florida*. Bulletin of the Bureau of American Ethnology no. 49, Smithsonian Institution, Washington, D.C.

Johannessen, Sissel
1984   Paleoethnobotany. In *American Bottom Archaeology*, edited by Charles J. Bareis and James W. Porter, 197–214. University of Illinois Press, Urbana.

Johnson, Ann F., and Michael G. Barbour
1990   Dunes and Maritime Forests. In *Ecosystems of Florida*, edited by Ronald L. Myers and John J. Ewel, 429–81. University of Central Florida Press, Orlando.

Johnson, G. Michael, and Timothy A. Kohler
1987   Toward a Better Understanding of North Peninsular Gulf Coast Florida Prehistory: Archaeological Reconnaissance in Dixie County. *Florida Anthropologist* 40: 275–86.

Johnson, Jay K.
1994   Prehistoric Exchange in the Southeast. In *Prehistoric Exchange Systems in North America*, edited by T Baugh and J. Ericson, 99–125. Plenum, New York.

Johnson, Kenneth W.
1987   *The Search for Aquacaleyquen and Cali: Archaeological Survey of Portions of Alachua, Bradford, Citrus, Clay, Columbia, Marian, Sumter, and Union Counties, FL*. Miscellaneous Project Report no. 33. Department of Anthropology, Florida State Museum, Gainesville.
1991   The Utina and the Potano Peoples of Northern Florida: Changing Settlement Systems in the Spanish Colonial Period. Ph.D. dissertation, Department of Anthropology, University of Florida, Gainesville.

Johnson, Kenneth W., and Bruce C. Nelson
1990   The Utina: Seriations and Chronology. *Florida Anthropologist* 43: 48–62.

Johnson, Robert E.
1988   Archeological Reconnaissance Survey of the St. Johns Bluff Area of Duval County, Florida. Report on file, Florida Division of Historical Resources, Tallahassee.
1996   An Intensive Archeological Survey of Florida Inland Navigation District Tract DU7, Duval County, Florida. Report on file, Florida Division of Historical Resources, Tallahassee.
1998   Phase II Archeological Investigations of Sites 8Du5544 and 8Du5545, Queen's Harbour Yacht and Country Club, Duval County, Florida. Report on file, Florida Division of Historical Resources, Tallahassee.

Johnson, William G.
1990   A Report on Investigations on the West Okeechobee Basin Archaeological Survey. Report on file, Florida Division of Historical Resources, Tallahassee.

Jones, B. Calvin
n.d.   Notes on the Markley Site. Ms. on file, Florida Division of Historical Resources, Tallahassee.
1982   Southern Cult Manifestations at the Lake Jackson Site, Leon County, Florida: Salvage Excavation of Mound 3. *Midcontinental Journal of Archaeology* 7: 3–44.
1990   A Late Mississippian Collector. *Soto States Anthropologist* 90: 83–86.

1992   November 1992 Septic Tank Survey at Lake Jackson Mounds State Park Archaeological Site, Leon County, Florida. Report on file, Florida Division of Historical Resources, Tallahassee.

1994   The Lake Jackson Mound Complex: Stability and Change in Fort Walton Culture. *Florida Anthropologist* 47: 120–46.

Jones, B. Calvin, John Hann, and John F. Scarry

1991   *San Pedro y San Pablo de Patale: A Seventeenth-Century Spanish Mission in Leon County, Florida.* Florida Archaeology no. 5. Bureau of Archaeological Research, Division of Historical Resources, Tallahassee.

Jones, B. Calvin, and John T. Penman

1973   Winewood: An Inland Fort Walton Site. *Bureau of Historic Sites and Properties Bulletin* 3: 65–90.

Jones, B. Calvin, and Louis Tesar

2001   1983–1995 Survey, Salvage and Mitigation of Archaeological Resources within the Mt. Royal Site (8PU35) Village Area, Putnam County, Florida. Bureau of Archaeological Research, Division of Historical Resources, Florida Department of State. Report on file, Florida Division of Historical Resources, Tallahassee.

Jordan, Douglas F.

1963   The Goodman Mound. In *Papers on the Jungerman and Goodman Sites, Florida*, edited by D. F. Jordan, E. S. Wing, and A. Bullen, 24–50. Contributions of the Florida State Museum Social Sciences 10. Gainesville.

Keigwin, Lloyd D.

1996   The Little Ice Age and Medieval Warm Period in the Sargasso Sea. *Science* 274: 1504–8.

Kelly, Arthur, and Fay-Cooper Cole

1931   Rediscovering Illinois. In *Blue Book of the State of Illinois, 1931–1932*, 318–41. Springfield.

Kelly, John E.

1980   Formative Developments at Cahokia and the Adjacent American Bottom: A Merrell Tract Perspective. Ph.D. dissertation, Department of Anthropology, University of Wisconsin, Madison.

1987   Emergent Mississippian and the Transition from Late Woodland to Mississippian: The American Bottom Case for a New Concept. In *The Emergent Mississippian*, edited by Richard A. Marshall, 212–26. Proceedings of the Sixth Mid-South Archaeological Conference, Starkville, Miss.

1990a   The Range Site Community Patterns and the Mississippian Emergence. In *The Mississippian Emergence*, edited by Bruce Smith, 67–112. Smithsonian Institution Press, Washington, D.C.

1990b   The Emergence of Mississippian Culture in the American Bottom Region. In *The Mississippian Emergence*, edited by Bruce Smith, 113–52. Smithsonian Institution Press, Washington, D.C.

1991   Cahokia and Its Role as a Gateway Center in Interregional Exchange. In *Cahokia and the Hinterlands: Middle Mississippian Cultures of the Midwest*, edited by Thomas E. Emerson and R. Barry Lewis, 61–82. University of Illinois Press, Chicago.

1996   Redefining Cahokia: Prince(ples) and Elements of Community Organization. *Wisconsin Archeologist* 77: 97–119.

2001   The Historical and Distributional Significance of Wells Incised Plates. Paper pre-

sented at the Fifty-eighth Annual Meeting of the Southeastern Archaeological Conference, Chattanooga, Tenn.
2002 The Pulcher Tradition and the Ritualization of Cahokia: A Perspective from Cahokia's Southern Neighbor. *Southeastern Archaeology* 21: 136–48.
2006 The Ritualization of Cahokia: The Structure and Organization of Early Cahokia Crafts. In *Leadership and Polity in Mississippian Society*, edited by Brian M. Butler and Paul D. Welch, 236–63. Center for Archaeological Investigations, Occasional Paper 33. Southern Illinois University, Carbondale.

Kelly, John E., and James A. Brown
2004 The Context of the Blocked-Line Motifs at Cahokia and Their Affinities with the Davis Rectangle Motif. Paper prepared for the Forty-sixth Annual Caddo Conference, Natchitoches, La.
2011 Cahokia: The Processes and Principles of the Creation of an Early Mississippian City. In *Making Ancient Cities: Studies of the Production of Space in Early Urban Environments*, edited by Kevin D. Fisher and Andrew Creekmore. Chapter submitted for review to Cambridge University Press.

Kelly, John E., Steven J. Ozuk, Douglas K. Jackson, Dale L. McElrath, Fred A. Finney, and Duane Esarey
1984 Emergent Mississippian. In *American Bottom Archaeology*, edited by Charles J. Bareis and James W. Porter, 104–27. University of Illinois Press, Urbana.

Kelly, John E., Steven J. Ozuk, and Joyce A. Williams
2007 The Range Site: The Emergent Mississippian, George Reeves and Lindeman Phase Components. ITARP, Transportation Archaeological Research Reports 18. University of Illinois, Urbana-Champaign.

Kelly, Lucretia S.
2001 A Case of Ritual Feasting at the Cahokia Site. In *Feasts: Archaeological and Ethnographic Perspectives on Food, Politics, and Power*, edited by Michael Dietler and Brian Hayden, 334–67. Smithsonian Institution Press, Washington, D.C.

Kennedy, William J., Ryan Wheeler, Linda Spears-Jester, James Pepe, Nancy Sinks, and Clarke Wernecke
1993 Archaeological Survey and Excavations at the Jupiter Inlet I Site (8PB34), DuBois Park, Palm Beach County, Florida. Report on file, Department of Anthropology, Florida Atlantic University, Boca Raton.

Kenworthy, C. J.
1883 Ancient Canals in Florida. *Smithsonian Institution Annual Report* 1881: 631–35.

Kidder, Tristram R.
2007 Contemplating Plaquemine Culture. In *Plaquemine Archaeology*, edited by Mark A. Rees and Patrick C. Livingood, 196–205. University of Alabama Press, Tuscaloosa.

Kimble, Elicia
2008 Rummaging Through Rubbish: Analysis of Feature 4 at Yon Mound and Village Site (8Li2). Undergraduate honors thesis, Department of Anthropology, University of South Florida, Tampa.

King, Adam
2003 *Etowah: The Political History of a Chiefdom Capital*. University of Alabama Press, Tuscaloosa.
2006 Leadership Strategies and the Nature of Mississippian Chiefdoms in Northern

Georgia. In *Leadership and Polity in Mississippian Society*, edited by Brian M. Butler and Paul D. Welch, 73–90. Center for Archaeological Investigations Occasional Paper no. 33. Southern Illinois University, Carbondale.

King, Adam (editor)
2007　*Southeastern Ceremonial Complex: Chronology, Content, Context*. University of Alabama Press, Tuscaloosa.

King, Adam, and Jennifer A. Freer
1995　The Mississippian Southeast: A World Systems Perspective. In *Native American Interactions: Multiscalar Analyses and Interpretations in the Eastern Woodlands*, edited by Michael S. Nassaney and Kenneth E. Sassaman, 266–88. University of Tennessee Press, Knoxville.

King, Adam, and Maureen S. Meyers (editors)
2002　Frontiers, Backwaters, and Peripheries: Exploring the Edges of the Mississippian World. *Southeastern Archaeology* 21: 113–226.

King, Adam, and Maureen S. Meyers
2002　Exploring the Edges of the Mississippian World. *Southeastern Archaeology* 21: 113–16.

King, John M.
2004　Grave-Goods as Gifts in Early Saxon Burials (ca. AD 450–600). *Journal of Social Archaeology* 4: 214–38.

Knight, Vernon J., Jr.
1984　Late Prehistoric Adaptations in the Mobile Bay Region. In *Perspectives on Gulf Coast Prehistory*, edited by Dave D. Davis, 198–215. University Press of Florida, Gainesville.
1989　Symbolism of Mississippian Mounds. In *Powhatan's Mantle: Indians in the Colonial Southeast*, edited by Peter H. Wood, Gregory A. Waselkov, and M. Thomas Hatley, 279–91. University of Nebraska Press, Lincoln.
1990　Social Organization and the Evolution of Hierarchy in Southeastern Chiefdoms. *Journal of Anthropological Research* 46: 1–23.
1991　Lake Jackson and Speculations on a Demographic Paradox. Paper presented at the Forty-eighth Annual Meeting of the Southeastern Archaeological Conference, Jackson, Miss.
1994　Ocmulgee Fields Culture and the Historical Development of Creek Ceramics. In *Ocmulgee Archaeology, 1936–1986*, edited by David J. Hally, 181–89. University of Georgia Press, Athens.

Knight, Vernon James, Jr., and Vincas P. Steponaitis
1998　*Archaeology of the Moundville Chiefdom*. Smithsonian Institution Press, Washington, D.C.

Kohler, Timothy A.
1979　Corn, Indians, and Spaniards in North-Central Florida: A Technique for Measuring Evolutionary Changes in Corn. *Florida Anthropologist* 32: 1–7.
1991　The Demise of Weeden Island, and Post–Weeden Island Cultural Stability, in Non-Mississippianized Northern Florida. In *Stability, Transformation, and Variation: The Late Woodland Southeast*, edited by Michael S. Nassaney and Charles R. Cobb, 91–119. Plenum, New York.

Kolianos, Phyllis E., and Brent R. Weisman (editors)
2005a　*The Florida Journals of Frank Hamilton Cushing*. University Press of Florida, Gainesville.

2005b *The Lost Florida Manuscript of Frank Hamilton Cushing.* University Press of Florida, Gainesville.

Kowalewski, Stephen A.
1995 Large-Scale Ecology in Aboriginal Eastern North America. In *Native American Interactions: Multiscalar Analyses and Interpretations in the Eastern Woodlands,* edited by Michael S. Nassaney and Kenneth E. Sassaman, 147–73. University of Tennessee Press, Knoxville.

Kozuch, Laura
1992 *Sharks and Shark Products in Prehistoric South Florida.* Institute of Archaeology and Paleoenvironmental Studies Monograph 2. University of Florida, Gainesville.
1998 Marine Shells from Mississippian Archaeological Sites (Illinois, Oklahoma, Georgia, Alabama). Ph.D. dissertation, Department of Anthropology, University of Florida, Gainesville.

Kroeber, Alfred L.
1927 Disposal of the Dead. *American Anthropologist* 29: 308–15.

Kroeber, Theodora
1961 *Ishi in Two Worlds. A Biography of the Last Wild Indian in America.* University of California Press, Berkeley.

Kushlan, James A.
1990 Freshwater Marshes. In *Ecosystems of Florida,* edited by Ronald L. Myers and John J. Ewel, 324–63. University of Central Florida Press, Orlando.

Lacquement, Cameron H.
2010 Recalculating Mound Volume at Moundville. *Southeastern Archaeology* 29: 341–54.

Lafferty, Robert H., III
1994 Prehistoric Exchange in the Lower Mississippi Valley. In *Prehistoric Exchange Systems in North America,* edited by Timothy G. Baugh and Jonathon E. Ericson, 177–213. Plenum, New York.
2008 The Diffusion of Shell-Tempered Pottery into the Baytown Area of the Northern Lower Mississippi Valley. *Southeastern Archaeology* 27: 172–92.

Lanham, J. F., and Alan Brech
2007 Summer Pentoaya: Locating a Major Ais Indian Town along the Indian River Lagoon, Florida. *Florida Anthropologist* 60: 21–38.

Larsen, Clark Spencer
2001 Bioarchaeology of Spanish Florida. In *Bioarchaeology of Spanish Florida,* edited by Clark Spencer Larsen, 23–51. University Press of Florida, Gainesville.

Larsen, Clark Spencer, Dale L. Hutchinson, Margaret J. Schoeninger, and Lynette Norr
2001 Food and Stable Isotopes in La Florida: Diet and Nutrition Before and After Contact. In *Bioarchaeology of Spanish Florida,* edited by Clark Spencer Larsen, 52–81. University Press of Florida, Gainesville.

Larsen, Clark Spencer, and Leslie Sering
2000 Inferring Iron-Deficiency Anemia from Human Skeletal Remains: The Case of the Georgia Bight. In *Bioarchaeological Studies of Life in the Age of Agriculture: A View from the Southeast,* edited by Patricia Lambert, 116–24. University of Alabama Press, Tuscaloosa.

Larson, Lewis H., Jr.
1958   Southern Cult Manifestations on the Georgia Coast. *American Antiquity* 23: 426–30.
1971   Archaeological Implications of Social Stratification at the Etowah Site, Georgia. In *Approaches to the Social Dimensions of Mortuary Practices*, edited by James A. Brown, 58–67. Memoirs of the Society for American Archaeology no. 25. Washington, D.C.
1980   *Aboriginal Subsistence Technology on the Southeastern Coastal Plain during the Late Prehistoric Period*. University Press of Florida, Gainesville.

Laudonnière, Rene de
1975 [1586]   *Three Voyages*. Translated by Charles E. Bennett. University Press of Florida, Gainesville.

Lazarus, William C.
1961   Ten Middens on the Navy Live Oaks Reservation, Santa Rosa County, Florida. *Florida Anthropologist* 14: 49–64.
1971   The Fort Walton Culture West of the Apalachicola River. *Southeastern Archaeological Conference Newsletter* 10: 40–48.

Lazarus, Yulee W.
1986   The Indianola Inn Shell Midden Mound, Fort Walton Beach, Florida. *Florida Anthropologist* 39: 253–63.

Lazarus, Yulee W., and Roger J. Fornaro
1986   Fort Walton Temple Mound, Further Test Excavations, DePaux 1973. *Florida Anthropologist* 18: 159–77.

Lazarus, Yulee W., William C. Lazarus, and Donald W. Sharon
1976   The Navy Live Oaks Reservation Cemetery Site. *Florida Anthropologist* 14: 103–17.

Leader, Jonathan M.
1988   Technological Continuities and Specialization in Prehistoric Metalwork in the Eastern United States. Ph.D. dissertation, Department of Anthropology, University of Florida, Gainesville.

Le Baron, J. F.
1884   Prehistoric Remains in Florida. In *Smithsonian Institution Annual Report for 1884*, 771–90. Smithsonian Institution, Washington, D.C.

Lee, Chung-Ho, and Deborah Joy
1989   *Archaeological Investigations at Bayside Property, Santa Rosa County, Florida*. University of West Florida, Office of Cultural and Archaeological Research, Report of Investigations no. 24. Pensacola.

Leonard, Irving A.
1936   The Spanish Re-exploration of the Gulf Coast in 1686. *Mississippi Valley Historical Review* 22: 547–57.

Le Page Du Pratz, Antoine S.
1947 [1774]   *The History of Louisiana or of the Western Parts of Virginia and Carolina: Containing a Description of the Countries That Lie on Both Sides of the River Mississippi: With an Account of the Settlements, Inhabitants, Soil, Climate, and Products*. T. Becket, London.

Lessure, Richard
1999   On the Genesis of Value in Early Hierarchical Societies. In *Material Symbols: Culture and Economy in Prehistory*, edited by John E. Robb, 23–55. Center for Archaeological Investigations, Occasional Paper no. 26, Carbondale, Ill.

Levy, R. S., D. F. Barton, and T. Riordan
1984 An Archaeological Survey of Cape Canaveral Air Force Station, Brevard County, Florida. Report on file, Florida Division of Historical Resources, Tallahassee.

Lewis, R. Barry, and Charles Stout (editors)
1998 *Mississippian Towns and Sacred Spaces: Searching for an Architectural Grammar.* University of Alabama Press, Tuscaloosa.

Lewis, R. Barry, Charles Stout, and Cameron B. Wesson
1998 The Design of Mississippian Towns. In *Mississippian Towns and Sacred Spaces*, edited by R. Barry Lewis and Charles B. Stout, 1–21. University of Alabama Press, Tuscaloosa.

Lewis, Thomas M. N., and Madeline Kneberg
1946 *Hiwassee Island.* University of Tennessee Press, Knoxville.

Lillios, Katina T.
1999 Objects of Memory: The Ethnography and Archaeology of Heirlooms. *Journal of Archaeological Method and Theory* 6: 235–62.

Little, Keith J., Cailup Curren, and C. Lee McKenzie
1988 *A Preliminary Archaeological Survey of the Blackwater Drainage, Santa Rosa County, Florida.* Institute of West Florida Archaeology, Report of Investigations no. 19, University of West Florida, Pensacola.

Lorenz, Karl G.
1996 Small-Scale Mississippian Community Organization in the Black River Valley of Mississippi. *Southeastern Archaeology* 15: 145–61.

Loucks, L. Jill
1976 Early Alachua Tradition Burial Ceremonialism: The Henderson Mound, Alachua County, Florida. M.A. thesis, University of Florida, Gainesville.
1979 Political and Economic Interactions between Spaniards and Indians: Archaeological and Ethnohistorical Perspectives of the Mission System in Florida. Ph.D. dissertation, Department of Anthropology, University of Florida, Gainesville.

Lowery, Lily E.
2002 Sedimentary Evidence of Coastal Response to Holocene Sea-Level Change, Blackwater Bay, Southwest Florida. http://keck.wooster.edu/archives/symposium/02/Florida01_pdfs/loweryabs.pdf.

Lozowski, Jennifer
1991 Shovel Testing at the Lake Jackson Site (8LE1) by Museum of Florida History Summer Campers, June 1991. Report on file, Museum of Florida History, Tallahassee.

Luer, George M.
1985 Some Comments on Englewood Incised, Safety Harbor Incised, and Scarry's Proposed Ceramic Changes. *Florida Anthropologist* 38: 236–39.
1989 Calusa Canals in Southwestern Florida: Routes of Tribute and Exchange. *Florida Anthropologist* 42: 86–130.
1993 A Safety Harbor Incised Bottle with Effigy Bird Feet and Human Hands from a Possible Headman Burial, Sarasota County, Florida. *Florida Anthropologist* 46: 238–50.
2002a Ceramic Bottles, Globular Vessels, and Safety Harbor Culture. In *Archaeology of Upper Charlotte Harbor, Florida*, edited by George M. Luer, 95–110. Florida Anthropological Society, Publication 15. Tallahassee.

2002b The Aqui Esta Mound: Ceramic and Shell Vessels of the Early Mississippian-Influenced Englewood Phase. In *Archaeology of Upper Charlotte Harbor, Florida*, edited by George M. Luer, 111–81. Florida Anthropological Society, Publication 15. Tallahassee.
2010 Ceremonial Metal Tablet #60: Stylistic and Compositional Analyses of a Lead-Iron Tablet from the Blueberry Site, Highlands County, Florida. *Florida Anthropologist* 63: 35–45.

Luer, George M., and Marion M. Almy
1981 Temple Mounds of the Tampa Bay Area. *Florida Anthropologist* 34: 127–55.
1982 A Definition of the Manasota Culture. *Florida Anthropologist* 35: 34–58.
1987 The Laurel Mound (8So98) and Radial Burials with Comments on the Safety Harbor Period. *Florida Anthropologist* 40: 301–20.

Luer, George M., and Ryan J. Wheeler
1997 How the Pine Island Canal Worked: Topography, Hydraulics, and Engineering. *Florida Anthropologist* 50: 115–31.

Lund, David C., and William B. Curry
2004 Late Holocene Variability in Florida Current Surface Density: Patterns and Possible Causes. *Paleoceanography* 19: PA4001: 1–17.

Magoon, Dane, Lynette Norr, Dale L. Hutchinson, and Charles R. Ewen
2001 An Analysis of Human Skeletal Materials from the Snow Beach Site (8WA52). *Southeastern Archaeology* 20: 18–30.

Mainfort, Robert C., Jr.
1988 Middle Woodland Ceremonialism at Pinson Mounds, Tennessee. *American Antiquity* 53: 158–73.
2001 The Late Prehistoric and Protohistoric Periods in the Central Mississippi Valley. In *Societies in Eclipse: Archaeology of the Eastern Woodland Indians, A.D. 1400–1700*, edited by David S. Brose, C. Wesley Cowan, and Robert C. Mainfort Jr., 173–89. Smithsonian Institution Press, Washington, D.C.

Mann, Michael E.
2000 Lessons for a New Millennium. *Science* 289: 253–54.

Marquardt, William H.
1987a Theoretical Issues I: The Analysis of Spatial Patterning. In *Regional Dynamics: Burgundian Landscapes in Historical Perspective*, edited by Carole L. Crumley and William H. Marquardt, 1–18. Academic Press, San Diego, Calif.
1987b The Calusa Social Formation in Protohistoric South Florida. In *Power Relations and State Formation*, edited by Thomas Carl Patterson and Christine Ward Gailey, 98–116. Archeology Section, American Anthropological Association, Washington, D.C.
1988 Politics and Production among the Calusa of South Florida. In *Hunters and Gatherers*, vol. 1, *History, Evolution, and Social Change*, edited by Tim Ingold, David Riches, and James Woodburn, 161–88. Berg Publishers, London.
1992a Dialectical Archaeology. In *Archaeological Method and Theory Volume 4*, edited by Michael B. Schiffer, 101–40. University of Arizona Press, Tucson.
1992b Recent Archaeological and Paleoenvironmental Investigations in Southwest Florida. In *Culture and Environment in the Domain of the Calusa*, edited by William H. Marquardt, 9–57. Institute of Archaeology and Paleoenvironmental Studies, Monograph 1. University of Florida, Gainesville.

1992c Shell Artifacts from Caloosahatchee Area. In *Culture and Environment in the Domain of the Calusa,* edited by William H. Marquardt, 191–228. Institute of Archaeology and Paleoenvironmental Studies, Monograph 1. University of Florida, Gainesville.
1999   Useppa Island in the Archaic and Caloosahatchee Periods. In *The Archaeology of Useppa Island,* edited by William H. Marquardt, 77–98. Institute of Archaeology and Paleoenvironmental Studies, Monograph 3. University of Florida, Gainesville.
2001   The Emergence and Demise of the Calusa. In *Societies in Eclipse: Archaeology of the Eastern Woodland Indians, A.D. 1400–1700,* edited by David S. Brose, C. Wesley Cowan, and Robert C. Mainfort Jr., 157–71. Smithsonian Institution Press, Washington, D.C.
2012   The Pineland Site Complex: Theoretical and Cultural Contexts. In *The Archaeology of Pineland: A Coastal Southwest Florida Site Complex, A.D. 50–1710,* edited by William H. Marquardt and Karen J. Walker, 1–22. Institute of Archaeology and Paleoenvironmental Studies, Monograph 4. University of Florida, Gainesville.

Marquardt, William H., and Carole L. Crumley
1987   Theoretical Issues in the Analysis of Spatial Patterning. In *Regional Dynamics: Burgundian Landscapes in Historical Perspective,* edited by Carole L. Crumley and William H. Marquardt, 1–18. Academic Press, Orlando, Fla.

Marquardt, William H., and Karen J. Walker
2001   Pineland: A Coastal Wet Site in Southwest Florida. In *Enduring Records: The Environmental and Cultural Heritage of Wetlands,* edited by Barbara A. Purdy, 48–60. Oxbow Books, Oxford, U.K.
2012   The Pineland Site Complex: An Environmental and Cultural History. In *The Archaeology of Pineland: A Coastal Southwest Florida Site Complex, A.D. 50–1710,* edited by William H. Marquardt and Karen J. Walker. Institute of Archaeology and Paleoenvironmental Studies, Monograph 4. University of Florida, Gainesville.

Marrinan, Rochelle A.
2005   Early Mississippian Faunal Remains from the Shields Mound (8DU12). *Florida Anthropologist* 58: 173–208.

Marrinan, Rochelle A., and Stephen C. Bryne
1986   Apalachee-Mission Archaeological Survey, vol. 1. Report on file, Florida Division of Historical Resources, Tallahassee.

Marrinan, Rochelle A., and Nancy Marie White
2007   Modeling Fort Walton Culture in Northwest Florida. *Southeastern Archaeology* 26: 292–318.

Marsh, Elan Tomkinson
2006   Fort Walton Burial Practices in the Apalachicola River Valley. Senior honors thesis in anthropology, University of South Florida, Tampa.

Marsh, Owen T.
1966   *Geology of Escambia and Santa Rosa Counties, Western Florida Panhandle.* Bulletin no. 46(7). Florida Geological Survey, Tallahassee.

Mauss, Marcel
1967   *The Gift: Forms and Functions of Exchange in Archaic Societies.* W. W. Norton and Company, New York.

Maxham, Mintcy D.
2000 Rural Communities in the Black Warrior Valley, Alabama: The Role of Commoners in the Creation of the Moundville Landscape. *American Antiquity* 65: 337–54.

McEwan, Bonnie G.
2004 Apalachee and Neighboring Groups. In *Handbook of North American Indians*, vol. 14, *Southeast*, edited by Raymond D. Fogelson, 669–76. Smithsonian Institution, Washington, D.C.

McGovern, Thomas H.
1994 Management for Extinction in Norse Greenland. In *Historical Ecology: Cultural Knowledge and Changing Landscapes*, edited by Carole L. Crumley, 127–54. School of American Research Press, Santa Fe, N.Mex.

McKern, William C.
1934 *Certain Culture Classification Problems in Middle Western Archaeology*. National Research Council, Committee on State Archaeological Surveys, Circular no. 17, Washington, D.C.

Mikell, Gregory A.
1990 The Sheephead Bayou Site (8BY150): A Single Component Fort Walton Hamlet Site in Northwest Florida. *Florida Anthropologist* 43: 198–208.
1992 The Fort Walton Mississippian Variant on the Northwest Florida Gulf Coast. *Southeastern Archaeology* 11: 51–65.
1995a Choctawhatchee Bay Fort Walton, the West Side Story. *Florida Anthropologist* 48: 120–32.
1995b Bell and Brooks Street: Two Fort Walton Village Sites on Choctawhatchee Bay. *Florida Anthropologist* 48: 97–119.

Milanich, Jerald T.
1971 *The Alachua Tradition of North-Central Florida*. Contributions of the Florida State Museum, Anthropology and History 17. Gainesville.
1972 Excavations at the Richardson Site, Alachua County, Florida: An Early Seventeenth Century Potano Indian Village (with Notes on Potano Culture Change). *Bureau of Historic Sites and Properties Bulletin* 2: 35–61.
1974 Life in a 9th Century Indian Household: A Weeden Island Fall-Winter Site on the Upper Apalachicola River, Florida. *Bureau of Historic Sites and Properties Bulletin* 4: 1–44.
1979 Origins and Prehistoric Distributions of Black Drink and the Ceremonial Shell Drinking Cup. In *Black Drink: A Native American Tea*, edited by Charles M. Hudson, 83–129. University of Georgia Press, Athens.
1994 *Archaeology of Precolumbian Florida*. University Press of Florida, Gainesville.
1995 *The Florida Indians and the Invasion from Europe*. University Press of Florida, Gainesville.
1996 *The Timucua*. Blackwell Publishers, Cambridge, Mass.
1997 Preface. In *Archaeology of Northern Florida, A.D. 200–900: The McKeithen Weeden Island Culture*, edited by J. T. Milanich, Ann S. Cordell, Vernon J. Knight Jr., Timothy A. Kohler, and Brenda J. Sigler-Lavelle, xv–xvi. University Press of Florida, Gainesville.
1998 Native Chiefdoms and the Exercise of Complexity in Sixteenth-Century Florida. In *Chiefdoms and Chieftaincy in the Americas*, edited by Elsa M. Redmond, 245–64. University Press of Florida, Gainesville.

1999   *Famous Florida Sites: Crystal River and Mount Royal*. University Press of Florida, Gainesville.
2002   Weeden Island Cultures. In *The Woodland Southeast*, edited by David G. Anderson and Robert M. Mainfort Jr., 352–72. University of Alabama Press, Tuscaloosa.

Milanich, Jerald T., Ann S. Cordell, Vernon J. Knight Jr., Timothy A. Kohler, and Brenda J. Sigler-Lavelle
1984   *McKeithen Weeden Island: The Culture of Northern Florida, A.D. 200–900*. Academic Press, New York. Reprinted in 1997 as *Archaeology of Northern Florida, A.D. 200–900: The McKeithen Weeden Island Culture*, University Press of Florida, Gainesville.

Milanich, Jerald T., and Charles H. Fairbanks
1980   *Florida Archaeology*. Academic Press, New York.

Milanich, Jerald T., and Charles Hudson
1993   *Hernando de Soto and the Indians of Florida*. University Press of Florida, Gainesville.

Milanich, Jerald T., Carlos Martinez, Karl Steinen, and Ronald Wallace
1976   Georgia Origins of the Alachua Tradition. *Florida Bureau of Historic Sites and Properties Bulletin* 5: 47–56.

Miles, Douglas
1965   Socioeconomic Aspects of Secondary Burial. *Oceania* 35: 161–74.

Miller, Christopher L., and George R. Hamell
1986   New Perspective on Indian-White Contact: Cultural Symbols and Colonial Trade. *Journal of American History* 73: 311–28.

Miller, James A.
1997   Hydrogeology of Florida. In *The Geology of Florida*, edited by Anthony F. Randazzo and Douglas S. Jones, 69–88. University Press of Florida, Gainesville.

Miller, James J.
1998   *An Environmental History of Northeast Florida*. University Press of Florida, Gainesville.

Mills, Barbara J.
2008   Remembering While Forgetting: Depositional Practices and Social Memory at Chaco. In *Memory Work: Archaeologies of Material Practices*, edited by Barbara J. Mills and William H. Walker, 81–108. School for Advanced Research Press, Santa Fe, N.Mex.

Milner, George R.
1990   The Late Prehistoric Cahokia Cultural System of the Mississippi River Valley: Foundations, Florescence, and Fragmentation. *Journal of World Prehistory* 4: 1–43.
1996   Development and Dissolution of a Mississippian Society in the American Bottom, Illinois. In *Political Structure and Change in the Prehistoric Southeastern United States*, edited by John F. Scarry, 27–52. University Press of Florida, Gainesville.
1998   *The Cahokia Chiefdom: The Archaeology of a Mississippian Society*. Smithsonian Institution Press, Washington, D.C.
2006   *The Cahokia Chiefdom: The Archaeology of a Mississippian Society*. University of Florida Press, Gainesville.

Milner, George R., David G. Anderson, and Marvin T. Smith
2001   The Distribution of Eastern Woodlands Peoples at the Prehistoric and Historic

Interface. In *Societies in Eclipse: Archaeology of the Eastern Woodlands Indians, A.D. 1400–1700*, edited by David S. Brose, C. Wesley Cowan, and Robert C. Mainfort Jr., 191–203. Smithsonian Institution Press, Washington, D.C.

Minar, Jill

2001 Material Culture and the Identification of Prehistoric Cultural Groups. In *Fleeting Identities, Perishable Material Culture in Archaeological Research*, edited by Penelope B. Drooker, 94–114. Center for Archaeological Investigation, Occasional Paper no. 28. Southern Illinois University, Carbondale.

Mitchell, Augustus

1875 Antiquities of Florida. In *Smithsonian Institution Annual Report for 1874*, 390–93. Washington, D.C.

Mitchem, Jeffrey M.

1986 Comments on Some Ceramic Pastes of the Central Peninsular Gulf Coast. *Florida Anthropologist* 39: 68–74.

1988 Some Alternative Interpretations of Safety Harbor Burial Mounds. *Florida Scientist* 51: 100–107.

1989 Redefining Safety Harbor: Late Prehistoric/Protohistoric Archaeology in West Peninsular Florida. Ph.D. dissertation, Department of Anthropology, University of Florida, Gainesville.

1996a The 1996 Field Season at Parkin Archeological State Park. Paper presented at the Fifty-third Annual Meeting of the Southeastern Archaeological Conference, Birmingham, Ala.

1996b The Old Okahumpka Site (8LA57): Late Prehistoric Iconography and Mississippian Influence in Peninsular Florida. *Florida Anthropologist* 49: 225–37.

1999 Clarence B. Moore's Work in Western and Central Florida, 1895–1921. In *The West and Central Florida Expeditions of Clarence Bloomfield Moore*, edited by Jeffrey M. Mitchem, 1–48. University of Alabama Press, Tuscaloosa.

2001 The Willcox Copper Plate from Florida. *Expedition: The Magazine of the University of Pennsylvania Museum of Archaeology and Anthropology* 43: 5–6.

2006 Unembossed Hawk Plates and Other Mississippian Copper Artifacts from Arkansas. Paper presented at the Sixty-third Annual Meeting of the Arkansas Archeological Society, Little Rock.

2008 Mississippian Influence on Weeden Island: Safety Harbor in the Greater Tampa Bay Region. Paper presented at the Seventy-third Annual Meeting of the Society for American Archaeology, Vancouver, B.C.

Moore, Clarence B.

1894a Certain Sand Mounds of the St. Johns River, Florida, Part I. *Journal of the Academy of Natural Sciences of Philadelphia* 10: 4–128.

1894b Certain Sand Mounds of the St. Johns River, Florida, Part II. *Journal of the Academy of Natural Sciences of Philadelphia* 10: 129–246.

1895 Certain Sand Mounds of Duval County, Florida. *Journal of the Academy of Natural Sciences of Philadelphia* 10: 448–502.

1899 A Cache of Pendant Ornaments. *Philadelphia Academy of Natural Sciences Journal* 11: 189–91.

1901 Certain Aboriginal Remains of the Northwest Florida Coast, Part 1. *Journal of the Academy of Natural Sciences* 11: 418–97.

1902 Certain Aboriginal Remains of the Northwest Florida Coast, Part II. *Journal of the Academy of Natural Sciences* 12: 126–355.

1903   Certain Aboriginal Mounds of the Apalachicola River. Reprinted 1999 in *The Northwest Florida Expeditions of Clarence Bloomfield Moore*, edited by David S. Brose and Nancy M. White, 359–412. University of Alabama Press, Tuscaloosa.
1907   Mounds of the Lower Chattahoochee and Lower Flint Rivers. *Journal of the Academy of Natural Sciences* 13: 426–56.
1915   Aboriginal Sites on Tennessee River. *Journal of the Academy of Natural Sciences of Philadelphia* 16: 431–87.
1918   The Northwestern Coast Revisited. Reprinted 1999 in *The Northwest Florida Expeditions of Clarence Bloomfield Moore*, edited by David S. Brose and Nancy White, 445–514. University of Alabama Press, Tuscaloosa.

Morse, Dan F., and Phyllis A. Morse (editors)
1980   Zebree Archaeological Project. Report submitted to Memphis District, U.S. Army Corps of Engineers by the Arkansas Archaeological Survey.

Morse, Dan F., and Phyllis A. Morse
1983   *Archaeology of the Central Mississippi Valley*. Academic Press, New York.
2010   A Fluorite Bead from Florida. *Florida Anthropologist* 63: 47–49.

Mueller, Bradley
2007   303 Arabian Road Parcel, Archaeological Monitoring Report, Town of Palm Beach, Palm Beach County, Florida. Archaeological and Historical Conservancy Technical Report 810.

Muller, Jon
1987   Salt, Chert, and Shell: Mississippian Exchange and Economy. In *Specialization, Exchange, and Complex Societies*, edited by Elizabeth M. Brumfiel and Timothy K. Earle, 10–21. Cambridge University Press, Cambridge.
1995   Regional Interaction in the Later Southeast. In *Native American Interactions: Multiscalar Analysis and Interpretations in the Eastern Woodlands*, edited by Michael S. Nassaney and Kenneth E. Sassaman, 317–40. University of Tennessee Press, Knoxville.
1997   *Mississippian Political Economy*. Plenum Press, New York.

Nassaney, Michael S.
1992   Communal Societies and the Emergence of Elites in the Prehistoric Southeast. In *Lords of the Southeast: Social Inequality and the Native Elites of Southeastern North America*, edited by Alex W. Barker and Timothy R. Pauketat, 111–44. Archaeological Papers no. 3. American Anthropological Association, Washington, D.C.

Nassaney, Michael S., and Charles R. Cobb (editors)
1991   *Stability, Transformation, and Variation: The Late Woodland Southeast*. Plenum Press, New York.

Nassaney, Michael S., and Kenneth E. Sassaman (editors)
1995   *Native American Interactions: Multiscalar Analysis and Interpretations in the Eastern Woodlands*. University of Tennessee Press, Knoxville.

National Aeronautic and Space Administration (NASA)
2000   Kennedy Space Center Master Plan. Report on file, Master Planning Office, Kennedy Space Center.

National Research Council (NRC)
2002   *Abrupt Climate Change: Inevitable Surprises*. National Academy Press, Washington, D.C.

Neuman, Robert W.
1961 Domesticated Corn from a Fort Walton Mound Site in Houston County, Alabama. *Florida Anthropologist* 14: 75–80.
Newell, H. Perry, and Alex D. Krieger
1949 *The George C. Davis Site, Cherokee County, Texas*. Memoirs of the Society for American Archaeology no. 5. Washington, D.C.
Newman, Christine L., and Louis D. Tesar
1997 Assessment of Cultural Resources on the Calusa Camp Resort and Adjacent Tropical Hammock Property, Including the Enigmatic Rock Mound, Monroe County, Florida. Report on file, Florida Division of Historic Resources, Tallahassee.
Newsom, Lee
1991 Archaeobotanical Analysis of Four Features from the 1990 South End Project at Fig Springs (8Co1), Columbia County, Florida. Report submitted to Jerald T. Milanich and John E. Worth, October 23, 1991. Ms. on file with the author.
Newsom, Lee, and Irvy R. Quitmyer
1992 Archaeobotanical and Faunal Remains. Appendix E to *Excavations on the Franciscan Frontier: Archaeology at the Fig Springs Mission*, by Brent R. Weisman, 206–33. University Press of Florida, Gainesville.
Nodine, Bruce K.
2006 A Phase I Cultural Resource Survey of the Dovetail Development Property, Alachua County, Florida. Report on file, Florida Division of Historic Resources, Tallahassee.
Northeast Florida Anthropological Society (NEFAS)
2000 Preliminary Results of Testing of the Wells Property (8Du14), Duval County, Florida. Report on file, Archaeology Laboratory, University of North Florida, Jacksonville.
Nyberg, Johan, Björn A. Malmgren, Antoon Kuijpers, and Amos Winter
2002 A Centennial-Scale Variability of Tropical North Atlantic Surface Hydrography during the Late Holocene. *Palaeogeography, Palaeoclimatology, Palaeoecology* 183: 25–41.
O'Brien, Greg
2009 Delusions of Chiefdoms: An Ethnohistorian's Viewpoint. *Native South* 2: 104–10.
Osborn, Timothy J., and Keith R. Briffa
2006 The Spatial Extent of 20th-Century Warmth in the Context of the Past 1200 Years. *Science* 311: 841–44.
O'Steen, Lisa D.
1999 Island in the Marsh: Zooarchaeological Analysis of 8Na59 and 8Na709, the Crane Island Sites, Nassau County, Florida. Report on file, Florida Division of Historical Resources, Tallahassee.
Parks, Lisa
2004 Spatial Distribution of Aboriginal Pottery on the Wells Property (8Du14). Report on file, Archaeology Laboratory, University of North Florida, Jacksonville.
Parsons, Alexandra
2008 The Grand Shell Ring: A Study of Site Seasonality, Hard Clam Exploitation, and Resource Scheduling. M.A. thesis, Department of Anthropology, Florida State University, Tallahassee.

Pauketat, Timothy R.
1983   A Long-Stemmed Spud from the American Bottom. *Midcontinental Journal of Archaeology* 8: 1–15.
1987   Mississippian Domestic Economy and Formation Processes: A Response to Prentice. *Midcontinental Journal of Archaeology* 12: 77–88.
1994   *The Ascent of Chiefs: Cahokia and Mississippian Politics in Native North America.* University of Alabama Press, Tuscaloosa.
1997   Specialization, Political Symbols, and the Crafty Elite of Cahokia. *Southeastern Archaeology* 16: 1–15.
2004   *Ancient Cahokia and the Mississippians.* Cambridge University Press, Cambridge.
2007   *Chiefdoms and Other Archaeological Delusions.* AltaMira Press, Walnut Grove, Calif.

Pauketat, Timothy R., and Susan Alt
2004   The Making and Meaning of a Mississippian Axe-Head Cache. *Antiquity* 78: 779–96.

Pauketat, Timothy R., and Thomas E. Emerson
1991   The Ideology of Authority and the Power of the Pot. *American Anthropologist* 93: 919–41.

Payne, Claudine
1981   A Preliminary Investigation of Fort Walton Settlement Patterns in the Tallahassee Red Hills. *Southeastern Archaeological Conference Bulletin* 24: 29–31.
1994   Mississippian Capitals: An Archaeological Investigation of Precolumbian Political Structure. Ph.D. dissertation, Department of Anthropology, University of Florida.
2002   Architectural Reflections of Power and Authority in Mississippian Towns. In *The Dynamics of Power*, edited by Maria O'Donovan, 188–213. Center for Archaeological Investigations, Occasional Paper no. 30. Southern Illinois University, Carbondale.
2006   The Foundations of Leadership in Mississippian Chiefdoms: Perspectives from Lake Jackson and Upper Nodena. In *Leadership and Polity in Mississippian Society*, edited by Brian M. Butler and Paul D. Welch, 91–111. Center for Archaeological Investigations, Occasional Paper no. 33. Southern Illinois University, Carbondale.
2010   The Disposal of Heirlooms and the End of Memory at Lake Jackson. Paper presented at the Seventy-fifth Annual Meeting of the Society for American Archaeology, St. Louis, Mo.

Payne, Claudine, and John F. Scarry
1982   Fort Walton Social Boundaries: Predicting Political Territories from Archaeological Data. Paper presented at the Thirty-fourth Annual Meeting of the Florida Anthropological Society, Tampa.
1990   Apalachee Prehistory: The Origins and Evolution of the Lake Jackson Phase. Paper presented at the Forty-seventh Annual Meeting of the Southeastern Archaeological Conference, Mobile, Ala.
1998   Town Structure at the Edge of the Mississippian World. In *Mississippian Towns and Sacred Spaces: Searching for an Architectural Grammar*, edited by R. Barry Lewis and Charles Stout, 22–47. University of Alabama Press, Tuscaloosa.

Peebles, Christopher S.
1974 Moundville: The Organization of a Prehistoric Community and Culture. Ph.D. dissertation, Department of Anthropology, University of California–Santa Barbara.

Peebles, Christopher, and Susan M. Kus
1977 Some Archaeological Correlates of Ranked Societies. *American Antiquity* 42: 421–48.

Penders, Thomas E.
2005 Bone, Antler, Tooth, and Shell Artifacts from the Shields Mound Site (8DU12). *Florida Anthropologist* 58: 239–55.

Penders, Thomas E., Bob Austin, Laura Barksdale, Eve Huggins, William Miller, Randall Parkinson, Vicki Rolland, D. Scott Taylor, and Vera Zimmerman
2009 Pine Island Conservation Area Archaeological Project 2003–2008, Merritt Island, Brevard County, Florida. Report on file, Florida Division of Historical Resources, Tallahassee.

Penton, Daniel T.
1968 Lake Jackson Site (8LE1). Ms. on file, Florida Division of Historical Resources, Tallahassee.
1970 Excavations in the Early Swift Creek Component at Bird Hammock (8Wa30). M.A. thesis, Department of Anthropology, Florida State University, Tallahassee.

Pepe, James
2000 An Archaeological Survey of St. Lucie County, Florida. Report on file, Florida Division of Historical Resources, Tallahassee.

Percy, George W., and Davis S. Brose
1978 Fort Walton Settlement Patterns. In *Mississippian Settlement Patterns*, edited by Bruce D. Smith, 81–114. Academic Press, New York.

Percy, George W., and M. Katherine Jones
1976 An Archaeological Survey of Upland Locales in Gadsden and Liberty Counties. *Florida Anthropologist* 29: 105–26.

Peregrine, Peter
1992 *Mississippian Evolution: A World System Perspective*. Prehistory Press, Madison, Wis.

Phillips, John C.
1989 *Archaeological Testing of the Hickory Ridge Site (8Es1280): A Mississippian Stage Cemetery in Escambia County, Florida*. Institute of West Florida Archaeology Report of Investigations no. 26. University of West Florida, Pensacola.
1995 Hickory Ridge: A Mississippian Period Cemetery in Northwest Florida. *Florida Anthropologist* 48: 72–95.

Phillips, John C., and Judith A Bense
1990 *Archaeological Assessment of Santa Rosa County*. University of West Florida Archaeology Institute, Report of Investigations no. 34. Pensacola.

Phillips, John C., and C. Lee McKenzie
1992 *Archaeology and the Geographic Resource Analysis Support System: An Evaluation of a Soil Conservation Service Model of Archaeological Site Locations in Santa Rosa County, Florida*. University of West Florida Archaeology Institute, Report of Investigations no. 47. Pensacola.

Phillips, Philip
1970   *Archaeological Survey in the Lower Yazoo Basin, Mississippi, 1949–1955.* Papers of the Peabody Museum of Archaeology and Ethnology vol. 60. Harvard University, Cambridge, Mass.

Phillips, Philip, and James A. Brown
1978   *Pre-Columbian Shell Engravings from the Craig Mound at Spiro, Oklahoma.* Peabody Museum of Archaeology and Ethnology, Cambridge, Mass.
1984   Pre-Columbian Shell Engravings from the Craig Mound at Spiro, Oklahoma, Part 2. Peabody Museum of Archaeology and Ethnology, Cambridge, Mass.

Phillips, Philip, James A. Ford, and James B. Griffin
1951   *Archaeological Survey in the Lower Mississippi Alluvial Valley, 1940–47.* Papers of the Peabody Museum of American Archaeology and Ethnology no. 25. Harvard University, Cambridge, Mass.

Platt, William J., and Mark Schwartz
1990   Temperate Hardwood Forests. In *Ecosystems of Florida*, edited by Ronald L. Myers and John J. Ewel, 194–230. University of Central Florida Press, Orlando.

Prentice, Guy
1986   Analysis of the Symbolism Expressed by the Birger Figurine. *American Antiquity* 51: 239–66.
1987   Marine Shells as Wealth Items in Mississippian Societies. *Midcontinental Journal of Archaeology* 12: 193–223.

Prewitt, Terry J., and Nichole Heintzelman
1998   Preliminary Report of Human Remains Investigated at 8OK780, Fort Walton Beach, Florida. Submitted to James Miller, Chief of Archaeological Research, Bureau of Archaeological Research, Department of Historical Resources, Tallahassee. Report on file, Department of Anthropology, University of West Florida, Pensacola.

Price, George, and Bryan Tucker
2003   New Data from the Cannon Site: A Thirteenth Century Burial from Lake Blackshear. *Early Georgia* 31: 5–22.

Price, James E., and Cynthia R. Price
1984   Phase II Testing of the Shell Lake Site, 23WE627, near Wappapello Dam, Wayne County, Missouri, 1984. St. Louis District Cultural Resource Management Report no. 11.

Priestly, Herbert J.
1928   *The Luna Papers: Documents Relating to the Expedition of Don Tristan de Luna Arellano for the Conquest of La Florida in 1559–1562.* Florida State Historical Society, Deland.

Pringle, Heather
1997   Death in Norse Greenland. *Science* 275: 924–26.

Puri, H. S., and R. O. Vernon
1964   *Summary of the Geology of Florida and Guidebook to the Classic Exposures.* Special Publication no. 5. Florida Geological Survey, Tallahassee.

Quitmyer, Irvy R.
1991   Preliminary Report of Zooarchaeological Findings. Letter report submitted to Jerald T. Milanich and John E. Worth, October 29, 1991. Report on file with the author.
1997   The Zooarchaeology of Yon Mound (8Li2) and the Sunstroke Site (8Li217): A

Preface to Fort Walton Subsistence in the Middle Apalachicola Valley, Northwest Florida. Report on file, archaeology lab, Department of Anthropology, University of South Florida, Tampa.

Radin, Paul
1923 [1990] *The Winnebago Tribe*. University of Nebraska Press, Lincoln.

Randolph, A. M.
1852 Survey of Township 1 North, Range 1 West. Survey notes and map on file, Bureau of Survey and Mapping, Title and Land Records Section, Tallahassee.

Reber, Eleanora A., John H. Blitz, and Claire E. Thompson
2010 Direct Determination of the Contents of a Ceramic Bottle from the Moundville Site, Alabama. *Midcontinental Journal of Archaeology* 35: 37–55.

Reilly, F. Kent III, and James F. Garber (editors)
2007 *Ancient Objects and Sacred Realms: Interpretations of Mississippian Iconography*. University of Texas Press, Austin.

Reitz, Elizabeth J.
1988 Evidence for Coastal Adaptations in Georgia and South Carolina. *Archaeology of Eastern North America* 16: 137–58.

Reyier, Eric A., Douglas H. Adams, and Russell H. Lowers
2008 First Evidence of a High Density Nursery Ground for the Lemon Shark, *Negaprion brevirostris*, near Cape Canaveral, Florida. *Florida Scientist* 71: 134–48.

Rodriguez, Nelson
2004 Contact/Mission Period and Depopulation in the Apalachicola River Valley, Northwest Florida. M.A. thesis, Department of Anthropology, University of South Florida, Tampa.

Rolland, Vicki
2004 Measuring Tradition and Variation: A St. Johns II Pottery Assemblage from the Shields Site (8DU12). M.A. thesis, Department of Anthropology, Florida State University, Tallahassee.
2005 An Investigation of St. Johns and Ocmulgee Series Pottery from the Shields site (8DU12). *Florida Anthropologist* 58: 209–35.

Romans, Bernard
1999 [1775] *A Concise Natural History of East and West Florida*. Edited by Kathryn Holland Braund. University of Alabama Press, Tuscaloosa.

Roosevelt, Anna C.
1995 Early Pottery in the Amazon: Twenty Years of Scholarly Obscurity. In *The Emergence of Pottery: Technology and Innovation in Ancient Societies*, edited by William K. Barnett and John W. Hoopes, 115–31. Smithsonian Institution Press, Washington, D.C.

Rosenthal, Erin
2010 A Comparative Study of Prehistoric Check-Stamped Pottery in Northwest Florida. Undergraduate honors thesis, Department of Anthropology, University of South Florida, Tampa.

Rouse, Irving
1951 *A Survey of Indian River Archeology*, Florida. Yale University Publications in Anthropology 44. Yale University Press, New Haven, Conn.

Rowlands, Michael
1993 The Role of Memory in the Transmission of Culture. *World Archaeology* 25: 141–51.

Russo, Michael
1985   *Zaremba: A Short-Term Use Malabar II Site.* Florida State Museum Miscellaneous Project and Report Series no. 25. Gainesville Department of Anthropology, Florida State Museum, Gainesville.
1988   Coastal Adaptations in Eastern Florida: Models and Methods. *Archaeology of Eastern North America* 16: 159–76.
1992a   Chronologies and Cultures of the St. Marys Region of Northeast Florida and Southeast Georgia. *Florida Anthropologist* 45: 107–26.
1992b   Subsistence, Seasonality and Settlement at Futch Cove. Report on file, Florida Division of Historic Resources, Tallahassee.
Russo, Michael, Ann Cordell, Lee Newsom, and Robert Austin
1989   Phase III Archaeological Investigations at Edgewater Landing, Volusia County, Florida. Report on file, Florida Division of Historical Resources, Tallahassee.
Russo, Michael, Ann S. Cordell, and Donna L. Ruhl
1993   *The Timucuan Ecological and Historical Preserve Phase III Final Report.* Southeast Archeological Center, National Park Service, Tallahassee.
Sabo, George, III, and Jerry E. Hilliard
2008   Woodland-Period Shell-Tempered Pottery in the Central Arkansas Ozarks. *Southeastern Archaeology* 27: 164–71.
Sahlins, Marshall
1972   *Stone Age Economics.* Aldine de Gruyter, New York.
Saitta, Dean J.
1994   Agency, Class, and Archaeological Interpretation. *Journal of Anthropological Archaeology* 13: 201–27.
1997   Power, Labor, and the Dynamics of Change in Chacoan Political Economy. *American Antiquity* 62: 7–26.
1999   Prestige, Agency, and Change in Middle-Range Societies. In *Material Symbols: Culture and Economy in Prehistory*, edited by John E. Robb, 135–49. Center for Archaeological Investigations, Occasional Paper no. 26. Carbondale, Ill.
Sampson, Kelvin W., and Duane Esarey
1993   A Survey of Elaborate Mississippian Copper Artifacts from Illinois. *Illinois Archaeology* 5: 452–80.
Sank, Karen, and Kelvin Sampson
1994   A Falcon from the Depths. *Illinois Antiquity* 29: 4–8.
Sassaman, Kenneth E., J. Christian Russell, and Jon C. Endonino
2000   St. Johns Archaeological Project Phase I: A GIS Approach to Regional Preservation Planning in Northeastern Florida. Report on file, Florida Division of Historical Resources, Tallahassee.
Saxe, Arthur A.
1971   Social Dimensions of Mortuary Practices in a Mesolithic Population from Wadi Halfa, Sudan. In *Approaches to the Social Dimensions of Mortuary Practices*, edited by James A. Brown, 39–57. Memoirs of the Society for American Archaeology no. 25.
Scarry, C. Margaret
2003   Food Plant Remains from Excavations in Mounds A, B, C, D, and L at Bottle Creek. In *Bottle Creek: A Pensacola Culture Site in South Alabama*, edited by Ian Brown, 114–29. University of Alabama Press, Tuscaloosa.

Scarry, John F.
1980   The Chronology of Fort Walton Development in the Upper Apalachicola Valley, Florida. *Southeastern Archaeological Conference Bulletin* 22: 38–45.
1984   Fort Walton Development: Mississippian Chiefdoms in the Lower Southeast. Ph.D. dissertation, Department of Anthropology, Case Western Reserve University, Cleveland, Ohio.
1985   A Proposed Revision of the Fort Walton Ceramic Typology: A Type-Variety System. *Florida Anthropologist* 38: 199–234.
1990   Mississippian Emergence in the Fort Walton Area: The Evolution of the Cayson and Lake Jackson Phases. In *The Mississippian Emergence*, edited by Bruce D. Smith, 227–50. Smithsonian Institution Press, Washington, D.C.
1994   The Apalachee Chiefdom: A Mississippian Society on the Fringe of the Mississippian World. In *The Forgotten Centuries: Indians and Europeans in the American South, 1521–1704*, edited by Charles M. Hudson and Carmen Chaves Tesser, 156–78. University of Georgia Press, Athens.
1995   Apalachee Homesteads: The Basal Social and Economic Units of a Mississippian Chiefdom. In *Mississippian Communities and Households*, edited by J. Daniel Rogers and Bruce D. Smith, 201–23. University of Alabama Press, Tuscaloosa.
1996   Stability and Change in the Apalachee Chiefdom. In *Political Structure and Change in the Prehistoric Southeastern United States*, edited by John F. Scarry, 192–227. University Press of Florida, Gainesville.
1999   How Great Were the Southeastern Polities? In *Great Towns and Regional Polities in the American Southwest and Southeast*, edited by Jill E. Neitzel, 59–74. Amerind Foundation, Dragoon, Ariz.
2007a Iconography and Value: Repoussé Copper from Mound 3 at the Lake Jackson Site. Paper presented at the Sixty-fourth Annual Meeting of the Southeastern Archaeological Conference, Knoxville, Tenn.
2007b The Materialization of Ritual and the Interpretation of Ritual Materials from Mound 6 at the Lake Jackson Site. Paper presented at the Sixty-fourth Annual Meeting of the Southeastern Archaeological Conference, Knoxville, Tenn.
Scarry, John F., and Bonnie G. McEwan
1995   Domestic Architecture in Apalachee Province: Apalachee and Spanish Residential Styles in the Late Prehistoric and Early Historic Period Southeast. *American Antiquity* 60: 482–95.
Schmidt, Walter
1997   Geomorphology and Physiography of Florida. In *The Geology of Florida*, edited by Anthony F. Randazzo and Douglas S. Jones, 1–13. University Press of Florida, Gainesville.
Schnell, Frank T.
1998   Ceramics in the Southern Half of the Chattahoochee Valley. *Journal of Alabama Archaeology* 44: 99–130.
Schnell, Frank T., Vernon J. Knight Jr., and Gail S. Schnell
1981   *Cemochechobee: Archaeology of a Mississippian Ceremonial Center on the Chattahoochee River*. University Press of Florida, Gainesville.
Schofield, Shanna
2003   A Model of Migration: The Alachua Culture. Nonthesis paper, Department of Anthropology, University of Florida, Gainesville.

Scudder, Sylvia
2012   Soils and Landscapes: Archaeopedology at the Pineland Site. In *The Archaeology of Pineland: A Coastal Southwest Florida Site Complex, A.D. 50–1710*, edited by William H. Marquardt and Karen J. Walker, 227–52. Institute of Archaeology and Paleoenvironmental Studies, Monograph 4. University of Florida, Gainesville.

Sears, William H.
1956   Melton Mound Number 3. *Florida Anthropologist* 9: 87–100.
1958   The Grant Site. *Florida Anthropologist* 11: 114–19.
1967   The Tierra Verde Burial Mound. *Florida Anthropologist* 20: 25–74.
1971   The Weeden Island Site, St. Petersburg, Florida. *Florida Anthropologist* 24: 51–60.
1973   The Sacred and the Secular in Prehistoric Ceramics. In *Variation in Anthropology: Essays in Honor of John C. McGregor*, edited by Donald W. Lathrap and Jody Douglas, 31–42. Illinois Archaeological Survey, Urbana.
1982   *Fort Center: An Archaeological Site in the Lake Okeechobee Basin*. University Press of Florida, Gainesville.
1992   Mea Culpa. *Southeastern Archaeology* 11: 66–71.

Sears, Elsie, and William H. Sears
1976   Preliminary Report on Corn Pollen from Fort Center, Florida. *Southeastern Archaeological Conference Bulletin* 19: 53–56.

Shahramfar, Gabrielle
2008   Determining Fort Walton Burial Patterns and Their Relationship within the Greater Mississippian. M.A. thesis, Department of Anthropology, University of South Florida (accessible online at USF libraries).

Shapiro, Gary
1986   Rivers as Centers, Rivers as Boundaries: Florida Variations on a Mississippian Theme. Paper presented at the Fifty-first Annual Meeting of the Society for American Archaeology, New Orleans.
1987   *Archaeology at San Luis: Broad-Scale Testing, 1984–1985*. Florida Archaeology no. 3. Bureau of Archaeological Research, Division of Historical Resources, Florida Department of State, Tallahassee.

Sheldon, Craig T., Jr.
2001   Introduction. In *The Southern and Central Alabama Expeditions of Clarence Bloomfield Moore*, edited by Craig T. Sheldon Jr., 1–114. University of Alabama Press, Tuscaloosa.

Shofner, Jerrell H.
1995   *History of Brevard County, Volume 1*. Southeastern Printing Company, Stuart, Fla.

Siddall, M., E. J. Rohling, A. Almogi-Labin, Ch. Hemleben, D. Melschner, I. Schmelzer, and D. A. Smeed
2003   Sea-Level Fluctuations during the Last Glacial Cycle. *Nature* 423: 853–58.

Sigler-Eisenberg, Brenda
1985   *Archaeological Site Types, Distribution, and Preservation within the Upper St. Johns River Basin, Florida*. Miscellaneous Project Report 27. Florida State Museum, Gainesville.
1988   Settlement, Subsistence, and Environment: Aspects of Cultural Development within the Wetlands of East-Central Florida. In *Wet Site Archaeology*, edited by Barbara Purdy, 291–306. Telford Press, Caldwell, N.J.

Sigler-Eisenberg, Brenda, and Michael Russo
1986   Seasonality and Function of Small Sites on Florida's Central-East Coast. *Southeastern Archaeology* 5: 21–31.

Sigüenza y Góngora, Don Carlos de
1693   Journal of Sigüenza y Góngora. In *Spanish Approach to Pensacola*, 152–92. Translated by Irving Leonard. Quivira Society Publications, Albuquerque, N.Mex.

Simpson, Terrance L. (editor)
1998   *The Narvaez/Anderson Site (8Pi54): A Safety Harbor Culture Shell Mound and Midden—AD 1000–1600*. Central Gulf Coast Archaeological Society, St. Petersburg, Fla.

Smith, Bruce D.
1978   Variations in Mississippian Settlement Patterns. In *Mississippian Settlement Patterns*, edited by Bruce D. Smith, 479–503. Academic Press, New York.
1985   Mississippian Patterns of Subsistence and Settlement. In *Alabama and the Borderlands: From Prehistory to Statehood*, edited by Reid R. Badger and Lawrence A. Clayton, 64–79. University of Alabama Press, Tuscaloosa.
1986   The Archaeology of the Southeastern United States: From Dalton to DeSoto (10,500–500 B.P.). *Advances in World Archaeology* 5: 1–92.

Smith, Bruce D.
2007   Preface to the New Edition. In *The Mississippian Emergence*, edited by Bruce D. Smith, xix–xxxi. University of Alabama Press, Tuscaloosa.

Smith, Bruce D. (editor)
1990   *The Mississippian Emergence*. Smithsonian Institution Press, Washington, D.C.

Smith, Greg C., Brent M. Handley, Keith H. Ashley, and Gregory S. Hendryx
2001   Archaeological Data Recovery and Mitigation at 8Du5544/45, Queen's Harbour Yacht and Country Club, Duval County, Florida. Report on file, Florida Division of Historical Resources, Tallahassee.

Smith, Hale G.
1948   Two Historical Archaeological Periods in Florida. *American Antiquity* 13: 313–19.
1956   *The European and the Indian*. Florida Anthropological Society Publications no. 4. Tallahassee.

Smith, Marvin T.
1989   Aboriginal Population Movements in the Early Historic Period in the Interior Southeast. In *Powhatan's Mantle: Indians in the Colonial Southeast*, edited by Peter H. Wood, Gregory A. Waselkov, and M. Thomas Hatley, 21–34. University of Nebraska Press, Lincoln.

Smith, Marvin T., and David J. Hally
1992   Chiefly Behavior: Evidence from Sixteenth Century Spanish Accounts. In *Lords of the Southeast: Social Inequality and the Native Elites of Southeastern North America*, edited by Alex W. Barker and Timothy R. Pauketat, 99–110. Archaeological Papers no. 3. American Anthropological Association, Washington, D.C.

Smith, Marvin T., and Erik Marks
2003   Timucuan Mission Ceramics of South Central Georgia. *Early Georgia* 31: 84–90.

Smith, Marvin T., and Julie B. Smith
1989   Engraved Shell Masks in North American. *Southeastern Archaeology* 8: 9–18.

Snow, Frankie
1977   An Archaeological Survey of the Ocmulgee Big Bend Region. Occasional Papers from South Georgia 3. South Georgia College, Douglas.

Solís de Merás, G.
1964 [1570]   Pedro Menéndez de Avilés, Adelantado, Governor, and Captain-General of Florida: Memorial. Facsimile reproduction of 1570 edition. University Press of Florida, Gainesville.

Sommerkamp, Cindy L.
2008   Along the Pathway of Souls: An Iconographic Analysis of the Hickory Ridge Cemetery Site (8ES1280) in Pensacola, Florida. M.A. thesis, Department of Anthropology, University of West Florida.

Southeastern Archaeological Center (SEAC)
n.d.   Naval Live Oaks Cemetery (8SR36) Database. Compiled from the Naval Live Oaks Reservation database. Gulf Islands National Seashore, National Park Service, Southeastern Archaeological Center, Tallahassee, Fla.

Stahle, D. W., M. K. Cleaveland, D. B. Blanton, M. D. Therell, and D. A. Gay
1998   The Lost Colony and Jamestown Droughts. *Science* 280: 564–67.

Stapor, Frank W., Jr., Thomas D. Mathews, and Fonda E. Lindfors-Kearns
1991   Barrier-Island Progradation and Holocene Sea-Level History in Southwest Florida. *Journal of Coastal Research* 7: 815–38.

Stein, Gil J.
1999   *Rethinking World-Systems*. University of Arizona Press, Tucson.
2002   From Passive Periphery to Active Agents: Emerging Perspectives in the Archaeology of Interregional Interaction. *American Anthropologist* 104: 903–16.

Steinen, Karl T.
1971   Salvage Excavations at 8Al(l)346, the Olster Site. Report on file, Florida Division of Historical Resources, Tallahassee.

Stephenson, D. Keith
1990   Investigation of Ocmulgee Cord-Marked Pottery Sites in the Big Bend Region of Georgia. M.A. thesis, Department of Anthropology, University of Georgia, Athens.

Stephenson, D. Keith, Adam King, and Frankie Snow
1996   Middle Mississippian Occupation in the Ocmulgee Big Bend Region. *Early Georgia* 24: 1–41.

Stephenson, D. Keith, and Frankie Snow
2004   Swift Creek to Square Ground Lamar: Situating the Ocmulgee Big Bend Region in Calibrated Time. *Early Georgia* 32: 127–60.

Steponaitis, Vincas P.
1983   *Ceramics, Chronology, and Community Patterns: An Archaeological Study at Moundville*. Academic Press, New York.
1986   Prehistoric Archaeology in the Southeastern United States, 1970–1985. *Annual Review of Anthropology* 15: 363–404.
1991   Contrasting Patterns of Mississippian Development. In *Chiefdoms: Power, Economy, and Ideology*, edited by Timothy Earle, 193–228. Cambridge University Press, Cambridge.

Sternberg, G. M.
1876   Indian Burial Mounds near Pensacola, Florida. *Proceedings of the American Association for the Advancement of Science* 24: 282–92.

Stickler, Justin
2006   A Phase 1 Cultural Resources Assessment Completion of the Fallschase Development Tract, Leon County, Florida. Report on file, Division of Historical Resources, Tallahassee.
Stirling, Mathew W.
1935   Smithsonian Archaeological Projects Conducted under the Federal Emergency Relief Administration, 1933–1934. In *Smithsonian Institution Annual Report for 1934*, 371–400. Smithsonian Institution, Washington, D.C.
1936   Florida Cultural Affiliations in Relation to Adjacent Areas. In *Essays in Anthropology in Honor of Alfred Louis Kroeber*, edited by Robert H. Lowie, 351–57. University of California Press, Berkeley.
Stokes, Anne V.
1997   A Cultural Resource Assessment Survey of the IFAS Horticultural Unit (Blocks II–IV), Alachua County, Florida. Report on file, Florida Division of Historical Resources, Tallahassee.
Stoltman, James B.
1978   Temporal Models in Prehistory: An Example from Eastern North America. *Current Anthropology* 19: 703–46.
1991   Ceramic Petrography as a Technique for Documenting Cultural Interaction: An Example from the Upper Mississippi Valley. *American Antiquity* 56: 103–20.
Storey, Rebecca
1993   Catalog of the Lake Jackson Mound 3 Skeletons. Report on file, Florida Division of Historical Resources, Tallahassee.
Stowe, Noel R.
1985   Pensacola Variant and the Bottle Creek Phase. *Florida Anthropologist* 38: 144–49.
Sturtevant, William C.
1978   The Last of the South Florida Aborigines. In *Tacachale: Essays on the Indians of Florida and Southeastern Georgia during the Historic Period*, edited by Jerald T. Milanich and Samuel Proctor, 141–62. University Press of Florida, Gainesville.
Sullivan, Lynne P.
2001   Those Men in the Mounds: Gender, Politics, and Mortuary Practices in Late Prehistoric Eastern Tennessee. In *Archaeological Studies of Gender in the Southeastern United States*, edited by Jane M. Eastman and Christopher Bernard Rodning, 101–26. University Press of Florida, Gainesville.
2006   Gendered Contexts of Mississippian Leadership in Southern Appalachia. In *Leadership and Polity in Mississippian Society*, edited by Brian M. Butler and Paul D. Welch, 264–85. Center for Archaeological Investigations, Occasional Paper no. 33. Southern Illinois University, Carbondale.
Sullivan, Lynne P., and Robert C. Mainfort Jr. (editors)
2010   *Mississippian Mortuary Practices: Beyond Hierarchy and the Representationalist Perspective*. University Press of Florida, Gainesville.
Surge, Donna M., Kyger C Lohmann, and Glenn A. Goodfriend
2003   Reconstructing Estuarine Conditions: Oyster Shells as Recorders of Environmental Change, Southwest Florida. *Estuaries, Coastal and Shelf Science* 57: 737–56.
Symes, M. I., and M. E. Stephens
1965   A-272: The Fox Pond Site. *Florida Anthropologist* 17: 65–72.

Tanner, William F.
1991   The "Gulf of Mexico" Late Holocene Sea Level Curve and River Delta History. *Transactions, Gulf Coast Association of Geological Societies* 41: 583–89.
1992   Late Holocene Sea-Level Changes from Grain-Size Data: Evidence from the Gulf of Mexico. *Holocene* 2: 249–54.
1993   An 8000-Year Record of Sea-Level Change from Grain-Size Parameters: Data from Beach Ridges in Denmark. *Holocene* 3: 220–31.
2000   Beach Ridge History, Sea Level Change, and the A.D. 536 Event. In *The Years Without Summer: Tracing A.D. 536 and Its Aftermath*, edited by Joel D. Gunn, 89–97. Archaeopress, Oxford, U.K.

Terzis, Lee A., and K C Smith
1990   Shovel Testing at the Lake Jackson Mounds Site (8LE1) by Museum of Florida History Summer Campers, July 1990. Report on file, Museum of Florida History, Florida Department of State, Tallahassee.

Tesar, Louis D.
1973   Archaeological Survey and Testing of Gulf Islands National Seashore, Part I: Florida. Report on file, Florida State University. Report prepared for the Southeastern Archaeological Center, National Park Service, Tallahassee, Fla.
1980   *The Leon County Bicentennial Survey Report: An Archaeological Survey of Selected Portions of Leon County, Florida, Section 2*. Miscellaneous Project Report Series no. 49. Division of Archives, History, and Records Management, Florida Department of State, Tallahassee.
2006   The Waddell's Mill Pond Site (8Ja65) Revisited: The Results of B. Calvin Jones' 1973–74 Investigation. Paper presented at the Fifty-eighth Annual Meeting of the Florida Anthropological Society, Stuart.

Tesar, Louis D., and B. Calvin Jones
2009   The Waddell's Mill Pond Site (8Ja65): 1973–74 Test Excavation Results. Florida Bureau of Archaeological Research, Tallahassee.

Tesar, Louis D., Brenda N. Swann, James J. Miller, Melanie Damour-Harrell, and Michael Lavender
2003   Results of the Letchworth Mound (8JE337) Archaeological State Park Auger and Topographic Survey with Management Recommendations. Florida Division of Historical Resources, Tallahassee.

Thomas, Daniel H.
1989   *Fort Toulouse*. University of Alabama Press, Tuscaloosa.

Thomas, David Hurst
2008   The "Guale Problem" Revisited: Farming and Foraging on St. Catherines Island (Cal A.D. 1300–1580). In *Native American Landscapes of St. Catherines Island, Georgia*, vol. 2, *The Data*, edited by David Hurst Thomas, 1095–1115. American Museum of Natural History, Anthropological Papers 88. New York.

Thomas, Prentice M., and L. Janice Campbell
1985   *Cultural Resources Investigation at Tyndall Air Force Base, Bay County, Florida*. New World Research, Inc., Report of Investigations no. 84. Prepared for Tyndall Air Force Base, Panama City, Fla.
1993   *Eglin Air Force Base Historic Preservation Plan: Technical Synthesis of Cultural Resources Investigations at Eglin and Santa Rosa, Okaloosa and Walton Counties,*

Florida. New World Research, Inc., Report of Investigations no. 192. Prepared for Eglin Air Force Base, Fla.

Thomas, Prentice M., L. Janice Campbell, and Erica Meyer
2007 *Delineation and Sampling, East Half of 8WL68 Walton County, Florida,* vols. 1 and 2. Prentice Thomas and Associates Report of Investigations no. 734. Prepared for Eglin Air Force Base, Fla.

Thunen, Robert L.
2005 Grant Mound: Past and Present. *Florida Anthropologist* 58: 253–61.

Thunen, Robert L., and Keith H. Ashley
1995 Mortuary Behavior along the Lower St. Johns: An Overview. *Florida Anthropologist* 48: 3–12.

Torrence, Corbett McP., Samuel J. Chapman, and William H. Marquardt
1994 Topographic Mapping and Archaeological Reconnaissance of Mound Key State Archaeological Site (8LL2), Estero Bay, Florida. Report prepared for Historic Resources Division, Lee County, Florida. Florida Museum of Natural History, University of Florida, Gainesville.

Torres y Ayala, Governor Laureano de
1693 Journal of Don Laureano de Torres y Ayala. In *Spanish Approach to Pensacola,* 228–55. Translated by Irving Leonard. Quivira Society Publications, Albuquerque, N.Mex.

Trocolli, Ruth
2002 Mississippian Chiefs: Women and Men of Power. In *The Dynamics of Power,* edited by Maria O'Donovan, 168–87. Center for Archaeological Investigations, Occasional Paper no. 30. Southern Illinois University, Carbondale.

Trubitt, Mary Beth
2000 Mound Building and Prestige Goods Exchange: Changing Strategies in the Cahokia Chiefdom. *American Antiquity* 675: 669–90.
2003 The Production and Exchange of Marine Shell Prestige Goods. *Journal of Archaeological Research* 11 (3): 243–77.
2005 Crafting Marine Shell Prestige Goods at Cahokia. *North American Archaeologist* 26: 249–66.

Tucker, Bryan D.
2007 The Ocmulgee/Blackshear People and the Middleman Hypothesis: An Isotopic Evaluation. *Southeastern Archaeology* 26: 124–33.

Turner, Bethany L., John D. Kingston, and Jerald T. Milanich
2005 Isotopic Evidence of Immigration Linked to Status during the Weeden Island and Suwannee Valley Periods in North Florida. *Southeastern Archaeology* 24: 131–36.

Virnstein, Robert W., and Dean Campbell
1987 Biological Resources. In *Indian River Lagoon Joint Reconnaissance Report,* edited by Joel S. Steward and Joel A. VanArman, 6.1–6.115. St. Johns and South Florida Water Management Districts, Palatka and West Palm Beach.

Vita-Finzi, Claudio, and Eric S. Higgs
1970 Prehistoric Economy in the Mt. Carmel area of Palestine: Site Catchment Analysis. *Proceedings of the Prehistoric Society* 36: 1–37.

Wainwright, R. D.
1918 Further Archaeological Exploration in Southern Florida, Winter of 1917. Paper II. *Archaeological Bulletin* 9: 43–47.

Walker, Karen J.
1992   The Zooarchaeology of Charlotte Harbor's Prehistoric Maritime Adaptation: Spatial and Temporal Perspectives. In *Culture and Environment in the Domain of the Calusa*, edited by William H. Marquardt, 265–366. Institute of Archaeology and Paleoenvironmental Studies, Monograph 1. University of Florida, Gainesville.
2000   The Material Culture of Precolumbian Fishing: Artifacts and Fish Remains from Coastal Southwest Florida. *Southeastern Archaeology* 19: 24–45.
2012   The Pineland Site Complex: Environmental Contexts. In *The Archaeology of Pineland: A Coastal Southwest Florida Site Complex, A.D. 50–1710*, edited by William H. Marquardt and Karen J. Walker, 23–52. Institute of Archaeology and Paleoenvironmental Studies, Monograph 4. University of Florida, Gainesville.

Walker, Karen J., and William H. Marquardt
2012   Excavations and Chronostratigraphy at Coastal Southwest Florida's Pineland Site Complex: 1988–1995. In *The Archaeology of Pineland: A Coastal Southwest Florida Site Complex, A.D. 50–1710*, edited by William H. Marquardt and Karen J. Walker, 53–154. Institute of Archaeology and Paleoenvironmental Studies, Monograph 4. University of Florida, Gainesville.

Walker, Karen J., Frank W. Stapor Jr., and William H. Marquardt
1994   Episodic Sea Levels and Human Occupation at Southwest Florida's Wightman Site. *Florida Anthropologist* 47: 161–79.
1995   Archaeological Evidence for a 1750–1450 BP Higher-Than-Present Sea Level along Florida's Gulf Coast. In *Holocene Cycles: Climate, Sea Levels, and Sedimentation*, edited by Charles W. Finkl Jr., 205–18. *Journal of Coastal Research*, Special Issue no. 17.

Walker, S. T.
1885   Mounds and Shell Heaps on the West Coast of Florida. *Annual Report of the Smithsonian Institution for the Year 1883*, 854–68. Smithsonian Institution, Washington, D.C.

Wallace, Jennifer A.
2012   The 1995 Excavations of Caloosahatchee II Deposits at Pineland's Old Mound and Randell Complex Mound 1. In *The Archaeology of Pineland: A Coastal Southwest Florida Site Complex, A.D. 50–1710*, edited by William H. Marquardt and Karen J. Walker, 746–66. Institute of Archaeology and Paleoenvironmental Studies, Monograph 4. University of Florida, Gainesville.

Wallis, Neill J.
2008   Networks of History and Memory: Creating a Nexus of Social Identities in Woodland Period Mounds on the Lower St. Johns River, Florida. *Journal of Social Archaeology* 8: 236–71.

Waring, Antonio J., Jr.
1968   The Southern Cult and Muskhogean Ceremonial. In *The Waring Papers: The Collected Works of Antonio J. Waring, Jr.*, edited by Stephen Williams, 30–69. Peabody Museum, Harvard University, Cambridge, Mass.

Waring, Antonio J., Jr., and Preston Holder
1945   A Prehistoric Ceremonial Complex in the Southeastern United States. *American Anthropologist* 47: 1–34.

Waselkov, Gregory A.
1989   Indian Maps of the Colonial Southeast. In *Powhatan's Mantle: Indians in the Co-*

lonial Southeast, edited by Peter H. Wood, Gregory A. Waselkov, and M. Thomas Hatley, 292–343. University of Nebraska Press, Lincoln.

Waselkov, Gregory A., and Bonnie L. Gums
2000   *Plantation Archaeology at Riviere aux Chiens, ca. 1725–1848*. Center for Archaeological Studies Monograph no. 7. University of South Alabama, Mobile.

Watson, Patty Jo
2005   WPA Excavations in the Middle Green River Area: A Comparative Account. In *Archaeology of the Middle Green River Region, Kentucky*, edited by William H. Marquardt and Patty Jo Watson, 515–628. Institute of Archaeology and Paleoenvironmental Studies, Monograph 5. University of Florida, Gainesville.

Wauchope, Robert
1950   The Evolution and Persistence of Ceramic Motifs in Northern Georgia. *American Antiquity* 16: 16–22.
1966   *Archaeological Survey of Northern Georgia, with a Test of Some Cultural Hypotheses*. Memoirs of the Society for American Archaeology no. 21.

Wayne, Lucy B., and Martin Dickinson
2002   Data Recovery Excavations, Ardisia Site, 8MR2722, SW 31st Street, Ocala, Marion County, Florida. Report on file, Florida Division of Historic Resources, Tallahassee.

Webb, William S.
1974 [1946]   *Indian Knoll*. University of Tennessee Press, Knoxville.

Webb, William S., and David L. DeJarnette
1942   *An Archaeological Survey of the Pickwick Basin in the Adjacent Portions of Alabama, Mississippi, and Tennessee*. Smithsonian Institution, Bureau of American Ethnology, Bulletin 129. U.S. Government Printing Office, Washington, D.C.

Weiner, Annette B.
1992   *Inalienable Possessions: The Paradox of Keeping-While-Giving*. University of California Press, Berkeley.

Weinstein, Richard A.
2006   Review of *Archaeological Survey in the Lower Mississippi Alluvial Valley, 1940–1947*, by Philip Phillips, James A. Ford, and James B. Griffin, with an Update of Subsequent Archaeological Research at PF&G'S Mississippi Sites. *Mississippi Archaeology* 40: 141–239.

Weisman, Brent R.
1992   *Excavations on the Franciscan Frontier: Archaeology at the Fig Springs Mission*. University Press of Florida, Gainesville.
2003   Why Florida Archaeology Matters. *Southeastern Archaeology* 22: 210–25.

Weisman, Russell M., S. Dwight Kirkland, and John E. Worth
1998   An Archaeological Reconnaissance of the Proposed Trail Ridge Mine, Charlton County, Georgia. Report submitted by Southern Research to Golder Associates, Inc.

Welch, Paul
1991   *Moundville's Economy*. University of Alabama Press. Tuscaloosa.

Welch, Paul D., and Brian M. Butler
2006   Borne on a Litter with Much Prestige. In *Leadership and Polity in Mississippian Society*, edited by Brian M. Butler and Paul D. Welch, 1–15. Center for Archaeological Investigations, Occasional Paper 33. Southern Illinois University, Carbondale.

Wheeler, Ryan J.
1995 The Ortona Canals: Aboriginal Canal Hydraulics and Engineering. *Florida Anthropologist* 48: 265–82.
1996a Ancient Art of the Florida Peninsula: 500 B.C. to A.D. 1763. Ph.D. dissertation, Department of Anthropology, University of Florida. Gainesville.
1996b Ornamental Bone Carving of Southern Florida: Some Late Styles and their Associations. *Florida Anthropologist* 49: 49–63.
1997 Report on Archaeological Sites at Calvin Browning Property, St. Lucie County, Florida. Report on file, Florida Division of Historical Resources, Tallahassee.
1998 Resource Group 8PB9636, the Spanish River Midden and Mound Complex. Site form on file, Florida Division of Historical Resources, Tallahassee.
1999 Report on Visit to Kings Mound (8SL9). Report on file, Florida Division of Historical Resources, Tallahassee.
2000a The Archaeology of Brickell Point and the Miami Circle. *Florida Anthropologist* 53: 294–323.
2000b *Treasure of the Calusa: The Johnson/Willcox Collection*. Monographs in Florida Archaeology 1. Rose Printing, Tallahassee.
2001 Williams Island Shell Gorgets from Florida. *Florida Anthropologist* 54: 67–74.
Wheeler, Ryan J., and Wesley F. Coleman
1996 Ornamental Bone Carving of Southern Florida: Some Late Styles and their Associations. *Florida Anthropologist* 49: 49–63.
Wheeler, Ryan J., William J. Kennedy, and James P. Pepe
2002 The Archaeology of Coastal Palm Beach County. *Florida Anthropologist* 55: 119–56.
Wheeler, Ryan J., and James P. Pepe
2002 The Jobé and Jeaga of the Palm Beach County Area. *Florida Anthropologist* 55: 221–42.
Wheeler, Ryan J., James P. Pepe, and William J. Kennedy
2002 The Archaeology of Jupiter Inlet 1 (8PB34). *Florida Anthropologist* 55: 157–98.
White, Nancy Marie
1981a *Archaeological Survey at Lake Seminole*. Cleveland Museum of Natural History Archaeological Research Report no. 29.
1981b The Curlee Site (8JA7) and Fort Walton Development in the Upper Apalachicola–Lower Chattahoochee Valley, Florida, Georgia, and Alabama. *Southeastern Archaeological Conference Bulletin* 24: 24–27.
1982 The Curlee Site (8Ja7) and Fort Walton Development in the Upper Apalachicola–Lower Chattahoochee Valley, Florida, Georgia, Alabama. Ph.D. dissertation, Department of Anthropology, Case Western Reserve University, Cleveland.
1994 *Archaeological Investigations at Six Sites in the Apalachicola River Valley, Northwest Florida*. National Oceanic and Atmospheric Administration Technical Memorandum NOS SRD 26. Marine and Estuarine Management Division, Washington, D.C.
1996 Test Excavations at the Yon Mound and Village Site (8Li2), Middle Apalachicola Valley, Northwest Florida. Report to the Florida Division of Historical Resources, Tallahassee. Department of Anthropology, University of South Florida, Tampa.
1999 Reflections and Speculations on Putting Women into Southeastern Archaeology. In *Grit-Tempered: Early Women Archaeologists in the Southeastern United States*, ed-

ited by Nancy Marie White, Lynne P. Sullivan, and Rochelle A. Marrinan, 315–36. University Press of Florida, Gainesville.
2000 Prehistoric and Protohistoric Fort Walton at Thick Greenbriar Site (8Ja417), Northwest Florida. *Florida Anthropologist* 53: 134–52.
2005a Archaeological Survey of the St. Joseph Bay State Buffer Preserve, Gulf County, Florida. Report to the Apalachicola National Estuarine Research Reserve, East Point, and the Division of Historical Resources, Tallahassee. Department of Anthropology, University of South Florida, Tampa.

White, Nancy Marie (editor)
2005b *Gulf Coast Archaeology*. University Press of Florida, Gainesville.

White, Nancy Marie
2007 Pierce Mounds: An Ancient Capital in Northwest Florida. Paper presented at the Fifty-ninth Annual Meeting of the Florida Anthropological Society, Avon Park.
2009 Northwest Florida Artifact Typology and Sorting Criteria. Ms. on file at the University of South Florida Department of Anthropology archaeology lab and the Florida Division of Historical Resources, Bureau of Archaeological Research Collections, Tallahassee.
2011 Middle Woodland and Protohistoric Fort Walton at the Lost Chipola Cutoff Mound, Northwest Florida. *Florida Anthropologist* 64 (3–4): 241–73.

White, Nancy Marie, Nelson D. Rodriguez, Christopher Smith, and Mary Beth Fitts
2002 St. Joseph Bay Shell Middens Test Excavations, Gulf County, Florida, 2000–2002. Report to the Department of State, Florida Division of Historical Resources, Tallahassee.

White, Sarah E.
2006 Lithic Production Trajectories and Precolumbian Settlement Pattern in the Northwest Florida Interior. M.A. thesis, Department of Anthropology, University of West Florida, Pensacola.

Widmer, Randolph J.
1988 *The Evolution of the Calusa: A Nonagricultural Chiefdom on the Southwest Florida Coast*. University of Alabama Press, Tuscaloosa.
1989 The Relationship of Ceremonial Artifacts from South Florida with the Southeastern Ceremonial Complex. In *The Southeastern Ceremonial Complex: Artifacts and Analysis; The Cottonlandia Conference*, edited by Patricia Kay Galloway, 166–82. University of Nebraska Press, Lincoln.
2002 The Woodland Archaeology of South Florida. In *The Woodland Southeast*, edited by David G. Anderson and Robert M. Mainfort Jr., 373–97. University of Alabama Press, Tuscaloosa.

Wilcox, Jennifer R.
2010 An Assessment of Archaic Hafted Biface Use in Mississippian Burial Contexts at the Mill Cove Complex. M.A. thesis, Department of Anthropology, State University of New York, Albany.

Willey, Gordon R.
1948 Culture Sequence in the Manatee Region of West Florida. *American Antiquity* 13: 209–18.
1949a *Archeology of the Florida Gulf Coast*. Smithsonian Miscellaneous Collections 113. Smithsonian Institution, Washington, D.C.
1949b *Excavations in Southeast Florida*. Publications in Anthropology 42. Yale University Press, New Haven, Conn.

1954   Burial Patterns in the Burns and Fuller Mounds, Cape Canaveral, Florida. *Florida Anthropologist* 7: 79–90.

Willey, Gordon R., and Philip Phillips
1958   *Method and Theory in American Archaeology*. University of Chicago Press, Chicago.

Willey, Gordon R., and R. B. Woodbury
1942   A Chronological Outline for the Northwest Florida Coast. *American Antiquity* 7: 232–54.

Williams, Joyce A.
2007   Georrge Reeves Phase Lithics. In *The Range Site 4: Emergent Mississippian George Reeves and Lindeman Phase Occupations*, edited by John E. Kelly, Steve J. Ozuk, and Joyce A. Williams, 141–70. ITARP, Transportation Archaeological Research Reports 18. University of Illinois, Urbana-Champaign. Williams, Mark
2008   The Lamar Tradition. *Early Georgia* 36: 119–28.

Williams, Mark, and Gary Shapiro
1990   *Lamar Archaeology: Mississippian Chiefdoms in the Deep South*. University of Alabama Press, Tuscaloosa.

Williams, Mark, and Victor Thompson
1999   A Guide to Georgia Indian Pottery Types. *Early Georgia* 27: 1–167.

Williams, Stephen
1990   The Vacant Quarter and Other Late Events in the Lower Valley. In *Towns and Temples along the Mississippi*, edited by David H. Dye and Cheryl A. Cox, 170–80. University of Alabama Press, Tuscaloosa.
2001   The Vacant Quarter Hypothesis and the Yazoo Delta. In *Societies in Eclipse: Archaeology of the Eastern Woodland Indians, A.D. 1400–1700*, edited by David S. Brose, C. Wesley Cowan, and Robert C. Mainfort Jr., 191–203. Smithsonian Institution Press, Washington, D.C.

Williams, Stephen, and John. M. Goggin
1956   The Long Nosed God Mask in the Eastern United States. *Missouri Archaeologist* 18: 1–72.

Wilson, Gregory D.
2001   Crafting Control and the Control of Crafts: Rethinking the Moundville Greenstone Industry. *Southeastern Archaeology* 20: 118–28.

Wing, Elizabeth
1963   *Vertebrates from the Jungerman and Goodman Sites near the East Coast of Florida*. Contributions of the Florida State Museum 10. Gainesville.
1977   Subsistence Systems in the Southeast. *Florida Anthropologist* 30: 3–7.
1978   Subsistence at the McLarty Site, Indian River County. *Florida Anthropologist* 31: 3–7.

Winter, Amos, Hiroshi Ishioroshi, Tsuyoshi Watanabe, Tadamichi Oba, and John Christy
2000   Caribbean Sea Surface Temperatures: Two-to-Three Degrees Cooler than Present during the Little Ice Age. *Geophysical Research Letters* 27: 3365–68.

Wise, J. B., G. Harasewych, and R. Dillon
2004   Population Divergence in the Sinistral Whelks of North America, with Special Attention to the East Florida Ecotone. *Marine Biology* 145: 1167–79.

Wood, W. Dean, Debra Wells, and Elizabeth W. Haywood
2004   The Indianola Site (8OK1012), Fort Walton Beach, Florida. Prepared by South-

ern Research Historic Preservation, Inc., for NWEC Development, LLC, Myrtle Beach, S.C.

Woodward-Clyde Consultants
1993 Physical Features of the Indian River Lagoon. Report on file, St. Johns River Water Management District, Palatka.

Worth, John E.
n.d. The Prehistory of Mission San Martín de Ayacuto: An Archaeological Exploration of the Suwannee Valley Culture, Ichetucknee Springs State Park, 1990. Draft manuscript on file with the author.
1990 Archaeology in the Timucua Mission Province: 1990 Excavations at Fig Springs (8Co1), South End Village. Paper presented at the Forty-seventh Annual Meeting of the Southeastern Archaeological Conference, Mobile, Ala.
1992a Revised Aboriginal Ceramic Typology for the Timucua Mission Province, A.D. 1597–1656. Appendix D to *Excavations on the Franciscan Frontier: Archaeology at the Fig Springs Mission*, by Brent R. Weisman, 188–205. University Press of Florida, Gainesville.
1992b *The Timucuan Missions of Spanish Florida and the Rebellion of 1656*. Ph.D. dissertation, Department of Anthropology, University of Florida, Gainesville.
1998a *Timucuan Chiefdoms of Spanish Florida*, vol. 1, *Assimilation*. University Press of Florida, Gainesville.
1998b *The Timucuan Chiefdoms of Spanish Florida*, vol. 2, *Resistance and Destruction*. University Press of Florida, Gainesville.
1999 Coastal Chiefdoms and the Question of Agriculture: An Ethnohistorical Overview. Paper presented at the Fifty-sixth Annual Meeting of the Southeastern Archaeological Conference, Pensacola, Fla.
2002 Spanish Missions and the Persistence of Chiefly Power. In *Transformation of the Southeastern Indian, 1540–1760*, edited by Robbie Ethridge and Charles Hudson, 39–64. University Press of Mississippi, Jackson.
2000 The Lower Creeks: Origins and Early History. In *Indians of the Greater Southeast: Historical Archaeology and Ethnohistory*, edited by Bonnie G. McEwan, 265–98. University Press of Florida, Gainesville.
2009 Ethnicity and Ceramics on the Southeastern Atlantic Coast: An Ethnohistorical Analysis. In *From Santa Elena to St. Augustine: Indigenous Ceramic Variability (A.D. 1400–1700)*, edited by Kathleen Deagan and David H. Thomas, 179–208. Anthropological Papers of the American Museum of Natural History no. 90. New York.
2012 Pineland during the Spanish Period. In *The Archaeology of Pineland: A Coastal Southwest Florida Site Complex, A.D. 50–1710*, edited by William H. Marquardt and Karen J. Walker, 767–92. Institute of Archaeology and Paleoenvironmental Studies, Monograph 4. University of Florida, Gainesville.

Wright, J. Leitch, Jr.
1986 *Creeks and Seminoles*. University of Nebraska Press, Lincoln.

Yuellig, Amber J.
2007 Fort Walton ceramics in the Perry Collection, Apalachicola Valley, Northwest Florida. M.A. thesis, Department of Anthropology, University of South Florida, Tampa.

Zeitlin, Robert
1996 Comment on Blanton et al., *A Dual-Processual Theory for the Evolution of Mesoamerican Civilization*. *Current Anthropology* 37: 64–65.

Contributors

Keith Ashley is coordinator of archaeological research in the Department of Sociology and Anthropology at the University of North Florida, Jacksonville.

Robert S. Carr is executive director of the Archaeological and Historical Conservancy, Inc., Miami.

Jeffrey P. Du Vernay is research associate with USF's Alliance for Integrated Spatial Technologies.

Norma Harris is research associate with the Archaeology Institute at the University of West Florida, Pensacola.

John E. Kelly is senior lecturer in archaeology in the Department of Anthropology at Washington University in St. Louis.

William H. Marquardt is curator of south Florida archaeology and ethnography at the Florida Museum of Natural History, University of Florida, Gainesville.

Rochelle A. Marrinan is associate professor in the Department of Anthropology at Florida State University, Tallahassee.

Jeffrey M. Mitchem is associate archeologist with the Arkansas Archeological Survey and research associate professor in the Department of Anthropology at the University of Arkansas.

Thomas E. Penders is cultural resources manager with the 45th Space Wing of the United States Air Force.

Vicki Rolland is research associate with the Archaeology Laboratory at the University of North Florida, Jacksonville.

Karen J. Walker is assistant scientist and collections manager of south Florida archaeology and ethnography at the Florida Museum of Natural History, University of Florida, Gainesville.

Nancy Marie White is professor of anthropology at the University of South Florida, Tampa.

John E. Worth is assistant professor of historical archaeology in the Department of Anthropology at the University of West Florida, Pensacola.

Amber J. Yuellig works at the Minnetrista Cultural Center in Muncie, Indiana, and is an archaeologist with Florea Environmental Services.

Index

Abbott, R. Tucker, 14
Abrupt change. *See* Environment
Acorns (*Quercus* sp), 168, 193, 253, 263, 281
Adams Mound site, Fla. *See* Pineland Site Complex
Aden Bayou site, Fla., 286, 290; ceramics, 286, 290
Africa, 33, 36
African contact, 308
Agriculture, 1, 6–7, 9–10, 14–15, 17–18, 22, 26–27, 29, 56, 58, 61, 65–66, 75, 126–27, 130, 139, 145–48, 173, 181, 185, 188, 192–95, 210, 226, 228–29, 231–33, 241, 263, 267–69, 277, 290–93, 300, 305; intensification, 148; preserved maize, 15; small-scale, 15; soils, 192. *See also* Alachua culture; Apalachee culture; Fort Walton culture; Pensacola culture; Timucua culture
Aguada X'caamal, 36
Ais, 24, 51, 81, 83, 86, 88, 91–92, 97–99; alliance with Calusa, 98; decline, 99; economy, 24; Hobe, 99; politics, 97; salvage, 24; settlement patterns, 88; social complexity, 99; subsistence, 97; tribute, 98. *See also* Indian River culture area
Alabama, 3, 180, 193, 231, 233, 263–64, 266, 276–78, 291, 293, 301; ceramics, 180, 238, 266, 275, 278, 283–88, 290, 307; greenstone, 301; Gulf coast, 293; Lamar culture, 266; Mobile delta region, 263; rivers, 276, 278, 291
Alabama-Georgia border, 231
Alabama River, 276, 278
Alachua Cob Marked. *See* Ceramics
Alachua County, Fla., 139, 142, 144
Alachua culture, 24, 128–48, 151; affinities with Suwannee Valley culture, 153–54; agriculture, 126–27, 130, 145–46; Alachua Cob Marked, 127, 130, 132, 145, 147; Alachua grit-tempered, 127; Alachua Net Marked, 132; Alachua Plaited or Twine Impressed, 132; Alachua sand-tempered, 127; arbitrary dates and lack of research, 127, 130; artifacts, 126; burial mounds, 141–44; ceramic distribution, 128; ceramics, 16, 24, 126–28, 130–32, 158; ceramics as markers, 130; Cholupaha (town), 145; chronology, 130; comparison with Mississippian world, 144; contrasts between Cades Pond, 144; cord-marked ceramics, 127, 147; correlation between upland sites and relict wetlands, 139; correlations between ceramics and hunter-gatherer lifestyle, 137; dental caries, 146; earthworks, 136, 148; economy, 24; emergence of simple chiefdom, 127; ethnohistorical account, 145; European contact, 126; exchange networks, 126; exotica, 148; exotica (lack of), 126; fishing, 140; Gainesville area sites, 129; grit-tempered ceramics, 132; historic period, 127; horticulture, 24; Ichetucknee point, 140; interregional networks, 126–27, 130, 133, 147; iron-oxide, 141–42; lack of village data, 144–46; Late Woodland, 24; lithic extractions sites, 140; lithic tool production, 140; maize, 25, 126–27, 130, 145–46; map of region, 128; Middle Woodland, 130; Mississippian material culture (lack of), 148; mortuary ceremonialism, 141, 148; mortuary goods, 140; mounds, 148; nonlocal mortuary goods (lack of), 126, 144; Phases, 128, 130; Pinellas point, 140; political economy, 140; political organization, 24–25, 127; Prairie Cord Marked, 127; Prairie-Punctated-over-Cord Marked, 161; preservation biases, 139; radiocarbon dates, 133, 134–35; sand mounds, 141; sedentism, 144; settlement patterns, 139, 144–45; shellfish, 140; similarities to Savannah River Valley cultures, 127; similarities to Suwannee Valley culture, 126; site patterns, 140; social stratification (lack of), 126; Spanish Mission period, 24; stable isotope analysis, 25; status, 127; St. Johns Check Stamped, 131; St. Johns Plain, 127; subsistence, 24–25, 126, 139–40, 145, 147; Suwannee Valley ceramics, 127; Tampa point, 140; ties to Weeden Island, 136; trade, 140. *See also* Alachua Phase; Hickory Pond Phase; Potano Phase

Alachua culture area, 183; ceramic distribution, 128; environment, 127–30; geographical boundaries, 127; hydrology, 128–29; maps, 128–29; Northern Highlands, 128; topography, 128
Alachua Net Marked. *See* Ceramics
Alachua Phase, 128, 130; Alachua Cob Marked, 133; Alachua Plain, 133; Cades Pond Plain, 133; ceramics, 133; Prairie Cord Marked, 133; radiocarbon dates, 133–34, 135. *See also* Ardisia site; Bolen Bluff site; Fox Pond site; Henderson Mound site; Law School Mound site; Rocky Point site; Woodward Mound and Village site
Alachua Plain. *See* Ceramics
Alachua Plaited or Twine Impressed. *See* Ceramics
Alachua Savannah. *See* Bartram, William; Paynes Prairie
Alachua Tradition, 151
Alachua Trail, 115
Alaqua Bayou, 284
Alexander, Michelle M., 202, 216–17
Allerton, David, 79
Alley, R. B., 32
Alliance for Integrated Spatial Technologies, University of South Florida, 363
Alliances. *See* Political organization
Alligator Lake site, Fla., map, 153
Alluvial: floodplains, 4, 17–18; soils, 231
Almy, Marion M., 55, 95, 175–76, 180
Alt, Susan, 301
Altamaha River, 117
Ambrose, Stanley H., 300
American Bottom, 114, 299–301
Anderson, David G., 34, 56, 61n5, 172, 237, 270–71, 308
Anderson site (Narvaez or Jungle Prada site), Fla., 176; ceramics, 176, 177; cultural continuity, 176
Andrews, Charles McLean, 86, 92, 98
Andrews, Evangeline Walker, 86, 92, 98
Angel Mound site, Ind., 298, 306
Anhaica. *See* Governor Martin–De Soto site
Anonymous, 217
Antler, 207, 223, 256
Apalache, 190, 217, 230n1, 292
Apalachee culture, 2, 15, 18, 26, 188, 195, 202, 216–18, 230n1, 266, 272; ceramics, 217–18; continuity with prehistoric Tallahassee Fort Walton, 26; early documents, 15; European contact, 26; farming, 15; sociopolitical organization, 218; trade, 218. *See also* Governor Martin–De Soto site; Lamar culture
Apalachee Province, 230n1
Apalachicola–lower Chattahoochee Valley Fort Walton culture, 26–27, 231–71; agency, 26; agriculture, 26, 241, 263, 267–69; aquatic resources, 263; beads, 258; Black-painted, 241; burials, 233, 236, 238–39, 243, 253, 255, 258, 261; cemeteries, 233, 236, 241, 252–53, 255–56, 262, 265; ceramics, 26, 231, 236–56, 258, 261, 273; ceramic sorting guide, 240; check-stamped, 249–50, 261; chiefdom, 270; cob-marked, 241, 251, 261, 263; communication, 268; competition, 272; Cool Branch Incised, 237–38, 240, 245; copper, 236, 253–55; craft production, 249; cultural continuity, 255; cultural diversity, 273; dates, 237; decline, 269, 274; decline of check-stamped, 251; depopulation, 26, 265, 272; European contact, 271, 274; faunal remains, 252, 258, 263; fish, 233, 258; five-pointed bowl, 262; fortifications, 235, 272; Fort Walton Incised, 238–39, 248–49, 262; geographical region, 231–32; grave goods, 241, 253–55; greenstone, 253, 255; habitation patterns, 235, 252, 256; heritage maintenance, 259; hipped stone, 26; historic period, 265; identity, 26, 231, 249, 265; in situ development, 267; interregional networks, 266–67, 273; Lake Jackson ceramic definitions, 241; Lake Jackson Incised, 237; Lake Jackson Plain, 237, 240; Lamar components, 232, 250–51, 256–57, 259–60, 265–67, 269; Late Woodland, 253, 263, 265, 267, 298; lithics, 253, 263, 265; maize, 233, 235, 241, 263–64, 267; map, 232; Marsh Island Incised, 238, 245, 251, 261; middens, 236; migration, 26; Mission-period, 26, 251, 260–61; mortuary ceremonialism, 265; mound centers, 233, 236, 252, 270–71; mounds, 26, 232–36, 243, 251–52, 256, 258, 264, 270–71; non-shell-tempered, 273; origins, 267–68; Pensacola Incised, 262; Pinellas point, 265; plazas, 251; Point Washington Incised, 238; political organization, 26; power, 26; projectile points, 265; protohistoric, 26; radiocarbon dates, 237, 241–44, 253, 255–56, 258, 260, 265; rank, 231; red-painted, 241; regional distinctiveness, 273; ritual, 235, 265; schematic of Fort Walton mound sites, 234; seasonality, 273; segmentation, 272; settlement patterns,

233, 252, 267–69; shell artifacts, 253, 255; shellfish, 233, 258; shell temper, 26, 231, 265; site patterns, 237; six-pointed bowl, 26, 251, 256, 259, 261; social complexity, 231, 237, 268–69, 273; social memory, 249; sociopolitical organization, 237, 267–68, 270, 273; Southeastern Ceremonial Complex (SECC), 236, 273; Spanish, 26, 265; status, 253; structures, 235; subsistence, 26, 233, 235, 253, 256, 258, 263, 270; temper, 246–49; temporal markers, 251; trade, 273; transportation, 268; villages, 241, 252–53, 256; warfare, 269; Woodland, 26, 251. *See also* Cayson site; Cemochechobee site; Ceramics: Lamar; Chattahoochee Landing site; Chipola Cutoff mound site; Corbin-Tucker site; Curlee site; J-5 site; Lighthouse Bayou site; Old Rambo Landing mound; Omussee Creek site; Pensacola culture; Perry Collection; Pierce site; Proto-Creek; Richardson's Hammock site; Rood culture; Thick Greenbriar site; Underwater Indian Mound site; Waddell's Mill Pond site; Yon site

Apalachicola River, 4, 27, 182, 193, 231–34, 246, 252, 257, 276, 307–8; delta, 273; preserved maize, 15; valley, 2, 15, 218, 229, 231, 266–67, 272, 274, 278, 283, 294, 298, 305

Appalachian Mountains, 13, 113, 114, 300, 307

Aquaculture, 23

Aquatic resources, 17, 23, 27, 38, 40–41, 43–44, 104, 167, 233, 263; environmental impacts, 42. *See also* Fish; Shellfish; Subsistence

Aqui Esta Mound, Fla., 55; ceramics, 55. *See also* Englewood Phase

Archaeobotanical analysis, 167

Archaeological and Historical Conservancy, Inc., 363

Archaeology Institute at the University of West Florida, 363

Archaeology of Precolumbian Florida (Milanich), 7

Archaic: bannerstones, 105; Early, 90, 235; Kentucky, 47; Late, 12, 69, 87, 133, 283; Middle, 17; projectile points, 109; Tennessee, 47. *See also* Shell Mound Archaic

Arch Creek, 64

Arch Creek site, Fla., 95. *See also* Glades II period; Indian River culture area

Ardisia site, Fla., 16, 135; ceramics, 135; dates, 135; lithics, 135; maize, 135

Arkansas, 77–78, 182, 223, 301

Ash, 200

Ashley, Keith H., 1–28, 56, 90, 93, 96, 100–125, 127, 132, 136–37, 152, 154–55, 172, 181–82, 185, 197, 295, 297, 299–300, 302, 363

Atlantic coast, 3–4, 13–15, 60, 117; of Florida, 14, 19, 23–24, 62, 75, 102, 104, 112, 132, 137, 305; of Georgia and South Carolina, 10, 132, 137

Atlantic Coastal Ridge, 63–64, 67, 73; map, 63

Atlantic Ocean, 3, 35, 63–65, 81

Aucilla River, 26, 155, 190, 276, 279

Austin, Robert J., 46, 75, 127–28, 130, 139–40, 142, 175–76, 185, 213, 215

Ayala, Torres y, 292

Aztalan, Wis., 116

Baker, Henry, 199
Balée, William, 44
Banana River, 81–82, 87, 90, 93
Baptising Spring site, Fla., map, 153
Barbour, Michael G., 4
Barker, Alex W., 10
Barley Barber site, Fla., 63, 72. *See also* Belle Glade culture area
Barrier islands, 3, 31, 38, 57, 64, 67, 70–71, 75, 82, 87–89, 94, 233, 267, 273, 280, 291; Cape Canaveral, 82; Cayo Costa, 38; Merritt Island, 82, 87, 89; Sanibel Island, 38; Santa Rosa, 280
Barton Incised. *See* Ceramics
Bartram, William, 129
Basalt, 296, 301
Basinger site, Fla., 63, 72
"Basket loading," 70
Bay County, Fla., 276, 279
"Bay of Pooy," 60n3. *See also* Tampa Bay
"Bay of Tampa," 60n3. *See also* Charlotte Harbor
"Bay of the Holy Spirit," 60n3. *See also* Tampa Bay
Bayshore Home site, Fla., 175
Bayview Phase, 174. *See also* Safety Harbor culture
Beads: association with burials, 115; Chevron, 290; fluorite, 307; glass, 202, 203, 219, 258, 264–65; Nueva Cadiz, 290; pearl, 205–9; shell, 14, 27, 47, 94, 106, 109, 115, 119, 143, 182, 205–8, 288, 303
Beans, 217, 281, 293, 300

Bear Grass site, Fla., 216; maize, 215; structures, 215
Bear Point 1 site, Ala., 276
Bear Point Phase, 286, 292. *See also* Pensacola culture
Beck, Robin A., Jr., 271
Belief systems, 8, 29, 45, 59, 67, 123, 181, 184–85, 191, 220, 225, 296, 304; origins, 220. *See also* Iconography; Southeastern Ceremonial Complex (SECC)
Belle Glade I, 72; dates, 72; earthworks, 72
Belle Glade II, chronology, 65
Belle Glade III, chronology, 65
Belle Glade IV, chronology, 65
Belle Glade culture area, 23, 39–46, 62, 63, 65–67, 71–72, 76, 79; agriculture, 66, 72; Belle Glade Plain, 39–40, 42–43, 65–66, 85, 175; Belle Glade Red, 39, 63, 72; burial mounds, 72; canals, 72; causeways, 66, 72–73; ceramics, 39–40, 42–46, 65–66; chronology, 65; defined by, 66; earthworks, 66–67, 71–72, 76; "effigy" pool, 71; exchange networks, 73; fish impoundments, 72; fishing, 76; "hand and eye motif," 78; influences, 67, 75; map, 63, 74; midden-mounds, 71–73; mounds, 71–73; mound complexes, 67, 71; platform mounds, 75; politics, 71–73; radiocarbon dates, 71–72; sand mounds, 71–73; settlement patterns, 67, 73; shell-mask gorget, 77; shell tools and ornaments, 75; silver disk, 78; social complexity, 76; Spanish, 76; subsistence, 23, 66, 72–75; trade, 73; weirs, 72, 75; Woodland period, 75. *See also* Barley Barber site; Basinger site; Belle Glade Mounds; Big Mound City site; Boynton Earthworks site; Boynton Mound; Clewiston Mound site; Everglades; Fort Center; Lake Okeechobee; Nicodemus site; Ortona Mound Complex; Pepper Mound site; Tony's Mound site
Belle Glade Mounds, Fla., 63, 72–73, 76; shell-mask gorget, 77
Belle Glade Plain. *See* Ceramics
Belle Glade Red. *See* Ceramics
Bellomo, Randy V., 86–87, 93
Bell Plain. *See* Ceramics
Bell site, Fla., 282; maize, 284; radiocarbon dates, 284
Belovich, Stephanie J., 233
Bense, Judith A., 7, 58, 87, 278–79, 285
Beriault, John G., 64–66, 68
Bicentennial Survey, 214–15
"Big Bang" (from Cahokia), 301, 303–4

Big Cypress Swamp, 65
Big Mound City site, Fla., 63, 72. *See also* Belle Glade culture area
Big River, 301; drainage, 301
Big Talbot Island, 110
Binford, Lewis R., 88, 104, 220, 227
Bird Hammock site, Fla., 193
Birds, 202. *See also* Iconography
Biscayne Bay, 64, 67–68
Bishop, Nicole, 125
Black drink, 273
Black Plague, 37
Blackwater River, 35, 37, 285
Blanchard, Charles E., 51
Bland, Myles C. P., 109
Blanton, Dennis B., 34, 37, 123
Blind Pass, 30
Blitz, John H., 8–10, 180, 228, 233, 237, 240, 246–47, 252, 262, 264, 266, 268–71, 307–8
Blue Goose Midden site, Fla., 86. *See also* Indian River culture area
Blue Ridge Mountains, Ga., 231
Boca Grande Pass, 30
Boca Raton Inlet, 67
Boca Raton site, Fla., 63
Bolen Bluff site, Fla., 145; map, 129
Bone, 16, 25, 79–80, 89, 94, 109, 111, 119–20, 139–41, 143, 146, 148, 167, 193, 199, 220, 243, 253–56, 258; arrow points, 265; awl, 143; beads, 109; covered with copper, 106; isotopic analysis, 146, 300; pendants, 109; perforator, 46; point/pins, 46, 78, 93, 106, 109, 120, 143, 207, 303; weight, 93
Borrow Pit site, Fla.: burials, 216; status, 216; village, 216
Bottle Creek site, Ala., 263, 277–78, 291, 294, 307; dates, 277; maize, 263; plazas, 277
Bourdieu, Pierre, 118
Bowfin. *See* Fish
Boyd, Mark F., 198, 215
Boynton Earthworks site, Fla., 72. *See also* Belle Glade culture area
Boynton Inlet site, 63
Boynton Mound, 63
Braden style. *See* Southeastern Ceremonial Complex (SECC)
Bradley, Raymond S., 34, 225
Branham, Charlie, 229–30
Brech, Alan, 83–85, 87–88, 90–92, 99
Breininger, David R., 83

Brevard County, Fla., 83
Bride: exchange, 218; wealth, 184
Briffa, Keith R., 34
Broecker, Wallace S., 34, 192
Brooks, H. Kelly, 64
Brooks, Mark J., 35
Brooks Street Mound site, Fla., 284
Brose, David S., 13, 188, 192–93, 195, 235, 256, 266–67, 272, 276–79
Broward County, Fla., 67
Broward–Palm Beach County line, 65, 67
Brown, Catherine, 223
Brown, Ian W., 249, 263, 277–78, 300
Brown, James A., 12–14, 100, 107, 115, 117, 127, 178, 220, 296, 302–3, 306–7
Brown, Randall B., 128
Brown's Complex. *See* Pineland Site Complex
Bryne, Stephen C., 192, 201
Buck Key Island, 38
Buck Key Low, 32, 42
Buck Key site, Fla., 30, 38, 42; whelk (*Busycon sinistrum*), 41–42
Buikstra, Jane E., 90, 121
Bullen, Adelaide K., 110
Bullen, Ripley P., 128, 130, 132, 135, 139, 141, 143–45, 183, 185, 214, 235–36, 240, 247, 259, 261–63, 264, 267
Burial, 10, 26, 44, 47, 78, 89–90, 93–96, 98, 106, 109–11, 115, 119–20, 122, 133, 135–36, 140–43, 146, 199, 204–9, 214, 216, 219–26, 233, 236, 238–39, 243, 252–53, 255–56, 258, 261, 283, 286, 290, 302; arc or radial ("wheel spoke"), 93–95; bundle, 143; children, 110, 143, 183, 216, 225, 255; cranial deformation, 293; dog, 200; extended, 143, 205–8, 216, 219; female, 26, 143, 183, 216, 222–25, 255; flexed, 205–6, 208, 216; furniture, 293; list of sites with arc or radial, 95; male, 143, 216, 225; map of sites with arc or radial arranged, 94; primary, 236; secondary, 236; semi-flexed, 206–7, 216. *See also* Cemeteries; Mortuary: goods
Burnham's Grove site. *See* Burns Mound site (Burnham's Grove)
Burns Mound site (Burnham's Grove), Fla., 89, 93, 95; ceramics, 93; ground stone celt, 93; notched stone weight, 93; silver cross, 93; Spanish olive jar, 93. *See also* Indian River culture area; Malabar II culture
Busk ceremony, 292
Busycon carica (knobbed whelk). *See* Whelk
Busycon contrarium. See Whelk

Busycon sinistrum (lightning whelk). *See* Whelk
Butcherpen Mound Complex, Fla., 287
Butler, Brian M., 29, 237, 271

Cabbage palm, 167–68, 263
Cabeza de Vaca, 188
Cades Pond culture, 126, 132–33, 135–36, 142, 145, 151; burial construction, 136; capped burial pits, 142; celts, 136; ceramics, 147; copper, 136; dates, 136; Deptford ceramics, 136; Dunns Creek Red ceramics, 139; earthworks, 136; fate of, 136; fishing, 140; grit-tempered ceramics, 130; identity, 136; interregional networks, 130, 132; "killed" vessels, 136; mica, 136; pigmented sand lenses, 142; projectile points, 136; sacred-secular ceramic dichotomy, 136; sand-tempered ceramics, 136; settlement pattern, 145; St. Johns Check Stamped, 136; subsistence, 140; Weeden Island association, 136; Weeden Island Incised, 136
Cades Pond Plain. *See* Ceramics
Caddo, 306
"Cahokia" lithic industry, 301
Cahokia mound site, Ill., 7, 14, 23, 27, 47, 58, 113–15, 117, 124–25, 182, 223, 296, 300–309; agriculture, 27, 58, 303; "Big Bang," 304; dates, 27; decline, 14, 124, 304; Early Mississippi period, 27, 301; European contact, 29; influence, 27; Mesoamerican influence, 304; Monks Mound, 303; mounds, 27, 303, 306; political organization, 27, 304; ritual, 47, 303; settlement patterns, 27, 303; shell, 47, 301, 303. *See also* Southeastern Ceremonial Complex (SECC)
Cahokia Side-Notched, 109, 114
Calaas. *See also* Calusa culture: king
Caldwell, Joseph R., 13, 172, 260
California, 265
Caloosahatchee I, 32, 39; ceramics, 45; cultural isolation, 45; sea-level fluctuations, 40; settlement, 40
Caloosahatchee IIA, 32, 38–40, 42, 45; ceramics, 45; cultural isolation, 45; sea-level fluctuations, 40; settlement, 40
Caloosahatchee IIB, 32–33, 38–42, 44–46, 57; Belle Glade Plain, 39, 41; Belle Glade Red, 39; canals, 40–41; ceramics, 39–41, 46; chronology, 32; correlation with MWP/La Costa High, 57; dates, 39;

Caloosahatchee IIB—*continued*
  dugout canoes, 41; elite demand, 41; faunal remains, 39; fishing, 39; interregional connections, 45–48; lightning whelk (*Busycon sinistrum*), 41; midden, 38–39; Mississippi period, 44; mounds, 39–41; radiocarbon dates, 39; sea-level, 40–41, 44, 57; settlement, 39–40, 44, 47; shell tools, 41; sociopolitical interaction, 41; St. Johns ceramics, 39, 46; subsistence, 38–39; trade, 41; Weeden Island ceramics, 39; *See also* Caloosahatchee Region: environmental change; Galt Island sites; Josslyn Island site; Mound Key site; Pineland Site Complex; Shell: tools
Caloosahatchee III, 32, 42–44, 46–47, 57; Belle Glade Plain, 42; bone tools, 46; Brown's Complex Mound 2, 46; ceramics, 42, 46; chert flake, 46; chronology, 32; coral biface, 46; correlation with LIA/Sanibel II Low, 57; dates, 42; dolomite, 46; environment, 42, 57; galena, 46; lightning whelk (*Busycon sinistrum*), 41, 47; Mississippi period, 44; mounds, 42, 46; ochre, 46; Pinellas Plain, 46; quartz, 46; ritual, 46; sandstone, 46; sea-level, 42, 44; settlement, 47; shark teeth, 46; shell net gauge, weights and tools, 46; St. Johns Check Stamped, 42, 46; structures, 46; subsistence, 42; technology, 42, 44; towns, 47; trade, 46–47; Weeden Island ceramics, 42. *See also* Buck Key site; Josslyn Island site; Pineland Site Complex
Caloosahatchee IV, 32, 42–44, 55; Belle Glade Plain, 43; Brown's Complex, 43; burial mounds, 55–56; ceramics, 43; chronology, 32; correlation with LIA/Sanibel II Low, 57; dates, 42–43; European contact, 43; Glades Tooled, 43; grog-tempered, 43; lightning whelk (*Busycon sinistrum*), 41, 47; Mississippi period, 44; mounds, 42; political organization, 43; radiocarbon dates, 42; Safety Harbor-related ceramics, 43, 55; sea-level, 42–44; settlement, 47; subsistence, 42, 44; technology, 44; towns, 47; trade, 43, 47; transportation, 43. *See also* Mark Pardo site; Pineland Site Complex
Caloosahatchee V, 32, 43, 48–49; capital (Calos), 49; *See also* Mound Key site
Caloosahatchee periods: chronology, 32. *See also* Caloosahatchee Region: environmental change
Caloosahatchee Region, 63, 65; cultural change, 38–44; environmental change, 31–38
Caloosahatchee River, 23, 30–31, 63, 67, 71, 73, 79; map, 63
Caloosahatchee River basin, 71
"Calos." *See* Mound Key site
Calusa culture, 175, 270, 309; burials, 41, 55–56; burial mounds, 56, 59; Calaas (Calusa King), 49; "Calos" (Mound Key), 47; canals, 49, 51, 56, 59; capital, 49; ceramics, 45, 56; change, 38–44, 58; Christianity, 29; chronology, 32; client polities, 51; decline, 58; domiciliary mounds, 57; earthworks, 23, 31; economics, 51, 55; environment, 23, 31–38, 54, 57–59; European contact, 29, 43, 54; fishing, 39, 56–57; gathering, 56–57; hereditary leadership, 29, 53; hierarchy, 53–54; historic period, 68; hunting, 56–57; ideologies, 54–55; interregional connections, 31, 45–47, 58–59; king, 49, 53–54, 58; lightning whelk (*Busycon sinistrum*), 47; maize agriculture (lack of), 23, 56; Mississippian influences, 54–57; mortuary behavior, 55; mounds, 47, 48, 49, 56; patron-client relations, 59; platform mounds (lack of), 23, 56, 59; political organization, 51, 53, 57, 59, 76; population loss, 57; priests, 54; region, 29–30; religion, 29, 53–54; ritual, 54; sedentism, 29; settlement, 29, 47, 57; shell-tempered ceramics (lack of), 23, 59; social complexity, 23, 29, 31, 53, 57, 76, 309; status, 29, 51, 54; structures, 49; subsistence, 19, 29, 31, 39–44, 54, 56–58; "Tampa" (Pineland), 47, 49, 60; ties with Mississippian world, 47; towns, 47; trade, 29, 41, 46–47, 54, 56–57, 59; transportation, 51; tributes, 19, 29, 53–54, 270; warfare, 58–59; warriors, 58–59. *See also* Buck Key site; Caloosahatchee IIB; Canals; Galt Island sites; Josslyn Island site; Large-scale communal construction projects; Mark Pardo site; Mound Key site; Mounds: midden; Pineland Site Complex; Useppa Island site
Calusa Heritage Trail, 61n4
Campbell, Dean, 83
Campbell, L. Janice, 87, 279–81, 283–86, 292, 295
Camp Walton site, Fla., 284
Canal Point, 77; shell-mask gorget, 77
Canals, 23, 40–41, 44, 49, 50–51, 56, 67, 71, 73, 76; feeder ponds, 49, 51; water-control structures, 49, 51

Cane, 263, 265; matting, 205–7; sheath, 207
Cannon site, Ga., 146
Canoes, 41
Canoe trails, 64, 67, 73, 79, 82, 96
Cantley, Charles E., 93
Cape Canaveral, 3, 82, 86, 88–89, 93, 99
Cape Canaveral Air Force Station (CCAFS), 86–87, 89
Cape Haze Peninsula, 30
Captiva Island, 30
Captiva Pass, 30
Carabelle Incised. *See* Ceramics
Carabelle Punctated. *See* Ceramics
Cariaco, 33, 35–36, 38
Caribbean, 11, 33, 97, 297, 307
Carlisle, Victor, 128
Carr, Robert S., 2, 18, 23, 62–80
Carter Complicated Stamped. *See* Ceramics
Carter Mound site, Fla., map, 153
Casuarina Mound site, Fla., 95; burial, 94; copper bead, 94; notched projectile point, 94; stone hone, 94; stone pendant, 94. *See also* Indian River culture area; Malabar II culture
Catchment areas, 11, 226–27
Causeways, 68, 71–73, 92
Causey, Philip D., 213, 215
Cayo Costa, 30, 38, 43
Cayson site, Fla., 232–33, 235, 252, 270; mound, 270
CCAFS. *See* Cape Canaveral Air Force Station
Celts. *See* Ground stone: celts
Cemeteries, 18, 27, 68, 71, 73, 123, 220, 228, 233, 236, 241, 252–56, 262–63, 265, 281, 283–84, 286–90, 292–93, 306
Cemochechobee site, Ga., 180, 184, 262
Central Pasture site, Fla. *See also* Pineland Site Complex
Central peninsular Gulf Coast, 172–85
Ceramics, 67, 113–14, 120, 127, 130, 133, 158, 184, 206, 209, 211, 236, 281, 283, 286–87, 290–93, 296, 305–6; Alachua Cob Marked, 16, 127, 130–33, 135, 137–38, 145, 158–59, 161–64, 168, 198, 216; Alachua grit-tempered, 127; Alachua Net Marked, 132; Alachua Plain, 133, 159; Alachua Plaited or Twine Impressed, 132; Alachua sand-tempered, 127; Amazonian, 20; as evidence of agriculture, 145; as symbol of fertility, 301; Barton Incised, 179; Baytown, 43; beakers, 259, 262; Belle Glade Plain, 39–43, 65–66, 85, 175–76; Belle Glade Red, 39; Bell Plain, 284–85, 291; Bell Plain, *variety* Hale, 287; black-painted, 241; bottles, 178, 238, 259, 262; bowls, 45, 108, 178, 206–7, 262, 273, 289, 301, 304, 306; brushed, 198; Cades Pond Plain, 133; Carabelle Incised, 132; Carabelle Punctated, 132, 165, 203, 213; carinated bowls, 203, 238; Carson Red on Buff, 179; Carter Complicated stamped, 155; casuela bowl, 239, 259; chalky, 39; Chattahoochee Brushed, 261, 281, 285, 291; check-stamped, 198, 239–41, 249–51, 253, 256, 259, 261, 300; cob-marked, 16, 24, 131–32, 145, 168, 193, 203, 241, 251, 259, 261, 263; Colonoware, 130; Colorinda, 102; Columbia Incised, 262; complicated-stamped, 203; Cool Branch Incised, 203, 237–38, 240, 245, 255; cordage traits, 138; cord-marked, 101, 127, 136–37, 139, 147, 154, 300; "crudware," 162; cylindrical beakers, 178; Dallas Incised, 237; decorative overtreatments, 161–62; decorative techniques, 55; Deptford, 136, 138; Deptford Linear Check Stamped, 250; discoidals, 207, 212; D'Olive Incised, 284, 290; D'Olive, *variety*, Arnica, 286–87; Dunns Creek Red, 139; effigy vessel, 179, 262, 288, 306; Englewood Incised, 177–78; erroneous classifications, 158; fabric-impressed, 261; fiber-tempered, 69; Fig Springs Incised, 159; Fig Springs Roughened, 158–59, 164; Fig Springs Roughened *variety* Ichetucknee, 161; Fig Springs Roughened *variety* Santa Fe, 161; five-pointed bowl, 262; flattened-globular bowls, 178; form-and-function analysis, 162; forms, 25–26, 45–46, 55, 132, 147, 158, 162, 178, 237, 256; Fort Walton, 27, 132, 195, 217, 249, 252, 256, 258–60, 281, 283, 293–94; Fort Walton Incised, 159, 198–200, 203, 211, 213, 216, 238–39, 241, 247–49, 251, 255, 259–62, 284, 288; Fort Walton Incised, *variety* Choctawhatchee, 288; Glades Plain, 85; Glades Tooled, 43, 65; Grassy Hole Pinched, 159, 165; grit and grog-tempered, 217, 238, 248; grit and sand-tempered, 248; grit-tempered, 132, 136, 159, 199, 202, 217, 239–40, 246–48, 261, 267, 290–91; grog and sand-tempered, 248; grog-tempered, 43, 55, 199, 213, 217, 238–40, 261, 291; heat absorption efficiency, 159–60; Hiwassee Island Red-on-Buff, 306; hooded bottles, 179–80, 262, 301, 304, 306; incised, 65, 261; jars, 178, 237–38, 259, 301, 304;

Ceramics—*continued*
  Jefferson, 251, 266, 284, 291; Jefferson Plain, 281; Jefferson Stamped, 198; Keith Incised, 256; "killed" vessels, 136; Lake Jackson, 241, 247–48, 253, 255, 259; Lake Jackson Fingernail Impressed, 198–99; Lake Jackson Incised, 159, 203, 213, 216, 237; Lake Jackson Plain, 198–99, 216, 237, 240, 281; "Lake Jackson" sherd-tempered, 42–43, 55; Lamar, 26–27, 217–18, 232–44, 250–51, 255, 258–60, 265–67, 291; Lamar Complicated Plain, 259; Lamar Complicated Stamped, 177, 198, 213, 217, 259, 284–85; L'Eau Noire Incised, *variety* Shell Bluff, 306; Lemon Bay Incised, 177; Leon Check Stamped, 195, 213, 250, 281, 284–85; limestone-tempered, 39, 159, 176, 179, 247; Little Manatee, 93, 95, 101, 114; Lochloosa Punctated, 130–32, 159, 158–59, 164–65; majolica, 202, 203; Marsh Island Incised, 198, 203, 238, 245, 251, 258–59, 261; McKeithen Weeden Island period, 164–66; mica inclusions, 203, 247; Mississippian influenced, 55; Mississippi Plain, 237, 284, 287, 290–91; Mississippi Plain, *variety* Warrior, 286–87; Mound Place Incised, 178, 284–85; Moundville Engraved, 283, 286–87, 307; Moundville Engraved *variety* Elliot's Creek, 307; Moundville Engraved, *variety* Hemphill, 286; Moundville Engraved, *variety* unspecified, 287; Moundville Incised, 238, 275, 284–88, 290; Moundville Incised, *variety* Moundville, 286–87; Moundville Incised, *variety* Snow's Bend, 286–87; Moundville Incised, *variety* unspecified, 286–87; mushroom, 253–54, 262; negative-painted, 306; Nodena Red-and-White, 179; Ocmulgee Cord Marked, 112, 117; Ocmulgee Fields Incised, 285; Papys Bayou, 101, 114; Parkin Punctated, 179; Pasco Plain, 39, 132, 138, 159; Pasco Roughened, 159; Pensacola, 27, 43, 249, 277, 281, 283, 290–91, 293–94; Pensacola Incised, 247, 262, 287, 290; Pensacola Incised, *variety* Bear Point, 286–87; Pensacola Incised *variety* Gasque, 286–87; Pensacola Incised, *variety* Moore, 286–87; Pensacola Incised, *variety* unspecified, 286–87; Pensacola Plain, 247; Pineland paste, 55; Pinellas Incised, 177–78, 198; Pinellas Plain, 46, 176, 179; Pinellas-style ticked rim, 43; Plain red, 198; plainwares, 66, 70, 84, 132, 253, 284; Point Washington Incised, 178, 238, 246, 256, 281, 284; Prairie Cord Marked, 127, 130–33, 135–36, 138–39, 158–59, 164; Prairie-Punctated-over-Cord Marked, 161; punctate, 65, 195; Punctate-over-Cord Marked, 130; Ramey Incised, 304–5; red-and-white painted, 179; red-filmed, 203, 301; red-on-buff, 179; red-painted, 241; Residual Plain, 198; Rhodes Incised, 179; rims, 43, 45, 131, 137, 162–63, 178, 203, 211, 236, 238, 240–41, 245, 247, 250, 261–62, 306; sacred-secular ceramic dichotomy, 136; Safety Harbor, 6–7, 42–43, 45–46, 55, 126, 132, 147, 165; Safety Harbor Incised, 177–78, 198; sand and grit-tempered, 213; sand-tempered, 39, 42, 55, 70, 132, 136, 159, 176, 217, 239, 261, 290, 292; sand-tempered plain, 42, 70, 179, 202, 246–48; San Luis Blue-on-White majolica, 199; San Pedro, 16, 132, 155; Sarasota, 93; Sarasota Incised, 114, 177–78; seed jars, 301; shell and limestone tempered, 247–48; shell-tempered, 9, 20–21, 23, 26–27, 29, 43, 56, 59, 70, 180, 198, 202, 231, 238–39, 245, 247, 249, 251, 253, 256, 262, 265, 268, 275, 278, 280, 284, 286–87, 290–92, 300; "sherd caps," 292; "simple stamped," 158; six-pointed bowls, 238–39, 249, 251, 256, 259, 261–62, 268, 288, 306; sorting guide, 246; Spanish wares, 130; spiculate tempered, 39, 179; St. Johns, 24, 39; St. Johns Check Stamped, 42, 46, 55, 65, 69–70, 84, 95, 101, 132, 136, 159, 176–77; St. Johns Plain, 66, 69, 101, 127, 132, 159, 176; St. Johns Red on Buff, 179; St. Mary's, 155; style as cultural identity, 150; "style zones," 150; surface obliteration, 132, 162; Surfside Incised, 65; Suwannee Valley, 127; Swift Creek, 138; temper, 179–80, 202, 239, 246–49, 291; Tippets Incised, 306; tools, 160; Trestle Point Shell Impressed, 159, 164; trowel, 262; Tucker Ridge Pinched, 165, 256; Wakulla Check Stamped, 195, 199–200, 203, 213, 249; Walnut Roughened, 291; Weeden Island, 39, 42, 46, 55, 114, 136, 138, 156, 158, 164–65, 175, 177–80, 184–85, 195, 213, 239, 249–50, 253, 256, 261, 267; Weeden Island V, 195; Weeden Island Incised, 136, 195; Weeden Island II, 159, 261; Z-twist, 138. *See also* Iconography; Motifs
Ceremonial centers, 189, 276, 294
Chacato (Indians). *See* Chatot (Indians)
Chaos theory, 302
Charles, Douglas K., 90, 121
Charles Spring site, Fla., map, 153

Charlotte Harbor, 29–31, 55, 60n3, 174–75, 307, 309
Charlotte Harbor–Pine Island Sound–San Carlos Bay estuarine system, 30
Charnel houses, 76
Chatot (Indians), 292
Chattahoochee Brushed. *See* Ceramics
Chattahoochee Landing site, Fla., 232–33, 236, 241, 252, 270; ceramics, 241, 247; mound, 241; mound center, 252; Woodland, 270
Chattahoochee River, 180, 182, 231–34, 238, 246, 260, 262, 266, 268–69, 276, 307; basin, 180, 231; valley, 229, 247, 279
Chen, Ellen, 4
Chenopodium sp., 299–300
Cherokee, 266
Chert, 46, 69, 207, 210, 261, 263, 286, 296, 301; Citronelle, 286; Tuscaloosa gravel, 286
Chesapeake Bay, 33, 36
Chiefdoms, 8–10, 17–20, 26–27, 29, 31, 45, 54, 56, 76, 97, 99, 117, 124, 126–27, 169–70, 173, 185, 189, 217, 231, 237, 269–72, 292, 307–8; cycling, 237, 270–71, 308; Florida overview, 17–20; hereditary, 237; lack of, 24, 169; nonagricultural, 270; size, 17. *See also* Apalachee culture; Cahokia mound site; Calusa culture; Fort Walton culture; Safety Harbor culture
Chinaberry, 167
Chinchacanab, 36
Chipola Cutoff mound site, Fla., 232–33, 247; ceramic mushroom, 262; European goods, 265
Chipola River, 233–34, 252
Chipped stone. *See* Lithics
Choctawhatchee Bay, 27, 249, 263, 276–77, 278–79, 280, 283–85, 288–95, 289–92, 294
Choctawhatchee River: basin, 263; valley, 279
Cholupaha (town), 145
Christianity, 29
Citronelle Formation, 275
Citrus County, Fla., 183
Citrus Ridge site. *See also* Pineland Site Complex
Claassen, Cheryl, 13, 181–82
Classic Mississippian Horizon, 305–8; "block-lined" motif, 306–7; ceramics, 305–6; plates, 306. *See also* Pensacola culture; Tallahassee Fort Walton
Clay, R. Berle, 186–87
Clearwater site, Fla., 174–75
Clewiston Mound site, 63

Climate, 4, 23, 31–38, 40–42, 45, 57, 59–60, 61n5, 172, 192; Little Ice Age (LIA), 32–34, 37–38, 42–44, 57–58; Maunder Minimum, 37, 43, 58; Medieval Warm Period (MWP) (Mississippian Optimum), 32, 34–35, 37–42, 46, 57–58, 192; paleo, 33; Roman Warm Period (RWP), 32, 34; sea-surface temperature (SST), 33, 36, 40; tropical storms, 40; Vandal Minimum (VM), 32, 34, 37–38, 41–42, 44, 46. *See also* Florida Straits records
Cloth, 205–9
Clothing, 209; mantle (cloak), 208–9
Coastal Lowlands, 275
Cobb, Charles R., 8–10, 12, 14, 17, 112, 117–18, 123, 235, 237, 269, 296
Cob-marked. *See* Ceramics
Cody Scarp, 190
Coker, William S., 292
Cole, Fay-Cooper, 114
Coleman, Wesley, 78
Coles Creek culture, 298, 301
Colonoware. *See* Ceramics
Colquhoun, Donald J., 35
Columbia County, Fla., 16, 128, 150, 193
Columbus, Christopher, 188
Communication, 154, 268
Conch (*Pleuroploca* sp), 181
Connerton, Paul, 225
Contact Period. *See* European: contact
Coosa, 308
Copper, 6–7, 9, 13, 24, 26–27, 76, 79, 94, 96, 105–7, 109–10, 112, 114–19, 122, 124, 126, 136, 148, 182–84, 205–8, 223–26, 236, 243, 253–55, 288, 293, 296, 300, 302–3, 305–6, 309; Appalachian Mountains, 13, 114; axe, 205–7, 224–25; baton, 183; beads, 94, 109; birds, 288; breastplate, 206; disk, 243, 253–55; ear plugs/spools, 105, 114, 116, 122, 182–83; gorgets, 288; Great Lakes region, 13, 114, 300; hair ornaments, 205–7; long-nosed maskettes (LNG), 24, 105, 114, 116, 122, 303, 305; pendants, 94, 205–6; plates, 24, 26, 183, 205–6, 223–26, 300, 305; repoussé plates, 6–7, 26, 105, 119, 122, 183, 204–8, 210, 222–24; spangles, 205–7
Coral, 36, 46
Corbin-Tucker site, Fla., 232–33, 238–39, 243, 251–53, 259, 262–63, 265; cemetery, 256; ceramics, 253, 255–56; Late Woodland, 253; radiocarbon dates, 253; six-pointed bowl, 259; subsistence, 253, 263; village, 256

Cordage traits. *See* Ceramics
Cordell, Ann S., 39, 42–43, 45, 55, 85, 104, 246
Cord-marked. *See* Ceramics
Corn. *See* Maize
Corporate identity, 24
Covey, Cyclone, 201
Craft: production, 107, 109, 119, 150, 249, 301; specialization, 44, 169, 182, 296
Craig. *See* Motifs
Cranial deformation, 293
Crawford, Catherine L., 226
Creeks, 32, 59, 261, 266
Crescent Hills quarry, 301
Cronin, T. M., 33
Crook, Morgan R., Jr., 15
Crowley, Thomas J., 34
Crumley, Carole L., 12, 44–45
Cuba, 170
Cultural continuity, 156, 164–65, 169, 175–76, 252, 255, 308
Culture hero, 220
Curlee site, Fla., 26, 232–33, 235, 238–40, 242, 249–50, 260, 262–64; cemetery, 233; maize, 264
Curry, William B., 33
Curtis, Jason H., 34, 36
Cushing, Frank, 53, 79
Cutler Mound Complex, 69, 95. *See also* Glades culture area; Glades II period
Cycling, 237, 270–71, 308

Dahlin, Bruce, 35
Daub, 199, 256
Davenport, Christopher, 75
Davidsson, Robert I., 97–98
Davis Rectangle. *See* Motifs
Deagan, Kathleen A., 152
Deanne Browning Midden site, Fla., 92. *See also* Indian River culture area
de Avilés, Pedro Menéndez. *See* Menéndez de Avilés, Pedro
Deer, 88, 139, 143, 167–68, 202, 204, 258, 281
deFrance, Susan D., 39, 42
DeJarnette, David L., 47
de León, Ponce. *See* Ponce de León
de Luna, Tristan. *See* Luna, Tristan de
deMenocal, P., 33
Deming, Joan, 86–87, 93
Democrat River, 73
de Narváez, Pánfilo. *See* Narváez, Pánfilo de
Dendrochronology, 34, 36. *See also* Climate; Environment
Denmark, 34–35, 37–38
Dental caries: as evidence of agriculture, 146
de Pez, Andrez, 292
Depopulation, 19, 26, 34, 44, 256, 265, 272–73, 308
DePratter, Chester, 18
Deptford culture, 250, 283
Deptford Linear Check Stamped. *See* Ceramics
De Soto, Hernando. *See* Soto, Hernando de
De Soto County, Fla., 175
DeSoto Groves Mound site, Fla., 89. *See also* Indian River culture area
Destin, Fla., 284–85
Deuel, Thorne, 8
Dextral. *See* Whelk
Diaz-Granados, Carol, 116, 302
Dickel, David N., 75, 83, 85, 87, 90, 92, 210–12, 229
Dickinson, Jonathan, 70, 86, 92
Dickinson, Martin, 16, 100, 134–35
Dietler, John E., 41
Dillenger culture, 299
Diplomacy. *See* Political organization
Direct historical approach, 188, 292
Discoidal. *See* Ceramics
Ditches. *See* Fish: weir and impoundment areas
Division of Historical Resources Collections, 194, 204, 210–13
DNA studies, 190
Dog burials, 200
D'Olive Incised, 284, 290
D'Olive, variety, Arnica. *See under* Ceramics
Dolomite, 46
Doran, Glen H., 83, 90, 287
Dothan-Orangeburg Soil Series, 192
Douglas, Marjorie S., 64, 68–69
Douglas, Mary, 222
Droughts, 34, 36. *See also* Climate; Environment
Dubois, Betsy W., 66, 70, 76
Dubois Midden site, 70. *See also* East Okeechobee culture area
Dunbar, James S., 108
Duncan, James R., 116, 302
Dunns Creek Red. *See* Ceramics
Duval County, 101
Du Vernay, Jeffrey, 26, 231–74

Earthworks, 19, 23, 47, 53, 56, 62, 64, 66–68, 71–74, 76, 81, 90, 92, 102, 104–5, 110, 136, 141–42, 148; circular ditch, 72;

crescent, 72. *See also* Canals; Fish impoundments; Mounds
Eastern Woodlands, 299–300
Eastern Woodlands site, Fla. *See* Pineland Site Complex
East Gulf Coastal Plain, 275
East Okeechobee II period, chronology, 65
East Okeechobee III period, 69; chronology, 65
East Okeechobee IV period, 69; chronology, 65
East Okeechobee culture area, 23, 62–63, 66–71, 75–76; burial mounds, 69–70; causeways, 71; ceramics, 69–70; chronology, 65, 71; copper ornaments, 76; defined as, 66; exchange networks, 73; fiber-tempered ceramics, 69; fishing, 76; ground stone celts and plummets, 66, 69–70; influences, 66–67, 75; interregional connections, 66; Late Archaic, 69; map, 63; mounds, 75; radiocarbon dates, 70; settlement patterns, 67; shell midden, 69–70; shell tools, 66; social complexity, 76; subsistence, 23, 75; trade, 76; trade goods, 66; Type X shell picks, 66. *See also* Boynton Inlet site; Ceramics: Belle Glade Plain; Ceramics: St. Johns Plain; Ceramics: St. Johns Check Stamped; Dubois Midden site; Jeaga; Jobe; Jupiter Inlet site; Palm Beach County; Riviera Complex; Spanish River Complex; Whelk
Eck, Christopher, 68
Economy, 10, 12, 17–18, 20, 25, 51, 60, 120, 137, 147–48, 150, 170, 191, 237, 268–70, 272–73, 278, 297, 305; autonomy, 120; questing, 11, 13, 115, 122. *See also* Prestige-goods economy
Eddy, Jack A., 37
Effigy, 179; bird, 286, 288, 303; bottles, 262; bowls, 306; handles, 199
"Effigy" pond, 71
Eglin Air Force Base, 279, 283–84, 286; Historic Preservation Plan of 1993, 283
Emergent Mississippian culture, 298, 300–301, 303; ceramics, 301; symbolic role of fertility, 301
Emerson, Thomas E., 123, 301, 304–5
Englewood Incised. *See* Ceramics
Englewood Phase, 55, 174–75, 185; ceramics, 55, 174, 184; contact with Mississippian culture, 174; cultural continuity, 174; dates, 55, 174. *See also* Clearwater site; Englewood site; Osprey site; Safety Harbor culture

Englewood site, Fla., 174; burial mound, 174
English, 58
Environment, 23, 31–42, 57–58, 69, 280, 285, 297; definition of abrupt change, 32; glacial advance, 37. *See also* Climate; Historical ecology; Sea-level
Esarey, Duane, 107, 114, 300
Escambia County, Fla., 276–77
Escambia River, 285, 291; valley, 293
Eschbach, Krista E., 291
Espenshade, Christopher T., 85
Estabrook, Richard W., 140
Estero Bay, 29–31, 40, 47, 60n2, 71
Estero Island, 30, 47
Estevez, Ernest D., 181
Estuaries, 18, 23, 27, 30–31, 35, 37, 41, 44–45, 57, 67, 75, 83, 86, 88, 104, 120, 122, 180, 276, 279, 280, 285–86, 290–91, 293–94
Estuarine resources, 23. *See also* Fish; Shellfish; Subsistence
Estuarine sites, 235, 272
Ethnohistorical: data, 220, 223; reconstructions, 149
Etowah Rogan plates, 208
Etowah site, Ga., 26, 51, 204, 207–8, 223, 269, 277, 307; source for copper plates, 223
European: contact, 8–9, 15–25, 28–29, 43–44, 54, 58–59, 65, 79, 81, 91, 96, 98–99, 125–27, 150, 156, 168–69, 174, 185, 188, 230n1, 265–66, 271, 290, 297, 300, 308; goods, 27, 68, 78–79, 94–99, 215; post-contact, 20; shipwrecks, 81, 97
Everglades, 63–65, 67–68, 72–73, 75, 78; draining, 64
Everglades area, 64–65. *See also* Glades culture area
Ewel, John J., 4–5
Ewen, Charles R., 218
Exchange networks, 8–9, 11–14, 42, 46, 54, 56, 73, 75, 79, 112, 121, 126, 183–84, 296–97. *See also* Trade
Exotic goods, 120, 148, 296

Fagan, Brian, 37
Fairbanks, Charles H., 7, 83, 114, 151, 193, 213–14, 217, 283; *Florida Archaeology*, 7
Falcon. *See* Iconography
Fandrich, Judith E., 87
Farming. *See* Agriculture
Farmsteads: Tallahassee Fort Walton, 196, 200–201, 214, 225, 233
Farnsworth, Kenneth B., 303

Faunal remains, 39, 167–68, 202, 205, 228, 252, 258
Feathers, 76
Feathers, James K., 20
Fenneman, N. W., 275
Fernandez, Steven, 274
Fertility, 301, 304
Fiber-tempered. *See* Ceramics
Fig Springs Incised. *See* Ceramics
Fig Springs Roughened. *See* Ceramics
Fig Springs site, Fla., 16, 150, 152, 156, 162–64, 166–68, 291; ceramics, 156, 158–61, 164–66, 168; comparison with McKeithen site, 166; decorative overtreatments, 161–62; faunal remains, 167–68; flora, 167–68; Franciscan Mission period, 170; maize, 16; map, 153; Mission-period, 167; pits, 166; posts, 166; radiocarbon dates, 156–57, 166; South End Village, 156–57, 160, 167–68; Spanish artifacts (lack of), 156; structural patterns, 166; subsistence, 167; utilitarian ceramic tradition, 162
Fireclay, 296, 301, 304
Fish, 38–39, 42–44, 139, 167–68, 204, 233, 235, 253, 281; bowfin, 204; gar, 253; human collection pressure, 19; mullet, 204; weir and impoundment areas, 23. *See also* Aquatic resources
Fisheating Creek, 64, 72
Fish impoundments, 72
Fishing, 2, 9, 15, 17, 23–24, 39, 42, 56, 61n5, 65, 76, 86–87, 97, 103–4, 120, 140, 167, 226, 258, 263, 270; hook-and-line, 39; hooks, 258; net-fishing, 39; weirs, 72. *See also* Fish impoundments
Fishing-gathering-hunting technology: *See* Fishing; Gathering; Hunting
Flint-Chattahoochee confluence, 241
Flint River, 231, 233, 252, 276
Flora (botanical remains), 167–68, 216, 252
Florida: Alachua County, 139, 142, 145; Alachua Trail, 115; Apalache, 190, 217, 230n1, 292; Aquifer, 129, 191; Bay County, 277, 279; biases in archaeology, 27; Big Cypress Swamp, 65; Biscayne Bay, 64, 67–68; Blind Pass, 30; Boca Grande Pass, 30; Boca Raton Inlet, 67; Broward County, 67; Cape Haze Peninsula, 30; Captiva Island, 30; Captiva Pass, 30; Cayo Costa, 30, 38, 43; Charlotte Harbor, 29–31, 55, 60n3, 174–75, 307, 309; Charlotte Harbor-Pine Island Sound-San Carlos Bay estuarine system, 30; Choctawhatchee Bay, 27, 249, 263, 276–80, 283–85, 288–95; Citrus County, 175; climate, 4, 23, 31, 35; Columbia County, 16, 128, 150, 193; conditions during Mississippian period, 4; De Soto County, 175; Duval County, 101; elevation, 4, 64; Escambia County, 276–77; Estero Bay, 29–31, 40, 47, 60n2, 71; Estero Island, 30; Everglades, 63, 64–65, 67–68, 72–73, 75, 78; Fisheating Creek, 64, 72; Florida Keys, 3–4, 63–65, 67–69; Fort Lauderdale, 68; Fort Myers Beach, 60n2; Franklin County, 191; Gainesville, 128, 144, 153; Gasparilla Island, 30; Gasparilla Pass, 30; geology, 3–4, 23; Hardee County, 175; Hogtown Prairie wetlands, 129; Indian Key Channel, 69; interaction with Mississippian world, 11; Jefferson County, 190; Jupiter Inlet, 63, 69–70, 73; Kramer Island, 75; Lake County, 128; Lake Okeechobee, 23, 39, 42–43, 45, 62–63, 67, 71, 73, 75, 77–79; Lake Worth, 64, 70; Leon County, 190, 195, 201; Levy Lake, 129; Little Gasparilla Island, 30; Manatee County, 55; maps of, 2, 5, 11, 30; Marion County, 128; Matlacha Pass, 51; Miami-Dade County, 67, 76; Monroe County, 67; Nassau County, 101; Newnan's Lake, 129; North Captiva Island, 30; northern border, 3; Northern Highlands, 128; Ocala, 135; Okaloosa County, 276–77; Orange Lake, 129; Palm Beach County, 66–67, 69, 77; Palm Beach Inlet, 70; panhandle, 1, 3–4, 6–7, 10, 15, 17–18, 20, 27, 81, 96, 114, 125, 240, 275–95, 297, 307; Paynes Prairie (Alachua Savannah), 129, 133; peninsula, 1, 3–4, 10–11, 14–17, 19, 25, 46, 60n1, 62, 81–83, 95, 115, 168, 172–73, 175, 180–81, 183–85, 246; Pensacola Bay, 27, 276–77, 279–80, 285–91, 294; Perdido Bay, 277; Pine Island, 30–31, 38, 40, 49, 51, 61n4, 71, 73; Pine Island Sound, 29–31, 38–39, 51, 58, 61n4; Pinellas County, 174–176; Polk County, 175; Punta Gorda, 55; Redfish Pass, 30; Ritta Island, 75; "River of Grass," 64; San Carlos Bay, 29–31; Sanibel Island, 30, 38; Santa Rosa County, 276–77; Sarasota County, 55, 174–75; shorelines, 3–4, 38–40, 44, 49, 53, 57, 87, 283; spatial boundaries and diversity, 3–5; St. Andrew Bay, 27, 276–77, 280–83, 290, 294; St. Johns County, 101; Taylor Creek, 64; Union County, 128; Van Swearingen Creek, 64; Wakulla County, 190; Walton County, 277. *See also* Agriculture; Caribbean; Fort Walton culture; Indian River culture area; Mill Cove Complex; Pensacola culture;

Safety Harbor culture; St. Johns II culture; Tallahassee Hills; Weeden Island culture
Florida Aquifer, 129, 191
Florida Archaeological Council, 274
Florida Archaeology (Milanich and Fairbanks), 7
Florida Atlantic University, 70
Florida Department of State, 215, 229
Florida Department of State Collections, 194, 210–12
Florida Keys, 3–4, 63–65, 67–69
Florida Master Site File, 87, 213–14, 230, 280–81, 285
Florida Museum of Natural History (FMNH), 48, 61n4, 131–32, 258
Florida Natural Areas Inventory, 4
Florida State University, 214
Florida Straits records, 33, 36. *See also* Climate
Fluorite, 296, 307
FNAI. *See* Florida Natural Areas Inventory
Fontaneda, Do. d'Escalante, 29, 73, 98
Foragers, 15, 26, 81, 87, 117, 120, 127, 193, 270
Ford, James A., 7–8, 298
Formative or pre-Mississippian Horizon: agriculture, 299; ceramics, 300; check stamped, 300; copper plates, 300; cultures, 298; lithics, 301; mound centers, 299; settlement patterns, 299; shell, 300–301
Fornaro, Roger J., 283
Fort Center, Fla., 63, 71–73, 76, 78. *See also* Belle Glade culture area
Fort Gaines, Ga., 262
Fortier, Andrew C., 301, 304
Fort Lauderdale, Fla., 68
Fort Myers Beach, Fla., 60n2
Fort Walton Beach, Fla., 276
Fort Walton Beach Heritage Park and Cultural Center, 295
Fort Walton Beach Indian Temple Mound Museum (Fort Walton Museum, Fort Walton Temple Mound Museum) 287, 289, 294
Fort Walton culture, 2, 6–8, 10, 15, 17–18, 20–21, 25–27, 55, 96, 114, 132, 147, 151, 155, 158–59, 163, 173, 177, 180, 182–84, 186–95, 280, 294, 299, 305–9; agriculture, 10, 15, 17, 26; burials, 10; ceramics, 20, 26, 147, 155, 163, 173–74, 213, 237–51, 280, 284; chiefdom, 26; copper plates, 26; dates, 6; iconography, 147; Leon-Jefferson, 26; matrilineal, 26; models, 26; mound centers, 252; mounds, 18, 26; political organization, 26, 268–74; protohistoric, 26; settlement, 26; shell middens, 17; shell-tempered ceramics (lack), 20; "Sneads" Phase, 283; Southeastern Ceremonial Complex (SECC), 26. *See also* Apalachicola–lower Chattahoochee Valley Fort Walton culture; Lake Jackson site; Tallahassee Fort Walton; Tallahassee Hills
Fort Walton Incised. *See* Ceramics
Fort Walton Landing site, Fla., 283
Fort Walton Temple Mound site, Fla., 188, 283, 293; burials, 283; ceramics, 283; Deptford component, 283; Early Woodland, 283; Late Woodland, 283; Middle Woodland, 283; Mississippi period, 283; platform mound, 283. *See also* Pensacola culture
Four Mile Point Phase, 284, 286, 292; ceramic ratios, 284. *See also* Pensacola culture
Fox Pond site, Fla., 129
Fradkin, Arlene, 141–44
Franciscan Mission period, 167, 170
Frankenstein, Susan, 118
Franklin County, Fla., 191
Freak wares. *See* Ceramics
Freer, Jennifer A., 13
French, 15, 18–19, 125, 170, 218; Revolution, 37
Freshwater resources, 23. *See also* Fish; Shellfish; Subsistence
Fritz, Gayle, 300
Fryman, Frank B., Jr., 196, 199, 202, 216–17, 225
Fuller, Richard S., 277–79, 286
Fuller Mound Group site, Fla., 89, 93, 95; bone pins, 93; burial mounds, 93; ceramics, 93; copper pendant with rattlesnake motif, 94; historic artifacts, 94; quartz pendant, 93; radial or wheel spoke burials, 93; stone weight and pendants, 93. *See also* Indian River culture area; Malabar II culture
Funerary *sacra*. *See* Mortuary: goods
Furey, John, 71
Futch Cove, Fla., 88. *See also* Malabar I culture

Gadsden County, Fla., 229
Gahagan, La., 116
Gainesville, Fla., 128, 144, 153
Galena, 46, 105, 112, 182–83, 207, 209, 309
Galinat, 264
Gallay, Alan, 58
Galloway, Patricia, 236
Galt Island sites, Fla., 30, 38–39, 41; dates, 41; radiocarbon dates, 41
Gar. *See* Fish

Garber, James F., 236
Gardner, William M., 235, 247, 262, 264
Garner, Michael S., 95
Garrow, Patrick H., 8–9, 112
Gasparilla Island, Fla., 30
Gasparilla Pass, 30
Gathering, 17, 23, 25, 42, 61n5, 65, 120, 126, 167, 193, 195, 210. *See also* Foragers
Georgia, 3, 10, 15–16, 34, 46, 108, 112, 115, 117, 127, 132, 137–39, 146, 152, 155, 158, 180, 191, 193, 204, 217–18, 231, 233, 251, 260–62, 266, 269, 276–77, 291, 299; Altamaha River, 117, 137; burials, 146; Cannon site, 146; ceramics, 108, 112, 138–39, 152, 158, 180, 217–18, 251, 266; Chattahoochee River, 4, 180, 231, 266, 269; coast, 16, 34; Creek Indians, 266; Cumberland Island, 132; drought, 34; Etowah site, 26, 51, 204, 207–8, 223, 269, 277, 307; Flint River, 231; Fort Gaines, 262; Fort Walton culture, 231, 233, 269; Guale Indians, 15; Kolomoki site, 299; Lamar culture, 217, 266; Macon Plateau, 218; maize, 16; mounds, 233, 260, 262, 299; Myakka River, 30; Ocmulgee Big Bend area, 137; Ocmulgee-Blackshear region, 117; Ocmulgee River, 117; Oconee River, 117; piedmont, 46; quartz, 46; Savannah River Valley, 127; University of, 260; Weeden Island culture, 193, 299; Wilmington-Savannah culture, 137; Withlacoochee River, 155. *See also* Cemochechobee site; Old Rambo Landing mound; Telfair site
Georgia Bight, 15
Gerber, John F., 4
Gifting, 114, 121, 184, 189, 302
Glacial advance, 37. *See also* Climate; Environment; Sea-level
Glades I period, 32
Glades II period (a,b,c), 32, 65, 70, 75, 78, 95; ceramics, 65, 75, 78; chronology, 65; exchange networks, 75; naturalistic art, 78; Woodland period, 75
Glades III period (a,b,c), 32, 65, 68, 70–71, 75, 78–79; ceramics, 75, 78; exchange networks, 75; naturalistic art, 78. *See also* Miami River Mound Complex; Riviera Complex
"Glades Cult." *See* Glades culture area; Motifs
Glades culture area, 23, 62–71, 75–79, 83, 85; agriculture (lack of), 65; boundaries, 65; Calusa, 68; canoe routes, 79; causeways, 68; cemeteries, 68; ceramics, 43, 65–69, 85; chert, 69; chronology 32, 65, 68; copper ornaments, 76; defined as, 64–65; earthworks, 68; environment, 69; European contact, 65, 68–69; Everglades tradition, 78; exchange networks, 73; fishing, 65, 75; gathering, 65; "Glades Cult," 79; Glades Tradition, 65; ground stone tools, 69, 76; hunting, 65; maize, 65; map, 63; middens-mounds, 68; mound complexes, 68–69; periods, 65; platform mounds, 75; politics, 73, 75–76; sand mounds, 68; Seminoles, 65; settlement patterns, 68–69, 73; shell gorget (vulture), 78; social complexity, 76; Spanish accounts, 76; subsistence, 23, 65, 76; Tequesta, 51, 67–68, 76, 78. *See also* Boca Raton site; Cutler Mound Complex; Key Largo Mound Complex; Madden's Hammock site; Matecumbe Complex site; Miami River Mound Complex; New River Mound Complex; Plantation Key Mound Complex; Sands Key Mound Complex site; St. Johns Check Stamped; St. Johns Plain; Stock Island Mound Complex
Glades Plain. *See* Ceramics
Glades Tooled. *See* Ceramics
Goad, Sharon L., 114
Goggin, John M., 6–7, 53, 64–66, 69–70, 75–76, 79, 83, 95, 101, 110, 114, 116, 130, 139, 152–54, 158, 174–75, 302
Goldstein, Lynne G., 220, 224
Goodman, Claire Garber, 183
Goodman Mound site, Fla.: map of location, 103; ritual, 116. *See also* St. Johns culture area; St. Johns II culture
Goody, Jack, 220
Gopher tortoise, 167–68
Gottschall rock shelter, Wis., 302
Gourds, 65, 162
Governor Martin–De Soto site (Anhaica), Fla., 218–19
Grand Shell Ring site, Fla., 103, 110; map location, 103; ring as center of settlement, 111; ritual, 111; sand burial mound complex, 110–11; settlement, 103; stratigraphy, 111
Grant Mound site, Fla. (Broward County), 90. *See also* Indian River culture area
Grant Mound site, Fla. (Duval County), 6–7, 24, 90, 104–11, 114–16, 118–19, 121–22, 302–3; absence of SECC motifs, 107; communal political economy, 124; copper long-nosed god maskettes, 105; copper plates, 105; copper-sheathed ear plug, 105; dates, 107; exotica, 105; galena, 105; ground stone celts, 105; interaction with Mississippian societies, 302; local artifacts, 105–6; map,

108; mica, 105; mortuary ceremonialism, 119, 122; mound construction, 106; quartz, 105; queen conch (*Strombus gigas*), 114; steatite, 105. *See also* Mill Cove Complex; St. Johns culture area; St. Johns II culture
Graphite, 110, 209
Grassy Hole Pinched. *See* Ceramics
Grave goods, 24, 70, 90, 96, 98, 109, 116, 119, 140, 195, 208–9, 221–24, 226, 236, 241, 271, 286; shell, 47, 302
Great Lakes region, 13, 114, 300
Greber, N'omi, 13
Greenland, 34
Greenstone, 236, 253, 255, 258–59, 286, 296, 301
Griffin, James B., 7–9, 13, 114, 173
Griffin, John W., 6–7, 64–65, 68, 76, 196, 198–200, 202, 204, 225, 227, 240, 246, 259, 298, 302
Griffin Award, 274
Grit-tempered. *See* Ceramics
Ground stone, 26, 66, 69–70, 76, 79, 109, 118, 122, 183; axe, 209, 301; celts, 66, 70, 76, 109, 118, 122, 183, 206–8, 236, 253, 255–56, 258–59; chunky stones, 288; cups, 205; hone, 94, 206; pendants, 70, 76, 94; plummets, 26, 66, 182–83
Guale, 15
Gulf Breeze Peninsula, 287
Gulf coast, 3–4, 6–7, 13–14, 23, 25, 46–47, 55–56, 59, 71, 73, 79, 114–15, 132–33, 172–73, 176, 180, 182–84, 190, 193, 275–76, 278–80, 285, 290, 292–94, 305, 309
Gulf Coastal Lowlands, 190
Gulf of Mexico, 3, 10, 14, 33, 35, 37, 60, 63–64, 188, 190–91, 231, 303
Gums, Bonnie L., 279, 292
Gunn, Joel D., 34–35, 60

Habitation patterns, 49, 166, 193, 225, 235, 252, 256, 283
Haeberli, Wilfried, 35, 37
Hair, 183, 205–7
Hale, H. Stephen, 14, 72
Hall, Joseph M., Jr., 13
Hall, Robert L., 13, 116, 302–5
Hally, David J., 13, 162, 217–18, 266, 271
Halsey, John R., 300
Hamilton, Henry W., 224–25
Hamlin, Jenna M., 306
Hammock islands, 64, 67, 78
"Hand and eye" design. *See* Motifs

Handley, Brent M., 86
Hann, John H., 15, 19, 29, 54, 56–57, 59, 60n3, 68, 73, 76, 79, 92, 97–98, 119, 126, 152, 170, 188, 218, 292
Harbor Branch Oceanographic Institution, 81, 83
Hardee County, Fla., 175
Hardin, Kenneth, 104
Harrington, Roswell, 77
Harris, Norma J., 2, 7, 18, 20, 27, 147, 188, 202, 238, 249, 262–63, 275–95
Harvard, 215, 264
Hawk dancer. *See* Iconography
Hawthorne Formation, 190
Head, Randy, 287–88
Head Collection, 288
Heckenberger, Michael J., 237
Heintzelman, Nichole, 284
Heirloom items, 222–23, 226
Helms, Mary, 305
Henderson Mound site, Fla., 95, 129, 133, 140–46; burial mound, 133; burials, 143; dental caries, 146; maize (lack of), 133; map 129; mortuary goods, 133; radiocarbon dates, 134. *See also* Alachua culture; Hickory Pond Phase
Hendry, Charles W., Jr., 190
Hendryx, Gregory S., 100, 107
Hereditary leadership, 17, 19, 29, 57, 237. *See also* Timucua culture
Heritage maintenance, 259
Hertz, Robert, 220
Hickory, 16, 139, 167–68, 202, 253, 263, 281
Hickory Pond Phase, 126; Alachua Cob Marked, 145; appearance of Cord-marked ceramics, 136–39; arbitrary dates and lack of research, 130; ceramics, 130; chronology, 130; Lochloosa Punctated, 130–32; origin hypothesis, 137–38; Prairie Cord Marked, 130–32, 138–39; Punctate-over-Cord Marked, 130; Rocky Point site, 138; Subsistence, 137. *See also* Alachua culture
Hickory Ridge, Fla., 286
Hickory Ridge site, Fla., 282, 290; ceramic table, 287; chert, 286; grave goods, 286; mica, 286; projectile point, 286; radiocarbon dates, 286, 290
Hierarchy. *See* Political organization
Higginbotham, Jay, 278
Higgs, Charles D., 88, 226
Hilgeman, Sherri L., 306
Hill, Louis, 199–200
Hillard, Jerry E., 20
Historical ecology, 44–45

Historic artifacts, 70, 78
Historic period, 32, 49, 53, 64–65, 67–68, 70–71, 75–76, 81, 83, 88, 98, 110, 127, 148–50, 152, 154–56, 169, 188–90, 220, 223, 255, 260, 265–67, 270–72, 281, 283, 285, 291–93, 304–5. *See also* Ais; Apalachee culture; Apalachicola–lower Chattahoochee Valley Fort Walton; Calusa culture; Potano Phase; Suwannee Valley culture; Timucua culture
Hiwassee Island Red-on-Buff. *See* Ceramics
Hiwassee Island site, 298
Hobe, 99. *See also* Ais
Hochunk, 302
Hodell, David A., 34, 36
Hogtown Prairie wetlands, 129
Holder, Preston, 7, 178, 224
Hollister, S. C., 60
Holmes, William, 298
Holmes Mound site, Fla., 89. *See also* Indian River culture area
Holzhauser, Hanspeter, 35, 37
Honey locust, 167–68
Hooded water bottle. *See* Ceramics: bottles
Hooks, 39. *See also* Fishing
Hopewell, 13, 75–76, 79. *See also* Woodland period
Horizons (Spatial), 298; definition, 298; Formative or Pre-Mississippian, 298; Pre-Classic, 300; styles, 298, 300
Horseshoe Plantation, 214
Horticulture, 24, 130, 145, 167, 300
Horvath, Elizabeth A., 86–87, 93
Huag, G. H., 33
Hudson, Charles, 145, 149, 152
Hughes, Gilbert H., 191
Humphreys, Jay, 4
Hunt, Charles B., 275
Hunter, Sue Ellen 50, 52
Hunter-gatherers, 2, 9, 23, 81, 90, 101, 113, 117, 137
Hunting, 23, 25, 42, 61n5, 65, 120, 126, 167, 193, 195, 210, 263
Hurricane Dennis, 286
Hutchinson, Dale L., 16, 146, 181, 183, 185
Hutto, Joe, 214
Hydrology, 191, 229

Iconography, 9, 27, 147, 149, 155, 169, 179, 204, 220, 222–25, 277, 279, 290, 293; bird, 286, 302; Braden-style raptor, 225; "Elder Hawkman," 207, 224; falcon, 224; hawk dancer, 224; long-nosed god, 116, 302; raptor, 222–23; Spiro-style "elder," 225. *See also* Motifs

Ideology, 54, 123
Illinois, 10, 27, 182, 300. *See also* Cahokia mound site
Illinois River Valley, 300
Indian Bayou Phase, 284; ceramic ratios, 284. *See also* Pensacola culture
Indian Field site, Fla. *See* Pineland Site Complex
Indian Key Channel, 69
Indianola Mound site, Fla., 283
"Indian Pond Complex." *See* Suwannee Valley culture
Indian Pond site, Fla., map, 153
Indian River, 24, 75, 79, 81, 87, 89–91, 94; map, 82; region, 14, 65–66, 81–86, 88–93, 95–96, 98. *See also* Ais; Indian River culture area; Malabar culture period
Indian River County, 86, 92
Indian River culture area: climate, 83; earthworks, 81; environment, 81–83; European contact, 81; European shipwrecks, 98–99; grave goods, 24, 98; influences, 96; interaction with St. Johns culture area, 96; interregional networks, 66, 81; maps, 82, 91; Merritt Island and Cape Canaveral, 82; monumental architecture, 90–93; mortuary practice, 93–96; nonlocal artifacts (lack of), 96–97; political boundaries, 82; radial or wheel-spoke burials, 93–96; residential vs. special-use, 87; sand-mounds, 89–90; sea-levels, 89; settlement-subsistence model, 86–89; site increase on barrier islands, 87; sociopolitical complexity, 81; subsistence, 24, 82, 86–89; Woodland period, 96. *See also* Ais; Blue Goose Midden site; Burns Mound site (Burnham's Grove); Deanne Browning Midden site; Kings Mound site; Malabar culture period; Sams site; Summer Pentoaya site; Trysting Stairs site
Indian River Lagoon, 24, 81–83, 87–88, 98–99
Ingles, Bunny, 177
Intermarriage, 11, 46
Interregional connections, 12, 31, 45–47, 64, 66, 85, 100, 154, 267, 273
Ioway, 302
Iron Oxide, 141–42. *See also* Ochre
Ishi, 265
Isotope analysis: bone, 16, 25, 117, 146, 181, 185, 193, 300; shell, 35, 37

Jeaga, 51, 67, 71, 98. *See also* Riviera site
Jefferson County, Fla., 190
Jefferson culture, 168; ceramics, 163, 251, 284

Jefferson Ware. *See* Ceramics
Jenkins, Ned J., 9, 180
Jennings, Jesse D., 95, 217
J-5 site (Chattahoochee River #1 village, 8Ja8), Fla., 235, 259, 261–64
Jobe, 70
Johannessen, Sissel, 300
Johnathan Creek site, 298
Johnson, Ann F., 4
Johnson, G. Michael, 127, 183
Johnson, Jay K., 12
Johnson, Kenneth W., 145, 151–54, 156, 158, 163
Johnson, Robert E., 72, 100, 107
Johnson site, Fla., 288
Jones, B. Calvin, 7, 15, 183, 189, 193–94, 196, 199–202, 204, 208–9, 216–17, 219, 222, 224, 227, 233, 235, 240–41, 252, 277
Jordan, Douglas F., 110
Josslyn Island site, Fla., 30, 38–42, 44; dates, 41; depopulation, 44; radiocarbon dates, 41
Joy, Deborah, 291
Jungle Prada site, Fla. *See* Anderson site
Jupiter Inlet site, Fla., 63, 69–70, 73, 76. *See also* East Okeechobee culture area

Karst topography, 129, 154, 190, 275
Keigwin, Lloyd D., 33
Keith Incised. *See* Ceramics
Kelly, A. R., 260
Kelly, Arthur, 114, 260
Kelly, John E., 27–28, 47, 107, 109, 114, 116, 125, 296–308
Kennedy, William J., 66, 70–71
Kentucky, 47
Kenworthy, C. J., 71
Kerber, Richard A., 107
Key Largo, Fla., 75
Key Largo Mound Complex, Fla., 69. *See also* Glades culture area
Key Marco cat, 79. *See also* Motifs
Key West, 69. *See also* Florida Keys
Kidd, Joby, 209
Kidder, Tristram R., 8
"Killed" vessels. *See* Ceramics
Kimble, Elicia, 258
Kimmerle, Erin, 254
King, Adam, 8–10, 13, 116, 173, 236, 269
Kings Mound site, Fla., 92. *See also* Indian River culture area
Kinship, 218
Kinzey's Knoll, 108, 114; activity patterns, 108; Burlington chert, 109; Cahokia Side-Notched, 109; ceramics, 108; construction, 109; copper, 109; craft production, 109; greenstone celt, 109; hematite, 109; human remains, 109; iron oxide, 109; map, 108; modified sharks teeth, 109; ritual activity, 109; role of nonlocal ceramics, 117; sandstone abraders, 109
Kissimmee River, 23, 62–64, 66, 71, 73, 79; map, 63
Kissimmee River–Lake Okeechobee watershed, 62
Kissimmee River Valley, 67, 71–72
Kneberg, Madeline, 307
Knight, Vernon J., Jr., 8, 124, 192, 195, 266–67, 272, 277
Kohler, Timothy A., 127, 130, 135–36, 145, 147, 175, 183
Koldehoff, Brad, 303
Kolianos, Phyllis E., 53
Kolomoki site, Ga., 193, 299
Kowalewski, Stephen A., 12
Kozuch, Laura, 14, 181, 303
Kramer Island, 75
Krause, Richard A., 9
Krieger, Alex D., 306
Kroeber, Alfred L., 220, 265
Kus, Susan M., 8, 277

Labor, 49, 59, 76, 117–18, 122, 189. *See also* Large-scale communal construction projects
La Costa High, 32, 35, 42, 57
Lacquement, Cameron H., 51
Lafayette Lake, Fla., 191
Lafayette site, Fla., 228
Lafferty, Robert H., III, 12, 300
Lake Alice, 145
Lake City, Fla., 218
Lake County, Fla., 128, 183
Lake Iamonia, Fla., 191, 226–28
Lake Iamonia site, Fla., mound, 213–14
Lake Jackson, Fla., 191, 214
Lake Jackson Incised. *See* Ceramics
Lake Jackson site, Fla., 7, 10, 26, 113, 146, 183, 187, 189–91, 194, 196–212, 214–19, 221–28, 246, 259, 271–72, 279, 305, 307–8; archaeological history of, 198–99; biases in interpretation, 202; burials, 26; center, 189; ceramics, 198–200, 202–3, 211, 213; ceremonial chiefdom, 196, 217; copper plates, 26, 210; cultural continuity, 308; dates, 201, 204; Fort Walton ceramics, 211–12; interregional networks, 196; labor, 189; maize, 202; map, 197; mica inclusion, 203; mortuary customs and data 3, 205–9, 221, 222–25; overview of mounds, 200;

Lake Jackson site—*continued*
  projectile points, 210, 214; radiocarbon dates, 194, 204; rank, 224; ritual, 200; salvage excavations by Calvin B. Jones, 7; settlement pattern, 201; site development and ceramic chronology, 203; site patterns, 196; status, 224; subsistence, 202, 204. *See also* Tallahassee Fort Walton
Lake Lafayette site, Fla., 213; ceramics, 215; mound, 213; village, 215
Lake Okeechobee, 23, 39, 42–43, 45, 62–67, 71, 73, 75, 77–79; basin, 64, 66–67, 71; map, 63
Lake Punta Laguna, 34, 36
Lake Worth, Fla., 64, 70
Lamar Complicated Stamped. *See* Ceramics
Lamar culture, 20, 180, 217–18, 232, 256–57, 259–60, 265–67, 269; ceramics, 163, 243–44, 250–51, 255, 258–60, 266–67; lithics, 265; migration, 217; shell-tempered ceramics (uncommon), 20; subsistence, 265
Language, 154, 296; Iroquoian, 266; Muskogean, 266
Lanham, J. F., 85, 87–88, 90–92, 99
Large-scale communal construction projects, 31, 45, 47–53, 57, 299, 307. *See also* Canals; Earthworks; Labor; Mounds; Shell: works
Larsen, Clark Spencer, 16, 146, 204, 207, 209, 223–24
Larson, Lewis H., Jr., 7, 146, 220
Late Archaic. *See* Archaic
Late Woodland. *See* Woodland period
Laudonnière, Rene de, 54
Laurel Mound site, Fla., 95. *See also* Safety Harbor culture
Law School Mound site, 141–44; burials, 143; map, 129
Lazarus, William C., 278–79, 283, 287–88
Leader, Jonathan M., 218, 223, 226
Leather, 206–8
L'Eau Noire Incised, *variety* Shell Bluff. *See* Ceramics
LeBaron, J. F., 93
Lee, Chung-Ho, 291
Lemon Bay Incised. *See* Ceramics
Leonard, Irving A., 292
Leon Check Stamped. *See* Ceramics
Leon County, Fla., 190, 195, 201, 229
Leon-Jefferson culture, 149, 156, 201, 217; ceramics, 213, 217. *See also* Mission-period; Suwannee Valley culture
Le Page Du Pratz, Antoine S., 218
Leslie Mound site, Fla., map, 153

Lessure, Richard, 118
Letchworth Mound site (Miccosukee Mound), 188, 213, 215, 228; mound, 213, 215
Levy, R. S., 93
Levy Lake, 129
Lewis, R. Berry, 18, 144, 233, 296, 306–7
LIA. *See* Climate: Little Ice Age
Lighthouse Bayou site, Fla., 244, 260, 265; radiocarbon dates, 265
Lightning whelk *(Busycon sinistrum)*. *See* Whelk
Lillios, Katina T., 226
Limestone, 206–7. *See also* Ceramics
Limestone-tempered. *See* Ceramics
Lithics, 135, 253, 256, 261, 281, 296; chipped stone, 235, 263, 265, 273; coral, 46; core, 209; extraction sites, 140; scrapers, 207, 209; tool production, 140. *See also* Chert; Projectile points; Stone tools
Little, Keith J., 285
Little Barley Brass, 300
Little Gasparilla Island, 30
Livingood, Patrick C., 270
Lochloosa Punctated. *See* Ceramics
Long-distance exchange, 1, 12, 112, 148, 182
Long-nosed god (Red Horn) (LNG), 6, 105, 107, 116, 122, 302–3, 305
Lopinot, Neal, 300
Lorenz, Karl G., 8–9, 180, 233, 237, 240, 246–47, 252, 262, 264, 266, 268–69, 307
Loucks, L., Jill, 128, 130, 133–35, 140–42, 144, 146, 152
Louisiana, 116, 276, 278, 299; copper long-nosed god maskettes, 116
Low Mound site, Fla. *See* Pineland Site Complex
Luer, George M., 49, 51, 55, 71, 79, 95, 175–76, 178–80, 185
Luna, Tristan de, 292
Lund, David C., 33

Machava, 170
Macon Plateau, 14, 113–14, 217–18; decline, 14, 124; site, 298, 302
Madden's Hammock site, Fla., 63, 75
Magoon, Dane, 219
Mainfort, Robert C., Jr., 56, 58, 220, 237, 252
Maize, 2, 9–10, 14–17, 22, 24–27, 29, 56, 58, 65–66, 72–73, 75, 80, 104, 119–27, 130, 132, 135, 139, 144–46, 149, 166–68, 173, 181, 185, 188, 192–93, 195, 201–2, 210, 214–16, 228–29, 235, 241, 263–64, 267, 269, 273–74, 277, 281, 284, 291–93, 296,

300, 305; cultivation dates, 16; cultures with absence of, 15, 56; Eastern Flint, 202; Northern Flint, 217, 264; preserved, 15, 25. *See also* Dental caries

Malabar culture period, 83–90, 96; beliefs, 90; burial mounds, 89–90; ceramics, 84–85; ceramics as temporal marker, 85; chronology, 85; defined by, 83; habitation settlement, 88–90; interregional networks, 97; middens, 86; north-south ceramics gradation, 85; post-archaic period, 84; ritual, 90; separation from St. Johns culture, 24; sociopolitical gathering, 90; status, 90; subsistence, 24, 86. *See also* Burns Mound site; DeSoto Groves Mound site; Fuller Mound Group site; Holmes Mound site; Indian River culture area; Norris Mound site

Malabar I culture, 83–85, 88–89, 96; ceramics, 84; Dunns Creek Red, 84; subsistence, 86–89

Malabar II culture, 24, 81, 83–87, 89, 96–99; arc, radial, or wheel-spoke burials, 93–96; burials, 95; cacique (king), 98; canoes, 82; ceramics, 84–85, 93; dates, 81, 84; Dunns Creek Red, 84; European contact, 24, 98; European shipwrecks, 97; fish, 86; fisheries, 86; fishing, 97; gathering, 97; Glades Plain, 85; grave goods, 98; hunting, 86, 97; impact of exotic goods, 98; interregional networks, 84; Late Woodland, 84; mortuary goods, 93; mound construction, 89; mounds, 89–90; north-south ceramics gradation, 85; "paired town model," 88; political organization, 97, 98; radiocarbon dates, 84; salvage, 97; sand-tempered plainwares, 84; settlement patterns, 87; shellfish, 86; status, 98; St. Johns, 84; St. Johns Check Stamped, 84–85; subsistence, 86–89, 97. *See also* Ais; Burns Mound site; DeSoto Groves Mound site; Fuller Mound Group site; Indian River Lagoon; Norris Mound site; Sams site; Summer Pentoaya site

Manasota culture, 25, 175, 180; ceramics, 175, 184; cultural continuity, 175; Pinellas Plain, 176; regional variant of, 175; St. Johns Check Stamped, 176; St. Johns Plain, 176. *See also* Bayshore Home site; Weeden Island culture

Manatee County, Fla., 55

Mangelsdorf, 264

Mann, Michael E., 34

Marginella, 13–14, 115, 303. *See also* Shell

Marion County, Fla., 128

Markley, Mark, 217

Markley-Sharer Road site, Fla.: ceramics, 217; mounds, 217

Mark Pardo site, Fla., 30, 43

Marks, Erik, 152, 155

Marquardt, William H., 2, 12, 18–19, 23, 29, 30, 31–51, 52, 53–61, 65, 69, 71, 76, 87, 92, 99, 120, 181, 192, 263, 266, 270

Marrinan, Rochelle A., 2, 6–7, 18, 26, 55, 100, 103–4, 108, 110, 113, 118, 146–47, 155, 163, 186–231, 233, 237, 240, 246, 249, 253, 255, 266–68, 271–72, 274, 278–79, 283

Marsh, Elan Tomkinson, 254

Marsh, Owen T., 275

Marsh clam (Rangia). *See* Shellfish

Marshelder, 300

Marshes, 4, 77, 83, 86–89, 120, 122, 128, 180, 190, 198

Marsh Island Incised. *See* Ceramics

Maskettes, 6, 24, 105, 107, 114, 116, 122, 302–3, 305

Matecumbe Complex site, Fla., 69. *See also* Glades culture area

Matlacha Pass, 51

Matrilineal societies, 26, 189, 218

Mauss, Marcel, 121

Maxham, Mintcy D., 9

Mayami, 51

Maygrass, 300

McCullin, James, 78

McElrath, Dale L., 301

McEwan, Bonnie G., 188, 214

McGovern, Thomas H., 34

McKeithen site, Fla., 193, 195, 151, 215, 218, 299; map, 153

McKeithen Weeden Island culture, 151, 156, 164–66; ceramics, 164–66

McKelvey culture, 299

McKenzie, C. Lee, 286

McKern, William C., 298

Medieval Warm Period (MWP). *See* Climate

Menéndez de Avilés, Pedro, 49, 58, 98

Meramec River, 301

Merritt Island, 82

Mexia, Alvaro, 88

Mexico, 27, 303

Meyers, Maureen S., 9–10, 173

Miami-Dade County, Fla., 67, 76

Miami River, 63–64, 68–69

Miami River Mound Complex, 68, 73, 76. *See also* Glades culture area; Tequesta

Mica, 136, 205, 207, 209, 286, 296

Miccosukee, 32, 191

Miccosukee Formations, 190
Michigan, 13
Midden, 17, 18, 23, 38–44, 47–49, 51, 53, 57, 61n4, 67–73, 78, 85–89, 91–92, 98, 103, 107–11, 113–14, 117–18, 120, 139–40, 142–43, 148, 176, 190, 193, 196, 198–201, 204, 219, 225, 233, 236, 241, 247, 249–51, 256, 258–59, 262, 264, 277, 281, 285, 287; circular, 281; linear, 281; ridges, 49, 287. *See also* Mounds
"Middle Mississippi," 298
Midwest, 28, 46–47, 56, 173, 181, 297, 298, 300, 302, 304, 308
Midwestern Taxonomic System, 298
Migration, 6, 11, 26, 137–39, 147, 164, 166, 192, 195, 202, 204, 217, 228–29, 237, 268, 303; Schofield migration hypothesis, 138
Mikell, Gregory A., 263, 279–82, 284, 292
Milanich, Jerald T., 5–7, 11, 14–15, 18–19, 42, 55–56, 65, 83–84, 86, 97–101, 115, 117, 119, 127–28, 130, 132–37, 139–40, 144–45, 151–54, 158, 161, 164, 166, 169–70, 172, 174–75, 180, 185, 193–95, 218, 252, 267, 277; *Archaeology of Precolumbian Florida*, 7; *Florida Archaeology*, 7; on Mississippian influence in Florida, 7
Miles, Douglas, 220
Mill Cove Complex, Fla., 6, 24, 100–108, 110–13, 115, 122–24, 299, 305, 307, 309; C. B. Moore, 104–5; ceramics, 107; chert, 107; communal political economy, 123–24; community cemeteries, 107; dates, 107; Early Mississippi period, 104; excavation data, 104–7; exotica, 105, 107–8, 116, 122; exotic craft production (lack of), 107; human burials, 106, 122; map, 102, 108; mound center, 102; Mt. Royal mound site, 6–7, 15, 24, 96, 102, 104, 110, 112–16, 118, 123–24, 182; sand mounds, 104, 122; settlement, 103–4; shared aspects with Mt. Royal, 112; shell artifacts, 106; shell as principal export, 115–17; status, 124. *See also* Ceramics; Grant Mound site; Kinzey's Knoll; Shell; Shields Mound site; St. Johns culture area; St. Johns II culture
Miller, Christopher L., 223
Miller, James A., 4–5
Miller, James J., 102
Miller's Landing site, Fla., 213, 226–28
Mills, Barbara J., 226
Milner, George R., 27, 58, 308
Minar, Jill, 136–38
Mirror frame, 209

Mission Patale site, Fla. *See* San Pablo de Patale site, Fla.
Mission-period, 16, 24, 68, 130, 164, 167–68, 170, 188, 191–92, 201, 216, 229, 251, 260–61, 267, 272, 287, 296–308; cemeteries, 146, 287; ceramics, 163; documents, 15; preserved maize, 15. *See also* Jefferson culture; Spanish
Mission Santa Cruz de Cachipile site, Ga., 155
Mississippi, 276, 291
Mississippian culture: agriculture, 2, 4–5, 9–10, 14–18, 22–23, 25–27, 29, 34, 54, 58, 104, 125–27, 137, 145, 147, 173, 181, 189, 196, 200–201, 214, 225, 231, 233, 241, 258, 263, 267–68, 270, 272–73, 277, 299, 301, 303; "Big Bang," 301, 303–4; burials, 7–8, 10, 24–26, 41, 44, 49, 55, 67, 69–73, 78–79, 87, 89–90, 93, 94–96, 98, 100–103, 106–7, 109–11, 115–16, 118–22, 133, 135–36, 141–44, 146–48, 174–77, 183–84, 193, 195, 200, 202, 204–9, 214–16, 219–26, 228, 233, 236, 238–39, 242–43, 252–56, 258–59, 261, 265, 270, 283–84, 286, 290, 293, 302; centers, 47, 58; ceramics, 9, 20–21, 23, 26–27, 29, 56, 59, 238–39, 245, 247, 249, 253, 256, 262, 268, 275, 278, 280, 284, 287, 290–92, 296, 300, 304–7; chiefdoms and variants, 8–10, 17–20, 26, 29, 31, 45, 54, 56, 76, 97, 99, 117, 124, 126, 169–70, 173, 185, 231, 237, 269–72, 292, 307–8; Classic, 27, 305–8; Columbia Incised, 262; complexity, 20; correlation with LIA/Sanibel II Low, 57; correlation with MWP/La Costa High, 57; dates, 27, 29; decline, 58, 179; direct contact with Safety Harbor, 185; Early, 18; early explanation of presence in Florida, 6–7; environmental influences, 58; Formative or Pre-Mississippian, 27, 298–301; horizons, 298–308; iconography, 9, 27, 147, 149, 155, 169, 204, 220, 222–25, 279, 290, 293, 302–4; influence, 27–28, 62; lithics, 296, 302; maize, 296; mortuary goods, 7, 118, 220, 222; mortuary practices, 237; motifs, 6, 9, 26–27, 78–80, 107, 178, 288, 290, 304–6; mounds, 29, 47, 58, 173, 296; nomenclature, 8, 172–73, 297–98; organization, 27; Post-Classic, 27, 308; Pre-classic, 302–5; prestige-related artifacts, 29; protohistoric phenomenon, 6; regional expressions, 187; ritual, 58, 296, 304; settlement patterns, 5, 13, 18–19, 22–23, 25–26, 40, 64, 68–69, 73–75, 86–88, 101–4, 109–11, 119, 127, 139–41, 144–45, 151–53, 171, 173, 176,

186, 189–90, 192, 201, 218–19, 226, 235, 268–69, 271, 279, 290–91, 293, 298, 303, 308; sites as redistribution centers, 66; social interaction, 150–51, 154; "Southern Cult," 6; status, 185, 188, 192–95, 202, 210, 235, 256, 258, 263, 265, 268, 271, 277, 281, 296, 305; subsistence, 5, 16–17, 19, 22–23, 25, 29, 42, 44, 54, 57, 61n5, 72, 75, 84, 86–89, 97, 99, 104, 115, 120, 135, 137, 139–41, 146, 148, 152, 167–69, 176, 181, 296; trade, 7, 12–13, 29, 46, 51, 62, 66, 94, 98, 100, 113–18, 140, 181, 184, 189–90, 195, 204, 290, 292, 297; use of qualifiers for Florida Mississippian sites, 7; warfare, 58–59. *See also* Apalachee culture; Cahokia mound site; Environment; Ceramics: shell-tempered; Exchange networks; Fort Walton culture; Mill Cove Complex; Mississippian world; Political organization; Pre-Classic Mississippian Horizon; Rood culture; Safety Harbor culture; Shell; Southeastern Ceremonial Complex; St. Johns II culture; Weeden Island culture

Mississippian Optimum. *See* Climate: Medieval Warm Period

Mississippi period, 133, 266, 280–81, 283, 286, 296–309; climate, 33–38; dates, 6, 8, 29, 302; definition, 8, 297; Early, 27, 179; Late, 179, 283, 285; Middle, 179, 278; research questions, 20–22. *See also* Cahokia mound site; Caloosahatchee region; Calusa culture; Horizons; Pensacola culture; Safety Harbor culture; Suwannee Valley culture

Mississippian world, 10, 14–15, 18, 20–21, 23–26, 47, 54, 56–57, 75, 77, 81, 96, 99, 101–2, 112, 116–17, 144, 147, 186, 231, 237, 249, 251, 265, 267, 273, 277, 279, 290, 296–309; map, 11

Mississippi Plain. *See* Ceramics

Mississippi River, 27, 276, 296, 303, 306

Mississippi River Valley, 6, 58, 147, 173, 178–82, 296, 298–99, 300–301, 303, 306

Missouri, 46, 302, 306

Missouri Botanical Gardens, 264

Mitchell, Augustus, 110

Mitchem, Jeffrey M., 2, 7, 13, 18, 25–26, 55, 112, 114–15, 125, 127, 144, 147, 165, 172–85, 246, 262, 273

Mobile, Ala., 277

Mobile Bay, 249, 275, 278–80, 285, 305

Mobile delta, 263, 291

Mobile-Tensaw Delta, 277, 294

Mollusks. *See* Shellfish

Monks Mound. *See* Cahokia mound site, Ill.

Monroe County, 67

Montgomery, Ala., 264

Monumental architecture, 126. *See also* Mounds

Moore, Clarence B., 6, 24, 100, 104–6, 109–10, 112, 114, 118–20, 122, 182, 233, 251, 256, 260, 262, 265, 283, 285, 287, 300, 303, 307

Morrell, Ross, 214

Morse, Dan F., 301, 307

Morse, Phyllis A., 301, 307

Mortuary: capital, 221; ceremonialism, 119–23, 141–42, 144, 188–89, 193, 219–25, 237, 265; debt, 221; goods, 7, 24, 43, 118, 120, 126, 133, 177, 204–9, 220–22

Motifs, 6, 9, 78–80, 107, 116, 147, 158, 178, 195, 217, 288, 290, 302, 304–6; alligators, 79; arrow, 205; arrowhead, 206; bifurcated crown, 302; birds, 79, 286, 288; block-lined, 306–7; complicated-stamped, 217–18; Craig, 308; cross, 79, 199; Davis Rectangle, 306; dot-in-circle eyes, 302–3; double arc punctation, 238; "eyelash punctations," 238; falcon, 205; feather-like plumes, 205; Gasque, 286; geometric, 78; guilloche (loop/scroll), 178, 238, 249, 250; "hand and eye" (weeping eye), 78; hawk, 206–8, 305; human hands, 178; incised, 101, 178, 195, 217, 237, 253, 262; incised-punctated, 249; knot-and-braid, 78; lizard, 206–7; maces, 178; notched, 240; panther, 79; punctated, 78, 101, 178, 237, 253, 262; quartered circle, 305; reptile, 286; snakes, 79, 94; spider, 182; sun burst, 306; "sun circle," 236; triforked eye, 205; whelk, 305; "Williams Island" (spaghetti-style), 236; zoned hatching, 78; zoned punctuates, 78. *See also* Key Marco cat; Southeastern Ceremonial Complex (SECC)

Mound centers/complexes, 17–18, 23, 26, 58, 66–73, 79, 96, 100, 102, 141, 144, 233, 236, 252, 268–71, 273, 278–79, 290, 298–99, 305, 308; redistribution centers, 66

Mound Island, Ala., 277

Mound Key site, Fla., 30, 40–41, 47, 48–49, 60n2, 73; "Calos," 47; canals, 49; as capital, 49; European contact, 49; map, 48; midden-mounds, 49; mound construction, 41; Park, 60n2; Pedro Menéndez de Avilés, 49; radiocarbon dates, 49

Mound Place Incised. *See* Ceramics
Mounds, 18, 23–27, 40, 47, 66–73, 219, 226–28, 281, 286, 290, 292, 299, 306; burial, 10–11, 24–25, 41, 44, 48–49, 55–56, 67, 69–73, 75–76, 79, 87, 89–90, 92, 96, 100–103, 109–11, 116, 118, 120–22, 133, 136, 141–44, 148, 174, 176–77, 183, 193, 195, 204, 213, 217, 219–20, 222, 233, 236, 252, 270; conical, 142, 188, 193, 233–35, 252, 260; construction, 189, 258, 292; decline, 218; domiciliary, 53, 56–57, 73, 75, 79, 92; elevated, 18, 73; flat-topped, 73, 213, 251, 258; habitation, 53, 56; linear, 40, 47, 53, 73; midden, 18, 23, 39–40, 42, 44, 47–49, 53, 57, 61n4, 68, 71–73; platform, 10, 18, 23, 25–26, 29, 47, 73, 75–76, 80, 90–92, 105, 142, 149, 153, 155, 166, 169, 171, 173, 176, 187, 189, 193, 195, 200, 203, 213, 214–15, 218, 233–36, 243, 251–52, 256, 259, 264, 283, 296, 299, 305; ramps, 75, 92; sand, 44, 47, 55, 68–69 71–73, 89–90, 94, 98, 104, 109, 111, 121–22, 140–41, 188, 193; temple, 6, 8–9, 47, 53–54, 59, 92, 126, 144, 213–14, 231, 233, 236, 241, 252, 267, 283, 287–89, 293–94; truncated pyramidal, 188–89. *See also* Mound centers/complexes; Pineland Site Complex: Brown's Complex Mounds; Randall Complex
Moundville Engraved. *See* Ceramics
Moundville Incised. *See* Ceramics
Moundville site, Ala., 7, 26, 51, 178, 275, 277, 286, 290, 307
Mount, Greg, 75
Mt. Royal Mound site, Fla., 6–7, 15, 96, 102, 104, 110, 112–16, 118, 123–24, 182; Cahokia side-notched point, 114; ceramics, 113; map, 102; mission-period, 15; shared aspects with Mill Cove, 112; shell as principal export, 115–17
Mueller, Bradley, 70
Mulatto Oaks site, Fla., 291
Muller, Jon, 9, 13, 237, 301
Mullet. *See* Fish
MWP. *See* Climate: Medieval Warm Period
Myakka River, 30–31
Myth. *See* Belief systems

Narváez, Pánfilo de, 26, 58, 176, 219, 266
Narvaez site. *See* Anderson site
Nashville basin, 306
Nassaney, Michael S., 9, 12, 14, 112
Nassau County, Fla., 101
National Aeronautic and Space Administration (NASA), 83

National Museum of the American Indian, 106, 125
National Park Service Naval Live Oaks Reservation, 287
National Park Service Southeastern Archaeological Center (SEAC), 287, 290
National Register of Historic Places, 60n2, 61n4
National Research Council (NRC), 31–32
Naval Live Oaks Cemetery site, Fla., 287–90, 293; burials, 290; cemetery, 287; ceramics, 287–88; SECC motifs, 288
Nelson, Bruce C., 151–53, 158
Nelson, Nels, 198
Net gauge, 46. *See also* Fishing
Net weights, 39, 46. *See also* Fishing
Neuman, Robert W., 264
Newell, 306
Newman, Christine L., 75
Newman, Marshall T., 95
Newnan's Lake, 129
New River, 64, 68
New River Mound Complex, Fla., 63, 68
New River Sound, 64
Newsom, Lee, 167–68
New Spain, 292
New World Research (NWR), 281
Nicodemus site, Fla., 73–74. *See also* Belle Glade culture area
Nodena Red-and-White. *See* Ceramics
Nodena site, 77
Nodine, Bruce K., 144
Norris Mound site, Fla., 89. *See also* Indian River culture area
Norse, 34
North Captiva Island, Fla., 30
Northeast Woods site, Fla. *See also* Pineland Site Complex
Northern Highlands, 128, 190
"North Utina." *See* Timucua culture
Northwest Pasture site, Fla. *See also* Pineland Site Complex
NRC. *See* National Research Council
Nyberg, Johan, 33

Oak, 141, 217, 253
Obion site, 302
O'Brien, Greg, 237
Ocala, Fla., 135
Ochre, 46, 205–7, 209; Georgia piedmont, 46
Ochlockonee River, 26, 190
Ocmulgee-Big Bend, 137
Ocmulgee-Blackshear region, 117
Ocmulgee Fields Incised. *See* Ceramics

Ocmulgee River, 117
Ocmulgee Territory, 113, 146
Oconee River, 117
Oddy, Donna M., 83
Oelsner Indian Mound site, Fla., 95. *See also* Safety Harbor culture; Weeden Island culture
Ohio, 13; Mississippi confluence, 296, 303
Okaloosa County, Fla., 276–77
Okeechobee basin. *See* Lake Okeechobee
Oklahoma, 10, 116, 204. *See also* Spiro, Okla.
Old Mound site, Fla. *See* Pineland Site Complex
Old Okahumpka site, Fla., 183
Old Rambo Landing mound, Ga., 232–33, 260; ceramics, 260–61; Creeks, 261; Late Woodland, 261; lithics, 261; mound, 260; Weeden Island II culture, 261
Olive (shell), 13, 115. *See also* Shell
Omussee Creek site (Mound near Columbia, Seaborn), Fla., 232–33, 264
Oneota culture, 308
Orangeburg Fine Sandy Loam, 192
Orange Lake, 129
Ormond Mound site, Fla., 95. *See also* St. Johns culture area
Ortona Mound Complex, Fla., 70–73. *See also* Belle Glade culture area
Osage, 304
Osborn, Timothy J., 34
Osprey site, Fla., 174–75
O'Steen, Lisa D., 104
Outina, 127, 154; ceramics, 155. *See also* St. Johns culture area
Oyster, 35, 37, 86, 92, 104, 285; midden, 108, 251, 281, 285
Ozarks, 300

Paint palette, 209
Paleoclimatology, 31, 33. *See also* Climate; Florida Straits records
Palisades, 18, 196, 228, 235, 292–93
Palm Beach County, Fla., 66–67, 69, 77
Palm Beach Inlet, Fla., 70
Panama City, Fla., 276, 278
Panzacola Indians, 292
Papys Bayou. *See* Ceramics
Parkin Punctated. *See* Ceramics
Parkin site, Ark., 182
Parks, Lisa, 107
Parsons, Alexandra, 101
Pasco Plain. *See* Ceramics
Pasco Roughened. *See* Ceramics

Pauketat, Timothy R., 9, 27, 114, 116, 123, 173, 182, 237, 301, 304–5
Payne, Claudine, 7, 10, 18, 47, 100, 113, 115, 117, 189, 194, 196–97, 199–204, 215, 219, 225–26, 228, 230, 233, 266, 272, 307
Paynes Prairie, Fla., 129, 133
Peabody Museum, 214
Peace River, 30–31
Peacock, Evan, 20
Peacock Lake site, Fla., map, 153
Pearls, 106. *See also* Beads
Pecan, 168
Peebles, Christopher S., 8, 220, 277
Penders, Thomas E., 2, 18, 24, 65, 81–99, 101, 109
Pensacola, Fla., 276, 286–87, 292, 307
Pensacola (Indians). See Panzacola Indians
Pensacola Bay, 27, 249, 276–77, 279–80, 285–91, 294
Pensacola Brushed. *See* Walnut Roughened
Pensacola culture, 7–8, 20, 27, 188, 202, 268, 275–95; abandonment, 27, 279, 293; agriculture, 15, 277, 284, 290–93; Bear Point Phase, 286, 292; Bell Plain, 284–85; Bell Plain, *variety* Hale, 287; Bottle Creek Phase, 286; burials, 27, 286; busk ceremony, 292; camps, 284–86; cemeteries, 27, 281, 283–84, 286, 292–93; ceramic ratios, 281, 284, 290; ceramics, 27, 147, 238, 249, 268, 277–78, 280–81, 284, 286–88, 290–94; Chattahoochee Brushed, 281, 285; coastal variant, 294; communication, 27, 292; connections to Mississippian world, 279; copper, 27, 288, 293; defined by Willey, 275; D'Olive Incised, 284; D'Olive *variety*, Arnica, 286–87; environment, 280, 285; ethnohistoric records (lack), 27; European contact, 27; evidence of coastal Mississippian variant, 280; faunal remains, 281; flora, 281; Fort Walton, 284, 291; Fort Walton Incised, 284; Fort Walton Incised, *variety* Choctawhatchee, 288; Four Mile Point Phase, 284, 286, 292; geographical boundaries, 275, 280; grave goods, 286; grit-tempered, 278, 284, 290–91; grog temper as marker, 291; grog-tempered, 291; habitation patterns, 283; historic period, 291, 293; iconography, 147, 277, 279, 290, 293–94; Indian Bayou Phase, 284; Jefferson Plain, 281; Jefferson ware, 284, 291; Lake Jackson Plain, 281; Lamar Complicated Stamped, 284–85; Lamar ware, 291; Late Archaic, 283; Late Mississippi, 283, 285; Leon Check Stamped, 281, 284–85;

Pensacola culture—*continued*
lithics, 281, 286; maize, 27, 281, 284, 291–93; map of geographic limits, 278; mica, 286; Middle-Mississippi, 278; Mississippian characteristics (lack of), 277; Mississippi-period sites, 280–81, 286; Mississippi Plain, 284; Mississippi Plain, *variety* Warrior, 286–87; motifs, 286, 290; mounds, 18, 27, 281, 286, 290, 292–93; Mound Place Incised, 284–85; Moundville Engraved, *variety* Hemphill, 286; Moundville Engraved, *variety* unspecified, 287; Moundville Incised, 284–85; Moundville Incised, *variety* Moundville, 286–87; Moundville Incised, *variety* Snow's Bend, 286–87; Moundville Incised, *variety*, unspecified, 287; nomenclature, 294; Ocmulgee Fields Incised, 285; oyster, 285; palisades, 292–93; Panzacola Indians, 292; Pensacola Incised, 284, 288; Pensacola Incised, *variety* Bear Point, 286–87; Pensacola Incised, *variety* Gasque, 286–87; Pensacola Incised, *variety* Moore, 287; Pensacola Incised, *variety* unspecified, 287; Pensacola Plain, 284; Point Washington Incised, 281, 284; population, 290; projectile point, 286; protohistoric, 27, 285, 291, 293; radiocarbon dates, 281–82, 284, 286, 290; *Rangia* (marsh clam), 285; relationship with Fort Walton, 275; ritual, 279, 288, 292–93; sand-tempered, 278, 284, 290; SECC motifs, 288; settlement patterns, 27, 279, 283–84, 290–93; shell beads, 27; shell middens, 281, 285; shell-tempered, 20–21, 27, 202, 275, 278, 284, 286–87; shell tools, 281; six-pointed bowl, 268, 288; social complexity, 277, 292; sociopolitical organization, 277; subsistence, 27, 277, 281, 293; trade, 290, 292–93; transportation, 27, 291; villages, 281, 284, 286, 292; Weeden Island, 279, 290, 292; Woodland, 283, 285. *See also* Bell site; Brooks Street Mound site; Butcherpen Mound Complex; Camp Walton site; Fort Walton Landing site; Fort Walton Temple Mound site; Hickory Ridge site; Indianola Mound site; Mulatto Oaks site; Naval Live Oaks Cemetery site; Sheephead Bayou site; Third Gulf Breeze site
Pensacola Incised. *See* Ceramics
Pensacola Plain. *See* Ceramics
Penton, Daniel T., 193, 196, 198, 225, 227
Pepe, James P., 70–71, 87
Pepper Mound site, Fla., 73. *See also* Belle Glade culture area
Percy, George W., 192–93, 195, 267, 277–79
Perdido Bay, 277
Peregrine, Peter N., 118
Perry Collection, 238–41, 245, 247, 249, 260–62
Persimmon, 281
Phelps, David, 219
Phillips, John C., 87, 178, 180, 277, 282, 285–87, 290, 295
Phillips, Philip, 8, 13, 100, 115, 117, 175, 178, 180, 245, 298, 302, 306
Piatek, Bruce J., 287
Picture Cave, Mo., 302
Piedmont, 307
Pierce site, Fla., 26, 232–33, 236, 243, 251, 270; Early Woodland, 251; midden, 251; Middle Woodland, 252
Pine, 202, 217, 243, 253
Pine Island, 30–31, 38, 40, 49, 51, 61n4, 71, 73; Canal, 41, 51; Sound, 29–31, 38–39, 50–51, 58–59, 61n4
Pineland paste, 55
Pineland Site Complex, Fla., 30, 38, 40–41, 49–50, 52–53, 57, 60n3, 61n4, 69, 71; abandonment, 41, 53; Adams Mound, 50; bone tools, 46; Brown's Complex Mounds, 1, 2, 42–43, 46, 49–50; burial mounds, 41, 44, 49, 55; canals, 40–41, 44, 49, 50–51; Central Pasture, 50; ceramics, 40–43, 45, 55; chert, 46; Citrus Ridge, 50; client polities, 51; comparison with Etowah and Cahokia, 51; coral, 46; craft specialization, 44; dates, 41; depopulation, 44; dolomite, 46; domiciliary mounds, 53; earthworks, 53; Eastern Woodlands, 50; habitation pattern, 49, 51, 53; linear mounds, 40–41, 44, 49, 53; Low Mound, 50; map, 50, 52; midden accumulations, 41, 51; mound complexes, 49–50; Northeast Woods, 50; Northwest Pasture, 50; ochre, 46; Old Mound, 50; quahog clam, 46; radiocarbon-dates, 40–41; Randall Complex Mound 1, 40, 50; ritual, 46; sand mounds, 44; sandstone, 46; sea-level fluctuations, 40–41; settlement, 39; shell net gauge, weight, and tools, 46; shell works, 51; Smith mound, 41, 50; soil analysis, 41; structures, 46; "Tampa," 49, 60n2; transportation, 51; vertical mounds, 40; water court, 40. *See also* Caloosahatchee IIB; Caloosahatchee III; Caloosahatchee IV; Labor
Pinellas County, Fla., 174, 176
Pinellas Phase, 174, 185. *See also* Safety Harbor culture

Pinellas Plain. *See* Ceramics
Pinellas-type point. *See* Projectile points
Pipes, 120, 199, 206; Chandler-style, 206–7; clay, 206–7; elbow, 206–7; lizard, 206; steatite, 206–7
Plains, 305
Plantation Key Mound Complex, Fla., 69. *See also* Glades culture area
Platform mound. *See* Mounds
Platt, William J., 128
Plazas, 18, 25, 144, 176, 196, 200–201, 228, 235, 251, 258, 277, 296, 299, 303, 306; criteria, 196
Plio-Pleistocene epoch, 275
Plummets. *See* Ground stone; Quartz
Point Washington Incised. *See* Ceramics
Pokrant, Marie E., 283–85
Political economy, 140
Political organization, 9, 20, 24–28, 31, 42, 51, 53, 56, 67, 124, 127, 144, 148, 169–70, 237, 267–74, 304; agency, 271; alliances, 11, 13, 19, 46, 73, 98–99, 113–14, 116–18, 121, 124, 184, 186, 192, 195, 308; chiefs, 26; complexity, 1, 18, 23; cycling, 237, 270–71, 308; diplomacy, 13, 46, 117, 122; matrilineal, 26; polities, 19–20, 49, 51, 114, 116, 186, 215, 228, 307–8; rank and hierarchy, 17, 25–26, 53, 98–99, 124, 169–70, 186, 189, 192, 204, 220, 224, 231, 237, 270–71; settlement hierarchy, 171; stratification, 270; women, 26. *See also* Chiefdoms
Polities. *See* Political organization
Polk County, Fla., 175
Pollen, 72, 229
Polygonum sp., 300
Ponce de León, 58, 81, 97
Ponds. *See* Fish: weir and impoundment areas
Population, 226, 290; depopulation, 19, 44, 57; environmental impact on, 19, 41–42, 44, 57; growth, 192, 267; levels, 19; movements, 57
Post-Classic Mississippian Horizon, 307; cultural continuity, 308; reorganization, 308; shell, 308
Post molds, 166, 235
Potano. *See* Potano Phase; Timucua culture
Potano Phase. *See* Alachua culture; Timucua culture
Pottery. *See* Ceramics
Poverty Point site, La., 299
Prairie Cord Marked. *See* Ceramics
"Prairie lakes," 191
Prairie-Punctated-over-Cord Marked. *See* Ceramics

Precipitation. *See* Climate
Pre-Classic Mississippian Horizon, 300, 302; agriculture, 305; copper, 302–3; long-nosed god (LNG) maskette, 302–3; mound centers, 305; settlement patterns, 303; shell, 303, 305
Prentice, Marie, 181, 220, 229
Prentice Thomas and Associates, 279, 286, 295
Presidios, 291
Prestige-goods economy, 8, 24, 100, 116–18
Prewitt, Terry J., 284
Price, Cynthia R., 300
Price, George, 146, 300
Price, James E., 300
Priestly, Herbert J., 292
Pringle, Heather, 34
Projectile points, 136, 206–7, 209–10, 213–14, 265, 286; Cahokia Side-Notched, 109; Ichetucknee, 140, 213–14, 219; Marion-type, 46; notched, 94; Pinellas-type, 107, 133, 140, 214, 265; Putnam-type, 46; side-notched point base, 263; Tampa, 140
Proto-Creek, 27
Protohistoric, 6, 26–27, 31–32, 48, 203, 219, 259–60, 281, 284–85, 287, 291, 293
Provancha, Jane A., 83
Puerto Rico, 33, 36–37
Pumice, 77
Punctated-over-Cord Marked. *See* Ceramics
Punta Gorda. *See* Florida
Puri, H. S., 276
Putnam County, Fla., 182

Quahog clam, 46, 86
Quartz, 46, 93, 96, 105, 183; plummet, 182
Queen conch (*Strombus gigas*), 114
Quitmyer, Irv R., 167–68, 258

Rabbit, 139, 204
Raccoon, 253, 258
Radin, Paul, 302
Radiocarbon dates, 16, 39, 40–41, 48, 70–72, 84–85, 133–35, 137, 141, 156–57, 174, 183, 188, 190, 194, 200, 204, 213, 215, 218, 227, 237, 241–42, 253, 255–56, 258, 260, 265, 281, 284, 288, 290–91
Raids. *See* Warfare
Ramey Incised. *See* Ceramics
Randall Complex, Fla., 40. *See also* Pineland Site Complex
Randell, Donald and Patricia, 61n4
Randell Research Center, 61n4
Randolph, A. M., 198

Range site, 303
Rangia (marsh clam). *See* Shellfish
Rank. *See* Political organization
Raptor. *See* Iconography
Reber, Eleanora A., 221
Red-and-white painted. *See* Ceramics
Redfish Pass, 30
Red Horn ("He-who-wears-human-heads-for-earrings"). *See* Iconography; Long-nosed god
Red Sea, 35
Reilly, F. Kent III, 236
Reitz, Elizabeth J., 15
Religion. *See* Belief systems
Reptiles, 281. *See also* Iconography; Motifs; Subsistence
Rhodes Incised. *See* Ceramics
Richardson's Hammock site, Fla., 236
Ricisak, John, 68–69
Riordan, T., 93
Ritta River, 75
Ritual, 10, 24, 29, 58, 90, 101, 104, 109–11, 118, 120–24, 136, 148, 189, 196, 218, 220, 225, 227, 235, 279, 288, 292–93, 296–97, 299, 303–4; adoption or alliance, 116; attendant, 221–22; Busk ceremony, 292; center, 124, 225, 303; ceramic styles, 144, 200; communal, 123; fertility, 301, 304; goods, 47, 220, 256, 296; knowledge, 123; mortuary, 24, 101, 108, 110, 112, 116, 120–23, 141–42, 147, 218–25, 265, 292–93; mound construction, 141, 299; purification, 200; rites of intensification, 225, 304–5; specialists, 29, 296; structures, 46–47; world renewal, 304
"River of Grass," 64
Rivers, 4, 17, 67; Alabama, 276; Altamaha, 117, 137; Apalachicola, 4, 27, 182, 193, 231–34, 246, 252, 257, 276, 307–8; Aucilla, 26, 155, 190, 276, 279; Big River, 301; Blackwater River, 35, 37, 285; Caloosahatchee, 23, 30–31, 63, 67, 71, 73, 79; Chattahoochee, 4, 180, 231, 238, 247, 252, 260, 262, 266, 268–69, 276; Chipola, 233–34, 247; Escambia River, 285, 291; Flint, 231, 233, 252, 276; Indian, 24, 75, 79, 81, 87, 89; Kissimmee, 23, 62–64, 66, 73, 79; map of Florida, 5; Meramec, 301; Miami, 63–64, 69; Myakka, 30–31; New, 63–64, 68; Ochlockonee, 190; Ocmulgee, 117; Oconee, 117; Peace, 30–31; Ritta, 75; Santa Fe 127, 145, 152; Savannah, 127; Shark 65; St. Francois, 301; St. Johns, 6, 15–16, 24, 85, 87–90, 95, 98, 100, 102–4, 110, 114–15, 154, 276, 299, 302, 305; Suwannee 19, 152–53, 276; Tombigbee, 276; Withlacoochee, 155, 175; Yellow River, 285
Riviera Complex, 71. *See also* Riviera site
Riviera site, Fla., 63, 70–71, 76
Rock art, 302
Rock Mound site, Fla., 75
Rocky Point site, Fla., 133, 138; dates, 133; inverted ceramic stratigraphy, 133; map 129; Pinellas points, 133; Woodland, 133
Rodriguez, Nelson, 264
Rogel, 54
Rolland, Vicki, 2, 16, 24–25, 100–101, 104, 108, 110, 113–14, 118, 120, 125–48, 150, 152–53, 155, 158, 162, 183, 228
Rollins Mound site, Fla., 213, 226, 228
Rollins Point, Fla., 214
Roman Warm Period (RWP). *See* Climate
Rood culture, 180, 183, 268; ceremonialism, 268; Early Rood, 268; ethnic differentiation, 268; shell-tempered, 268; subsistence, 268. *See also* Cemochechobee site; Rood's Landing site
Rood's Landing site, Ga., 268
Roosevelt, Anna C., 20
Rosenthal, Erin, 250
Rouse, Irving, 24, 66, 83–89, 93–96
Rowlands, Michael, 118, 226
Russo, Michael, 83, 86–88, 104
RWP. *See* Climate: Roman Warm Period

Sabo, George, III, 20
Sacred-secular ceramic dichotomy. *See* Ceramics
Safety Harbor. *See* Ceramics
Safety Harbor, Fla., 307
Safety Harbor culture, 6–8, 15, 18, 25–26, 45–46, 55–56, 59, 95, 126–27, 132, 144, 147, 165, 172–85, 198, 246, 262, 273, 307, 309; agriculture, 7, 15, 25, 181, 185; burials, 25, 176; ceramics, 6–7, 25, 42–43, 55, 126, 132, 147, 165, 173–74, 176–80; chiefdoms, 26, 185; copper, 26; craft specialization, 182; cultural continuity, 176; dates, 6, 55–56; differences from Mississippian; economy, 25; Englewood Incised, 177–78; environment factors, 180; geographical boundaries, 175–76; ground stone, 26; iconography, 147; ideology, 55; influences, 7, 179–80; interregional networks, 126; map, 173; Mississippian influence, 25, 172–74, 178–79; mortuary ceremonialism,

184; mounds, 8, 18, 25, 176; phases, 174; plazas, 18, 25, 176; politics, 26; regional variants, 174; "sacred vs. secular," 177; settlements, 25–26, 127, 173, 175–76; shell, 26; specialized localities vs. habitation sites, 176; subsistence, 25, 181; sustained direct interaction, 179; temper, 179–80; trade, 25–26, 181–82; villages, 176. *See also* Anderson site; Bayview Phase; Englewood Phase; Manasota culture; Pinellas Phase; Tatham Phase
Safety Harbor Incised. *See* Ceramics
Sahlins, Marshall, 121
Saitta, Dean J., 117–18, 120, 123, 307
Salinity, 36–37, 285. *See also* Climate; Sea-level
Salvage excavations, 7, 222, 287
Sampson, Kelvin W., 107, 114, 300, 303
Sams site, Fla., 86–87
San Carlos Bay, 29, 30–31
Sand mounds. *See* Mounds: sand
Sands Key Mound Complex, Fla., 69. *See also* Glades culture area
Sandstone, 46, 205, 275
Sand-tempered. *See* Ceramics
Sanibel II Low, 32, 37, 42–43, 57
Sank, Karen, 303
San Pablo de Patale site, Fla., 201; ceramics, 216
San Pedro. *See* Ceramics
Santa Fe River, Fla., 127, 145, 152
Santa Fe site, Fla., map, 153
Santa Maria site, Fla., 291
Santa Rosa (island), Fla., 280
Santa Rosa County, Fla., 276–77
Santa Rosa culture, 285
Santa Rosa site, Fla., 291
Santa Rosa Sound, 283
Sarasota County, Fla., 55, 174–75
Sarasota Incised. *See* Ceramics
Sargasso Sea, 33, 36
Sassaman, Kenneth E., 12, 102
Savannah River Valley, 34, 308; agriculture, 34; climate, 34
Savannah River Valley cultures, 127
Saw palmetto, 168, 217
Saxe, Arthur A., 220
Scarry, C. Margaret, 263
Scarry, John F., 10, 18, 100, 113, 115, 117, 152, 155, 163, 189, 196, 199–200, 214–15, 218, 220, 226, 240, 256, 266–67, 272, 277, 279, 283
Schmidt, Walter, 3

Schnell, Frank T., 180, 262
Schofield, Shanna, 133–34, 136, 138
Schwartz, Mark, 128
Science, 298
Scudder, Sylvia, 41
Seaborn site (Mound near Columbia). *See* Omussee Creek site
SEAC. *See* National Park Service Southeastern Archaeological Center
SEAC. *See* Southeastern Archaeological Conference
Sea-level, 3, 23, 32–44, 56–58, 69; models, 33. *See also* Buck Key Low; La Costa High; Sanibel II Low; Wulfert High
Sears, Elsie, 72
Sears, William H., 66, 72, 78, 84, 136, 177, 184, 193, 240–41, 245
Seasonality, 88, 103, 190, 273
Sea-surface temperature. *See* Climate
SECC. *See* Southeastern Ceremonial Complex
Seeds, 16, 167, 253, 299–300
Seminole, 32, 65, 266
Settlement hierarchy, 19, 171
Settlement patterns, 67, 72, 75, 145, 176, 201, 219, 226–27, 233, 252, 267–69, 279, 283–84, 291–93, 299, 303, 306
Shahramfar, Gabrielle, 236, 271
Shapiro, Gary, 21, 181, 217
Shark: jaw knife, 209; spangle, 209; teeth, 46, 76, 106
Shark River, 65
Sheephead Bayou site, Fla., 281–82
Sheldon, Craig T., Jr., 180, 264
Sheldon, E., 264
Shell, 114, 181, 236, 263, 296; adzes, 66; beads, 14, 27, 47, 94, 106, 109, 115, 119, 143, 182, 205–8, 288, 301, 303; cups, 47, 206, 209, 253, 255, 303; demand, 14; goods, 9, 13–14, 26–28, 47, 54, 66, 75, 94, 96, 106–7, 109, 111, 114–15, 117, 119–20, 148, 181–84, 236, 253, 273, 288, 296, 300, 302–3, 305–9; gorgets, 13–14, 77–78, 80, 182, 205–6, 236, 303, 308; hair pin, 207; mask, 13–14, 77, 80, 302, 308; middens, 17, 68–70, 85, 92, 107–11, 233, 247, 251, 281, 285, 287; net gauge, 46; net weights, 46; pendant, 47, 78–79, 109, 205–7, 223–24, 303; picks, 66, 75; tools, 13–14, 46, 120, 158, 160–62, 165, 181, 206, 209, 253, 273, 281, 303, 308; works, 23, 53. *See also* Ceramics; Marginella; Olive; Quahog clam; Trade; Whelk

Shellfish, 2, 9, 19, 24, 31, 38–39, 42, 57, 86, 88, 104, 120, 129, 140, 233, 235, 258, 263, 281; coquina, 86; cross barred venus, 86; crown conch, 86; environmental pressure, 38; human pressure, 38; mollusks, 253, 263; moon snail, 86; oyster, 86; quahog clam, 46, 86; *Rangia* (marsh clam), 251, 285; snails, 253. *See also* Environment; Sea-level; Whelk
Shell Mound Archaic, 47
Shell-tempered. *See* Ceramics
Shields Mound site, Fla., 6–7, 18, 24, 104–11, 117–22; bannerstones, 105; copper artifacts, 105; dates, 107; galena, 105; ground stone celts, 105; hematite sand with burials, 109; local artifacts, 105–6; map, 103, 108; mica, 105; mortuary ceremonialism, 116, 122; mound construction, 106; platform mound, 105; projectile points, 105; quartz, 105; spatulate celts, 105–6. *See also* Kinzey's Knoll; Mill Cove Complex; St. Johns culture area; St. Johns II culture
Shipwrecks, 70, 78
Siddall, M., 35
Sigler-Eisenberg, Brenda, 83, 86–88
Sigler-Lavelle, Brenda, 151
Sigmann, Samuella, 13, 181
Sigma Xi, 274
Sigüenza y Góngora, Don Carlos de, 292
Silver disk, 78
"Simple-stamped." *See* Ceramics
Simpson, Terrance L., 176
Sinistral. *See* Whelk
Sinkers, 39. *See also* Fishing
Siouan myth, 302, 304
SITE, Inc., 264
Sites, Fla.: 8Al273 site, 129, 132; 8Bd87 site, 68; 8Br49–50 site, 90; 8Da1081 site, 78; 8Du52 site, 103; 8Du58 site, 103, 109, 110; 8Du97 site, 103; 8Du238 site, 103; 8Du276 site, 103; 8Du626 site, 103; 8Du1542 site, 103; 8Du5545 site, 103; 8Es1052 site, 286; 8PB28 site, 70; 8PB29 site, 70; 8SR17 site, 286; 8Wl119 site, 284–85. *See also* East Okeechobee culture area; Glades culture area; Indian River culture area; New River Mound Complex; Pensacola culture; St. Johns culture area; St. Johns II culture
Six-pointed bowl. *See* Ceramics
Slave-raiders, 59
Sloth Hole site, Fla., 191
Smith, Bruce D., 8–9, 17–18, 112, 144, 269, 277

Smith, Gregory S., 100–101, 107, 308
Smith, Hale G., 193, 213–15, 217, 266
Smith, Julie Barnes, 77, 153
Smith, K C, 199, 219
Smith, Marvin T., 13, 77, 101, 150, 155
Smith, Rebecca, 83
Smith Mound site, Fla. *See* Pineland Site Complex
Smithsonian Institution, 106, 125, 305
Snails. *See* Shellfish
Snakes, 204, 258. *See also* Motifs
Snow, Frankie, 137
Snow Beach site, Fla., 219; beads, 219; burials, 219; Ichetucknee points, 219; mounds, 219
Social complexity, 23, 45, 53–54, 76, 228, 237, 268–69, 277, 292, 309
Social inequality, 9, 17, 124, 237
Social memory, 121, 219, 221–22, 225–26, 249
Social stratification, 126
Sociohistorical structures, 45
Sociopolitical organization, 41, 204, 218, 237, 267–68, 270, 273, 277, 305, 307. *See also* Political organization
Solís de Merás, G., 29, 49, 56, 185
Sommerkamp, Cindy L., 286, 294
Soto, Hernando de, 8, 26, 58, 145, 188, 218, 266, 308
South Carolina, 10, 35, 37, 127, 137, 266, 276; sea level, 35, 37. *See also* Lamar culture
Southeast, 1–2, 6–10, 12–15, 17, 19, 21, 27–28, 32–33, 35, 38, 45, 56–59, 62, 80–81, 84, 99–100, 104, 113, 115, 117, 121, 124, 126–27, 138, 148–49, 165, 172–73, 178, 181, 185, 187, 218, 233, 235, 247, 252, 262, 269–70, 293, 297, 299, 302, 306–8
Southeast cultural chronology, 32. *See also* Protohistoric; Woodland period
Southeastern Archaeological Conference (SEAC), 21, 287
Southeastern Ceremonial Complex (SECC), 6–8, 26, 79, 107, 184, 224–25, 236, 273, 288, 300, 302–3, 306–7; artifacts, 6–7, 24, 105, 107, 114, 116, 122, 301–3, 305–6; Braden style, 302; similarities with South Florida Ceremonial Cult, 79; stylistic motifs, 6, 79, 302
"Southern Cult," 6. *See also* Southeastern Ceremonial Complex
South Florida: earthworks, 64; habitation and settlement, 64; mound centers,

66–73; prairies, 64, 67; topography, 64; tree islands, 64
South Florida Ceremonial Complex ("Glades Cult"), 79
Spall cache, 209
Spanish, 16, 18–19, 24–26, 29, 49, 54, 58, 68–69, 73, 76, 88, 97, 99, 101, 125–26, 130, 132, 135, 145, 147, 149, 155–56, 168–70, 185, 191, 201, 219, 264–65, 290–91; contact with Ais, 24; contact with Alachua, 24; contact with Apalachee, 26; contact with Apalachicola/lower Chattahoochee Fort Walton culture, 265; contact with Calusa, 29; contact with Safety Harbor culture, 185; contact with Suwannee Valley culture, 25, 149, 155. *See also* Mission-period
Spanish River, 64, 71
Spanish River Complex, 63, 71–72. *See also* Belle Glade culture area
Spatulate celts, 6, 24, 105, 107, 114, 116, 301
Spiro, Okla., 113, 116, 178, 204, 224–25, 306; copper long-nosed god maskette, 116
Sproul, Charles R., 190
Squash, 300
SST. *See* Climate: sea-surface temperature
Stahle, D. W., 37
St. Andrew Bay, 27, 276–77, 280–83, 290, 294
Stapor, Frank W., Jr., 33, 35, 37
Status, 17, 19, 124, 127, 169, 170–71, 186–87, 189, 195–96, 216, 218, 220–21, 224, 227, 237, 241, 253, 271, 296, 307
St. Augustine, Fla., 132, 170
Stein, Gil J., 10, 12
Steinen, Karl T., 135–36
Stephenson, D. Keith, 9, 127, 137–38
Steponaitis, Vincas P., 8–9, 17–18, 60, 178, 307
St. Francois Mountains, 301
St. Francois River, 301
Stickler, Justin, 213, 215
Stirling, Mathew W., 64, 93, 173
Stirrup-spout bottles. *See* Ceramics: bottles
St. Johns Check Stamped. *See* Ceramics
St. Johns County, Fla., 101
St. Johns culture area, 126, 147; agriculture, 15–16; aquatic resources, 103–4; burial mounds, 56; ceramics, 24, 102; Corinda culture, 101–2; Early Mississippi period, 22; Early Woodland St. Johns I, 56; interregional networks, 100, 154; Late Woodland, 101–2; social landscape, 101–2
St. Johns Plain. *See* Ceramics
St. Johns River, 6, 15–16, 24, 85, 87–90, 95, 98, 100–104, 110, 114–15, 154, 299, 302, 305; valley, 24, 101
St. Johns II culture, 7, 14, 24, 101–25, 155, 158, 299, 309; abandonment, 124; alliances, 113, 116; alternative views on nonlocal grave goods, 116–18; cemeteries, 109; ceramics, 101, 112–14, 120; child burials, 110; communication, 112; connection to the Mississippian World, 24; copper, 7; cord marked ceramics, 101; corporate identity, 24; dates, 101, 116; decline in Early-Mississippi period interactions, 124; distribution of exotica, 107–9, 120–22; earthworks, 102–10; economy, 24, 120; emulation, 112; European contact, 125; exchange networks, 112–16, 120; exotica/grave goods, 24, 96, 100, 105, 108–11, 116, 118–19; exotic stone, 7; fish, 104; fishing, 103, 120; gathering, 103; hunting, 103, 120; interregional networks, 66, 114, 126, 133, 154; labor, 117–18, 122; long-nosed maskettes, 24, 116; macroregional shell demand, 112; maize, 104, 119–25; map of Mill Cove Complex and Mt. Royal, 102; map of St. Johns II sites, 103; midden deposits, 103; Mississippianization, 111–12; mortuary customs, 119–23; mortuary goods, 24; motifs, 116; *Northeastern Florida as defined by Ashley*, 101; Outina, 127; oysters, 104; paucity of data, 100; pipes, 120; "pluralistic creation of Mississippian identities," 112; political economy, 101, 116–24; production of shell artifacts, 115; queen conch (*Strombus gigas*), 114; ritual, 116, 118, 122–23; sand burials, 103; sand mounds, 120; settlement, 101–4, 111, 113; shell as principal export, 115–17; shellfish, 104, 120; shell suppliers, 14; shell tools, 120; social memory, 121; spatulate celts, 24; stone tools, 120; subsistence, 24, 103–4, 115, 120; Timucua, 110; views of economy, 100, 116–18; warfare, 119; wild plants, 104. *See also* Ceramics: Papys Bayou; Ceramics: Ocmulgee Cord Marked; Ceramics: St. Johns Check Stamped; Ceramics: St. Johns Plain; Goodman Mound site; Grand Shell Ring site; Grant Mound site; Kinzey's Knoll; Mill Cove Complex; Mt. Royal Mound site; Prestige-goods economy; Shields Mound site; Timucua culture
St. Joseph Bay, 260, 273
St. Mary's. *See* Ceramics

Stock Island Mound Complex, Fla., 69. *See also* Glades culture area
Stokes, Anne V., 132
Stoltman, James B., 173
Stone, Earl, 128
Stone tools, 120. *See also* Lithics
Storey, Rebecca, 204, 207, 209, 222, 224
Stout, Charles, 18, 144, 233, 306
Stowe, Noel R., 277-79, 286
Strombus gigas. *See* Queen conch
Structures, 193, 216-17, 227, 235, 286
Sturtevant, William C., 53-54, 57, 76
Subsistence, 15-17, 20, 23-25, 31, 38-39, 57, 61n5, 65, 120, 126, 140, 145-47, 167-69, 181, 188, 192-93, 195, 210, 226, 233, 235, 253, 256, 258, 263, 265, 277, 293. *See also* Agriculture; Foragers; Gathering; Hunting
Sullivan, Lynne P., 220, 223, 237, 271
Summer Pentoaya site, Fla., 90. *See also* Indian River culture area
Sunflower, 217, 300
Surface obliteration. *See* Ceramics
Surge, Donna M., 35, 37
Surpluses, 15, 118, 120, 170
Suwannee River, 19, 152-53, 276
Suwannee Valley, 14, 126, 150-51, 155, 237; map, 153
Suwannee Valley culture ("Indian Pond Complex") 25, 126-27, 149-71; affinities with Alachua, 153-54, 164; Alachua Cob Marked, 158-59, 161, 162, 164, 168; Alachua Plain, 159; ceramics, 150, 152, 154-56, 158-59, 160-62; ceramics as "marker," 158; chronological parameters, 156; chronological perspective on ceramics, 163-64; comparison with McKeithen Weeden Island, 164-65; complexity, 25; contrasts with Mississippian culture, 163, 169; cord-marked ceramics, 154; cultural boundaries, 154-55; cultural continuity, 156, 164-66, 169; decoration vs. heat absorption efficiency and function, 159-60; decorative overtreatments, 161-62; definition, 150-52; early nomenclature, 151-52; ethnohistoric accounts, 170; evidence for chiefdom, 169; evidence for maize cultivation, 168; Fig Springs Incised, 159; Fig Springs Roughened, 158-59, 161, 164; Fig Springs Roughened *variety* Ichetucknee, 161; Fig Springs Roughened *variety* Santa Fe, 161; Fort Walton Incised, 159; geographical boundaries, 152-53; gourds, 162; Grassy Hole Pinched, 159; grit-tempered, 159; habitation patterns, 166; hereditary chiefdoms, 237; household craft production, 150; identification with historic Timucua, 149-50; interregional networks, 126, 150, 153-58; Lake Jackson Incised, 159; language, 154; limestone-tempered, 159; Lochloosa Punctated, 158-59, 161, 164-65; maize, 166; map of related sites, 153; material culture, 158-66; Mission-period, 155, 170; motifs, 158; Pasco Plain, 159; Pasco Roughened, 159; pits, 166; political organization, 25; posts, 166; Prairie Cord Marked, 158-59, 161, 164; pre-{#}and post-European data sets, 150; radiocarbon dates, 156, 166-68; sand-tempered, 159; settlement patterns, 152, 171; sociopolitical structure, 167-71; Spanish, 25, 149, 155; St. Johns Check Stamped, 159; St. Johns Plain, 159; structural patterns, 166; subsistence, 167-69; surface obliteration, 132, 162; surface treatment, 165; trade, 159; Trestle Point Shell Impressed, 159; utilitarian ceramic tradition, 162; warfare, 154; Woodland, 149; Yustaga region, 154. *See also* Alligator Lake site; Baptising Spring site; Carter Mound site; Charles Spring site; Fig Springs site; Indian Pond site; Jefferson culture; Leslie Mound site; McKeithen site; McKeithen Weeden Island culture; Peacock Lake site; Santa Fe site; Timucua culture; Weeden Island culture; Weeden Island II culture
Sweet gum, 217
Swift Creek. *See* Ceramics
Swift Creek culture, 285
Sycamore site, Fla., 194; habitation patterns, 193; maize, 193; Northwest Florida Cob Marked, 193; residential structures, 193; subsistence, 193
Symbol badges, 205-6, 224

Tallahassee, Fla., 251, 266, 305, 308
Tallahassee Fort Walton, 25-26, 55, 183, 186-230, 266; agriculture, 188, 210, 228-29; burials, 216, 220; ceramics 184, 188, 195, 206, 209, 211-12, 216-17, 227-28, 246; continuity with historic Apalachee, 26, 188, 191; cultural continuity, 195; dates, 188; decline, 217; exchange networks, 183; export shell, 183; farmstead, 214; future research, 227-28; gathering, 210; geographical boundaries, 190-91; hunting, 210; iconography, 222-24; identity,

223–25; interaction with Safety Harbor culture, 183; maize, 202, 210, 215–16, 228–29; migration vs. in situ development, 192, 204, 228; Mission-period, 229, 266; mortuary ceremonialism, 219–25; mortuary data, 204–9; mortuary goods, 204–9; mounds, 213, 214–15, 217–18, 220, 226–28; nomenclature, 188, nonmound sites, 215–17; radiocarbon dates, 188, 190, 204, 215; rank, 204; relationship with Etowah and Spiro, 204; ritual, 218, 220; seasonality data, 190; settlement patterns, 219, 226–27; site density, 190; social identity, 202; social memory, 219, 221–22, 225–26; sociopolitical organization, 204; Southeastern Ceremonial Complex (SECC), 224–25; status, 216; structures, 220, 227; subsistence, 188, 195, 202, 210; trade, 190, 204, 224; villages, 213–14, 216; Weeden Island predecessor, 193, 195; Woodland-Period Base, 192–96. *See also* Bear Grass site; Borrow Pit site; French; Lake Iamonia site; Lake Jackson site; Lake Lafayette site; Letchworth Mounds site; Markley-Sharer Road site; Miller's Landing site; Rollins Mound site; Snow Beach site; Velda site; Winewood site

Tallahassee Hills, 15, 26, 183, 186–229, 230n1, 246, 272, 279–80, 294; map, 191; mound sites in area, 213, 246; preserved maize, 15

Tallahassee Red Hills. *See* Tallahassee Hills

Tallahassee Tertiary Highlands. *See* Tallahassee Hills

Tampa, Fla., 262

"Tampa" (Pineland). *See* Pineland Site Complex

Tampa Bay, 25–26, 175–76, 305, 307

Tampa Bay area, 18, 26, 55–56, 172–85, 262

Tampa point. *See* Projectile points

Tanner, William F., 34–37, 43

Tatham Mound site, Fla., 177, 181–82; ground stone celt, 182; radiocarbon dates, 183

Tatham Phase, 174. *See also* Safety Harbor culture

Taylor Creek, 64

"Tekesta" subarea, 64. *See also* Glades culture area

Telfair site, Ga., 146

Temper. *See* Ceramics

Temple Mound I and II. *See* Mississippi period

Temple mounds. *See* Mounds

Tennessee, 47, 223, 306

Ten Thousand Islands, Fla., 43, 63, 65

Tequesta, 51, 67–68, 76, 78. *See also* Glades culture area; Miami River Mound Complex

Terminal Glades Complex. *See* South Florida Ceremonial Complex

Terrapin, 139

Terzis, Lee A., 199, 219

Tesar, Louis D., 15, 75, 188, 192, 195–96, 202, 213–17, 233, 235, 240, 252, 272, 277, 279, 287

Theory, 22, 172, 302

Thick Greenbriar site, Fla., 264; European goods, 265

Third Gulf Breeze site, Fla., 287

Thomas, Daniel H., 279

Thomas, David Hurst, 15–16, 34, 37, 230

Thomas, P., Jr., 83, 87, 279–81, 283–86, 292, 295

Thompson, Victor, 152

Thousand Islands, Fla., 82

Thunen, Robert L., 56, 101, 104–5, 107, 111

Timucua culture ("North Utina"), 2, 15–17, 19–20, 99, 110, 119, 125–26, 148–55, 165, 169–71; agricultural intensification, 148; agriculture, 126; Alachua Cob Marked, 130; alliances, 19; anthropological vs. archaeological perspectives, 19; Carabelle Incised, 132; Carabelle Punctated, 132; ceramics, 130, 132; characteristics of Mississippi-period sites, 126; chronology, 130; Colonoware, 130; contact-period, 19; demographic collapse, 170; European contact, 125; farming, 15; Fort Walton ceramics, 132; hereditary leadership, 17, 19; identification with Suwannee Valley culture, 149, 165; identity, 226; language, 154; Machava, 170; maize, 16, 19, 126; Pasco Plain, 132; political organization, 19–20, 148; Potano, 16; Prairie Cord Marked, 130; raiding, 125, 148; Safety Harbor ceramics, 132; settlement hierarchy, 19; settlement pattern, 226–27; simple chiefdom, 19, 126; sociopolitical organization, 170; Spanish contact, 132, 149; Spanish wares, 130; St. Johns Check Stamped, 132; St. Johns Plain, 132; subsistence, 16–17; warfare, 119, 127, 154. *See also* Mission-period; Mission Santa Cruz de Cachipile site; Outina; Suwannee Valley culture

Tippets Incised. *See* Ceramics

Tobacco, 300

Tocobaga, 55–56, 59
Tombigbee River, 276, 278
Tony's Mound site, Fla., 63, 72. *See also* Belle Glade culture area
Toqua site, Tenn., 223
Torrence, Corbett, 48–49, 50
Towns, 18, 47–58, 73, 88, 189, 201, 219, 306
Trace element analysis, 114
Trade, 11–13, 29, 41, 43, 46, 66, 73, 75, 94, 98, 100, 113–15, 117–18, 124–25, 140, 154, 159, 181–84, 189–90, 192, 195, 204, 218, 221, 273, 290, 292–93, 296–97, 300, 303, 305–8; beads, 27, 47, 94, 106, 115, 119, 182; bride, 195; Calusa, 46; copper, 13; galena, 46; goods, 51, 66, 94, 100, 140, 184, 189–90, 293, 300; lithics, 140; networks, 204, 224, 273, 292, 296, 305; periods of florescence, 12; prestige-goods model, 117–18; quartz, 46; routes, 62, 98, 115, 124–25, 204; shell, 13–14, 26–28, 47, 54, 66, 75, 77, 96, 106, 109, 112, 114–15, 117, 119, 124–25, 181–84, 273, 300, 302–3, 306–9; tied to labor, 117; wares, 113–14, 117, 159; with interior Southeast, 7, 12–13, 181, 204, 302; with Midsouth and Midwest, 46, 181, 302, 308. *See also* Exchange networks
Tradition, 298
Transportation, 27, 40–41, 51, 79, 268, 291
Tree islands. *See* Hammock islands
Trestle Point Shell Impressed. *See* Ceramics
Tributes, 19, 53, 76, 98, 263. *See also* Exchange networks
Trocolli, Ruth, 223
Trubitt, Mary Beth, 181–82, 307
Trysting Stairs site, Fla., 90. *See also* Indian River culture area
Tucker, Bryan D., 117, 146
Tucker Ridge Pinched. *See* Ceramics
Tukabatchee, 223
Turkey, 281
Turner, Bethany L., 193, 218
Turner River, 65
Turtle, 88, 139, 167–68, 202, 204, 235, 253
Tyndall Air Force Base, 281

UGA. *See* University of Georgia
Underwater Indian Mound site, Fla., 232–33
Union County, Fla., 128
Unionid mussel, 204
University of Arkansas, Department of Anthropology, 363

University of Georgia (UGA), 260–61
University of South Florida (USF), 254; archaeology lab, 243
University of West Florida (UWF), 276–79, 286, 288–89, 291, 295
Useppa Island site, Fla., 30, 38–39, 57; shell ridge, 39
USF. *See* University of South Florida
UWF. *See* University of West Florida
UWF Archaeology Institute, 277–78

Vacant Quarter Hypothesis, 308
Vandal Minimum. *See* Climate
Van Swearingen Creek, 64
Velda site, Fla., 216, 228; farmstead, 214; maize, 215; mound, 213–14; radiocarbon dates, 215; village, 213–14
Venezuela, 33
Vernon, Richard, 114, 276
Villages, 18–19, 61, 87–89, 91, 97, 99, 103, 107, 110, 117–18, 124, 129, 132, 135–36, 139–40, 144–45, 156–57, 160, 167–68, 176, 189, 193, 196, 198, 284, 286; Apalachicola/lower Chattahoochee Fort Walton, 231, 233, 235, 237, 241, 252–53, 256–60, 263, 274; Calusa, 47, 53, 61; Contact period, 17, 19; East Okeechobee, 67, 73; Formative or Pre-Mississippian 299, 301; Glades, 69, 71, 73; Mission period, 16; Pensacola, 281, 284, 286, 292; Safety Harbor, 18; Tallahassee Fort Walton, 26, 200–202, 204, 213–16, 225–27
Virnstein, Robert W., 83
Vita-Finzi, Claudio, 226
VM. *See* Climate: Vandal Minimum

Waddell's Mill Pond site, Fla., 146, 232–33, 235, 262, 264; burials, 233; ceramic mushroom, 262; mounds, 233, 252; Woodland, 233
Wakulla Check Stamped, 249
Wakulla County, Fla., 190
Wakulla Springs, Fla., 193
Walker, Karen J., 2, 18–19, 23, 29–61, 65, 69, 71, 87, 92, 120, 181, 192, 263, 266, 270
Walker, S. T., 283
Wallace, Jennifer A., 40
Wallis, Neill J., 90
Walnut, 168
Walnut Roughened. *See* Ceramics
Walton County, Fla., 277
Warfare, 11, 18, 58–59, 98–99, 119, 125, 148, 170, 221, 237, 269, 292. *See also* Palisades
Waring, Antonio J., Jr., 7, 178, 224

Waselkov, Gregory A., 12, 279, 292
Washington County, Fla., 275, 279
Washington University in St. Louis, Department of Anthropology, 363
Water travel. *See* Canals; Canoes
Waterways. *See* Canals; Canoe trails; Rivers
Watson, Patty Jo, 47
Wauchope, Robert, 217
Wax myrtle, 253
Wayne, Lucy B., 16, 100, 134–35
Webb, William S., 47
Weed, C., 83, 87
Weeden Island culture, 6, 25, 39, 42, 46, 55, 76, 95, 114, 136, 147, 149, 151, 156, 159, 164–66, 174–80, 184–85, 193, 195, 213, 215, 218, 228, 239, 249–50, 253, 256, 261, 263, 267–69, 279, 290, 292, 299, 305; agriculture, 193; belief systems, 184–85; burial ceremonialism, 55, 147; ceramics, 39, 42, 46, 55, 114, 136, 138, 147, 149, 156, 158, 164–66, 175, 177–80, 184–85, 193, 195, 213, 239, 249–50, 253, 256, 261, 267; cultural continuity, 195; dates, 193; exchange, 76; habitation patterns, 193; Late, 55, 268; lithics, 253; mortuary traditions, 193; mounds, 55, 95, 166, 215, 292, 299; relation to, 195; sacred/secular dichotomy, 184; settlement, 19, 268–69, 279, 290; subsistence, 181, 193, 195. *See also* Kolomoki site; Manasota culture; McKeithen site; McKeithen Weeden Island culture; Suwannee Valley culture; Weeden Island II culture; Woodland period
Weeden Island Incised. *See* Ceramics
Weeden Island II culture, 151, 156, 159, 261
Weiner, Annette, 224
Weinstein, Richard A., 252
Weirs, 72, 76
Weisman, Brent R., 2, 16, 53, 150, 152, 156–57, 163, 166
Welch, Paul D., 29, 237, 271, 301
West Jefferson culture, 299
Wetlands, 4–5, 23, 61, 64, 73, 75, 77, 129, 136, 139, 180, 263, 273
Wheeler, Ryan J., 48–49, 51, 68–71, 78–79, 92, 236
Whelk, 13–14, 26, 41–43, 47, 60n1, 86, 106, 115, 181–82, 236, 253, 255, 273, 300, 303, 305–6, 308; associated with burials, 47; *Busycon carica* (knobbed), 14; *Busycon contrarium*, 60n1; *Busycon perversum*, 60n1; *Busycon sinistrum* (lightning), 14, 41–43, 47, 60n1, 236, 273, 303; demand, 14; dextral, 14, 26; manufacture, 21, 47, 182, 301; nomenclature, 60n1; sinistral, 14, 26, 60n1, 72, 303; symbolism, 14; tools, 41, 106, 308. *See also* Shell; Trade
White, Nancy Marie, 1–28, 42, 55, 115, 125, 146–47, 155, 163, 172, 177, 181, 185, 188, 192, 202, 218, 223, 229, 231–74, 278–79, 283, 295, 297, 299, 306
Widmer, Randolph J., 19, 51, 53, 76, 79
Wilcox, Jennifer R., 122
Wild plants, 65, 104, 167, 235
Willey, Gordon R., 6–8, 55, 72, 76, 93–96, 114, 151–52, 155, 158, 163–64, 172–75, 178, 188, 192–93, 195–96, 198, 213–15, 217, 225, 227, 231, 236, 239–41, 246, 250–51, 259, 266, 275–76, 279, 281, 283, 285, 287, 294, 298; explanation of Mississippian in Florida, 6
Williams, Mark, 21, 152, 266, 303
Williams, Stephen, 7, 58, 116, 302, 308
Wilmington-Savannah cultures, 137
Wilson, Gregory D., 301
Windover site, Fla., 90
Winewood site, Fla., 217; burials, 216; ceramics, 216; maize, 216
Winnebago, 116, 302
Winter, Amos, 36
Wise, J. B., 60n1
Withlacoochee River, 155, 175
Wood, 281, 284; axe handle, 205–7; boards, 205–9; carvings, 78; litter poles, 206–7; plate backing, 205; split logs, 205, 207
Wood, W. Dean, 283
Woodbury, R. B., 173, 188, 198
Woodland period, 6, 12–14, 24–26, 33, 56, 65, 75–76, 79, 84, 96, 101–2, 111–12, 126–27, 129–30, 132–33, 135–36, 138–40, 142, 149, 151, 156, 164, 166, 192–96, 233, 235–36, 249, 251–53, 261, 263, 265, 267, 269–70, 273, 283, 285, 299, 301–2; agriculture, 193, 301; Alachua culture, 24; alliances, 192; American Bottom, 301–2; belief systems, 184; burial mounds, 56; ceramics, 135–36, 138, 164, 249, 253, 261, 267; Choctawhatchee Bay, 285; Early, 56, 249, 251, 283; exchange networks, 14, 76, 111–12; habitation patterns, 193; Hopewell, 13, 75–76, 79; Late, 14, 24, 33, 65, 84, 101–2, 111–12, 126, 130, 133, 139–40, 156, 193, 239, 253, 261, 263, 265, 267, 269, 283, 298–99, 302; maize, 193, 267; McKeithen regional subdivision, 151, 156, 164–66; Middle, 12, 56, 79, 130, 135, 142, 193, 233, 235–36, 252, 267, 283, 285; mounds, 166, 236, 252, 270, 283; points, 140, 265;

Woodland period—*continued*
political organization, 195; sea-levels, 263; subsistence, 181, 193; Suwannee Valley culture, 156; trade, 13, 192–93; Weeden Island II, 151, 156, 159; West Jefferson culture, 299. *See also* Cades Pond culture; McKeithen Weeden Island culture; Weeden Island culture; Weeden Island II culture
Woodstock culture, 299
Woodville Karst Plain, 190
Woodward Mound and Village site, Fla., 95, 134, 139, 141–44; burials, 143; ceramics, 135; dates, 135; greenstone celt, 135; maize (lack of), 135; map, 129; projectile points, 135. *See also* Alachua culture area; Alachua Phase
Women, 26, 117, 216, 222–23, 271; burials of, 216, 222–23, 271; chiefs, 26; potters, 117
Works Progress Administration, 174, 298
Worth, John E., 2, 15–17, 19, 25, 53, 60n3, 119, 126–28, 132, 148–71, 237, 266, 270
WPA. *See* Works Progress Administration
Wright, J. Leitch, Jr., 292
Wulfert High, 32

X-ray fluorescence analysis, 260

Yahi Indians, 265; Ishi, 265
Yamassee, 59
Yankeetown culture, 299
Yaupon, 115, 273
Yellow River, 285
Yon site, Fla., 26, 232–33, 238, 242, 251, 256, 260, 262–63, 265, 269, 274; antler, 256; basket loading, 280; bead, 258; bone tools, 256; ceramics, 256, 258–59, 263; daub, 256; faunal remains, 258; fish hooks, 258; fishing, 258; groundstone, 256, 258; habitation patterns, 256, 259; Lamar component, 256–57, 259; lithics, 256; map, 257; mound, 256, 258; mound construction, 258; radiocarbon dates, 256, 258, 265; subsistence, 256, 258, 263
Yucatán, 34–36, 38, 60n1
Yuellig, Amber J., 26, 231–74
Yustaga region, 154; ceramics, 155

Zebree site, Ark., 301
Zeitlen, Robert, 9
Zoomorphic motifs. *See* Motifs
Z-twist. *See* Ceramics

RIPLEY P. BULLEN SERIES

FLORIDA MUSEUM OF NATURAL HISTORY

Tacachale: Essays on the Indians of Florida and Southeastern Georgia during the Historic Period, edited by Jerald T. Milanich and Samuel Proctor (1978)

Aboriginal Subsistence Technology on the Southeastern Coastal Plain during the Late Prehistoric Period, by Lewis H. Larson (1980)

Cemochechobee: Archaeology of a Mississippian Ceremonial Center on the Chattahoochee River, by Frank T. Schnell, Vernon J. Knight Jr., and Gail S. Schnell (1981)

Fort Center: An Archaeological Site in the Lake Okeechobee Basin, by William H. Sears, with contributions by Elsie O'R. Sears and Karl T. Steinen (1982)

Perspectives on Gulf Coast Prehistory, edited by Dave D. Davis (1984)

Archaeology of Aboriginal Culture Change in the Interior Southeast: Depopulation during the Early Historic Period, by Marvin T. Smith (1987)

Apalachee: The Land between the Rivers, by John H. Hann (1988)

Key Marco's Buried Treasure: Archaeology and Adventure in the Nineteenth Century, by Marion Spjut Gilliland (1989)

First Encounters: Spanish Explorations in the Caribbean and the United States, 1492–1570, edited by Jerald T. Milanich and Susan Milbrath (1989)

Missions to the Calusa, edited and translated by John H. Hann, with an introduction by William H. Marquardt (1991)

Excavations on the Franciscan Frontier: Archaeology at the Fig Springs Mission, by Brent Richards Weisman (1992)

The People Who Discovered Columbus: The Prehistory of the Bahamas, by William F. Keegan (1992)

Hernando de Soto and the Indians of Florida, by Jerald T. Milanich and Charles Hudson (1993)

Foraging and Farming in the Eastern Woodlands, edited by C. Margaret Scarry (1993)

Puerto Real: The Archaeology of a Sixteenth-Century Spanish Town in Hispaniola, edited by Kathleen Deagan (1995)

Political Structure and Change in the Prehistoric Southeastern United States, edited by John F. Scarry (1996)

Bioarchaeology of Native Americans in the Spanish Borderlands, edited by Brenda J. Baker and Lisa Kealhofer (1996)

A History of the Timucua Indians and Missions, by John H. Hann (1996)

Archaeology of the Mid-Holocene Southeast, edited by Kenneth E. Sassaman and David G. Anderson (1996)

The Indigenous People of the Caribbean, edited by Samuel M. Wilson (1997; first paperback edition, 1999)

Hernando de Soto among the Apalachee: The Archaeology of the First Winter Encampment, by Charles R. Ewen and John H. Hann (1998)

The Timucuan Chiefdoms of Spanish Florida, by John E. Worth: vol. 1, *Assimilation*; vol. 2, *Resistance and Destruction* (1998)

Ancient Earthen Enclosures of the Eastern Woodlands, edited by Robert C. Mainfort Jr. and Lynne P. Sullivan (1998)

An Environmental History of Northeast Florida, by James J. Miller (1998)

Precolumbian Architecture in Eastern North America, by William N. Morgan (1999)

Archaeology of Colonial Pensacola, edited by Judith A. Bense (1999)

Grit-Tempered: Early Women Archaeologists in the Southeastern United States, edited by Nancy Marie White, Lynne P. Sullivan, and Rochelle A. Marrinan (1999)

Coosa: The Rise and Fall of a Southeastern Mississippian Chiefdom, by Marvin T. Smith (2000)

Religion, Power, and Politics in Colonial St. Augustine, by Robert L. Kapitzke (2001)

Bioarchaeology of Spanish Florida: The Impact of Colonialism, edited by Clark Spencer Larsen (2001)

Archaeological Studies of Gender in the Southeastern United States, edited by Jane M. Eastman and Christopher B. Rodning (2001)

The Archaeology of Traditions: Agency and History Before and After Columbus, edited by Timothy R. Pauketat (2001)

Foraging, Farming, and Coastal Biocultural Adaptation in Late Prehistoric North Carolina, by Dale L. Hutchinson (2002)

Windover: Multidisciplinary Investigations of an Early Archaic Florida Cemetery, edited by Glen H. Doran (2002)

Archaeology of the Everglades, by John W. Griffin (2002)

Pioneer in Space and Time: John Mann Goggin and the Development of Florida Archaeology, by Brent Richards Weisman (2002)

Indians of Central and South Florida, 1513–1763, by John H. Hann (2003)

Presidio Santa Maria de Galve: A Struggle for Survival in Colonial Spanish Pensacola, edited by Judith A. Bense (2003)

Bioarchaeology of the Florida Gulf Coast: Adaptation, Conflict, and Change, by Dale L. Hutchinson (2004)

The Myth of Syphilis: The Natural History of Treponematosis in North America, edited by Mary Lucas Powell and Della Collins Cook (2005)

The Florida Journals of Frank Hamilton Cushing, edited by Phyllis E. Kolianos and Brent R. Weisman (2005)

The Lost Florida Manuscript of Frank Hamilton Cushing, edited by Phyllis E. Kolianos and Brent R. Weisman (2005)

The Native American World Beyond Apalachee: West Florida and the Chattahoochee Valley, by John H. Hann (2006)

Tatham Mound and the Bioarchaeology of European Contact: Disease and Depopulation in Central Gulf Coast Florida, by Dale L. Hutchinson (2006)

Taino Indian Myth and Practice: The Arrival of the Stranger King, by William F. Keegan (2007)

An Archaeology of Black Markets: Local Ceramics and Economies in Eighteenth-Century Jamaica, by Mark W. Hauser (2008; first paperback edition, 2013)

Mississippian Mortuary Practices: Beyond Hierarchy and the Representationist Perspective, edited by Lynne P. Sullivan and Robert C. Mainfort Jr. (2010; first paperback edition, 2012)

Bioarchaeology of Ethnogenesis in the Colonial Southeast, by Christopher M. Stojanowski (2010; first paperback edition, 2013)

French Colonial Archaeology in the Southeast and Caribbean, edited by Kenneth G. Kellyand Meredith D. Hardy (2011; first paperback edition, 2015)

Late Prehistoric Florida: Archaeology at the Edge of the Mississippian World, edited by Keith Ashley and Nancy Marie White (2012; first paperback edition, 2015)

Early and Middle Woodland Landscapes of the Southeast, edited by Alice P. Wright and Edward R. Henry (2013)

Trends and Traditions in Southeastern Zooarchaeology, edited by Tanya M. Peres (2014)

New Histories of Pre-Columbian Florida, edited by Neill J. Wallis and Asa R. Randall (2014)

Discovering Florida: First-Contact Narratives from Spanish Expeditions along the Lower Gulf Coast, edited and translated by John E. Worth (2014)

Constructing Histories: Archaic Freshwater Shell Mounds and Social Landscapes of the St. Johns River, Florida by Asa R. Randall (2015)

Archaeology of Early Colonial Interaction at El Chorro de Maíta, Cuba, by Roberto Valcárcel Rojas (2016)

Fort San Juan and the Limits of Empire: Colonialism and Household Practice at the Berry Site, edited by Robin A. Beck, Christopher B. Rodning, and David G. Moore (2016)

Rethinking Moundville and its Hinterland, edited by Vincas P. Steponaitis and C. Margaret Scarry (2016)

Animal Symbolism in the Early Ceramics of the Pre-Columbian Caribbean by Lawrence Waldron (2016)

Paleoindian Contexts in the Thermal Enclave of the Coastal Southeast by James S. Dunbar (2016)

Gathering Places: nfHunter-Gatherer History and Interaction at Florida's Late Archaic Shell Mounds by Zackary I. Gilmore (2016)

Cuban Archaeology in a Circum-Caribbean Context, edited by Ivan Roksandic (2016)

www.ingramcontent.com/pod-product-compliance
Lightning Source LLC
Chambersburg PA
CBHW020217240426
43672CB00006B/339